ENGLISH PLACE-NAME SOCIETY

SUPERNUMERARY VOLUME FOR 2012

General Editor

RICHARD COATES

PERCEPTIONS OF PLACE

TWENTY-FIRST-CENTURY INTERPRETATIONS OF ENGLISH PLACE-NAME STUDIES

THE SURVEY OF ENGLISH PLACE-NAMES
UNDERTAKEN WITH THE APPROVAL AND SUPPORT OF
THE ARTS AND HUMANITIES RESEARCH COUNCIL
AND
THE BRITISH ACADEMY

PERCEPTIONS OF PLACE

TWENTY-FIRST-CENTURY INTERPRETATIONS OF ENGLISH PLACE-NAME STUDIES

edited by
Jayne Carroll and David N. Parsons

NOTTINGHAM

ENGLISH PLACE-NAME SOCIETY

2013

Published by the English Place-Name Society,
School of English, University of Nottingham
Nottingham NG7 2RD

Registered Charity No. 257891

ISBN 978-0-904889-86-4

Typeset by Jayne Carroll and printed in Great Britain
by 4word, Bristol.

Contents

Abbreviations

English counties (preceding the reorganisation of 1974)

Bd	Bedfordshire	Li	Lincolnshire
Brk	Berkshire	Mx	Middlesex
Bu	Buckinghamshire	Nb	Northumberland
Ca	Cambridgeshire	Nf	Norfolk
Ch	Cheshire	NRY	North Riding of Yorkshire
Co	Cornwall	Nth	Northamptonshire
Cu	Cumberland	Nt	Nottinghamshire
D	Devon	O	Oxfordshire
Db	Derbyshire	R	Rutland
Do	Dorset	Sa	Shropshire
Du	Durham	Sf	Suffolk
ERY	East Riding of Yorkshire	So	Somerset
Ess	Essex	Sr	Surrey
Gl	Gloucestershire	St	Staffordshire
Ha	Hampshire	Sx	Sussex
He	Herefordshire	W	Wiltshire
Hrt	Hertfordshire	Wa	Warwickshire
Hu	Huntingdonshire	We	Westmorland
K	Kent	Wo	Worcestershire
La	Lancashire	WRY	West Riding of Yorkshire
Le	Leicestershire	Y	Yorkshire

acc.	accusative
AHRC	Arts and Humanities Research Council
AN	Anglo-Norman
ASC	The Anglo-Saxon Chronicle, with letter indicating manuscript.
BAR	British Archaeological Reports
Bede	(As source) the Latin version of Bede's *Historia Ecclesiastica*.
CDEPN	V. Watts, *Cambridge Dictionary of English Place-Names* (Cambridge: Cambridge University Press, 2004).
CMCS	Cambrian Medieval Celtic Studies
Co.	County
CPNE	O. J. Padel, *Cornish Place-Name Elements*, EPNS 56–57 (Nottingham: EPNS, 1985).
d.	died
Dan.	Danish
dat.	dative
DB	Domesday Book
DEPN	E. Ekwall, *The Concise Dictionary of English Place-Names*, 4th edn (Oxford: Clarendon, 1960).
DPNW	H. W. Owen and R. Morgan, *Dictionary of the Place-Names of Wales* (Llandysul: Gomer, 2007, repr. with corrections 2008).
DR	L. Jacobsen and E. Moltke, with A. Bæksted and K. M. Nielsen (eds), *Danmarks Runeindskrifter* I–II (Copenhagen: Munksgaard, 1941–42).
e	early (i.e. e11 is early 11th century)
EPNE	A. H. Smith, *English Place-Name Elements*, 2 vols, EPNS 25–26 (Cambridge: Cambridge University Press, 1956).
EPNS	English Place-Name Society; when followed by county abbreviation, the EPNS county Survey volumes.
f., fem.	feminine
fl.	*floruit* 'flourished'
Fr.	French
G, Gael	Gaelic
GDB	Great Domesday Book, The National Archives E31/2.
Germ	Germanic
gen.	genitive
Hy2; Hy3	Dated to the reign of Henry II, 1133–89; Henry III, 1207–72.
IE	Indo-European
IPN	A. Mawer and F. M. Stenton (eds), *Introduction to the Survey of English Place-Names*, EPNS 1.i (Cambridge: Cambridge University Press, 1924).
Ir.	Irish
JEPNS	*Journal of the English Place-Name Society*
l	late (i.e. l11 is late eleventh century)
m	mid- (i.e. m11 is mid-eleventh century)

m., masc.	masculine
ME	Middle English
MGH	Monumenta Germania Historica
Ms	manuscript
n., neut.	neuter
NGR	National grid reference
nom.	nominative
ODan	Old Danish
OCo	Old Cornish
OE	Old English
OEBede	The Old English version of Bede's *Historia Ecclesiastica.*
OED	*Oxford English Dictionary*, online edition <www.oed.com>.
OFr	Old French
OHG	Old High German
ON	Old Norse
OS; OSNB	Ordnance Survey; Ordnance Survey Name-Books
OSax	Old Saxon
OSwed	Old Swedish
PNI	*The Place-Names of Northern Ireland* (Belfast: The Queen's University Belfast, 1992–).
PNRB	A. L. F. Rivet and C. Smith, *The Place-Names of Roman Britain* (London: Batsford, 1979).
PRO	Public Record Office; now The National Archives
r.	reigned
S	P. Sawyer, *Anglo-Saxon Charters: An Annotated List and Bibliography* (London: The Royal Historical Society, 1968). An electronic version (2006), rev. by R. Rushworth is available at <http://www.esawyer.org.uk/>.
s.a.	*sub anno* 'under the year'
Sc.	Scots
s.n.	*sub nomine* 'under the name'
SSE	Scottish Standard English
s.v.	*sub verbo* 'under the word'
SkO	*Skånes ortsnamen* (Lund: Institutet för Språk och Folkminnen, Dialekt- och Ortnamnsarkivet, 1958–).
TNA	The National Archives
vb	verb
VEPN	D. Parsons, T. Styles with C. Hough, *The Vocabulary of English Place-Names* I *(Á–Box)* (1997); Parsons and Styles, *The Vocabulary of English Place-Names* II *(Brace–Cæster)* (2000); Parsons, *The Vocabulary of English Place-Names* III *(Ceafor–Cock-pit)* (2004).
W	Welsh

Contributors

Jayne Carroll is Director of the Institute for Name-Studies at the University of Nottingham, Honorary Secretary of the English Place-Name Society, and co-editor of the journal *Nomina*. She has published on place-names, Old English and Old Norse poetry, and the Anglo-Saxon Chronicle. She directs, with David N. Parsons, the AHRC-funded project, The Place-Names of Shropshire (2013–16).

Thomas Owen Clancy holds the Chair of Celtic at the University of Glasgow, and is Research Convener of the School of Humanities. His publications range across the field of Celtic Studies, as well as the history of early Scotland. He has led several major projects on Scottish place-names, funded by both the AHRC and The Leverhulme Trust. He is convener of the Scottish Catholic Historical Association.

Richard Coates is Professor of Linguistics / Professor of Onomastics at the University of the West of England, Bristol. He is county editor for Hampshire for the Survey of English Place-Names, and has been Honorary Director of the Survey since 2003. He has published widely on place-names and other onomastic and philological topics.

Paul Cullen is a Research Associate on the AHRC-funded 'Family Names of the United Kingdom' project, based at the University of the West of England, and an Honorary Visiting Fellow in the Institute for Name-Studies at the University of Nottingham. He is county editor for Kent for the Survey of English Place-Names, and co-author with Richard Jones and D. N. Parsons of *Thorps in a Changing Landscape* (2011).

Gillian Fellows-Jensen was formerly Reader in Name-Studies at the Department of Name Research in the Institute of Scandinavian Research at the University of Copenhagen, and she still has a desk there. She is particularly interested in Scandinavian place-names as a source of information about settlement in the Viking period and has published four books on Scandinavian place-names or personal names in England.

Carole Hough is Professor of Onomastics at the University of Glasgow. She has published extensively in the field of name-studies, and is a former editor of the journal *Nomina*. She is currently President of the International Congress of Onomastic Sciences, and Convener of the Scottish Place-Name Society.

John Insley is retired *außerplanmäßiger* Professor of English Language (earlier periods of the History of English) at the Ruprecht-Karls-Universität Heidelberg. He is the author of *Scandinavian Personal Names in Norfolk* (1994) and co-author with the late Kenneth Cameron of *The Place-Names of Lincolnshire*, Part VII: *The Wapentake of Lawress* (2010).

Kay Muhr grew up in East Anglia and read Celtic Studies (MA and PhD) in Edinburgh. After re-locating to Ireland she was from 1987 to 2010 Senior Research Fellow of the Northern Ireland Place-Name Project in Queen's University, Belfast. Her research interests include place-names and identity, place-names and archaeology, and the use of place-names in Gaelic narrative literature and mythology.

Hywel Wyn Owen is Professor Emeritus at Bangor University where he was Director of the Welsh Place-Name Research Centre. A former President of the Society for Name Studies in Britain and Ireland, he is Honorary Vice-President of the English Place-Name Society and a founder member of the Welsh Place-Name Society. He has published and broadcast extensively on the place-names of Wales, and was co-author of the authoritative *Dictionary of the Place-Names of Wales* (2007). He advises national bodies in Wales on matters relating to place-names.

Oliver Padel is currently President of the English Place-Name Society, and was formerly Reader in Cornish and Celtic in the University of Cambridge. He is county editor for Cornwall for the Survey of English Place-Names, and author of *Cornish Place-Name Elements*, English Place-Name Society 56/57 (1985) and *A Popular Dictionary of Cornish Place-Names* (1988).

David N. Parsons is Senior Research Fellow at the Centre for Advanced Welsh and Celtic Studies at the University of Wales and Deputy Director of the Survey of English Place-Names. He has published widely on English place-names and their constituent languages, and on medieval inscriptions, and now directs the AHRC-funded project, *The cult of saints in Wales*, and co-directs, with Jayne Carroll, *The place-names of Shropshire*, also funded by the AHRC.

Matthew Townend is Reader in the Department of English and Related Literature, and the Centre for Medieval Studies, at the University of York. His research interests include language and literature in Viking Age England, Old Norse poetry, and nineteenth- and twentieth-century medievalism. His books include *Language and History in Viking Age England* (2002) and *The Vikings and Victorian Lakeland: the Norse medievalism of W.G. Collingwood and his contemporaries* (2009).

Acknowledgements

We owe thanks to a number of people for helping in various ways with the production of this volume, particularly members of the Institute for Name-Studies in Nottingham. Rebecca Gregory made the initial compilation of items for the bibliography, Christine Hickling helped with index-checking, John Baker read a number of the chapters and did some last-minute checking, and Paul Cavill saw the volume off to the printers. Warm thanks are due to Sarah Beach for her meticulous proof-reading, her editing of the bibliography, and her help in pulling things together in the very final stages of production. Any errors, omissions, and oversights which remain are of course the fault of the editors. Ian and Diana Whaley provided the beautiful image, of Cheviot, for the cover.

We are very grateful to the Arts and Humanities Research Council and to the British Academy – the work of the English Place-Name Society would not be possible without their continuing support.

Finally, heartfelt thanks to our contributors for their sterling work and their patience.

Perceiving place through time: English place-name studies, 1924–2013

Jayne Carroll

The first part of the *Introduction to the Survey of English Place-Names* was published in 1924, the year after the English Place-Name Society (EPNS) was established to conduct the Survey. Its purpose was to set out 'the present state of our knowledge and indicate the lines along which the possibilities of further progress lay'.[1] In the ninety years since the birth of the Society and the Survey, which saw its first county volume—Buckinghamshire—published in 1925, the material available for English place-name study has increased enormously. Of the Survey series alone, eighty-nine volumes have so far been published: twenty-five of England's historical counties have complete surveys (with varying levels of detail), eight are partly published, and work is underway on the remaining seven.[2]

The volumes of the English Place-Name Society's survey are indicated by EPNS + county abbreviation as given in note 2.

[1] Quoted in the preface to A. Mawer and F. M. Stenton (eds), *Introduction to the Survey of English Place-Names*, English Place-Name Society 1.i (Cambridge: Cambridge University Press, 1924) [IPN], pp. vii–viii (p. vii). Accounts of the establishment and subsequent history of the EPNS are to be found in D. Whitelock, 'The English Place-Name Society 1923–1973', *Journal of the English Place-Name Society* 5 (1972–73), 5–14, in A. M. Armstrong, M. Gelling, and K. Cameron, 'Some notes on the history of the English Place-Name Society', *Journal of the English Place-Name Society* 25 (1992–93), 1–8, and in M. Gelling, 'English place-name studies: some reflections', *Journal of the English Place-Name Society* 35 (2002–03), 5–16.

[2] There are complete surveys for Bedfordshire (Bd), Berkshire (Brk), Buckinghamshire (Bu), Cambridgeshire (Ca), Cheshire (Ch), Cumberland (Cu), Derbyshire (Db), Dorset (Do), Essex (Ess), Huntingdonshire (Hu), Gloucestershire (Gl), Middlesex (Mx), Northamptonshire (Nth), Nottinghamshire (Nt), Oxfordshire (O), Rutland (R), Surrey (Sr), Sussex (Sx), Warwickshire (Wa), Westmorland (We), Wiltshire (W), Worcestershire (Wo), and the three ridings of Yorkshire (ERY, NRY, WR). Volumes offering partial county coverage are available for Cornwall (Co) Durham (Du), Leicestershire (Le), Lincolnshire (Li), Norfolk (Nf), Shropshire (Sa), and Staffordshire (St), and further volumes are currently in progress for Co, Du, Le, Li, and Sa. Work is underway for Hampshire (Ha), Kent (K), Lancashire (La), and Suffolk (Sf), and though Somerset (So) lacks a county Survey editor, a one-volume dictionary is in preparation. The Survey of

Given the growth in material to work with, it is inevitable that much has changed in place-name study since the Society was established and the *Introduction* published. Not only is there now coverage for most of England's counties, the level of detail within each Survey volume has increased over this period. The Buckinghamshire Survey comprises a single volume of 274 pages, giving relatively concise explanations of the linguistic origins of names collected from Ordnance Survey 1″ and 6″ maps, and with minimal introductory material and general commentary. Coverage of field- and minor names is limited to a brief selection at the end of the volume (EPNS Bu, pp. 257–61) illustrating their elements and the Old English and Old Norse personal names used in their composition. Back in 1925, field-name material was seen primarily as an aid to dialect and language study: the Buckinghamshire editors, Sir Allen Mawer and Sir Frank Stenton, justified their summary coverage of field-names thus: 'many of them are without much interest, consisting largely of forms which are common in all field-names'.[3] The potential that field- and minor names offer for the study of all types of history—local, agricultural, social, ecclesiastical, administrative, landscape, and not just linguistic—was not fully acknowledged therein. Within a decade, though, Mawer had written an essay which sought to demonstrate how field- and minor names might enable identification of the sites of hundredal (and other) meeting-places, indicate the extent of land-units in the early and later medieval periods, contribute to discussions of settlement history, and add substantially to our knowledge of the historical lexicon and of dialectal usage.[4]

Mawer's essay was published in 1933, the year in which the EPNS Survey of Northamptonshire appeared. EPNS Nth treated field- and minor names in greater detail than had previous volumes, albeit still tucking them away at the end of the volume. It offered greatly expanded coverage of early name-forms, arranged by 'their most significant element', but, perhaps more significantly, it evidenced a shift away from

English Place-Names is a British Academy Research Project, and the EPNS gratefully acknowledges the Academy's ongoing support, which has made possible—and continues to make possible—many of these publications. The eighty-nine volumes include the *Introduction* itself, A. H. Smith's *English Place-Name Elements* (1956), and Oliver Padel's *Cornish Place-Name Elements* (1985).

[3] EPNS Bu, p. 257. In place-name study, the term 'field-names' covers not just the names of areas of enclosed land, but those of woods, heath- and marsh-land, hills, and so on.

[4] A. Mawer, 'The study of field-names in relation to place-names', in J. G. Edwards, V. H. Galbraith, and E. F. Jacob (eds), *Historical Essays in Honour of James Tait* (Manchester: printed for subscribers, 1933), pp. 189–200.

the view that the forms common in modern field-names were without interest, with a new section treating elements found only or mainly in modern names, and another which gave modern names (and, where possible, their earlier forms) arranged by hundred and parish. This greater level of coverage had been made possible through the assistance of around 200 schools in collecting the twentieth-century and historical forms of these names,[5] and similar collaborative exercises produced the same arrangement for the next nine counties to be surveyed. The publication of the three-volume Cumberland Survey, however, marked a further shift: field- and minor names were treated within the body of the Survey, after the major names of each parish (and township). With this, the form of the EPNS Survey volume more or less as we know it today was established, although a continuing move towards exhaustive coverage can be observed in recently edited county volumes. The latest Survey volume at the time of writing, that for 2011, is the sixth in a projected ten-part Survey of Shropshire;[6] there are 1594 pages of Shropshire material published so far, covering around two thirds of the county. Here, we find comprehensive coverage of the field-names within each township or parish, and street- and building-names are also treated.

Scholarship on the place-names of England's neighbours has also flourished. In 1924, Scandinavia already had state-supported place-name surveys in progress, but the *Introduction*'s authors had little to draw upon from Wales, Scotland, and Ireland. Much has changed. It can no longer be said that the 'place-names of Wales are on the whole *terra incognita*',[7] and in Scotland place-name study has in the last decade entered something of a golden age.[8] Place-name volumes for four of the six

[5] See EPNS Nth, pp. vi–vii.

[6] This is Margaret Gelling's EPNS Sa **6**, published posthumously in 2012. The Shropshire Survey is being completed by an editorial team of six, working at the Institute for Name-Studies, University of Nottingham, and the Centre for Advanced Welsh and Celtic Studies, University of Wales, and funded by the Arts and Humanities Research Council (2013–16).

[7] E. Ekwall, 'The Celtic element', IPN, pp. 15–35 (pp. 15, 16). See H. W. Owen and R. Morgan, *Dictionary of the Place-Names of Wales* (Llandysul: Gomer, 2007; reprinted with corrections 2008) [DPNW]. The Welsh Place-Name Society was established in 2011. There are published surveys for Pembrokeshire, Cardiganshire, and parts of Glamorganshire and Flintshire. See below, pp. 3–4, and ch. 11 (particularly pp. 321–23). The recently-launched website, 'My Place in Wales' <http://lle.llgc.org.uk/>, is intended to 'act as a hub for a group of related projects concerned with recording and understanding the place-names of Wales'.

[8] Surveys of Fife and the Isle of Bute have recently been completed, and ones for Berwickshire, Kinross-shire, Clackmannanshire, and Menteith are underway, funded by

counties of Northern Ireland are available,[9] and the Republic of Ireland Civil Service has a Placenames Branch, whose research is disseminated through the website, <www.logainm.ie>.[10]

Much work underpinning the historical-linguistic foundations of place-name study has been done since 1924, and major reference works have appeared. Kenneth Jackson's *Language and History in Early Britain* was published in 1953 and Alistair Campbell's *Old English Grammar* in 1959.[11] The multi-volume *Middle English Dictionary* was completed in 2001; the final volume of the first edition of *Geiriadur Prifysgol Cymru*, the historical dictionary of Welsh, appeared in 2002; the *Oxford English Dictionary* is into its third (online) edition;[12] and the ongoing Toronto *Dictionary of Old English* is gradually replacing Bosworth and Toller's *Anglo-Saxon Dictionary*.[13] The *Linguistic Atlas of Early Middle English* is now available in electronic form, joining its predecessor on Late Middle English, first published in 1986 and now in revised form also available electronically.[14]

the Arts and Humanities Research Council. See ch. 10; a summary of this recent work, as well as older survey work, can be found on pp. 283–86. The Scottish Place-Name Society was established in 1996.

[9] See the references on p. 355 below. The Ulster Place-Name Society was founded in 1952.

[10] Work also progresses further afield. The following recent and reliable national dictionaries for France, Germany, and the Netherlands contain useful bibliographies: P.-H. Billy, *Dictionnaire des noms de lieux de la France* (Paris: Errance 2011); D. Berger, *Geographische Namen in Deutschland. Herkunft und Bedeutung der Namen von Ländern, Städten, Gerben und Gewässern*, 2nd edn (Mannheim: Bibliographisches Institut, 1999); G. van Berkel and K. Samplonius, *Nederlandse Plaatsnamen*, 3rd edn (Utrecht: Het Spectrum, 2006).

[11] K. Jackson, *Language and History in Early Britain* (Edinburgh: Edinburgh University Press, 1953); A. Campbell, *Old English Grammar* (Oxford: Clarendon, 1959). The latter has been supplemented, although not superseded, by R. M. Hogg and R. D. Fulk, *A Grammar of Old English*, 2 vols (Oxford: Wiley-Blackwell, 1992–2011).

[12] Now complemented by C. Kay et al., *Historical Thesaurus of the Oxford English Dictionary*, 2 vols (Oxford: Oxford University Press, 2009).

[13] H. Kurath et al., *Middle English Dictionary*, 14 vols (Michigan: University of Michigan Press, 1952–2001); R. J. Thomas et al., *Geiriadur Prifysgol Cymru*, 4 vols (Cardiff: University of Wales Press, 1950–2002); J. Simpson (ed.), *Oxford English Dictionary* [OED Online <www.oed.com>]; A. Cameron et al., *Dictionary of Old English – A–G on CD-ROM* (Toronto: University of Toronto, 2008).

[14] A. McIntosh, M. L. Samuels, and M. Benskin, A *Linguistic Atlas of Late Middle English, 1350–1450* (Aberdeen: Aberdeen University Press; Edinburgh: Mercat Press, 1986); the revised online edition [*eLALME*, 2013] is available at <www.lel.ed.ac.uk/ihd/elalme/elalme.html>. *A Linguistic Atlas of Early Middle English* can be found at <www.lel.ed.ac.uk/ihd/laeme1/laeme1.html>.

In the decades which have seen such progress in the collection and analysis of the place-names of England—mainly but not solely under the auspices of the EPNS Survey[15]—and in the work on their constituent languages, key critical works have revolutionized the wider interpretation of place-names within the historical disciplines. Publications from the 1960s and later have challenged and sometimes overturned the orthodoxies of the 1924 volume: the accepted chronology for early English name-types which provided the framework for Stenton's chapter on 'The English element' was dealt a near-fatal blow;[16] the premise of large-scale Scandinavian settlement which underlies a number of Eilert Ekwall's points in his chapter on 'The Scandinavian element' is still a matter for debate (although a less fierce one now than a decade or two ago);[17] and the picture sketched in 'The French element', by R. E. Zachrisson, of English towns whose schools, clergy, and administration were dominated by speakers of French even into the fourteenth century

[15] Significant reference publications include, on the national level, E. Ekwall, *The Concise Oxford Dictionary of English Place-Names* (Oxford: Clarendon, 1st edn 1936, 4th edn, 1960); A. D. Mills, *A Dictionary of English Place-Names* (Oxford: Oxford University Press, 1st edn 1991, 2nd edn 1998); V. Watts, *The Cambridge Dictionary of English Place-Names* (Cambridge: Cambridge University Press, 2004). Non-Survey county and regional studies include J. K. Wallenberg, *Kentish Place-Names* (Uppsala: A.-B. Lundequistska Bokhandeln, 1931); J. K. Wallenberg, *The Place-Names of Kent* (Uppsala: Appelberg, 1934); J. Field, *The Place-Names of Greater London* (London: Batsford, 1980); O. J. Padel, *A Popular Dictionary of Cornish Place-Names* (Penzance: Alison Hodge, 1988); R. Coates, *The Place-Names of Hampshire* (London: Batsford, 1989; B. Coplestone-Crow, *Herefordshire Place-Names* (Oxford: BAR, 1989); A. D. Mills, *The Place-Names of the Isle of Wight* (Stamford: Paul Watkins, 1996); A. D. Mills, *A Dictionary of London Place-Names* (Oxford: Oxford University Press, 1st edn 2004, 2nd edn 2010); D. Horovitz, *The Place-Names of Staffordshire* (Brewood: the author, 2005). See also EPNS non-Survey publications: K. Cameron, *A Dictionary of Lincolnshire Place-Names* (Nottingham: English Place-Name Society, 1998); V. Watts, *A Dictionary of County Durham Place-Names* (Nottingham: English Place-Name Society, 2002); B. Cox, *A Dictionary of Leicestershire and Rutland Place-Names* (Nottingham: English Place-Name Society, 2006); D. Whaley, *A Dictionary of Lake District Place-Names* (Nottingham: English Place-Name Society, 2006). A. Mawer, *The Place-Names of Northumberland and Durham* (Cambridge: Cambridge University Press, 1920) and E. Ekwall, *Place-Names of Lancashire* (Manchester: Manchester University Press, 1922) were published before the EPNS was founded, but foreshadowed in their conventions those of the Survey of English Place-Names.

[16] J. McN. Dodgson, 'The significance of the distribution of the English place-name in *-ingas*, *-inga-* in south-east England', *Medieval Archaeology* 10 (1966), 1–29; B. Cox, 'The significance of the distribution of English place-names in *-hām* in the midlands and East Anglia', *Journal of the English Place-Name Society* 5 (1973), 15–73.

[17] A premise famously challenged by Peter Sawyer in his *The Age of the Vikings* (London: Arnold, 1962); see below, pp. 107–11.

has faded.[18] On the other hand, Ekwall's comment in his chapter, 'The Celtic element', that '[t]he view often held that the British population was exterminated or swept away, seems to have lost ground of late years'[19] now seems prescient, even though his seeming acceptance of the idea that the relative paucity of surviving British village-names might be explained by a British preference for uplands and an Anglo-Saxon one for river-valleys and lowlands does not (IPN, p. 32).

Later-twentieth-century landmark scholarship in place-names responded to the shifting perspectives on these central issues. Margaret Gelling, Kenneth Cameron, and Gillian Fellows-Jensen met these challenges to traditional interpretations and accepted, rejected, or modified the conclusions which arose from them. For each of these scholars, new frameworks for interpretation had to be tested against detailed analysis of the evidence of the names, and the resulting publications have become fundamental to subsequent scholarship in these areas, both by place-name specialists and those working in related fields.[20] The late twentieth century also saw Gelling's reassessment of topographical settlement-names (those which define settlements through their landscape surroundings), 'revolutionising [...] our detailed understanding of the words used in [place-names].[21]

[18] C. Clark, 'Towards a reassessment of "Anglo-Norman influence on England place-names"', in P. Sture Ureland and G. Broderick (eds), *Language Contact in the British Isles: Proceedings of the Eighth International Symposium on Language Contact in Europe, Douglas, Isle of Man, 1988* (Tübingen: Niemeyer, 1991), pp. 275–95; C. Clark, 'The myth of "the Anglo-Norman scribe"', in M. Rissanen et al. (eds) *History of Englishes: New Methods and Interpretations in Historical Linguistics* (Berlin: Mouton de Gruyter, 1992), pp. 117–29.

[19] E. Ekwall, 'The Celtic element', IPN, pp. 15–35 (p. 17).

[20] Key works are Gelling's *Signposts to the Past*, 3rd edn (Chichester: Phillimore, 1997); the essays by Cameron collected in *Place-Name Evidence for the Anglo-Saxon Invasion and Scandinavian Settlements* (Nottingham: English Place-Name Society, 1987); and Fellows-Jensen's volumes on *Scandinavian Settlement Names in Yorkshire* (Copenhagen: Akademisk forlag, 1972), *Scandinavian Settlement Names in the East Midlands* (Copenhagen: Akademisk forlag, 1978), *Scandinavian Settlement Names in the North-West* (Copenhagen: C. A. Reitzels forlag,1985). Publication lists for, respectively, Cameron (to 1985) and for Fellows-Jensen (to 2006) can be found in *Leeds Studies in English* 28 (1987), 267–69 and P. Gammeltoft and B. Jørgensen (eds), *Names through the Looking Glass* (Copenhagen: C. A. Reitzels forlag, 2006), pp. 322–50.

[21] Thus the assessment of Padel and Parsons in their preface to *A Commodity of Good Names: Essays in Honour of Margaret Gelling* (Donington: Shaun Tyas), p. viii. The revolution took the form of two related monographs, *Place-Names in the Landscape* (London: Dent, 1984), and *The Landscape of Place-Names* (Donington: Shaun Tyas, 2000).

An overarching reassessment of the state of English place-name studies, and of the effects of the changing landscapes of the disciplines that draw on and contribute to the subject, is therefore due, and it was with this in mind that this volume was first conceived. Some of the contributors to this book were invited to author chapters which, broadly speaking, were modelled on, or written in response to, the contributions to the 1924 volume. Six of the book's twelve chapters, those on the Brittonic, Anglo-Saxon and Scandinavian elements in the English name-stock and those on archaeology and personal names, originated in this way, with each of the six contributors responding differently to his or her 1924 predecessor chapter. It is testament to the scholarship of the *Introduction*'s authors that, despite the intervening years' exponential increase in place-name material and seismic shifts in history and archaeology occasioned by advances in theory and technology, each contributor finds something to admire in the earlier work.

For Oliver Padel (chapter 1), while it is Kenneth Jackson's *Language and History in Early Britain* (1953) which provides the basis for modern scholarship on Brittonic names in England, Ekwall's take on 'The Celtic element' 'remains useful' (p. 1). Many of Ekwall's topics—the extreme difficulty of the evidence, the characteristics of Brittonic names in England, the varying distribution over the country of particular types of Brittonic name—are revisited by Padel, with the benefit of nearly ninety years of accrued scholarship. Work in the intervening years has established and refined a chronology of linguistic change for the Brittonic languages (albeit one which should be used cautiously), and provided surveys of other (once-)Brittonic areas, supplying comparanda which may suggest, strengthen, or cast doubt on Brittonic derivations for English names. Many of Ekwall's suggestions for further research—systematic work on *w(e)alh* and *Brettas*, for example[22]—have been taken

[22] *W(e)alh* alone has generated a considerable body of scholarship. The following is only a sample: J. R. R. Tolkien, 'English and Welsh', in *Angles and Britons* (Cardiff: University of Wales Press, 1963), pp. 1–41; M. L. Faull, 'The semantic development of Old English *wealh*', *Leeds Studies in English*, n. s., 8 (1975), 20–44; K. Cameron, 'The meaning and significance of Old English *walh* in English place-names', *Journal of the English Place-Name Society* 12 (1979–80), 1–53; J. Insley, 'The continental evidence: OHG *wal(a)h*, OSax *walh*', *Journal of the English Place-Name Society* 12 (1979–80), 50–53; M. Todd, 'The archaeological significance of place-names in *walh*', *Journal of the English Place-Name Society* 12 (1979–80), 47–50; S. Draper, 'Old English *Wīc* and *Walh*: Britons and Saxons in Post-Roman Wiltshire', *Landscape History* 24 (2002), 27–43; J. Insley, 'Wealh', *Reallexicon der Germanischen Altertumskunde* 33 (2006), 319–22; M. Blake, '*W(e)alh tūn*: balancing the probabilities', in R. Jones and S. Semple (eds), *Sense of Place in Anglo-Saxon England* (Donington: Shaun Tyas, 2012), pp. 284–300.

up, often in discussions of how the place-name evidence might contribute to the historical debates surrounding the Anglo-Saxon settlement of the fifth to seventh centuries and its effects on the resident British-speaking population. Very often this research has demonstrated quite how intractable some of this evidence can be. The example of *eccles* serves to illustrate. In 1924, Ekwall was able to state that the majority of *Eccles*-names are 'derived from a Brit. form of Lat. *ecclesia*' (IPN, p. 23). In 2013 Padel observes, 'it is still uncertain which language the *Eccles*-names were originally given in, let alone their significance' (pp. 24–25). The survival and status of British speakers, after the coming of the Anglo-Saxons, is for many likely to remain 'the greatest problem in the history of England' (p. 1) for the foreseeable future, despite the new genetic evidence, once seen as a potential 'magic bullet' but which at present cannot offer definitive answers.

David Parsons's essay on 'place-names and early English society' (chapter 2) is more explicitly a response to Sir Frank Stenton's 1924 chapter. This chapter, though bearing a very general title, 'The English element', was intended to give 'an indication of the way in which the evidence supplied by place-names can be brought to bear upon the study of Early English society' (IPN, p. 36). Research in place-names, history, and archaeology over the course of the twentieth century has overturned some of the fundamental assumptions upon which Stenton based his account of the early Anglo-Saxon period: the chronology of the earliest names which saw in *-ingas* place-names derived from folk-names (Reading, Woking and so on) groups of migration-period settlers; the early origins of the English village; the early and lord-less 'communal' origins of the Charltons which pepper the map of England; the belief that most of the place-names which defined settlement with reference to landscape were of little interest. With so many of these beliefs rejected by more recent work, it would be easy to dismiss altogether Stenton's analysis of the historic import of Anglo-Saxon place-names. He was, however, the twentieth century's pre-eminent Anglo-Saxon documentary historian, and Parsons shows that, where he invoked contextual detail in support of his interpretations of particular name-types, it is worth returning to them, as they may usefully refine more recent, now generally accepted, readings. The lesson conveyed by Stenton's chapter and what might usefully be gleaned from its conclusions, nearly ninety years on, is of the importance of context – onomastic, linguistic, documentary, archaeological, topographical. Parsons's methodological thrust is that the interrogation of place-names as a source for history (of any place and period) is undertaken most profitably with reference to all available contextual material. His examples, from the late Anglo-Saxon period, illustrate its application, and show how combining different sorts of evidence may illuminate corners of history left dark by a narrow disciplinary approach, or provide new perspectives on events which are prominent in the documentary record and seemingly already well understood.

Ekwall's second contribution to IPN, on the 'Scandinavian element', is at thirty-seven pages considerably longer than his chapter on Celtic names. This reflects both the greater amount of scholarship available in 1924 on Scandinavian place-names, in the homelands and in England, and the particular interest of the Vikings, as great in the early twentieth century as in the early twenty-first. This emphasis is matched here: the Scandinavian 'element' has proven mitotic, generating two chapters in this volume (and lengthy comment in a number of the others): one on the Scandinavian background as well as one on Scandinavian place-names in England. The question of how place-names in the Scandinavian homelands might throw light upon Scandinavian names in England was not systematically treated by Ekwall, although comments on the matter are scattered throughout his chapter. Here, a more methodical treatment is offered by Gillian Fellows-Jensen, who gives an overview of the early evidence for Danish place-names of the Viking Age and earlier, before comparing the early-recorded name-types with Scandinavian place-names in England. Some of these name-types are shared (those in *-bý* and *-þorp*, and with elements denoting clearings), some are not (either because they fell out of use before the Viking Age or had meanings inappropriate to an Anglo-Scandinavian context), and some are complicated by the existence of Old English cognates (*-tūn*; the same might be said of *-þorp*). Fellows-Jensen demonstrates how consideration of the Scandinavian background—again, the importance of context—contributes to assessments of the chronology and significance of names in England.

Much of Ekwall's analysis of Scandinavian place-names was intended to elucidate their significance as a source for settlement history. Matthew Townend seeks to shift the focus somewhat from this question, which has remained at the centre of Scandinavian place-name scholarship since 1924 (and even earlier). While Townend adds his voice to those who affirm that the place-name evidence points to significant numbers of Scandinavian settlers in England, he also suggests that the late-twentieth-century's heated debate on scale of settlement has checked other, equally important approaches to the material, and has in fact limited the range of material examined. Social history has for decades trumped linguistic history, and attention has been directed towards settlement-names at the expense of topographical names, hydronyms, minor names, and street-names, although field-names have, particularly in recent years, proven fertile ground for analysis (p. 123, n. 75). Work in these less cultivated fields is, of course, likely to bear fruit to feed the settlement debate: the full onomastic context is necessary to interpret securely the evidence of the settlement-names.

The authorship of two chapters in the *Introduction*—and the ease with both Celtic and Germanic languages demonstrated therein—reflects Ekwall's titanic status within place-name studies. Stenton too wielded his pen a second time, writing a chapter on personal names which John Insley regards as having 'stood the test of time very well' (p. 209). Insley, enjoying the benefit of modern editions and extensive published research on both English and Continental names, expands on and refines many of Stenton's points, rather than refuting them. In the first section of his chapter, Stenton commented briefly on the Germanic tradition from which Old English personal names derived and gave a concise account of the structure of mono- and dithematic names (names with one or two 'themes', or elements). He divided the former into two categories: 'descriptive' names (adjectives, animal-names, indications of ethnicity); and short forms of dithematic names – one of a name's two elements, with or without a suffix (Brūn or Brȳni for Brūnheard, for example), or a shortened form which incorporated the first element and the beginning of the second (Tubba for Tūnbeald), both types potentially affected by assimilation or gemination. Insley provides a much fuller account of the ways in which the Germanic tradition of dithematic names worked, and situates it within the wider Indo-European context. He then gives details of the main elements found in the Old English dithematic tradition, providing an extensive corpus of personal name elements, with protothemes divided into semantic categories. Old English monothematic names are categorized in eighteen sub-groups, which is perhaps an alternative response to what led Stenton to state, '[i]t is difficult to bring [shortened names] under any express rule of general validity' (IPN, p. 170).

That is not to say that there are no significant differences in approach or opinion to be found. Stenton chose to emphasize, for example, that in the Old English tradition from earliest times the sense of the elements in dithematic names was, at the point at which they were combined to form a name, largely irrelevant. For Insley, on the other hand, semantic motivation is one of the characteristics of the 'primary' dithematic tradition. He sees lack of semantic connection, such as that resulting from the use of alliteration or patterns of elements to reflect a particular lineage, as secondary, if widespread. Stenton's evident scepticism about the existence of lall-names (name-forms originating in the phonologically simplifying speech of children; IPN, p. 174) is not shared by Insley.

In his conclusion, Stenton claimed that '[a]t the present time it is difficult to say anything in general terms about the history of English personal nomenclature' (IPN, p. 188). He had though, in the preceding pages, said much on this subject. He outlined an early stratum of English naming which shared much with the Germanic tradition, followed by gradual divergence from Continental practice (certain elements falling out of use, others coming into use). He made clear the vigour of a specifically Anglo-Scandinavian tradition in those parts of the country most affected by the incursions of the Viking Age, and illustrated the stereotyped aristocratic tradition of late Anglo-Saxon England, marked by the repeated use of a very small number of elements. His source-critical sketch has endured. To it, Insley adds not just the level of detail which makes this new chapter an invaluable work of reference, but also a more specifically toponymic examination: his analysis of the personal names appearing in habitative names in *-hām*, *-ingas*, *-tūn*, and *-bý* has been made possible by the existence of near-nationwide EPNS Survey coverage.

Much is shared between the paired chapters discussed above: the authors working in 1924 sought to answer the same or similar questions, with recognizable or related methodologies, to those working in 2013 – but with far fewer resources. This cannot precisely be said of the chapters on archaeology and linguistics. Here, the academic disciplines in question were at an early stage of development in the early twentieth century, and the work of the last ninety years has resulted in significant conceptual shifts in what it is to 'do' archaeology or linguistics.

In 1924, the discipline of medieval archaeology barely existed, and for this reason the gulf between O. G. S. Crawford's chapter and that of Richard Jones yawns wide. Crawford was clear that archaeologists could help place-name scholars in defining more closely the meaning of particular elements, and the corollary, that place-names may signal much of interest to archaeologists, is implicit. However, Crawford had something quite specific in mind – '"archaeological" elements', as he calls them, those which refer to pre-historic features in the landscape. The interest, in 1924, was not primarily in the period in which the names had their origin. Jones's is a world much changed – by the advent of medieval archaeology as a discipline in its own right, by the wholesale reassessment, in the 1960s and 70s, of village origins, and by the changes in theoretical perspective that have marked the subsequent decades. During this time, the bringing together of archaeological and place-name evidence has led to radical shifts in the interpretation of particular name-types: the 1960s saw the eruption of the *-ingas* debate. It has, however, also provided support for long-held beliefs: the test-pitting of more recent times seems to confirm what written record and distribution suggest, that most settlements bearing names in *-hām* have considerably earlier origins than those with names in *-tūn*. Place-names have contributed, and continue to contribute, to the question of village formation, and they are central to discussions of that part of individual or group identity which has come to be known as 'sense of place'. For Jones, as for Parsons, it is multidisciplinary approaches which hold the most promise – the number of studies listed on pp. 188–91 suggests that the '[c]alls from the late 1950s for fuller integration of historical, archaeological and place-name evidence' (p. 184) are at last being answered by scholars from all these disciplines, with exciting results.

The 1924 chapter by Henry Cecil Wyld (with Mary Sergeantson), 'Place-names and English linguistic studies', has as its subject English historical dialectology, now a small but vigorous sub-discipline of modern 'English linguistic studies'. He had a specific aim: 'to urge that information of an important kind may be derived from an investigation of the distinctive dialect features displayed by the forms of [place-names] recorded during the M[iddle] E[nglish] period or earlier' (IPN, p. 134). England's place-names provide a corpus of linguistic material whose geographical provenance is precise and indisputable, though complicated by the varying provenance of the documents in which the names are recorded. Old and Middle English texts, particularly literary texts, are rarely localizable to the same extent. How best, then, should philologists exploit the potential of the 'rich, well-authenticated material' (IPN, p. 142) which the new Survey promised to deliver, for a 'line of research [...] as yet in its infancy' (IPN, p. 140)?[23] Here was an opportunity to set out a manifesto, to offer guidelines for the use of place-name evidence in

[23] For work on Middle English dialectology in the decade preceding the publication of IPN, see G. Kristensson, *A Survey of Middle English Dialects 1290–1350:* I *The Six Northern Counties and Lincolnshire* (Lund: C. W. K. Gleerup, 1967), p. x. Place-names had of course been used before in historical dialectology, notably by Ekwall in his *Contributions to the History of Old English Dialects* (Lund: C. W. K. Gleerup, 1917).

historical-dialectological research. For Wyld, the broader documentary and linguistic contexts were crucial; he rightly emphasized that individual place-name forms are likely to depend upon the status of the text, local or national, in which they are found, and that place-name forms should be studied in conjunction with other textual evidence of relevant (and secure) provenance. His chapter offers a kind of checklist of considerations for the scholar, considerations that remain valid, and are in fact fundamental to modern dialectological study: that there are no firm dialect boundaries; that the language variety of any one place will combine dialectal features associated with a number of varieties (i.e. individual isoglosses do not correspond with broad dialect areas, but a preponderance of shared isoglosses distinguishes a dialect area); that attention should be paid to proportions of particular forms used, rather than individual instances; that copying introduces different dialectal features, and may eliminate original 'local' characteristics.

Wyld's envisaged application of his guidelines and considerations was, though, somewhat limited. He provided a set of questions, 'which we desire to see answered in respect of every area' (IPN, p. 136), whose answers would form the basis of 'a detailed survey of the dialect characters of M[iddle] E[nglish], which should show the typical grouping of these, county by county, and an even minuter analysis of the linguistic features within the larger areas' (IPN, p. 133). While this was an enormously practical way to encourage the filling of the perceived gap, Wyld's questions were solely concerned with the realization of Old English vowels in Old and Middle English: lexis, morphology and syntax, along with consonants, went unmentioned. It is immediately obvious that place-name evidence can contribute to discussion of variation in lexis, rather less so (though nonetheless true) that it can also contribute to discussion of morphological and syntactical variation. Wyld's focus was consistent with the concerns of historical dialectology at the time, and subsequent studies which privilege place-name evidence, such as those by Sundby and Kristensson, have also tended to focus on phonology.[24] Kristensson's volumes offer in fact just the kind of detailed

[24] Sundby and Kristensson both use name-material from securely provenanced Middle English texts: Sundby treats vowels in detail and consonants briefly and partially, Kristensson offer comprehensive coverage of both vowels and consonants. B. Sundby, *Studies in the Middle English Dialect Material of the Worcestershire Records* (Bergen and Oslo: Norwegian Universities Press, 1963); G. Kristensson, *A Survey of Middle English Dialects 1290–1350*, 5 vols (Lund: C. W. K. Gleerup, 1967; Lund University Press, 1987–2002).

analysis desired by Wyld: his distribution maps show phonological variation between and within counties across England. Other forms of variation than phonological tend to be treated in works not explicitly or only concerned with dialect. Notes on the distribution of a wider range of linguistic features can be found in the Survey volumes and in other place-name dictionaries; comments on the geographical distribution of particular elements form part of those elements' entries in Hugh Smith's two-volume *English Place-Name Elements* (1956) [EPNE], and the ongoing *Vocabulary of English Place-Names* (1997–) [VEPN].[25] Work on Scandinavian linguistic influence in northern and eastern areas of the country naturally contributes to the study of the dialects of those areas. Margaret Gelling's work on topographical settlement names has highlighted the restricted distribution of certain elements—sometimes the result of variations in landscape rather than language—and the complementary distribution of particular elements within the same semantic field.

In 2013 we have an extraordinarily wide range of material to bring to bear on the matter. With the work of LALME and LAEME (see note 14 above), we have the comparative evidence of a wide range of Middle English texts, each dated and located and assigned a 'linguistic profile'. Peter Kitson continues to mine the corpus of Anglo-Saxon charter boundaries, whose landscape descriptors complement, indeed meld into, place-name evidence, producing information on distinctive phonological, lexical, and syntactical features.[26] Much has been done and much is in progress, and the possibilities for further research are expanding: advances in technology are aiding the searching and comparison of disparate records, not only making ever more material freely available,

[25] A. H. Smith, *English Place-Name Elements*, English Place-Name Society 25–26 (Cambridge: Cambridge University Press, 1956); D. Parsons and T. Styles with C. Hough, *The Vocabulary of English Place-Names* I *(Á–Box)* (Nottingham: Centre for English Name-Studies, 1997); D. N. Parsons and T. Styles, *The Vocabulary of English Place-Names* II *(Brace–Cæster)* (Nottingham: Centre for English Name-Studies, 2000); D. N. Parsons, *The Vocabulary of English Place-Names* III *(Ceafor–Cock-pit)* (Nottingham: English Place-Name Society, 2004).

[26] P. R. Kitson, 'The nature of Old English dialect distributions, mainly as exhibited in charter boundaries', in J. Fisiak (ed.), *Medieval Dialectology* (Berlin and New York: Mouton de Gruyter, 1995), pp. 43–135; Kitson, 'Quantifying qualifiers in Anglo-Saxon charter boundaries', *Folia Linguistica Historica* 14 (1993), 29–82 ; Kitson, *A Guide to Anglo-Saxon Charter Boundaries* (Nottingham: English Place-Name Society, forthcoming).

but—crucially—more functionally accessible.[27] Information to provide the contextual support so important to Wyld for the dialectological analysis of place-names is now abundant and relatively easy of access.

The point underlying Wyld's conviction that place-name material can contribute much to the study of historical phonology is that, '[a]part from occasional irregular changes introduced by analogy or popular etymology, it may be said that the forms of English p.n. have a normal, and regular phonetic development just as the other words have' (IPN, p. 133). In other words, place-names are subject to the same set of sound changes as ordinary vocabulary items. The twenty-first-century perspective would modify this somewhat: names do not necessarily behave in precisely the same way as ordinary words, and their value as evidence for linguistic change has to be assessed with care and with reference to their special status.[28] It is this special status—the particular properties of place-names (and more generally names of all kinds)—which is the primary subject of Richard Coates's chapter, 'Place-names and linguistics'. After briefly considering the (relatively well understood) role of place-names within historical linguistics, Coates considers in more detail a range of issues which arise when 'interrogating place-name data in ways shaped by linguistics' (p.137), the following amongst them: sense vs. etymological understanding; etymology (the linguistic origin and constituent elements of a name) vs. motivation (why those elements were used); and the process by which a place gets its name, either through the evolution of a descriptive phrase or through an act of deliberate naming. Place-name study, at least historically and as practised within Britain, has rarely considered these matters, but their potential importance is clear. The very different implications of evolved vs. bestowed names, for example, are explored by Townend in relation to the question of Scandinavian settlement (pp. 111–13), by Cullen in relation to recurrent names such as Acton (pp. 168–69), and are implicit in Jones's interpretation of the Southwell estate-names (pp. 202–05).

While Coates's chapter does not cover precisely the same ground as Wyld's it does consider the role of place-names within historical linguistics (pp. 130–37), and ponders questions fundamental to that role. There are chapters though, in the present volume, that lack entirely a

[27] See, for instance, Manuscripts Online, <www.manuscriptsonline.org> (accessed July 2013), which has pulled together primary and secondary resources for the period 1000 to 1500 and created structured indices for each source, so that integrated searches across the entire collection are possible with the minimum of technological know-how.

[28] See pp. 130–34.

1924 precursor. Paul Cullen's assessment of 'English place-names and landscape terminology' is one of them. Inevitably, the focus of Cullen's chapter is upon the ground-breaking work of Margaret Gelling, whose work on topographical settlement-names revealed 'hitherto unsuspected depths of subtlety and significance' in the precise topographical naming-system of the Anglo-Saxons,[29] and led to a reassessment of their date—potentially very early—and their origins and usage – quasi-habitative, denoting from the start settlements as well as landscape features. Here we are a world away from the 1924 volume, whose contributors largely overlooked the potential of topographical names (see below, pp. 161–63). Gelling has established their value in the intervening years beyond any doubt, but as Cullen makes clear much remains to be done: later and minor topographical names remain underexploited; the gaps in Gelling's otherwise nationwide system—'from Kent to Northumberland and from the east coast to Offa's Dyke'[30]—deserve a closer look; and the very spread of the system raises questions about chronology and usage which remain unanswered.

A second chapter lacking a predecessor is that by Carole Hough, on 'Women in place-names'. While the 1924 volume had no such chapter, one of its editors had a marked interest in this topic. Stenton's 1942 presidential address to the Royal Historical Society was on 'The historical bearing of place-name studies: the place of women in Anglo-Saxon society',[31] and a number of the questions addressed therein are addressed also by Hough, both here and in her earlier work on the subject.[32] Hough, like Stenton, interrogates place-names as evidence of the position of women in pre-Conquest England supplementary to that

[29] Gelling and Cole, *Landscape of Place-Names*, p. xiii.

[30] Gelling and Cole, *Landscape of Place-Names*, p. xv. For caveats regarding Gelling's purportedly early, national system, see below, pp. 174–78.

[31] F. M. Stenton, 'The historical bearing of place-name studies: the place of women in Anglo-Saxon society', *Transactions of the Royal Historical Society*, 4th series 25 (1943), 1–13.

[32] See particularly C. Hough, 'Women in English place-names', in C. Hough and K. A. Lowe (eds), *'Lastworda Betst': Essays in Memory of Christine E. Fell with her Unpublished Writings* (Donington: Shaun Tyas, 2002), pp. 41–106, which presents an extremely useful county-by-county corpus for feminine personal names in English place-names, with indices of these names and of the second elements they combine with. The corpus is preceded by a clear assessment of the methodological challenges of identifying women's names in place-names and a discussion of their possible significance. Additions to the corpus are listed below, p. 259; see also J. Jesch, 'Scandinavian women's names in English place-names', in Padel and Parsons (eds), *A Commodity of Good Names*, pp. 154–62.

provided by the Anglo-Saxon legal and diplomatic record. Laws are fragmentary and ambiguous, and charters 'have little to tell about the inheritance of unprivileged land'[33] – 'unprivileged' land which bore names no less than did the great estates of the period. Both Stenton and Hough emphasize the ambiguity of the evidence provided by place-names which incorporate a woman's name—what kind of association with the named place might this imply?—but both agree it points to prominent roles for Anglo-Saxon women throughout society. While Stenton was concerned, here as elsewhere, primarily with habitative major names, Hough demonstrates the value of topographical names, major and minor, for this matter.

Hough's work also shows very clearly how the increasing mass of evidence resulting from the work of the EPNS Survey sheds new light on enduring questions. Quantitative analysis and work on varying distributions of the place-names in question is possible now, but was not for Stenton in 1924. Hough's chapter also reflects the increasing weight given over to minor and field-names in the Survey, and shows the kinds of analysis, social and linguistic, that this facilitates.

Three further chapters without 1924 precursors extend the remit of this volume even further beyond that of the *Introduction*: they are contributions on the English (or Scots) place-names of England's immediate neighbours Wales, Scotland, and Ireland (both sides of the present-day border). Hywel Wyn Owen, Thomas Clancy, and Kay Muhr provide surveys of the influence of the English language—and by extension English power and politics—on the place-nomenclature of the adjacent regions.[34]

While the work of the EPNS Survey is limited to the historical counties of England, 'all workers in the field are aware that distribution-maps of English names are misleading if they stop at the modern [Anglo-Scottish] Border'.[35] This statement applies equally well to England's border with Wales – parts of Shropshire are, from the perspective of language history, 'Welsher' than parts of Wales. Our national borders are not those of earlier periods, and in any case languages rarely respect political boundaries. The *bý*-names of Dumfriesshire, for example, are

[33] Stenton, 'The historical bearing', p. 2.

[34] Clancy's focus is on the south-west of Scotland, but his analysis has the main general aim of illustrating 'a number of features of the [linguistic] strata and contexts of varieties of English in Scottish toponymy' (p. 291).

[35] The comment is Padel's (p. 5).

part of a group which stretches north from northern Cumberland, and analysis which treats only the 'English' or the 'Scottish' names in this group is partial. The inclusion of these 'new' chapters not only underlines the point that borders move and reflect non-linguistic aspects of social organization, it also demonstrates that the evidence of English language-origin place-names beyond England's borders can further our understanding of English place-names in general, as well as being of intrinsic interest. Thomas Clancy is explicit in his aim to 'give insight into the potential advantages of cross-border comparative work' and to demonstrate how investigation of the use of particular English name-elements in south-western Scotland 'can inform and inflect our understanding of their usage in Scotland as a whole, and also in England' (p. 299). His analysis of Preston-, Monkton-, and Bishopton-names, for example, shows how their use in south-western Scotland might affect their interpretation in other areas. It also serves to remind us that names 'should be treated individually and circumspectly' (p. 300), even when they appear to belong to a particular type. The message is methodological, as much as historical-linguistic.

The chapters on Ireland and Wales by Muhr and Owen provide surveys of the English-language and anglicized material, facilitating the kind of cross-border comparison advocated by Clancy. In Ireland, as in south-western Scotland, centuries of varying and intermittent contact with English have resulted in a linguistic admixture of particular complexity. Muhr's essay illustrates the effects on Ireland's essentially Gaelic place-nomenclature of Scandinavian activity, of Anglo-Norman colonization, of Elizabethan conquest and Plantation, and of the complex Anglo-Irish relationship of the subsequent centuries, and shows how the English influence can be teased out only through a detailed knowledge of the tortuous routes travelled by very many individual names.[36] Owen's survey is based upon the 24% of places treated in DPNW which have English, Scandinavian, or anglicized names. The chapter discusses their characteristics, distribution, phonological transformations, and relations to Welsh names. It updates the work of B. G. Charles and Gwynedd Pierce on the non-Welsh language element in Welsh place-names,[37] and provides the first extended discussion of Scandinavian place-names in

[36] The final two examples cited by Muhr on pp. 396–97 give a good idea of just how tortuous those routes might have been.

[37] See p. 321, nn. 1–3.

Wales since that in Loyn's 1976 Dorothea Coke lecture, *The Vikings in Wales*.[38]

While some of the chapters herein lack a predecessor in the 1924 volume, conversely some of the chapters from the 1924 volume lack a successor. Those by Zachrisson and Tait have no exact—or even approximate—equivalent in this book, and both are concerned with the influence of the Normans upon England's place-name stock.[39] The present volume's principal focus upon the major names of England's pre-Conquest period has resulted in the Norman influence on its name-stock being treated only in passing. In fact, it receives more treatment in the chapters on place-names in areas outside England, and in particular in Ireland, where the English contribution to the place-name stock was entirely a post-Conquest phenomenon (see Muhr, below, pp. 356–60). Nevertheless, outlines of Zachrisson's and Tait's chapters are given here, with details of major subsequent work in the areas and indications of future lines of research.

Zachrisson's contribution to IPN, 'The French element', drew upon his University of Lund thesis, published in 1909 as *A Contribution to the Study of Anglo-Norman Influence on English Place-Names*.[40] Zachrisson treats sparingly the few settlement-names given in French (largely to strongholds and monasteries which spawned villages), and focuses instead upon phonological changes to existing place-names, purportedly 'the chief result [...] of the Norman influence' (IPN, p. 94). The changes discussed at some length in the 1924 chapter were:

1. the substitution of /ʦ/ (> /s/) for /ʧ/, invoked particularly as an explanation of certain pronunciations of modern forms of names in OE *cæster* (e.g. Worcester);
2. the simplification of initial consonant clusters, either through loss (e.g. /sn/ > /n/ in Nottingham) or through insertion of an epenthetic vowel (e.g. /kn/ > /kæn/ in Cannock);
3. the substitution of /ʤ/ for /j/ (e.g. Jarrow (Du), for OE *Gyrwe*);
4. the substitution of <au> for <a> (and corresponding diphthong-ization) before a nasal (e.g. Staunton for Stanton);

[38] H. Loyn, *The Vikings in Wales* (London: Viking Society for Northern Research, 1976), pp. 8–11. See also M. Redknap, *Vikings in Wales: An Archaeological Quest* (Cardiff: National Museums and Galleries of Wales, 2000), pp. 19–22.

[39] R. E. Zachrisson, 'The French element', in IPN, pp. 93–114; J. Tait, 'The feudal element', in IPN, pp. 115–32.

[40] R. E. Zachrisson, *A Contribution to the Study of Anglo-Norman Influence on English Place-Names* (Lund: University of Lund, 1909).

5. the interchange of /l/ /n/ /r/ in cases of dissimilation or assimilation (Salisbury, earlier *Sares-*);
6. difficulties in the pronunciation of /θ/ and /ð/ which led in certain contexts to their replacement by /t/ and /d/ (e.g. Turnworth for *Thorn-*), or to loss.

The pervasive influence suggested by Zachrisson was attributed to extensive and long-lasting use of French as one of England's conversational languages, and to its key position as the language of instruction and administration for centuries (IPN, pp. 93, 96),[41] and was—as characterized by Cecily Clark—based on the 'assumption of an enduring inability [of these Anglo-Norman speakers] to get their tongues round English place-names'.[42] This theory of 'Anglo-Norman influence', as outlined by Zachrisson, was—and is—regularly invoked to explain un-English-looking forms or developments of names.[43] Zachrisson's approach was comprehensively challenged by Clark, who pointed out that the evidence suggests (1) that Anglo-French pronunciation was influenced by English, rather than the other way around, (2) that the use of French as a vernacular was short-lived, and (3) that there was very little French lexical influence on post-Conquest place-names, even in medieval street-names (excepting the use of common vocabulary absorbed into English).[44] Many of the 'Anglo-Norman' name-forms do not represent a change in pronunciation, but reflect the Latin documentary context of the form: the use of <t> and <d> for /θ/ and /ð/, for example, cannot be taken to reflect difficulty in pronouncing dental spirants, only a particular set of spelling conventions associated with Latin text. Where there *are* permanent phonological developments, Clark suggested that many of these should be attributed not to external influence, but to the 'unchecked operation of general native tendencies' in name-material, which tends to develop more freely than does ordinary

[41] It should be noted that Zachrisson himself added the cautionary observation that '[i]t is sometimes extremely difficult to tell if the alterations in a name are due to French or dialectal English sound-change' (IPN, p. 98).

[42] C. Clark, 'Towards a reassessment of "Anglo-Norman influence on England place-names"', in P. Sture Ureland and G. Broderick (eds), *Language Contact in the British Isles: Proceedings of the Eighth International Symposium on Language Contact in Europe, Douglas, Isle of Man, 1988* (Tübingen: Niemeyer, 1991), pp. 275–95 (p. 279).

[43] See the comments cited in C. Clark, 'The myth of "the Anglo-Norman scribe"', in M. Rissanen et al. (eds) *History of Englishes: New Methods and Interpretations in Historical Linguistics* (Berlin: Mouton de Gruyter, 1992), pp. 117–29 (p. 117).

[44] Clark, 'Towards a reassessment'; see also Clark, 'The myth of "the Anglo-Norman scribe"'.

vocabulary: in short she invoked 'onomastic sound-change'—an alien concept in 1924—as a more satisfactory explanation.[45]

While certain of Zachrisson's specific points of Anglo-Norman phonological influence have been examined in detail and systematically refuted,[46] in general they are still cited to explain sound changes found in place-names, and Clark's conclusions remain under-investigated by place-name scholars. In the Introduction to EPNS Sa **1**, Margaret Gelling refers to the 'time-honoured practice, common throughout EPNS publications' (EPNS Sa **1**, p. xviii) of ascribing changes in name-forms to Anglo-Norman pronunciation. Writing in 1990, she gave notice of the 'formidable challenge' posed by Clark's forthcoming 'Reassessment', and seemed to indicate that she wished to reconsider her frequent recourse to Norman French pronunciation as a factor in the development of name-forms. However, her statement from the first edition of *Signposts to the Past* (1978), that the Normans 'brought about violent changes by their efforts to render English names pronounceable', stands unrevised in the 1997 third edition.[47] Kenneth Cameron, in *English Place-Names*, listed in some detail Zachrisson's points of influence, but preceded this with a strong caveat: 'it must be clearly understood that some are now much better explained as being sporadic developments due to local English conditions'.[48] The matter is a knotty one, but evidence for the changes listed in the 1924 chapter, as fleshed out in Zachrisson's

[45] Clark, 'Towards a reassessment', p. 287. See also p. xxvii above and Coates, pp. 130–34.

[46] To take one example, the *æðel/ægel/ail* variation found in *Æthel-* personal names was explained by Zachrisson as 'Norman substitution of *ægel*, *ail* for *æðel*' (IPN, p. 111; see also *Anglo-Norman Influence*, pp. 100–07, O. von Feilitzen, *The Pre-Conquest Personal Names of Domesday Book* (Uppsala: Almqvist and Wiksell, 1937), pp. 105–06, and A, Campbell, *Old English Grammar* (Oxford: Clarendon, 1959), pp. 195, n. 5). Ekwall, noting that /ð/ > /j/ or Ø, is found also in Danish, saw it as a native English sound-change, possibly associated with hypocorism (*Early London Personal Names* (Lund: C. W. K. Gleerup, 1947), p. 197). Fran Colman defined the context of the change as 'between two vowels, second one of which is followed by /l/', and independent of hypocorism ('The name-element *Æðel-* and related problems', *Notes and Queries*, n.s. 28 (1981), 295–301, (p. 297)). Colman's take on evidence from moneyers' names on late Anglo-Saxon coins was further refined by Veronica Smart, who pointed to administrative origins for the abrupt shift to <ÆGEL> *c.* 1023 ('Variation between *ÆTHEL-* and *ÆGEL-* as a name-element on coins', *Nomina* 7 (1983), 91–96).

[47] M. Gelling, *Signposts to the Past*, 3rd edn (Chichester: Phillimore, 1997), p. 240. The 'Addenda to chapter nine: Scandinavian and French place-names' (pp. 261–63) adds nothing to her discussion of French names.

[48] K. Cameron, *English Place Names*, new edn (London: Batsford, 1996), pp. 91–93 (p. 91).

1909 thesis, is very uneven, and the intervening century has provided a wealth of information with which to reconsider his hypotheses, even if that reconsideration results not in conclusions but in an appreciation of the complexity of the matter.

French settlement-names, largely untouched by Zachrisson, were treated in James Tait's contribution, 'The feudal element', a title to balk at but glossed as 'the Norman or Anglo-Norman additions to our place-nomenclature which arose out of, or at least reflect, the manorial system and military arrangements based upon land' (IPN, p. 115), or as Gelling put it, 'the effect on place-names of the advent of a foreign aristocracy unaccompanied by a body of peasant settlers'.[49] Tait discussed the names of settlements, castles and monasteries, place-names with personal names introduced to England after the Conquest, and names with manorial affixes (appended Norman family- and personal names). His enumeration of the relevant names was sound, but can be supplemented by the French names listed in Survey volumes from EPNS Nth (1933) on,[50] and by the county-by-county list of place-names with manorial affixes in Cameron's *English Place Names*.[51] Some of Tait's comments on the French settlement names appear rather dated. Few scholars today would interpret the preponderance of *bel-* and *beau-* names as evidence of the Normans' 'feeling for natural beauty' (IPN, p. 115)[52] – compare Gelling's reading of them as 'stereotyped', 'deliberate creations of the builders of the castle or manor house [rather than] spontaneous descriptions of the site which arose in local speech'.[53] Most of his chapter, though, is given over to the affixes which appeared (mostly) between the thirteenth and fifteenth centuries. These are helpfully categorized, and Tait's examination of their form, characteristics, and distribution remained the most extensive and authoritative on the subject throughout the twentieth century. Only very recently have these names been reviewed with anything like the same level of detail. Richard Jones's 2012 essay on manorial affixes discusses their numbers and distribution, chronology and survival, function and purpose, offering both general reasons for their use (a means for distant,

[49] Gelling, *Signposts to the Past*, p. 236.

[50] French settlement-names extracted from Survey volumes which appeared between 1933 to 1976 are listed in Gelling, *Signposts*, pp. 236–37.

[51] Cameron, *English Place Names*, pp. 112–13.

[52] Zachrisson too saw the *Beau-*, *Bel*-names as indicating the Norman 'taste for places with beautiful surroundings' (IPN, p. 93).

[53] *Signposts to the Past*, p. 237. Gelling goes as far as to characterize some of these names as 'boastful' (p. 238).

central-government administrators of differentiating places with common names) and, through detailed case study, more specific ones (a reflection of seigneurial investment and intervention in the fabric of certain villages).[54] Jones's case studies in particular illustrate the potential of combining prosopographical and archaeological approaches to determine the range of reasons why places gained and retained—or lost—manorial affixes. Context and interdisciplinarity are (again) key here.

By way of working towards a conclusion, I turn to the very first chapter in the *Introduction*, on the methodology which underlies its chapters and the Survey volumes which were to come.[55] The methods W. J. Sedgefield outlined therein form the basis of place-name scholarship as much today as in 1924: the arrangement of place-names within their parishes, with their early forms arranged broadly chronologically but grouped according to spelling, followed by linguistic analysis undertaken with an eye to the history and topography of the area. Sedgefield's insistence on the fundamental importance of a run of early spellings, interpreted within the historical-phonological framework established for the development of English and the other constituent languages of England's place-nomenclature, is a given for any serious present-day student of place-names. His non-technical descriptions of sound-changes such as assimilation, consonant insertion, and lengthening and shortening of vowels illustrate effectively to non-specialists the care and phonological expertise necessary 'to guide the investigator in his efforts to establish the original form of a place-name' (IPN, p. 9), and thence—where possible—to its linguistic origins and its meaning at the point it came into existence. This most basic of tenets pertaining to place-name study bears repeating: it is not uncommon to find non-specialists disregarding it, and instead suggesting interpretations for place-names which are not supported by the early spelling evidence, but which fit—or are believed to fit—a particular model of settlement history favoured by the interpreter.[56]

Another of Sedgefield's givens, that '[w]e must bring to bear upon [an individual name] the evidence of all names containing the same or similar elements' (IPN, p. 2), chimes with the emphasis on context which is

[54] R. Jones, 'Thinking through the manorial affix', in R. Silvester and S. Turner (eds), *Life in Medieval Landscapes: People and Places in Medieval England* (Oxford: Oxbow Books, 2012), pp. 251–67.

[55] W. J. Sedgefield, 'Methods of place-name study', IPN, pp. 1–14.

[56] See, for example, the letters in *Current Archaeology* 260 (p. 5), 263 (p. 4), 265 (pp. 4–5), 267 (p. 5), 268 (p. 5), and Padel's comments in chapter 1, pp. 35–37.

found again and again in the chapters of the present volume. It lies behind Smith's *Elements* and VEPN, and indeed much work dating back to the very beginnings of place-name study in England.[57] It could be argued, though, that this approach has reached maturity relatively recently, and perhaps not in precisely the way Sedgefield—or indeed Smith—anticipated. Neither Sedgefield nor Smith could have anticipated the results of Margaret Gelling's reassessment, element by element, of topographical settlement-names. Similarly comprehensive approaches have recently been urged for place-names which define a settlement with a term for habitation. As Richard Jones and Sarah Semple comment in their introductory chapter to the volume *Sense of Place in Anglo-Saxon England*:

> If an analogy is drawn from the topographical names which have revealed place-names to be precise readers of the landscape; one must suspect that a similar level of precision and specificity was applied when making decisions regarding whether a place saw, say, a *cot* or a *stoc*, a *worth* or a *burh*.[58]

While treating names which share particular habitative elements as groups is by no means only a recent pursuit, current approaches illustrate the benefit of undertaking them within a thoroughly interdisciplinary environment, alongside insights offered from history, archaeology, and historical geography.[59]

The scholarship of the 1924 volume was grounded on the fundamentals of place-name study outlined by Sedgefield – that sound interpretation and evaluation is based upon the informed analysis of early forms of names, and upon the consideration of an individual name within the wider context provided by others in its group. For this reason, a remarkable number of its conclusions have been borne out by the

[57] The tradition of name-group studies is as old as the discipline itself, and includes, of course, the revisionist articles of the 1960s and 70s, on *-ingas, hām*, and *-ingahām*, which turned on its head the chronological framework espoused in the chapters of the *Introduction*.

[58] R. Jones and S. Semple, 'Making sense of place in Anglo-Saxon England', in R. Jones and S. Semple (eds), *Sense of Place in Anglo-Saxon England* (Donington: Shaun Tyas, 2012), pp. 1–15.

[59] The study of names in *þorp* and *þrop* by Paul Cullen, Richard Jones, and David Parsons is the most developed version to date of this interdisciplinary approach: their study assembles an exhaustive corpus of *thorps* and examines it with the historical and, where available, archaeological evidence for settlement activity in each place. P. Cullen, R. Jones, and D. N. Parsons, *Thorps in a Changing Landscape* (Hatfield: University of Hertfordshire Press, 2011). See further pp. 65–69, 197.

accumulated evidence of place-name scholarship in subsequent years, much of it provided by the Survey which the *Introduction* launched. The present volume is similarly grounded in those fundamentals. It is intended not only to update, modify, expand upon, and revise the content of the *Introduction*, but also to celebrate the erudition of its authors and editors, who did so much to ensure the lasting vigour of English place-name studies, in their contributions to the 1924 volume, in the EPNS Survey volumes that followed, and elsewhere. The health of the discipline in 2013 should be clear in the pages that follow, not least in the many paths they open for future enquiry.

1

Brittonic place-names in England

O. J. Padel

The topic of Celtic place-names in England is particularly beset by the kinds of difficulties for which place-name studies generally are well known. Such names have, by definition, come down to us mediated through another language, in which the names had to be modified phonologically; and most of them will have been etymologically opaque to their English users for some time, often for several centuries, before the date of their earliest attestation. This problem of mediation is not present, or far less so, for English, Scandinavian, or French names in England; thus for Celtic names there is an extra layer of uncertainty in anything said about them, as well as additional skills required for studying them. Moreover, the topic is intimately related to another one, still the greatest problem in the history of England, the question of what happened in the fifth to the seventh centuries, when the invading Anglo-Saxons encountered the indigenous British. The intractability of that related topic, for which place-names constitute major evidence, adds to the problems of studying the Brittonic names.

A history of the scholarship on Brittonic place-names in England would not usually, today, need to discuss much work from before Kenneth Jackson's *Language and History in Early Britain* (1953), since that book provided a new and secure phonological framework for the subject and still forms the basis for any work in it.[1] However, Eilert Ekwall's essay on the topic, published at the beginning of the Survey of English Place-Names in 1924, remains useful; and his book on one

The volumes of the English Place-Name Society's Survey are indicated by EPNS + county abbreviations as given on p. vi above. Anglo-Saxon charters are indicated by S + the number in P. H. Sawyer, *Anglo-Saxon Charters: An Annotated List and Bibliography* (London: The Royal Historical Society, 1968) and the electronic version of S 1–1602 by S. E. Kelly, rev. by R. Rushworth (2006) at <http://www.esawyer.org.uk/>.

[1] K. Jackson, *Language and History in Early Britain* (Edinburgh: Edinburgh University Press, 1953).

important group of these names, those of rivers and streams, remains the standard authority on the subject, although there has subsequently been valuable further work.[2]

Since 1953 the subject has naturally advanced in many areas. The Survey itself has continued, adding further examples of Brittonic names, and providing greater detail and understanding concerning those already known. Hugh Smith's *English Place-Name Elements* (1956) provides a useful survey of the chief Brittonic words, though important corrections to their forms were subsequently made by Jackson, and of course Smith's work is now superseded for those elements which have appeared to date in the fascicles of the *Vocabulary of English Place-Names*.[3] Succinct introductions to the topic have been provided in a chapter by Kenneth Cameron, 'Celtic place-names and river-names', and two chapters by Margaret Gelling, on Romano-British place-names and later evidence for Brittonic survival.[4] There is a full treatment of the place-names of Roman Britain.[5]

Richard Coates and Andrew Breeze have published a book on the specific topic of Celtic place-names in England, plus additional individual articles;[6] and Coates has separately discussed the significance of these names.[7] Patrick Sims-Williams has re-examined Jackson's work

[2] E. Ekwall, 'The Celtic element', in A. Mawer and F. M. Stenton (eds), *Introduction to the Survey of English Place-Names*, English Place-Name Society 1.i (Cambridge: Cambridge University Press, 1924), pp. 15–35; Ekwall, *English River-Names* (Oxford: Clarendon, 1928).

[3] A. H. Smith, *English Place-Name Elements*, English Place-Name Society 25–26 (Cambridge: Cambridge University Press, 1956) [EPNE]; Addenda and corrigenda by K. Jackson, *Journal of the English Place-Name Society*, 1 (1968–69), 43–52; 2 (1969–70), 73–74; 3 (1970–71), 50; and 6 (1973–74), 52; D. Parsons and T. Styles with C. Hough, *The Vocabulary of English Place-Names* I *(Á–Box)* (Nottingham: Centre for English Name-Studies, 1997); D. N. Parsons and T. Styles, *The Vocabulary of English Place-Names* II *(Brace–Cæster)* (Nottingham: Centre for English Name-Studies, 2000); D. N. Parsons, *The Vocabulary of English Place-Names* III *(Ceafor–Cock-pit)* (Nottingham: English Place-Name Society, 2004) [VEPN].

[4] K. Cameron, *English Place-Names* (London: Batsford, 1961 and subsequent editions), ch. 2; M. Gelling, *Signposts to the Past: Place-Names and the History of England* (London: Dent, 1978, and subsequent editions), chs 2 and 4.

[5] A. L. F. Rivet and C. Smith, *The Place-Names of Roman Britain* (London: Batsford, 1979) [PNRB].

[6] R. Coates and A. Breeze, *Celtic Voices, English Places: Studies of the Celtic Impact on Place-Names in England* (Stamford: Shaun Tyas, 2000); for subsequent articles see the yearly bibliographies in *Nomina* and *Journal of the English Place-Name Society*.

[7] R. Coates, 'The significances of Celtic place-names in England', in M. Filppula and

on the phonology of Brittonic place-names borrowed into English.[8]

For Brittonic names in specific geographical areas, the major work by Alan James on the elements of Brittonic place-names in northern England and southern Scotland, though not yet fully published, is available in electronic form.[9] A fine survey of the county of Fife has now made its place-names, including Brittonic ones, fully available in their onomastic context.[10] My own *Cornish Place-Name Elements* is of some use for all Brittonic areas, since it gives details of Welsh and Breton cognates and usages of the elements, and also cites parallel place-names in other English counties.[11]

Within Wales, the completion of the historical dictionary of Welsh has provided ready access to the toponymic usage of individual Welsh words, since it often includes place-name evidence within its citations.[12] Welsh river-names have been well treated.[13] There is now a historical dictionary of Welsh place-names, aiding comparison westwards across the border;[14] and two Welsh counties now have complete published surveys, alongside partial surveys of two others.[15] The publications of Melville Richards

others (eds), *The Celtic Roots of English* (Joensuu: Joensuu University Press, 2002), pp. 47–85; R. Coates, 'Invisible Britons: the view from toponomastics', in P. Cavill and G. Broderick (eds), *Language Contact in the Place-Names of Britain and Ireland* (Nottingham: English Place-Name Society, 2007), pp. 43–55.

[8] P. Sims-Williams, 'Dating the transition to Neo-Brittonic: phonology and history, 400–600', in A. Bammesberger and A. Wollmann (eds), *Britain 400–600: Language and History* (Heidelberg: Carl Winter, 1990), pp. 217–61 (esp. pp. 237–44 and map, p. 261).

[9] A. James, 'Brittonic language in the Old North' <www.spns.org.uk/bliton/blurb.html>.

[10] S. Taylor and G. Márkus, *The Place-Names of Fife*, 5 vols (Donington: Shaun Tyas, 2006–12).

[11] O. J. Padel, *Cornish Place-Name Elements*, English Place-Name Society 56–57 (Nottingham: English Place-Name Society, 1985) [CPNE].

[12] R. J. Thomas, G. Bevan et al. (eds), *Geiriadur Prifysgol Cymru*, 4 vols (Cardiff: University of Wales Press, 1950–2002); fuller treatment of letters A–B is still appearing.

[13] R. J. Thomas, *Enwau Afonydd a Nentydd Cymru* (Cardiff: University of Wales Press, 1938), covers names based upon vocalic suffixes in *-a-* to *-o-*; supplemented by his article, 'Enwau afonydd â'r ôl-ddodiad *-wy*', *Bulletin of the Board of Celtic Studies* 7 (1933–35), 117–33, and 8 (1935–37), 27–43.

[14] H. W. Owen and R. Morgan, *Dictionary of the Place-Names of Wales* (Llandysul: Gomer, 2007).

[15] B. G. Charles, *The Place-Names of Pembrokeshire*, 2 vols (Aberystwyth: National Library of Wales, 1992); I. Wmffre, *The Place-Names of Cardiganshire*, 3 vols (Oxford: Archaeopress, 2004); G. O. Pierce, *The Place-Names of Dinas Powys Hundred* [Glamorganshire] (Cardiff: University of Wales Press, 1968); H. W. Owen, *The Place-Names of East Flintshire* (Cardiff: University of Wales Press, 1994).

have made Welsh place-names generally more accessible;[16] and his extensive collection of historical forms of Welsh place-names is accessible on-line as a searchable database.[17]

For Brittany, the work of Bernard Tanguy in particular has provided material of great value for comparative purposes in Britain: he has published surveys of the major names in two of the four departments, and a classified list, with examples, of the elements used in topographical names.[18] There is also now a convenient one-volume dictionary of Continental Celtic place-names, building upon considerable recent work in that area.[19]

In 1924 it was possible for Ekwall to survey the whole subject of Celtic place-names in England within twenty pages. For reasons of length this chapter deals only with certain aspects of the topic. It largely ignores those few parts of England which have significantly greater density of Brittonic place-names, either because they were less thoroughly settled by the Anglo-Saxons (notably Cornwall and parts of Herefordshire), or because of re-immigration at various dates – Cumberland in the tenth century, and part of Shropshire around Oswestry in the central Middle Ages.[20]

With regret, this study stops at the Scottish Border, except for occasional glances into southern Scotland, although all workers in the

[16] Bibliography in *Onoma* 18 (1974), 619–25; note especially M. Richards, *Welsh Administrative and Territorial Units* (Cardiff: University of Wales Press, 1969).

[17] Archif Melville Richards Database <www.e-gymraeg.co.uk/enwaulleoedd/amr>.

[18] B. Tanguy, *Dictionnaire des noms de communes, trèves et paroisses du Finistère* (Douarnenez: Le Chasse-Marée, 1990); *Dictionnaire des noms de communes, trèves et paroisses des Côtes d'Armor* (Douarnenez: Le Chasse-Marée, 1992); *Les Noms de lieux bretons*, I, *Toponymie descriptive* (Rennes: Centre Régional de Recherche et de Documentation Pédagogiques, 1975).

[19] A. Falileyev et al., *Dictionary of Continental Celtic Place-Names* (Aberystwyth: CMCS, 2010); other recent work by Falileyev and others is referred to in the introduction and bibliography.

[20] K. Jackson, 'Angles and Britons in Northumbria and Cumbria', in H. Lewis (ed.), *Angles and Britons: O'Donnell Lectures* (Cardiff: University of Wales Press, 1963), pp. 60–94; A. James, 'A Cumbric diaspora?', in O. J. Padel and D. N. Parsons (eds), *A Commodity of Good Names: Essays in Honour of Margaret Gelling* (Donington: Shaun Tyas, 2008), pp. 187–203; B. G. Charles, 'The Welsh, their language and place-names in Archenfield and Oswestry', in Lewis (ed.), *Angles and Britons*, pp. 85–110 (pp. 99, 105, 110); Ll. Beverley Smith, 'Yr Iaith Gymraeg cyn 1536', in G. H. Jenkins (ed.), *Y Gymraeg yn ei Disgleirdeb* (Cardiff: University of Wales Press, 1997), pp. 15–44 (p. 19 and references).

field are aware that distribution-maps of English names are misleading if they stop at the modern Border. The work of Alan James is making the Brittonic names in that region more accessible, but it is still not easy to examine these names in terms of their historical documentation and onomastic context, except in Fife.

Sims-Williams's re-examination of the phonology of Brittonic place-names in England is so thorough that the topic does not need detailed treatment here. Naturally it is not the last word on the subject: some of his datings of Brittonic sound-changes may be on the early side, being based on evidence which ultimately amounts to very few forms which need not be decisive.[21] Moreover, Sims-Williams was revisiting Jackson's chronology specifically with a view to elucidating the development of the Brittonic languages, using Jackson's own evidence and methods but in the light of subsequent scholarship in those areas. His treatment therefore prepares the ground for further work studying the Brittonic place-names from the perspective of Old English diachronic phonology.

There is room for slight reservation, too, concerning one of the basic methods used by Jackson and Sims-Williams, even though it remains an essential tool. Brittonic names borrowed into English, when plotted geographically, show chronological progression from east to west across England in their contrasting representations of Brittonic sounds. The later a name was borrowed, the later the Brittonic phonology that it is likely to reflect. This progression can be used to chart the advance of English across the country, and also to provide relative datings for the chronological sound-changes which are frozen into the place-names. But it would be dangerous to expect this principle to be applicable too rigidly at a small scale among the small numbers of names available in most of England. Within the south-western peninsula alone there is an uncomfortable disparity between the borrowed tribal name of Devon itself, *Deofenas*, showing Brittonic lenis *m* in its later, lenited, form giving Old English [v], contrasting with some names to the west of Devon which show the same sound borrowed in its earlier (pre-lenition) form, as [m], for example in the name of the River Tamar and indeed some lesser places within eastern Cornwall itself.[22] It is virtually

[21] O. J. Padel, 'Aneirin and Taliesin: sceptical speculations', in A. Woolf (ed.), *Beyond the Gododdin: Dark Age Scotland in Medieval Wales* (St Andrews: University of St Andrews Press, 2013), pp. 115–52 (pp. 118–19).

[22] For example, Hammett, Hampt, Hamatethy, all correspond to Welsh Hafod 'shieling';

inconceivable that these and other names showing [m] were actually borrowed into Old English significantly earlier than the name of Devon itself, or any earlier at all; and this uncomfortable fact must make us wary of trying to generalize too rigidly from the limited corpus of names showing these kinds of contrasts. Similarly, the forms of place-names ascribed to Brittonic **crūg*, including Crook (D), Creech (Do), Creek, Crook- and Crutch- (all in Sr), Crich (Db), and Crutch (?), Church- and Crook- (all in Wo) are incompatible with regular chronological progression.[23]

Given the small numbers of Brittonic place-names existing in most of England, occasional inconsistencies in the behaviour of words (perhaps especially names), when borrowed between languages with rather different phonological systems, may make it difficult to achieve a fine-tuned geographical chronology of sound-changes. Of course the attempt to use the data in this way must still be made: a broad geographical and chronological progression can be detected, and most names do not show a phonological free-for-all. Sims-Williams, following Jackson, has successfully constructed a chronology from them; but at smaller geographical scales the low numbers of names may create limits to how exactly this chronology can be applied.

Brittonic river-names are not examined in detail here, since that section of the subject has remained largely static since Ekwall's thorough study, in the sense that the corpus has changed little. However, within the corpus there has been fresh work. Peter Kitson has examined British river-names in the context of the theory that many river-names, in Europe and beyond, are 'Old European', an essentially undifferentiated Indo-European language attested in river-names over much of the area of the later language-groups of the family; he has suggested that some river-names in Britain can be better understood as Old European names which were reinterpreted as Brittonic, before being subsequently borrowed by the Anglo-Saxons.[24] Andrew Breeze has shown that better interpretations

CPNE, p. 127.

[23] Coates and Breeze, *Celtic Voices*, pp. 290, 292, 294, 336 etc.; D. Probert, 'Mapping early medieval language change in south-west England', in N. Higham (ed.), *Britons in Anglo-Saxon England* (Woodbridge: Boydell, 2007), pp. 231–44, has attempted to reconcile this material; see also D. N. Parsons, 'Sabrina in the thorns: place-names as evidence for British and Latin in Roman Britain', *Transactions of the Philological Society* 109 (2011), 113–37 (pp. 129–30); and below, pp. 22–23 and 30–31.

[24] P. Kitson, 'British and European river-names', *Transactions of the Philological Society* 94 (1996), 73–118.

for known Brittonic river-names in England can sometimes be obtained by considering types of river-names found in later Brittonic areas, particularly Wales; some Brittonic river-names in England can be interpreted as based on words for weapons, tools, and animals and birds. Examples include Laughern Brook (Wo), equivalent to Welsh *llywern* 'fox';[25] and the River Poulter (Nt), equivalent to Welsh *paladr* 'spear';[26] however, neither *llywern* nor *paladr* seems actually to be attested as a Welsh stream-name.

English place-names in Irish or Scottish Gaelic, occurring mostly in northern counties, are not considered here. They constitute a different kind of topic, arising from immigration, mostly in about the tenth century and by people who were probably of mixed Norse-Irish background.[27] However, these names also provide a reminder that some Brittonic names in England may also have arisen through inward migration by speakers of Welsh or Cumbric in the central Middle Ages.[28]

The present chapter is therefore limited to three specific aspects of Brittonic place-names in England. First, the extent to which areas within England differ from one another in the density of Brittonic names which they contain. Second, the types of Brittonic name which have survived across most of England, and also the types of places which have Brittonic names, since that dimension provides an important tool for assessing whether a particular name is likely to be Brittonic. Finally, that group of names which consist of a single Brittonic element, either on its own (e.g. Liss or Avon), or combined with an English one, sometimes tautologically (e.g. Chetwood, Bredon), since these single-element Brittonic names form an important sub-group, of which the precise significance is still unclear.

[25] Coates and Breeze, *Celtic Voices*, pp. 67–69, repeating a suggestion of Henry Owen, in G. Owen, *The Description of Penbrokshire*, ed. H. Owen, 4 vols (London: Honourable Society of Cymmrodorion, 1892–1936), II, p. 288, n. 9; compare Ystumllywern 'fox's bend' SO4313, Monmouthshire, on the River Troddi.

[26] Coates and Breeze, *Celtic Voices*, pp. 74–76.

[27] Coates and Breeze, *Celtic Voices*, pp. 234–62 and 265–66. See now D. N. Parsons, 'On the origin of "Hiberno-Norse inversion-compounds"', *Journal of Scottish Name Studies* 5 (2011), 115–52.

[28] For example, James, 'A Cumbric diaspora?', and F. Edmonds, 'A twelfth-century migration from Tegeingl to Lancashire', in T. M. Charles-Edwards and R. J. W. Evans (eds), *Wales and the Wider World: Welsh History in an International Context* (Donington: Shaun Tyas, 2010), pp. 28–56.

Varying densities of names

The overall scarcity of Brittonic place-names in England has not altered significantly since Jackson's or even Ekwall's time.[29] The publications of Coates and Breeze, and others, have made a few valuable additions to the corpus;[30] but in a judicious review of *Celtic Voices*, Alan James pointed out that the authors of that work had not significantly increased the corpus itself: typically their contributions offer fresh interpretations of names which were already considered Brittonic, or of uncertain language.[31]

In 1953 Jackson published his well-known map of Brittonic names of rivers and streams, on which four zones across England and Wales show an increasing density of Brittonic names from east to west.[32] The map was based on Ekwall's *River-Names*, and it has been often cited and reprinted; since the corpus has changed little since Ekwall's time, the map remains valid today, and agrees rather well with more recent maps showing Brittonic settlement-names (below). However, Stephen Yeates has raised the important question of when changes in river-names may have occurred, especially the replacement of Brittonic names by English ones.[33] He has quite rightly pointed out that as late as the sixteenth century river-names were less stable than they are now, and he cites examples of rivers which can be shown to have had different names for parts of their courses, or which changed from an ancient name to an (Old?) English one in the late-medieval or early-modern period. Only one of Yeates's examples was not already listed in Ekwall's *River-Names*, so these issues do not invalidate Jackson's map; but they are extremely important. The chief implication is that it would be desirable to revisit the river-names in their own right, not for their derivations, but rather to consider the comparative attestation of English and earlier names in

[29] Map 2 in EPNE; Gelling, *Signposts*, ch. 4; O. J. Padel, 'Place-names and the Saxon conquest of Devon and Cornwall', in Higham (ed.), *Britons in Anglo-Saxon England*, pp. 215–30.

[30] Coates and Breeze, *Celtic Voices*; P. Brotherton, 'Celtic place-names and archaeology in Derbyshire', *Derbyshire Archaeological Journal* 125 (2005), 100–37, may have added one or two in that county.

[31] A. James, review of Coates and Breeze, *Celtic Voices*, *Nomina* 27 (2004), 147–50.

[32] Jackson, *Language and History*, p. 220; Gelling, *Signposts*, p. 89.

[33] S. Yeates, 'River-names, Celtic and Old English: their dual medieval and post-medieval personalities', *Journal of the English Place-Name Society* 38 (2006), 63–81.

historical records, both over time and (crucially) the kinds of records and contexts in which the various names occur.

Brittonic names of settlements and estates can be less confidently plotted. One difficulty is the lack of even coverage across England as a whole, since the detail of the individual county surveys has deepened during their ninety years. However, the increase in detail is mostly in minor names and field-names, which (it is suggested below) are the categories least likely to contain Brittonic names in most of England; so the uneven coverage may not be a major problem. Another difficulty in compiling a map of all Brittonic names in England is the varying status of the names. A Brittonic river-name obviously has a different kind of significance from an estate-name, but there are also estates named from a river, and especially in the south-west there are sometimes numerous estates all named from a single river.[34] It is difficult to know how to plot such estate-names, since some of them may have been created by subdivision during the Anglo-Saxon period, or even the original estate-name may have been created in that period from the borrowed river-name. A third difficulty is that a simple Brittonic name may have different significance from one combined with an English second element, for example, Creech (Do) versus Creechbarrow (So); but often it may be uncertain whether an English element has been added subsequently to a Brittonic name now known only in a combined name.[35] Given these difficulties, it is understandable that the authors of *Celtic Voices* were cautious about providing general distribution-maps of Celtic names in England, although the county-maps form an essential part of that volume.[36] On a single map it would be difficult to show the various types of name, and the various types of features that they denote, without making it undesirably complex or even misleading.

These maps of Brittonic names (excluding river-names) in individual counties show the overall westward increase in density which is generally recognized, similar to that of the river-names. The counties can be approximately (and impressionistically) classified into three groups: those showing hardly any Brittonic place-names, those with a slightly richer

[34] For example, at least eight different manors in Domesday Book, all called *Clist*(*e*) or *Clistone*, and named from the River Clyst: EPNS D, pp. 573–74, 577–78 and 584–86.

[35] On Creechbarrow see below, pp. 30–31.

[36] Coates and Breeze, *Celtic Voices*, pp. 275, 357 and 368–92.

density, and those with slightly more again. The first group, where Brittonic names are extremely scarce, includes the whole of the east of the country south of approximately the River Humber, extending westwards into the central Midlands: the eighteen counties of Bedfordshire, Buckinghamshire, Cambridgeshire, Essex, Hertfordshire, Huntingdonshire, Kent, Leicestershire, Lincolnshire, Middlesex, Northamptonshire, Nottinghamshire, Oxfordshire, Rutland, Suffolk, Surrey, Sussex, and Warwickshire.[37] Some of these counties are even sparser than others: Kent is slightly richer than its two western neighbours, and East Anglia particularly poor.[38] But in none of them is there more than a light scatter. Independently of this observation, a recent survey has identified at most about 100 pre-English settlement-names (including doubtful ones, but not rivers) in the sixteen south-eastern counties, an average of about six per county.[39] This area includes two counties (Hampshire and Berkshire) which are here classified in the next group; the average would be lower still without them. In addition County Durham, in the north-east, is also very light compared with its neighbours to south and north (Yorkshire, Northumberland).

The second group, with a slightly greater, though still sparse, showing of Brittonic names, comprises three adjacent counties in the south (Berkshire, Hampshire including the Isle of Wight, and Wiltshire), and four northern counties (Staffordshire, Yorkshire especially the West Riding, Westmorland, and Northumberland), which form less of a discrete block than the three southern counties. Finally, eleven western counties show slightly greater density again: Cheshire, Cumberland, Derbyshire, Devon, Dorset, Gloucestershire, Herefordshire, Lancashire, Shropshire, Somerset, and Worcestershire. Even here, however, the

[37] Surrey looks denser than Sussex on the maps in Coates and Breeze, *Celtic Voices*, p. 389, but several of the Surrey names are doubtful, to varying degrees; see V. Watts, *The Cambridge Dictionary of English Place-Names* (Cambridge: Cambridge University Press, 2004) [CDEPN], entries for Caterham, Coulsdon, Leatherhead, and Merrow.

[38] To the names in Kent listed in Coates and Breeze, *Celtic Voices*, pp. 315–16, add now Winfield Bank: P. Cullen, '*Vagniacis* and Winfield: the survival of a British place-name in Kent', in Padel and Parsons (eds), *A Commodity of Good Names*, pp. 95–100; and perhaps Pennyquick, Kent (*Penycrek*, *Penecrek* 1502, *Pennycrych* 1574), if that is 'head of the tumulus', **penn* + **crūg* (compare Penkridge, St): J. K. Wallenberg, *The Place-Names of Kent* (Uppsala: Appelbergs boktryckeriaktiebolag, 1934), p. 556; my thanks to Paul Cullen for help with this name.

[39] Parsons, 'Sabrina', p. 123: south and east of a line embracing Norfolk, Northamptonshire, Oxfordshire, Berkshire and Hampshire.

overall numbers of Brittonic names constitute a very small proportion even of the major names (parishes and manors): these counties, including even Cumberland, are denser only in comparison with others further east, not when compared with the thoroughly Brittonic areas of Cornwall and Wales.[40] Even in all the counties of this third group the overall density of Brittonic names is much closer to that of eastern counties, such as Essex or Durham, than to that of Cornwall. The only areas showing true density of Brittonic names are parts of certain counties bordering on Wales, notably Shropshire and Herefordshire, where spoken Welsh survived until Tudor times, and where minor names and even field-names in Modern Welsh are found.[41]

Within these three broad categories the densities are not even. Ekwall, in 1924, had already pointed out the differential survival of Brittonic names in different areas;[42] and Margaret Gelling has also discussed the topic briefly.[43] Ekwall's examples were at a broad level, and mainly exemplified the increasing numbers found by moving westwards across England. One area which he noted was Dorset and adjoining parts of Wiltshire; his other areas were Devon and Somerset, western parts of Gloucestershire and Worcestershire, and Herefordshire and Shropshire 'in a position of their own'.

Subsequent work on the Survey has made greater detail possible. Hence one can note areas of slightly greater density such as north-western Derbyshire, running into north-eastern Cheshire and south-eastern Lancashire; and eastern Hampshire as contrasted with the near-desert of Sussex and Surrey.[44] Coates has suggested that the phonology of a few names in north-west Wiltshire may suggest the survival of Brittonic speech into the seventh century there.[45] In Westmorland there is a difference between the south, largely devoid of Brittonic names, and the

[40] Padel, 'Place-names and the Saxon conquest'.

[41] Charles, 'Archenfield and Oswestry'; the areas (but not all of the names) are shown on the maps in Coates and Breeze, *Celtic Voices*, pp. 379–80 and 388.

[42] Ekwall, *Introduction*, pp. 27–31.

[43] Gelling, *Signposts*, pp. 60–62, 90 and 101, with reference to Map 2 in EPNE.

[44] Map 2 in EPNE; Gelling, *Signposts* (1978), p. 90; Coates and Breeze, *Celtic Voices*, pp. 377 and 389.

[45] Coates and Breeze, *Celtic Voices*, pp. 112–16; several of the names are only doubtfully Brittonic.

north, dividing at Shap Fell.[46] However, even these clusters tend to consist each of only about half a dozen names.

Even assuming that local clustering exists and is significant, there has not been much discussion of what it means. There is probably a general assumption that such clusters indicate ethnic enclaves, places where a community of Brittonic-speakers survived, within a context where other people round about were speaking Old English. A case could probably be made for some of these apparent clusters (for example, that of north-west Derbyshire) being located on land which is less desirable for agriculture. If these clusters are significant in terms of Brittonic survival, then the blanks, the much larger areas in between the clusters, presumably mean something different in terms of such survival, or the lack of it.

Types of name, types of places

The chief types of name which have survived are well known. Single-element names (discussed below) are common. Names composed of two elements are usually true compounds, having the qualifying element in first position as in the Germanic languages, for example Malvern 'bare-hill' (Wo), Candover 'fair-waters' (Ha), Lich(field) 'grey-wood' (St). These compounds stand in contrast with the name-phrases which provide the overwhelming majority of place-names in all the Neo-Celtic regions (Wales, Cornwall, Brittany, Ireland, much of Scotland, and the Isle of Man), and which have the generic element in first position, and the qualifying one second.[47] It is generally accepted that, since almost all names from Roman Britain and Ancient Gaul are true compounds (with the chief exception of names in *Duro-*: PNRB, pp. 346–47), and the great majority from Neo-Celtic areas are name-phrases, there was a change in how place-names were made, in all the Celtic languages, in about the fifth to sixth centuries; the implication is that the type of a name therefore provides some indication of when it was created. Exceptions to this principle, in both directions, are sufficiently well attested to make it dangerous if applied rigidly;[48] but as a rough guide it remains useful.

Overall, the Brittonic names in England are very different from those appearing in any later Brittonic area. One of the two crucial tools of

[46] My thanks to Alan James for pointing out this distinction.

[47] CPNE, pp. xv–xvi.

[48] CPNE, pp. xvi–xvii.

place-name study, equal in importance to the need for early spellings of names, is the comparative method. The existence of a convincing comparison or parallel within the Brittonic world greatly strengthens a suggested derivation, just as a lack of such a parallel weakens it; but many Brittonic settlement-names in England lack close parallels in Wales or Cornwall. Comparisons between Wales and Ancient Gaul seem to be almost easier to find than between Wales and England.[49] However, the known Roman-period place-names in Wales (a small sample, perhaps not very representative) also fail to show a great deal in common with later Welsh place-names, so the lack of correspondence between Brittonic names in England and Wales may be partly due to the poorness (or partially unrepresentative nature?) of the Roman-period sample, and to subsequent changes in naming habits within Brittonic.

Parallels do exist, providing precious evidence of some continuity in Celtic naming habits. For example, the compound *Branodunum* 'crow-fort' or 'fort of **Branos*' in Norfolk is paralleled by the name-phrase Dinbren (also called Dinas Brân) in Denbighshire; by Caer Brân (Co), with the same personal name qualifying a different word for 'fort'; and by early Irish *Dún mBrain* and *Ráith brain*.[50] Second, there are recurrent compounds, such as Mellor in Lancashire and Derbyshire, both corresponding to the Welsh examples of Moelfre 'bald-hill' (*moel* + *bre*); likewise Mulfra, Mulvra and Mulberry in Cornwall;[51] and Tulketh (La), *Tolchet* (So), and Olchard (D) are paralleled by Tyllgoed 'hole-wood' in Wales (*twll* + *coed*), Tolgus (Co), and *Toulgoat* in medieval Brittany.[52] There are also a very few parallels of name-phrases, including Pentridge (Do) and Pentrich (Db), 'boar's head', with their equivalents in Pentyrch (Wales) and Penterc'h (Finistere), for which in turn the several Irish examples of *Cenn tuirc* 'boar's head' constitute essential comparanda for their interpretation.[53] Similarly Penge 'wood's end' (Sr), *Paunsett* (W), Penketh (La) and Penquit (D) are paralleled by Pencoed (Wales) and

[49] M. Richards, 'Some Welsh place-names containing elements which are found in Continental Celtic', *Études celtiques* 13 (1972–73), 364–410.

[50] CPNE, p. 29.

[51] CPNE, p. 167; Mellor in Cheshire (Coates and Breeze, *Celtic Voices*, p. 279) is the same place as Mellor in Derbyshire, EPNS Db, p. 144n.

[52] CPNE, pp. 219–20; O. J. Padel, 'Two Devonshire place-names', *Journal of the English Place-Name Society* 41 (2009), 119–26 (pp. 119–22).

[53] CPNE, p. 222.

Penquite, Pencoose (Co).[54] As a name-phrase in the far east of England, Penge provides valuable evidence that such a name could be created presumably before the sixth century, although it is of the phrasal type considered to be later in date.

The general lack of correspondence leaves some suggested derivations for Brittonic names in England unparalleled in the Brittonic world. Although this situation is not impossible, it is a cause for concern. Some Brittonic explanations generally accepted for difficult names in England have a strained appearance. Even with changes in naming-habits, if the Brittonic names within England were typical of the naming-habits of the language in the period down to the fifth century, one might expect some similar older names to have survived within Wales or Cornwall. In Appendix I a sample list is given of some fifteen place-names in England for which Brittonic derivations have been suggested, but no close parallel in the Brittonic world has yet been found. Doubt concerning the Brittonic derivations which have been suggested for these names need not mean that their pre-English nature is altogether questionable; merely that a convincing derivation has not yet been produced, and that Brittonic may not necessarily offer one. But good parallels may yet be found for some of these names, as work proceeds in the Brittonic areas themselves.

Conversely, there is also a lack of parallels in the other direction, common Brittonic types of name which might be expected to have occurred in Anglo-Saxon England. Such absences could be due to a particular type of name having arisen in the Brittonic world after the language had died out in most of England (for example, phrasal names incorporating the definite article, as in west-Cornish Pen-an-vounder 'the head of the lane').[55] One type of name which is common in all Brittonic areas, but largely absent in England, is the type consisting of a single element, usually a plant-name but sometimes another natural resource such as a mineral, plus the adjectival ending *-āco-*, Welsh *-og*, Cornish *-ek*. In place-names this ending usually means 'growing with' or 'abounding in' (a plant or a substance). The Brittonic place-names in England include a high proportion of single-word place-names; such names incorporate no syntax or morphology, unlike compound and phrasal names, so they were more easily borrowed. Therefore one might

[54] CPNE, p. 181.

[55] CPNE, pp. 5–7 and references.

have expected single-word names using this suffix to be well represented in England; but there are few such names outside Cumberland, and those that exist are atypical. There are half a dozen instances from Roman Britain.[56] York, *Eburacum*, contains this suffix, possibly with a plant-name but more probably with a personal or god-name, which makes this name a good example of a parallel between a Romano-British place-name and a common Gaulish type;[57] but this use of the suffix (personal name + *-āco-*) is not well attested in the later Brittonic areas, though Tudweiliog (Caernarfonshire) and Pebidiog (Pembrokeshire) are two Welsh examples.[58] Romano-British *Vagniacis* also contains the suffix; it probably survives as the first syllable of Winfield Bank (K). The base-noun here is probably British **wāgn-* 'marsh', a usage closer to the later Brittonic type, though still not quite the same.[59]

Chideock in Dorset and Dunchideock in Devon both contain the suffix in an adjectival form of **kɛd* 'wood', Welsh *coed*; but in the Brittonic world the adjective of that particular word seems to be rather unusual, so these two English names are themselves slightly atypical, though not in doubt.[60] Quantock and Berk(shire), like Bannock in the Scottish Midlands, all containing this suffix, are names of hill-ranges; in all three names, both the words to which the suffix has been added, and also the use of the formation to denote a hill-range, are again atypical of the names with this suffix in the main Brittonic regions. In the north-west and Scotland there are lesser names of similar type, such as Barrock (Cu), Charnock (La), and Bannock(burn) (Stirlingshire); but still very few containing plant-names.[61] One reason for the general lack of parallels in the use of this suffix may be that in Wales and Cornwall the botanical place-names with this adjectival suffix are mostly names of rather minor places, whereas in most of England it tended to be the names of more

[56] P. Russell, 'The suffix *-āko-* in Continental Celtic', *Études celtiques* 25 (1988), 131–73 (pp. 155–56).

[57] PNRB, pp. 355–7; Russell, 'Suffix *-āko-*', pp. 139–54.

[58] Owen and Morgan, *Dictionary of the Place-Names of Wales*, p. 478; Charles, *Place-Names of Pembrokeshire*, p. 197, and other examples cited there.

[59] Cullen, '*Vagniacis* and Winfield'.

[60] Note also Quethiock, Cornwall: O. J. Padel, *A Popular Dictionary of Cornish Place-Names* (Penzance: Alison Hodge, 1988), p. 146; Tanguy, *Noms de lieux bretons*, p. 100, cites Roscoëdec and Linhouëdec, both containing the adjectival form.

[61] Coates and Breeze, *Celtic Voices*, pp. 281 and 316; James, 'Brittonic language in the Old North', s.v. *-og*.

important places, such as *Eburacum*, that were borrowed. So perhaps this use of the suffix existed in England but such names have not survived.

Another lack in most of England is Brittonic names containing habitative elements. They are almost entirely absent from names attested in the Roman period. The ancestors of Welsh *caer* 'fort' and *tre* 'farmstead' are both unattested; that of *bod* 'dwelling' is considered to occur only in *Botis*, the island of Bute (PNRB, p. 273). Among English names of later attestation a very few examples do appear: one instance of **lïs* 'court' (Liss, Ha); and two or three possible examples of compounds containing *tre* have been suggested, standing beside a considerable number of such names in southern Scotland.[62] On the other hand, neither of the two suggested instances of **tïγ* 'house', Priddy (So) and Minety (W), is convincing: Priddy, if Brittonic at all, could be a derivative of **prïð* 'clay', rather than a compound of that word with **tïγ*; and Minety is more likely to be English 'mint-island', OE *minte* + *īeg*.[63]

The types of places preserving Brittonic or older names in England are well established. Rivers are the best known, along with some other major natural features, such as large woods (Savernake in Wiltshire; Wyre in Worcestershire; *Andred* in early Sussex and Hampshire, a former settlement-name later attached to a natural feature; and probably Arden in Warwickshire), and major hills or ranges, such as Chiltern (Bu), Quantock and Mendip (So), Berk(shire), Malvern (Wo), Pen-y-Ghent (Y), Mam (Tor) (Db), Helvellyn and Blencathra (Cu), and also Cheviot (Nb), since it is presumably pre-English, although without a convincing Brittonic derivation.

Among settlements having Brittonic names, less attention has been given to the types of places to which these names belong. Nearly forty known names of Roman towns and forts have survived, mostly in very reduced form. What has happened to the majority of these names is regular enough to be called a pattern. It is exemplified by the names Manchester (*Mamucium*) and Wroxeter (Sa; *Viroconium*), in which a

[62] Chitterne, Wiltshire (Coates and Breeze, *Celtic Voices*, p. 85); and possibly Kinder and Findern, Derbyshire (Brotherton, 'Celtic place-names in Derbyshire'), but there are reservations concerning both of these: Kinder as a river-name is more likely to contain *-duvr* 'water'. Scottish examples of *tre* are listed by James, 'Brittonic language in the Old North', s.v. *treβ*.

[63] EPNS Gl **1**, p. 81; EPNS W, p. 61: there was a noted abundance of wild mint there in the seventeenth century.

Romano-British name has survived, but reduced to a single syllable (usually its first), and followed by *-cæster* as an English generic. Appendix II (pp. 40–41) gives a list of these names within England, and of the smaller number of other Romano-British names of settlements and forts which have also survived, but without the addition of *-cæster*. These names are obviously of the highest interest; the discussion of them by Colin Smith remains especially useful.[64] The reduction of the Romano-British names to a single syllable has occurred rather irregularly (note the disyllabic survival in Cirencester, though there exist pronunciations of that name which reduce it further); Margaret Gelling has pointed out that where early evidence exists (before the tenth or eleventh century), it suggests that Romano-British names were originally borrowed in fuller form, and the reduction happened subsequently within Old English, not at the stage of borrowing.[65] The fact that *-cæster* is itself a disyllabic generic may have contributed to the subsequent reduction of the Romano-British names, since the composite names were more complex than a monosyllabic generic would give. However, in the case of Lich(field) and Win(field) the Romano-British names have likewise been reduced to a single syllable, even though the English generic (*feld*) is a monosyllable.

The frequency of the Manchester type suggests that it could be useful to re-examine those *-cæster* names which lack a recorded Romano-British ancestry, in case some may also have a Brittonic first element. The parallel of Alcester (Wa, from Romano-British *Alauna*) suggests that Alchester in Oxfordshire could be such an example, although it has no Romano-British attestation.[66] Dorchester (O) is another such example, though *Dorcic-* there might be a river-name.[67] The extent of the reduction which has usually occurred in the qualifying element of such names would make these later-attested *-cæster* names difficult to analyse, lacking the Roman-period forms which might provide derivations; but it

[64] A. H. A. Hogg, 'The survival of Romano-British place-names in southern Britain', *Antiquity* 38 (1964), 296–99; C. Smith, 'The survival of Romano-British toponymy', *Nomina* 4 (1980), 27–40.

[65] Gelling, *Signposts*, pp. 54–55.

[66] EPNS O, p. 241 and **1**, p. xvi n. 2, suggests (following Richmond and Crawford) that Alchester is *Alauna* in the Ravenna Cosmography; but Rivet and Smith identify that *Alauna* doubtfully as Alcester (Wa) (PNRB, pp. 207 and 244).

[67] EPNS O, p. 152; compare rivers called *Dorce in Surrey and Wiltshire, Ekwall, *River-Names*, pp. 128–29; but see R. Coates, 'The pre-English name of Dorchester on Thames', *Studia Celtica* 40 (2006), 51–62.

might be fruitful to examine them, not with a view to suggesting fresh derivations, but merely with a view to identifying those which lack a convincing derivation in Old English. Where so much is uncertain, collecting the data and perhaps identifying patterns is a necessary preliminary to attempts to solve individual problems.

What is evident from the two lists given in Appendix II is that survival of Romano-British settlement-names is well established, albeit in reduced form. However, it was not the norm, for the total of these survivals is at most 39 out of approximately 180 fort- or settlement-names attested in Roman-period England. (Wales and Scotland are not included in these figures, since they raise such different questions of continuity; nor are Romano-British names of rivers and other major natural features in England included, unless they seem to have survived as settlement-names in their own right.) So although these lists provide respectable and important evidence for survival of names, the rate of survival is not high, and as Colin Smith has noted, no name of a Roman villa or estate has survived as a place-name. Since we know the names of so few of those, that is not surprising, but the lack still forms an important part of the whole picture, and stands in marked contrast with Gaul.[68]

Among the names which do show continuity, one point that sometimes occurs in discussion of them is some problem in the phonology which makes the development of the name irregular. Occasionally the problem might be resolved if we could posit written influence upon the transmission of the name. Names where that hypothesis might help include Binchester (*Vinovium*), Brougham (*Brocavum*) and Catterick (*Cataractonium*); also Loughor (*Leucarum*), in Wales (PNRB, pp. 504, 284, 304 and 388). There may be no more than half a dozen such names, but combined they might make a case for not ruling out entirely the possibility of written influence.[69] But in most surviving names such influence is unnecessary.

Ten of the *-cæster* names showing survival of a Romano-British name, listed at the end of Appendix II (i) (pp. 40–41), are known only from medieval documents, and have not survived to modern times, being replaced mostly by names lacking *-cæster*. In three of these names (York, Reculver, Richborough) the Romano-British name has survived, but

[68] Smith, 'Survival of Romano-British toponymy', p. 27.

[69] Compare remarks of Smith, 'Survival of Romano-British toponymy', pp. 32–33.

without *-cæster*; in the other seven cases the Romano-British name has been lost (Bath, Chester-le-Street, Canterbury, Pevensey, Tadcaster, St Albans, and Bradwell-on-Sea). The history of these seven names could be taken to suggest that the Anglo-Saxons originally borrowed rather more in the way of place-names from the British, but subsequently lost or replaced them; and, hence, that the replacement of Brittonic by Germanic names occurred not at the period of settlement but at a later date. However, there are other interpretations of this limited material. Some of the ten names showing temporary survival are found primarily or solely in Bede. It is possible that he could have created them himself, knowing the written forms and using the parallels which existed; his purpose might have been to steer the onomasticon so as to create a continuity between the Roman past and the Anglo-Saxons. For some other places Bede used the Latin name itself, such as *Eboracum* for York. He seems to have had access to written sources for some places, mainly in northern England, for which he used Romano-British names, such as *Campodunum* near Leeds, *Calcaria* (Tadcaster), *Cataracta* (Catterick), and *Durobriva* (Rochester, K) (PNRB, pp. 293 and 348).[70]

A similar question of continuity arises from the important corpus of names published by Barrie Cox, those place-names recorded in Anglo-Saxon sources down to 731, including Bede.[71] The material listed by Cox contains a comparatively high proportion of Brittonic (or partly Brittonic) place-names, 32 out of 224 names, or 14%.[72] The question therefore arises whether this material suggests that the Anglo-Saxons originally borrowed a larger number of Brittonic names than we now have. Cox did not draw that conclusion himself, and he pointed out that the high proportion of ecclesiastical sites named in these earliest sources may have caused an imbalance towards Brittonic names in the list, compared with a comparable selection of secular names.

Moreover, it has already been noted that the Anglo-Saxons borrowed names of important towns and other existing settlements; since the names in these earliest records include many of the most important places, such

[70] Similarly Gelling has suggested that *Acemannesceastre* for Bath, found only in the Anglo-Saxon Chronicle, was a learned form, not in local use (*Place-Names in the Landscape* (London: Dent, 1984), p. 13).

[71] B. Cox, 'The place-names of the earliest English records', *Journal of the English Place-Name Society* 8 (1975–76), 12–66.

[72] Cox, 'The place-names of the earliest English records', pp. 53 and 56–57.

as London, York and Lincoln, the list would be expected to show a high proportion of Brittonic names, compared with a list including typical quantities of lesser place-names. In terms of demonstrating continuity from British to Anglo-Saxons, the name of a major town is less significant than the name of a lesser estate.

Thirdly, owing to the uneven coverage of these earliest English sources, Cox's corpus of names is uneven in its distribution, with hardly any examples in East Anglia; even the names of the Saxon-Shore forts in that region are absent from Cox's list, although present in other areas. East Anglia is also very lacking in Brittonic names. If more names from that very Germanic area had been present in the material, they might have reduced the proportion of Brittonic names in the corpus, giving it a higher proportion of Germanic ones. Overall, therefore, the list of names recorded down to 731 does not lend support to a hypothesis that higher numbers of Brittonic names were borrowed to begin with, to be gradually replaced later.

Alan James has suggested a refinement of such a hypothesis, based upon changes in settlement-patterns which occurred in much of (especially lowland) Britain in the eighth to twelfth centuries.[73] He suggests that initially the Anglo-Saxons may have borrowed many more Brittonic place-names, replacing them with Germanic ones only during these later centuries because of the changes in settlement at that period. However, at present it is not clear that Cox's data would support this theory either. As already seen, only 14% of his pre-731 settlement-names were Brittonic, so the corpus does not indicate extensive borrowing in the early period. Moreover, of the 194 settlement-names in Cox's corpus, at most about 43 have now been lost (including ones which refer to settlements still inhabited, but now known by other names). These figures mean that changes in settlement during the Anglo-Saxon period did not involve loss of settlement-names on a scale sufficient to suggest that the overall onomasticon would have looked very different before the eighth century. Clearly more work is needed on this interesting suggestion, but at present it does not account for the absence of Brittonic names in most of England.

The types of places in England having Brittonic names are not

[73] A. James, review of Cavill and Broderick (eds), *Language Contact in the Place-Names of Britain and Ireland* in *Journal of Scottish Name Studies* 3 (2009), 135–58 (pp. 145–47), with reference to Coates, 'Invisible Britons'.

restricted to major natural features and Roman towns and forts. Among lesser places with clearly Brittonic names, it is still mainly ones of some administrative or economic significance which appear, such as Anglo-Saxon estates, Domesday manors, and parishes. This suggested principle, that Brittonic names tend to belong to places of some administrative significance, means that the type of place to which a name belongs is one factor to be considered in deciding whether a name is likely to be Brittonic.[74] If a place was not of administrative significance in the central Middle Ages, then the burden of proof for a suggested Brittonic derivation is greater; for example, good parallels within the Brittonic world itself. There may be a danger of circular reasoning here: in order to have a convincing Brittonic derivation, a name must usually be well attested in the written record; but places which are well attested were usually ones of some administrative significance. However, the documentary record does contain some names of lesser places, and when these occasionally have a good Brittonic derivation there may be particular circumstances to explain the exception.

The principle is not uniformly applicable. It probably applies most strongly in the south and east, and less clearly in parts of the north-western counties, where there are examples of a few minor settlement-names and even field-names which may be Brittonic.[75] There may be several reasons for this variability, including the later immigration, already mentioned, by speakers of Cumbric into north-west England. In Lancashire such names can alternatively sometimes be attributed to Welsh immigration in the central Middle Ages. The minor settlement-name Alkincoats (in Whalley parish), if it is Brittonic at all, would be proclaimed by its form to be such a Welsh import, though it is not in the area of known Welsh settlement;[76] however, it is more likely to belong with the other (English) names in *-coat*(*s*), etc., in the same parish and elsewhere in Lancashire.[77]

A Brittonic place-name recently suggested in Devon, Olchard ('hole-wood', *toll* + **kɛd*), flouts this principle, since medieval documentation for it is lacking at present, and its first known appearance is as a local

[74] Compare Ekwall, *Dictionary*, pp. xxii–xxiii.

[75] Coates and Breeze, *Celtic Voices*, pp. 281–86, 316–19 and 338.

[76] Coates and Breeze, *Celtic Voices*, pp. 218–19; Edmonds, 'Twelfth-century migration'.

[77] E. Ekwall, *The Place-Names of Lancashire* (Manchester: Manchester University Press, 1922), p. 9.

surname in 1332 (Walter *Tolchet*), which is far from the kind of attestation to be expected of a convincing Brittonic place-name.[78] However, in this instance the Brittonic parallels are excellent (Welsh Tyllgoed 'hole-wood', and comparable names in Cornwall, Lancashire, Somerset and Brittany); the topography suits the suggested derivation; the location itself is typical of an ancient settlement, similar to those of Domesday manors in Devon and Cornwall; and it may be the lack of recent work on medieval records in Devon, and perhaps the corruption that the name has undergone, which are responsible for its lack of a recorded history at present.

Two other names which appear to violate this suggested principle are Winfield Bank (K), probably the *Vagniacis* of the Antonine Itinerary (British **wāgn-* 'marsh' + OE *ge-fall* 'fall, (?) felled area'), and *Chetwde*, given as a lost field-name in Yorkshire.[79] In making his suggestion about Winfield Bank, Cullen has noted that it is a rarity in that respect;[80] since Winfield is attested in 1199 and again in the thirteenth century, it might be interesting to note what kind of place it was at that period. Similarly with *Chetwde* 12th (Brittonic **kɛd* 'wood' + OE *wudu*): lost names classified under 'field-names' in the volumes of the Survey can include names of important places, now disappeared. Here it would be desirable to ascertain whether the name referred to a major wood, like Chute Forest in Wiltshire and Hampshire, or to a settlement (now lost) as Chetwode (Bu) does. Or the name may belong with the greater incidence of minor places having Brittonic names in the north-western counties. Overall, more work is needed on the kinds of places to which definite Brittonic names refer, in order to ascertain the validity of this suggested principle in different parts of the country.

There can be other reasons why Brittonic elements appear at the level of field-names and minor settlement-names, without necessarily violating the general principle. The frequency of minor settlement-names containing Crook, Creech, etc., usually ascribed to Brittonic *crūg*, suggests that this word was borrowed into English dialect, perhaps only for naming purposes. Judging by the variety of forms, it may even have

[78] Padel, 'Two Devonshire place-names', pp. 119–22.

[79] Cullen, '*Vagniacis* and Winfield'; EPNS WRY **4**, p. 122 (not in Coates and Breeze, *Celtic Voices*, p. 344); Pennyquick (K) may be a third such name (note 38, above).

[80] Cullen, '*Vagniacis* and Winfield', p. 99.

been borrowed into English more than once in different areas, or once borrowed have spread into areas which also show it in another form.[81] The element *penn* 'head' also appears in a considerable number of minor settlement-names in western counties; these are discussed below (pp. 32–33).

The name Idover (W) appears once as an ancient stream-name (now Brinkworth Brook), and ten times as separate nineteenth-century field-names, two of them on that particular stream.[82] The pattern of attestations suggests that this was a single ancient Brittonic stream-name (presumably containing **duvr* 'water'), which subsequently spread, perhaps in the early-modern period, by re-application as either a field-name or a stream-name. The pattern would be similar to that of Delabole, in east Cornwall (SX0784), a Domesday manor (*Deliov*) with a large and well-known slate-quarry. Its full name is attested from 1284 *Delyou Bol*, and it recurs as a field-name in at least twenty-eight Cornish parishes, mainly in the eastern half of the county, from the late sixteenth century onwards.[83] The reason for the re-application is not clear: although lesser slate quarries might have been named after the famous one, it is unlikely that all these fields did contain small slate quarries. In the case of Idover (W) some comparable modern re-application of the ancient stream-name may be responsible for the recurrent later field-name.

One outstanding exception to the general principle is the name of a pass in Cumberland, Trusmadoor, which has been convincingly explained by Diana Whaley as equivalent to Welsh **Drysfa* 'door-place' (plus English *door*). The earliest attestation so far found for this name is no older than 1867.[84] This probable Brittonic name is wholly exceptional in the lateness of its appearance; but the greater incidence, already noted, of

[81] See above, p. 6; compare Gelling, *Place-Names in the Landscape*, pp. 137–39; M. Gelling and A. Cole, *The Landscape of Place-Names* (Stamford, Shaun Tyas, 2000, repr. with corrections, 2003), pp. 159–63; Coates and Breeze, *Celtic Voices*, pp. 269 and 350; Probert, 'Mapping early medieval language change', map on p. 236, shows south-western examples of **crūg*.

[82] Coates and Breeze, *Celtic Voices*, pp. 93–94 and map on p. 116; further local detail in EPNS W, pp. 2–4, 69 and 74, and Ekwall, *River-Names*, pp. 208–09.

[83] Padel, *Popular Dictionary*, p. 78; O. J. Padel, 'Fields called *Denabole*', *Devon and Cornwall Notes and Queries* 36 (1987–91), 145–47.

[84] D. Whaley, *A Dictionary of Lake District Place-Names* (Nottingham: English Place-Name Society, 2006), pp. 348–49 and plate 1; Whaley, 'Trusmadoor and other Cumbrian "pass" words', *Nomina* 24 (2001), 77–95; there do not seem to be comparable examples of **Drysfa* 'door-place' from Wales itself or from other Brittonic areas.

Brittonic minor names generally in Cumberland provides a context.

Thus in order to assess whether a particular name in England is likely to be a Brittonic one (whether ancient or due to medieval in-migration), it has to be studied, not as an isolated phonological specimen, but in the context of the other names of the area in which it occurs, including even the field-names in some cases. Factors which may help to classify a name may usually include the kind of place to which it refers, in the context of kindred information for other Brittonic names (if any) in the same area, and the kind of documentation in which the name appears, as well as the frequency, type and phonology of other Brittonic names in the same area.

Single-element Brittonic names

Many of the accepted Celtic names within England consist of a single Brittonic element, or one combined with an Old English generic, sometimes tautologically or roughly so: for example, Chute (Forest), Bre(don), the Rivers Avon, the various places called Crich, Crook, etc., Liss (Ha), and names in *Eccles*(-). To understand these names one looks first to the Brittonic regions. There are few parallels for such names in Cornwall (two places called Bray, and two called Brea, but none called *Pen*, *Cos*, *Cruk* or *Eglos*);[85] in Wales some of these single-element names are paralleled, others not: there are no examples of simplex Afon, Bre, or Pen, but there are numerous woods, and a few farms or hamlets, called Coed, tumuli called (Y) Crug, and a dozen places called Llys 'court'. These names tend to be first attested in the nineteenth century and do not seem likely to be much older. The simplex names suggested by the English names Avon, Pen- and Eccles seem to be unparalleled in the Brittonic world. The paralleled and unparalleled names imply different types of explanation for the English names. In addition, some of these single-word Brittonic names in England form a special category, since the very words were used apparently in different ways from their known Brittonic uses.

Theoretically some of these simplex names might have arisen from common nouns (appellatives) in Brittonic which were mistaken for names by the Anglo-Saxons, rather than having been simplex Brittonic place-names in their own right. However, these two alternatives are not the only possibilities. In the case of **eglēs* it is still uncertain which language the

[85] CPNE, pp. 30, 67, 74 and 91.

Eccles- names were originally given in, let alone their significance. As for *penn*, some English place-name authorities consider that this Brittonic element has the meaning 'hill' in England; if so, this word had a different meaning as well as usage in English from that of the Brittonic languages (see below).

Richard Coates has suggested an intermediate position for some of these names:

> the English took over monomorphemic Brittonic words for landscape features as if they were proper names, possibly many times over, in such a way that no new lexical item of the relevant form entered English. [...] most items that were borrowed were understood as being used in order to make reference, but not as denoting; they named, but had in most instances no lexical status.[86]

This subtle approach is very helpful; the suggestion is that these words were not necessarily encountered as names in Brittonic, but were used by the Anglo-Saxons to form names. That is not the same thing as saying that the Anglo-Saxons mistakenly thought that they were Brittonic names, although that too is possible in some cases: rather, a Brittonic word was borrowed and used in Old English as a simplex name, sometimes differently from its usage in Brittonic, but it did not become available for use in any other way in Old English. It was because **Bre* did not mean 'hill' to the Anglo-Saxons, or only so as a Brittonic word, that it was available to them as a simplex name. Thus such names, according to this analysis, would be ones given by speakers of Old English, but deliberately using a 'native' word. One can envisage colonists in Africa or Australia doing something similar with topographical terms used by the indigenous peoples: getting the right meaning, or approximately so, but applying it slightly differently to make their own names: the use of 'loch' in standard English to refer to specific sites in Scotland, or the Australian adoption of 'billabong' might provide approximate parallels, though in both these cases the words are used as (specialized) appellatives. Closer still might be the way in which Celtic generics were used, sometimes with Latin personal names, to coin names for Roman places, such as *Caesaromagus* (Chelmsford, Ess) and (on the Continent) *Augustodunum*

[86] Coates, 'The significances of Celtic place-names', pp. 72–73; Coates, 'Invisible Britons', pp. 48–49.

(PNRB, pp. 22–23 and 287–88).[87]

The situation is slightly more complicated for words which do occur widely as simplex names in Wales, notably *coed* and *crug* of the elements found thus in England. Even within a single language there can be uncertainty about what precisely constitutes a proper name (e.g. 'the street corner'; see Coates below, pp. 138–43), and the precise status of the numerous examples of Coed and (Y) Crug in Wales, referring to a wood or a tumulus, is open to question. It seems likely that these are mostly very recent names, and dependent upon the living language to serve as casual local descriptions. For this purpose Cornwall stands in an intermediate position between Wales and most of England, since the Brittonic language has been dead there for several centuries in most of the western half, and for rather longer in the east; so there are no examples at all of *cos* 'wood' or *cruc* 'tumulus' as simplex names, presumably because in the seventeenth and eighteenth centuries the language was already too weak to create or use minor names of this type, such that they could have been recorded as place-names by the surveyors in about 1800.[88]

However, Coates explicitly excluded some single-element Brittonic names from his discussion, recognizing that his explanation need not apply to all such formations. Avon is an example: in Welsh this word means 'river', but it never occurs as a name; the river-name occurs in south-west England and central Scotland.[89] In this case it has been significantly pointed out that if we are dealing with a common noun which was mistaken as a name by the Anglo-Saxons, then the Romans made the same mistake, since we find one example of *Abona*, both river and settlement, in Roman Britain.[90] Furthermore, the full word *avon*, including the suffix *-on-*, does not seem to have cognates outside

[87] A. L. F. Rivet, 'Celtic names and Roman places', *Britannia* 11 (1980), 1–19.

[88] There is one farm now called Engoyse 'the wood' (Wendron parish), reduced from older *Coiscuntell* 1556 'gathering-wood'; and two farms called Crugoes, Cregoe (plural **Crugou* 'tumuli'): CPNE, pp. 67, 76 and 74.

[89] See the map in PNRB, p. 239; also James, 'Brittonic language in the Old North', s.v. *āβ*. It is unclear whether early forms make the Scottish names definitely Brittonic **avon*, not Gaelic *abhainn*: J. B. Johnston, *Place-Names of Scotland*, 3rd edn (London: Murray, 1934), p. 94.

[90] VEPN I, p. 3; Rivet and Smith, PNRB, p. 239, say that the river-name also occurs in Gaul 'though little mentioned in the classical sources' – seemingly not at all, in fact.

P-Celtic, as either a word or a name.[91] This fact, combined with the pre-English existence of *Abona* as a name, suggests that this word may actually have originated as a river-name, from the wider-occurring Indo-European root *ab-* plus the Celtic suffix *-on-*; and that it was only later that it became generalized in Welsh (less clearly in Cornish and Breton) to give a common noun meaning 'river'.[92] This theory would be compatible with the various pieces of evidence. However, I have not found any close parallels to the suggestion that a recurrent place-name might have become a common noun.

The *Eccles* names are odd in several ways, both the simplex examples and the names in which it is compounded with an English word. It may be doubted whether they all have the same derivation, and it is open to question whether the names usually cited as examples of this element do all represent Brittonic **eglēs* or an Old English reflex of that.[93] In Cornwall at least it is doubtful whether the word was used to form place-names, either simplex or qualified, in the early post-Roman centuries, as it would need to have been elsewhere in England in order to have entered into Brittonic place-names.[94] The repeated nature of some of the English compounds in *Eccles-*, particularly the four examples in which it is compounded with Old English *halh* 'nook, corner' (Eccleshall, etc.), is

[91] Gaelic *abhainn* is not etymologically equivalent, and was originally the dative case of Old Irish *ab* 'river': W. J. Watson, *The History of the Celtic Place-Names of Scotland* (Edinburgh: Blackwood, 1926), p. 430; R. Thurneysen, *A Grammar of Old Irish* (Dublin: Dublin Institute for Advanced Studies, 1946), p. 213; J. Vendryes and others, *Lexique étymologique de l'irlandais ancien* (Dublin and Paris: Dublin Institute for Advanced Studies and Centre National de la Recherche Scientifique, 1959–), pp. A4–5.

[92] This suggestion replaces the account given in CPNE, pp. 13–14; in Cornish and Breton the common-noun *avon* occurs only in glossaries, and the usual Breton word for 'river' is *stêr*.

[93] K. Cameron, 'Eccles in English place-names', in K. Cameron (ed.), *Place-Name Evidence for the Anglo-Saxon Invasion and Scandinavian Settlements* (Nottingham: English Place-Name Society, 1975), pp. 1–7; Gelling, *Signposts* (1978), pp. 83 and 96–99; C. Hough, 'Eccles in English and Scottish place-names', in E. Quinton (ed.), *The Church in English Place-Names* (Nottingham: English Place-Name Society, 2009), pp. 109–24; A. James, '**Eglēs/Eclēs* and the formation of Northumbria', in Quinton (ed.), *The Church in English Place-Names*, pp. 125–50.

[94] A. Preston-Jones, 'Decoding Cornish churchyards', *Cornish Archaeology* 33 (1994), 71–95 (p. 81); O. J. Padel, 'Christianity in medieval Cornwall: Celtic aspects', in N. Orme (ed.), *Victoria County History of Cornwall* II: *Religious History to 1560* (Woodbridge: Boydell and Brewer for the Institute of Historical Research, 2010), pp. 110–25 (p. 119a); and the word is virtually unknown as a formative element in Brittany, where it might have been expected to occur if it was in use in Britain at an early date.

suspicious.[95]

Names in Eccles were omitted from the maps in *Celtic Voices*, on the grounds that **eglēs* was considered, along with *penn* and one or two other elements, to be among the few words actually borrowed into Old English.[96] Without necessarily endorsing that suggestion, it is suggested here that *Eccles* names have actually received too much attention as possible Brittonic names. There is a recurrent stream-name in England of this form, appearing in two Ecclesbournes;[97] two lost instances of *Eclesbroc*;[98] Ecchinswell in Hampshire;[99] Eccleswall (i.e. 'well') in Herefordshire;[100]; *Ecles cumb* in Somerset;[101] *Ecclesdo* c. 1180, a stream in Yorkshire;[102] and in County Durham Eggleston (*Egleston'* 1197) and Eggleshope (*Egleshope* c. 1160×85) are on a stream called *Egesburne* (*sic*) in *c.* 1160×83, now Great and Little Eggleshope Beck and Eggleston Burn.[103] Although Ekwall cited only five of these nine names, he observed, 'The common occurrence of *Eccles-* in stream-names is remarkable'. He considered possible English derivations for the names, including a personal name **Eccel* and OE *ecels* 'additional land', along with Brittonic **eglēs*, but no derivation explains the recurrence in stream-names.[104] There is also a River Egel in Glamorganshire.[105] If *-es-* were an

[95] Gelling and Cole, *Landscape of Place-Names*, p. 130: the four instances are 'perhaps not beyond the bounds of coincidence'.

[96] Coates and Breeze, *Celtic Voices*, pp. 272–73.

[97] EPNS Db, p. 7; that in EPNS Sx, p. 507, has late and variable forms; note also Ecclesden (not nearby), EPNS Sx, p. 165, where an OE personal name **Eccel* is accepted, though a name in **eglēs* has been suggested by R. Coates, *Toponymic Topics: Essays on the Early Toponymy of the British Isles* (Brighton: Younsmere, 1988), pp. 48–51.

[98] In Worcestershire 8th (11th–12th) S 142 (also in S 1372), and in Middlesex 962 S 702, at Ashford, *Ecelesford* 969 (*c.*1100), EPNS Mx, pp. 11–12.

[99] *Eccleswelle* 1086; situated on *Ec(e)lesburna* in 931 (12th), S 412: R. Coates, *The Place-Names of Hampshire* (London: Batsford, 1989), p. 70.

[100] B. Coplestone-Crow, *Herefordshire Place-Names* (Oxford: BAR, 1989), p. 130.

[101] In the bounds of Corston in 956 (12th) S 593.

[102] EPNS WRY **2**, p. 229; *-do* is obscure.

[103] NY9531 to NY9825; derived by V. Watts, *A Dictionary of County Durham Place-Names* (Nottingham: English Place-Name Society, 2002), p. 39, from the genitive of the personal name *Ecgwulf.*

[104] Ekwall, *English River-Names*, p. 141; E. Ekwall, *Concise Oxford Dictionary of English Place-Names*, 4th edn (Oxford: Clarendon, 1960), s.v. Ecchinswell.

[105] SN7107: Breeze in *Celtic Voices*, pp. 142–44, suggests that these English names contain the name of a supposed Celtic hero *Echel*, in an English genitival form.

English genitive in these names, one could compare the syntax of *Auenes broc* 'stream called *Aven*' in Dorset;[106] but it would be most improbable for a stream-name to appear in the genitive so consistently in all these various names.

Kenneth Cameron excluded these stream-names from his discussion of *Eccles* names, and they have remained largely divorced from that corpus in subsequent discussion;[107] but he also pointed out that even the names in his reduced corpus are all located close to rivers or streams, except for one on the coast.[108] In the context of these stream-names some of the names in Cameron's corpus might deserve to be reconsidered, for instance the Eccleshalls. Gelling and Cole cite some examples of *halh* compounded with river-names, though no repeated examples;[109] and they additionally say that a high proportion of *halh* names have obscure first elements, depending upon how charitable one is about possible personal names which also appear in many *halh* names.[110] Perhaps a better understanding of *halh*, and of other English words compounded with *Eccles*, might help with understanding *Eccles* itself; the conclusions in the most recent account of *halh* do not suggest an explanation of why it should regularly have been combined with a word meaning 'British church';[111] and one recent suggestion of the meaning of **eglēs*, 'land belonging to a (British) church', seems to have developed partly out of the 'administrative' sense of *halh* invoked by Margaret Gelling, 'piece of land projecting from, or detached from, the main area of its administrative unit'.[112] Taking the whole corpus together, it is at least worth considering whether some or most of the names currently considered to derive from Brittonic **eglēs* contain instead some English word, perhaps a personal name or stream-name.

For some one-word Brittonic place-names another suggestion can be

[106] 10th (14th) S 573, EPNS Do **1**, p. 30.

[107] Cameron, 'Eccles in English place-names', p. 3.

[108] Cameron, 'Eccles in English place-names', p. 4.

[109] Gelling and Cole, *Landscape of Place-Names*, pp. 129–30.

[110] Gelling and Cole, *Landscape of Place-Names*, pp. 127–28.

[111] P. Stiles, 'Old English *halh*, "slightly raised ground isolated by marsh"', in A. R. Rumble and A. D. Mills (eds), *Names, Places and People: An Onomastic Miscellany in Memory of John McNeal Dodgson* (Stamford: Paul Watkins, 1997), pp. 330–44.

[112] James, '**Eglēs/Eclēs* and the formation of Northumbria'; Gelling, *Place-Names in the Landscape*, pp. 100 and 109.

made, perhaps especially for those with a tautologous English element added, the Chetwood and Bredon types. The explanation arises from a phrase in a Somerset charter purportedly of the seventh century, where a hill now called Creechbarrow (ST247255), outside Taunton, is specified by two names:

> Et tres cassatos in australi parte amnis Tan ad insulam juxta collem qui dicitur brittannica lingua **Cructan** apud nos **Crycbeorh**, et hec pars telluris evidentissimis cingitur limitibus, habet enim ab austro Blacanbroc, ab aquilone Tan.[113]

> And three hides [of land] on the south side of the River Tone, at the island by the hill called *Cructan* in the British language, *Crycbeorh* among us, and this piece of the land is surrounded by very visible bounds, for it has Black Brook on the south, Tone on the north.

The charter, in its sixteenth-century copy, is not beyond question, but this clause within it must presumably be derived from an early text. The contrast seen in *brittannica lingua ... apud nos ...* is unparalleled in England, though there is an approximate parallel in eighth-century Scotland, *in loco qui sermone Pictorum Peanfahel, lingua autem Anglorum Penneltun appellatur* 'in the place called *Peanfahel* in the speech of the Picts, but *Penneltun* in that of the Angles'.[114] This uniqueness within England is itself symptomatic of the general Anglo-Saxon reluctance to engage fully with Brittonic place-names. The clause does not necessarily constitute evidence that Brittonic was still a living language in that part of Somerset in the later seventh century, though it does suggest that it had been so fairly recently, within the previous two or three generations.

It is the names within the phrase that are especially illuminating. The Brittonic name here is a standard two-element name-phrase, with the generic element, *crūg, in first position, and the qualifier, the river-name Tone, in second. The structure means that the name inevitably incorporates a certain amount of Brittonic syntax, and in English such a name has a foreignness and awkwardness which discourages its adoption

[113] '672' (for 682?) (16th), S 237; W. de Gray Birch, *Cartularium Saxonicum*, 4 vols (London: Whiting, 1885–99), no. 62 (Glastonbury); Gelling and Cole, *Landscape of Place-Names*, pp. 159 61, with illustrations.

[114] Bede, *Historia Ecclesiastica Gentis Anglorum*, I, 12; B. Colgrave and R. A. B. Mynors (eds), *Bede's Ecclesiastical History* (Oxford: Clarendon, 1969), p. 42; now Kinneil, West Lothian, NS9880; compare Watson, *Celtic Place-Names of Scotland*, pp. 346–48.

as a name in its entirety. It is stressed on the second syllable, not because individual Brittonic words were stressed on the final syllable (although they were at that date), but because the qualifying element takes the stress, irrespective of the stress in polysyllabic words. *Cruc Tan* is really two separate words, and probably sounded so, rather than as a unified name. The Saxons seem to have borrowed only the first word, **crūg*, then added their own word, *beorh*, which in this case, whether by chance or intention, is synonymous or nearly so. The fact that the Anglo-Saxons recognized the second word as the local river-name might have helped to make the syntax clear, which might in turn have made that element seem separable and encouraged its omission. Partial adoption of this kind might be considered to explain some other tautologous compounds, and perhaps other single-element names as well. The term 'grudged' or 'reluctant borrowing' might describe this type of partial adoption. Such borrowing is quite distinct from the reduced forms of some polysyllabic Romano-British names, since (as seen earlier) in those names the reduction of the original name to a single syllable seems to have taken place long after the date of borrowing, whereas in *Cructan* becoming *Crycbeorh* the dropping of the second Brittonic element seems to have been inherent in the act of borrowing.

It is also worth noting that in this case the single word, **Crūg* or **Cryc*, does not seem ever to have existed as a name in its own right. It went straight from being the first (generic) element in a Brittonic name-phrase, *Cruc Tan*, to become the first (specific) element in an Old English name, *Crycbeorh*. Thus the latter name does not mean 'hill near to (a settlement called) **Cryc*', but 'hill which we [the Saxons] call *Cryc-*' (note the hyphen). Such an interpretation is compatible with Coates's suggestion, that common generic elements were sometimes adopted, perhaps comprehendingly, for the purposes of forming English names but without being borrowed as ordinary words into the language; and such partially-borrowed names would constitute a particular sub-type within Coates's general scheme of words borrowed for name-forming purposes.

There are two cautions concerning such an extrapolation from this unique name. It does not help with the Avon names, since even if Primitive Welsh **avon* did actually mean 'river', it is very unlikely that rivers were named as *Avon X* in Brittonic at this early period, although that has previously been suggested:[115] such names do not appear in Wales until the late Middle Ages.[116]

Second, the question would remain whether this type of borrowing applied particularly to tautologous compounds (as in Creechbarrow), or also to other names in which a single Brittonic element is used on its own. This question raises additionally the difficult one of English names containing *Pen*. As mentioned earlier, some English authorities think that this word has the sense 'hill' in England, or at least 'high ground', perhaps 'ridge'.[117] If so, and names such as Pendle (La; *Pen-* + *hyll*), Inkpen (Brk), and Hackpen (D, W) support the idea, then the word was used in a sense not known in the Brittonic languages, where the word means not 'hill' but 'head, top, end', corresponding to Old English *hēafod*, not to *hyll* or *dūn*, and does not occur as a simplex place-name. The *pen* element in such names can hardly, as it stands, have been a Brittonic place-name, for Brittonic *penn* on its own does not make good sense as a name: describing a place as a 'head' or 'end' begs the question, of what.[118] It might make sense to hypothesize that *Pen-* in some names was originally the generic word in Brittonic name-phrases of which the qualifier was dropped (as in *Cructan*, above). The kind of name in which this could be envisaged happening is *Peon mynet* 'the end of the hill', found in an eleventh-century charter-text for Culmstock, in north-east Devon.[119] One can envisage such a name being half-borrowed, along the lines of *Crycbeorh*, to become English *Pen Hill, although no such name is known in that area.

However, that explanation would still not necessarily account for the frequency of the specific combination *penn* + *hyll*, of which there are at least ten instances, including some minor and field-names.[120] We should

[115] Henry Bradley, cited in Ekwall, *River-Names*, p. 23.

[116] Thomas, *Enwau Afonydd*, pp. 125 and 164, and 'Enwau afonydd â'r ôl-ddodiad *-wy*', p. 131; also loose compounds in poetry: *Byrri avon*, *Certenhin avon* (Thomas, *Enwau Afonydd*, pp. 130 and 203).

[117] Gelling and Cole, *Landscape of Place-Names*, pp. 210–13.

[118] Similarly OE *hēafod* (EPNE, I, p. 237) and Irish *cenn* seem not to occur as simplex place-names.

[119] S 386; EPNS D, pp. 612n., 617; Cornish Penmenna etc., CPNE, pp. 163 and 178. The charter is attributed to King Athelstan but dated 670 (!); *Peon mynet* itself probably referred to Culmstock Beacon ST110150.

[120] Coates and Breeze, *Celtic Voices*: Pen Hill (Gl, three, p. 299), Pendle(-) (La, two, p. 319), Penhill (Y, two, pp. 343 and 345), perhaps Penhill (D, p. 293), Pen Hill (Do,

need to suppose, either that the English often part-borrowed Brittonic **Penn minið* 'end of the hill', but not other names in *Penn-* such as **Penn coid* 'wood's end' or **Penn nant* 'head of a valley', where *hyll* would not have been a natural word to add; or that the English did misunderstand *penn* in such part-borrowed names as meaning 'hill', and added their own supposedly synonymous term. Alternatively, Brittonic *penn* may have been borrowed by the English as a formative element in the (incorrect) sense 'hill', and used by them to create tautologous place-names. It is notable that all of the names in *penn* + *hyll*, although they were created (perhaps entirely) by English-speakers, occur towards the western side of England, in counties where other Brittonic names are reasonably well attested, not in the eastern counties where Brittonic names are particularly rare. However, the areas where Brittonic names are better attested are also the hillier parts of the country, thus more likely to have names referring to hills; and, in addition, Gelling and Cole have suggested that perhaps *hyll* was not in use in the earliest period of the Anglo-Saxon settlement, which could also have contributed to the absence of these names from eastern counties. The names in *penn* + *hyll* may not all be of the same kind.

The unlocated place-name in eastern Devon or western Somerset or Dorset, found in the Chronicle (*s.a.* 658) as *æt Peonnum* 'at the *Pen*s', is instructive in this context. *Pen* is used here as an Old English word, in an inflected plural simplex name, a thoroughly Anglo-Saxon formation, as if understood in some sense; but, in accordance with Coates's analysis, that need not mean that it was actually borrowed into Old English as an ordinary word.

Other Brittonic words for 'hill' provide clearer examples of tautologous compounds. There are three or four instances of **bre* plus *dūn*;[121] but only one, very uncertain, instance of **bre* plus *hyll*;[122] **crūg* recurs with *hyll* and *beorh*, but there is only one instance of it with *dūn*.[123]

p. 295), and *Penhul* (field, Db, p. 289).

[121] Breadon Lane (D), Breedon on the Hill (Le), Bredon (Wo), and possibly Brydonhill, field (Cu): Coates and Breeze, *Celtic Voices*, pp. 285, 292, 320 and 341.

[122] Brill (Bu): Coates and Breeze, *Celtic Voices*, p. 278.

[123] Crook Hill and perhaps *the Cruckhill*, field (Db), Church Hill (Gl), Crouch Hill (O), Churchill (Wo, two), and perhaps Crook Hill (W), Coates and Breeze, *Celtic Voices*, pp. 288, 298, 325, 339 and 341; Creechbarrow (So) and Crookbarrow Hill (Wo), Coates and Breeze, *Celtic Voices*. pp. 332 and 341; Churchdown (Gl), Coates and Breeze, *Celtic Voices*, p. 298.

There seems to be no example of a name composed of *penn* + *dūn*.[124] Whether or not the names in *Pen* + *hyll* suggest that *hyll* was felt (by the English) to be a suitable generic for names in *Pen-*, at any rate *dūn* apparently was not. It is possible that further study of the differences between the various words for 'hill' in Old English might illuminate the meaning ascribed (by speakers of Old English) to Brittonic *penn*.

Thus the names in England which contain a single Brittonic topographical word, often one which is used widely as a generic in Brittonic name-phrases, are not all of one kind. Various processes were involved in the borrowing and use of these names and words by the Anglo-Saxons, and these processes, although not fully understood, make the names some of the most illuminating data for considering such limited linguistic interaction as the evidence suggests between the two peoples.

Attitudes to Brittonic names

The final matter to be considered is different attitudes to Brittonic place-names in England, especially as evidence for the Anglo-Saxon settlement and possible Brittonic survival. Approaches to the place-names will be affected by opinions concerning that wider issue. There have been many attempts to assert that there are rather larger numbers of Brittonic place-names in England than have generally been recognized. The claim can take two main forms. The extreme one is that large numbers of English-looking place-names are actually folk-etymologized Brittonic names, reinterpreted as English (for instance, that English *-ton* is actually Modern Welsh *ton* 'grassland', or that names in OE *-dūn* are derived from Brittonic *din* 'fort'). Much more reasonably, the suggestion has been made that since English toponymists usually, and necessarily, come to their research from a background in English philology, they will try to explain a difficult name within Germanic, rather than looking to Brittonic.[125]

The more extreme claim hardly needs refuting. It involves ignoring the basic methods of place-name study, the use of early spellings and the comparative principle. Margaret Gelling's later work provides important

[124] Pendown (Co) SW760488 is a nineteenth-century creation, on land which was still downs (rough grazing) in the seventeenth century.

[125] For example, Coates, 'Significances', p. 48.

confirmation that for most names the long-established English etymologies are correct: the precise and consistent shades of meanings which she has established for different topographical elements in Old English would not exist, if many of the names in which they appear were actually reinterpreted corruptions of earlier Brittonic names. Additional refutation of such wayward theories is obtained from examining the qualifying (specific) elements in the names, which mostly are consistently meaningful words in Old English, or attested or reasonably reconstructed personal names; and is also shown by the implausible nature of the Brittonic names which are hypothesized, when compared with genuine names from the Celtic world, ancient and modern.

The more reasonable assertion can be answered, first, by suggesting that there has also been a counter-tendency to ascribe to Brittonic any name that cannot easily be explained as English; the strained appearance, to a Celticist, of some of the names appearing in Appendix I (pp. 38–39) is symptomatic of this tendency. The choice whether to struggle within Germanic or Celtic to explain a difficult name may be due as much to individual preference as to academic background. Second, efforts over the last two decades to redress the balance of Brittonic names in England have produced few convincing examples of completely new Brittonic names previously considered to be Old English, again suggesting that the established results of the survey have been broadly accurate. Within any language there will be a few names which arise from irrecoverable, sometimes near-random, processes in which whim or other unknowable human factors may have played a part, producing names which are entirely opaque to subsequent generations, and not capable of being analysed by the rigorous methods necessary within onomastics. The nicknames of a children's playground may include one or two such names, and place-names can sometimes arise similarly. Not all obscure place-names in England are necessarily pre-English.

Conversely, one recent work has suggested that Brittonic names have never existed in the east of England, that area having been Germanic, rather than Celtic, from at least the Neolithic period.[126] This extraordinary claim seems to have arisen out of taking seriously the opinion expressed by some archaeologists, that there was no significant change in the population of England in the fifth and sixth centuries. Stephen

[126] S. Oppenheimer, *The Origins of the British* (London: Robinson, 2006).

Oppenheimer, who at least takes account of the linguistic evidence, has taken that position to its logical conclusion for a geneticist. He is (perhaps necessarily) imprecise about where in England the supposed boundary (genetic or linguistic) lay between Germanic and Celtic;[127] and also about when the Germanic peoples arrived: at times it seems to be the Neolithic, several millennia BC, or even the Mesolithic, earlier still.[128] However, his discussion of place-name evidence implies that many Roman-period place-names of England are of uncertain language, although he cites work which makes it clear that where identifiable they are thoroughly Celtic, and that none at all are Germanic.[129] The use which Oppenheimer makes of the linguistic evidence will make a non-scientific reader uneasy about his interpretation of the genetic evidence, especially in the knowledge that the same genetic data have also been interpreted very differently.[130] Perhaps the science of DNA-typing is still too young for its exciting and important conclusions to be applied confidently at present in relation to other disciplines. In the early days of an extremely important analytic tool, theories naturally have to be tried out; but this particular tool may not yet be able to offer more than speculations for use in other disciplines.[131]

The concluding question, therefore, is why many people would like there to be more Celtic place-names in England than scholars have generally recognized. There is something romantically attractive in the idea that names can be extremely ancient, placing us in verbal contact

[127] Welsh border, *Origins of the British*, pp. 4, 175, 301 and 405; Wessex and Stonehenge, pp. 272, 308–09 and 328; but Cornwall received both eastern and western genetic input, p. 308.

[128] Bronze Age or Neolithic, Oppenheimer, *Origins of the British*, pp. 105–06 and 355; Neolithic, pp. 232–33, 250–51, 269 and 382; Neolithic or earlier, pp. 213–14, 228–29, 301 and 308; Mesolithic, p. 245.

[129] Oppenheimer, *Origins of the British*, pp. 323–29; see also Gelling, *Signposts*, ch. 2, and D. N. Parsons, 'Classifying Ptolemy's English names', in D. N. Parsons and P. Sims-Williams (eds), *Ptolemy: Towards a Linguistic Atlas of the Earliest Celtic Place-Names of Europe* (Aberystwyth: CMCS, 2000), pp. 169–78.

[130] Oppenheimer, *Origins of the British*, pp. 172 and 399–443.

[131] In this rapidly-developing interdisciplinary topic the remarks of Patrick Sims-Williams remain sound: 'Genetics, linguistics, and prehistory: thinking big and thinking straight', *Antiquity* 72 (1998), 505–27, supplemented now by his 'Bronze- and Iron-Age Celtic-speakers: what don't we know, what can't we know, and what could we know? Language, genetics and archaeology in the twenty-first century', *The Antiquaries Journal* 92 (2012), 427–49.

with remote periods, as some names unquestionably do; and all onomasts are susceptible to the appeal of that concept. Additionally, many people do not like to think that the foundation of England may have been, in part, a violent process.[132] The extent of native survival must have varied from region to region, yet the absence of any convincing evidence for significant linguistic influence of Brittonic upon Old English (e.g. syntax, vocabulary) suggests a lack of extensive linguistic intercourse between the populations.[133] In archaeological circles, for half a century, there has been a dominant assumption that Brittonic survival was widespread, that the archaeological evidence for it only needs documenting, and that the Anglo-Saxon invasions were limited to 'small groups of Germanic lifestyle advisers'.[134] Partly that attitude was a reaction against an earlier overuse of simplistic invasion models. Perhaps it also arose out of misunderstanding or misrepresentation of contrary models of large-scale migrations, as if they must entail complete elimination of the population: yet in places where ethnic cleansing by colonists is attested within the historic period, such as (in different ways) the Americas and Australia, there has also been plenty of survival, with mixed marriages and other forms of intercourse; so evidence for survival is not evidence against a violent Anglo-Saxon settlement.[135]

[132] For example, Coates, 'Significances', p. 47, 'expiation for the sins of my forefathers', has light-heartedly captured a widespread, if usually unspoken, thought among English scholars.

[133] For unconvincing attempts to find syntactic influence see H. Tristram, 'Why don't the English speak Welsh?' in Higham (ed.), *Britons in Anglo-Saxon England*, pp. 192–214, and references given there; contrast R. Coates, 'Invisible Britons: the view from linguistics', in Higham (ed.), *Britons in Anglo-Saxon England*, pp. 172–91.

[134] H. Härke, 'The debate on migration and identity in Europe' (review), *Antiquity* 78 (2004), 453–56 (p. 455).

[135] My warm thanks to Richard Coates, Alan James, and David Parsons for their comments upon this chapter, saving me from errors and omissions; they are naturally not responsible for remaining inaccuracies and infelicities.

Appendix I: Some suggested Brittonic derivations lacking parallels in the Brittonic world

A sample of Brittonic derivations which have been suggested for place-names in England, but for which no convincing parallel in the Celtic world has been found. The list is merely a selection of such names, and good parallels for some of these names may yet be found. For further detail and references, see Coates and Breeze, *Celtic Voices*. English derivations, some similarly doubtful, have also been suggested for several of the names: see the entries in Ekwall, *Dictionary*, and CDEPN.

Arlosh (Cu): 'facing burnt (land)' (?) or 'very-burnt (land)' (?); compare Losk 'burnt (land)' (?) (Db): compare Welsh *llosg* 'burning'?

Beccles (Sf): **Bach-lys* 'small-court' (?) (or OE *Bec-læs* 'stream-pasture')

Brailes (Wa): **bre* + *lys* 'hill-court' (?) (but Ekwall, *Dictionary*, suggests an English derivation; **bre-lys* rejected by Jackson, EPNS Db **3**, p. viii, and by Gelling, *Signposts*); or compare Breazle (below)?

Breazle (D), *Breulishill*, *Brewlleshull* 1238: **Breu-lys* 'generous-court' (Modern Welsh *brau* 'frail, refined, generous'), or **Briw-lys* 'shattered-court' (Modern Welsh *briw* 'shattered'), or **Bryw-lys* 'strong-court' (Modern Welsh *bryw* 'lively, strong') (?) (all + OE *hyll*). For this name compare Brûlis (Morbihan, Brittany: 2 miles north of Muzillac, south-east of Vannes), spelt *Breulis*, *Broulis*, *Broolis* 11th–12th: Bernard Tanguy, in *Cartulaire de Redon*, edited by H. Guillotel and others, 2 vols (Rennes: Amis des Archives Historiques du diocèse de Rennes, Dol et Saint-Malo, 1998–2004), II, 69a.

Chard (So), *Cerdren* 1065 (15th–16th): Welsh *cerdinen* or *cerddinen* '(one) rowan-tree' (?)

Charles (D), *Carmes* 1086, *Charnes* 1242 etc., *Charles* 1244 etc.: **Carn-lys* 'rock-court' (?)

Chinnock (So): compare Welsh *ciniog* 'tattered' (?)

Coslany (Nf): compare Welsh *cystlynedd* 'relationship, kindred' (?)

Croyde (D): compare Welsh *crud* 'cradle' (?)

Doult(ing) (So): Welsh *dylad* 'flood' (+ *-ing*[2]) (?)

Minety (W): Welsh *min* 'edge, lip' or *myn* 'kid' + *tŷ* 'house'(?)

Ower(moigne) (Do): compare (only?) (Bwlch) Oerddrws '(gap of) the cold-door' (Merionethshire, SH7917); but an English derivation is suggested by Watts, CDEPN

Priddy (So): Welsh *pridd* + *tŷ* 'clay-house(s)' (?)

Tarnock (So): compare Tarnac (France) < **tarnāco-* ‘dry-place (?)’

Trusham (D): compare Welsh *drys* (OCo *dreis*) + *ma* ‘brambles-place’? More plausibly perhaps compare Welsh **drysfa* ‘door-place, pass’ (cf. Trusmadoor, Cu)? But still with (different) problem in the vowel

Watchet (So): compare Welsh *go-* + *coed* ‘sub-wood’ (?)

Appendix II: Surviving Romano-British settlement-names

See the discussion (above, pp. 16–19). The list includes a few uncertain examples (Smith, 'Survival of Romano-British toponymy', pp. 31–32). Further details of the Romano-British names are given in PNRB, and of the later names in CDEPN.

(i) Survivals with OE **-cæster** added (28 or 29 examples)

Alauna (PNRB, p. 244): Alcester (Wa); compare Alchester (O; but no Romano-British name known there)

(?) *Bannovalium* 'horn-strong (?)' (PNRB, p. 265): Horncastle (Li; seemingly part-translated)

Branodunum (PNRB, p. 274): Brancaster (Nf)

Calleva (PNRB, p. 291): Silchester (Ha; Coates, *Toponymic Topics*, pp. 39–47)

Colonia (PNRB, p. 312): Colchester (Ess)

Corinium (PNRB, p. 321): Cirencester (Gl)

**Coriosopitum* (PNRB, p. 322): Corchester (Nb; also Corbridge)

Danum (PNRB, p. 329): Doncaster (Y)

Durnovaria (PNRB, p. 345): Dorchester (Do)

Durobrivae (PNRB, p. 346): Rochester (K)

Glevum (PNRB, p. 368): Gloucester

Isca (PNRB, p. 378): Exeter (D)

Longovicium (PNRB, p. 398): Lanchester (Du)

Mamucium (PNRB, p. 409): Manchester (La)

Manduessedum (PNRB p. 411): Mancetter (Wa)

Sorviodunum (PNRB, p. 461): Salisbury (W)

Venta (PNRB, p. 492): Winchester (Ha)

Vinovium (PNRB, p. 504): Binchester (Du)

Viroconium (PNRB, p. 505): Wroxeter (Sa)

Anderitum (PNRB, p. 250): *Andredescester* 890s ASChronicle A, *s.a.* 491 (= Pevensey, Sx)

Aquae Sulis (PNRB, p. 255): (*on*) *Acemannesceastre* 973 ASChronicle A (= Bath; Coates, *Toponymic Topics*, pp. 24–30)

Calcaria (PNRB, p. 288): *Kælcacaestir* 8th Bede (= Tadcaster, Y)

Concangis (PNRB, p. 314): *Kuncacester c.* 700 (9th) Anonymous Life of St Cuthbert (= Chester-le-Street, Du)

Durovernum (PNRB, p. 353): *Dorwitceaster* 1120s ASChronicle E, *s.a.* 604 (= Canterbury, K)

Eburacum (PNRB, p. 355): *Eoforwicceaster* (etc.) 890s+ ASChronicle ABC, Orosius, OEBede (= York)

Othona (PNRB, p. 434): *Ythancaestir* 8th Bede, *Effecestre* 1086 DB (= Bradwell-on-Sea, Ess)

Regulbium (PNRB, p. 446): *Raculfcestre* 784 (12th) S 38 (= Reculver, K)

Rutupiae (PNRB, p. 448): *Reptacaestir* 8th Bede (= Richborough, K)

Verulamium (PNRB, p. 497): *Verlamacaestir* 8th Bede (= St Albans, Hrt)

(ii) Survivals without OE **-cæster** (10 or 11 examples)

Brocavum (PNRB, p. 283): Brougham (We)

Cataractonium (PNRB, p. 302): Catterick (Y)

(?) *Cilurnum* (PNRB, p. 307): Chollerton (Nb; but the connection is doubted in PNRB, and not mentioned in CDEPN, pp. 137a and 139b)

Dubris (PNRB, p. 341): Dover (K)

Letocetum (PNRB, p. 387): Lich(field) (St)

Lindum Colonia (PNRB, p. 393): Lincoln

Londinium (PNRB, p. 396): London

Luguvalium (PNRB, p. 402): (Car)lisle (Cu); note Brittonic *Cair-* in the modern name, corresponding elsewhere to *-cæster*: Welsh *Caerlleon* = Chester (Bede's *Legacæstir*), and Old Welsh *Cair Daun* (*Historia Brittonum*) = Doncaster

Pennocrucium (PNRB, p. 437): Penkridge (St)

Spinis (PNRB, p. 462): Speen (Brk)

Vagniacis (PNRB, p. 485): Win(field) (K; Cullen, '*Vagniacis* and Winfield')

2

Churls and athelings, kings and reeves: some reflections on place-names and early English society

David N. Parsons

In the 1924 *Introduction to the Survey* Sir Frank Stenton wrote on 'The English element' in English place-names.[1] The present chapter is in some ways an equivalent to that one, and covers a good deal of the same ground, though both the approach and the topic are rather different. The scope of Stenton's title was ambitious, to say the least, although clearly there was no intention to encompass all aspects of English language and history, since further contributions to the volume addressed others, including a second chapter by Stenton himself on 'Personal names in place-names', which concentrated largely on Anglo-Saxon material. Indeed, since all place-names in modern England are in one sense English, the title was never a completely happy one. In context, however, the 'English element' was lined up beside the 'Scandinavian element' and the 'Celtic element', where it made a degree of sense, though 'Anglo-Saxon' might have been a better label, and 'early Anglo-Saxon' an even better one, to describe the chapter that Stenton wrote. He concentrated on the very earliest English centuries and—like the contributors on Celtic and Scandinavian names—focused principally on the potential of place-names to add to an understanding of historical, rather than primarily linguistic, questions; questions which were, inevitably for the time,

The volumes of the English Place-Name Society's Survey are indicated by EPNS + county abbreviation as given on p. vi. Anglo-Saxon charters are indicated by S + the number in P. H. Sawyer, *Anglo-Saxon Charters: An Annotated List and Bibliography* (London: The Royal Historical Society, 1968) and the electronic version of S 1–1602 by S. E. Kelly, rev. by R. Rushworth (2006) at <http://www.esawyer.org.uk/>. VEPN = D. Parsons and T. Styles with C. Hough, *The Vocabulary of English Place-Names* I *(Á–Box)* (Nottingham: Centre for English Name-Studies, 1997); D. N. Parsons and T. Styles, *The Vocabulary of English Place-Names* II *(Brace–Cæster)* (Nottingham: Centre for English Name-Studies, 2000); D. N. Parsons, *The Vocabulary of English Place-Names* III *(Ceafor–Cock-pit)* (Nottingham: English Place-Name Society, 2004).

[1] F. M. Stenton, 'The English element', in A. Mawer and F. M. Stenton (eds), *Introduction to the Survey of English Place-Names*, English Place-Name Society 1.i (Cambridge: University Press, 1924), pp. 36–54.

framed in terms of societies defined linguistically, and to an extent racially. The present article follows Stenton in its emphasis on the history of early England, and revisits most of the aspects of early medieval society that he discussed, before extending the timescale into the later Anglo-Saxon or Anglo-Scandinavian period. The approach adopted here, however, is mainly methodological. While Stenton's was a survey of what he believed place-names could add to the earliest English history, the aim here is to reflect upon how historical information can fairly be drawn from place-names, and what kind of history results.

A justification of this approach should be implicit in what follows, but one clear reason for it is simply the matter of scale: to attempt a full modern survey of work relevant to the early Anglo-Saxon centuries, let alone the whole pre-Conquest period or beyond, could by now hardly be encompassed in anything less than a book-length study – and such a book would surely have to start with some consideration of the nature of the evidence. Though that book is not planned, it is hoped that these remarks will be of some interest to any scholars tempted to draw on place-name evidence to supplement other historical materials, whether their interests are in such early periods or are focused elsewhere – for many of the challenging and problematic characteristics of place-name evidence remain largely constant whether the names were coined during, before or after the Anglo-Saxon period, traditionally *c.* 410–1066.

Although place-names in England span twenty centuries and more, there is every reason to be drawn, as was Stenton, to the study of the early middle ages, for the names of the great majority of significant places in most of England—modern cities, towns, villages, a good many hamlets and farmsteads, not to mention the names of major topographical features of all kinds—were clearly established before the Norman Conquest, and, outside parts of the far west, they had passed through Anglo-Saxon transmission even where Old English was not the language of origin. Since surviving documentary historical sources for the pre-Conquest period are relatively few and very biased towards particular regions, periods and concerns, it is natural to look to place-names to help supply some of the gaps in our knowledge, both of language and of history.

This potential was already fully appreciated by the scholars of the early twentieth century, Stenton among them. His chapter, in fact, concentrated specifically on the hidden corners—or the hidden swathes—of Anglo-Saxon history, that, it might be hoped, place-names could help illustrate. Names, after all, are found in every corner of the country, and are thus not limited to the areas of cultural and/or political ascendency that dominate the written record. Moreover, it is very likely that a good many of our surviving English-language names were coined in the first dark centuries that followed the collapse of Roman rule in Britain, when English-speakers were first settling and asserting political control – a period for which narrative sources are almost wholly absent. And as well as appearing everywhere, and potentially carrying information of an early date, place-names have a third attribute, which might be termed register: 'obscurity hangs most thickly,' Stenton observed, 'over just the agrarian field in which the student of place-names is especially interested'.[2] Place-names, many of them, are concerned with the everyday business of growing crops, keeping animals, making a living – the commonplaces of life with which narrative historical sources rarely engage.

Stenton's essay, therefore, explored the society of early England: how the country was colonized by the Germanic-speaking immigrants who divided up the land and over time exploited and developed its economic potential. Most of this belongs to the pre-historic period of English history in terms of documentary records, and place-names were drawn upon to create a picture of a society essentially, at the first, free and communal and equitable, though gradually, over the centuries, constricted by private and institutional interests.[3]

How did Stenton draw this picture from place-names? His central evidence was the class of names in *-ingas*, first of all the Hastings and Woking type, originally folk-names which denote groups descended from or associated with some eponymous ancestral leader; secondly the Birmingham and Nottingham type, in which we appear to have the

[2] 'English element', p. 36. These categories of ubiquity, chronological range and register overlap with, and could be thought to complement, the 'abundance, ubiquity and internal consistency' stressed by Margaret Gelling: 'Towards a chronology for English place-names', in D. Hooke (ed.), *Anglo-Saxon Settlements* (Oxford: Blackwell, 1988), pp. 59–76 (p. 59). Her 'internal consistency' is a major aspect of the interpretational context discussed further below.

[3] This is something of a caricature of Stenton's views, of course, and in 'English element', as in other works, he wrestled with the relationship between free peasant and nobility. Nonetheless, his general estimation was certainly along these lines – cf. the specific arguments from place-names, discussed below, and the interim conclusions: '[I]t is necessary to remember that the *ceorls* formed the basis of the community and that their independence was not affected by the relationship in which they stood to the great man of their village' and 'the familiar features of later manorial society must not be carried back to the remote age in which village communities arose' ('English element', p. 44). For some comments on Stenton's views of the free peasantry see J. Campbell, 'Stenton's *Anglo-Saxon England*, with special reference to the earlier period', in D. Matthew (ed.), *Stenton's* Anglo-Saxon England *Fifty Years On*, Reading Historical Studies 1 (Reading: University of Reading, 1994), pp. 49–59 (pp. 55–56).

enduring 'homesteads' of such groups. Such names, he argued, take us back to 'the time following the migration' of the Anglo-Saxons, and—in their nature, as plural group-names—'they suggest that the original settlement of at least the eastern third of England was the work of communities rather than of individuals'.[4] In support of the communality of early English society he pointed also to the recurrent name Charlton, a settlement of *ceorlas* or 'free, non-noble' peasants; and he contrasted these with names like Ednaston, '*Ēadnōð*'s *tūn*', where a personal name appears to indicate an individual owner. This latter type of name belonged, he believed, to 'a late phase' of pre-Conquest history, the ninth to eleventh centuries.[5]

Besides this grand narrative, Stenton made various incidental observations in the course of his chapter. He had a section, for instance, on what he called 'descriptive names', where he made three substantive points. One, that occasionally such names can be historically informative, as in the case of a group of names in *feld* in Berkshire which, he said, 'undoubtedly suggest that the Saxon settlement of this region was only made possible by the clearance of woodland'.[6] Two, that the most interesting descriptive names are those relating to the beliefs of the heathen period: thus 'if the great earthwork called Wansdyke was not regarded as [Woden's] work, it was at least sacred to him'.[7] But three—which in fact took priority in his formulation—that descriptive names on the whole tell us 'nothing of importance for social history', and are 'intrinsically trivial'.[8]

Thus Stenton's assessment in 1924. Perhaps we should not be surprised that in the nearly ninety years that have since passed practically every aspect of his interpretation should have been doubted, challenged, modified or rejected, at least as far as the name-evidence goes. Most fundamentally, the significance and chronology of group-names in *-ingas* was turned on its head by John Dodgson, Barrie Cox and others in the 1960s and 70s:[9] the names do not correlate with early Anglo-Saxon

[4] 'English element', pp. 53–54.

[5] 'English element', p. 43.

[6] 'English element', p. 37.

[7] 'English element', p. 38.

[8] 'English element', pp. 36–37. Another point that Stenton took up for discussion in his chapter, the nature of place-names in the earliest Anglo-Saxon records, is considered further in D. N. Parsons, *The Pre-Viking Place-Names of Northamptonshire*, 26th Brixworth Lecture (Leicester, forthcoming).

[9] J. McN. Dodgson, 'The significance of the distribution of the English place-name in

archaeology in a straightforward way, and it has been proposed that—rather than representing the earliest boatloads of immigrants—they derive from a secondary phase of settlement, close to, if not within, the Christian period. And as part of this reassessment it was argued that names in *-hām*, simply, are probably earlier than the *-ingahām* type, which in turn could well be earlier than the *-ingas* type: a complete reversal of the earlier thinking.[10] Given that very many names in *-hām* are interpreted as containing an Anglo-Saxon personal name as first element, then Stenton's primary conclusion, that the earliest names favour the settlement of communities over individuals, is thrown into question.

Similar doubts attend the chronology, if not the ultimate implication, of the Charlton names. Scholars have tended naturally to relate this name-type in some way to the practice of open-field farming, in which a village community made use of a shared agrarian system: huge common fields, worked in separate strips by individual farmers. Stenton was, of course, familiar with this arrangement, which continued into the early modern period in much of the country, and in common with others of his generation, he saw such communal husbandry, with its attendant village settlements, as a system introduced by the 'free' Anglo-Saxon settlers. He would have been utterly astonished to learn what modern archaeology and landscape-history has taught us, that open-field farming appears to be an innovation—an agricultural revolution—of the central Anglo-Saxon period, beginning around the ninth century.[11] More recent commentators,

-ingas, *-inga-* in south-east England', *Medieval Archaeology* 10 (1966), 1–29; B. Cox, 'The significance of the distribution of English place-names in *-hām* in the midlands and East Anglia', *Journal of the English Place-Name Society* 5 (1973), 15–73. These two studies were reprinted in K. Cameron (ed.), *Place-Name Evidence for the Anglo-Saxon Invasion and Scandinavian Settlements* (Nottingham: English Place-Name Society, 1975), pp. 27–54 and 55–98 respectively. Further contributions on similar lines were J. McN. Dodgson, 'Place-names from *hām*, distinguished from *hamm* names, in relation to the settlement of Kent, Surrey and Sussex', *Anglo-Saxon England* 2 (1973), 1–50; J. Kuurman, 'An examination of the *-ingas*, *-inga-* place-names in the east midlands', *Journal of the English Place-Name Society* 7 (1975), 11–44.

[10] The debate was reviewed in some detail, and the reversal of the chronology embraced, by K. Cameron, 'The significance of English place-names', *Proceedings of the British Academy* 62 (1976), 3–23 (pp. 5–15), and by M. Gelling, *Signposts to the Past*, 3rd edn (Chichester: Phillimore, 1997), pp. 108–14.

[11] T. Rowley (ed.), *The Origins of Open-Field Agriculture* (London: Croom Helm, 1981); D. Hall, *The Open Fields of Northamptonshire* (Northampton: Northamptonshire Record Society, 1995), pp. 125–39; C. Lewis, P. Mitchell-Fox and C. Dyer, *Village, Hamlet and Field: Changing Medieval Settlements in Central England*, 2nd edn (Macclesfield: Windgather, 2001); T. Williamson, *Shaping Medieval Landscapes: Settlement, Society, Environment* (Macclesfield: Windgather, 2003), pp. 1–27, 180–85. Cf. Jones below, pp. 191–98.

like H. P. R. Finberg and Ros Faith, have argued that the coining of Charlton place-names is to be sought in its wake—in the context of late Anglo-Saxon processes of manorialization and settlement-nucleation—an interpretation which then, of course, has implications for the nature and origins of the freedom of the *ceorlas* concerned.[12]

In other ways too the paradigm has changed, or at least shifted, since the 1920s. That Berkshire's *feld*-names imply the clearance of woodland by the Anglo-Saxon immigrants evokes a picture of the penetration of primordial forest somewhat at odds with the prevailing modern view of a landscape extensively cleared in the Neolithic, and under widespread cultivation in the Roman period.[13] Margaret Gelling understood *feld* quite differently, arguing that to the earliest Anglo-Saxons it denoted 'open land', unencumbered by forest, marsh or mountain.[14] Indeed, Gelling interpreted much of Stenton's material quite differently. She worked extensively on the 'heathen' Anglo-Saxon place-names, for instance, and the problems of their interpretation.[15] Names of ancient earthworks that apparently recall the god Woden, she suspected, could be Christian-period coinages for constructions supposed to have been built in the legendary past: at any rate, it could not simply be assumed that they bore

[12] R. Faith, *The English Peasantry and the Growth of Lordship* (London: Leicester University Press, 1997), pp. 150–51; H. P. R. Finberg, 'Charltons and Carltons', in his *Lucerna: Studies of some problems in the early history of England* (London: Macmillan, 1964), pp. 144–60.

[13] Lewis, Mitchell-Fox and Dyer, *Village, Hamlet and Field*, p. 67: 'The suggestion that Saxon incomers in the fifth and sixth centuries found a "virgin country" of forest and marshes has been refuted by archaeological evidence [...] much of England had been largely cleared of woodland, farmed and settled in a process which began as early as 4000 BC'. Note that later woodland is not necessarily a good guide to earlier conditions: the medieval Whittlewood Forest in the south-east midlands was in the Roman period 'largely an open landscape of arable and pasture': R. Jones and M. Page, *Medieval Villages in an English Landscape: Beginnings and Ends* (Macclesfield: Windgather, 2006), p. 106.

[14] M. Gelling, *Place-Names in the Landscape* (London: Dent, 1984), pp. 235–37; M. Gelling and A. Cole, *The Landscape of Place-Names* (Stamford: Shaun Tyas, 2000), pp. 269–72. For the specific group of Berkshire *feld*-names discussed by Stenton she proposed 'a belt of open heath-land [...] used as common pasture' by the early Anglo-Saxons (*Signposts to the Past*, p. 128). Compare Scarfe's treatment of the adjacent parishes of Bradfield, Cockfield and Stanningfield in Suffolk – he argued that they were indeed arable cleared from woodland, but that the clearance belonged to the Roman period: N. Scarfe, *Suffolk in the Middle Ages* (Woodbridge: Boydell, 1986), pp. 76–77.

[15] M. Gelling, 'Place-names and Anglo-Saxon paganism', *University of Birmingham Historical Journal* 8 (1961), 7–25; 'Further thoughts on pagan place-names', in F. Sandgren (ed.), *Otium et Negotium: studies in onomatology and library science presented to Olof von Feilitzen* (Stockholm: Norstedt, 1973), pp. 109–28, reprinted in Cameron (ed.), *Place-Name Evidence*, pp. 99–114; *Signposts to the Past*, pp. 148–50, 158–61.

direct witness to pagan practice or belief.[16] The Devil's Dyke or Devil's Punchbowl, after all, are not usually interpreted as evidencing modern pockets of devil-worship.

Then there are those 'intrinsically trivial' descriptive names. Gelling devoted much of the last quarter century of her prolific career to a defence, a promotion, of such descriptive names. She argued that they take us into the minds of the ordinary folk who tilled the soil, and that such perceptions are of immense value to the student of the social and agrarian history of the early middle ages.[17] Indeed, for good measure, she proposed that topographical names are likely to form the earliest stratum of names given to settlements by the Anglo-Saxons, often earlier than all Stenton's *-ingas* and *-ingahāms*.[18]

In her University of Nottingham Cameron lecture, in 2002, Gelling went so far as to characterize Stenton's introductory chapters to the early county-volumes as nowadays seeming 'largely misguided'.[19] That is perhaps a little harsh, at least with regard to his chapter in the *Introduction to the Survey*; but the observations so far, combined with her judgement, prompt some questions. If Stenton's conclusions are wrong, why are they wrong? Is it simply a question of the accumulation of

[16] It should be conceded that although she preferred the Christian-period interpretation for some instances of Grimsditch and Grim's Dyke—where *Grīm* is a nickname for Woden—Gelling was troubled by the origin of the name Wansdyke itself. She accepted archaeological indications that the earthworks were post-Roman, and she thought that therefore the Anglo-Saxons ought to have known of their man-made origins. In consequence she did in this case entertain Stenton's interpretation, while noting 'no solution has been found which is wholly convincing': Gelling, 'Place-names and Anglo-Saxon paganism', pp. 11–13; *Signposts to the Past*, pp. 148–49 (quotation p. 149).

[17] E.g. Gelling and Cole, *Landscape of Place-Names*, pp. xii–xiii. Cf. Stenton's own conclusion, similarly expressed yet diametrically opposed at the same time: '[t]hese earliest English place-names were created by men who as yet thought less of the land itself than of the groups of people settled on it. And this indication of men's habits of thought deserves to be considered in any attempt to understand the social conditions of the centuries which followed the migration' ('English element', p. 54). See further Cullen below, pp. 161–79.

[18] This suspicion, in fact, is evidently what drew her to the study of topographical names in the first place: Gelling, *Place-Names in the Landscape*, p. 6; *Signposts to the Past*, pp. 116–29. As she noted, Dodgson ('The significance of the distribution', p. 29) and Cameron ('The significance of English place-names', p. 15) also proposed or endorsed the suggestion that the first names may have been topographical, while Cox's analysis of the earliest sources gave it an evidential and statistical basis: B. Cox, 'The place-names of the earliest English records', *Journal of the English Place-Name Society* 8 (1975–76), 12–66. See Cullen below, pp. 164–65.

[19] M. Gelling, 'English place-name studies: some reflections', *Journal of the English Place-Name Society* 35 (2002–03), 5–16 (p. 7).

knowledge over time – do we know more about the names than he did? Or is it a function of his approach or reasoning? Is it somehow an almost inevitable outcome of the passing of time in any discipline?

Stenton's understanding of the names that he selected, at one level, is wholly unexceptionable. The group-names, or folk-names, in *-ingas* are still understood as such today.[20] Charlton names, all agree, denote settlements of *ceorlas*, churls, a kind of middle-ranking Anglo-Saxon peasant (though the nature and extent of their 'free' status is controversial[21]). *Feld*-names denote open land. Wansdyke is 'Woden's dyke or earthwork'. But in each case, to flesh out historical significance from the literal interpretation, Stenton drew inferences that might be questioned. Most obviously, interpretation of *feld* as not just 'open land', but 'open land newly cleared from woodland', is pure assumption. Similarly, to infer that the name Wansdyke necessarily dates from a period of active heathenism, involves, as it were, a leap of faith. And there are, arguably, similar leaps in the interpretation of the *-ingas* and Charlton groups, though these cases are rather more complicated, because here Stenton introduced evidence beyond the mere fact of the name.

Thus when Stenton argued that *-ingas* names were early in the settlement sequence, he pointed to the facts that they can often be equated with the large *provinciae* of early accounts, and that the documentation indicates that they were already ancient by the seventh/eighth-century horizon of the earliest sources: evidently, as he argued, they 'belong to a phase of local organization earlier than the division of the land into shires'.[22] Linguistic analysis, moreover, shows that many of the first elements—apparently personal names—are paralleled in early continental documents, but not in English ones.[23] And further, the distribution map

[20] No one disputes the fact that there are hundreds of *-ingas* group-names in the place-names of southern and eastern England, even if some individual names have been reanalysed: a significant example is Mucking, site of a notable early Anglo-Saxon settlement and cemetery complex, which Gelling reinterpreted as a stream-name, with a distinct singular *-ing* suffix (*Signposts to the Past*, pp. 119–21). Cf. Jones below, p. 184.

[21] Faith, *English Peasantry*, p. 127, suggested that *ceorl* was 'a large and loosely defined social category [...], which included all those who were neither unfree nor of aristocratic birth'; and that it 'may preserve vestiges of a social class of a type which escapes our modern typologies, a class in which both peasant farmers and lesser landowners were to be found'. Discussion and further references in VEPN, III, p. 19.

[22] 'English element', p. 48.

[23] 'English element', p. 51. So also, e.g., A. H. Smith, *English Place-Name Elements*, 2 vols (Cambridge: Cambridge University Press, 1956) [EPNE], I, p. 300; cf. Insley below, pp. 239–40.

places them in the southern and eastern part of the country, where the Anglo-Saxons undoubtedly settled first. There is a good deal to go on here, and it would be very unfair to say that Stenton had simply jumped to conclusions.

Similarly with Charlton. Stenton did not know what we have been taught by modern archaeology, and when he thought about the communality implied by a 'settlement of churls', he rather naturally wanted it to be original, and to make it part of the same narrative as the folk-names. As in the Britain of the later twentieth century: a phase of communal ownership gave way to subsequent privatization. For the Anglo-Saxon period the archaeologists have certainly complicated this with regard to common-field farming. But, again, as with the *-ingas* groups, Stenton was able to put forward more than a mere hunch: he drew attention to one of the earliest surviving English laws, issued in the name of the late seventh-century king of the West Saxons, Ine. There is a famous clause here which begins: 'if churls have common meadow or other share-land to enclose, and some have enclosed their share, others not, and beasts eat of their common acres or grass', then—to paraphrase—woe betide the churl who left the gap.[24] The word Stenton translated as 'meadow' here is a kind of *tūn*, a *gærstūn*, literally a 'grass-enclosure'; so here we have churls holding a *tūn* within a system of communally held share-land, which includes both grass, i.e. pasture, and acres, i.e. arable ploughland, by the end of the seventh century. The elements of a *ceorla-tūn* thus sound as if they are in place long before the archaeologists' open-field revolution, which is a point that might have received rather more attention in recent scholarship than it has.[25]

[24] Stenton, 'English element', pp. 41–42. The clause is printed in Old English in F. Liebermann, *Die Gesetze der Angelsachsen*, 3 vols (Halle: Max Niemeyer, 1903–16), I, 106, and in English translation in D. Whitelock (ed.), *English Historical Documents c. 500–1042*, 2nd edn (London: Eyre Methuen, 1979), p. 403; text and translation are also given in VEPN, III, p. 21.

[25] The passage was noted in connection with the origin of open fields by Williamson, *Shaping Medieval Landscapes*, p. 6 – he observed, quite reasonably, that it does not establish that such fields existed in all the places or forms that they are later found; he did not discuss the name Charlton. In the discussions of the name-type by Faith and Finberg (above, n. 12), Ine's text is not introduced. Another point generally overlooked in consideration of the name (omitted also from the discussion in VEPN, III, pp. 20–22) is the tenth-century evidence for open-field farming (intermingled strips) in the phrasing of two charters relating to a place, or two distinct places, called Charlton in Berkshire: S. E. Kelly (ed.), *Charters of Abingdon Abbey, Part II*, Anglo-Saxon Charters 8 (Oxford: British Academy, 2001), p. 292 (no. 69 = S 634), p. 461 (no. 118 = S 839).

If Stenton was wrong over *-ingas* and Charltons, it may be that he was only partially wrong, and that in both cases there is a distinction to be drawn, which he did not draw, between the social organization and the place-names. Thus *-ingas* groups may well have been prominent amongst the earliest migrants and in giving name to the earliest territories. It is another question how those names came to survive, attached to individual places, generally parish-sized units, probably much smaller than their earlier extent.[26] Stenton thought they would over time 'have become restricted to the place where habitation was thickest, or where the original settlement had been made'.[27] This may well be the weak point in the argument. The force of modern work may be to suggest that the names persisted best on the edges of the territories, or perhaps sometimes even applied to detached appurtenances. Hence, possibly, the paradox that one of the oldest name-types seems not to correlate in detail with the oldest archaeology.[28] Similarly, perhaps, with Charltons. If the surviving names derive, as Finberg thought, from the breakup of large Anglo-Saxon estates towards the end of the period, that does not preclude the possibility that the concept of a *ceorla-tūn*—at an early date perhaps generally a constituent part of a larger, otherwise named, estate—may, as Stenton believed, have very deep roots. While the survival of individual instances as place-names, and their geographical distribution around the country, could be due to the circumstances of the ninth to eleventh centuries, it is possible that the underlying settlement-type predates this by centuries.[29] Such an example (an hypothesis only, of course) illustrates

[26] This suggestion could be seen as the extension of a notion proposed by Barrie Cox: 'Logically one would suppose names in *-ingas* to have preceded place-names formed from its genitive plural *-inga-* + *hām*. In fact they did so; but not as place-names' (Cox, 'Significance of the distribution', p. 48; quoted also by Cameron, 'Significance of English place-names', p. 13). The contention is thus that, as group-names (and societal phenomena) *-ingas* names are early, but that they became attached to individual settlements relatively late in the naming sequence. The view might be thought to contrast with Dodgson's explicit argument that *-ingas* groups as a phenomenon, as well as the place-names derived from them, were products of a secondary, post-immigration, phase in the Anglo-Saxon settlements (Dodgson, 'Significance of the distribution', p. 40, echoed by Gelling, *Signposts to the Past*, p. 109).

[27] 'English element', p. 47.

[28] This question is given further consideration in Parsons, *Pre-Viking Place-Names*.

[29] For a fuller treatment of the Charlton debate, with further references, see VEPN, III, pp. 19–23. More recently Carole Hough has suggested that the place-name may emphasize the functional, legal status of the holding, which seems entirely reasonable, though her implication that it need not be distinctive in this respect from neighbouring holdings seems to me doubtful (C. Hough, 'Commonplace place-names', *Nomina* 30 (2007), 101–20 (pp. 117–19)).

the potential complexity of place-name evidence, and highlights a key recurrent difficulty for the historian: establishing the likely date of a name's coining.

Gelling's verdict on the early place-name historians, amongst whom Stenton was pre-eminent, was sharp: 'they looked for evidence to support the views they already held. They did not let the names speak for themselves'.[30] My reading of the 'English element' chapter from the *Introduction to the Survey* would modify that. Sometimes Gelling clearly has a point: the vision of Berkshire settlers cutting *feld* places out of the primordial forest is straight from Stenton's imagination, albeit that the view of a heavily wooded land would have been widely held at the time. In other instances, also, further study has complicated conclusions which seemed clear in the 1920s. But some of those judgements, as we have seen, were buttressed with contextual evidence which has not gone away, and the acceptance of the new indications sometimes seems to have been at a price. Stenton was above all a documentary historian: he knew better than most of us the texts, English and Latin, that relate to the history of early medieval England. Some of the connections he made between these sources and place-names are invaluable, and cannot be overlooked, even if their implications are not straightforward.

The discussion so far is intended primarily to have been methodological, with a view to addressing three questions: how does Stenton's contribution stand up? why does it fall down when it does? how can we derive history from place-names? The remainder of this article will concentrate on expanding upon the third. But we shall move away from Stenton's agenda, because—as he himself put it at the beginning of his concluding remarks—'[t]he earliest English place-names are difficult material to handle for historical purposes. They lead to much inconclusive discussion, and they yield few assured results'.[31] The particular topic of the Anglo-Saxon settlements, and the prehistoric developments between the fifth and seventh centuries inevitably remain difficult and controversial. Indeed Stenton chose not to touch at all, in 'The English element', on the aspect of this period which remains the most controversial: the size of that element – the extent to which Anglo-Saxon incomers lived alongside the settled British population, or the extent to which they drove them away.[32] Rather than become entangled in

[30] Gelling, 'English place-name studies', p. 16.

[31] 'English element', p. 54.

[32] For the range of views see the various contributions to N. Higham (ed.), *Britons in*

this thorny conundrum, it is a relief to shift attention for much of the rest of this chapter to later periods, a little better evidenced.

The thrust of what follows is simple, perhaps simplistic: that the key to understanding place-name evidence is context, and that the robustness of the context needs constantly to be assessed and reassessed. Individual place-names can be notoriously misleading. Old English *Eoforwīc*, York, is clearly to be interpreted as a farm supplying the local economy with pork (OE *eofor* 'boar', *wīc* 'specialized farm'), until it is recalled that the Romano-British name of the place was *Eburācon*, perhaps 'place of (a man called) Eburos' or 'place abounding in yew-trees'. Whether by linguistic chance or conscious recasting place-names can give a false impression, and secure linguistic interpretation requires not only thorough documentary research and expertise in the likely languages of origin, but also some kind of contextual grounding – sometimes in the topography, often in the name-type.[33] And the first impressions of a plausible context may not be enough, as the instance of York, which would seem to have good Old English parallels, demonstrates.[34] Even a recurrent compound which appears wholly linguistically transparent may not yield up its origins without a struggle.

An excellent example of this is provided by recent work on the name Kingston, the 'king's *tūn*'. Given, perhaps, the circumstance that one Kingston—Kingston upon Thames in Surrey—is known to have been a prominent royal centre where successive kings were crowned, the (largely tacit) assumption has always been that the sixty or more further places that bear the same name were also important royal manors, estates where the king may have a residence, from which he might exercise his

Anglo-Saxon England (Woodbridge: Boydell, 2007). See also Padel above, pp. 35–37. There is a worrying tendency to polarization between place-name specialists on the one hand and archaeologists on the other: there remains room for a critical assessment of the limitations of method, on both sides.

[33] This argument is made at greater length in L. Abrams and D. N. Parsons, 'Place-names and the history of Scandinavian settlement in England', in J. Hines, A. Lane and M. Redknap (eds), *Land, Sea and Home* (Leeds: Maney, 2004), pp. 379–431 (pp. 393–94).

[34] It is possible to fit *Eoforwīc* into two Old English place-name sequences: recurrent *Eofortūn*, Everton, on the one hand, and all the *wīc*-names that imply specialised food-production, including Spitchwick in Devon, perhaps with OE *spic* 'bacon', on the other (see EPNE, I, pp. 153–54; II, pp. 137, 262). This underlines the point that, whereas strong patterns of names—like the Charltons and the various *-ingas* types—can be wholly convincing, the etymologies of individual place-names generally fall short of absolute certainty. Where there is a strong pattern, of course, a similar, but ultimately unrelated, name may well be altered by analogy to conform to it (Abrams and Parsons, 'Place-names and the history', pp. 393–94).

power. Yet investigation of the sites renders this improbable.[35] Kingstons are characteristically small and not valuable when first recorded; around half the names are not recorded in Domesday Book, and many first appear in documents of the twelfth and thirteenth centuries; they have a tendency to survive as the name of hamlets or houses more often than of parishes or villages; Kingston upon Thames apart, there is no historical record suggesting any royal centrality, though in some cases they are positioned close to known royal centres – Kingston Maurward beside Dorchester (Do), for instance. Add to this the observation that several groups of Kingstons appear regularly spaced, around ten miles apart, along known Roman roads, and a case emerges for a Kingston as something functional, with origins probably relatively early in the Anglo-Saxon period, and concerned with the reach and administration of royal power, but not with the status and lodging of the royal person.

All of this can be deduced, as Jill Bourne has shown, from a careful analysis of the place-names in their documentary and landscape context. When such an analysis dovetails neatly with an examination of *cyninges tūn* in Old English usage, the argument becomes particularly compelling. In the laws of Æthelberht of Kent, putatively of the early seventh century, there is a clause detailing the punishment for murder in a *cyninges tūn*, while a law of King Alfred, three hundred years later, specifies imprisonment in a *cyninges tūn* for oath-breakers.[36] Finally, the Anglo-Saxon Chronicle, under the year 787 (for 789), records the futile attempts of a Dorset reeve to compel the earliest-known Viking visitors to England to accompany him to the *cyninges tūn*.[37] While in each of these examples

[35] J. Bourne, 'The Place-Name Kingston and its Context', unpublished PhD thesis (University of Nottingham, 2012); Bourne, 'Kingston – the place-name and its context', in R. Jones and S. Semple (eds), *Sense of Place in Anglo-Saxon England* (Donington: Shaun Tyas, 2012), pp. 260–83. These works supersede Bourne's preliminary study 'Kingston place-names: an interim report', *Journal of the English Place-Name Society* 20 (1987–88), 13–37. See also D. Probert, 'Towards a reassessment of "Kingston" place-names', *Journal of the English Place-Name Society* 40 (2008), 7–22.

[36] Liebermann, *Die Gesetze* I, 3, 48; Whitelock, *English Historical Documents*, pp. 391, 409 (in each case translating *cyninges tūn* as 'king's estate'). The significance of these texts for the interpretation of the place-name was first emphasized by C. Hough, 'The place-name Kingston and the laws of Æthelberht', *Studia Neophilologica* 69 (1997), 55–57; see also Probert, 'Towards a reassessment', pp. 14–15, Bourne, 'Kingston', p. 271.

[37] J. M. Bately (ed.), *The Anglo-Saxon Chronicle: A Collaborative Edition. Volume 3 MS A* (Cambridge: D. S. Brewer, 1986), p. 39; D. Whitelock (ed. and trans.), with D. C. Douglas and Susie I. Tucker, *The Anglo-Saxon Chronicle: A Revised Translation* (London: Eyre and Spottiswoode, 1961), p. 35. Complications in interpreting the passage arise from Æthelweard's late-tenth-century Latin version of the text: he was able to add the information that the reeve was called out from the *oppidum* of Dorchester, and wanted

'royal estate' is just about a conceivable gloss (though there would be doubts about whether the semantic range of *tūn* would extend to encompass 'estate, manor' in such potentially early instances), an alternative—in the light of the place-name patterns—seems more likely. A 'kingston', in the first half of the Anglo-Saxon period, looks as if it may have been the 'king's enclosure' or even 'compound', functioning as a local lockup, and, quite possibly also, the local focus of various aspects of royal administration, such as the collection of renders, as well as providing a link in a chain of communication stretching around the kingdom. This suggestion is not wholly new: Finberg wrote on related lines in 1972,[38] while Stenton himself had been well aware of the documentary record of *cyninges tūn*,[39] as we might expect, though neither discussed the recurrent place-name in this connection. It has, however, bypassed the main lines of English place-name scholarship, and only now—with the work on the status and distribution of the names—does it crystallize, in my view, as a probability rather than a possibility.

to drive the incomers to the *regiam uillam*. Not unnaturally, *regia villa* has here been interpreted as the 'royal town' of Dorchester, but that need not follow: it may or may not be what Æthelweard himself understood, but in either case *regia villa* may here simply be a translation for original *cyninges tūn*, even though the two are perhaps usually to be kept apart (see below, n. 39). See also Bourne, 'Kingston', p. 271.

[38] H. P. R. Finberg (ed.), *The Agrarian History of England and Wales: volume I, ii A.D. 43–1042* (Cambridge: Cambridge University Press, 1972), pp. 456–57: 'Justice would normally be done at the nearest *cyninges tun*—we shall hardly be coining a word if we call it a Kingston—one of those domains which the king owned in every shire. The kingston, managed for him by a reeve, was a fundamental unit in the Old English organization of justice and finance. [...] to the kingston the tillers of the soil would deliver the produce which made up the monarch's food-rent'. Though the adoption of a common noun 'kingston' clearly shows that Finberg made the connection, he does not appear to have studied the Kingston place-names in light of his understanding of the term.

[39] F. M. Stenton, *Anglo-Saxon England*, 3rd edn (Oxford: Clarendon Press, 1971), p. 482 (the passage is substantially unaltered from pp. 474–75 of the first edition of 1943). Stenton explicitly conflated *cyninges tūn* with *regia villa*, regarding the institution as the very early 'predecessor of the royal manor, [...] a fundamental unit in the organization of justice and finance'. The force of modern work has been to separate the early Old English *cyninges tūn*, surviving in the place-names, from the later Anglo-Saxon Latin use of *regia villa*, *villa regalis*, etc. Imprisonment was evidently an aspect of the former; it might be suspected that other practical functions attributed to the royal manor/*regia villa*, such as the collection of food-rents, were also handled at the *cyninges tūn*. It may be possible that we have here a chronological sequence: that the early Kingstons were superseded by richer royal manors which took over their functions. The label *cyninges tūn*, denoting perhaps a purpose-built enclosure, may have been inappropriate for such later estates, which would help explain why known *regiae villae* do not bear the name. It is nonetheless strange that more Kingstons did not survive in the lands, or as appurtenances, of known later *regiae villae*.

In this example the patterns made by the place-names, their distribution across time, space and documents, can be set alongside a handful of valuable textual records. Elsewhere 'context'—admittedly a broad and sometimes slippery term—comes in other forms and in differing proportions. In the instance which follows the accent is placed particularly on the surviving written record, the nexus of narrative accounts and administrative documents like wills, law-codes and royal diplomas, which, in the right circumstances, can combine to illustrate each other and to bathe some parts of Anglo-Saxon England in a relative flood of light. Written sources are particularly rich, of course, for the affairs of the West Saxon royal house between the ninth and early eleventh centuries; yet place-name evidence, it will be shown, can have something to add even here.

We begin at one of the most famous points in the history of early England. By the winter of 877 the 'Great Army' of the Vikings, having made significant conquests over recent years in the kingdoms of Northumbria, Mercia and East Anglia, had turned its attention to Alfred's Wessex. The Vikings overwintered at Chippenham in Wiltshire, and the Anglo-Saxon Chronicle relates that they:

> occupied the land of the West Saxons and settled there, and drove a great part of the people across the sea, and conquered most of the others; and the people submitted to them, except King Alfred [who] journeyed in difficulties through the woods and fen-fastnesses with a small force.[40]

Alfred's biographer Asser gave more detail:

> King Alfred, with his small band of nobles and also with certain soldiers and thegns, was leading a restless life in great distress amid the woody and marshy places of Somerset. He had nothing to live on except what he could forage by frequent raids, either secretly or even openly, from the Vikings as well as from the Christians who had submitted to the Vikings' authority.[41]

So Alfred spent the winter, but at Easter 878 he constructed a stronghold at Athelney, a place which, according to Asser, 'is surrounded by swampy, impassable and extensive marshland and groundwater on every side'.[42] From this base, somewhat miraculously, the small force struck

[40] Whitelock, *Anglo-Saxon Chronicle*, p. 49.

[41] S. Keynes and M. Lapidge (trans.), *Alfred the Great: Asser's* Life of King Alfred *and other contemporary sources* (Harmondsworth: Penguin, 1983), p. 83 (ch. 53).

[42] Keynes and Lapidge, *Alfred the Great*, p. 103 (ch. 92).

out and won a great battle at Edington in Wiltshire, such that the Vikings were defeated and their leader, Guthrum, was forced to come to terms and to accept Christian baptism. The Vikings remained a threatening presence for decades to come, but the tide had turned, and the history of the following century can be seen—and was certainly presented by these clearly partial sources—as the gradual flowering of the West Saxons, from the low point in the swamps of Athelney, to recovery, and then to conquest of new lands, resulting ultimately in an England politically united for the first time. The turning-point quickly became embroidered: not much more than a century later *The Life of St Neot* described Alfred's journey to Athelney as a lone traveller, taking refuge in a swineherd's cottage and—of course—burning the cakes.[43]

Even Asser, writing in 893, and unaware of the longer-term outcome, doubtless presented the events of 878 for maximum effect: Alfred's subsequent success thrown into all the greater relief by the depths of his earlier predicament. Nonetheless, even if we suspect hyperbole, it would be a brave historian who rejected the fundamental nature of the crisis of 877–78, and Alfred's retreat to the swamps. That there is a little more to this most famous of stories than meets the eye, however, seems highly likely from the place-name, though this has rarely been noted,[44] and deserves some expansion here since it connects to a wider onomastic pattern.

Athelney, Old English *Æðelinga-ēg*, is transparently 'the island of the princes', of the athelings, the king's sons.[45] It surely cannot be

[43] Keynes and Lapidge, *Alfred the Great*, pp. 197–202.

[44] The following point is hinted at by Dorothy Whitelock, in her introduction to the reprint of Stevenson's Asser (D. Whitelock, 'Recent work on Asser's *Life of Alfred*', in W. H. Stevenson (ed.), *Asser's Life of King Alfred* (Oxford: Clarendon Press, 1904; repr. 1959), pp. cxxxii–clii (p. cxxxv)) and by D. N. Dumville, 'The ætheling: a study in Anglo-Saxon constitutional history', *Anglo-Saxon England* 8 (1979), 1–33 (pp. 5–6). Recently Ryan Lavelle has usefully begun to develop it (R. Lavelle, 'Geographies of power in the Anglo-Saxon Chronicle: the royal estates of Anglo-Saxon Wessex', in A. Jorgensen (ed.), *Reading the Anglo-Saxon Chronicle: Language, Literature, History* (Turnhout: Brepols, 2010), pp. 187–219 (pp. 202–03). Nonetheless, there is no note in any of the standard editions or translations of the Alfredian Chronicle, and so general accounts usually fail to pick up the potential significance.

[45] The earliest spellings, from manuscript A of the Chronicle, copied *c.* 900, are *æt Ęþelingaeigge* and *wiþ Ęþelinggaeige* (Bately, *Anglo-Saxon Chronicle*, pp. 50–51); Asser's form, potentially as early but surviving only in an early modern transcript of a manuscript of *c.* 1000, is *Æthelingaeg* (Stevenson (ed.), *Asser's Life of King Alfred*, pp. 44, 79). The place-name dictionaries are unanimous on the interpretation, though none speculates on the implications: E. Ekwall, *The Concise Oxford Dictionary of English Place-Names*, 4th edn (Oxford: Clarendon, 1960) [DEPN], p. 18; A. D. Mills, *Dictionary*

coincidence that a site bearing this name was the scene of a remarkable royal event, but how does the connection work? An early speculation was roundly rebuffed by W. H. Stevenson in 1904:

> Bishop Clifford, in his fantastic manner, explained the name as meaning 'isle of the royal children', because Alfred hid his wife and children in it in 878 (which is a mere guess), or because he permitted his nobles to accompany him thither.[46]

Yet Stevenson's preferred alternative, that the name should rather be derived from 'some person whose name began with the stem *Æthel*' is itself implausible,[47] and his further assertion that the 'isle of the royal children' or 'isle of the princes' 'is a very unlikely Old English local name' ignores contextual parallels.[48]

The most promising such parallel, a place-name recorded in the Anglo-Saxon Chronicle which combines athelings and a topographical generic, proves to bring with it something of a detective story of its own. After a respite during the second half of the tenth century, Viking raids

of English Place-Names, 2nd edn (Oxford: Oxford University Press, 1998), p. 18; V. Watts, *The Cambridge Dictionary of English Place-Names* (Cambridge: Cambridge University Press, 2004) [CDEPN], p. 26. Dumville, 'The ætheling', establishes that the sense 'prince of the royal house' is the active one throughout at least the second half of the Anglo-Saxon period – a more general 'nobleman', found in Germanic cognates and in Old English poetry, seems less likely to be relevant to the place-names, especially given the context that follows.

[46] Stevenson, *Asser's Life*, p. 259, n. 4. He cited Clifford's contributions to the *Somerset Archaeological and Natural History Society's Proceedings* for 1876 and 1877. Note that Clifford's influence is not extinguished: A. P. Smyth, *King Alfred the Great* (Oxford: Oxford University Press, 1995), caption to plate 15, accepts that the name 'may derive from the fact that King Alfred kept his family about him there for safety' in 878.

[47] Certainly the recorded forms do not allow it. Conceivably an original name involving an *Æðelrīc*, or the like, could have been transformed by the weight of popular tradition in the years immediately following 878, but this is open to the same objection as Bishop Clifford's speculations: since the contemporary records of Asser and the Chronicle do not recount a story in which athelings play any role, they offer evidence against the currency of such a story before 900. Incidentally, it should be conceded that the suffix in *æðeling* is closely related to that of the *-ingas* names, and that the plural makes it formally identical with such a group-name. However, the rival claims of the common Old English noun, plus the distribution-map—Somerset is otherwise lacking *-ingas* names—and the contextual parallels, effectively exclude a 'conventional' *-ingas* type.

[48] Stevenson, *Asser's Life*, pp. 259–60, n. 4. The note draws attention to early evidence for explanations of the name as *regalis insula* and *clitonum insula* (with Anglo-Latin *clito*(*n*) 'atheling', on which see Dumville, 'The ætheling', pp. 7–10) in versions of the Life of St Neot (see above, n. 43), and in a spurious charter to Athelney minster (S 343, W. de Gray Birch, *Cartularium Saxonicum*, 4 vols (London: Whiting, 1885–99), no. 545). Despite spelling out the meaning of the name, these sources do not build narratives upon it, which reinforces the point made about Asser and the Chronicle in n. 47, above.

started again during the reign of Æthelred the Unready. In 1001, according to the Chronicle, a fleet ravaged and burnt widely along the coasts, before heading inland to *Æthelingadene*, 'the valley of the princes', where they fought and won a pitched battle with the Hampshire militia.[49] By a notable coincidence the only other pre-Conquest record of a place with the same name is in a charter of the following year, 1002, when King Æthelred granted *Æthelingadene* to the nunnery of Wherwell in Hampshire.[50] There is a good case to be made that the two instances refer to a single place, and that this place is to be identified with the modern parishes of East Dean and West Dean, near the Hampshire boundary in the far west of Sussex.[51] Indeed, Mark Gardiner and Richard Coates were able to confirm the long-suspected identification in 1987, by showing that the fuller Anglo-Saxon form survived, as modern Ellingsdean, applied to a rabbit warren just to the south of the modern parishes.[52] In the Anglo-Saxon period it would seem that there was a large estate at *Dene*, OE *denu* 'valley', here, and that it was of some royal significance: it was, for instance, the place that the Welshman Asser first met King Alfred. And when Alfred died in 899 his will seems to indicate that he bequeathed *Dene* to his younger son, the atheling Æthelweard.[53]

[49] Bately, *Anglo-Saxon Chronicle*, p. 79 (the form is *to Æþelingadene*); Whitelock, *Anglo-Saxon Chronicle*, p. 85.

[50] S 904; J. M. Kemble, *Codex diplomaticus ævi Saxonici* (London: English Historical Society, 1839–48), no. 707.

[51] EPNS Sx **1**, p. xlv; Keynes and Lapidge, *Alfred the Great*, p. 319, n. 41; S. E. Kelly (ed.), *Charters of Selsey* (Oxford: British Academy, 1998), p. 28.

[52] M. Gardiner and R. Coates, 'Ellingsdean, a Viking battlefield identified', *Sussex Archaeological Collections* 125 (1987), 251–52. The forms they assemble, including *Elingeden' c.* 1230, *Ellingdeane* 1612, show a clear link with the Anglo-Saxon forms, though by the sixteenth century the medial *-s-* of Ellingsdean had appeared; it is apparently intrusive. The fact that Ellingsdean Warren lies in Binderton parish, just south of West Dean, and that East Dean is separated from West Dean by the parish of Singleton, all tends to confirm the suggestion, first made in EPNS Sx **1**, p. xlv, that there has been considerable alteration to the administrative pattern here, and that the large royal estate of *Dene* had been incorporated, by the end of the Anglo-Saxon period, in the still larger Domesday manor of Singleton. I should like to thank Richard Jones for obtaining the Gardiner and Coates article for me, twice.

[53] 'Seems to' because there is something of a proliferation of places called 'Dean' in the early record and, indeed, Alfred bequeaths two distinct properties, one to his elder son (probably West Dean in Wiltshire according to Keynes and Lapidge, *Alfred the Great*, p. 320) and the other to his younger. The identification of *Æthelingadene* with one of these places, and with the Dean in Sussex where Asser met Alfred, is likely enough and is the consensus view; it should be noted, however, that any lingering doubts about an association with one of Alfred's sons do not affect the following argument about Æthelred's athelings.

So at the end of the ninth century a royal estate called *Dene* appears to have passed into the ownership of a known atheling. But there is a further step in examining the name *Æthelingadene*, 'valley of the princes', plural. When Æthelred granted the estate to Wherwell Abbey, he did so for the good of the soul of his recently-departed mother, Ælfthryth. *Dene*, says the charter, was formerly in her personal use, that is, presumably, her home (or one of them).[54] It is then interesting to find that Æthelred's eldest son noted in his will that he was brought up by Ælfthryth, his grandmother.[55] Moreover, he had no fewer than seven atheling brothers, all of them quite possibly also brought up by their grandmother: certainly Ælfthryth and her grandsons were close, and not just in a domestic context, but together in a family block they witness many of King Æthelred's charters.[56] There is here an alternative late tenth-century context for *Æthelingadene* as 'the valley of the princes' or, probably better, 'the royal estate of Dene where the princes are being raised', which is difficult to resist. The jigsaw of place-names and historical references is not quite complete, but it is tantalisingly nearly so. At the very least it gives an insight into what the Vikings were up to in 1001. Their dart inland was not a random excursion—as the Chronicle account could imply—it was presumably a strike at a significant royal estate.

There is still further telling documentary evidence. In another charter of Æthelred, probably from 999, the king specifically alluded to a group of estates given over to the use and maintenance of athelings.[57] Their status received comment because the estates had been 'illegally' granted away to Abingdon Abbey by his father, King Edgar; they had since been reclaimed for the athelings, and the purpose of the charter was to confirm the legality of the restoration, and also to compensate Abingdon with alternative estates. Both the arrangement, and the names of the athelings' estates, are worthy of note: Hurstbourne (Tarrant, Ha), Bedwyn (W) and Burbage (W), like the Dean of East/West Dean, do not bear explicit witness to their status. There is then an interesting contrast with a further set of names which seem likely to belong somewhere in this same story:

[54] This point, and all the connections in the present paragraph, were first made in S. Keynes, *The Diplomas of King Æthelred 'the Unready' 978–1016: A Study in their Use as Historical Evidence* (Cambridge: Cambridge University Press, 1980), p. 187.

[55] S 1503; D. Whitelock, *Anglo-Saxon Wills* (Cambridge: University Press, 1930), no. 20.

[56] Keynes, *Diplomas*, Table 1 (in pocket at back), summarises the subscriptions of the athelings.

[57] S 937; Kelly, *Charters of Abingdon Abbey, Part II*, p. 506 (no. 129); Whitelock, *English Historical Documents*, no. 123.

those which combine *æðeling* with *tūn*, as Allington (at least three examples) and Athelington.[58] This small group is crying out for further study; possible interpretations are not hard to suggest. One would be that these are estates, like Bedwyn and Burbage, set aside for the athelings. Their functional name would then perhaps be best paralleled by the Buckland type: Buckland is generally OE *bōc-land*, 'land held by charter', yet estates which bear the name are a tiny fraction of lands known to have been so held.[59] The explanation for this is not certain, but Alex Rumble made the plausible suggestion that the place-name might sometimes have arisen on the relatively rare occasions that a wholly new unit of land was created by the charter.[60] Similarly, perhaps a place that gained the name *Æðelingatūn* was land for the athelings' use newly carved out of an earlier estate arrangement; contrasting with examples where ancient estates, bearing older names, were wholly apportioned to the same purpose. An alternative possibility comes to mind, however, in light of the earlier discussion of Kingston. For, as Hough emphasized, a *cyninges tūn* is not the only functional *tūn* which appears in Anglo-Saxon law – there is an apparently parallel usage of *eorles tūn* in Æthelberht's early Kentish code.[61] No equivalent *æðelinga tūn* is on record, it is true, but the possibility that there may have been compounds or 'offices' for the management of princes' interests as well as kings' should perhaps not be dismissed without investigation.

To return to Athelney. No certainty here is possible: there are not enough pieces of the jigsaw. But there is good context for royal land set aside for, and specifically used by, princes. It is an attractive conjecture that when Alfred retreated here in the winter of 877–78 he was retiring

[58] Place-name scholars have shown a marked reluctance to investigate the names, beyond offering a short gloss on the presumed sense, as 'farmstead or estate of the princes' or the like. For Allington Do see EPNS Do **4**, p. 468; Allington W, EPNS W, p. 311; for Allington Li, see K. Cameron, *A Dictionary of Lincolnshire Place-Names* (Nottingham: English Place-Name Society, 1998), p. 2; for Athelington Sf, see DEPN, p. 18, CDEPN, p. 26. Investigation is carried no further in EPNE, I, p. 7 or VEPN, I, p. 35. Probert, 'Towards a reassessment', p. 12, includes *æðeling* + *tūn* on his map of types that can be compared with Kingston, which is a start. It should be noted that the forms are not always sufficient entirely to guarantee the etymology: here an *-ingtūn* type, with personal name *Æthel*(*e*) or a dithematic name, beginning with *Æthel-* but with obscured second element, offers an alternative sometimes more plausible than in the case of Athelney.

[59] VEPN, I, p. 120.

[60] A. Rumble, 'Old English *Bōc-land* as an Anglo-Saxon estate name', *Leeds Studies in English* 18 (1987), 219–29. Hough is not convinced by this interpretation: 'Commonplace place-names', p. 117.

[61] Hough, 'The place-name Kingston', p. 56.

not to a barren swamp populated only by the odd swineherd, but to an existing royal estate. Lavelle has noted that the site has now revealed archaeological evidence for Iron-Age occupation.[62] Perhaps—to stretch a parallel to its limit—Alfred and his siblings had spent time in the place as children, just as Æthelred's sons may have been raised at (Ellings)Dean. However that may be, it is tempting to suggest that the estate may once have been known as *Ēg*, equivalent to the various surviving instances of Eye. *Æðelingaēg*, like *Æðelingadene*, would have been a secondary development, a result of the estate's royal status. There could be a relatively straightforward, mechanical, linguistic explanation why the *æðeling* affix sometimes or always survived with these simplex names, whilst it is not found with the compound names Hurstbourne, Bedwyn and Burbage, which may have been of equivalent functional status.

The example of these atheling names is a good one to illustrate various aspects of the nature of place-name evidence. At one end of the spectrum, stories – medieval and modern; at the other some relatively solid historical contextual evidence. *Æðelingadene* is as secure an instance as we are likely to find (if not quite absolutely precise); while the further evidence of estates set aside for *æðeling*s surely establishes the principle (and offers a likely context for the recurrent Allington type). All of this establishes a pattern which offers context for further examples. Though in a single instance—however good the story—there tends to be some room for doubt, and it is not suggested otherwise in the case of Athelney itself.

Intersections with written documents, of course, only offer one kind of context, though in the nature of things such context will tend to be key if place-names are to be related to such 'headlines' of early history as battles and the movements and affairs of royal families. Two recently discussed examples, however, may serve to illustrate how place-name interpretation can combine with other evidence to add potentially significant information about prominent events and periods. The first of these takes us straight back to Sussex during the reign of Æthelred. The huge ramparts of Cissbury Ring, north of Worthing, are a monumental construction from the Iron Age; they almost certainly also played a part in events *c.* 1010, for Anglo-Saxon coin-evidence suggests that the ancient hill-fort was pressed into service as an emergency minting-place at this time.[63] Since 1929 the first element of the name Cissbury has been

[62] Lavelle, 'Geographies of power', p. 203.

[63] The case is considered in full in J. Carroll, 'Coins and the Chronicle: mint-signatures,

explained as antiquarian wishful thinking, providing a link between the venerable site and *Cissa*, the legendary founder of Chichester and the South Saxons.[64] As long ago as 1957, however, it was shown that coins bearing forms of the legend SIÐ(M)ESTEB[YRIG] should be attributed here.[65] Early in the eleventh century, with those renewed Viking raids in Sussex and elsewhere in southern England, there was evidently disruption to administrative life. Indeed, there is very clear parallel evidence from Somerset that the Iron-Age fort of South Cadbury was used as an emergency mint: the moneyers who had been signing coins at Ilchester, Bruton and Crewkerne, decamped to Cadbury. It is likely that Cissbury was similarly a retreat from Hastings, Lewes and/or Chichester. Its coin-sequence begins in or after 1009, and the Chronicle has Vikings again burning and harrying in Sussex in that year.[66] The identification, which makes good sense of the spellings, despite a five hundred year lacuna between attestations, is highly likely, and adds local detail to the narrative of Viking threat and Anglo-Saxon response in the early eleventh century. Beyond that, the apparent implication of the name itself is remarkable. *Siðmestebyrig* is the 'last stronghold', with a temporal superlative which is highly unusual, if not unique in English place-names. 'Last resort' is the modern collocation that comes to mind, and if that is what was intended, or understood, by the place-name, it would add a note of urgency and colour rare amongst toponymic evidence.[67]

The second example does not in fact involve events prominent in records of their own time, but rather a discovery famous in ours. The 'Staffordshire hoard' made national headlines in 2009, as the richest cache of Anglo-Saxon precious metalwork found since Sutton Hoo.[68]

history, and language', in Jorgensen (ed.), *Reading the Anglo-Saxon Chronicle*, pp. 243–73 (pp. 246–51); see also J. Carroll and D. N. Parsons, *Anglo-Saxon Mint-Names: I. Axbridge – Hythe* (Nottingham: English Place-Name Society, 2007), pp. 97–98.

[64] EPNS Sx **1**, pp. 197–98. The explanation was repeated as late as 2004 in CDEPN, p. 140. For doubts about Cissa at Chichester—and quite possibly, therefore, any historical foundation for his legend—see Carroll and Parsons, *Anglo-Saxon Mint-Names*, pp. 95–96.

[65] R. H. M. Dolley and F. Elmore Jones, 'The mints "Æt Gothabyrig" and "Æt Sith(m)estebyrig"', *British Numismatic Journal* 28 (1957), 279–82.

[66] Whitelock, *Anglo-Saxon Chronicle*, p. 89.

[67] It is difficult to see what else might be understood by the name. The 'last stronghold before reaching the coast' is an unconvincing alternative: if places were named like that in Anglo-Saxon England, one might expect numerous parallels. The principal alternative, for such a prominent ancient monument, is that *siðmest*, and *siðest* (both are attested), are somehow a 'rationalization' of an older name no longer understood. This may be so, though suggestions for such an original are not forthcoming.

[68] K. Leahy and R. Bland, *The Staffordshire Hoard* (London: British Museum Press,

Less remarked, even when the exact findspot was made public, was the significance of place-name evidence to an understanding of the find. The hoard was buried, in perhaps the seventh century, on the edge of the parish of Hammerwich, a name loaded with resonance. Although the only Hammerwich on record, it has many congeners. The element *wīc*, applied to a specialized site of production and/or trade, has already been mentioned. Amongst the specialisms pursued at *wīc*-settlements elsewhere was metal-smithing, witness Smethwick St and Ch, and a lost *Smithwick* in Sussex.[69] At Hammersmith Mx, the smithy was defined by its characteristic tool, just as at a lost *Lootwic*, near Droitwich Wo, the salt-makers' rake or 'loot' characterized the site.[70] The discovery of important metalwork adjoining Hammerwich is striking. The nature of the hoard—weapon and helmet fittings of gold and silver, all carefully detached from the more mundane iron of the remainder of the objects (e.g. sword-blades)[71]—then excites particular attention. The inference that the iron had been stripped from the precious metal at, and/or for re-use in, the smithy at Hammerwich seems irresistible, though to date archaeologists generally appear to have been able to resist it.

Such instances, whilst they illustrate how place-name evidence can amplify and extend interpretations in concert with archaeological finds and historical records, are essentially exceptional: rare windows on individual places and events. For more substantial historical information relating to wider society, and to everyday experience across regions, we should turn to widespread recurrent compounds and name-types, which bring with them extensive opportunities for interdisciplinary study. The examples of Charlton and Kingston have been discussed; as, briefly, has the complex of *-ingas*, *-hām* and *-ingahām*. The final extended example

2009). A number of expert contributions on different aspects of the find are published online at <http://finds.org.uk/staffshoardsymposium/>, the proceedings of a conference held in March 2010. One of these is D. N. Parsons, 'The name "Hammerwich"', which expands a little on the matter of this paragraph.

[69] EPNE, II, pp. 130–31.

[70] *Lootwic* is the subject of an extended investigation in D. N. Parsons, 'Old English **lōt*, dialect *loot*, a salt-maker's "ladle"', in C. Hough and K. A. Lowe (eds), *'Lastworda Betst': Essays in Memory of Christine E. Fell* (Donington: Shaun Tyas, 2002), pp. 170–88.

[71] Cf. K. Leahy, 'The contents of the hoard': '[T]here are no sword blades; there is no Anglo-Saxon iron at all. Every bit had been stripped, not only from the swords but also from the helmet(s). Some of the Pressblech foils have got traces of iron corrosion on the underside, and the process of stripping might explain why so much of the silver is in small fragments' <http://finds.org.uk/staffshoardsymposium>.

of this chapter takes names coined with a single generic element – it is argued that in its distributional, archaeological and documentary contexts, this name-type may possibly illustrate a key development in the social and economic history of much of England.

The element is *thorp*, which I shall use as a shorthand for Old Norse *þorp*, Old English *þrop* (part of the argument is that these two cognate terms, as they are evidenced in place-names in England, form a contemporary continuum of usage).[72] The major development to which *thorp*-names may be linked is the 'open-field revolution' that would have so disturbed Sir Frank Stenton's view of early Anglo-Saxon social organization: the discovery that the communal agriculture so characteristic of much of medieval and early modern England, and especially of the midlands, was not brought across by the settlers of the migration age, but was a revolution of the mid-Anglo-Saxon period. The archaeology appears clear: in counties like Northamptonshire and Leicestershire an earlier pattern of scattered farmsteads was swept away to be replaced by large central villages surrounded by arable lands organized into great fields, cropped in rotation, and farmed in individual strips allocated across the community.[73] The mechanics of this revolution—which must have ousted many thousands from their homes, rehoused them in planned surroundings and provided them, apparently, with a new social ethos—are completely lost to history. We can pick up traces in the records, as we shall shortly see, but there is no description of, or reaction to, the process: nothing from the ninth century comparable to John Clare in the nineteenth lamenting the process of enclosure, which in effect marked the end of this same agricultural system.

It might fairly be asked whether, if there was a movement that so fundamentally affected agriculture, settlement and the management of the land, it should not be visible in the place-name record. The early medieval settlement-pattern is, after all, what English place-names seem so faithfully to reflect. Yet the open-field revolution has been largely unreflected by place-name studies. There are precious references in Anglo-Saxon charters to some of the technicalities of the open-field system: the furlongs, strips and headlands of the ploughlands;[74] and there

[72] The case is set out in full in P. Cullen, R. Jones and D. N. Parsons, *Thorps in a Changing Landscape* (Hatfield: University of Hertfordshire, 2011). For the argument for the continuum between Norse and English usage, see pp. 73 75. For the archaeologist's view of the collaboration see Jones below, p. 197.

[73] See above, n. 11.

[74] See, e.g., D. Hooke, 'Open-field agriculture: the evidence from the pre-Conquest

are some late name-types which seem to reflect the patterns of ancient countryside as opposed to those where nucleation took hold.[75] Save for some tendency for names in *tūn* to cluster in the central zone of open fields and nucleations—and there are far too many *tūn*-names elsewhere for the type to be considered diagnostic of these developments in the landscape—no specific correlation between groups of major place-names and the agricultural upheaval has previously been proposed.[76] But with *thorp* there is a case to be made.

The first indication that there might be a link simply arises from the overall distribution of evidence.[77] The major area of open-field farming, attested by archaeology, documentary record and the morphology of settlements, comprises a midland belt extending some way into the south west and East Anglia, but falling short of the far south-west, the south-east, much of the west midlands and the north-west. The distribution of some 900 *thorp*-names in England is remarkably similar. Further, the evidence of modern land-use maps tends to suggest a close association with farmland used for arable, rather than livestock. Settlements with *thorp*-names are typically small, simple and linear in plan,[78] which accords with the observation that—while, in some parts, there are many villages and hamlets with names in *thorp*—they never develop into modern places of substance. Only Scunthorpe is today of any size, and that is a product of the Industrial Revolution, not its early status. *Thorps* are simple, small, insignificant places in the zone characterized by open-field agriculture.[79]

To these observations can be added documentary and quantitative analysis. Above all, this goes to emphasize that *thorps* were characteristically small, secondary, subsidiary.[80] There are a number of ways of reckoning this: some early documents describe *thorps* as outlying dependencies; and later medieval ecclesiastical arrangements often reveal

charters of the West Midlands', in Rowley, *Origins*, pp. 39–63; Kelly, *Charters of Abingdon Abbey, Part II*, p. 372. And see above, n. 25, and below, pp. 68–69.

[75] V. Watts, 'Some place-name distributions', *Journal of the English Place-Name Society* 32 (1999–2000), 53–72, with reference to later settlement-names with generics *street*, *end* and *green*. Watts draws in particular on the work of the historical geographer Brian Roberts.

[76] Watts, 'Some place-name distributions', p. 60 and map 14 (p. 69).

[77] Cullen, Jones and Parsons, *Thorps*, p. 142 and map, p. 143.

[78] Cullen, Jones and Parsons, *Thorps*, pp. 97–107.

[79] Cullen, Jones and Parsons, *Thorps*, pp. 88–97.

[80] Cullen, Jones and Parsons, *Thorps*, pp. 37–68.

them to be; moreover, when compared with other place-name types, *thorp*-settlements are more likely to disappear during the Middle Ages, and they are less likely to have become parishes.

The net result, therefore, is that *thorps* are typically minor or secondary settlements:[81] but they are found in areas where nucleated villages are generally thought to have swept away lesser settlements. Moreover, for various reasons they seem to be datable to late in the Anglo-Saxon period, if not still later. A survey of archaeological evidence from their settlement-cores produces practically nothing earlier than the ninth century; a very large number of *thorps* in the east and north are combined with Scandinavian first elements which would not be expected to pre-date the late ninth century; in addition a significant number combine with post-Conquest elements, words and names that were introduced by the Norman French. There is, then, a dichotomy. *Thorps* take their place in a landscape that is characterized, from the middle of the Anglo-Saxon period onwards, by centralized, nucleated village settlements, where outliers were swept away. Yet they themselves appear to be outliers. One attractive solution to this conundrum is that *thorps* are something of a missing link: it is possible that in origin they may have been temporary settlements, perhaps seasonal, accommodating ploughmen working in the new open fields, which can be at some distance from the central village.[82]

However this may be, there is in this case again a precious tie-up with pre-Conquest documentation which gives some greater precision to the hypothesis. The earliest secure reference to a *thorp* comes in a Mercian diploma of AD 869, a charter which gives us remarkable contextual information.[83] It concerns a place called *Upþrop*—which unfortunately cannot be identified—but the document makes clear (a) that it is a small part of larger estate, and (b) that the pasture, woodland *and ploughland* of this estate was held in common. Such an arrangement inevitably brings to

[81] Cognate usage in other Germanic languages indicates that this sense is inherited and to be expected: how far a particular function in open-field farming might be matched by usage overseas remains to be established.

[82] Cullen, Jones and Parsons, *Thorps*, pp. 149–51. The possibility is noted there that every great field may once have had its *thorp* – the suggestion arises in the light of Leicestershire material which Barrie Cox has recently brought to light in his work on the EPNS survey for the county. Amongst the open fields of Kirby Bellars, for instance, were an *Esthorp*, *Medilthorpe* and *Westhorp*; while *Thorpe on le toftis*, in Belgrave, was a 'tillage', an arable farm, in 1278. See further Cullen, Jones and Parsons, *Thorps*, pp. 27–28.

[83] Cullen, Jones and Parsons, *Thorps*, pp. 83–84, 145–46; the charter is S 214.

mind open-field farming, and it appears to establish a *throp* place-name within that regime, somewhere in Mercia, in the generation before Scandinavian settlements are believed to have begun in eastern England. It is tempting to see *thorps* as part of the open-field process, beginning in the English midlands by the middle of the ninth century, and thence adopted within Scandinavian England over the following centuries.

Whether or not this hypothesis is acceptable, the simple point is that profitable, secure and interesting interpretations of place-names tend to arise out of the intersections between a name and further evidence, whether that is documentary, topographical, archaeological, or some combination of the three.[84] In 1924 Stenton did not approach his task methodologically, or methodically, but mixed together contextualized and uncontextualized place-name interpretations. As shown, it is the latter that are particularly vulnerable – speculation on the basis of linguistic interpretation tends to remain just that, speculation. Where other evidence can be introduced—a body of other names, documentary record, archaeological context—the ground usually becomes firmer. That is not to say that it may not shift over time: it would be depressing if advances were not made in any of these fields. But my contention would be that the conclusions Stenton drew from *-ingas* names and from the Charlton-type in 1924 may still have more to offer than some recent scholarship has recognized, because the documentary and comparative context that he supplied remains valuable.

These are simple observations, and they are hardly new. When Ken Cameron addressed the British Academy in a 1976 lecture on 'The significance of place-names', his starting-point was that whilst occasionally an individual name can carry significance beyond its immediate etymology, real advances were going to come through 'the wider study of the types, the distribution, and the topographical situations of place-names derived from a particular element, or from groups of elements'.[85] In fact, similar observations can be traced right back to the beginning. The very first publication to bear the imprint of the Survey of English Place-Names was a lecture by Allen Mawer, delivered in Newcastle in 1922,[86] which makes a very interesting companion to

[84] Jones below, pp. 188–91, details a number of recent works which make a success of integrating place-names with landscape history and archaeology.

[85] Cameron, 'Significance of English place-names', p. 3. It is, of course, a considerable irony that one of Cameron's extended examples in this lecture involved *thorp* which we are now trying to explain rather differently.

[86] A. Mawer, *Place-Names and History*, Robert Spence Watson Memorial Lecture,

Stenton's chapter of two years later. Mawer ranged much more widely across periods and subjects, but still managed to comment extensively on Anglo-Saxon themes; and he did so in sections that correspond rather closely to points made in this chapter. He discussed legends and stories that arise from names, and contrasted them with the 'exact science' that can be expected from detailed linguistic analysis.[87] One might cavil, perhaps, at the absolute exactness of the science, but Mawer observed that it was in patterns of names that we could learn so much, and he made a series of observations that remain valid. Some of them have been thoroughly probed since, such as the association of *wīchām* with Roman remains, widely and correctly regarded as a major contribution by Margaret Gelling,[88] but substantially foreshadowed already in 1922.[89] Other points, we should perhaps be ashamed to admit, have not yet been fully taken up – the observation, for instance, that names in *worth* are very frequently qualified by personal names, while those in *wīc* are very rarely so qualified,[90] indicates a significant distinction between two types of settlement that tend to be grouped together, not unlike *thorp*, as minor and dependent. The qualifiers suggest a quite different pattern of holding, which remains uninvestigated in any systematic way.[91]

Mawer was wholly persuaded of the value of what is now called interdisciplinarity. Beyond the documentary evidence, which had 'for the most part been worked until it [was] threadbare',[92] he recognized two sources of information: archaeology and place-name study. 'When these two fields have been fully explored,' he wrote, 'we may hope to have a fresh store of historical facts of the utmost value, not only in themselves, but also because with their aid we shall be able to go back once more to our documents and we shall find in the light of our fuller knowledge of the facts that many dark places are now clear, [and] many of the gaps in

published for the Survey of English Place-Names (Liverpool: University Press of Liverpool, 1922).

[87] Mawer, *Place-Names and History*, pp. 6–9.

[88] M. Gelling, 'English place-names derived from the compound *wīchām*', *Medieval Archaeology* 11 (1967), 87–104; reprinted in Cameron (ed.), *Place-Name Evidence*, pp. 8–26.

[89] Mawer, *Place-Names and History*, p. 16.

[90] Mawer, *Place-Names and History*, pp. 15–16.

[91] Though *worth* has been the subject of some recent landscape-based investigations: J. English, '*Worths* in a landscape context', *Landscape History* 24 (2002), 45–52; R. Faith, 'Worthys and enclosures', *Medieval Settlement Research Group Annual Report* 21 (2006), 9–14.

[92] Mawer, *Place-Names and History*, p. 12.

our documentary evidence have been made good.'[93]

Mawer talked of potential, Stenton tried—ambitiously, and perhaps prematurely—to weave a narrative out of the place-name evidence available to him. It is tempting to suggest that relatively little has changed in the last ninety years, in that (1) the linguistic interpretation of most major place-names, the names of towns and villages, has not radically changed in that time; and (2) the methodological lines, implied in particular by Mawer's essay of 1922, can still very much be endorsed today. Many details of the kind that he envisaged can be filled in, while the extent of contextual evidence that can be brought to bear—as evidenced by the recent work on *thorp*, and in earlier work, since the 1960s, by the likes of Dodgson, Cox, Cameron, Gelling and Fellows-Jensen—is perhaps greater than Mawer and Stenton could have envisaged. There have also been some significant changes of emphasis: Gelling's demonstration of the importance, and potential historical significance, of topographical names is undoubtedly the most notable. But my principal reaction, having given some consideration to the views of our predecessors setting out on a great project, is that their interpretation, understanding and expectations were remarkably modern.

However, if progress at one level has been incremental—for the very good reason that it started from an intelligent and sophisticated base—there have been immense advances at another level. While most of the major names of England were pretty well understood already in the 1920s, and certainly by the first publication of Ekwall's *Dictionary of English Place-Names* in 1936, the 'minor' names—those of hamlets, farms, fields, woods and meadows—have made up a huge proportion of the material gathered over the decades by the Survey of English Place-Names. Most of this was still quite unknown in the 1920s, and—as well as being of enormous value to local history, and to the study of all later periods—it frequently adds to our understanding of the early medieval centuries.[94] One such example, newly brought to light, will serve as a suitable tailpiece to the chapter, an illustration of the continuing potential of place-name study.

One of Ken Cameron's favourite examples of a place-name that brought history to life was Lawress wapentake in Lincolnshire.[95] The

[93] Mawer, *Place-Names and History*, p. 13.

[94] Cf. the *thorp* field-names in Leicestershire (above, n. 82), and Ellingsdean, the rabbit-warren in Sussex (above, p. 60).

[95] K. Cameron, *Scandinavian Settlement in the Territory of the Five Boroughs: the Place-Name Evidence* (Nottingham: University of Nottingham, 1965); reprinted in Cameron

wapentake, *vápnataki*, was a unit of administration introduced by the Scandinavian settlers of the Danelaw in the later ninth and tenth centuries. Lawress was named after the *hrís*, the copse, of a man called *Lag-Ulfr*, 'Law-Wolf', a type of name echoed in medieval Norse sources, indicative of the local administrator, or law-man. *Lag-Ulfr* presumably held sway, *c*. 900, in the district north of Lincoln which continued to be called Lawress for nearly a millennium thereafter. Where within the large wapentake the meeting-place lay—the copse of the name—was uncertain until, amongst the material originally collected by Cameron and then analysed by John Insley, was a field-name of *c*. 1234, siting *Laolf Ris*, surely *Lag-Ulfs hrís*, in Reepham parish, just north-east of Lincoln.[96] This identification is intriguing because Reepham is the 'reeve's homestead', where 'reeve', Old English *ge-rēfa*, denotes a senior official of Anglo-Saxon government.[97] Indeed, a recent archaeological and landscape survey of the area of Lawress wapentake, by David Stocker and Paul Everson, has made a case that Reepham was a major administrative centre in the area, controlling a large estate that goes back to the early Anglo-Saxon period, if not beyond.[98] They have identified a large enclosure that may be the dwelling of the reeve himself. That Reepham should subsequently have become the base for the Norse law-giver, during the period of Scandinavian rule in the Danelaw, would be a coincidence hard to overlook. A fascinating continuity is implied, and it is implied in large part by a linguistic understanding of the major place-names (Lawress, Reepham), combined with the documentary discovery of a thirteenth-century field-name, and the independent work of modern landscape archaeologists. In this chapter an attempt has been made to show that the continued collection and analysis of place-name records, particularly when this is carried out alongside the examination of historical documents, archaeological remains and the landscape, will continue to breathe new life into some of our earliest historical periods.[99]

(ed.), *Place-Name Evidence*, pp. 115–29 (pp. 117–18).

[96] EPNS Li **7**, p. 80.

[97] EPNS Li **7**, p. 76.

[98] P. Everson and D. Stocker, *Custodians of Continuity? The Premonstratensian Abbey at Barlings and the Landscape of Ritual* (Sleaford: Heritage Trust of Lincolnshire, 2011), pp. 204, 385–90. The authors note (at p. 204) the potential significance of the new field-name, but its discovery came towards the completion of their volume, and they had already written up the case for the traditional meeting-place, at Riseholme (pp. 233–34; cf. p. 250, n. 1). As they observe, there are questions to resolve here.

[99] An earlier version of this chapter was delivered as the third Cameron Lecture in the University of Nottingham, January 2011.

3

The Scandinavian background to English place-names

Gillian Fellows-Jensen

Introduction

The earliest more or less permanent settlements in Denmark can now be shown to date from the Neolithic period, i.e. 3000–1500 BC, but none of the surviving settlement names in the country can be as old as this. That southern Scandinavia has escaped lasting occupation by people speaking a foreign tongue for the last couple of thousand years, however, is shown by the fact that written evidence reveals an uninterrupted development of settlement in Denmark by people speaking the same language. This evidence is, however, scanty. Roman sources can only tell us the names of the Germanic tribes who arrived in Denmark from further north, together with a few names of major natural features such as islands and waterways. Archaeological evidence for dating Roman imports, however, has at least made it impossible to claim, as did Andreas M. Hansen over a century ago, that settlements in Denmark with names in *-lev*, *-løse* and *-inge*, for example, might date from the same period as the Neolithic graves.[1] Philologists and archaeologists have pointed out that it is vital to distinguish between evidence such as finds of movable artefacts that can help to date settlements and evidence that can contribute to the dating of the formation of the names of these settlements.[2]

On account of the scantiness of the surviving written material there is little firm evidence to show which of the surviving names can be assumed to have existed in Denmark at the time when the Danes first began their attacks on

[1] A. M. Hansen, *Landnåm i Norge* (Kristiania [Oslo]: Fabritius, 1904), pp. 102, 105.

[2] J. Kousgård Sørensen, 'Place-names and settlement history', in P. H. Sawyer (ed.), *Names, Words, and Graves: Early Medieval Settlement* (Leeds: School of History, 1979), pp. 14–17; T. Grane, 'Did the Romans really know (or care) about Southern Scandinavia? An archaeological perspective', in T. Grane (ed.), *Beyond the Roman Frontier: Roman Influences on the Northern Barbaricum* (Roma: Edizioni Quasar, 2007), pp. 19–25.

England at the end of the eighth century or when they were partitioning out land in the Danelaw in the last quarter of the ninth century or when the Viking Age in England petered out, as William the Conqueror gradually established control over his kingdom after the Norman Conquest in 1066.

The earliest record?

I shall begin with a brief look at the earliest evidence for a place-name in Denmark. Recent discussion by my colleagues in Copenhagen has concluded that the earliest written evidence for a place-name proper is to be ascribed to the Roman historian Pliny the Elder, who died in the pursuit of scientific knowledge while studying an eruption of Vesuvius in 79 AD. Pliny had served as an officer in Roman *Germania* in the late AD 40s and in his *Naturalis Historia* 4.97 he mentions an expedition to the *promontorium Cimbrorum* 'the promontory of the Cimbri tribe', which must be Jutland, where he refers to a peninsula projecting far out into the sea as *Tastris*.[3] This would seem to be the jutting headland that is now known as Skagen or in English 'the Skaw'. The Latin name is in the locative case but I have not been able to find any translation of it and cannot propose a satisfactory one of my own. It can hardly be a settlement name.

Ohthere and Wulfstan's narratives

The earliest literary text to contain forms of Danish place-names is the late ninth-century account of the mariners known to posterity as Ohthere and Wulfstan. The text survives in two tenth-century manuscripts, where it is interpolated in the anonymous Old English paraphrase of Orosius's *Historia Adversus Paganos*, a Latin work compiled in the early fifth century.[4] The narrative contains a number of Scandinavian place-names but these are mostly the names of islands and provinces. Only three of them are the names of settlements and only one is Danish. In the Viking period the geographical frontiers of Denmark extended over a much wider area than they do today, and included Skåne and some of the adjoining parts of Sweden, as well as South Schleswig, the land between the present frontier with Germany and the river Ejder. The Danish place-name which occurs in the late ninth-century Old English source is that of the prosperous port of *æt Hæþum*, to which Ohthere

[3] H. Rackham (ed. and trans.), *Pliny: Natural History. II Libri III–VII*, Loeb Classical Library (London: Heinemann, 1942), p. 194.

[4] J. Bately (ed.), *The Old English Orosius* (London: Oxford University Press for the Early English Text Society, 1980), pp. lxxi–lxxii, 13–18.

sailed from *Halgoland* and from where Wulfstan set sail on his Baltic voyage. *Æt Hæþum* 'at the heaths' is presumably an English translation (OE *hǣð* 'heath') of an older form of the name that later became known as Hedeby, now in South Schleswig.[5] Many of the earliest settlement names in both England and Denmark would seem to have begun life as topographical descriptions of the site, often, as is the case with *Æt Hæþum*, in a prepositional compound with the dative plural ending *-um*. In his late tenth-century chronicle the English ealdorman and historian Æthelweard notes that the port of Hedeby was known in the Saxon language as *Slesuuic* but by the Danes as *Haithaby*.[6] This suggests that the port on the Slie was first called **Heiðum*, then **Heiðabý* and finally, when it was transferred to a site across the Slie, **Slesvík*.

Runic inscriptions

The numerous personal names contained in inscriptions on Viking Age rune stones in Denmark might lead one to believe that many place-names would also be found there but this is not the case. The name of the country itself, *Danmark* 'the boundary forest of the Danes', is inscribed on the two Jelling-stones.[7] The phrase **tanmarkaʀ : but** 'Denmark's adornment' on DR 41 is now considered to be a term of praise referring to Thyre, the wife of King Gorm and mother of King Harald, while Harald's boast on DR 42 includes the words **sa | haraltr [:] ias : sąʀ · uan · tanmaurk** 'that Harald who won the whole of Denmark for himself'.[8] The name *Danmark* is also found on some Swedish rune stones and that this name was known to the English is suggested both by its mention by Wulfstan in the above-mentioned report to King Alfred, where he notes that Langeland and Lolland and Falster and Skåne all belong *to Denemearcan* 'to Denmark',[9] and by the occurrence of the name *Danmark* as that of a now-extinct settlement in Mumby in Lincolnshire. The earliest record of this name is dated to 1259 and it was probably recycled in memory of the home country

[5] J. Bately, 'Ohthere and Wulfstan in the Old English Orosius', in J. Bately and A. Englert (eds), *Ohthere's Voyages*, Maritime Cultures of the North 1 (Roskilde: The Viking Ship Museum in Roskilde, 2007), pp. 10–58 (p. 53).

[6] A. Campbell, *The Chronicle of Æthelweard* (London: Nelson, 1962), p. 9.

[7] L. Jacobsen and E. Moltke, with A. Bæksted and K. M. Nielsen (eds), *Danmarks Runeindskrifter* I–II (Copenhagen: Munksgaard, 1941–42), nos. 41–42. Subsequent references to this work in the present text are in the form of DR + number.

[8] E. Moltke, *Runes and their Origin: Denmark and Elsewhere* (Copenhagen: The National Museum of Denmark, 1985), pp. 206–07.

[9] Bately, 'Ohthere and Wulfstan', p. 48.

of the Danes.[10]

Among all the relevant Danish runic inscriptions I have only found two settlement names in Sjælland and one in Skåne, each of which occurs once, and one name from south of the present-day Danish border that occurs three times. The oldest of these inscriptions is on a stone from Snoldelev parish, Tune herred, Sjælland (DR 248). Together with the swastika and the triskele of three drinking horns the inscription can be dated to before the end of the eighth century, while the carved sun-wheel is prehistoric. The inscription reads **kun · uAltstAin · sunaR · ruHalts · þulaR · ąsalHauku[m]** 'Gunvald's stone, son of Roald, the orator at Salløv'. The name of the settlement Salløv, which is situated in Snoldelev parish, is a plural name in *-um* and means 'at the mounds (*haugum*) at the temple or magnate's house (*sal*)'. This *sal* may be the same first element as that found in the place-name Selby in Yorkshire (*Salebi* GDB 302c).[11]

The second runic inscription from Sjælland is more than two centuries younger than that from Snoldelev. It is on the stone known as Sandby 3 from Sandby parish, Tybjerg herred (DR 229). Its text is defective but the phrase **i sbalklusu** is clear and means 'in Spragelse'. This pre-Viking township, which lies in Sandby parish, would seem to contain as its specific a word related to *spjælke* 'splint', while the generic is *løse* 'glade'.

The third inscription that contains a Danish settlement name is found on the Hyby stone 1 in Hyby parish, Bara Härad in Skåne (DR 264). This stone is decorated on the A face with a crossed cross and the image of a stag, showing it to be a Christian memorial and thus relatively young. The inscription on the B face, which is defective, probably commemorates the wealthy owner of the estate: **fulukui:a:huk[bi]** 'Folkvi owns (or perhaps the preposition 'in') Hy(by)'.[12] The settlement name is to be explained as 'settlement on or at the mound (*haug*)' and may be linguistically identical with the name Huby in Yorkshire (*Hobi* GDB 222a).

Three other inscriptions all contain early records of the name Hedeby. The stones now referred to as Haddeby 1 and 3 were both set up in the immediate neighbourhood of Hedeby. Haddeby 3 was raised by a Sven to commemorate his retainer Skarde, who fell at Hedeby: **uarþ:tauþr:at:hiþa:bu** (DR 3), while

[10] G. Fellows Jensen, *Scandinavian Settlement Names in the East Midlands* (Copenhagen: Akademisk Forlag, 1978), pp. 167–68.

[11] Here and elsewhere below GDB refers to Greater Domesday Book, The National Archives E31/2.

[12] Moltke, *Runes and their Origin*, pp. 266–67.

Haddeby 1 was raised by one of this Sven's men in memory of a man who died: **þą + trekiaʀ satu + um + haiþa + bu** 'when warriors besieged Hedeby' (DR 1). External evidence dates these two inscriptions to the 980s or later[13] and Sven is thus probably to be identified with Sven Forkbeard (d. 1014), although the date of the siege remains uncertain. Sven could have captured the fortress after the death of the Emperor Otto in 983, when he may already have become joint-king in Denmark, or he may have re-conquered the port from the Swedish king Erik Segersäl in about 1000.[14] The later date would perhaps fit with the use as a fire-ship of the great Hedeby longship, constructed about 985, in an attack on Hedeby between 990 and 1010.[15] A third victim of the same siege may have been commemorated in a fragmentary inscription ending with the name **hiþabu** on a stone known as Århus 1 (DR 63), which was found in the structure of the town's earliest church.[16] The multiple occurrence of this place-name both around Hedeby as well as much later in runic inscriptions in Sweden may mean, as suggested by Lerche Nielsen,[17] that the siege of Hedeby was a far-famed event.

From the point of view of the dating of the name-form in the three Danish inscriptions Moltke claims that Haddeby 3 must be younger than Haddeby 1 because the place-name there retains the unmonophthongized form of the diphthong **ai** /æi/ as opposed to the monophthongized form **i** /e:/ in Haddeby 1 and Århus 1.[18] Both the Haddeby stones, however, show monophthongized **i** instead of **ai** in other words, i.e. **suin**, **stin** and **him-** (*Sven*, *sten* and *hem-*), while the fragmentary Århus 1 has no other instances of the relevant monophthong. Both Haddeby stones show the unmonophthongized form of the diphthong **au** in the word **tauþr**, however. The variation between the

[13] M. Stoklund, 'Chronology and typology of the Danish runic inscriptions', in M. Stoklund et al. (eds), *Runes and their Secrets: Studies in Runology* (Copenhagen: Museum Tusculanum Press, 2006), pp. 355–83 (pp. 367–68).

[14] A. E. Christensen and E. Moltke, 'Hvilken (kong) Svend belejrede Hedeby', *Historisk Tidsskrift* 12 Række V, Hæfte 2 (1971), 297–326 (p. 310); Moltke, *Runes and their Origin*, p. 200.

[15] O. Crumlin-Pedersen, *Viking-Age Ships and Shipbuilding in Hedeby/Haithabu and Schleswig*, Ships and Boats of the North Volume 2 (Schleswig and Roskilde: Archäologisches Landesmuseum and The Viking Ship Museum, 1997), pp. 94–95.

[16] E. Roesdahl and D. M. Wilson, 'The Århus rune-stones', in P. Gammeltoft and B. Jørgensen (eds), *Names through the Looking-Glass. Festschrift in honour of Gillian Fellows-Jensen* (Copenhagen: Reitzel, 2006), pp. 208–29 (p. 210).

[17] M. Lerche Nielsen, 'Runefund fra Hedeby og Slesvig', *Enogtyvende tværfaglige Vikingesymposium* (Højbjerg: Forlaget Hikuin, 2002), pp. 53–71 (p. 62).

[18] Moltke, *Runes and their Origin*, p. 201.

monophthongized and unmonophthongized forms probably reflects the fact that monophthongization was still in a state of flux at the end of the tenth century and the carver of Haddeby 1 may simply have been using a conservative spelling.

The search for settlement names from Denmark recorded on runic inscriptions has admittedly not been very rewarding and that for nature-names there even less so. There is only one possible primary nature-name in a runic inscription and this instance is somewhat uncertain. This is on a now-lost stone that was originally set up in Torup in North Jutland by Ase in memory of Tóki, a huskarl who was killed on **aufu : hiþi** (possibly *Ove Hede*) (DR 154). There is no other documented record of an *Ove Hede* in the neighbourhood of Torup but Hvidbjerg Å runs into Ovesø not far from there and an old river-name **Ava* might conceivably lie behind the names of both the river and the uncertainly recorded **aufu : hiþi**.[19] Although this identification is certainly feasible, it seems unwise to rely too much upon it.

Inscriptions on Danish coins

Some interesting inscriptions are found on eleventh-century coins. In the early part of that century in particular coins struck in Denmark were strongly influenced by the well-organized Anglo-Saxon coinage and almost half of the moneyers in the reign of Knut the Great seem from their names to be English. Most of the inscriptions are in Latin lettering but in the period from approximately 1065 to 1074 runic letters were used in coin inscriptions from Lund and Roskilde, possibly in connection with a monetary reform.[20] On the reverse of the Danish coins stand the name of the moneyer and that of the mint. Most of the place-names on the coins are those of old and important settlements.[21] These include:

from the reign of Knut the Great 1018–35: LVND (Lund, Skåne), RICZTA (Ringsted, Sjælland), OÐSVI (Odense, Fyn), VIBERG (Viborg, Jutland), ORBEC (probably the village of Ørbæk, near the small town of Løgstør

[19] J. Kousgård Sørensen, *Danske sø- og ånavne*, 8 vols (Copenhagen: Akademisk Forlag, 1968–96), I, pp. 100–01.

[20] M. Lerche Nielsen, *Vikingetidens personnavne i Danmark belyst gennem runeindskrifternes personnavne og stednavne på* -torp *sammensat med personnavneforled* (Copenhagen: Københavns Universitet, 1997), p. 57; J. S. Jensen, 'The introduction and use of runic letters on Danish coins around the year 1065', in Stoklund et al. (eds), *Runes and their Secrets*, pp. 159–68 (p. 167).

[21] *Stednavne i tekster*, udgivet af Institut for Navneforskning (Copenhagen: Gyldendal, 1971), p. 21.

on the Limfjord in Jutland), RIHBIIR (Ribe, Jutland);

from the reign of Harthaknut 1035–42: ROSCLDE (Roskilde, Sjælland), SLAHLOV (Slagelse, Sjælland), AROSII (Århus, Jutland);

from the reign of Sven Estridsen 1047–74: **lunt** (Lund);

from the reign of St Knut 1080–86: BVRHI (Borgeby, Skåne), ALEBURH (Ålborg, Jutland); RANDROS (Randers, Jutland).

Most of the mint-sites bear topographical names. The coin inscriptions embrace the simplex names Lund (*lund* 'grove') and Ribe (*ripa* 'strip'), and the compound names Viborg (*wī* 'shrine' + *bjerg* 'hill, mound', Roskilde (pers.n. *Rōir* + *kilde* 'spring'), Slagelse (*slag* 'hollow' + *løse* 'glade'), Århus (gen.sg. *år* 'river' + *ōs* 'mouth') and Randers (*rand* 'edge' + *ōs* 'mouth' or **rūs* 'heap of stones'). Two of the names of the mint-sites denote a cultural feature, namely Ringsted (*ring* 'stone circle' + *sted* '(settlement) place') and Odense (the name of the heathen god *Óðin* + *wǣ* 'shrine'). The only habitative names among the mint-sites are Borgeby containing *bý* and Ålborg containing *borg* 'stronghold'.

Place-names recorded in St Knut's deed of gift of 1085

To gain an impression of what Danish settlement names looked like at the time when Domesday Book was being compiled in England it is convenient to look at the deed of gift made by the Danish king later known as St Knut on 21st May 1085 to the as yet unfinished church of St Lars in Lund in Skåne.[22] This charter survives in a transcript from before 1123. The land concerned is said to have been paid to the crown in penance by an Œpi filius Thorbiorn of Lund. Of the twenty-five named settlements fourteen are situated in Skåne, while there are ten in Sjælland and one on the island of Amager.

Seven of the names are topographical. In Skåne these include the name of the soon-to-be cathedral city of Lund (*lund* 'grove', probably with sacral significance), as well as three names in *haug* 'grave-mound or natural elevation' (Skälshög, Flädie, Hilleshøg), and one name each in *ager* '(small) field' (Uppåkra) and *lyng* 'ling, heather' (Skättiljunga). Stefan Brink has suggested tentatively that the name Uppåkra, originally a simplex name **Åker*, might have been borne by a central place, for the same element is sometimes

[22] E. Kroman, *Necrologium Lundense*, Medieval manuscript 6 in the University Library Lund, facsimile in *Corpus Codicum Danicorum* I (Hafniae [Copenhagen]: Munksgaard, 1960), fols 1v–2v.

compounded with the name of a heathen god in Uppland.[23] In Sjælland there is just one topographical name, Skenkelsø, which consists of the original name of a now dried-up lake **skænkil* 'little shank', referring to its shape, and the epexegetic generic term *sjó* 'lake'.[24]

Two of the settlement names in Sjælland would seem to have a cultural significance. They involve the Old Danish word **wǣ* 'heathen shrine': Onsved containing the name of the god Óðinn, and *Winningavve* whose specific is the name of the settlement Vindinge, whose own name is the common noun **winning* in the sense 'cultivation', while the site of the shrine is marked by the disused settlement of Wesby (1257) in which the originally simplex name has been linked in genitive form to the generic *-bý*.[25]

Seven of the habitative names contain generics which probably antedate the Viking period. There are three names in Skåne containing plural *-staðir*, Herrestad, Håstad and Søvestad, while Brønneslöv contains the word *lev* meaning 'inheritance'. There is another *lev*-name in Sjælland, namely Skuldelev, whose specific is the common noun *skuld* meaning 'debt' or 'tax', while there are two names in *-heim* in Sjælland, Øm and Smørum, whose specifics are the common nouns *ø* 'island' and *smør* 'butter' respectively.

The most striking fact about the primary settlement names in the deed of gift, however, is that the generic in no fewer than six of the names is *bý* 'settlement'. Three of these are in Skåne, namely Sandby containing *sand*, Västra Karaby (SkO A7, 106)[26] or Östra Karaby (SkO A14, 323) or Karlaby in Järrestads härad, all containing the gen.pl. of *karl* 'churl, peasant', while Lomma is recorded in the charter in the form *Lumaby*, in which the old Danish river-name **Luma* 'the tepid one' has received an explanatory *bý* to show that the name refers to a settlement.[27] The three *bý*s across the Sound are Tjæreby containing *tjara* 'tar, resin' and Brøndby(vester) containing *brunn* 'spring' in Sjælland, and Sundby(vester) in Amager containing the word *sund* 'sound, strait'. With the exception of the river-name in Lomma, the specifics in these

[23] S. Brink, 'Land, bygd, distrikt och centralort i Sydsverige: Några bebyggelsehistoriska nedslag', in L. Larsson and B. Hårdh (eds), *Central Platser Centrala Frågor* (Stockholm: Almqvist and Wiksell, 1998), pp. 297–326 (p. 322).

[24] Kousgård Sørensen, *Danske sø- og ånavne*, VI, p. 116.

[25] B. Jørgensen, *Danske Stednavne*, 3rd edn (Copenhagen: Gyldendal, 2008), pp. 220, 334; L. Eilersgaard Christensen, *Stednavne som kilde til yngre jernalders centralpladser* (Copenhagen: Det Humanistiske Fakultet, 2010), p. 137.

[26] The abbreviation SkO A here and below stands for *Skånes ortsnamen*, Serie A. Bebyggelsenamn, 1 ff. (Lund: Institutet för Språk och Folkminnen, Dialekt- och Ortnamnsarkivet i Lund, 1958 ff.).

[27] Kousgård Sørensen, *Danske sø- og ånavne*, IV, p. 342.

bý-names are all common words in the Danish vocabulary.

There are just three other habitative names mentioned in the deed of gift which probably originated in the Viking period or later. Helsingborg in Skåne, whose specific is the same term for inhabitants 'the dwellers at the neck' as that found in Elsinore across the Sound, has the generic *borg* presumably in the sense 'fortification', although this name might conceivably be topographical, with the generic *borg* in its original sense 'hill' (SkO A12, 456–62). The second name contains the next most frequently occurring Viking-period generic in England, namely *thorp* 'secondary settlement'. This is Tollerup in Oppe-Sundby parish in Sjælland, containing the late Danish hypocoristic personal name *Tolli*.[28] The third name is Børstingerød in Sjælland. The specific **byrstingar* is probably a term for inhabitants, 'the men with bristly hair', while the generic is *ryði*, a derivative of the Old Danish word *ruð* meaning 'clearing'.[29]

Names probably current in the Viking period: *bý*

Even though the twenty-five names recorded in the deed of gift are hardly representative of the corpus of Danish settlement names as a whole, they can suggest some significant characteristics of the Danish settlement names likely to be current in the Viking period, if they are considered together with the names recorded in the other early sources. I shall begin by discussing the name-types that not only occur in many of the early sources but also played a role in the formation of Nordic place-names in England. Attention is naturally drawn first and foremost to the place-names in *-bý* .

There are over 700 names in England containing this generic and it seems likely that in some instances the *bý*-names replaced earlier names when the Danes took over the settlements in question. This would have taken place in a similar way as when the older Danish name represented in the narratives of Ohthere and Wulfstan as **Hæþum* 'at the heaths' was replaced by a form of the name Hedeby, presumably **Heiðabý*, in which the appellative *heið* in the plural, denoting stretches of wasteland, forms the specific of the new name. The only documented example of a possible replacement of an Old English place-name by a Danish name in *-bý* is that in a statement in the late tenth-century chronicle of Æthelweard to the effect that the place that was known to the English as *Norðweorðig*, was referred to by the Danes by a completely

[28] K. Hald, *Personnavne i Danmark II. Middelalderen* (Copenhagen: Dansk Historisk Fællesforenings Håndbøger, 1974), p. 94.

[29] Jørgensen, *Danske Stednavne*, p. 239.

unrelated name, *Deoraby*.[30] The Danish name may reflect the presence of a deer-park in the immediate vicinity, perhaps because Derby's neighbouring settlement bears the English name Darley (*dēor-lēah* 'deer clearing').[31]

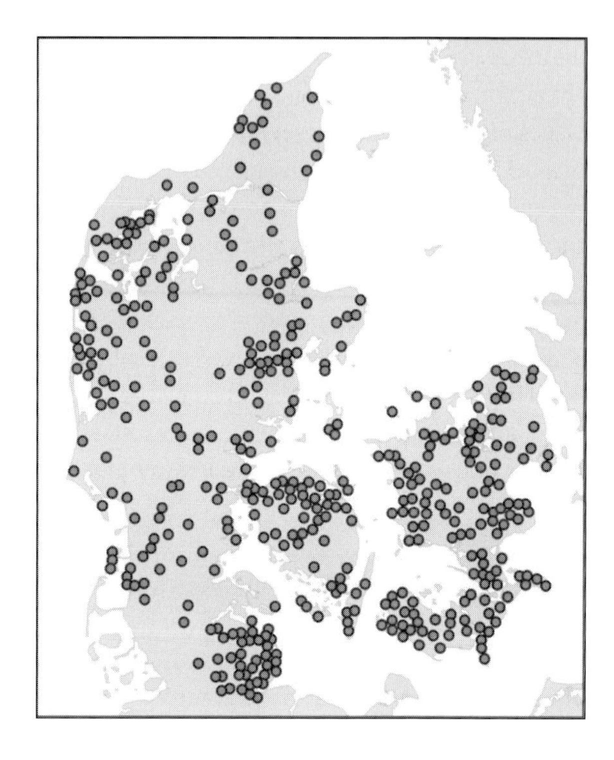

Fig. 1. The distribution of place-names in *-bý* in Denmark. Map prepared by Peder Dam after the map in P. Skautrup, *Det danske sprogs historie* I (Copenhagen: Gyldendal, 1968), p. 41.

A significant fact about the six names in *-bý* in the Danish deed of gift is that five of the names are common appellatives. Bent Jørgensen has pointed out that in many parts of Denmark the names in *-bý* are borne by settlements which can be shown by their location, size and archaeological status to have a central position in the cultural landscape in spite of the fact that their names are not only generally lexically transparent but also contain as their specifics words for very basic conditions, thus belying the apparent antiquity of the settlements in question.[32] Jørgensen would explain this fact by suggesting that the *bý*-names arose in a situation in which an attempt was being made to emphasize the habitative nature of the place-names, possibly pointing to redistribution of

[30] Campbell, *Chronicle of Æthelweard*, p. 37.

[31] K. Cameron, *The Place-Names of Derbyshire*, 3 vols (Cambridge: Cambridge University Press, 1959), pp. 443, 446. Cf. below, p. 103.

[32] B. Jørgensen, 'The degree of onomastic coverage within various categories of denotata', in E. Brylla and M. Wahlberg (eds), *ICOS 2002*, I (Uppsala: Språk- och folkminnesinstitutet, 2005), pp. 196–206.

both the settlements and their affiliated resources.

The term 'redistribution of settlement' applies well to the Danish partitions of land in the Danelaw, where place-names in *-bý* are exceptionally common. This fact tempted me to look again at earlier explanations of the distribution of the *bý*-names in England. When I was young and naive, there was a tendency to believe that the distribution pattern of these names reflected the planting by the Danes of new settlements on land that had previously been heavily wooded or in need of draining and clearance. A pioneering study was L. W. H. Payling's study of Scandinavian place-names in the light of local topography and surface geology in Kesteven, Lincolnshire.[33] His lead was followed by Kenneth Cameron, who considered that the *bý*s in the East Midlands must have been established on the best available vacant land.[34] To begin with I came to a similar conclusion in my study of the names in Yorkshire, although I pointed out that there must have been pre-English settlements at several of the sites with names in *-bý* in that county.[35] Peter Sawyer had shown that assessments for the collection of tributes in England recorded in the eighth and ninth centuries were statements not of potential but of real capacity and that land resources must often have been fully exploited before the arrival of the Vikings.[36] He consequently suggested that since vast tracts of fertile land could not have been left unoccupied before this time, the best explanation for the dissemination of the names in *-bý* in England is that settlements hitherto dependent on large estates were re-named when they passed into the possession of new Danish smallholders.[37] By the time that I had begun work on the names in North-West England, I realized that there must have been at least two strata of names in *-bý* in England. The first of these must have arisen at the end of the ninth century or the beginning of the tenth, when the Danish settlers in eastern England took over a large number of pre-existing English settlements, to many of which they gave names in *-bý* whose specifics were common nouns such as *dal* 'valley' in Dalby, *haug* 'mound' in Huby, and *kirkja* 'church' in Kirkby,

[33] L. W. H. Payling, 'Geology and place-names in Kesteven (S. W. Lincolnshire)', *Leeds Studies in English* 4 (1935), 1–13.

[34] K. Cameron, *Scandinavian Settlement in the Territory of the Five Boroughs: The Place-Name Evidence* (Nottingham: University of Nottingham, 1965).

[35] G. Fellows-Jensen, *Scandinavian Settlement Names in Yorkshire* (Copenhagen: Akademisk Forlag, 1972), pp. 175–77, 218–28.

[36] P. H. Sawyer, 'Baldersby, Borup and Bruges: the rise of Northern Europe', *The University of Leeds Review* 16 (1973), 75–96 (p. 90).

[37] P. H. Sawyer, *From Roman Britain to Norman England* (London: Methuen, 1978), pp. 161–63.

that is names of the same type as the majority of the *bý*-names in Denmark. Probably at a slightly later date, some of the settlers in the Danelaw proper began to make their way up the river valleys and across the Pennines to Amounderness and the Lune valley and down the Eden valley towards Carlisle. In these regions, too, they gave names in *-bý* to the settlements they took over, giving names of the same type, for example with specifics such as *horn* 'horn' or **horni* 'spit of land' in Hornby and *kross* 'cross as a religious symbol' in Crosby. From Carlisle there was a further expansion northwards into Dumfriesshire, marked by names such as Bombie (*bóndi* 'farmer') and Esbie (*eski* 'place growing with ash-trees'), and southwards along the coastal plain of Cumberland to Man and back across the sea to Wirral and south-west Lancashire, where there are names such as Raby (*rá* 'boundary mark') and Ribby (*rygg* 'ridge').

It was perhaps rather later than this anticlockwise movement westwards, or maybe concurrently with it, that the Danish settlers in eastern England began to break up old estates into small independent agricultural units, many of which may have begun life as dependent secondary settlements. In Yorkshire and the East Midlands this fragmentation resulted in settlements whose names consisted of a Danish personal name and *-bý*, for example *Eymund* in Amotherby (Yorkshire), and *Saksulf* and *Ásfrith* in Saxelby and Asfordby (Leicestershire). Since over 80% of the personal names compounded with *-bý* in English place-names are of Nordic origin, it seems likely that most of these names were formed while there was still a distinct Danish community that retained its own customs of personal naming and perhaps also its own language.[38] The use of personal names as specifics in *bý*-names would seem to have been a novelty in Denmark, however, and this practice does not seem to have made its appearance there until late in the Viking period. It is almost only in the southern part of the country that anthroponymical specifics occur and only a few of the names involved are of Christian origin, e.g. *Johannes* in Jensby (see Fig. 2). It was suggested by Kristian Hald that the development of this type of name might have owed its development to the popularity of the formation personal name plus *-bý* in the Danelaw[39] but it is not typically

[38] See Fellows Jensen, *Scandinavian Settlement Names in Yorkshire*, pp. 12, 242 and Fellows Jensen, *Scandinavian Settlement Names in the East Midlands*, p. 278; also L. Abrams and D. N. Parsons, 'Place-names and the history of Scandinavian settlement in England', in J. Hines, A. Lane and M. Redknap (eds), *Land, Sea and Home: Proceedings of a Conference on Viking-Period Settlement, at Cardiff, July 2001* (Leeds: Maney, 2004), pp. 379–431 (pp. 397–98).

[39] K. Hald, *Vore Stednavne*, 2nd edn (Copenhagen: Gad, 1965), p. 113.

Anglo-Danish forenames that occur in the Danish names in *-bý*.[40]

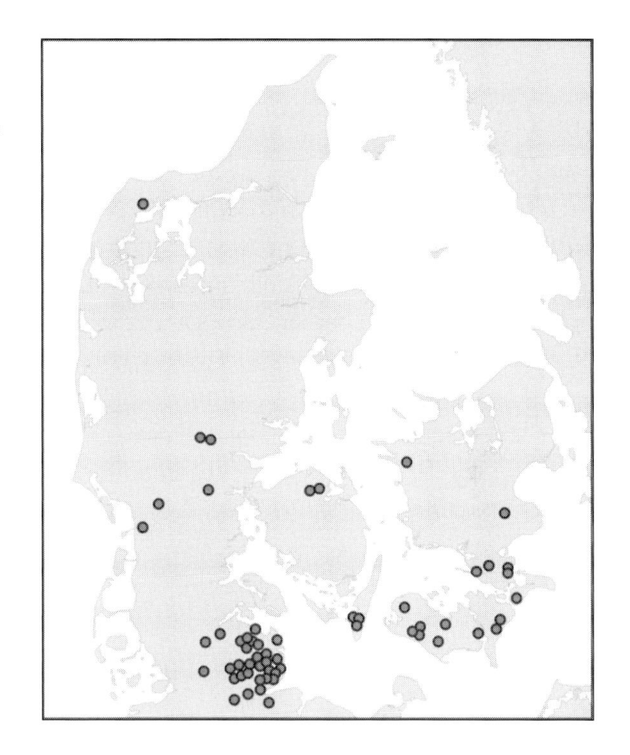

Fig. 2. The distribution of place-names in *-bý* with anthroponymical specifics in Denmark. Map prepared by Peder Dam after Pedersen, 'Bebyggelses-navne på -bý', p. 11 and Hald, *Vore Stednavne*, p. 109.

With the advent in England of *bý*-names containing personal names of Norman or Breton origin we come to what I would consider to be a third stratum of *bý*-names. This probably began towards the end of the Viking period, for we only find three such names recorded in the East Midlands. These are Grimoldby and Hagnaby (Li), and Serlby (Nt). These estates must have been held by men called *Grimald*, *Hagen* and *Serlo*, who presumably received their lands from Knut the Great or his sons early in the eleventh century or perhaps from Edward the Confessor, who brought Norman followers with him when he returned from exile in 1042. I think that these place-names must have replaced earlier ones, possibly names in *-bý*. There are six place-names in *-bý* in north-eastern England containing Norman personal names that are first recorded in sources younger than Domesday Book: Halnaby, Jolby, Fockerby and Huby (Y), containing *Halanant*, *Johel*, *Folkward* and *Hugo*, and Follingsby and Raisby (Du), containing *Folet* and *Raco*. The date of formation

[40] B. Hjorth Pedersen, 'Bebyggelsesnavne på -bý sammensat med personnavn', in *Ti Afhandlinger. Udgivet i anledning af Stednavneudvalgets 50 års jubilæum* (Copenhagen: Gad, 1960), pp. 10–46.

of these six surviving place-names is uncertain but their earliest records suggest that they arose in the twelfth century.[41] Across the Pennines there are twenty-eight place-names containing personal names of Norman origin, all of which can be presumed to have been borne by men who were established there by the Norman king after William Rufus had garrisoned the castle in Carlisle in 1092.[42]

It was earlier thought that the *bý*s in the North-West represented the longest survival of *bý* as a place-name forming generic in England.[43] This type of name also occurs in Central Scotland, however, where many of the *bý*-names have exact parallels in the Danelaw, and it seems likely to me that most such names there were formed by analogy with similar names in the Danelaw, probably in replacement for older names, by men brought north by the Scottish kings or other great landowners at one period or another.[44] An analogical formation Sorbie in Fife, for example, was first recorded as late as in the mid-nineteenth century.[45]

Names in *-thorp*

Next after *bý* the most frequently occurring Danish generic from the Viking period in England is *thorp*, of which there are well over 500 examples. Among the early Danish sources I have discussed here, however, there is only the single instance of Tollerup in Sjælland in the deed of gift from 1085, although there are now at least 2,500 instances of names in *-thorp* in Denmark, spread fairly evenly over the whole of the country except Bornholm (see Fig. 3).[46]

[41] Fellows Jensen, *Scandinavian Settlement Names in Yorkshire*, pp. 7–8, 28; V. Watts, *A Dictionary of County Durham Place-Names* (Nottingham: English Place-Name Society, 2002), pp. 45, 101.

[42] G. Fellows-Jensen, *Scandinavian Settlement Names in the North-West* (Copenhagen: Reitzel, 1985), p. 15.

[43] E. Ekwall, 'The Scandinavian element', in A. Mawer and F. M. Stenton (eds), *Introduction to the Survey of English Place-Names*, English Place-Name Society 1.i (Cambridge: English Place-Name Society, 1924), pp. 55–92 (p. 91).

[44] G. Fellows-Jensen, 'Scandinavians in Southern Scotland', *Nomina* 13 (1989–90), 41–60 (pp. 54–55).

[45] S. Taylor, 'Scandinavians in Central Scotland – *bý*-place-names and their context', in G. Williams and P. Bibire (eds), *Sagas, Saints and Settlements* (Leiden and Boston: Brill, 2004), pp.125–45 (p. 145).

[46] Hald, *Vore Stednavne*, p. 137.

Fig. 3. The distribution of place-names in *-thorp* in Denmark in 1688. Map prepared by Peder Dam after P. Dam, 'De nordiske -torper', in G. Kváran et al. (eds), *Nordiska namn – Namn i Norden: Tradition och förnyelse*, NORNA-Rapporter 84 (2008), p. 76.

The meaning of the element *thorp* is generally agreed to be something like 'dependent, secondary settlement'. One of the reasons for its frequency of occurrence in England is possibly that the generic found in the English names may sometimes have been the cognate Old English word *throp*. The fact that Danish personal names such as *Viðfari* in Weaverthorpe and *Hjalp* in Helperthorpe in Yorkshire and *Gunnhild* or *Gunni* in Gunthorpe in Nottinghamshire are so predominant among the specifics of the *thorp*-names in England, representing 177 out of a total of 265 personal names involved, points not to the colonization of unused land by raiding Danes, however, but rather, as suggested long ago by Niels Lund, to the take-over of existing settlements already called something plus *-throp* or *-thorp*, perhaps in connection with an intensification of cultivation.[47] I have wrestled with the problem of the origin of the *thorps* in England on three occasions.[48] Although I

[47] N. Lund, '*Thorp*-names', in P. H. Sawyer (ed.), *Medieval Settlement: Continuity and Change* (London: Arnold, 1976), pp. 223–25.

[48] G. Fellows-Jensen, 'Place-names in *-þorp*: in retrospect and turmoil', *Nomina* 15 (1991–92),

have to admit that changes of specific often did take place in place-names in *-thorp*, it is equally true that many of the *thorp*-names with English specifics, at least 52 of them personal names, can have been coined after the end of the Viking period proper, when the English language had once again become dominant in England. I would certainly agree with Karl Inge Sandred that the many *thorp*-names in Norfolk in particular cannot form the basis for mapping Scandinavian settlement there but that it is at the very least a reflection of a very strong Danish influence on the process of naming.[49] To some extent the same may be true of the *thorp*-names in Yorkshire and the East Midlands. I would argue that a clear demarcation should be drawn in England between the *thorps* containing Danish specifics on the one hand and the simplex *thorps* and those with English specifics on the other.[50]

Significant for the dating of the *thorp*-names in Denmark is the fact that Viking-period names such as the by-name *Dragmál* in Drammelstrup in Jutland and compound names such as *Ásketil* in Eskildstrup, *Sigmund* in Simmendrup and *Steinketil* in Stenkelstrup, all in Sjælland, do occur in Danish *thorps* but comparatively rarely, while more numerous Danish *thorp*-names contain Christian personal names such as *Peder* in several Pederstrups, formations that are known to have been particularly popular in the thirteenth century.[51] Further, the Middle Low German personal names that first became popular after about 1400 are only weakly represented, for example *Lambert* in Lammestrup.[52]

Names denoting clearings

There is one other name in St Knut's deed of gift which points to a period of currency in the Viking period, namely Børstingerød in north-eastern Sjælland.

35–51; '*Torp*-navne i Norfolk i sammenligning med *torp*-navne i andre dele af Danelagen', in P. Gammeltoft and B. Jørgensen (eds), *Nordiske torp-navne*, NORNA-rapporter 76 (Uppsala, 2003), pp. 47–59; 'A few more words on place-names in *thorp* in England', in P. Dam et al. (eds), *Torp som ortnamn och bebyggelse*, Tvärvetenskaplig torp-konferens Malmö, 25–27 april 2007 (Lund: Dialekt- och ortnamnsarkivet i Lund, 2009), pp. 43–53. For a different approach to *thorp*-names in England see above, pp. 65–69, and below, p. 197.

[49] K. I. Sandred, 'Nordiskt i Norfolk. Ortnamn och bebyggelsehistoria i en del av Danelagen', *Kungl Humanistiska Vetenskaps-Samfundet I Uppsala Årsbok* (1994), 129–54 (pp. 141–42).

[50] Fellows-Jensen, 'A few more words', pp. 49–52.

[51] Lerche Nielsen, *Vikingetidens personnavne i Danmark*, pp. 110–11.

[52] Hald, *Personnavne i Danmark* II, p. 22.

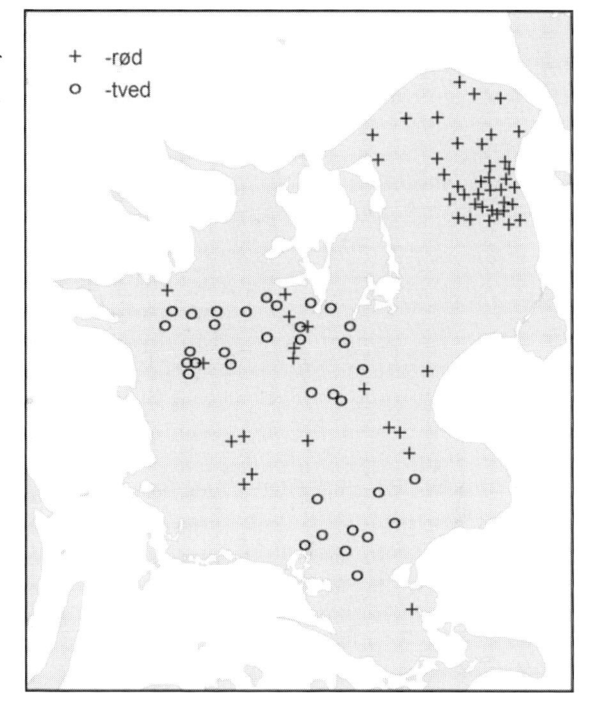

Fig. 4. The distribution of place-names in *-rød* and *-tved* in Sjælland. Map prepared by Peder Dam after Hald, *Vore Stednavne*, p. 165.

The generic is a derivative form of Old Danish *ruð* 'clearing', namely *ryði*. There is a marked concentration of the distinctive dialectal north-east Sjælland form *-rød* < *-ruð* in place-names in Sjælland and this form later became an independent element in Danish.[53] There are no instances of *ruð* as a generic in England but Routh in Yorkshire (*Rutha* GDB 304b) may be an instance of a side-form *rūð* as a simplex name, and *ruð* may occur as a specific in Rudby (*Rodebi* GDB 305d) and a now-lost *Rud(e)torp* (*Rvdtorp* GDB 326d, 381d, *Rudetorp* GDB 373c) in the same county. There is a second Danish generic denoting clearings in woodland which appears more frequently in England but this is not found among the names recorded in the earliest Danish sources. It is *thveit*, which appears in Denmark as *tved*. It is particularly common in a broad belt that runs roughly north-west/south-east from Hordaland in Norway, through Telemark, across Skagerrak to Vendsyssel and Djursland, and across Kattegat to north-western, central and southern Sjælland, for example Løgtved (*løg* 'bulb'), Bregentved (**brækni* 'bracken') and Ortved (*wara* 'uncultivated area'). Names in *-thveit* are completely absent from north-eastern Sjælland and comparatively rare in Skåne and Sweden. They are, however, comparatively well represented in England, where there are over 250 examples, for example

[53] Hald, *Vore Stednavne*, p. 162.

Bassenthwaite and Thackthwaite in Cumberland and Crostwight in Norfolk, as well as in Normandy, where there are at least 88 instances, for example Blaquetuit,[54] and there are scattered instances in Shetland and Orkney, for example Twatt in Orkney.[55]

I would argue that it is the names containing Danish words for clearing that are the best indicators of areas that were first cleared for occupation by Viking settlers. Since the Danish word *thveit* was adopted into the local English dialects and remained in use in some of these for a long period, however, the names need not all reflect Viking settlement. Names in *-thveit* are particularly frequent in remote and inaccessible areas such as the Cumbrian Dome and the Yorkshire Moors and quite common in Cumberland, Westmorland, northern Lancashire and the North and West Ridings of Yorkshire. Elsewhere in England they are not common but they are to be found even as far south as Norfolk.[56] Kristian Hald has suggested that the greater popularity of *thveit*-names than *ruð*-names in England may suggest that the Vikings did not come from those parts of Scandinavia where the generic favoured for names of clearings was *ruð*[57] but it is perhaps more likely that the currency of *ruð* simply culminated after the period of Viking settlements.

Pre-Viking-period names

Having discussed the Danish generics in place-names in England which would seem to have flourished in and after the Viking period, I should like to explain briefly why some other generics that are recorded in place-names in early Danish sources do not occur in England. One such element is the Old Danish word **lø̄sa*, now generally referred to in Danish as *løse* and often appearing in place-names as *-(e)lse*, for example Spragelse.[58]

[54] Å. K. Hansen, *Språkkontakt i gammelt koloniområde. En studie av normannerbosetningens stedsnavn, med særlig vekt på navnegruppa* -tuit (Bergen: Universitetet i Bergen, 1998), pp. 112–87.

[55] G. Fellows-Jensen, 'Little Thwaite, who made thee?', in W. F. H. Nicolaisen (ed.), *Proceedings of the 19th International Congress of Onomastic Sciences. Aberdeen, August 4–11, 1996*, II (Aberdeen: University of Aberdeen, 1998), pp. 101–06.

[56] K. I. Sandred, 'Language contact in East Anglia: some observations on the Scandinavian place-names in *-thwaite* in Norfolk', in E. M. Närhi (ed.), *ICOS 1990 Helsinki. Proceedings of the XVIIth International Congress of Onomastic Sciences* (Helsinki, University of Helsinki, 1990), pp. 310–17.

[57] Hald, *Vore Stednavne*, p. 168.

[58] Jørgensen, *Danske Stednavne*, p. 189.

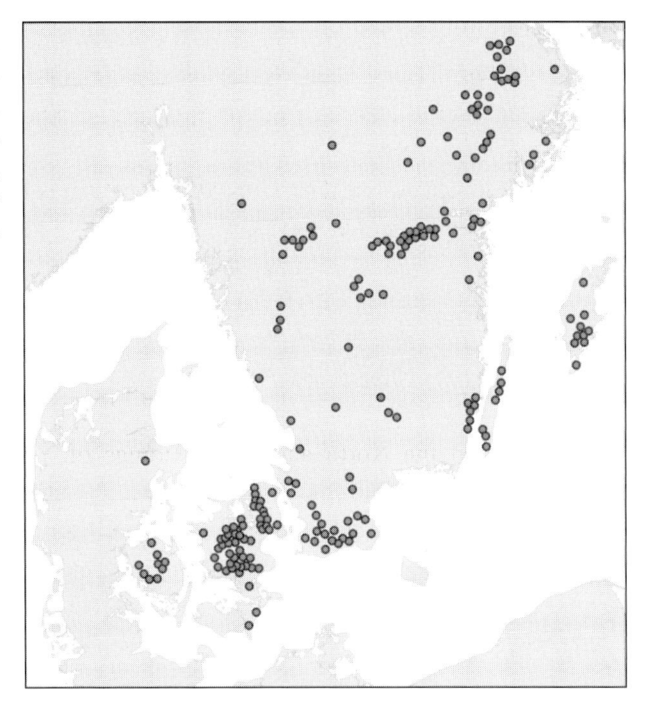

Fig. 5. The distribution of place-names in *-løsa* in Denmark and southern Sweden. Map prepared by Peder Dam after Skautrup, *Det danske sprogs historie* I, p. 28.

It would seem to have had a sense such as 'glade'. It was apparently current as a naming element in Denmark in the first half of the first millennium but then seems to have dropped out of use. The majority of the names containing it are found in Skåne and Sjælland but there are also instances in Fyn. The specifics in the names are often rather obscure. The two instances in the early Danish sources are both from Sjælland and, although their earliest records are from the eleventh century, both names are certain to be older than this. Spragelse in the form **sbalklusu** is inscribed in runes on the Sandby 3 stone,[59] while Slagelse is stamped in capital letters as SLAHLOV and SLAHLUS on coins of Hartheknut.[60] The Danish specifics are a word related to *spjælke* 'splint' and *slag* meaning 'hollow in the ground'. There are no instances of the generic *løse* in place-names in England.

The absence of place-names in the Danish element *-lev* in England may be for a different reason. It is generally thought to have been current as a naming element in Denmark between about 300 and 800 so it may well have dropped out of currency in the Viking period. The reason for its absence from English place-names, however, is most probably that its meaning is something like

[59] Jørgensen, *Danske Stednavne*, p. 268.

[60] Jørgensen, *Danske Stednavne*, p. 260.

'that which is left behind', as in the Modern Danish word *levninger*, which means 'leftovers'.

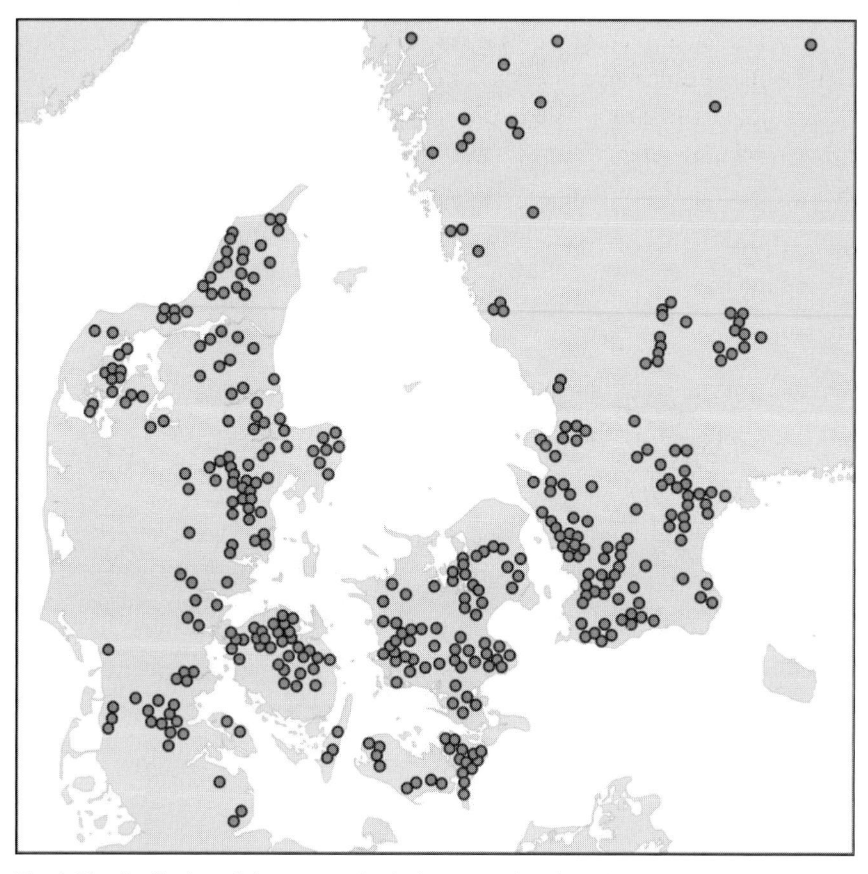

Fig. 6. The distribution of place-names in *-lev* in Denmark and southern Sweden. Map prepared by Peder Dam after A. Bach, *Deutsche Namenkunde* II, *Die deutschen Ortsnamen 2* (Heildelberg: Carl Winter, Universitätsverlag, 1954), p. 334.

The absence of instances of *lev* in the early Danish sources I have discussed, however, may perhaps be because it is most widespread in Jutland, where surviving written records are rather scanty. On the other hand, in place-names such as Gørslev in Sjælland *lev* probably meant 'inherited property', 'Gøtar's inheritance', and this would have rendered it inappropriate for forming names for property that had been either seized or bought.[61]

For two other old Danish elements, *-heim* meaning 'home, homestead' and *-sted* (plural *steder*) meaning 'place', as well as for various forms of the

[61] Jørgensen, *Danske Stednavne*, p. 104.

derivative ending *-ing-*, the situation is greatly complicated because of the existence of related elements in England that must have been introduced by the Anglo-Saxons before the Viking period. There is, for example, no reason to think that a name such as Ringstead in Norfolk (*Rincsteda* GDB 173b) is a Danish place-name or a name which might have been influenced by the Danes, even though it is almost identical in form with Danish Ringsted and both names probably refer to a place associated with a stone circle as a meeting-place. The Ringsteads in England are simply English place-names.[62]

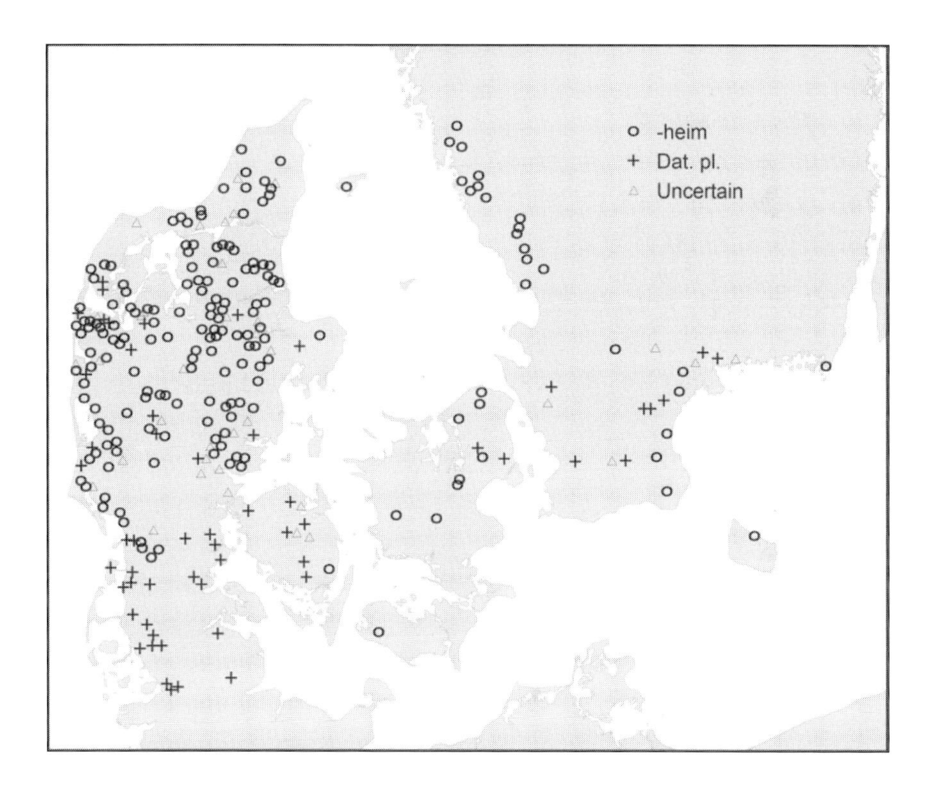

Fig. 7. The distribution of place-names in *-heim* in Denmark. Map prepared by Peder Dam after K. Hald, *De danske Stednavne paa -um* (Copenhagen: J. H. Schultz Forlag, 1942), p. 141.

In the case of the Danish element *-heim*, however, there is a difference in spelling between this word and its cognate English element *-hām* so it is possible to distinguish between the Danish and English place-names. In Denmark it is also frequently difficult to determine from the surviving forms

[62] K. I. Sandred, *English Place-Names in -stead* (Uppsala: Almqvist and Wiksell, 1963), p. 103.

whether a place-name originated as a compound formation in *-heim* or a dative plural formation in *-um*. Similar confusion can sometimes arise in the case of English names in *-hām*. There are a number of instances in which English place-names in *-hām* display isolated spellings in *-heim*, showing that Danish speakers recognized the identity of the two elements.

Such erratic Scandinavianization is much more characteristic of the document dating from between 1115 and 1118 that is known as the Lindsey Survey than of Domesday Book.[63] There are no fewer than 14 names in *-hām* in the Lindsey Survey whose generic is replaced by *-heim* in some or all of the forms, e.g. Haltham on Bain (GDB *Holtham* 339a, Lindsey Survey *Holteim* 26).[64] It would seem that the *heim*-forms in the Lindsey document represent a deliberate attempt by the scribe to give the names a more Danish appearance. Very occasionally there are instances of such Scandinavianization in Domesday Book, e.g. Middleham in Yorkshire (*Medelai* GDB 311c), where all later forms suggest that the name was originally a compound of the two English words *middel* and *hām*, that were replaced in Domesday Book but not elsewhere by their Scandinavian cognates *meðal* and *heim*.

Tune and the English names in *-tūn*

The last of the early Danish generics that I want to discuss is one that was also current in the Viking period, namely *-tūn*. The history is not very lengthy and to some extent it is enigmatic. It has, however, long had a lurking fascination for me, since I have lived for over 38 years in Tune *herred* 'hundred', and in the course of the two years that my husband was in and out of hospital before he died in 2009, I travelled regularly on the yellow buses from my home in Karlslunde to Roskilde, changing buses at Tune church, where I spent a good deal of time thinking about the significance of the name Tune. The village of Tune was not one of those involved in St Knut's deed of gift but that the place-name was certainly current at that period in Denmark is shown by the fact that the deed explicitly states that the site of the shrine there referred to as *Winningavve* was located in Tune *herred* (*Tuna herathi*). From other documents we know that Tune (where the generic *tūn* stands as a simplex name in plural form) was an important settlement in the *herred* of the same name.

The element *tūn* is not of common occurrence in Denmark but in central Sweden the plural form *Tuna* occurs quite frequently and the core area of

[63] G. Fellows Jensen, 'The scribe of the Lindsey Survey', *Namn och Bygd* 57 (1969), 58–74 (pp. 64–69).

[64] Fellows Jensen, *Scandinavian Settlement Names in the East Midlands*, pp. 200–02.

distribution of these names is the Mälar region. In his dissertation on the generic Karl Axel Holmberg argued that it had no specific significance but just meant 'fence' or 'enclosure'.[65]

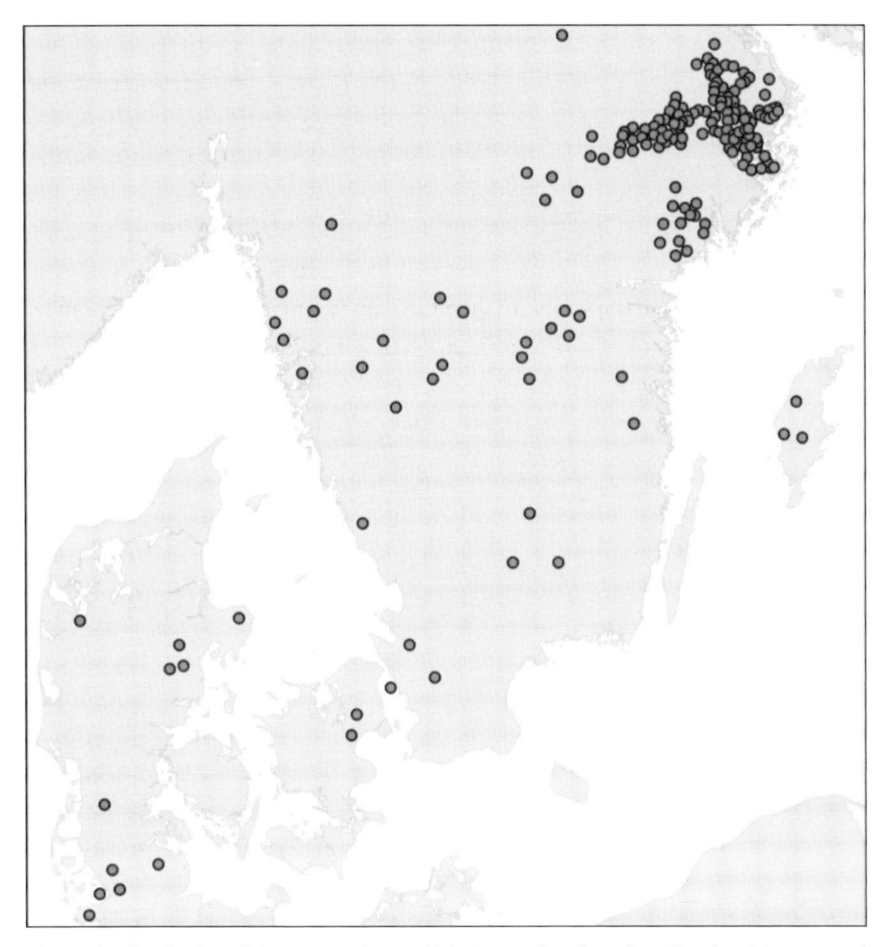

Fig. 8. The distribution of place-names in *-tun(a)* in Denmark and southern Sweden. Map prepared by Peder Dam after Holmberg, *De svenska Tuna-namnen*, Bild 14, and J. Udolph, *Namenkundliche Studien zum Germanenproblem* (Berlin and New York: Walter de Gruyter, 1994), p. 699.

Other scholars have found this explanation unlikely and Thorsten Andersson has considered that it was important to study whether the names might not have denoted central places and whether *Tuna* was perhaps even a kind of technical term.[66] The frequency of occurrence in Sweden of *Tuna* as a simplex name

[65] K. A. Holmberg, *De svenska Tuna-namnen* (Uppsala: AB Lundequistska Bokhandel, 1969), p. 260 and illustration 14.

[66] T. Andersson, '*Tuna*-problem', *Namn och Bygd* 56 (1968), 88–124 (pp. 121–22); 'The

certainly suggests that it may have been employed there during a period of administrative reorganization of settlement, perhaps replacing older names in the tenth or eleventh centuries.[67] An examination of the dissemination of the generic in Sweden shows that the Danish *Tuna*-names in Skåne and Sjælland form the very tail end of the spread of the plural names from central Sweden. Although a close examination of the onomastic and archaeological background for Tune in Sjælland has not revealed unambiguous evidence that it was a central place of the same kind as the *Tuna*-names in Sweden, the topic seems worthy of further study.[68] The plural form of the name Tune only occurs once elsewhere in present-day Denmark and this is as the specific in a field-name *Tunemose* in eastern Sjælland whose significance remains unexplained.

The few remaining relevant Danish settlement names containing *-tūn* are found in eastern Jutland. They are all compound names with *-tūn* in the singular and the generic can generally be translated as 'enclosed plot of land', for example in two Galtens containing the animal term *galt* 'hog', Nøtten probably containing the adjective 'new', and Orten containing *wara* 'outlying field'.[69] Since some of the names seem to be old and well established, they can probably be assumed to have acquired a general meaning 'farm'.

The Danish word *tūn* has an Old English cognate which must originally have had the same significance, namely 'enclosed plot of land'. This word is not common in the earliest English sources, where Barrie Cox found only six instances from before *c.* 730,[70] although names containing the element occur rather frequently in the Anglo-Saxon Chronicle, where they are often the names of royal residences or places of some standing.[71] It may simply have been the familiarity of the Danes with the singular form *tūn* that lay behind the coining of so many settlement names of the Grimston-type to indicate Danish reorganization of settlement. I have calculated that less than a quarter of the place-names in *-tūn* in most parts of England have personal names as their

origin of the *Tuna*-names reconsidered', in I. Wood and N. Lund (eds), *People and Places in Northern Europe 500–1600: Essays in honour of Peter Hayes Sawyer* (Woodbridge: The Boydell Press, 1991), pp. 197–204.

[67] Å. Hyenstrand, *Centralbygd – Randbygd*, Acta Universitatis Stockholmiensis. Studies in North-European Archaeology 5 (1974), p. 103.

[68] Eilersgaard Christensen, *Stednavne som kilde*, pp. 135, 150.

[69] Jørgensen, *Danske Stednavne*, pp. 89, 217, 221.

[70] B. Cox, 'The place-names of the earliest English records', *Journal of the English Place-Name Society* 8 (1975–76), 12–66 (p. 63).

[71] J. Campbell, 'Bede's words for places', in P. H. Sawyer (ed.), *Names, Words, and Graves: Early Medieval Settlement* (Leeds: University of Leeds, 1979), pp. 34–51 (pp. 48–50).

specifics and this suggests that it was not particularly common for an Old English place-name to contain the name of an owner or tenant. The reason why the English did not often change the form of an existing place-name to incorporate the name of a new lord or tenant is probably that land was not simply bought and sold in the Anglo-Saxon period.[72] In the tenth century, however, individual owners began to acquire small parcels of land all over England and this habit of buying and selling property may well have developed as a result of Danish activity. This is reflected not only in the popularity of personal names as specifics in names in *-bý* and *-thorp* but also in the names generally referred to as Grimston-hybrids which contain Nordic personal names. The same probably applies to what may be referred to as Carlton-hybrids, where the specifics are common words of Danish origin.[73] The spread of both types of name outside the Danelaw proper cannot, of course, be said to reflect Viking settlement but rather Danish influence on the personal nomenclature and lexicon of English-speaking settlers.

English *cot*(*e*) and Danish names like Koldkaad

Finally, I shall make a brief attempt to explain why the originally English generic *cot* n. 'hut, cottage', which occurs frequently in the plural forms *-cotum* and secondary *-cotes* in England, makes some scattered appearances in Denmark. From the point of view of the relationship between Denmark and England in the Viking period interest is concentrated on the compound formation which appears in forms such as Caldecote and Caldecott in England. Such names are comparatively widespread and probably denote 'unheated shelter for animals or men'. This name occurs in Denmark in forms such as Koldkaad, Kollekolle and Kalleko[74] and in the parts of Normandy where English influence was prominent in the Viking period in forms such as *Caudecote*, *Caude-Cote* and *Côte-Côte*.[75] The compound formation would seem likely to have originated in England and been carried back to both Denmark and Normandy by Vikings who had spent time in England. Louis

[72] T. M. Charles-Edwards, 'The distinction between land and moveable wealth in Anglo-Saxon England', in Sawyer (ed.), *Medieval Settlement*, pp. 180–87; Fellows Jensen, *Scandinavian Settlement in the East Midlands*, pp. 282–86.

[73] On the *tūn* compounds in England see also Townend below, pp. 117–20.

[74] Hald, *Vore Stednavne*, p.160.

[75] J. Adigard des Gautries, 'Études de toponymie Normannique II. Les *Caudecote*', *Études Germaniques* 8 (1953), 1–5; L. Musset, 'Pour l'étude comparative de deux fondations politiques des vikings: le royaume d'York et le duché de Rouen', *Northern History* 10 (1975), 40–54 (p. 50).

Guinet has objected to this suggestion because in Old English there are two forms of the English word, *cot* n. and *cote* f., while Danish *kot* is a neuter word and the nine relevant place-names in Normandy all have the element in the feminine gender.[76] The change of gender is not, however, an insuperable obstacle to assuming a relationship between the elements in England and Denmark.[77] The Caldecote, Caudecote, Koldkaad names are, however, of no direct relevance for a discussion of the Danish background for English place-names.

Conclusion

The comparative paucity of the surviving records of place-names in Denmark before and during the Viking period means that it is necessary to base my conclusions primarily on the names found in England, merely drawing support for my claims where possible from such Danish names that do make a comparatively early appearance. Most significant is the popularity of the generic *-bý*. It now seems clear that the names in *-bý* must have replaced older names to mark a change in the administrative and taxable status of the settlements. This would seem to have happened in England at three different periods. Firstly came the names that resemble most closely those in Denmark, where the specifics are common nouns of everyday relevance, for example Derby, Kir(k)by and Dalby, and probably indicate that the names now became independently taxable for the first time. Secondly came the names in which the specifics are personal names of Nordic origin, marking the splitting off of parcels of land from the larger estates and the granting of these to Danish smallholders. Thirdly came the arrival of personal names of Norman, Breton and Celtic origin as specifics in the *bý* names and these probably mark the closing of the Viking period. There are comparatively few names of this type in England, where the use of the generic *-bý* would seem to have dropped out of use quite early, but such names continued to be formed analogically in Scotland for a much longer period. The Danes must also have made a considerable contribution to the popularity of the names in *-thorp* in England but, when mapping areas of Danish settlement, it seems imperative only to take into account compound names whose specific is of Scandinavian origin. The best evidence for Danish settlement in areas newly brought under cultivation would

[76] L. Guinet, *Contribution à l'étude des établissements saxons* (Caen: Publications de la Faculté des lettres et sciences humaines de l'université de Caen, 1967), pp. 49–54.

[77] G. Fellows-Jensen, 'Les noms de lieux d'origin scandinave et la colonisation viking en Normandie. Examen critique de la question', *Proxima Thulé* 1 (1994), 63–103 (pp. 96–97).

seem to be the names containing the generic *-thveit* but it must be remembered that this only applies to names in the areas of dense Danish settlement and not to the areas where the word *thwaite* entered into the local dialects. The last major contribution by the Danes to English place-names would seem to be the Grimston-type names in which Nordic personal names are compounded with the English element *-tūn* and probably also the less numerous Carlton-type names in which the specifics are Nordic common nouns.[78]

[78] For help and advice in the preparation of this paper for publication I am much indebted to Peder Gammeltoft, Bent Jørgensen and Bo Nissen Knudsen.

4

Scandinavian place-names in England

Matthew Townend

Comment on the Scandinavian element in English place-names, from both the English and Scandinavian sides, dates back to the medieval period itself. In a famous passage in his late tenth-century *Chronicon*, a Latin adaptation of the *Anglo-Saxon Chronicle*, ealdorman Æthelweard tells us that in 871 the body of a certain Æthelwulf 'was carried away secretly, and was taken into Mercia, to the place called *Northworthig*, but in the Danish language Derby'.[1] And Snorri Sturluson, in his early thirteenth-century *Heimskringla*, writes that:

> Northumbria is reckoned a fifth part of England. Eiríkr had taken residence in York, where, men say, the sons of Loðbrók had previously resided. After the sons of Loðbrók conquered the land, Northumbria was mostly settled by Norwegians. And after control of the land had been taken away from them, Danes and Norwegians often harried there. Many place-names there are in the Norse language, such as *Grímsbœr* [Grimsby] and *Hauksfljót* [?] and many others.[2]

In terms of more recent comment, though, continuous scholarship on Scandinavian place-names in England effectively begins with the Danish archaeologist Jens Worsaae, whose 1852 *Account of the Danes and Norwegians in England, Scotland, and Ireland* (first published in Danish the previous year) contains an insightful chapter on 'Danish-Norwegian

[1] A. Campbell (ed.), *The Chronicle of Æthelweard* (London: Nelson, 1962), p. 37 ('abstrahitur furtim, adduciturque in Merciorum prouinciam in loco qui Northuuorthige nuncupatur, iuxta autem Danaam linguam Deoraby').

[2] Bjarni Aðalbjarnarson (ed.), *Heimskringla*, 3 vols, Íslenzk Fornrit 26–28 (Reykjavík: Íslenzka Fornritafélag, 1941–51), I, 152–53 ('Norðimbraland er kallat fimmtungr Englands. Hann [i.e. Eiríkr blóðøx] hafði atsetu í Jórvík, þar sem menn segja, at fyrr hafi setit Loðbrókarsynir. Norðimbraland var mest byggt Norðmǫnnum, síðan er Loðbrókarsynir unnu landit. Herjuðu Danir ok Norðmenn optliga þangat, síðan er vald landsins hafði undan þeim gengit. Mǫrg heiti landsins eru þar gefin á norrœna tungu, Grímsbœr ok Hauksfljót ok mǫrg ǫnnur.'). See also Bjarni Einarsson (ed.), *Ágrip af Nóregskonunga Sǫgum. Fagrskinna – Nóregs Konunga Tal*, Íslenzk Fornrit 29 (Reykjavík: Íslenzka Fornritafélag, 1985), p. 76.

Names of Places'.[3] An early, regional application of Worsaae's work by an antiquarian enthusiast was Robert Ferguson's *The Northmen in Cumberland and Westmoreland* (1856), but Ferguson's linguistic skills were limited, and his place-name etymologies did not prove enduring.[4] A similar regional study, somewhat better informed, was made by G. S. Streatfeild for Lincolnshire in 1884.[5] None of these pioneering figures were philologists, however, and it was in the last two decades of the nineteenth century that place-name studies as a whole were put on a new footing by figures such as Henry Bradley and W. W. Skeat. Come the twentieth century, and building on these new, philological foundations, it was two Swedish scholars—Harald Lindkvist and Eilert Ekwall—who took forward in new and sustained ways the study of Scandinavian place-names in England. For his doctoral dissertation at Uppsala, in 1912 Harald Lindkvist (1881–1974) produced his *Middle-English Place-Names of Scandinavian Origin: Part I*. Lindkvist's place-names are 'Middle English' in the sense that they are primarily preserved in post-Conquest sources, and his choice of the term signals the linguistic orientation of his approach (Part II, never published, was to treat of 'place-names as are proved by consonantic criteria to be Scandinavian').[6] Although the corpus of Lindkvist's names remains incomplete, his monograph was the first work to survey the Scandinavian place-names in England on a nationwide basis and with a fully rigorous, philological methodology. In his introduction he was also the first scholar to discriminate, from the distribution of the place-name evidence, the Scandinavian settlement of England into a number of distinctive zones, which he labels the East Anglian division, the Midland division, the

[3] J. J. A. Worsaae, *An Account of the Danes and Norwegians in England, Scotland, and Ireland* (London: Murray, 1852), pp. 65–76.

[4] R. Ferguson, *The Northmen in Cumberland and Westmoreland* (London: Longman, 1856). On Ferguson see further M. Townend, *The Vikings and Victorian Lakeland: The Norse Medievalism of W. G. Collingwood and his Contemporaries*, Cumberland and Westmorland Antiquarian and Archaeological Society Extra Series 34 (Kendal: Cumberland and Westmorland Antiquarian and Archaeological Society, 2009), esp. pp. 24–26.

[5] G. S. Streatfeild, *Lincolnshire and the Danes* (London: Kegan Paul, Trench and Co, 1884). On Streatfeild see further A. Wawn, 'Hereward, the Danelaw and the Victorians', in J. Graham-Campbell et al. (eds), *Vikings and the Danelaw: Select Papers from the Proceedings of the Thirteenth Viking Congress, Nottingham and York, 21–30 August 1997* (Oxford: Oxbow, 2001), pp. 357–68 (p. 360).

[6] H. Lindkvist, *Middle-English Place-Names of Scandinavian Origin: Part I* (Uppsala: Uppsala University Press, 1912).

North-Eastern division, and the North-Western division.[7] As for Eilert Ekwall (1877–1964), he was, of course, one of the twentieth-century giants of the discipline. His *Scandinavians and Celts in the North-West of England* (1918) and (especially) *The Place-Names of Lancashire* (1922) were major works, and it was he who was invited to write the chapter on 'The Scandinavian Element' for the collection of state-of-the-art essays that launched the English Place-Name Society.[8] Three further scholars, from the course of the twentieth century, may be picked out for mention. The EPNS county surveys of A. H. Smith and Kenneth Cameron illuminated the Scandinavian place-names of, respectively, Yorkshire and the East Midlands; and Smith also produced the most famous map in the history of place-name studies.[9] Outside of the EPNS, Gillian Fellows-Jensen's three major volumes have supplied overview and analysis on a regional basis.[10] There have been many other workers too, of course, making countless contributions to our ever-developing knowledge and understanding of the Scandinavian element in English place-names.

This is a rich heritage, and what we owe to such scholarship is immense. At the level of national history—whether that history be political, social, linguistic, or whatever—it is place-name study that has done as much as any discipline to bring us knowledge about the Scandinavian episode in England's past; the history of the Danelaw

[7] Lindkvist, *Middle-English Place-Names*, pp. xxxix–l.

[8] E. Ekwall, *Scandinavians and Celts in the North-West of England* (Lund: Gleerup, 1918); *The Place-Names of Lancashire* (Manchester: Manchester University Press, 1922); and 'The Scandinavian element', in A. Mawer and F. M. Stenton (eds), *Introduction to the Survey of English Place-Names*, English Place-Name Society 1.i (Cambridge: Cambridge University Press, 1924), pp. 55–92. For the early history of the EPNS see A. M. Armstrong, M. Gelling, and K. Cameron, 'Some notes on the history of the English Place-Name Society', *Journal of the English Place-Name Society* 25 (1992–93), 1–8.

[9] A. H. Smith, *The Place-Names of the North Riding of Yorkshire* (Cambridge: Cambridge University Press, 1928) [EPNS NRY], *The Place-Names of the East Riding of Yorkshire and York* (Cambridge: Cambridge University Press, 1937) [EPNS ERY], and *The Place-Names of the West Riding of Yorkshire*, 8 vols (Cambridge: Cambridge University Press, 1961–63) [EPNS WRY], K. Cameron, *The Place-Names of Derbyshire*, 3 vols (Cambridge: Cambridge University Press, 1959) [EPNS Db], and (with J. Field and J. Insley), *The Place-Names of Lincolnshire*, 7 vols so far (Nottingham: English Place-Name Society, 1985–2010) [EPNS Li]. Smith's map is in A. H. Smith, *English Place-Name Elements*, 2 vols, English Place-Name Society 25–26 (Cambridge: Cambridge University Press, 1956), map 10 'The Scandinavian Settlement'.

[10] G. Fellows-Jensen, *Scandinavian Settlement Names in Yorkshire* (Copenhagen: Akademisk forlag, 1972), *Scandinavian Settlement Names in the East Midlands* (Copenhagen: Akademisk forlag, 1978), and *Scandinavian Settlement Names in the North-West* (Copenhagen: C. A. Reitzel, 1985).

would be unwritable without it. And at the regional or local level it is place-name studies that have allowed many individuals or communities to respond with excitement, imagination, and perhaps even identification, to the glamour of Scandinavian origins in their own patch of the country. As Robert Ferguson wrote, evocatively, in 1856: 'the land is dotted over with little individual histories'.[11] If we like, we can—and as scholars, we should—attempt to join the dots, but across northern and eastern England, over the past 150 years, many have thrilled to the romance of local etymologies.[12] Study of the Scandinavian place-names in England has played a significant role in both the understanding of national history and the making of regional and personal identities.

In this paper I shall not attempt a blow-by-blow review of the various debates and discussions that have animated the study of Scandinavian place-names in the 90 years since Ekwall published his EPNS introduction, not least because a number of excellent reviews already exist.[13] In particular, the 2004 article by Lesley Abrams and David Parsons should be commended as offering both the most thorough and acute literature review available, and also the most telling contribution to debate in the last decade or so.[14] Abrams and Parsons re-affirm, as a 'bottom-line' interpretation of the Scandinavian element in English place-names, that the evidence indicates 'sizeable communities of Norse speakers in parts of eastern England', who played a significant role as land-holders, and who gave names to places in their own language.[15]

These may hardly seem controversial assertions; but in the last half-century there has been no aspect of the interpretation of the Scandinavian element that has not, in some way or other, been queried by sceptics of various stripes, and there is, of course, one publication in particular that has been responsible for spreading uncertainty. Hackneyed though it may be in a review of this kind, even after all these years there is no way of

[11] Ferguson, *Northmen in Cumberland and Westmoreland*, p. 227.

[12] For a study of one cluster of enthusiasms see Townend, *Vikings and Victorian Lakeland*.

[13] See for example G. Fellows-Jensen, 'The Vikings in England: a review', *Anglo-Saxon England* 4 (1975), 181–206, and D. M. Hadley, *The Vikings in England: Settlement, Society and Culture* (Manchester: Manchester University Press, 2006), pp. 1–27.

[14] L. Abrams and D. N. Parsons, 'Place-names and the history of Scandinavian settlement in England', in J. Hines, A. Lane and M. Redknap (eds), *Land, Sea and Home: Proceedings of a Conference on Viking-Period Settlement, at Cardiff, July 2001* (Leeds: Maney, 2004), pp. 379–431.

[15] Abrams and Parsons, 'Place-names and the history of Scandinavian settlement', esp. p. 405.

bypassing a consideration of Peter Sawyer's 1962 book *The Age of the Vikings*.[16]

This is one of those seminal books whose arguments, perhaps, have not proved particularly enduring, but whose effects most certainly have. Famously, what Sawyer argued with regards to the Vikings in England was that Scandinavian armies were small—to be numbered in the low hundreds rather than in the thousands—and that it should not be assumed that the Old Norse place-names in England were given early, by substantial populations of Norse speakers; they might have been given late, by English speakers, whose language had been influenced by a small Norse elite. Such claims had in fact been made by Sawyer a few years earlier, in an article which was more polemical and closely argued than the 'Settlements' chapter of *The Age of the Vikings*; but it is the briefer and less assertive treatment in the monograph which has since received most attention.[17] (Oddly, the 1957 paper is not referenced in *The Age of the Vikings*, suggesting that Sawyer had perhaps already begun to reconsider some of his more extreme formulations.)

It would be an error to see the supporters and opponents of Sawyer as having split simply along disciplinary lines—historians (and archaeologists) for him, and linguists against—as suggested for example in Margaret Gelling's weary sigh that 'it seems likely that there will always be historians who do not believe that the appearance of a large number of place-names in a new language is evidence of a large-scale settlement by the speakers of the new language'.[18] For a simple disciplinary split is not what happened. To begin with, we should remember that Sawyer's position was advanced in opposition to the prevailing views of both linguists and historians, above all in opposition to the views of Sir Frank Stenton.[19] And it can hardly be said that the most eminent Anglo-Saxon historians of the last fifty years all lined up to stand shoulder-to-shoulder with Sawyer in his iconoclastic views: Dorothy Whitelock reportedly took a critical view of his work, while

[16] P. H. Sawyer, *The Age of the Vikings* (London: Arnold, 1962).

[17] P. H. Sawyer, 'The density of the Danish settlement in England', *University of Birmingham Historical Journal* 6 (1957), 1–17.

[18] M. Gelling, *Signposts to the Past: Place-Names and the History of England*, 2nd edn (Chichester: Phillimore, 1988), p. 220.

[19] Stenton's views can be found in, for example, 'The Danes in England', *Proceedings of the British Academy* 13 (1927), 203–46.

Patrick Wormald remained conspicuously unpersuaded.[20] Sawyer's arguments about the size of Viking armies were most effectively answered by Nicholas Brooks.[21] The original reviews of the book also make interesting reading. For example, Michael Wallace-Hadrill, no small figure in the world of early medieval history, ended his cool review with the advice that 'Mr Sawyer could plainly write a really good Viking book if he would give himself space and time. Until he does, he will just have to wait in the queue where he appears to place Sir Frank Stenton, Sir Thomas Kendrick and the rest by whom, it is to be inferred, "the Viking period has been fabricated"'.[22] As for the response of an archaeologist, David Wilson handed out a stern rebuke for Sawyer's handling of both the textual and material sources, and observed that when it came to the philological evidence 'even the layman can detect certain exaggerations [...] and these do not make his arguments any more convincing'.[23] I quote these comments not so much to pass judgement on the quality of Sawyer's book but rather to point out, first, that the book's reception was not split on a disciplinary basis, and second, that, although the book had an immediate and lasting impact, this was due more to its provocative qualities than to instant acclamation as a classic.

It would thus be a misrepresentation to depict the response to Sawyer's work, and the development of Scandinavian place-name studies in the post-Sawyer period, in terms of a simple opposition between historians and archaeologists on one side, and linguists on another, resulting in a frustrating cross-disciplinary impasse. It would also be an error to see Sawyer's book as somehow bringing an abrupt end to a pre-lapsarian period of consensus, in which everyone believed in a maximalist view of Scandinavian place-names and settlement; Ekwall wrote as far back as 1936 that 'it is often stated that the Scandinavian settlers in the Danelaw cannot have been very numerous, and that they

[20] See R. I. Page, review of I. Wood and N. Lund (eds), *People and Places in Northern Europe 500-1600: Essays in Honour of Peter Hayes Sawyer*, *Saga-Book of the Viking Society* 23 (1993), 529–35 (p. 535), C. P. Wormald, 'Viking Studies: whence and whither?', in R. T. Farrell (ed.), *The Vikings* (Chichester: Phillimore, 1982), pp. 128–53 (pp. 134–37).

[21] N. P. Brooks, 'England in the ninth century: the crucible of defeat', *Transactions of the Royal Historical Society*, 5th Series, 29 (1979), 1–20.

[22] J. M. Wallace-Hadrill, review of P. H. Sawyer, *The Age of the Vikings*, *English Historical Review* 79 (1964), 818 19 (p. 819).

[23] D. M. Wilson, review of P. H. Sawyer, *The Age of the Vikings*, *Saga-Book of the Viking Society* 16 (1962), 103–08 (p. 105).

soon became assimilated to the English population' (he immediately added, however, that 'even place-names tell us that this cannot be correct').[24] In other words, there has always been a debate about numbers. Nonetheless, it was linguists who replied most fully to Sawyer's interpretation of the place-name evidence, and above all Kenneth Cameron, whose three papers of 1965, 1970, and 1971 provided for the next generation the essential theorization, and the most powerful demonstration, of the processes that gave rise to Scandinavian place-names in England.[25] Although his systematic foregrounding of drift geology was an innovative move, Cameron was essentially restating what one might term the traditional philological view on the Scandinavian place-names of England, as articulated, for example, in Ekwall's 1924 EPNS chapter (in which he had, incidentally, foreshadowed Cameron by invoking, albeit only in passing, the importance of geology as a factor).[26] It is an irony, though, that it was Cameron's acceptance of Sawyer's arguments for the small size of Viking armies that led him, at least partly, to propose that 'in addition to the settlements made by men from the invading army in and after 877, an immigration from Scandinavia into the north-eastern Midlands took place behind the protection provided for at least two generations by the armies of the Five Boroughs'.[27] It is also important to note that, at least in this influential, first formulation, Cameron does not talk about a 'peasant' migration, though this term has

[24] E. Ekwall, 'The Scandinavian settlement', in H. C. Darby (ed.), *An Historical Geography of England Before AD 1800: Fourteen Studies* (Cambridge: Cambridge University Press, 1936), pp. 133–64 (p. 160). See also E. Ekwall, 'The proportion of Scandinavian settlers in the Danelaw', *Saga-Book of the Viking Society* 12 (1937–45), 19–34 (p. 19).

[25] K. Cameron, *Scandinavian Settlement in the Territory of the Five Boroughs: The Place-Name Evidence*, Inaugural Lecture (Nottingham: University of Nottingham, 1965), 'Scandinavian settlement in the territory of the Five Boroughs: the place-name evidence, part II, place-names in thorp', *Mediaeval Scandinavia* 3 (1970), 35–49, and 'Scandinavian settlement in the territory of the Five Boroughs: the place-name evidence, part III, the Grimston-hybrids', in P. Clemoes and K. Hughes (eds), *England Before the Conquest: Studies in Primary Sources Presented to Dorothy Whitelock* (Cambridge: Cambridge University Press, 1971), pp. 147–63. These are helpfully reprinted in K. Cameron (ed.), *Place-Name Evidence for the Anglo-Saxon Invasion and Scandinavian Settlements* (Nottingham: English Place-Name Society, 1975), pp. 115–71, and it is to this reprint that reference will be made here.

[26] See Ekwall, 'Scandinavian element', pp. 58, 79, 83, 84. The most important precursor to Cameron's work was L. W. H. Payling, 'Geology and place-names in Kesteven (S.W. Lincolnshire)', *Leeds Studies in English and Kindred Languages* 4 (1935), 1–13.

[27] Cameron (ed.), *Place-Name Evidence*, pp. 120–21.

repeatedly been attributed to him by his critics.[28] For it is the case that, for his hypothesis of a secondary, unrecorded civilian migration, Cameron has been singled out for sharp criticism from some quarters. In my view, however, such criticism is unjustified: first, because such a hypothesis was by no means restricted to Cameron (it had been suggested, for example, by Lindkvist half a century earlier, and raised also by Ekwall in his 1924 EPNS chapter);[29] second, because the hypothesis actually fitted the linguistic evidence very well; and third, because the hypothesis was consonant with other tenth- or eleventh-century evidence indicating that the movement of Scandinavians into England was not a once-for-all event of the ninth century, but rather an ongoing process that lasted the best part of two centuries.[30] One might also add that the huge number of non-elite metalwork finds in the last couple of decades agrees better with Cameron's interpretation than that of his critics.[31] If one conceptualizes this secondary migration (or ongoing migration, as one might prefer to call it) in terms of households, or dependents, of lords or tenants entering the country—or indeed in terms of new lords or tenants—and not in terms of poor peasants making their independent way, then it does not seem to me to be exceptionable. This is

[28] See for example D. M. Hadley, '"And they proceeded to plough and to support themselves": the Scandinavian settlement of England', *Anglo-Norman Studies* 19 (1997), 69–96 (pp. 70–71), and S. Trafford, 'Ethnicity, migration theory, and the historiography of the Scandinavian settlements of England', in D. M. Hadley and J. D. Richards (eds), *Cultures in Contact: Scandinavian Settlement in England in the Ninth and Tenth Centuries* (Turnhout: Brepols, 2000), pp. 17–39 (pp. 20–21). See, however, K. Cameron, 'Stenton and place names', in D. Matthew (ed.), *Stenton's Anglo-Saxon England Fifty Years On: Papers given at a Colloquium held at Reading 11–12 November 1993* (Reading: University of Reading, 1994), pp. 31–48 (p. 43), where the phrase 'peasant farmers' is used.

[29] See Lindkvist, *Middle-English Place-Names*, pp. xliv–xlv ('The original stock of Scand. settlers here in the late 9th cent. must have been considerably reinforced through additional immigration of their countrymen during the next two centuries'), and Ekwall, 'Scandinavian element', p. 82 ('it is somewhat difficult to believe that the army can have been numerous enough to account for the very extensive Scandinavian colonisation in England, and a reinforcement by later settlers from Denmark is plausible').

[30] See M. Townend, *Scandinavian Culture in Eleventh-Century Yorkshire*, Kirkdale Lecture 2007 (Kirkdale: The Trustees of the Friends of St Gregory's Minster, 2007), pp. 4–6.

[31] See for example K. Leahy and C. Paterson, 'New light on the Viking presence in Lincolnshire: the artefactual evidence', in Graham-Campbell et al. (eds), *Vikings and the Danelaw*, pp. 181–202, and J. F. Kershaw, 'Culture and gender in the Danelaw: Scandinavian and Anglo-Scandinavian brooches', *Viking and Medieval Scandinavia* 5 (2009), 295–325.

a point I will return to below.

I do not intend to add—unnecessarily—to the voices querying Sawyer's interpretation of the place-name element. Rather, in the light of the debate that his contributions have generated over the last fifty years, I want to examine a number of inter-related themes or areas in place-name studies that seem important, and to consider how these have fared since Ekwall published his 1924 chapter. Have they helped to determine the field, loomed large in debate, and brought us to where we are now? Or have they fallen by the wayside, and hence failed to prevent certain developments in the subject?

I want to begin with the question of how places acquire names – how place-names are 'coined', to use the most common word. In an article published in 2000 I suggested that 'there could well be a greater consideration of what exactly is meant by reference to the "coining" of place-names, as it is an expression regularly employed in the study of Scandinavian settlement', and I further proposed that 'a distinction might be drawn between the "coining" of major settlement names on the one hand, and of minor names and topographical names on the other'.[32] Happily, some incisive discussion on precisely this topic has since been offered by Abrams and Parsons,[33] but it is still worth reviewing the implications for the study of Scandinavian place-names of the varying assumptions and arguments that have obtained concerning the 'coining' of place-names.

As Abrams and Parsons note, there have been essentially two models proposed for the coining of Scandinavian place-names in England, though I shall suggest that one might distinguish a third model as well.[34] The older, more traditional view is that place-names are normally given not by the residents of a place, but rather by their neighbours. This is firmly the view espoused in the 1924 EPNS volume. So for example, Frank Stenton, in discussing Old English names, affirmed that 'the spontaneous origin of place-names is the fundamental fact which governs their interpretation'.[35] Ekwall's opinion, in his chapter on 'The

[32] M. Townend, 'Viking Age England as a bilingual society', in Hadley and Richards (eds), *Cultures in Contact*, pp. 89–105 (p. 100).

[33] Abrams and Parsons, 'Place-names and the history of Scandinavian settlement', pp. 401–03.

[34] Abrams and Parsons, 'Place-names and the history of Scandinavian settlement', p. 401.

[35] F. M. Stenton, 'The English element', in Mawer and Stenton (eds), *Introduction to the Survey of English Place-Names*, pp. 36–54 (p. 44).

Scandinavian element', is worth quoting at length:

> In the period of the Scandinavian invasions place-names were not generally, as now, given deliberately by the inhabitants of the places themselves. They arose spontaneously, unconsciously [...] At first alternative names might be used, but one would soon oust the others. The names would be given rather by neighbours than by the inhabitants of places. Place-names thus indicate the predominant nationality of the population of a district [...] A single Scandinavian place-name indicates a Scandinavian district, not the settlement of an isolated Scandinavian or Scandinavian household.[36]

Such a view has formed the customary assumption in studies of the Scandinavian place-names in England; indeed, in *The Age of the Vikings* Peter Sawyer also stressed that 'it is very important to recognise that settlement names [...] are not given by the people who live in the farms and villages but by their neighbours',[37] and such a view was echoed, for example, by Kenneth Cameron (though Cameron does, however, add that 'of course, it does not follow that all names were given in this way').[38] And as Ekwall explains, one corollary of this position is that the place-name evidence is usually held to indicate a large community of Old Norse speakers.

The alternative view that has been advanced is that the Scandinavian place-names in England did not arise 'spontaneously, unconsciously' at all, but rather very deliberately, very self-consciously, by those in a position of authority, with the power to select a name and impose its usage on the general populace. This view is associated with what one might term the 'fragmenting estates' paradigm (as later espoused by Peter Sawyer, for example), in which it is argued that 'the Scandinavian names reflect the fragmentation of estates rather than settlement'.[39] As is evident, one corollary of this position is that (in theory) communities of Norse speakers are not required to give rise to Norse place-names, and the position has normally been adopted by scholars who downplay the extent and influence of Scandinavian settlement.[40]

[36] Ekwall, 'Scandinavian element', pp. 71–72; see also 'Scandinavian settlement', p. 139.

[37] Sawyer, *Age of the Vikings*, p. 152.

[38] Cameron (ed.), *Place-Name Evidence*, p. 116.

[39] P. H. Sawyer, *Kings and Vikings: Scandinavia and Europe AD 700–1100* (London: Routledge, 1982), p. 104.

[40] See for example the comments in J. D. Richards, *Viking Age England*, rev. edn (Stroud: Tempus, 2000), p. 47.

No doubt there is some justification for both positions, though this is not to say that they are likely to have acted as equal causes in the creation of Scandinavian place-names in England. A worthwhile exercise would be to gather together all the stories and anecdotes contained in pre-Conquest texts (such as Bede's *Historia Ecclesiastica*) that give accounts of how places gained their names; my strong suspicion is that such an exercise would lend considerable support for the first position, but not for the second (for which documentary evidence is harder to come by). But a third position—again, not to be preferred exclusively—is also possible, which is that Scandinavian settlement names were indeed given by inhabitants rather than neighbours, but not in a process of top-down, bureaucratic labelling through the fragmenting of estates. As Kenneth Cameron pointed out, the Icelandic *Landnámabók* or 'Book of Settlements' contains many accounts of how places gained their names.[41] Most commonly the narrative just states that places were named after their occupants, and such names may well have come into being spontaneously and unconsciously. But sometimes *Landnámabók* pictures the settlers of Iceland deliberately bestowing names upon the places where they made their homes (and it is of course the general patterns presented by *Landnámabók* that are important, not whether this or that process really happened in this or that individual case). So, for example, Helgi Hrólfsson 'discovered a fjord and found a harpoon [*skutill*] on the shore; he called it Skutilsfjǫrðr; he lived there afterwards'; or Þormóðr inn rammi 'came with his ship into Siglufjǫrðr and sailed up to Þormóðseyri, and for that reason he called it Siglufjǫrðr [...] and he settled at Siglunes'.[42] Reviewing the three models in reverse order, one might say that the third (names given by occupiers) is analogous to the modern giving of house-names, the second (names given by those in authority) to the modern giving of street-names, and the first (names given by those resident in the vicinity) to the early origin of major river-names.

It is worth digressing a little more about *Landnámabók*, to make the point that it is, arguably, the single most neglected source for the study of

[41] Cameron (ed.), *Place-Name Evidence*, p. 116.

[42] Jakob Benediktsson (ed.), *Íslendingabók. Landnámabók*, Íslenzk Fornrit 1 (Reykjavík: Íslenzka Fornritafélag, 1968), p. 187 ('Hann fann fjǫrð einn ok hitti þar skutil í flœðarmáli; þat kallaði hann Skutilsfjǫrð; þar byggði hann síðan'), pp. 244, 246 ('Hann kom skipi sínu í Siglufjǫrð ok sigldi inn at Þormóðseyri ok kallaði af því Siglufjǫrð [...] ok bjó á Siglunesi').

Scandinavian settlement abroad. In the early days of scholarship, *Landnámabók* was gleefully seized upon as supplying, by a sort of analogy or parallelism, the unrecorded cultural details of Scandinavian settlement in England.[43] But even if one hesitates fully to resurrect such a procedure, the text still has an obvious pertinence to the much-debated 'numbers' question: put simply, the settlement of Iceland by Scandinavians in the ninth and tenth century demonstrates that in the Viking Age migrations did happen, potentially to the tune of thousands and thousands of settlers. Estimates for the population of Iceland by the close of the settlement period (mid-tenth century) range as high as 60,000 to 80,000, resulting from the actual migration of perhaps 10,000 to 20,000 individuals.[44] In recent decades a whole school of thought in history and (perhaps especially) archaeology has arisen that minimizes the extent and significance of migration in the early medieval world, and prefers elite emulation as the prime explanation for cultural change (including linguistic change).[45] But the sheer fact of the settlement of Iceland, and its commemoration in *Landnámabók*, may have served to prevent Old Norse scholars from subscribing to such a school of thought; and in a recent book the historian Peter Heather has launched a full-scale counterblast.[46] In social studies there is now a whole field, thoroughly theorized and researched, of 'migration studies', and this has much to teach Viking scholars about how best to formulate the question of numbers. For as Heather helpfully points out, the concept of 'mass migration' is primarily to be defined qualitatively, not quantitatively:

> To encompass [a] variety of situations and avoid numerical quibbling, migration studies have come to define 'mass' migration as a flow of

[43] See for example the antiquarian works of Thomas Ellwood (1838–1911), rector of Torver in Lancashire (now Cumbria): *The Landnama Book of Iceland as it illustrates the Dialect, Place Names, Folklore, & Antiquities of Cumberland, Westmorland and North Lancashire* (Kendal: Wilson, 1894) and (trans.), *The Book of the Settlement of Iceland, translated from the original Icelandic of Ari the Learned* (Kendal: Wilson, 1898).

[44] See for example Sturla Fridriksson, 'Grass and grass utilization in Iceland', *Ecology* 53 (1972), 785–96 (p. 789), R. F. Tomasson, *Iceland: The First New Society* (Minneapolis: University of Minnesota Press, 1980), p. 58, Gunnar Karlsson, *Iceland's 1100 Years: The History of a Marginal Society* (London: Hurst, 2000), p. 15, and J. Byock, *Viking Age Iceland* (Harmondsworth: Penguin, 2001), p. 9. I am grateful to Pragya Vohra for advice on this point.

[45] See for example Trafford, 'Ethnicity, migration theory, and the historiography of the Scandinavian settlement'.

[46] P. Heather, *Empires and Barbarians: Migration, Development and the Birth of Europe* (London: Macmillan, 2009).

> human beings (whatever the numbers involved) which changes the spatial distribution of population at either or both the sending and the receiving ends, or one 'which [often] gives a shock to the political or social system', again at either end or both.[47]

With the disappearance of Anglo-Saxon kingdoms, bishoprics, manuscripts and treasures, profound effects on the English language (and English toponymy), and the creation of new social, political, and administrative structures, there can be little question that—as Heather observes—the Viking impact on England can be regarded as a case of mass migration.[48] *Landnámabók* also provides ample indication that in the Viking Age migration was not an individual exercise: lords and land-takers took with them their households and dependents, as well as stimulating side-by-side settlement by other members of their kin-group.[49] Moreover, the example of Iceland indicates that, if resources are available, populations increase in the period after settlement. In other words, the time at which there will have been the greatest number of people of Scandinavian culture, language, and descent in England is not at the initial point of settlement, but perhaps one or two generations after that point.

The next issue I want to address, which picks up on some of my comments about the reception of *The Age of the Vikings*, is the disciplinary basis of place-name studies. One of the striking things about the 1924 *Introduction to the Survey of English Place-Names* is the disciplinary balance among the contributors, between historians and linguists. This balance is epitomized by the volume's two editors (who were also the Society's General Editors): Allen Mawer (1879–1942) and Frank Stenton (1880–1967). Mawer was a linguist with considerable historical expertise, Stenton a historian of great linguistic distinction.[50] The creative interfusion of history and linguistics is of course one of the

[47] Heather, *Empires and Barbarians*, pp. 31–32; the quotation is from R. King and S. Öberg, 'Introduction: Europe and the future of mass migration', in R. King (ed.), *Mass Migrations in Europe: The Legacy and the Future* (London: Belhaven Press, 1993), pp. 1–4 (p. 2).

[48] Heather, *Empires and Barbarians*, pp. 495–97.

[49] See P. Vohra, 'Kinship in the Viking Diaspora: Icelanders and their Relations across the North Atlantic', unpublished PhD thesis (University of York, 2008).

[50] For obituaries see F. M. Stenton, 'Sir Allen Mawer', *Proceedings of the British Academy* 29 (1943), 433–39, and D. M. Stenton, 'Frank Merry Stenton', *Proceedings of the British Academy* 54 (1968), 315–423. See also Cameron, 'Stenton and place names'.

defining features of place-name studies, and of its rise as a distinctive discipline; it is, perhaps, no coincidence that Abrams and Parsons' 2004 article, a thorough-going collaboration between a historian and a linguist, made such an incisive contribution to the subject. In terms of overarching theory and discipline, however, it may be more helpful in some regards to think of the particular field of historical linguistics as being primarily aligned with, and a subtype of, history rather than linguistics.[51] We might therefore better describe the meeting of disciplines in place-name studies as being between linguistic history and—as a convenient umbrella term—social history (that is, the history of society, as broadly defined), rather than more crudely between history and linguistics per se; place-name studies thus form part of the grand enterprise of historical study, through which, as the philosopher R. G. Collingwood argued, individuals and societies grow in self-knowledge.[52] Do place-name studies, then—using these terms of reference—incline more naturally towards social history or linguistic history? This is, of course, a false dichotomy, for they partake of both. Nonetheless, it is, I would suggest, worthwhile to consider whether, in the study of the Scandinavian place-names in England, social history or linguistic history has at certain times gained the upper hand – and if so, when, why, and whether this matters.

One way of approaching this question is to consider the principles of arrangement adopted by place-name volumes. We are now so familiar with the county-by-county, hundred-by-hundred, parish-by-parish organization of the EPNS Survey—patterned, to a large degree, on important fore-runners such as Ekwall's *Place-Names of Lancashire*—that it seems a self-evident format; but of course it is not. Ferguson and Streatfeild, for example, organized their material according to the type of feature named: settlements, mountains, rivers, fields. Gillian Fellows-Jensen's regional surveys are organized according to the type of settlement name—place-names in *-bý*, Grimston-hybrids, and so on—and in this she follows Cameron's subdivisions in his studies of the 1960s and

[51] See the discussion in J. J. Smith, *Sound Change and the History of English* (Oxford: Oxford University Press, 2007), p. 160, responding to comments in R. D. Fulk, 'Old English poetry and the alliterative revival: on Geoffrey Russom's "The evolution of Middle English alliterative meter"', in A. Curzan and K. Emmons (eds), *Studies in the History of the English Language II: Unfolding Conversations* (Berlin: Mouton de Gruyter, 2004), pp. 305–12 (p. 310).

[52] R. G. Collingwood, *The Idea of History*, rev. edn (Oxford: Oxford University Press, 1993).

early 1970s. But if we go back to Lindkvist's 1912 monograph, we find that he structures his book not by geographical unit, or landscape feature, or name-type, but by phonology: place-names containing the Old Norse diphthong *ei* are in one chapter, those containing the diphthong *au* in another chapter, and so on. In doing this, Lindkvist was no doubt modelling his practice on that of his doctoral supervisor, Erik Björkman, in his *Scandinavian Loan-Words in Middle English*, published ten years earlier.[53] Lindkvist's organization now seems curious, and hard to use for modern scholarly purposes; but this very curiosity, to a modern reader at least, is an index of how far the study of Scandinavian place-names has moved away from the linguistic history end of the scale, and towards the social history one, where the material is organized on non-linguistic principles.

But let us see what happens when we think about one famous class of names, the Grimston-hybrids, from the point of view of linguistic history rather than social history. Traditionally, of course, these names have been interpreted as representing pre-existing English villages, in some way taken over, and re-named, by Scandinavians, with the first element's Old Norse personal name indicating the new Scandinavian lord of the place.[54] I do not intend to cast any doubt on the main points of this interpretation. But the 'hybrid' part of their label is worth pondering further. To quote Kenneth Cameron: 'we can [...] be confident that the Grimston-hybrids are what they have always been considered to be, hybrids, part Scandinavian, part English'.[55] So, whatever the first element may have been, the second element of these place-names is assumed, in the pre-Viking period, to have been OE *tūn*. More recently, however, David Parsons has made an extremely suggestive observation:

> If this [i.e. the traditional] approach is substantially correct, it has always seemed to me strange that Viking conquerors took over, and partially renamed, so very many places that bore names in *tūn*, and so very few with other English habitative elements, like *hām*, *worð* and *wīc*. Indeed, given this observation, it seems to me far more likely that if the Vikings were responsible for the names, they must have adopted into their vocabulary the element *tūn*, perhaps with a notional sense 'English

[53] E. Björkman, *Scandinavian Loan-Words in Middle English*, Studien zur englischen Philologie 7 (Halle: Niemeyer, 1900–02).

[54] For a helpful review see J. Insley, 'Grimston-hybrids', in *Reallexikon der Germanischen Altertumskunde* 13, 49–56.

[55] Cameron (ed.), *Place-Name Evidence*, p. 158.

village'.[56]

This is a very interesting idea. Parsons notes, however, that there is another possible explanation for the names, which is to see them as *tūn* names which were partially re-named by the English-speaking population rather than the Norse-speaking (in which case Grimston-hybrids would not really be Scandinavian place-names at all, or even hybrids, but just English place-names with Scandinavian personal names as their first element).[57] There are reasons, however, to reject this second possibility. First, the presence, for some Grimstons, of a Norse genitive inflexion on the Norse personal name that forms the first element suggests that a Norse-speaking population was involved in the naming practice in some way, though it is the case that (unlike *bý*-names in England) the Grimstons preserve no examples of a Norse genitive in the more distinctive *-ar*, only in *-s*.[58] Second, and more tellingly, Parsons' observation about the oddity of hybridization applying only to names in *-tūn* would apply equally, but perhaps even more implausibly, in the other direction, if the English-speaking population was responsible: why should the English-speaking population have only replaced the first element of names in *-tūn*, and not those in *hām*, *worð* and *wīc*? The so-called Carlton hybrids are presumably a different case, at least on the whole, as their first elements are thought to be Scandinavianizations of Old English words, implying that they may indeed have been Old English place-names in *-tūn*.[59]

If we see the Grimston-hybrids as being 'Scandinavian' place-names, given or re-shaped by a Norse-speaking community, then Parsons' main argument seems to me incontrovertible. There is no reason why the second element of such names, in the pre-Viking period, must have been OE *tūn*. It is just as likely that the original Old English second element may have been something else, or even that some of the place-names may have been simplexes, or Celtic in origin. The antecedent Old English

[56] D. N. Parsons, 'How long did the Scandinavian language survive in England? Again', in Graham-Campbell et al. (eds), *Vikings and the Danelaw*, pp. 299–312 (p. 308). See also, briefly, P. Cullen, R. Jones, and D. N. Parsons, *Thorps in a Changing Landscape* (Hatfield: University of Hertfordshire Press, 2011), p. 87 n. 8.

[57] Parsons, 'How long did the Scandinavian language survive in England?', pp. 308–09.

[58] See for example Fellows-Jensen, *Scandinavian Settlement Names in Yorkshire*, pp. 192, 240, and *Scandinavian Settlement Names in the East Midlands*, pp. 272–74.

[59] See for example Fellows-Jensen, *Scandinavian Settlement Names in Yorkshire*, pp. 112–21, and *Scandinavian Settlement Names in the East Midlands*, pp. 179–80.

place-name could have been almost anything, and the place was re-named by Old Norse speakers as 'X's *tún*', with *tún* having the active sense of 'English village' (or more precisely, 'English village transferred into Scandinavian lordship', or even, conceivably, 'English village transferred into Scandinavian lordship and now assuming a new, nucleated form'). Such re-naming is certainly paralleled by another group of Scandinavian place-names in England, the 'Kirkby' group (where ON *kirkjubý* has traditionally been interpreted as meaning 'English village with a (stone?) church').[60] In such an interpretation, then, Grimstons are not hybrids at all, English place-names 'partially renamed' by speakers of Old Norse; rather, they are wholly Norse names for pre-existing English settlements. The only coherent alternative to this scenario would be to see the Grimstons as representing a Viking Age re-naming by English speakers of pre-existing settlements with originally different names (that is, different in both generic and specific), with *tūn* again bearing the sense 'English village transferred into Scandinavian lordship'. Perhaps, even, this re-naming of pre-existing villages now under Scandinavian lordship took place among both speech communities in the Danelaw at the same time, using a mutually transparent term of reference; the existence of variant genitives for the first element (with some names showing OE *-es*, some ON *-s*, and some both in varying forms) might be taken to support this. But what is hard to accept, from a linguistic perspective, is the traditional idea that these are 'hybrid' names, with one element contributed by each speech community.

One reason, perhaps, why the view suggested here, of Grimstons as wholly Norse names, has not been entertained previously is because scholars of Scandinavian place-names in England have been conscious that, although it was used in Viking Age Norway and the Atlantic colonies, ON *tún* 'settlement' was not an active place-name element in Viking Age Denmark;[61] and so they have tended to rule out the idea that the Grimstons, mostly found in supposedly Danish-settled parts of England, may be wholly Norse names. But although pre-existing ON *tún*

[60] See G. Fellows-Jensen, 'The Vikings' relationship with Christianity in the British Isles: the evidence of place-names containing the element *kirkja*', in J. E. Knirk (ed.), *Proceedings of the Tenth Viking Congress: Larkollen, Norway, 1985* (Oslo: Universitetets Oldsaksamling, 1987), pp. 295–307.

[61] See for example Fellows-Jensen, *Scandinavian Settlement Names in the East Midlands*, pp. 175–76, and *Scandinavian Settlement Names in the North-West*, pp. 180–82, and above pp. 96–99.

may not have been imported into England by Danish settlers as an active element, that is no reason why the Old English word *tūn* may not have entered the Old Norse language in England, and have been re-interpreted and re-used.

One could push this admittedly speculative interpretation even further. Kenneth Cameron and others have commented on the irregular distribution of the Grimstons; Cameron notes, for example, that there are only eleven in the whole of Lincolnshire, compared to 217 names in *-bý*.[62] The explanations given to account for this tend to be drawn from social history, in terms of the presence or absence, or relative density, of Scandinavian settlers. No doubt such explanations have much truth to them. But conceivably, the patterns could also be explained in terms of linguistic history: in some areas of the Danelaw the Old Norse word *tún*, borrowed from OE *tūn*, may have enjoyed wider currency than in other areas, or perhaps in some areas it did not enter Old Norse at all. (Or alternatively, in some areas the English-speaking population re-named villages now under Scandinavian lordship as 'X's *tūn*', and in some areas they did not.) What we would then be seeing on the distribution maps are not so much settlement patterns as linguistic isoglosses.

This is far from impossible. Old Norse as spoken in Scandinavian England must have shown considerable elements of variation. All languages do.[63] But traditionally, scholars have conceived of variation within the Old Norse language in England in terms of pre-existing variation, imported unchanged from the Scandinavian homelands – most obviously, in the (very worthwhile) search for Old East Norse and Old West Norse 'test-words'.[64] But in the centuries in which Old Norse was spoken in England—and in some places we are dealing with centuries, not just decades—the language must have developed new features of variation, most obviously through contact with Old English, so that as a result the Old Norse language in England may have varied not only from its homeland varieties (as most colonial languages do), but also within itself, from region to region.[65] The few Norse runic inscriptions in

[62] Cameron (ed.), *Place-Name Evidence*, pp. 161–62.

[63] See for example M. Barnes, 'Standardisation and variation in Migration- and Viking-Age Scandinavian', in Kristján Árnason (ed.), *Útnorður: West Nordic Standardisation and Variation* (Reykjavík: University of Iceland Press, 2003), pp. 47–66.

[64] See for example G. Fellows-Jensen, 'To divide the Danes from the Norwegians: on Scandinavian settlement in the British Isles', *Nomina* 11 (1987), 35–60.

[65] On linguistic contact see M. Townend, *Language and History in Viking Age England:*

England seem to suggest, tantalizingly, some local developments,[66] and the same variability is found, not surprisingly, in the Norse language's influence on English in the Danelaw.[67]

So, the example of the Grimstons suggests that it may be fruitful to think a little more about the nature of the Old Norse language in England, and to adopt a little more often a more linguistic approach to these names (and by linguistic I mean, broadly, sociolinguistic, rather than etymological). A common assumption has often been that social history is the key variable, and the factor that explains the distribution and history of Scandinavian place-names in England; but this is not necessarily the case.

The same tendency, to think in terms of social history rather than linguistic history, is seen much more starkly, and obviously, in the topic that has been at the heart of most study of Scandinavian place-names in the last 50 years: Scandinavian settlement. It is, I think, not only remarkable, but positively odd, how in the last half-century the study of Scandinavian place-names in England has all too often been confined to this one topic. Again, when one goes back to the early publications on the Scandinavian place-names of England, from the late nineteenth century and early twentieth, one is struck by the fact that the full range of types of names are discussed. Worsaae, Ferguson, Streatfeild, and Lindkvist all consider other types of names, such as field-names, mountain names, river-names, street names – not just settlement names. To turn to the post-Sawyer publications is to observe a certain shrinking of the scholarly range of focus, so that just one class of names—settlement names—dominates the discussion. There are exceptions, of course, as I shall go on to discuss, but the general point is true. There are many reasons for this narrowing of range. One is that, naturally enough, people have always been most interested in discovering the etymology of their town or village, and the typographical formatting of EPNS volumes, in terms of

Linguistic Relations between Speakers of Old Norse and Old English (Turnhout: Brepols, 2002).

[66] See M. P. Barnes and R. I. Page, *The Scandinavian Runic Inscriptions of Britain* (Uppsala: Uppsala Universitet, 2006).

[67] See for instance the Aldbrough (ERY) inscription, where Old Norse *hanum* 'him' seems to have been borrowed into the local form of Old English (see for example E. Okasha, *Hand-list of Anglo-Saxon Non-Runic Inscriptions* (Cambridge: Cambridge University Press, 1971), p. 47, and M. Townend, 'Contacts and conflicts: Latin, Norse, and French', in L. Mugglestone (ed.), *The Oxford History of English* (Oxford: Oxford University Press, 2006), pp. 61–85 (pp. 79–80)).

font size and mise-en-page, has appropriately reflected this. Another is that settlement names have usually been the currency for plotting on distribution maps – as in Smith's map of 1956.[68] (But this need not be the case, as demonstrated by Kenneth Jackson's celebrated map of Celtic river-names.[69]) And another reason, I think, is Peter Sawyer. In his 1957 article Sawyer argued that 'it is important to limit the discussion to place-names that are recorded in Domesday Book or earlier'.[70] In numerical terms, this would exclude the vast majority of Old Norse place-names in England; but even those who were in disagreement with Sawyer were, on the whole, willing to follow this suggestion.

My point here is two-fold: first, that the study of settlement names has been preferred overwhelmingly to the study of other types of names; and second, that settlement names themselves have been examined predominantly for the purposes of settlement history, when they have much else to offer as well. To discuss, briefly, the second point first. One could certainly argue that settlement names might be deployed a little more for the writing of other forms of social history. The question usually asked of Scandinavian place-names in England is: what can they tell us about where the Scandinavians settled, and how many of them there were? Less frequently asked, at least in recent times, is: what can place-names reveal about the society of Viking Age England after the settlers had settled? As inspiring examples of such work, one might think of the light cast on agricultural history through the study of names suggesting transhumance and other early farming practices;[71] or the light cast on legal and administrative history through the study of names indicating assemblies or things;[72] or even the light cast on the history of sport through Mary Atkin's celebrated article on names that seem to indicate Old Norse race-courses.[73] Gillian Fellows-Jensen's study of 'Kirkby'

[68] Smith, *English Place-Name Elements*, map 10.

[69] K. Jackson, *Language and History in Early Britain* (Edinburgh: Edinburgh University Press, 1953), p. 220.

[70] Sawyer, 'Density of the Danish settlement', p. 10.

[71] See for example M. Higham, 'The *-erg* place-names of northern England', *Journal of the English Place-Name Society* 10 (1977–78), 7–17, and G. Fellows-Jensen, 'A Gaelic-Scandinavian loan-word in English place-names', *Journal of the English Place-Name Society* 10 (1977–78), 18–25. For an impressive early example see W. G. Collingwood, *Scandinavian Britain* (London: SPCK, 1908), pp. 193–95.

[72] See G. Fellows-Jensen, 'Tingwall, Dingwall and Thingwall', *North-Western European Language Evolution* 21/22 (1993), 53–67.

[73] M. Atkin, 'Viking race-courses? The distribution of *skeið* place-name elements in

names illuminates the Scandinavian settlers' attitudes towards the physical, institutional church.[74] There is much still to be learned about the early culture of Viking Age England through a creative engagement with place-name material.

Similarly, it is worth reflecting on the sorts of possibilities that might be available if one were to consider other types of names than settlement names. We can do this most easily by reviewing what other types of names have in fact received some attention in recent decades, and top of the list, of course, come field-names. There is a distinguished tradition of the study of Norse field-names in England, to which scholars such as Fellows-Jensen, Cameron, and Parsons, among others, have made important contributions.[75] The historical perspective opened up by field-name study is very different from that of settlement name study: it encourages us to think in terms of a more extended chronology, and a more nuanced localism. It brings us closer to the full extent of the impact of Old Norse on the English language, and implies a more bottom-up process for the giving of names.[76]

The corpus of street names is, inevitably, both smaller and geographically more restricted, but for a number of Danelaw towns, above all York, this type of name offers an otherwise unparalleled means of accessing information about certain aspects of urban development and culture in the Viking Age – for instance, about trades and crafts, property-owning, and urban geography. To take two York street names as examples: Bootham (ON *búðum* 'at the booths') seems to reveal to us an early market site set up just outside the city walls, possibly to avoid taxes that would otherwise be levied; and Goodramgate raises possible issues about women's property-owning and urban role (the early forms seem to alternate between the male name Guðrum and the female name Guðrún,

northern England', *Journal of the English Place-Name Society* 10 (1977–78), 26–39.

[74] Fellows-Jensen, 'Vikings' relationship with Christianity'.

[75] See for example G. Fellows-Jensen, 'English field-names and the Danish settlement', in P. Andersen et al. (eds), *Festskrift til Kristian Hald: navneforskning, dialektologi, sproghistorie* (Copenhagen: Akademisk forlag, 1974), pp. 45–55, K. Cameron, 'The Scandinavian element in minor names and field-names in north-east Lincolnshire', *Nomina* 19 (1996), 5–27, and D. N. Parsons, 'Field-name statistics, Norfolk and the Danelaw', in P. Gammeltoft and B. Jørgensen (eds), *Names through the Looking-Glass: Festschrift in Honour of Gillian Fellows-Jensen, July 5th 2006* (Copenhagen: C. A. Reitzel, 2006), pp. 165–88 (this last item in particular contains a helpful bibliography).

[76] See, in general terms, J. Field, *A History of English Field-Names* (London: Longman, 1993).

and the latter would presumably be the *lectio difficilior*).[77] The pioneering work on York street names was done by Harald Lindkvist; further major contributions have come from A. H. Smith and Gillian Fellows-Jensen.[78]

It is, perhaps, names for topographical features that have lost out most in recent decades. Even the landmark work on topographical terms—Margaret Gelling's *Place-Names in the Landscape*—is actually a study of settlement names that are derived from topographical features.[79] Let us consider, for example, mountain names and river-names. Naturally enough, there was a strong interest in mountain names among the early scholars of the place-names of Cumbria, who were eager to uncover the earlier human history of the Lakeland fells; W. G. Collingwood, for example, argued that the toponymic evidence suggests that 'the opening up of the fells seems to date from the coming of the Vikings, who as especially sheep-farmers would be able to take advantage of the pastures they afforded, and would become acquainted with the mountain-land'.[80] Such names do receive attention in the county surveys for the area, and in Diana Whaley's regional *Dictionary*, but it is hard to think of any recent study of the Scandinavians in England that pays much attention to the possible value of such names.[81] As for river-names, their neglect is even more puzzling. River-names are arguably the type of place-names that possess the greatest linguistic inertia, so that, in spite of successive strata of linguistic change and linguistic history, names given in earlier languages continue to survive: many of the major river-names of England

[77] For forms see EPNS ERY, p. 289.

[78] See H. Lindkvist, 'A study on early medieval York', *Anglia* 50 (1926), 345–94, EPNS ERY, p. 280–300, and G. Fellows-Jensen, 'The Anglo-Scandinavian street-names of York', in R. A. Hall et al., *Aspects of Anglo-Scandinavian York* (York: York Archaeological Trust, 2004), pp. 357–71.

[79] M. Gelling, *Place-Names in the Landscape* (London: Dent, 1984). The work was later revised as M. Gelling and A. Cole, *The Landscape of Place-Names* (Stamford: Shaun Tyas, 2000).

[80] W. G. Collingwood, 'Mountain-names', *Transactions of the Cumberland and Westmorland Antiquarian and Archaeological Society* New Series 18 (1918), 93–104 (p. 104). See also, for example, Ferguson, *Northmen in Cumberland and Westmoreland*, pp. 77–99, and W. P. Haskett Smith, 'Wastdale Head 600 years ago', *The Climbers' Club Journal* 5 (1903), 3–15.

[81] For county and regional surveys see Ekwall, *Place-Names of Lancashire*, A. M. Armstrong et al., *The Place-Names of Cumberland*, EPNS 20–22 (Cambridge: Cambridge University Press, 1950–52) [EPNS Cu], A. H. Smith, *The Place-Names of Westmorland*, EPNS 42–43 (Cambridge: Cambridge University Press, 1967) [EPNS We], and D. Whaley, *A Dictionary of Lake District Place-Names* (Nottingham: English Place-Name Society, 2006).

are, of course, Celtic or even pre-Celtic. So it is striking that the arrival of a Norse speech community in England had such a conspicuous effect on river-names in areas of Scandinavian settlement. The basic corpus of material is readily to hand in Ekwall's *English River-Names*, and a fuller listing of Norse river- and stream-names in the northern counties has also been assembled by Gillian Fellows-Jensen.[82] The range of names in, particularly, Yorkshire and Cumbria is very interesting. We find, for instance, rivers named for their appearance (such as the Greta 'rocky river' in Cumberland and Brathay 'broad river' in Westmorland);[83] rivers named for their geographical position (such as the Winster 'the left (river)' in Lancashire and Westmorland, and Roe Beck 'boundary stream' in Cumberland);[84] and rivers named in an evaluative mood (such as the Gaunless 'the useless (river)' in County Durham, and Costa Beck 'the choice stream' in Yorkshire).[85] Intriguingly, a number of rivers have personal names as their first element, such as Snary Beck in Cumberland ('Snarri's stream', and an inversion compound, *Becsnari*, in its earliest form), Arkle Beck ('Arnkell's stream') in Yorkshire, and Thordesay Beck in Yorkshire ('Þórdís' river', a woman's name, with 'Beck' later added).[86] Some preserve features of Old Norse grammar, suggesting early coinage, such as the Brennand in Yorkshire, apparently from a present participle *brennandi* 'burning' (perhaps 'burning cold').[87] And scattered all over northern England, of course, are innumerable small streams with the second element 'Beck' (ON *bekkr*).

This rich body of material remains understudied, except in Fellows-Jensen's catalogue and in atomistic fashion within the pages of county surveys and Ekwall's great book. What might it tell us about the history of Norse speakers in England? How are we to account for the distribution of names, and the evident replacement of names in earlier languages? Margaret Gelling argued that 'a major factor governing the loss or survival of names in a language which has been superseded is likely to be

[82] E. Ekwall, *English River-Names* (Oxford: Clarendon Press, 1928), G. Fellows-Jensen, 'Danish lake- and river-names in England', in V. Dalberg and G. Fellows-Jensen (eds), *Mange Bække Små: Til John Kousgård Sørensen på tresårsdagen 6.12.1985* (Copenhagen: C. A. Reitzel, 1986), pp. 59–74.

[83] Ekwall, *English River-Names*, pp. 49, 185, EPNS Cu, p. 16, EPNS We **1**, p. 5.

[84] Ekwall, *English River-Names*, pp. 346, 463, EPNS We **1**, p. 15, EPNS Cu, p. 25.

[85] Ekwall, *English River-Names*, pp. 99, 169–70, EPNS NRY, p. 2.

[86] Ekwall, *English River-Names*, pp. 16, 374, 406, EPNS Cu, p. 27, EPNS NRY **7**, p. 295.

[87] Ekwall, *English River-Names*, p. 51, EPNS WRY **6**, p. 211, **7**, p. 121.

the number of people who were using the names at the time of the language change', and she pointed specifically towards stream- and river-names as an index of continuity, or lack of continuity, between successive speech communities.[88] Does the presence of Norse river-names in an area therefore suggest the occupation of uncolonized or deserted land, or does it tell us something about the relative proportion of Norse speakers in comparison to speakers of other languages?

For one crucial point to note is that it is the non-settlement names, more varied and numerically greater than the settlement names, that have the greatest potential (in alliance with loanword evidence) to give us a full and true idea of the extent and history of the Old Norse language in England; and this, paradoxically but very importantly, would then put us in a much better position to make sense of the settlement names (with due attention to linguistic history as well as social history). It is simply not possible—as Sawyer wished to do—to exclude non-settlement names from consideration, and then hope to make a reliable interpretation of the settlement names themselves. Certainly, an awareness of the full range of types of names means that it is impossible to adopt either the 'fragmenting estates' paradigm as the main explanation for the coining of Scandinavian place-names in England or, arguably, the 'elite emulation' model as the main explanation for Scandinavian linguistic influence.

So this is where I would like to end: with an expression of deep and proper gratitude for the remarkable, and permanently valuable, work that has been done on Scandinavian settlement names and settlement history; but also with an aspiration that work in the coming decades might concentrate a little less exclusively on settlement names, and settlement history, and might re-widen the focus a little, so as to engage with the full range of Scandinavian place-names in England, and the full possibilities for historical investigation that they permit.[89]

[88] M. Gelling, 'Anglo-Norse place-names on the Yorkshire Wolds', in Gammeltoft and Jørgensen (eds), *Names through the Looking-Glass*, pp. 85–93 (p. 90).

[89] I am grateful to participants at the 'Perceptions of Place' conference for discussion, and to Lesley Abrams and Richard Dance for their comments on an earlier written version.

5

Place-names and linguistics

Richard Coates

When the introductory volume of the Survey of English Place-Names was published in 1924,[1] covering philological and interdisciplinary themes in place-name study, the discipline of linguistics as we know it today had barely come into existence. The fountainhead of linguistics is Ferdinand de Saussure's *Cours de linguistique générale*, assembled posthumously out of notes taken at the author's lectures by his students Charles Bally and Albert Sechehaye, and published in Paris in 1916.[2] Before this revolutionary book, linguistics[3] had been an essentially historical discipline whose main goals were to explain systematic change in languages and, using the principle that change was systematic, to reconstruct the unattested ancestor languages out of which the families of attested languages had evolved. After Saussure, academic linguistics absorbed what had until then been the province of grammar, i.e. the study of the systems of languages at particular points or periods in time and the (crude) theory of the structures and processes which constituted them. That is, languages could be viewed as disconnected from their histories and understood as autonomous objects, met by linguists on exactly the same terms as those on which their newly-born native speakers meet them. The novelty implicit in Saussure's work was that a synchronic (non-historical) approach to language theory was possible, and that it did not need to take as its point of departure the rigid framework of formal

The volumes of the English Place-Name Society's Survey are indicated by EPNS + county abbreviation as given on p. vi.

[1] A. H. Mawer and F. M. Stenton, *Introduction to the Survey of English Place-Names* English Place-Name Society 1.i (Cambridge: Cambridge University Press, 1924).

[2] F. de Saussure, *Cours de linguistique générale*, ed. by C. Bally and A. Sechehaye (Paris: Payot, 1916).

[3] The corresponding French word, in the singular form *linguistique*, appears in French in 1826, the German *Linguistik* in the 1840s, and the English also in the 1840s, always at first with reference to historical, philological, *wissenschaftlich* 'scientific' study as practised mainly in German universities (see *Oxford English Dictionary* [OED], online edn).

categories and meanings postulated from time immemorial for the description of Latin and Ancient Greek. In other words, questions could be asked about language structure which might expect a richer response than the 1500-year-old catechism based on the work of the Roman grammarians Donatus and Priscian whose impact can easily be discerned in such early-modern English grammars as those of Christopher Cooper and Robert Lowth, in Fowler's *The King's English* of 1906, and in popular works even today.[4] In other words, a new general or theoretical study of language was possible, and especially of language considered as a mental faculty, or (in Saussure's case) a social construct, rather than as a historical product. By insisting on a strict dichotomy between diachronic (historical) and synchronic study, Saussure arguably missed an important trick, but there is a way to resolve the problem which we will see a hint of when we deal with the role of *analogy* (below, pp. 147, 157). We will accept the distinction in the meantime, and focus mainly on proper names (hereafter simply *names*) in synchronic linguistics, avoiding questions solely relating to the history and philology of names, which are treated by at least five other papers in this volume.

Diachronic (historical) linguistics

Before embarking on the past and present contribution of synchronic linguistics to name-study, which is likely to be less familiar, let us rehearse fairly briefly the relationship that has evolved between name-study and the historical discipline. The main issues can be distinguished as the *microlinguistic* and the *macrolinguistic*.

Microlinguistics

The principal microlinguistic issue has been the status of names as evidence in reasoning about language change. The formulation of the Leipzig or *Neogrammarian* doctrine[5] that sound-change operates exceptionlessly (regularly), and more or less simultaneously across the entire vocabulary of a language, subject to well-understood but relatively

[4] C. Cooper, *Grammatica linguae anglicanae* (London, 1685; repr. Menston: Scolar Press, 1968); R. Lowth, *A Short Introduction to English Grammar* (London, 1762; repr. Menston: Scolar Press, 1967); F. G. Fowler, *The King's English* (Oxford: Clarendon, 1906).

[5] H. Osthoff and K. Brugmann, *Morphologische Untersuchungen auf dem Gebiete der indogermanischen Sprachen* (Leipzig: Hirzel, 1878).

minor qualifications,[6] immediately calls into question the status of names as evidence. It has always been known that names are semantically, i.e. synchronically, different from regular vocabulary-words to some degree, a point which will be developed in full below, but for the moment let us simply note that the distinction between *proper* and *common names* is present even in the earliest known works of Greek grammar. As abnormal linguistic objects, what kind of light can they shed on the behaviour of normal ones? Should onomastic evidence be discarded, or at least treated with caution? The kind of issue which has been thought troublesome is that names have often seemed to show evidence for particular changes appreciably before those changes were observable in the general vocabulary, or perhaps even for changes restricted to names. A change operating under conditions which were not purely phonological would run counter to the Neogrammarian hypothesis.

Fran Colman notes,[7] in relation to personal names, the possibility that name-elements can be exempt from sound-changes, reminding us of Alistair Campbell's observation that the name-element *Ælf-* in West Saxon seems to be systematically excepted from the general change [æ] > [ie] before [l] before another consonant;[8] it is presumably preserved by being identified with the [æ] which is preserved in other phonetic environments, though readers will register the oddity of this idea and perhaps wonder whether it is really a scribal phenomenon rather than a phonological one. It is odd because it suggests that a pronunciation which has become "impossible" is preserved only in names. Imagine the regular disappearance of preconsonantal [r] in the accents of the standard dialect except in place-names; it would vanish in *sportsman* but not in *Portsmouth* and worse still in *barking* but not in *Barking*. If the phenomenon were real, we could perhaps interpret it as an attempt to

[6] It is now universally accepted that the strongest interpretation of this hypothesis is false. The progression of a change through a society can often be observed and plotted to show that it has dimensionality: its progress may be influenced by age, social group (class and gender) and speech style, as the work of those following William Labov and Peter Trudgill has conclusively demonstrated for almost fifty years. But the notion of regularity is still widely influential in the guise of the idea that sound-changes tend to proceed to completion unless the social and cultural circumstances in which they are proceeding change radically. It is a useful provisional hypothesis in particular cases, and it will readily be understood that linguistic reconstruction is near-impossible unless one accepts that it is broadly true.

[7] F. Colman, *Money Talks: Reconstructing Old English* (Berlin and New York: Mouton de Gruyter, 1992), p. 15.

[8] A. Campbell, *Old English Grammar* (Oxford: Clarendon Press, 1959), §200 (1), fn. 4.

maintain or mimic a conservative local pronunciation at the place so named. (We shall see below that such things do really happen, but that the issue is not the preservation in names of historically out-of-place sounds, but their conditional preservation in *certain* names – that is, they lack systematicity, and in any case they are constrained by the phonology of the receiving dialect.)

A distinct but related issue is whether there can be sound-changes whose operation is limited to names, or which operate in names earlier, or more radically, than in other words.[9] As far as place-names are concerned, it seems inescapable that changes of a reductive kind are more frequent and more radical in names than in the common vocabulary. The record includes such notorieties as /'(w)ulzəri/ 'Woolfardisworthy' (D), /'heizbrə/ 'Happisburgh' (Nf), /'ilsn/ 'Ilkeston' (Db) and /'hɑ:niʃ/ 'Hardenhuish' (So).[10] But these have evidential value only if it can be shown that phonologically parallel words in the relevant local dialect which are not names do not reduce to the same extent, and such comparative evidence is by no means easy to come by or to establish an analysis for. Nevertheless the notion is widely believed to be true, on the basis of an argument from first principles, presented here in a simplified form and papering over some difficulties. Take the word *pen*. It needs to be kept distinct from *pan*, *pin*, *pun*, *pain*, *pawn*, *pine*, etc. Precision as regards the articulation of its vowel is therefore crucial. Now take the place-name *Penn* (St).[11] No such precision is required since there are no phonologically similar place-names (and if there were, they might be far distant from Penn and unknown to the conversational participants, like for instance the village in Greece called *Pan*, or *Pernes* in the Pas-de-Calais in an English mouth). Therefore, in principle, the articulation of the vowel is free to wander into the space of other vowels without compromising successful communication. In practice, this idea interacts with the principle of phonological sufficiency. In a historically complex name such as most English ones are, their job of identifying a place is

[9] Colman, *Money Talks*, pp. 59–67; C. Clark, 'Towards a reassessment of "Anglo-Norman Influence on English Place-Names"', in P. Jackson (ed.), *Words, Names and History: Selected Papers of Cecily Clark* (Cambridge: Brewer, 1995), pp. 144–55 (pp. 150–52), originally published in P. Sture Ureland and G. Broderick (eds), *Language Contact in the British Isles: Proceedings of the Eighth International Symposium on Language Contact in Europe, Douglas, Isle of Man, 1988* (Tübingen: Max Niemeyer, 1991), pp. 275–95.

[10] These can be checked in K. Forster, *A Pronouncing Dictionary of English Place-Names* (London: Routledge, 1982).

[11] D. Horovitz, *The Place-Names of Staffordshire* (Brewood: the author, 2005), p. 433.

likely to be done before the utterance of the full name is complete. If I say *I'm going to Wolverhampton*, you have probably established where I am going with reasonable probability by the /v/ and with certainty by the /æ/, especially if we are conversing in the West Midlands. Any material after what psycholinguists studying language processing call the *decision point*,[12] which will usually be unstressed in English names (including *Wolverhampton* for some), can be articulated indistinctly or even lost without seriously affecting communication unless the hearer is a formalistic pedant. The obsolete local pronunciation "Wolverton"[13] shows the theory in action, as does the more deliberately crafted local alternant "Briz" for *Brislington* (in Bristol).[14]

However, it is hard to sustain the idea that there are really sound-changes whose operation is literally restricted to names. Clark prefers the formulation that names may be subject to what she calls 'the unchecked operation of general native tendencies': processes that play out less vigorously in expressions other than names.[15] She uses this to account for the radical consonant cluster reductions seen in certain names like *Exeter*, so to speak "Exe-chester", and in *Cirencester*, formerly /'sisitə(r)/ and now pronounced "as spelt", after the stressed vowel (and no doubt after the decision point). In these names, a process of consonantal dissimilatory loss affecting a succession of [s] (in combination with other processes) takes place, but with more drastic effects than are seen in English words where, for example, a succession of [r] is dissimilated (*library*, *secretary*).

Once we recognize that sound-change is, in part, a matter of geographical ebb and flow, it is possible to use place-name material as, or in support of, claims about the former geographical extent of certain phonological features. The conspicuous voicing of initial fricatives of the English south and west has all but disappeared in the living language, but the persistence of such place-names as *Vobster* (So)[16] and *Zeal* (D)[17] gives a clue to its former extent, which has also been perseveringly traced

[12] W. D. Marslen-Wilson, 'Functional parallelism in spoken word recognition', *Cognition* 25 (1987), 71–102.

[13] Forster, *Pronouncing Dictionary*, p. 260, quoting A. Schröer, though this pronunciation is not mentioned in Horovitz, *Staffordshire*.

[14] Writer's local knowledge.

[15] Clark, 'Towards a reassessment', p. 152.

[16] V. Watts, *Cambridge Dictionary of English Place-Names* (Cambridge: Cambridge University Press, 2004) [CDEPN], p. 642b.

[17] EPNS D, p. 450 (and several other places with the same name).

in nationwide personal-name and place-name data (along with many other linguistic features) by Gillis Kristensson.[18] Phonological survivals of the *Vobster* and *Zeal* kind recall the onomastic exemptions from sound-changes that we dealt with above (pp. 131–32), but in the present context we are able to see them for what they are: they are "accidental" survivals, i.e. features of individual names, as seen from the fact that other names in Somerset and Devon now have "standard" initial /f/: *Frome*, *Farleigh*, *Fiddington*, *Filleigh*, *Farway*. And examples such as these make it clear that the retention process is more a sociolinguistic one than a psycholinguistic one: regional initial /v/ and /z/ can be preserved by any speaker who already has both /f/ and /v/, and /s/ and /z/, contrasting in initial position: that is any speaker from outside the south-west who has acquired vocabulary originating in e.g. French (*value*, *village*, *zest*), Latin (*valid*, *vast*) or Greek (*zone*, *zeal*), or any south-western speaker who has acquired non-regional pronunciations (i.e. excluding those consistent dialect speakers who failed to acquire the newly fashionable ones).

Macrolinguistics

The historical macrolinguistic importance of names has resided in the fact that names may provide the only evidence for the prior existence of some language, or at any rate for the existence of a known language in a previously uncharted area. This may happen when ancient places are mentioned in documents written in languages of record. In the British Isles, for example, it is clear that there are long-established names which cannot be explained from the vocabulary of the known Celtic and Germanic languages, or Latin, or French, though they are preserved in, for example, Latin documents. What is it reasonable to do with them? They may be examined to see whether they have characteristics in common which might lead to the conclusion that they were formulated in some language whose characteristics can be defined by the onomastic evidence, and that language may or may not be identifiable. But it may be possible to ascribe that language to some historically known group of people or to a known linguistic lineage. Thus some names in the British Isles have been ascribed to Pictish (whatever lineage that may belong

[18] G. Kristensson, *A Survey of Middle English Dialects* (Lund: New Society of Letters, 1967–2002).

to)[19] or to North-West Semitic,[20] both of which ideas have proved controversial at least to some degree.

The same sorts of reasoning can be applied in the case of names which, although formulated in a relevant language whose characteristics are well known, appear to be out of place. For example, the very small scatter of Celtic place-names in Devon can be taken as evidence that the language ancestral to Cornish was once spoken east of the Tamar;[21] more broadly, it is universally accepted on the basis of place-name evidence that present-day England was once an area where British Celtic and Latin were spoken, and fortunately that chimes with everything which is known from works of history from the most ancient times onwards. The important methodological point here is that there is absolutely no textual, non-onomastic, evidence for British at the relevant period except for a few recently discovered graffiti from, for example, Bath;[22] names otherwise constitute all the evidence. On a similar basis, and with varying amounts of other historical evidence in support, we know that Welsh was once spoken in western Herefordshire and Shropshire[23] and a language very closely related to it (generally distinguished as Cumbric) in southern Scotland and northern England,[24] and that Irish was spoken in Wirral, alongside Scandinavian.[25] It is remarkable also that there is rather little

[19] E. Sutherland, *In Search of the Picts: A Celtic Dark Age Nation* (London: Constable, 1994), pp. 200–03; W. F. H. Nicolaisen, *The Picts and their Place Names* (Rosemarkie: Groam House Museum, 1996); K. Forsyth, *Language in Pictland: The Case against Non-Indo-European Pictish* (Utrecht: de Keltische Draak, 1997).

[20] R. Coates, 'A glimpse through a dirty window into an unlit house: names of some north-west European islands', in W. Ahrens et al. (eds), *Names in Multi-lingual, Multi-cultural and Multi-ethnic Contact: Proceedings of the 23rd International Congress of Onomastic Sciences* (Toronto: York University, 2009), pp. 228–42 (available only on CD-ROM ISBN 978-1-55014-521-2).

[21] For mapped facts, see O. J. Padel, 'Place-names and the Anglo-Saxon conquest of Devon and Cornwall', in N. J. Higham (ed.), *Britons in Anglo-Saxon England* (Woodbridge: Boydell, 2007), pp. 215–30 (pp. 215–17).

[22] R. S. O. Tomlin, 'Was ancient British Celtic ever a written language? Two texts from Roman Bath', *Bulletin of the Board of Celtic Studies* 34 (1987), 18–25.

[23] See R. Coates and A. Breeze, *Celtic Voices, English Places* (Stamford: Shaun Tyas, 2000), maps on pp. 379–80 and 388.

[24] K. H. Jackson, *Language and History in Early Britain* (Edinburgh: Edinburgh University Press, 1953), pp. 9–10 and 219.

[25] J. Jesch, 'Scandinavian Wirral', in P. Cavill, S. E. Harding and J. Jesch (eds), *Wirral and its Viking Heritage* (Nottingham: English Place-Name Society, 2000), pp. 1–10 (p. 2); R. Coates, 'The sociolinguistic context of Brunanburh', in M. D. Livingston (ed.), *The Battle of Brunanburh: A Casebook* (Exeter: University of Exeter Press, 2011), pp. 365–84 (pp. 379–80).

textual evidence for the use of Scandinavian in England; apart from works of historical report which record the presence of Vikings, the bulk of the very considerable amount of evidence derives from names, and largely from place-names.[26]

Such matters are part of the staple of historical onomastics in continental Europe, where issues like the position and movement through the centuries of the great linguistic boundaries, for example, between Germanic and Romance, and between Slavic and Germanic, remain subject to the liveliest study.[27] The spread of Celtic in central and southern Europe and western Asia, as revealed by its place-name residue, has been thoroughly revisited recently by Patrick Sims-Williams.[28]

These matters mean that names can be understood as the footprints of a language, preserved as if archaeologically among later deposits. Their relation to the limb that left those prints is an interesting philosophical matter to which we return below (pp. 155–57).

I have recently pointed to the phonological anomaly of *chester*, the generic element meaning 'Roman walled town' (later also applied to other structures), which occurs in place-names throughout England even though its form is appropriate only to an origin in strict West Saxon Old English and "should not" therefore occur in the Midlands or North.[29] It is clear that understanding the geographical spread of this microlinguistic feature may require an element of cultural interpretation. Some genuinely

[26] I acknowledge that there is Old Norse skaldic verse clearly composed in England about English subjects; see J. Jesch, 'Skaldic verse in Scandinavian England', in J. Graham-Campbell et al. (eds), *Vikings and the Danelaw: Selected Papers from the Proceedings of the Thirteenth Viking Congress, Nottingham and York, 21–30 August 1997* (Oxford: Oxbow, 2001), pp. 313–25.

[27] See for example W. Haubrichs, 'Geschichte der deutsch-romanischen Sprachgrenze im Westen', article 214 in W. Besch et al. (eds), *Sprachgeschichte: ein Handbuch zur Geschichte der deutschen Sprache und ihrer Erforschung*, 2nd edn, 4 vols (Berlin and New York: Walter de Gruyter, 1998–2000), IV, pp. 3331–46; H. Scheuringer, 'Geschichte der deutsch-ungarischen und der deutsch-slawischen Sprachgrenze im Südosten', article 216 in the same volume, pp. 3365–79; and the many writings of Martina Pitz on the former situation.

[28] P. Sims-Williams, *Ancient Celtic Place-Names in Europe and Asia Minor* (Oxford: Blackwell, for the Philological Society, 2006).

[29] R. Coates, 'Chesterblade, Somerset, with a reflection on the element *chester*', *Journal of the English Place-Name Society* 38 (2006), 5–12 (pp. 9–10). This is like the *Ælf-* case mentioned above.

highly localized linguistic features found only in place-names in the south-east have been plotted in other recent work.[30]

Synchronic linguistics

What general questions might linguistics raise, then, about names and naming, and about place-names and place-naming in particular? Has our own practice of toponomastics in Britain approached these questions, and if so how? We shall explore a range of issues with no claim to being comprehensive.

A little autobiography is regrettably necessary to explain the general approach that I adopt, but I will keep it short. I do not attach myself to any -ism, except functionalism in a broad sense. I was trained in the Chomskyan paradigm. My PhD dissertation was about how one might use historical phonology as a testing-ground for generative phonological theory (exemplified by Chomsky and Halle's *The Sound Pattern of English*).[31] Part-way through the enterprise, I concluded that this entailed rejecting some of the most characteristic aspects of generativism itself: the testing done by others at this time as well as me appeared to be testing to destruction. This rejection had as one consequence the firm belief that a linguistics which was not founded squarely on language use was useless. This position is what underlies my belief that some key notions involved in constructing a theory of names and naming are (or should be) grounded in language use, rather than in structural categories imposed on languages. One of those key notions is **properhood** itself, i.e. the state of being proper, which is not about *sorts of noun* (proper vs. common), but about *ways of referring*. We shall examine this in detail, and some consequences will play out below.

This section is about interrogating place-name data in ways shaped by linguistics. I do not intend to imply that scholars usually fail to address *some of* the issues I mention below, but there are some areas which are often skated over or not theorized at all, and some pertinent questions that are not routinely or systematically asked at all. Here are some of the key questions about names in general before we address the subject of place-names in particular:

[30] R. Coates, 'Microdialectological investigations in the English south-east', *Locus Focus: Forum of the Sussex Place-Names Net* 7:1/2 (2003–07), 62–80.

[31] R. Coates, 'The Status of Rules in Historical Phonology', unpublished PhD thesis (University of Cambridge, 1977); N. Chomsky and M. Halle, *The Sound Pattern of English* (New York: Harper and Row, 1968).

- What is a name? [perhaps meaning, What sort of a noun phrase is a name?, or How is a noun phrase used in order to be a name?]
- What do names mean? vs How do names mean?
- How does an expression which is not a name become a name, and vice versa?
- What is the relation, in names, between meaning and etymology, and between etymology and the motivation for the bestowal or the direction of evolution of names?
- Can names have more than one sort of meaning, for example some sort of core meanings vs conveyed meanings (associations, connotations, non-logically implied meanings)? and if so what does that entail?
- Are names part of any particular language?

Readers are warned that what follows may come across as unusually difficult and hair-splitting for a work in a collection of this kind, but it is important to avoid the terminological confusions and pitfalls which are endemic in the onomastic literature, and also in linguistics more generally.

In Britain, though not in the rest of Europe, place-name study is largely restricted to the diachronic question of the *etymology* of individual names and the historical significance of name-types, which is sometimes not clearly distinguished from the enterprise dealing with the *motivation* of names (on which distinction more later, pp. 150–53). Despite its dominating position among the issues addressed in British place-name scholarship, etymology is not the only question of linguistic interest.

Properhood (or namehood)

Let us examine first the question of how names in general, and place-names in particular,[32] work as items in a functioning language system (if indeed names can justifiably be said to be part of a language-system, a matter to which we shall return, pp. 155–57). Two characteristics have generally been thought crucial in their definition. Firstly, their main

[32] A particularly interesting question that will have to be passed over here is that raised by T. Thrane, *Referential-Semantic Analysis: Aspects of a Theory of Linguistic Reference* (Cambridge: Cambridge University Press, 1980), p. 214: namely that of whether a name carries any semantic information at all about the category of the thing it denotes, a more fraught issue that might be suspected. This is related to some of the issues raised by the works mentioned in n. 48.

purpose is *reference*, i.e. picking out individuals (individual persons, individual places, and so on; below, I shall simply say *individuals*) in particular contexts on real occasions of use. Secondly, they have *no synchronic semantic content*. These two notions are fundamental, and I believe that between them they serve to define *name*, provided that they are themselves both tightly defined. There is much scope for unclarity and confusion, which has actually occurred and which has historically obscured their essential correctness. I have tried to remove the potential for confusion in a series of articles,[33] and I give here a very brief account of precisely how they need to be understood, bringing the two notions together in a slogan at the end of this section.[34]

- Names are devices which **refer to** individuals. This means that they are defined by their primary functional or conversational role, namely reference, which is defined as the **act** of picking out some individual (the **referent**) in a context of use. They perform the range of roles performed by noun phrases or determiner phrases (the term used depends on one's theoretical framework), though their internal structure can consist of any material whatsoever.[35]
  - Caution 1: names have often been presented as devices which **denote** individuals, i.e. unique potential referents. That would mean that they are devices for identifying a unique potential referent in any context, and that they do so independently of any context of use. Some names do indeed have this property (for example, to the best of my knowledge, *Droylsden*, *Hove* and *Immingham* are only ever used to refer to particular unique places

[33] Especially 'Singular definite expressions with a unique denotatum and the limits of properhood', *Linguistics* 38:6 (2000), 1161–74; 'Properhood', *Language* 82:2 (2006), 356–82; 'Some consequences and critiques of The Pragmatic Theory of Properhood', *Onoma* 41 (2006), 27–44; 'A strictly Millian approach to the definition of the proper name', *Mind and Language* 24:4 (2009), 433–44; '*to þære fulan flóde óf þære fulan flode*: on becoming a name in Easton and Winchester, Hampshire', in D. Denison et al. (eds), *Analysing Older English* (Cambridge: Cambridge University Press, 2011), pp. 28–34.

[34] These issues have been discussed in an immense and conflicting literature, mainly in philosophy, but also in linguistics (see esp. Coates, 'Properhood'). I do not have the space here to draw attention to every reservation or qualification that seems to need to be made, but I am satisfied that the two crucial bullet-points made in the text are robust.

[35] That is, they have the same external distribution as noun/determiner phrases. But *Pity Me* (Du) is a bona fide place-name despite having the form of a subjectless sentence (CDEPN, p. 474b). *Severn-break-its-neck*, a waterfall in Montgomeryshire, is even more problematic in this regard; its name seems to be a grammatically indeterminate calque on a non-sentential Welsh expression amounting to *Severn breaking [its] neck* (*Hafren-torri-gwddf*).

- Connotation(s): disjoint sets having to do with food preparation and consumption, surgery, violent attack, etc. (e.g. association with the right hand through the etiquette requiring knives to be placed at a diner's right hand; association with infirmity through metonymy for surgery in general, as in *going under the knife*; association with criminality because preferred by certain types of criminal for body-cutting)
- Reference: to refer to a particular knife, the word needs to be embedded in a construction which works as a referring expression, e.g. *this knife*, *the old knife with the bone handle*, *that thug's knife*, etc.; unique reference may be finally established by context of situation: *Richard's just dropped a knife* (visual evidence identifies it uniquely)

7. A **name** is fully equipped to refer without any extra qualifying linguistic material (*Brighton* does not need to be embedded in more elaborate expressions in order to refer successfully to some place called *Brighton*)
   - Denotation: any individual (e.g. place) which bears the name in question (there is more than one *Brighton*: in Sussex, Cornwall, Michigan, South Australia, and so on; it also exists as a surname)
   - Sense: none (*Brighton* has no sense of its own as a linguistic item, in terms of the current English language, and has no operative lexical parts that might construct one)
   - Connotation: can work as with a regular word (e.g. the place Brighton (Sx) and therefore the name *Brighton* has the encyclopedic attributes of a pebbly beach and veteran car displays on the first Sunday of November, and the public connotations of dirty weekends and sexual politics, i.e. facts and stereotypes; also "personal" "meanings", i.e. those derived from a person's own life-experiences and judgements, such as sunny childhood outings, an unusual secondary-school-place allocation system (in 2010) or a large population of bulldogs; its form might suggest association with *bright* in a way useful for the tourist industry)

The meaning of names is nothing, if by that we mean that they have no sense, leading to the corollary that such meanings as they do possess are all external to themselves: their denotation (the things they could be used to refer to), and their connotations (understandings of the nature of the individuals, e.g. places, that they denote which are dependent on the perception(s) of the user, including common knowledge), as well as the individuals that they are actually used to refer to on particular occasions.

The synchronic relevance of the etymology of names

Etymology is not usually an issue in the everyday use of expressions which are not names. A grasp of it is not required to understand the sense of an expression, except in this one very restricted scenario: it may be a help in the case of those expressions which are of transparent structure but which you have never previously encountered: e.g., in my case, on real occasions, *(a) language revitalizer*, *(to) budgie-sit*, *(a/the) toilet duck*. When faced with such expressions for the first time, you may work out the origin "online" from their constituent parts and construct the, or a, probable sense, or you will continue to flounder through the conversation. But it is totally unnecessary to do this with established expressions like *greenhouse*, *sweetbread*, *pantomime dame*, *cloud nine*; in fact, in such cases, which are fully sense-bearing in their own right at the level which includes all their elements, an etymological approach to sense may prove to be misleading, at least in part: these do not have to do literally with *house*, *bread*, *dame* or *cloud* in their basic senses. Such material is enough to establish, in any event, that etymology is not the same as sense. Let us work to dispel any lingering impression that names may have sense, because we might be tempted to argue that there is a cline or gradient of sensefulness. No-one will dispute that synchronically opaque names have no sense: *Brill* (Bu), *York*, *Mancetter* (Wa), *Brenzett* (K), *Auckland* (Du), *Levenshulme* (La), *Ogbourne* (W), *Congleton* (Ch). Any impression of sense-bearing depends on a decidedly non-linguistic property: the etymological sophistication of the user. An individual user of these names may acquire the philological knowledge that the ancestor of *bourne* once meant 'stream', that that of *-ton* once meant 'farm, village', and that *land* still exists with a sense partly comparable with its original Old English one. That knowledge may be treacherous, because the *-land* in *Auckland* originally had nothing whatever to do with *land*,[37] and one would find it difficult to establish suitable terrain on which to fight for the cause that *land* synchronically means 'land' in this name. *Chelmsford* (Ess) appears more or less transparently to be 'ford across the (river) Chelmer', and according to one possible, and current, understanding that is what it is, but it is an understanding that has arisen through a topographer's intervention, whether mistaken, or deliberate and

[37] CDEPN, pp. 9–10.

transformative,[38] and that understanding does not reflect the "sense" of the elements out of which the name was originally constructed because the river-name has been carved out of the place-name by backformation.[39] Any argument that etymological transparency is a surrogate for sense founders on examples like these, and even less forcefully can it be argued that transparency is the same as sense.

What about names with an undeniably transparent etymology? Can it be credibly claimed that such names as *Longbridge* (Wo), *Broadstairs* (K), *Newtown* (Montgomeryshire), *Redhill* (Sr) and *Woodhall* (Li) have sense? Surely not, not even here where the transparent form is etymologically trustworthy. As a functioning place-name, *Longbridge* entails (i.e. logically requires) nothing, not even the existence of a bridge, let alone a long one. Given a set of usual assumptions about names (except in cases of copying from one place to another), it must entail the existence of a long bridge at the long-gone moment of naming, otherwise British place-name scholars would not be doing what they do professionally, namely recovering the sense of the expression which gives rise to the name. But the bridge's continued existence or its disappearance is of no *linguistic* relevance at all. That does not mean that a name like *Longbridge* is incapable of conveying anything. It conveys that there may very well have been a significant bridge there and that maybe there still is, but that inference does not amount to synchronic linguistically-based knowledge of the place. Getting on a bus to Longbridge (Wo) does not allow you to believe with the logical security afforded by lexical semantics that on arrival you will find a bridge there. Some such sort of expectation is admissible, but it is defeasible, that is, it can be abandoned without a logical disaster in the face of evidence which undermines it. Notice also that Longbridge is not a bridge but an inhabited place, and the widely-applied schema of metonymy which gives rise to the place-name (an object or feature gives its name to an adjacent inhabited place) may have lost its factual grounding, in much the same way that the metonymy which gave rise to the place-name *Newchurch* is necessarily undermined by the passing of time. So if you want to see the long bridge at Longbridge, you had better make sure there

[38] Christopher Saxton's map of 1576; the topographer William Harrison, who puts *Chelme* in his contribution to Holinshed's *Chronicles* in 1577 (EPNS Ess, p. 5). Saxton's form won out.

[39] EPNS Ess, pp. 5 and 245.

is one there, using sound non-linguistic information, before you get on the bus. (There isn't, but it is possible to work out where it was.)

In the face of the kind of evidence under inspection here, we can conclude that apparent sense in names is not really sense but (correct or incorrect) etymological understanding, and the two are not to be equated. They are divided by the logical (in)security of the inferences to which they may give rise. *A/The long bridge* is what is perceived by the senses, whilst *Longbridge* does not necessarily reveal anything comparable. In names, a transparent etymology amounts in linguistic terms to a connotation or conveyed meaning, not an asserted one, i.e. one with no secure logical status; putting it more loosely, a meaning may be suggested, but is not entailed (logically required). We can also conclude that "How does a name mean?" is a better question than "What does a name mean?" The former is the only question of synchronic linguistic importance, and it is to be understood as "How does a name identify a referent in a context of use?" The answer is the perhaps pompous-sounding "Through shared knowledge of an arbitrary but stable and rigid association of a linguistic form with an individual".[40] The corresponding diachronic question is: "What did a name mean?" – note the crucial past tense of the verb.

Getting a name

How do names become associated with or attached to what they denote? There are two processes or procedures. The first process is evolution from fully meaningful (sense-bearing) referring expressions with the loss of any sense of those expressions. This is routine. We know what *Acton* (Sa and Mx), *Keswick* (We and Nf), *Bristol* (Gl) and *Morpeth* (Nb) once meant through having done etymological work. Attrition from such expressions sometimes leaves phono-morphological evidence of the definiteness which is characteristic of expressions referring to individuals (i.e. expressions including *the* and its associated grammar), e.g. the medial <n> in *Newnham* (Ca) and *Hendon* (Mx), which have clearly descended from expressions meaning 'at the new estate' and 'at the high hill'.[41] Where this can be demonstrated, we can call the process of

[40] The word *rigid* is in here as an acknowledgement of the philosophical position of S. Kripke, *Naming and Necessity*, 2nd edn (Oxford: Blackwell, 1980). According to him, a proper name is a *rigid designator*, that is it names the same individual in all possible worlds. I accept this but do not pursue its ontological implications here.

[41] EPNS Ca, p. 43; EPNS Mx, p. 56.

association *nomination by evolution*. The second procedure is naming by formal act, *nomination by bestowal*. We know from documentary evidence that modern *Peacehaven* (Sx), *Peterlee* (Du) and *Telford* (Sa) were deliberately named, in some cases ceremonially, at a particular instant. There is rarely if ever any external evidence for the bestowal of ancient place-names, but it can sometimes be suspected. Could Old English compound constructions such as the recurrent *Higham* or most instances of *Acton*, which show no overt sign like that in *Newnham* of the definite usage typical of referring expressions, be names which were bestowed at a particular moment, rather than evolving from a fully articulated referring expression? It is likely that the difference between evolution and bestowal is an onomastically important distinction, because evolved names might be evidence for a site not important enough to receive the culturally significant act of name-bestowal (or to retain any name bestowed).

It is not always easy to apply the distinction between evolved names and bestowed ones. The many names such as *Branston* 'Brand's farm',[42] with the name of the owner or holder in the genitive case, are in origin grammatically articulated like the indisputable evolved names such as *Newnham* '(at) the new estate' (see above), and they are therefore phrasal, consisting of a noun preceded by a modifying expression, but both types are prosodic compounds (i.e. with the first element stressed), presumably as a result of conversationally deaccenting the generic where 'farm' or 'estate' can be taken for granted in the context of use, as happens when we speak of *going to Sárah's house* unless we are drawing special contrastive attention to the fact that we are going to her house, not her shed, garage, etc. It is therefore particularly hard to apply the distinction to them. *Kingston* names never show any definiteness marking, not even in elaborated expressions such as *Kingston upon Hull* (with the very late exception of 1487 *the Kingis town opon Hull*).[43] Given Jill Bourne's assessment that by no means all places called *Kingston* were examples of a *cyninges tūn*,[44] a 'king's farm', this recurrent name-type may give the impression of set of systematically bestowed names rather than evolved ones, as may the more than 60 instances of *Upton* for

[42] EPNS Li **1**, pp. 195–96.

[43] EPNS ERY, p. 210.

[44] J. Bourne, 'Kingston place-names: an interim report', *Journal of the English Place-Name Society* 20 (1987–88), 13–37 (p. 36); see also J. Bourne, 'The Place-name Kingston and its Context', unpublished PhD thesis (University of Nottingham, 2012).

unmanaged 'wild' land in an estate.[45] Both may simply represent a lexical compound (i.e. a grammatically normal expression) applied to places where descriptively appropriate and evolving into a name, but *Upton* does not appear in the record with a definite article and that fact appears to suggest repeated bestowal as a 'ready-made' name.

But whether through bestowal or through evolution in use, the elements in a name lose the capacity to mean by virtue of their original sense. That is what is critical for being a name. It is especially important theoretically, because it means that an expression, on becoming a name, is attached to an individual which is capable of being taken to represent a *type* (e.g. female given name, hill-name, business-name). Further names may evolve or be bestowed on the analogy of those which already exist, leading to an impression of systematicity which is, however, not systematicity in the constraining sense endemic in structural(ist) linguistics. Onomastic "systematicity" is fuzzy and partial, and that is because analogy, not structure, is the driving-force. We return to this point at the very end of the chapter (p. 157). The same loss of sense is what enables a name originally naming an individual of a certain type to become attached to individuals of other types. It is not always metonymy which achieves this. A much more arbitrary mechanism is suggested by the fact that I can, with impunity, apply what was originally a place-name to an arbitrary human being (e.g. *Shirley*), an animal (e.g. the celebrated racehorse *Arkle*), or a group of musicians (e.g. *Boston*). It is this that enables us to assert that names do not carry any categorial meaning unless one builds in the notion of a prototype. But the fundamental weakness of *any* claim that names essentially represent a type or category, with or without prototypy, is obvious. At the individual level, if I have never heard of a place called *Boston*, but know of the band, then *Boston* is a musical ensemble-name – and analogously throughout a range of such examples.

Synchronic transparency and name stability

That assertion immediately makes us confront another difficult question. A logical consequence of the position I have been arguing for so far is that when any expression is used to refer without the use of lexical

[45] R. Jones, 'Hunting for the meaning of the place-name *Upton*', in R. Jones and S. Semple (eds), *Sense of Place in Anglo-Saxon England* (Donington: Shaun Tyas, 2012), pp. 301–15.

senses, it is by definition a proper name.[46] Can that be true of an expression like *The North Sea*? Is it a name or not? The necessary answer seems to be that the responsibility is thrown back on the speaker or writer.[47] At the moment of use, is s/he using it with the senses of the words and the grammar intact, or not? Does s/he intend to identify by linguistic means some sea in or of the north, or does s/he intend to identify only some map-location by means of what is synchronically, in effect, an arbitrary label? The most naïve of neurolinguistics will suggest that using an expression as a name (in the way defined above) has fewer processing costs, seeing that a level of sense does not need to be involved: if one refers by a direct association of an expression with a place it should be literally quicker to do so than by a mediated route. It has long been known that, in normal cases, personal names are processed quicker than descriptions of persons, and this generalizes to all names. It follows that to use an expression as a name is adaptive, and that the option of using an expression which is ambiguous as regards namehood with all its semantic baggage intact will usually be a counterproductive option. Putting it more simply, once a language-user has used an expression as a name, i.e. without appealing to its sense, the system within which it functions will find no advantage in going back, and the status of namehood is automatically reinforced by each further use.[48]

Having no sense is the guarantee of a name's stability. When we consider such names as *High and Over*,[49] *Saddleworth*[50] and *Ryhall*,[51] if we have the relevant philological knowledge we can see that they contain

[46] This is the single most important factor that distinguishes The Pragmatic Theory of Properhood from previous approaches.

[47] This is the compromise referred to above, p. 141.

[48] In the recent important book by W. Van Langendonck, *Theory and Typology of Proper Names* (Berlin and New York: Walter de Gruyter, 2007), pp. 202–04, the author appears to support the view that transparent elements like *Sea* in the above example, and analogous ones elsewhere in this chapter, continue to function as synchronic classifiers, and he introduces a typological hierarchy of names with varying degrees of "classifierhood". See also J. M. Anderson, *The Grammar of Names* (Oxford: Oxford University Press, 2007), pp. 106–07, 114–16, and 305. This seems to me to be semantically wrong, though I do not have the space here to defend fully what may appear perverse. My view is more like that of Gottfried Kolde, whom Van Langendonck cites, and for me what the user performs in such cases is an act of etymological recovery, not of semantically normal lexical usage. A key issue is where one thinks the proper name begins in cases like *lake/Lake Windermere* and *the river/River Avon*.

[49] EPNS Sx, p. 416.

[50] EPNS WRY **2**, p. 310.

[51] EPNS R, pp. 160–61.

elements which no longer have their etymological senses: OE *ofer* 'bank, slope', *worð* 'smallholding', *halh* 'hale, nook, etc.'. These words lack their senses quite radically: they no longer exist in English in their original applications. If the Old English names had maintained their sense into later periods of the language, in order to maintain meaningfulness the obsolescent elements in question would have needed to be replaced by some which supported the intended sense, e.g. *bank*, *farm*, *corner*. This is a knock-down argument in favour of the senselessness of names: as these elements disappear in the language at large, at some critical point the old names can evidently, even in principle, no longer transmit the required senses. The old elements can survive in these names only because they communicate no sense. Senselessness is also a guarantee of name stability even if the place named moves, a notable case in point being the Welsh *Aberystwyth* 'mouth of the [river] Ystwyth' which was founded at a place appropriately described in that way, was moved lock, stock and castle to the mouth of the river Rheidol, and became appropriately named again when the Ystwyth was diverted to flow into the Rheidol at Aberystwyth in the nineteenth century.[52] These cases show that names do not *become senseless through their use as names*; they are senseless already through being used as a name.

An interesting perspective is offered by the names *Irby in the Marsh* and *Irby on Humber* in Lindsey. *Irby in the Marsh* is a name if and only if the user is not logically committed to anything that follows from the name at the moment of using it, e.g. if s/he says "I live at Irby in the Marsh" and does not *intend* at the moment of speaking to convey "I live in the marsh"; if s/he did intend to convey this s/he might well say "I live at Irby, in the marsh", which differs at least prosodically. *Irby on Humber* is a name by anyone's reckoning, because it conveys a literal falsehood; if someone says "I live at Irby on Humber", s/he cannot be committed to the truth of "I live on the [river] Humber" since the village is 5½ miles or so from the Humber (a fact not drawn attention to in the Survey volume for this area).[53]

[52] H. W. Owen and R. Morgan, *Dictionary of the Place-Names of Wales* (Llandysul: Gomer 2007), pp. 12–13; J. G. Jenkins, *Ceredigion: Interpreting an Ancient County* (Llanrwst: Gwasg Carreg Gwalch, 2005), pp. 57–58.

[53] EPNS Li **5**, p. 125.

Nonlinguistic meaning-relations

We have just seen that names carry no sense, and are therefore not connected by sense-relations, as the term is usually understood in linguistics. Nevertheless, there are cases where names have undoubtedly influenced each other in a way reminiscent of the type of analogical reformation which some linguists call, in a somewhat puritanical way, *contamination.*[54] This is seen in vocabulary in the case of *female*, whose form has been influenced by the semantically closely related *male*; *female* was originally Middle English *fēmēle*. Place-names undoubtedly influence each other too.[55] *Misterton* (So) and *Mosterton* (Do), etymologically, have nothing whatever to do with each other. *Misterton* derives from OE *mynster* 'minster-church' + *tūn*;[56] *Mosterton* is OE **Mortes þorn* 'Mort's thorn-tree'.[57] The obvious reason for their influencing each other (or perhaps better, for *Misterton*'s influencing *Mosterton*) is that the two villages are only a mile and a half apart, despite being separated by a county boundary. Distance on the ground, an extremely non-linguistic property, may act as a surrogate for a semantic relation. Examples such as these demonstrate that for names to be organized in a conceptual system, e.g. that of any individual user of the language, they do not require the cocoon of linguistic organization. Denotation of individual places, held in place cognitively by and within geographical knowledge, may suffice to influence linguistic form. One could hardly ask for a clearer demonstration that language is not an isolated semiotic system but takes its very important place within a broader framework for knowledge representation and communication.

Etymology and motivation

Now we move to a distinction drawn explicitly by many European scholars between the two stages or processes of **name-interpretation**,

[54] See, for example, R. Anttila, *Historical and Comparative Linguistics*, 2nd edn (Amsterdam and Philadelphia: John Benjamins, 1989), p. 76; H. H. Hock, *Principles of Historical Linguistics* (Berlin: Walter de Gruyter, 1986), p. 197.

[55] R. Coates, 'Pragmatic sources of analogical reformation', *Journal of Linguistics* 23 (1987), 319–40. This influence was first suggested in a published lecture by G. P. R. Pulman, *Local nomenclature* [etc.] (London: Longman [etc.], 1857), p. 136, but his etymology is wrong.

[56] CDEPN, p. 417b.

[57] EPNS Do **4**, pp. 308–09.

i.e. establishing the **etymology** of a name and its **motivation**.[58] This distinction is not regularly drawn by British scholars either in methodological discussions or in the interpretation of individual names. Etymology, the practice of discovering the linguistic origin of words and names, involves the recognition of linguistic elements present in a name at the moment of its bestowal or at the outset of its evolution. Motivation involves establishing the reason for the use of those elements in a particular name on a particular occasion. Motivation is not always obvious, in a variety of ways, even where etymology is. It may be hard to explain what a *Westborough* or *Westbury* is west of; or to explain why one place is more deserving of the name *Cliff(e)* or *Trentham* than another nearby; or to identify the nature of the "prepositional" relationship between two nominal elements as 'on', 'at', 'near', 'constituting', or whatever. The same structural type accounts for the village-names *Fenton* where the relationship may be 'farm near a fen' or 'in', maybe even 'exploiting a fen', *Welton* where it is likely to be 'farm at' or 'near a well', or 'having a well', *Honiton* where it is probably 'farm producing honey', *Stibbington* where it may be 'farm consisting of [a stretch of cleared land]' and *Acton* where it may be 'farm at oak(s)' or 'marked by' or 'for', i.e. 'producing' – a notorious unresolved problem of motivation.[59] Another relation, categorial elucidation, is offered by *Slade Hollow*,[60] where the second element is an elucidation of the meaning of the first, which was probably obsolete when the modern name was

[58] The term *motivation* requires care, though, because German *Motivation* is used in a somewhat different sense by, for example, E. Ronneberger-Sibold, 'Warennamen', in A. Brendler and S. Brendler (eds), *Namenarten und ihre Erforschung: Ein Lehrbuch für das Studium der Onomastik* (Hamburg: Baar-Verlag, 2004), pp. 557–603 (pp. 573–75), where it appears tantamount to 'etymological transparency', especially in the context of the psychology of brand-name creation. The sense I have in mind is closer to that of *Namengebungsanlass* literally 'name-giving cause' as used by E. Weber, 'Hausnamen', in Brendler and Brendler (eds), *Namenarten*, pp. 469–90 (p. 471), and in cases of deliberate name-bestowal to that of *Namegebungsakt* as used by E. Hoffman, 'Namen politischer Ereignisse', in Brendler and Brendler (eds), *Namenarten*, pp. 655–70 (p. 657). However, W. Wenzel, 'Familiennamen', also in Brendler and Brendler (eds), *Namenarten*, pp. 705–42 (p. 721) appears to use *(Namen-)motivation* in much the sense I have in mind.

[59] Discussed most recently in EPNS Sa **1**, pp. 1–4; R. Coates, '"Agricultural" compound terms and names in *tūn* like *Acton* and *Barton*', in Jones and Semple (eds), *Sense of Place*, pp. 211–37 .

[60] EPNS Db, p. 572.

coined.[61] More fundamental difficulties attach to the problem of identifying the hill in the etymology supplied by Ekwall for *Carburton* (Nt),[62] the road or the brook accounting for *Stradbroke* (Sf),[63] or the snout for *Wroot* (Li),[64] or to the problem of explaining why *Canterbury* does not contain *chester* but *bury*. These are perfectly reasonable onomastic questions anyway, about the motivation for the (non-)application of names of a certain shape in their contexts.

The etymologies of *Hedon* and *Howden*[65] are interestingly problematic in this respect. Beyond reasonable doubt they originally contain the OE elements *hēah* 'high' + *dūn* 'hill' and *hēafod* 'head' + *denu* 'valley' respectively, but the topographical motivation for the application of the last three terms to these places is difficult to decide, which leads to a questioning of the accepted etymological meanings of these words, and therefore, productively, to a possible refinement of philological knowledge.

Scholars have often conflated (though it would be unfair to say "confused") etymology and motivation. To give just one example among many, Cameron analyses *Clifton* etymologically as "**clif**, **tūn**: 'farm on a hill-slope'".[66] In making this ex-cathedra judgement, he does not acknowledge a problem in proceeding directly from the Old English elements to aspects of the geography of the place, namely the possible extension of the meaning of *clif* from 'cliff' (as no doubt in other *Clifton*s)[67] into a more generic type of slope, for which Old English has other words anyway, nor the consequent problem of the implicit required shift of the "prepositional" meaning of the compound from 'near' to 'on'. It is a moot point whether this Clifton is appropriately described as "on a hill-slope". Gelling and Cole say that *clif* "is regularly used of slopes

[61] Exactly how accurate such elucidations are or need to be is a separate matter. Essentially the same process accounts for the modern proliferation of "elucidated" semi-official name-forms such as *Rottingdean Village*.

[62] EPNS Nt, p. 71.

[63] CDEPN, p. 584a

[64] R. Coates, 'Reflections on some major Lincolnshire place-names, part 2: Ness Wapentake to Yarborough', *Journal of the English Place-Name Society* 41 (2009), 57–102 (pp. 93–94).

[65] EPNS ERY, pp. 39, 244 and 250.

[66] EPNS Db, p. 432. Identification of the elements is the etymological stage; the gloss represents or subsumes the author's view of the motivation.

[67] E.g. EPNS Nt, p. 246, EPNS Gl **3**, p. 97.

which are 45° or steeper",[68] in contrast with (non-West Saxon) *helde* for shallower slopes, which makes Cameron's analysis of the Derbyshire name, taken at face value, a problematic one.

A further instructive problem is where a single etymological name-form has been explained in more than one way, as noted for example by Hough about *Bampton* in her review of CDEPN.[69] There are places of this name in Cumberland and Oxfordshire. For both of them the etymology is uncontroversially established as OE *bēam* + *tūn*.[70] In CDEPN, the Cumberland name is glossed 'tree farmstead', simply translating the elements established etymologically, whilst the Oxfordshire one is glossed more fully, cautiously and evaluatively as 'Probably "the homestead by the tree" or possibly "made of beams"'. Victor Watts's untimely death in 2002, inevitably compromising consistency across the vast range of names treated, is not the real issue here: the deeper issue is the methodological one of whether we systematize our responses to questions like the one this name-form raises, fully distinguishing etymology and motivation in so doing.

Polyonymy

Many places have more than one simultaneously current name, usually one official and at least one unofficial one (allowing also for differences of pronunciation such as *Southwell* /'sauθwel/, /'suðəl/, /'sʌðəl/ (Nt),[71] *Shrewsbury* /'ʃru:zbri/, /'ʃrouzbri/ (Sa)[72]), a situation which may result from a complex interaction of dialect and accent, modal difference (i.e. speech vs writing), and sociological factors. A good example of modern work leading towards a rich socio-onomastics is the work of Terhi Ainiala and her collaborators.[73] English place-name scholars do not on

[68] M. Gelling and A. Cole, *The Landscape of Place-Names* (Stamford: Shaun Tyas 2000), p. 153.

[69] C. Hough, review of CDEPN, *Nomina* 27 (2004), 133–42 (p. 139). Hough notes a similar problem with two *Buttermere*s.

[70] CDEPN, p. 33b.

[71] EPNS Nt, p. 175, where only the third form, the recessive received pronunciation used by the BBC in its horse-racing commentaries, is given.

[72] EPNS Sa **1**, pp. 267–70.

[73] E.g. T. Ainiala, 'Place names in the construction of social identities: the uses of names of Helsinki', in W. Ahrens et al. (eds), *Proceedings of the 23rd International Congress of Onomastic Sciences* (Toronto: York University, 2009), pp. 67–75; J. Vuolteenaho and T. Ainiala, 'Slang toponyms in early Twentieth century Helsinki', in Ahrens et al. (eds),

the whole systematically deal with the fact of variation or alternation, except in those instances where the alternation has been a matter of record for a very long time, as in *Iwerne Courtney* alternating with *Shroton*;[74] cf. Jones' manorial specifier alternation.[75] Typically, their focus is on the name, or rarely names, which has or have become official. Many radical name alternations are not treated in the EPNS Survey, whether because the volume editor judged them to be too recent, or too trivial and not worth mentioning, being unclear. But such alternations are genuinely part of the toponymic repertoire of their users, and a complete synchronic onomastics will pay them proper attention, especially since the different alternants are likely to be culturally loaded with different connotations.

A particularly striking instance of what I have in mind is afforded by *Cleethorpes* ~ *Meggies*. *Meggies* is widely used as an informal alternative name for Cleethorpes (Li), especially in the Grimsby area.[76] Another is *Devonport* ~ *Guz*,[77] where the second is particularly associated with the usage of members of the Royal and Merchant Navies. The precise cultural value and the exact patterns of usage of the informal alternant have not been determined, but the new spoken-corpus methodology of De Stefani and Pepin, evaluating the whole gamut of topographical expressions used in a context, offers a model for such investigations.[78]

Other alternations typically involve morphological derivatives of the official name. *Doncaster* ~ *Donny*[79] are related by truncation and suffixation; *Lawrence Weston* ~ *El Dub*[80] by initialism and then

Proceedings. pp. 1030–35 [available only on CD-ROM, see note 20]; and several papers from *Onoma* 42 (2007) on urban toponymy.

[74] EPNS Do **3**, p. 37.

[75] R. Jones, 'Thinking through the manorial affix', in R. Silvester and S. Turner (eds), *Life in Medieval Landscapes: People and Places in Medieval England* (Oxford: Oxbow, 2012), pp. 251–67.

[76] See R. Coates, 'Reflections on some major Lincolnshire place-names, part 1: Algarkirk to Melton Ross', *Journal of the English Place-Name Society* 40 (2008), 35–95 (pp. 53–54), for a possible etymology.

[77] E. Partridge, *A Dictionary of Slang and Unconventional English*, 8th edn rev. P. Beale (London: Routledge, 1984, repr. 2003), p. 516, though I suspect Partridge's suggested etymology, from *guzzle*, may be wrong, as the entry for that word itself suggests.

[78] E. De Stefani and N. Pepin, 'Une approche interactionniste de l'étude des noms propres: Les surnoms de famille', *Onoma* 41 (2006), 131–62.

[79] Common knowledge.

[80] Writer's local knowledge.

truncation of the resulting expression. In most cases, where there is a clearly unofficial form it can be simple-mindedly characterized as the form used by local people with local people in a way which conveys and reinforces their shared identity and community values; that is, the official and unofficial names have different associations or connotations (conveyed meanings). Any unofficial form may operate in the named community alone, or over a wider region (for example, the relevant county) or user-group, representing the possibility of different levels or criteria of self-identification (thus *Donny*, mainly local and also among railway enthusiasts, vs *Guz*, mainly among seafaring professionals).

Where are names?

I promised above (p. 138) to deal with one more fundamental question: Are names part of a language? This is a harder question to deal with than might be imagined. Names can be formulated in a language; in that sense *Southport* (La)[81] is English, i.e. etymologically English, and so is the now-obscure *Shrewsbury*. They can be used in an area where a particular language dominates, irrespective of their linguistic origin; in that sense the above two, *Beaulieu* (Ha; etymologically French)[82] and *Skegby* (Nt; etymologically Scandinavian)[83] are English. Does that make them synchronically part of the English language? This is an important question, because if the answer is no it entails that there are some linguistic objects which are not part of some language, which has the whiff of paradox about it (though it is perfectly intelligible). It entails that people who know names do not necessarily thereby know (any aspect of) a language.

Certainly (place-)names have the appearance of detachability from their language, under either of these two interpretations. A typical place-name is language-neutral. I can light on the reasonably obscure village called *Falsterbo* in Sweden,[84] and be reasonably confident that I would need to use the same form to refer to it whatever language I was speaking, with only the phonological adjustments required by my native pronunciation. This may become progressively less true the more

[81] CDEPN, p. 562a. Note however that its transparent etymology does not make its motivation any clearer, as Watts explains.

[82] CDEPN, p. 44b.

[83] Two places, EPNS Nt, pp. 133 and 190.

[84] M. Wahlberg, *Svenskt Ortnamnslexikon* (Uppsala: SOFI, 2002), p. 71b.

prominent or cosmopolitan a place is. *Saint* (or *St*) *Petersburg* is a specifically English name; for Russians, its full name is *Sankt-Peterburg* (deriving from an etymologically German form). The Arabic-speaking city of *al-Jazā'ir* is *Dzayer* for Berber-speakers, *Algiers* for English (with an etymologically French *-s*) and *Argel* for Portuguese. *Copenhagen* looks like an English name (cf. *København* for the Danes).

There are, then, clearly some instances that it seems appropriate to associate with a particular language, like *Copenhagen*. No great harm seems to be done by speaking of "English names" and meaning those (proto)typically used when speaking English, but do I "lapse into Swedish" in mid-utterance when saying *I have seen photos of Falsterbo*, or does it become English in the saying within an English sentence? We may occasionally face even profounder paradoxes. *Neithvrane* is a hamlet in Cornwall[85] which is normally associated with English-speaking, its source-language Cornish having died out. It is therefore an English name if *Beaulieu* and *Skegby* are. But it contains a medial consonant cluster /ðvr/ which is inadmissible in English and is in that sense not English.

Where does that leave us? It seems best to say that, synchronically speaking, a place-name is indeed language-neutral if it does not alternate with other forms; and where it does alternate it seems best to say that each form is (prototypically) associated with a language or range of languages. Speaking English, I may refer to a town in Finland with no "English" name as *Nystad* or *Uusikaupunki*, and I would do best to say, for convenience, that I *use the Swedish name* or *use the Finnish name*. But arguably I would mean that I *use the name associated with Swedish/Finnish*.

A practical lexicographical issue arises at this point. If (place-)names are, so to speak, semi-detached from individual languages, to what extent, if at all, should they be drawn upon to elucidate such issues as the first record of a word in a language? If the first record of some word is in a place-name, should that be discounted since it is arguably not evidence for the language in question? In practice, the problem vanishes, since it is only likely to arise in historical dictionaries. It is current policy to admit name evidence in the OED, in some circumstances as quotation evidence,

[85] For the first element, see O. J. Padel, *Cornish Place-Name Elements*, English Place-Name Society 56–57 (Nottingham: English Place-Name Society, 1985), p. 172, and for the second, p. 29.

and in others as supporting documentation in etymologies.[86] The justification is that the first record of a place-name acts as a surrogate for the moment of its creation or evolution into a name, i.e. the last moment at which it was fully sense-bearing, which will not normally be recoverable.

A final issue raised briefly above, which we lack the space to deal with comprehensively, is whether place-names and other names (may) represent types which are valid constructs in the system of the language in whose territory they are used; and/or whether names form systems. The trouble is that names are obviously not fully systematic: there are plenty of names that defy categorization (could we know from the form, without specialized historical knowledge, whether *Blean* or *Marten* or *Leeds* was the name of a village, mountain, river or family?); and there are names which are not obviously fully unsystematic: there are plenty of lake-names, for example, which include the word *Lake*. The account I have given above tends to deny a theoretical place to systematicity altogether. This issue intersects with the issue of the transparency of names, i.e. the recoverability of their origin from their form. A recent dissertation by Antti Leino (2007) on Finnish lake-names suggests a sophisticated dynamic model which cuts the Gordian knot:[87] within a framework of Construction Grammar[88] modified to allow analogy based on prototypes (as Leino explains it, a notion fully dependent on *usage* by real people in real contexts), analogy is acknowledged to be a driving force in the creation and maintenance of names without the awkward need to suggest that there is a kind of rigid embracing system in place for sets of names which are mainly, but not fully, etymologically transparent.

Conclusion

We have now examined the relations which toponomastics has enjoyed with general historical linguistics, and the place which it, and the data which inform it, occupy in current synchronic linguistics. Let us finish by repeating the main conclusions we have come to about the linguistic

[86] Stated on the authority of Dr Philip Durkin; see also <http://public.oed.com/aspects-of-english/shapers-of-english/place-names-in-the-oxford-english-dictionary/>.

[87] A. Leino, *On Toponymic Constructions as an Alternative to Naming Patterns in Describing Finnish Lake Names* (Helsinki: Finnish Literature Society, 2007).

[88] W. Croft, *Radical Construction Grammar: Syntactic Theory in Typological Perspective* (Oxford: Oxford University Press, 2001).

nature of names in general and place-names in particular, and about the way the issues have been treated in English place-name studies:

1. Names are senseless, and to be a proper name is to (be used to) refer senselessly; etymology (transparency) in names is a conveyed "meaning" and not a sense.
2. Place-names may evolve or be bestowed.
3. The motivation of a place-name is a different matter from its etymology, and methodologically the relation between the two is not straightforward, though etymology, the formal identification of the elements from which the name is constructed, is logically prior. Scholars have not always clearly distinguished the two enterprises.
4. The semantic relation between a name and the category of things it denotes is not one of logical *entailment* but a probabilistic and historically insecure one amounting to a species of conveyed meaning *(implicature)*, partly because of the sense-killing nature of naming events and partly because of processes such as metonymy.
5. In British, especially English, toponymic work, alternation in place-names is suppressed, or often reduced to a consideration of the relation between a historical pronunciation and a current, often spelling-based, one.
6. The relation between names, particularly place-names, and the languages in whose culture they are embedded is a complex one where intuitions may falter. The evolution or a bestowal of a place-name deprives it of sense, and thereby arguably takes it outside the language in which it was formulated.
7. The partial systematicity of some categories of name, which seems to undermine point 1 from some perspectives, can be accommodated within a dynamic, as opposed to a structural(ist), approach to linguistics.

6

English place-names and landscape terminology

Paul Cullen

In the English Place-Name Society's introductory volume of 1924 the topic of landscape terminology receives scant attention.[1] Frank Stenton offers some observations on the cluster of names containing Old English *feld* 'open country' in south-east Berkshire,[2] and Eilert Ekwall, listing examples, asserts that 'Scandinavian elements are particularly common among so-called nature-names, a great many of which, however, have developed into names of villages or homesteads',[3] but beyond this there is little more than a single paragraph, under the subheading *Importance of topography*, which appears in W. J. Sedgefield's opening chapter on methodology.[4]

Sedgefield does not examine the niceties of topographical vocabulary as such, but he makes two main pertinent points. The first, basic but important, is that 'in many cases a knowledge of configuration will be of great help. It may enable us to decide, for example, between confused suffixes. Thus when early forms leave us in doubt whether the original suffix was *-hale* or *-hill*, a knowledge of the actual local conditions may resolve our hesitation at once. In the past, failure to remember this precaution has led to some mistakes on the part of place-name students'.[5]

The volumes of the English Place-Name Society's Survey are indicated by EPNS + county abbreviation as given on p. vi.

[1] A. Mawer and F. M. Stenton (eds), *Introduction to the Survey of English Place-Names, Part 1*, English Place-Name Society 1.i (Cambridge: English Place-Name Society, 1924) [IPN].

[2] F. M. Stenton, 'The English element', in IPN, pp. 36–54 (pp. 37–38).

[3] E. Ekwall, 'The Scandinavian element', in IPN, pp. 55–92 (p. 59).

[4] W. J. Sedgefield, 'Methods of place-name study', in IPN, pp. 1–14 (p. 11).

[5] We would now avoid the term *suffix* for the generic element in a compound place-name. Sedgefield is not alone in this use; it is also employed in the second part of the introductory volume: A. Mawer (ed.), *Introduction to the Survey of English Place-Names, Part 2: The Chief Elements used in English Place-Names*, English Place-Name Society 1.ii (Cambridge: English Place-Name Society, 1924), p. vi.

This principle of checking name against landscape is sound enough, although (particularly given Sedgefield's choice of OE *halh* as an example) we will have to return to the question of what might be meant by 'configuration' in such an exercise. His second point, applicable to all categories of place-name, is that a 'satisfactory investigation and explanation of any individual place-name involves the study of all the other names of the district. In practice this is not always sufficient, for there are many cases where light is thrown on the origin of a name by the early forms of places in distant parts of the country'. Context of two types, both local and systematic, is indeed essential, and accordingly the regional study of place-names undertaken by the EPNS on a county-by-county basis has from the start been accompanied by some form of countrywide key to the vocabulary involved, from the pioneering handlist of Allen Mawer, through the much more substantial two volumes edited by Hugh Smith, to the near exhaustive ongoing *Vocabulary of English Place-Names*.[6] But it is in two inter-related monographs, Margaret Gelling's *Place-Names in the Landscape* (1984) and, with Ann Cole, *The Landscape of Place-Names* (2000), that rigorous investigation of topographical place-names has been revolutionized and put onto a sound footing.[7]

Gelling's work has been pioneering in tackling a category of place-name which had been not merely neglected but largely misunderstood. She took issue with the sometimes derisory attitude towards topographical names expressed by earlier scholars whose interests tended to focus on various other types of names which were considered to have more to tell us about the earliest Anglo-Saxon settlers (an attitude well illustrated by such dismissive remarks as 'Names of the descriptive type in general bear a very trivial character [...] Oxford is only the most famous of many names in this quarter which carry a strong smack of the farmyard', quoted by Gelling from Stenton's 1911 study of Berkshire

[6] Mawer, *Chief Elements*; A. H. Smith, *English Place-Name Elements*, English Place-Name Society 25–26 (Cambridge: English Place-Name Society, 1956); D. Parsons and T. Styles with C. Hough, *The Vocabulary of English Place-Names* I *(Á–Box)* (Nottingham: Centre for English Name-Studies, 1997); D. N. Parsons and T. Styles, *The Vocabulary of English Place-Names* II *(Brace–Cæster)* (Nottingham: Centre for English Name-Studies, 2000); D. N. Parsons, *The Vocabulary of English Place-Names* III *(Ceafor–Cock-pit)* (Nottingham: English Place-Name Society, 2004) [VEPN].

[7] M. Gelling, *Place-Names in the Landscape* (London: Dent, 1984); M. Gelling and A. Cole, *The Landscape of Place-Names* (Stamford: Shaun Tyas, 2000; reprinted with corrections, 2003).

place-names).[8] She also questioned prevailing beliefs or assumptions about the way in which the 'descriptive type' of village-names were coined, and beliefs or assumptions that they were as a category somehow less 'early' than other types of English-language place-name. In the introduction to his *Concise Oxford Dictionary of English Place-Names*, Ekwall begins a chapter on 'Original nature-names' with the observation that '[m]any names of villages or homesteads originally denoted a natural object, or more rarely some product of human activity near which, or sometimes in which, the place was situated. Names of this kind, when used of inhabited places, are elliptical or metonymical. Oxford at first designated a ford over the Thames. When a village grew up at the ford it was named from the ford, and Oxford, when used of the village, originally meant "the village at Oxford"'.[9] Though we know that Ekwall was well aware of the peoples and languages (and relevant chronologies) of early medieval England, he seems in this account almost to depopulate the country and to envisage the Anglo-Saxons arriving in and naming a landscape devoid of existing settlements. This is not how Gelling understands the naming process behind most of the names of towns and villages in England, whose locations must in many cases have involved many centuries of continuity of settlement and of farming practices. She does not necessarily deny an element of ellipsis or metonymy at work in all manner of English place-names over many centuries, but in the topographical settlement-names of the early Anglo-Saxons she sees the name-bestowal as applying, surely often simultaneously, to both the topography and to the (often pre-existing) settlement in its topographical, social, and administrative context; hence her use of the term 'quasi-habitative' for 'many landscape terms which occur in names of places where geography dictates that that is where people would choose to live'.[10]

Gelling's appreciation of the significance and precision of names

[8] Gelling, *Place-Names in the Landscape*, p. 5; F. M. Stenton, *The Place-Names of Berkshire: An Essay* (Reading: University College, 1911), p. 19. Stenton's view of 'descriptive' (i.e. topographical) names remained uncharitable in the 1924 EPNS introductory volume: 'It may at once be admitted that the greater number of English place-names tell nothing of importance for social history [...] many place-names of this [descriptive] kind are intrinsically trivial' (Stenton, 'The English element', pp. 36–37). See also Parsons above, pp. 46, 48–49.

[9] E. Ekwall, *The Concise Oxford Dictionary of English Place-Names*, 4th edn (Oxford: Clarendon, 1960), pp. xviii–xxi.

[10] Gelling and Cole, *Landscape of Place-Names*, p. xvii.

derived from natural features is evident right from the start, even before she had begun any systematic study. As early as 1952, in what I believe to be her first published paper, she notes that 'certain elements have a curiously regional distribution, which cannot always be explained. [... It] is difficult to see why so many names in Bedfordshire and Huntingdonshire end in *-hoe*, *-oe*, etc., representing *hōh*, one of the many Old English words for a hill. On the other hand, it is easy to understand why *hyrst*, meaning something like "wooded hill", should be particularly frequent in the Weald. The characteristic place-name endings of the Chilterns are *-ore*, from *ōra* "slope", and *mere* [...] "a small pool". These small pools occur in the Chilterns where there is a fairly thick deposit of clay over the chalk; they are still a noticeable feature of the landscape, and it is easy to understand their importance to the Anglo-Saxon settlers, which led to their being mentioned so frequently in the place-names of the region'.[11] The rather obvious point, that if a topographical feature were truly of little importance to the Anglo-Saxons it would hardly merit specifying by name (let alone stand a chance of giving rise to a settlement-name), is actually a crucial insight and something of a fresh open-minded approach. Gelling is prepared to allow the names to speak for themselves and thereby reveal what mattered to those who coined them, rather than choosing to sift the corpus in the hunt for a few name-types of pre-selected 'historical' interest.

From this initial awareness, various ideas emerge. One is an inkling of the potential chronological importance, and thus status, of topographical settlement-names. In a series of articles in the 1970s, aided by innovative distribution maps, she develops the notion that '[o]ne possibility [...] is that the type of name which consists of a statement about the site of the settlement, the topographical as opposed to the habitative type of name, may sometimes be the earliest in a district'.[12] Keen to give credit where it is due, she notes in several publications that 'The true status of

[11] M. Gelling, 'Place-names as clues to history', *The Amateur Historian* 1:2 (1952), 51–59 (p. 55). It is noteworthy that the vehicle for Gelling's first publication should be *The Amateur Historian*. Her desire to bring the subject, and its inherent interest, merits, nuances and difficulties, to the attention of the general public is already evident.

[12] M. Gelling, 'Some notes on Warwickshire place-names', *Transactions of the Birmingham and Warwickshire Archaeological Society* 86 (1974), 59–79 (p. 63); also developed in Gelling, 'The chronology of English place-names', in T. Rowley (ed.), *Anglo-Saxon Settlement and Landscape* (Oxford: BAR, 1974), pp. 93–101, and Gelling, 'Topographical settlement-names', *The Local Historian* 12:6 (1977), 273–77, as well as in EPNS Brk, pp. 800–47.

topographical settlement-names was hinted at by John Dodgson in his paper of 1966' (on place-names containing the OE 'folk-name' element *-ingas*), when discussing 'which kinds of English place-names are likely to be the oldest in use in England'.[13] Dodgson's suspicion was that '[i]t might turn out that quite ordinary nature-names, such as *burna*, "a stream", *lēah*, "a wood", *feld*, "open land", are the first to be used by settlers in a new land, and that habitative terms such as *hām* and *tūn*, and place-names formed from the personal-names and folk-names of the inhabitants, only come into use when the pattern of settlement and society has evolved to a stage at which the need for identification is felt, and recognition by neighbours is established'.[14] Although some questions concerning the absolute and relative chronology of Anglo-Saxon place-name formation will probably always remain unanswerable, Gelling has at the very least succeeded in demonstrating that topographical settlement-names are 'specially characteristic of areas where the English are known to have established themselves at a particularly early date, and that in such areas the more important settlements, the ones which became the centres of large estates, are more likely to have topographical names than habitative ones'.[15]

A second aspect to Gelling's reappraisal of the topographic corpus is her conviction that the material lends itself to (and is deserving of) proper quantification. In a paper written in 1981 she bemoans the lack of precision, especially statistical precision, underlying the use of terms such as 'common' and 'rare' in Ekwall's *Dictionary* and Smith's *Elements*, and stresses the need to sort and analyse the mass of evidence properly, daunting though this task may be: 'It seems legitimate to criticize Smith for not quantifying his material and for not making a systematic analysis of first elements, because that can be done from reference books and is not inordinately time consuming. It would be less fair to criticize him for not doing much topographical research, because that is so time consuming as to be impossible on a large scale for any one worker, even

[13] Gelling, *Place-Names in the Landscape*, p. 6.

[14] J. McN. Dodgson, 'The significance of the distribution of the English place-name in *-ingas*, *-inga-* in south-east England', *Medieval Archaeology* 10 (1966), 1–29 (p. 5).

[15] M. Gelling, 'The effect of man on the landscape: the place-name evidence in Berkshire', in S. Limbrey and J. G. Evans (eds), *The Effect of Man on the Landscape: the Lowland Zone*, Research Report 21 (London: Council for British Archaeology, 1978), pp. 123–25 (p. 124).

if done with maps and unsupported by field work'.[16] Impossible it may have seemed, but in *Place-Names in the Landscape* and, with Cole, *The Landscape of Place-Names*, she went ahead and did it anyway. The material upon which these studies are based is restricted primarily to Ekwall's corpus of 'major' names (i.e. 'a certain category of settlement-name for which, thanks to Ekwall's Dictionary, country-wide coverage is available'), and there is no attempt to include 'the vast category of what are loosely designated "field" names, or [...] names of landscape features which are not referred to in settlement-names, though such material is drawn upon in discussion of some generics'.[17] A key difference between the two books is the inclusion of Cole's sketches (line-drawings, based on photographs, executed with great clarity), the first of which appeared in 1998 illustrating a paper by Gelling on 'Place-names and landscape', others having since been employed by Victor Watts in the glossary to his *Cambridge Dictionary of English Place-Names*.[18]

Cole's pictures do much to paint the thousand words demanded by yet another aspect of Gelling's investigations: the discovery that the terminology of the topographical settlement-names of England is immensely rich, far from trivial, and above all precise (seemingly to the near preclusion of synonyms). 'In many cases [...] there is no equivalent modern term, and a lengthy periphrasis is required to translate the Old English word. There is not much left of the ancient variety and subtlety in the topographical vocabulary of modern English'.[19] Although, to modern perceptions, these typically non-phrasal, two-element compound English place-names may convey 'a spurious impression of simplicity and shallowness of meaning' ('fern hill', 'long valley', and so on), Gelling's hypothesis resurrects their informativeness enormously: 'The key to Anglo-Saxon topographical naming lies, however, in the precise use of words which get blanket translations like "hill" and "valley" in the impoverished modern English vocabulary. The Anglo-Saxons had a vast and subtle topographical vocabulary which can be decoded by field-work. [...] In addition to the richness and variety of the generics there is infinite

[16] M. Gelling, 'On looking into Smith's *Elements*', *Nomina* 5 (1981), 39–45 (p. 43).

[17] Gelling and Cole, *Landscape of Place-Names*, p. xxiii.

[18] M. Gelling, with illustrations by A. Cole, 'Place-names and landscape', in S. Taylor (ed.), *The Uses of Place-Names* (Edinburgh: Scottish Cultural Press, 1998), pp. 75–100; V. Watts, *The Cambridge Dictionary of English Place-Names* (Cambridge: Cambridge University Press, 2004), pp. xlii–xlix.

[19] Gelling, *Place-Names in the Landscape*, p. 7.

scope for fine tuning in the qualifiers of compound names'.[20]

I shall not attempt here to reproduce or rehearse the painstaking argumentation and careful observations which underlie Gelling's two *Landscape* books. Her repeated demonstrations that correlations between landscape features and place-name elements are not accidental, and synonyms are rare or absent, have won wide acceptance, and it is no longer adequate practice to gloss cavalierly any number of topographical terms as simply 'hill' or 'valley' or the like in anything but the most minimalist dictionary format, if at all. Even the supremely terse 'Glossary of some common elements' in David Mills's *Dictionary of British Place-Names* finds space for some of the refinements proposed by Gelling and Cole in glossing *brōc* 'brook, stream, often used of muddy streams', *burna* 'stream, often used of clear streams', *cumb* 'coomb, valley, used particularly of relatively short or broad valleys', *denu* 'valley, used particularly of relatively long, narrow valleys', and *dūn* 'hill, used particularly of low hills with fairly level and extensive summits'.[21] And even at this middling level of detail, the wordiness jars: there is no way to keep the glosses at once accurate and idiomatic, or even concise, when we have no modern idiom to match the intimate topographical knowledge possessed by (or concerns expressed by) an Anglo-Saxon land-working peasant. How best, for instance, to render into Modern English the OE **wæsse* convincingly explained by Gelling as 'land by a meandering river which floods and drains quickly'?[22] This striking phenomenon, observable by twentieth-century field-work, is as real today as in the Anglo-Saxon period, but the vocabulary to do it justice is long gone.

A new appreciation of the subtleties of topographical naming allows the reassessment of some earlier evaluations. Unsurprisingly, a lack of such appreciation and of field-work is evident in many pre-Gelling EPNS county surveys. The medieval spellings assembled for Farndon in Nottinghamshire, for example, indicate clearly that it derives from OE *fearn* 'fern' + *dūn* 'hill', to the puzzlement of the county editors, for whom '[t]he chief difficulty in interpreting the name lies in the second element. There is no semblance of a hill here and it may be that we must interpret *dūn* simply as denoting open land' (EPNS Nt, pp. 213–14).

[20] Gelling, 'Place-names and landscape', pp. 75–76.

[21] A. D. Mills, *A Dictionary of British Place-Names* (Oxford: Oxford University Press, 2003), pp. 521–27.

[22] Gelling and Cole, *Landscape of Place-Names*, pp. 63–64.

Actually the village partly sits upon a very low but nevertheless typical *dūn* in Gelling's terms, and, though *dūn* is a rare term in the major names of Nottinghamshire, a definition 'large (but not particularly high) flattish-topped hill' works consistently well, both as generic element in Farndon and Headon and as qualifier in Dunham (EPNS Nt, pp. 48 and 52; see Figs 1–3).

Fig. 1. Farndon, Nottinghamshire

Fig. 2. Headon, Nottinghamshire

The fact that Gelling and Cole's work covers topographical terms employed as qualifiers as well as generics should not be overlooked. In particular, a recognition of the uneven yet often coherent distributions of certain recurring compounds of topographical qualifier with habitative generic (Acton, Draycot, Eaton, Merton, Wootton, and many more) is groundbreaking, and allows a strong case to be made that such name-types are not merely ad hoc visual descriptions but are more likely to reflect the role and function of the places so named.[23]

Fig. 3. Dunham, Nottinghamshire

Other scholars besides Gelling have of course contributed to our understanding of particular topographical terms, or have shown how profitable use can be made of them in related disciplines. We might note, for instance, the studies by Dodgson and Karl Inge Sandred on *hamm*, and the detailed use of place-name evidence by historical geographers and landscape historians such as H. C. Darby, Harold Fox, Alan Everitt, and Della Hooke.[24] In particular, the many pioneering articles by Cole are of great importance.[25] Nevertheless, the prefatory comments in Gelling's

[23] EPNS Sa **1**, pp. 1–7; A. Cole, 'The Anglo-Saxon traveller', *Nomina* 17 (1994), 7–18 (pp. 11–12); Gelling and Cole, *Landscape of Place-Names*, pp. 14–15 and 258; A. Cole, 'Distribution and use of the Old English place-name *mere-tūn*', *Journal of the English Place-Name Society* 24 (1991–92), 30–41.

[24] J. McN. Dodgson, 'Place-names from *hām*, distinguished from *hamm* names, in relation to the settlement of Kent, Surrey and Sussex', *Anglo-Saxon England* 2 (1973), 1–50; K. I. Sandred, 'The element *hamm* in English place-names: a linguistic investigation', *Namn och Bygd* 64 (1976), 69–87; H. C. Darby, 'Place-names and the geography of the past', in A. Brown and P. Foote (eds), *Early English and Norse Studies Presented to Hugh Smith* (London: Methuen, 1963), pp. 6–18; H. Fox, *Dartmoor's Alluring Uplands: Transhumance and Pastoral Management in the Middle Ages* (Exeter: Exeter University Press, 2012); A. Everitt, *Continuity and Colonization: the Evolution of Kentish Settlement* (Leicester: Leicester University Press, 1986); A. Everitt, 'Common land', in J. Thirsk (ed.), *The English Rural Landscape* (Oxford: Oxford University Press, 2000), pp. 210–35; D. Hooke, *The Landscape of Anglo-Saxon England* (London: Leicester University Press, 1998).

[25] An incomplete list includes A. Cole, 'Topography, hydrology, and place-names in the

Festschrift are fair: she 'has achieved this "landscape revolution" largely single-handedly'.[26]

A fuller consideration of the landscape terms used in 'minor' or 'later' place-names is an obvious next step. It is encouraging to learn that the work of Gelling and Cole has inspired Terhi Nurminen to adopt their methodological framework and employ extensive field-work and map-work in undertaking an investigation of hill-terms in the place-names of Northumberland and County Durham.[27] Nurminen sets out to employ consistent and clearly-defined terminology in her assessment of the relationship between topographical terms and the landscape features to which they refer, and to examine the semantics (including positive or negative connotations) of the elements with which the hill-terms are compounded. Her corpus of over 2000 names, based on the current Ordnance Survey Landranger series and as such not restricted to major names or to names of Old English origin, should allow an examination of the precision and consistency with which hill-terms in names of later coinage may have been applied.[28] Careful map-work and awareness of fluctuating geographical conditions also underpin a number of recent studies of curiously recurrent topographical place-names, such as those by Peter McClure on *Lindrick* ('lime-tree ridge'), Richard Coates on

chalklands of southern England: *cumb* and *denu*', *Nomina* 6 (1982), 73–87; 'Topography, hydrology and place-names in the chalklands of southern England: **funta*, *ǣwiell* and *ǣwielm*', *Nomina* 9 (1985), 3–19; 'The distribution and usage of the OE place-name *cealc*', *Journal of the English Place-Name Society* 19 (1986–87), 45–55; 'The meaning of the Old English place-name element *ōra*', *Journal of the English Place-Name Society* 21 (1988–89), 15–22; 'The origin, distribution and use of the place-name element *ōra* and its relationship to the element *ofer*', *Journal of the English Place-Name Society* 22 (1989–90), 26–41; '*Burna* and *brōc*: problems involved in retrieving the Old English usage of these place-name elements', *Journal of the English Place-Name Society* 23 (1990–91), 26–48; 'The distribution and use of *mere* as a generic in place-names', *Journal of the English Place-Name Society* 25 (1992–93), 38–50; '*flēot*: distribution and use of this OE place-name element', *Journal of the English Place-Name Society* 29 (1996–97), 79–87; '*cisel*, *grēot*, *stān* and the four U's', *Journal of the English Place-Name Society* 31 (1998–99), 19–30; '*Ersc*: distribution and use of this Old English place-name element', *Journal of the English Place-Name Society* 32 (1999–2000), 27–40; '*Weg*: a waggoner's warning', in O. J. Padel and D. N. Parsons (eds), *A Commodity of Good Names: Essays in Honour of Margaret Gelling* (Donington: Shaun Tyas, 2008), pp. 345–49.

[26] Padel and Parsons, *Commodity of Good Names*, p. viii.

[27] T. Nurminen, 'Hill-terms in the Place-Names of Northumberland and County Durham', unpublished PhD thesis (Newcastle University, 2012).

[28] Details from an interim report presented to the Twentieth Annual Conference of the Society for Name-Studies in Britain and Ireland, 15th 18th April 2011, at the University of Kent, Canterbury.

Dumball ('pasture subject to occasional tidal flooding'), and Barrie Cox on *Dimmingsdale* ('valley which darkens quickly').[29] Successful elucidation of this kind of precise terminology would not be achievable by any other method.

Of all the categories of vocabulary to which place-name study can make a contribution, landscape terminology must be one of the most significant. Place-names offer an insight into a word-stock, even a register, which is under-represented in literary and other sources – that is the vocabulary, view-point, and concerns of medieval people who got their hands dirty, the land-working peasantry. As well as topographical terms which are unknown to the standard dictionaries of English, whose existence and application can be demonstrated through place-name study alone, there are many items of English vocabulary already catalogued in a range of dictionaries, and whose senses might be quite well known, but whose precise application can be still better understood and visualized through topographic investigation and field-work. Take the word *doke*, for instance, which the *Oxford English Dictionary* defines as 'a hollow, depression; a dint; a dimple', supported by citations dating from 1615 ('The doke or dimple in the middest of the chin') to 1866 ('The little doke in the end of the nose').[30] This is best explained as a development, via a form *dolk*, of the word *dalk* which *OED* defines as 'a hole, hollow, depression', with citations beginning much earlier, from about 1325 ('a dalk in the nekke'). The *Middle English Dictionary* includes *dalk* 'a glen or gully; a groove or dimple; a hollow', and the *English Dialect Dictionary* has *doke* 'a hollow, depression, the impression of a body in a bed, etc.; the indentation from a blow upon anything soft; a dimple', also 'a bruise; a flaw in a boy's marble; a small brook, stream'.[31] Despite hints of some confusion with reflexes of OE *dolh* 'a wound, a scar' (compare OED *dolk*), the chief sense of *dalk* and its variant *doke* is clearly 'a hollow, a depression', and we must be dealing with a diminutive of OE

[29] P. McClure, 'Names and landscapes in medieval Nottinghamshire, with particular attention to Lindrick and lime woods', in Padel and Parsons (eds), *Commodity of Good Names*, pp. 395–409; R. Coates, 'South-West English *dumball*, *dumble*, *dunball* "pasture subject to (occasional) tidal flooding"', *Journal of the English Place-Name Society* 39 (2007), 59–72; B. Cox, 'Dimmingsdale', in Padel and Parsons (eds), *Commodity of Good Names*, pp. 350–51.

[30] J. Simpson (ed.), *The Oxford English Dictionary*, 3rd edn, online at <www.oed.com>.

[31] H. Kurath and S. M. Kuhn (eds), *Middle English Dictionary* (Ann Arbor: University of Michigan Press, 1952–2001); J. Wright (ed.), *The English Dialect Dictionary* (London: Henry Frowde, 1898–1905).

dæl 'a hollow' (in its open-syllable stem form *dal-* when followed by a back vowel), i.e. **daluc* 'a small hollow' > **dalc* > Middle English *dalk*, *dolk*. The place-name evidence for this term is very limited indeed, but is nevertheless worthy of observation. The 1839 Tithe Award for Eastry parish in Kent records the field-name *The Doke* (at NGR TR 309559) and, adjacent to the south, *Fellings Doke*.[32] The latter is earlier recorded as *Phillenden Dolke*, *Fyllenden Doke*, and *Fyllend Doke* in 1545–46, usefully confirming a development from *dolke* to *doke*.[33] A visit to the site reveals a shallow, gently-contoured hollow, the philtrum-proportioned linearity of which is rather evocative of the 'impression of a body in a bed' which we met in the *English Dialect Dictionary* (Fig. 4).

Fig. 4. The Doke in Eastry, Kent.

In Bodiam parish in Sussex there is a field called Dokes Field (at NGR TQ 782257) with a very pronounced 'U'-shaped dry valley right down the middle. It was formerly divided into two parts, recorded as *The Farther Doke*, *The Doke Next South Hill* in 1730 and *Inner Dokes Field*, *Outer Dokes Field* in 1839, and it appears to be another example of our 'linear depression' term (see Fig. 5).[34] There is further scope for field-work in Leicestershire, where Doak Close in Gumley parish must be connected with the earlier-recorded field-names *banland doake* (1674), *Freemans doake* (1703), and *the Open Doke* (1707) (EPNS Le **4**, pp. 89–

[32] Eastry Tithe Award of 1839 (Public Record Office [National Archives] IR/29/17/120), plots 42 and 43; plots 44a, 45 and 46.

[33] A. Hussey, 'Eastry wills', *Archaeologia Cantiana* 39 (1927), 77–90 (p. 81), and 40 (1928), 35–47 (p. 45).

[34] 'A MAPP of a farm of William Tempest Esquire called the Courtlodge in the Parish of Bodiam and County of SUSSEX Mary Walker widdow tenant' by Robert Wraight of Cranbrook, dated 1730 (East Sussex Record Office AMS 6454/6/1); Bodiam Tithe Award of 1839 (East Sussex Record Office TD/E 99), plots 67 and 69.

92).

Fig. 5. Dokes Field in Bodiam, Sussex

Ideally, studies of minor names and Gelling's work on major names will need also to be integrated with the work of Peter Kitson on Anglo-Saxon charter boundaries, which is very much informed by map-work and by careful statistical, distributional, and dialectal analysis.[35] The charter-boundary material is for the most part highly detailed and, when the course of a survey is correctly pinpointed, one great advantage is that it usually permits the land-form referred to by any given boundary point to be identified precisely. There will always be occasions when a judgement needs to be made about which nearby feature is the referent, but the problem is minimal compared to the same task when studying the names of 'major' settlements and parishes. It is clear that there is many a topographical term which behaves consistently across the place-name and charter corpora, but equally there are some which present as yet unresolved mismatches. To some extent, VEPN acts as a unifying repository, digesting work on major, minor, and charter-boundary names (see, for instance, the entries *brōc*, *burna*, *clif*, and *cnoll*), and aiming to achieve a keener and more systematic awareness of details of local topography, dialect, and statistical significance than did Smith's *Elements*.

Onomastic context may help to shed light on the etymology of topographical terms of uncertain derivation, and also inform our understanding of such vocabulary when it appears in medieval literature, as demonstrated by Thorlac Turville-Petre's analysis of the word 'road',

[35] P. Kitson, *A Guide to Anglo-Saxon Charter Boundaries* (Nottingham: English Place-Name Society, forthcoming); Kitson, 'Quantifying qualifiers in Anglo-Saxon charter boundaries', *Folia Linguistica Historica* 14 (1993), 29–82; Kitson, 'The nature of Old English dialect distributions, mainly as exhibited in charter boundaries', in J. Fisiak (ed.), *Medieval Dialectology* (Berlin and New York: Mouton de Gruyter, 1995), pp. 43–135.

which takes as a starting point the investigations by Kitson and Gelling into OE *rodu* 'linear clearing' in charter-bounds and place-names respectively, and applies their findings to a crux in the Middle English poem *Patience*.[36] Gelling herself makes a useful excursion into literary territory, clarifying some of the relatively obscure diction of the Anglo-Saxon epic *Beowulf*.[37] By applying her precise fieldwork-deduced definitions of three topographical terms to their occurrences in the poem, she elicits the menacing overtones which would once have been conveyed by the poet's choice of *hlið* 'concave hill-slope, hill with a recess or hollow' (not simply 'slope', as it is usually translated), *hop* 'remote, secret place' (not 'valley' or 'lair'), and *ge-lād* 'hazardous water-crossing' (not simply 'path, track' or 'passage across water', but something decidedly treacherous and unpredictable).

Before concluding, I must avoid giving the impression that everything in the realm of 'major' topographical terminology is now done, dusted, decoded, and resolved. Various questions remain. When Gelling justifiably claimed in 1998 that '[t]he naming system which has been deciphered by our field-work has been found valid in most of England', she added: 'I shall not attempt to deal with the historical, linguistic and philosophical questions raised by the fact that with few exceptions this vocabulary is used in the same way from Kent and Dorset to Northumberland and Westmorland'.[38] Two years later, in *The Landscape of Place-Names*, while remaining 'reluctant to pronounce upon' the problem of how such a system could arise, she does begin to offer some suggestions, pointing to the remarkably varied nature (on a compact scale) of the English landscape, which immigrants from northern Europe, employing shared vocabulary, may have dealt with in the same way 'when faced with the same visual challenges in Kent and Northumberland'.[39] Kitson, in a paper which he presents as 'a fleshing out of implications of something important' in Gelling's work, is the first to respond to the problem, noting that the interdialectal uniformity which she finds in topographic elements as used in place-names seems not to be mirrored in Old English usage at large.[40] He asks whether, for some

[36] T. Turville-Petre, 'The etymology of *road*', *Notes and Queries* 55:4 (2008), 405–06.

[37] M. Gelling, 'The landscape of *Beowulf*', *Anglo-Saxon England* 31 (2002), 7–11.

[38] Gelling, 'Place-names and landscape', pp. 76–77.

[39] Gelling and Cole, *Landscape of Place-Names*, p. xv.

[40] P. Kitson, 'Fog on the Barrow-Downs?', in Padel and Parsons (eds), *Commodity of*

components in Gelling's country-wide system, 'a narrow place-name meaning was primary or secondary, i.e. whether it was the lexical meaning of the word when the names originated, broader literary senses being loose usage, or whether the lexical meaning was the broad one and the narrow place-name sense is due to a process of selection after the names had been coined'. He argues that the latter situation is more likely than the former in a number of cases, such as that of OE *beorg* ('an eminence with a continuously rounded profile' in the Gelling and Cole toponymicon), a reflex of Common Germanic **bergaz* 'mountain' which, in Kitson's view, retained its position as the general word for a hill or eminence in early Old English, only secondarily correlating during the Old English period with the rounded profiles which English terrain offers in abundance.[41] Not the immediate response of immigrants from northern Europe, then, but a process evolving over many succeeding generations.

A second notion which Gelling cautiously airs, in partial answer to those 'historical, linguistic and philosophical questions' posed by the surprisingly widespread uniformity of terminology, is that of 'the Anglo-Saxon traveller'.[42] This personification is tied in with the discovery that '[s]ome landform terms show a more than accidental relationship to known ancient routes', Gelling and Cole's somewhat awkward position being that '[t]ravellers' perceptions would probably not initiate a naming system, but they could have played a major part in its development and stabilisation'.[43] Once more it is only Kitson who has responded in print, and his concern is again chronological: if the perceptions of travellers did indeed play a part in establishing a country-wide system of place-names, 'that can only have been after the warlike chaos of the *adventus Saxonum* had subsided, and something like country-wide conquest had been attained'.[44]

Answers to philosophical questions regarding the motivation behind ancient name-bestowal might be near impossible to come by, but if we assume that everyone agrees that an Anglo-Saxon traveller is unlikely to be responsible for coining the settlement-names along his route himself, it

Good Names, pp. 382–94 (p. 393).

[41] Kitson, 'Fog on the Barrow-Downs?', pp. 383 and 386–87.

[42] The chief ideas behind the concept, and some useful distribution maps, are conveniently to be found in Cole, 'The Anglo-Saxon traveller', *Nomina* 17 (1994), 7–18.

[43] Gelling and Cole, *Landscape of Place-Names*, p. xvi.

[44] Kitson, 'Fog on the Barrow-Downs?', p. 392.

is necessary to wonder who the well-organized local folk might be, across the land, who have apparently done so much onomastically to facilitate his wanderings, or to wonder whether such a name-system could or would be imposed by a central authority. Or perhaps to wonder whether, given a sizeable but restricted register-specific vocabulary to work with (which in any historical period will inevitably include a ready-made cliché-rich name-stock), people in district after district simply name their surroundings with, on the whole, relatively little imagination or originality, so that when one steps back many components of the pattern can be seen to repeat and repeat, with no input (either stabilizing or disruptive) from travellers required. There is endless scope for musing, but it is easy to sympathize with Gelling's reluctance to do so.

Further investigation of topographical naming practices is required in the parts of England where Gelling and Cole acknowledge that the precision evident elsewhere fizzles out. Devon is one such area: 'The naming system [...] does not work so well in Devon, and this combines with other evidence to indicate that the full glory of the topographical vocabulary belongs to the earliest centuries of Old English speech', and '[t]he general distinction between "major" and "minor" names is less relevant in Devon than elsewhere'.[45] North-west Derbyshire is another: 'In the northern tip of Derbyshire and regions north of that it seems necessary to postulate other meanings [for OE *ēg* 'island'] such as "hill jutting into flat land" and "patch of good land in moor".'[46] As there are good reasons to believe that the Anglo-Saxon takeover in Derbyshire, as in Devon, was relatively late, we could ascribe to the same chronological considerations any lack of correspondence between landscape terminology here and the widespread norms. It certainly seems clear that there is a lack of precision in terms for 'valley' in Devon, where OE *cumb* greatly predominates and is applied fairly indiscriminately to valleys of various shapes, at the expense of other terms such as *denu* and *slæd*, though with a compensatory increase in the frequency of landform-describing qualifiers in compound place-names where *cumb* is the generic.[47] There is nothing quite so clear-cut in Derbyshire, but it is noticeable that the basic hill-terms, especially OE *dūn* and *beorg* which

[45] Gelling, 'Place-names and landscape', pp. 76–77; Gelling and Cole, *Landscape of Place-Names*, pp. 45–46.

[46] Gelling and Cole, *Landscape of Place-Names*, p. 37 (similarly p. 39).

[47] Gelling and Cole, *Landscape of Place-Names*, p. 106.

Gelling and Cole identify as contrasting with each other over so much of England, operate differently here. The locations of those 'major' names in the north-west of the county which contain *dūn* suit the general pattern well enough: 'upland expanse' is an appropriate description at Chelmorton, Hartington, Great and Little Longstone, and Nether and Over Haddon (along with adjacent Sheldon, which is probably named from the same feature as the Haddons), although these upland expanses are not so much flat-topped as distinctly undulating, except at Sheldon where the striking flatness is reflected in the qualifying element OE *scelf* 'shelf' (see Fig. 6).[48]

Fig. 6. Sheldon, Derbyshire

But not a single 'major' name in Derbyshire contains *beorg* ('rounded hill' in Gelling's terms), and it is rare in 'minor' names too. I suspect the chief contrast in hill-type which merits mentioning in this landscape is not so much 'large and flattish' (*dūn*) versus 'small and roundish' (*beorg*) but rather 'green and usable, i.e. for ploughing or pasture' (*dūn*) versus 'rocky and unusable' (OE *ecg* 'edge', *clif* 'cliff', *torr* 'rocky outcrop', *clūd* 'mass of rock', and so on). The terminology is not less precise than elsewhere, it is just precise in a different way. Chronological and toponymic considerations go hand in hand in explaining this difference: the terrain is difficult, the Anglo-Saxon settlement of the area is accordingly late, and the topographical vocabulary required to name and distinguish settlements has to function in these particular circumstances.

A further concern or two before concluding. There is a large, grey, overlapping area between what might be strictly called landscape terminology and the terminology of farming practices, animal husbandry, and various forms of land exploitation. It is not always clear (to me, at least) where the boundary between the two broad, long-established classes known as 'topographical names' and 'habitative names' should be drawn. Gelling believes that some topographical terms convey inherent

[48] EPNS Db, pp. 74, 106–07, 138–39, 141, 164, 364–65, 368, and 370–71.

aspects of a site's settlement potential (thus a *denu*, a long meandering valley, offers greater opportunities for expansion of settlement and for attracting passing trade than does a *cumb*, a squat dead-end valley). The useful concept of 'quasi-habitative' topographical names drifts uneasily into the grey area, as do countless terms for routes of communication and structures of industrial, religious, social, or agricultural use (part of the problem being simply that 'habitative names', if taken at face value, is too narrow and exclusive a classification). Establishing the remit of this chapter is problematic, and it could justifiably be defined in a variety of ways, all of them admittedly more expansive than the rather limited hills-and-valleys material which I have concentrated on here while ignoring Gelling and Cole's impressive body of work on woods, clearings, rivers, roads, marshland, ploughland, and pasture. One trap which the investigator of landscape terminology must not fall into is to expect to answer topographical questions solely at the level of physical surface geography. An awareness of the historic settlement process behind the topography is vital: the toponymist needs to learn to view the landscape with the eyes of a landscape historian, perhaps especially an agricultural historian. The point made by Sedgefield in 1924 with which we began ('in many cases a knowledge of configuration will be of great help') would not really have got him very far if he were trying to work out just what an OE *halh* was by studying the austere physical geography of contour lines. The usual gloss is 'nook', and it has been ascertained that in place-names the term seems sometimes to refer to a physical depression (an irregularly-shaped hollow), sometimes to land between rivers (or in a river-bend), sometimes to slightly raised ground in marsh (the lowest eminence on which settlement is possible), and sometimes to an administrative oddity (such as an angle or pan-handle in a parish boundary).[49] A baffling array, all of which might be revealed by very careful map-work. But what the relevant agrarian, settlement or woodland factors behind the names have in common is arguably the single concept of a subsidiary, relatively minor, slightly obscure or hidden settlement. Any of the various types of 'nook', whether in a wooded valley or a common or a marsh, is a *halh* because, in terms of historic settlement

[49] Gelling, *Place-Names in the Landscape*, pp. 100–11; Gelling and Cole, *Landscape of Place-Names*, pp. 123–33; P. V. Stiles, 'Old English *halh*, "slightly raised ground isolated by marsh"', in A. R. Rumble and A. D. Mills (eds), *Names, Places and People: An Onomastic Miscellany in Memory of John McNeal Dodgson* (Stamford: Shaun Tyas, 1997), pp. 330–44.

processes, it is out of the way.

The study of landscape terminology in English place-names has clearly advanced considerably since 1924, and in particular since 1952 when, as mentioned above, Gelling was on the trail but as yet found it 'difficult to see why so many names in Bedfordshire and Huntingdonshire end in *-hoe*, *-oe*, etc., representing *hōh*, one of the many Old English words for a hill'. By 1984, she had not only done the preliminary sorting and quantifying of major-name material and the map-work necessary to establish a definition decidedly sharper than 'hill', she had also begun to envisage the settlement and colonization conditions under which names containing *hōh* 'heel' might have been coined (taking into account the observations of the regional historian Everitt).[50] And by 2000 she and Cole had undertaken sufficient field-work to determine a specialized, anatomically-precise use of the element for 'ridges which rise to a point and have a concave end' (contrasting with the 'level ridges with convex shoulders' for which *ofer* and *ōra* are used) alongside a looser 'spur of land' application, supporting their findings with a page of illustrations.[51] The way forward must be to build on Gelling's successes by meticulously extending these approaches, with due chronological awareness, to minor names and to ever more place-name elements.[52]

[50] Gelling, *Place-Names in the Landscape*, pp. 167–69; A. Everitt, 'Place-names and *pays*: the Kentish evidence', *Nomina* 3 (1979), 95–112.

[51] Gelling and Cole, *Landscape of Place-Names*, pp. 186–90, explaining *hōh* in terms of human anatomy ('the shape is in fact that of the foot of a person lying face down, with the highest point for the heel and the concavity for the instep'). For a compatible development of this idea in terms of equine anatomy ('the external profile of the horse's upper hind leg down to the calcaneus bone of the ankle or hock-joint') see R. Coates, 'Heel your ho, boys....', *Locus Focus: Forum of the Sussex Place-Names Net* 4:1 (2000), 16.

[52] Thanks go to Casper Johnson and Pam Combes for alerting me to Dokes Field in Bodiam, to Barrie Cox for alerting me to the field-names in Gumley, and to Jayne Carroll for ensuring that there was a little more to this paper than four field-names. I am also grateful to Stephen McKibbin for improving the quality of the photographs.

7

Settlement archaeology and place-names

Richard Jones

When O. G .S. Crawford wrote his contribution to the *Introduction to the Survey of English Place-Names* little was known about the origins and development of early medieval rural settlements.[1] Indeed many places whose names were recorded in early written sources but whose location was uncertain—Maurice Beresford's evocative 'lost villages'—still awaited identification on the ground.[2] In fact Crawford himself played an important role in their discovery. He is credited with taking the first aerial photograph of a deserted village even though he initially believed he was recording a Roman camp before correctly identifying the cropmarks as the house platforms and streets of Gainsthorpe (Li).[3] And it was under his direction that the Ordnance Survey began to depict hachure plans of upstanding earthworks other than hillforts and barrows of the prehistoric period on their maps, providing us with some of the first accurate surveys of a great number of manorial complexes, moated sites, fishponds and other medieval settlement remains that survive across the English landscape. But Crawford's aerial sorties and cartographic innovations came after Mawer and Stenton's invitation to consider the relationship between place-names and archaeology: Gainsthorpe was captured on film in 1925, Ordnance Survey conventions changed in the 1930s.

Moreover, and arguably more significantly, Crawford's chapter also predated the advent of medieval archaeology as a recognized scholarly sub-discipline. Archaeology in the 1920s was essentially that which had been established by the late nineteenth century: an enquiry squarely focused on the material evidence of the prehistoric and Roman periods.

[1] O. G. S. Crawford, 'Place-names and archaeology', in A. Mawer and F. M. Stenton (eds), *Introduction to the Survey of English Place-Names*, English Place-Name Society 1.i (Cambridge: Cambridge University Press, 1924), pp. 143–64.

[2] M. Beresford, *Lost Villages of England* (London: Lutterworth Press, 1954).

[3] O. G. S. Crawford, 'Air photograph of Gainsthorpe, Lincolnshire', *Antiquaries Journal* 5 (1925), 432–33.

Few medieval-period sites had been well studied and even where they had these tended to be prominent landmarks of high status such as monasteries and castles.[4] More mundane settlements in the English landscape—the villages, hamlets, and farmsteads which represented, of course, the great majority of places bearing names coined in the medieval period—still remained to be investigated. Mid-nineteenth-century excavations on the deserted village of Woodbury (O) were thus unusual, and even here its excavators were dismissive of their findings, suggesting that they offered little interpretative assistance in reconstructing the life of the place or its occupants.[5] Unusual too were plans of settlement earthworks such as those recorded at Bingham (Nt) in the first decade of the twentieth century.[6]

Thus, for lack of empirical data, sensible discussion of the possible relationship between place-names and settlements with probable early medieval origins was near impossible in 1924. And this lacuna certainly helps to explain what might now appear to be the rather idiosyncratic approach that Crawford took to his subject. For although he derived much information from Anglo-Saxon charters and their appended boundary clauses—indeed more space was devoted to the discussion of the minor names that these contained than the major names recorded in Domesday Book and other sources—Crawford was not concerned with relating these to the actual landscape and settlements which they described. Instead, and perhaps not unsurprisingly, he was far more interested in linking the onomastic evidence that early medieval written sources offered with surviving prehistoric and Roman archaeology, the two periods where significant advances in understanding had already been made, and the very material he was then trying to chart systematically on what would become the Ordnance Survey maps of prehistoric and Roman Britain.[7] Consequently, his introductory chapter focused on two principal

[4] C. Gerrard, *Medieval Archaeology: Understanding Traditions and Contemporary Approaches* (London and New York: Routledge, 2003), pp. 59–65.

[5] J. Wilson, 'Antiquities found at Woodperry', *Archaeological Journal* 3 (1846), 116–28.

[6] A. H. Allcroft, *Earthwork of England* (London: Macmillan, 1908), pp. 550–53.

[7] Throughout the 1920s Crawford was publishing papers on prehistoric remains for the Ordnance Survey, e.g. *Notes on Archaeological Information Incorporated in the Ordnance Survey Maps, Part 1: Long Barrows and Stone Circles*, OS Professional Paper 6 (London: HMSO, 1922); *Notes on Archaeological Information Incorporated in the Ordnance Survey Maps, Part 2: Long Barrows and Megaliths*, OS Professional Paper 8 (London: HMSO, 1924).

categories of names: those referring to enclosures (*ceaster*, castle, *stodfald, tun-steall*, *burh*, and *briga*) where associations with hillforts, Roman military camps and walled towns could be most easily established; and those associated with mounds (heathen 'burials', *beorh*, *hlaw*, *haugr*, tump, *aad*, ball, butt, and moot),[8] allowing connections to be made between names and prominent prehistoric funerary monuments. Further to these Crawford offered shorter observations on a whole range of associated subjects: the place-name element *flōr* and its connection, when found in combination with *fāg* 'variegated', to mosaic pavements; 'harbour' names; the relationship between *sēað*-names and spring ponds found in proximity to Roman sites and 'Celtic' villages; and an extended section devoted to names alluding to devils and giants.

What catches the eye when looking back at this early attempt to bring material and linguistic evidence together is the absence of any meaningful discussion of the thousands of English rural settlements whose names would be so thoroughly studied in the county survey volumes of the English Place-Name Society that followed the *Introduction*. Crawford's contribution, then, was a product of its time; a work of synthesis driven by his own particular interests and the more general archaeological concerns then current. At first sight it would appear to have been superseded and rendered redundant by subsequent scholarship, to remain a curio but nothing more. However, in one respect, as we shall see, Crawford's treatment of his material precociously anticipated archaeological engagements with place-names that have evolved in the last few years.

Place-names and archaeology (1925–1990)

Crawford concluded his chapter by identifying how and where archaeological studies might bring further clarification for the study of place-names. This message was clearly heard by the onomasts, for whom consideration of the archaeological record quickly became standard practice. By contrast, Crawford's observations seem to have had little impact on the archaeological community. Perhaps this was because nearly a quarter of a century would elapse before archaeologists had their medieval epiphany; perhaps because when they did, their attention was drawn to the very places Crawford had not discussed – villages and

[8] The element-forms are Crawford's; 'Place-names and archaeology', p. 145.

hamlets not castles and towns; and perhaps because initial interest focused on the later medieval experience of these places, in particular their route to desertion, a subject upon which place-names seemed to offer little extra information. Whatever the explanation, the effect was profound. Because place-names found no place in the constitution of the new medieval archaeology, the two subjects—place-name studies on the one hand, archaeology on the other—were destined to develop largely independently during the middle decades of the twentieth century.[9]

Calls from the late 1950s for fuller integration of historical, archaeological and place-name evidence to aid early medieval settlement studies were thus timely.[10] Important studies which signalled what could be achieved by adopting such a multidisciplinary approach began to appear in the late 60s, notably two articles in successive issues of *Medieval Archaeology*, first John Dodgson's ground-breaking study of *-ingas*-names followed by Margaret Gelling's exploration of the compound *wīchām*.[11] But by the mid-70s tensions were beginning to emerge. The situation was exacerbated when the place-name Mucking (Ess), previously considered to belong to the *-ingas* folk-name group,[12] and where recent excavation had revealed an important early Anglo-Saxon settlement of the very sort that might be expected to be associated with such a place-name formation, was questioned and where it was instead proposed that it belonged to a different, toponymic group *-ing* referring to a stream, without implications of an early date.[13] As etymologies of this kind were queried, so an atmosphere of mutual distrust developed: archaeologists began to doubt the fundamental utility

[9] Looking back with hindsight, Chris Gerrard was certainly correct when he stated that place-name analysis would become a 'critical foundation stone for the future study of medieval settlement'; it is simply that this took some time to realize (Gerrard, *Medieval Archaeology*, p. 79).

[10] See for example W. G. Hoskins, *Local History in England* (London: Longmans, 1959); F. T. Wainwright, *Archaeology and Place-Names and History: An Essay on Problems of Co-ordination* (London: Routledge, 1962).

[11] J. M. Dodgson, 'The significance of the distribution of the English place-name in *-ingas*, *-inga-* in south-east England', *Medieval Archaeology* 10 (1966), 1–29; M. Gelling, 'English place-names derived from the compound *wīchām*', *Medieval Archaeology* 11 (1967), 87–104. Gelling revisited this compound together with other archaeologically significant place-name elements in 'Latin loan-words in Old English place-names', *Anglo-Saxon England* 6 (1977), 1–13.

[12] P. H. Reaney, *The Place-Names of Essex* (Cambridge: Cambridge University Press, 1935), p. 163.

[13] M. Gelling, 'The place-names of the Mucking area', *Panorama* 19 (1975), 7–20.

of place-names to inform, for instance, on questions of major historical importance such as the nature and scale of early Anglo-Saxon settlement when place-name scholars appeared to be so unsure of what their material meant; whilst place-name scholars were keen both to counter what they perceived to be the mishandling of philological material by non-linguists, and to work beyond what they saw as limiting historical and archaeological paradigms.[14]

Inevitably it was Margaret Gelling, herself a major protagonist in this fierce debate, who looked to establish order and chart a way forward. It is impossible to underestimate the impact of her 1978 publication *Signposts to the Past* on the archaeological community.[15] While the book showed with great clarity how place-names might be used to guide archaeological investigation and to inform interpretation—and thus encouraged the sharing of ideas across disciplinary boundaries—a second message continued to warn archaeologists of the inherent dangers that place-name analysis presented for the unwary and imprudent. Because of their complexities, Gelling argued, place-names should be treated with care. Establishing etymologies was a task only competent linguists and philologists should undertake. If misused by non-specialists 'catastrophic misunderstandings' and 'embarrassment' would follow.[16] In these carefully chosen words and phrases, and whether by design or as an unfortunate consequence, the effect of *Signposts* on the next generation of archaeologists seems to have been simply to frighten many away from using place-names at all.

For the few brave or foolhardy archaeologists who did continue to

[14] A useful account of the uncomfortable relations between archaeology and place-name scholarship is provided by S. Draper, 'Language and the Anglo-Saxon landscape: towards an archaeological interpretation of place-names in Wiltshire', in N. J. Higham and M. J. Ryan (eds), *Place-Names, Language and the Anglo-Saxon Landscape* (Woodbridge: Boydell, 2011), pp. 85–104 (pp. 85–88).

[15] M. Gelling, *Signposts to the Past* (London: Dent, 1978).

[16] Gelling would return to this theme later when her disapproval of the misuse of place-name evidence was not limited to archaeologists. She was particularly scathing, for instance, of the historical ecologist Oliver Rackham who had dared to suggest in his book *The History of the Countryside* (1986) that there was a 'tradition among place-name scholars of not admitting ignorance, clutching at straws, and reading into place-names more than they say'. Gelling's response was forthright: 'The later pages of *The History of the Countryside* are copiously sprinkled with wrong etymologies and false conclusions based on them'; M. Gelling, 'The historical importance of English place-names', in J.-C. Boulanger (ed.), *Proceedings of the XVth International Congress of Onomastic Sciences* (Quebec: Université de Laval Press, 1990), pp. 85–104, (p. 100, n. 2).

work with place-names post-*Signposts*, the book appears to have influenced the way they approached place-name evidence in more subtle and rarely acknowledged ways. They took from its title the idea that the primary function of a place-name was to point them towards a particular place in the landscape where they might find something of interest. Archaeologists got into the habit of using names, particularly minor names, as a means to an end; a way of locating lost settlements, for instance, using field-names such as *dunstall* and *tunstall*, or furlong-names in -*worð* or -*wīc*. Place-names simply came to be seen as tools to aid initial archaeological prospection. Viewed thus, once a site has been found the place-name was considered to have largely fulfilled its role. Thereafter archaeological evidence took precedence. The field-names of Shapwick (So), the focus of intensive fieldwork across the 1990s, provide a salient case in point.[17] The collection of this material was exhaustive and proved critical to the identification of elements of the pre-village settlement pattern which were subsequently excavated. Beyond this, however, the rich description of the landscape and its people which might equally have been read off these field-names was largely ignored in the account of the development of the parish. And when published, the field-name corpus was allowed to languish without further analysis in an appendix to the main report.[18] Treatment of this kind, however, is nothing unusual. The place- and furlong-names of Raunds (Nth), where extensive field survey and excavation were undertaken from 1985 to 1994, remain under-analysed in the final report of this major landscape research project or its sister publications.[19] Some use was made of major place-names in the reconstruction of the developing landscape of Whittlewood Forest, the subject of intensive investigation from 2000 to 2005, but the minor names remained largely unutilized despite their collection.[20] This kind of

[17] C. Gerrard with M. Aston, *The Shapwick Project, Somerset: A Rural Landscape Explored* ([London]: Society for Medieval Archaeology, 2007).

[18] M. Costen, 'The field names of Shapwick', in Gerrard with Aston, *The Shapwick Project*, pp. 1078–83.

[19] D. N. Hall, 'The open fields of Raunds and its townships', in S. Parry, *Raunds Area Survey: An Archaeological Survey of the Landscape of Raunds, Northamptonshire, 1985–94* (Oxford: Oxbow, 2006), pp. 116–26; D. N. Hall, R. Harding, and C. Putt, *Raunds: Picturing the Past* (Raunds: March, 1988), pp. 312–15.

[20] R. Jones and M. Page, *Medieval Villages in an English Landscape: Beginnings and Ends* (Macclesfield: Windgather, 2006). The place-names of Whittlewood were the subject of a PhD undertaken at the same time as the field project and archival research. See E. Forward, 'Place-Names of the Whittlewood Area', unpublished PhD thesis

treatment (or lack thereof) is symptomatic of a second, and again perhaps inadvertent, legacy of *Signposts*, which encouraged archaeologists to use place-names in narrowly proscribed ways. A tradition developed following Gelling that saw place-names solely as her eponymous 'signposts' guiding investigators elsewhere, rather than as village signs that might say something about the settlements and communities where particular place-names were coined, applied, and used. The rather perfunctory way in which landscape archaeologists have come to view and use place-names is perhaps summed up best in the final report on the excavations and field survey at Yarnton (O):

> All three settlements within the study area have Old English *tun* suffixes, 'enclosed piece of ground, homestead, village' (Gelling 1954, 469). Such names are sparse in documents predating the early 8th century, but become common thereafter (Cox 1999, 225). Yarnton comes from a personal name, Earda, 'Earda's farm'. Cassington and Worton both have prefixes describing vegetation in those localities '*tun* where the cress grows' and 'herb or vegetable enclosure' (Gelling 1954, 252–3). There are records of some early field names in these parishes, for example *Francwordy* near to Purwell Farm, but the majority of known names are of post-enclosure date. *Where they shed light on land use they are discussed below*. [my italics][21]

Archaeology and place-name study in the early twenty-first century

Despite appearances, the last decade has seen more harmonious relations begin to develop between place-name scholars and medieval archaeologists. Interdisciplinary dialogue has been encouraged by a number of important multidisciplinary conferences and workshops whose proceedings have just begun to appear in press.[22] But this is not to underestimate the gulf which still divides these two disciplines. It is

(University of Nottingham, 2007). Such compartmentalization of efforts is symptomatic of the problems of achieving full integration of materials and approaches even within research frameworks which claim, and indeed have the opportunity to realize, true interdisciplinarity.

[21] G. Hey, *Yarnton: Saxon and Medieval Settlement and Landscape* (Oxford: Oxford Archaeology, 2004), p. 23.

[22] For example, N. J. Higham and M. J. Ryan (eds), *The Landscape Archaeology of Anglo-Saxon England* (Woodbridge: Boydell, 2010); Higham and Ryan (eds), *Place-Names, Language and the Anglo-Saxon Landscape*; R. Jones and S. Semple (eds), *Sense of Place in Anglo-Saxon England* (Donington: Shaun Tyas, 2012).

surely telling, for example, that in a recent retrospective assessment of the first fifty years of the activities and achievements of the Society for Medieval Archaeology written by acknowledged leaders in this academic field, place-names do not even warrant a mention in the index.[23] Reassuringly, but perhaps dispiritingly sparingly, place-name evidence is at least drawn upon by a minority of contributors to a recent volume examining the history of, and prospects for, the study of medieval rural settlement in British and Irish perspective.[24] Yet the absence of any discussion of place-names in the greater majority of the regional and national reviews that this book contains continues to remind us that landscape history, landscape archaeology, and historical geography are still divided between those practitioners who foreground place-name material and those for whom it remains of background significance.[25]

While it is easy to dwell on failure, examples of successful integration of onomastic and material evidence deserve to be highlighted. Sarah Semple's work on Anglo-Saxon responses to prehistoric burial mounds in the early medieval landscape, *hearg*-named places and their long-term significance as foci for ritual or religious practice from the prehistoric period onwards, and other aspects of the numinous landscape epitomize new archaeological approaches to place-name evidence.[26] Sam Turner's studies of early settlement and ecclesiastical provision in the south-west take full account of both the landscape and the names that it contains.[27]

[23] R. Gilchrist and A. Reynolds (eds), *Reflections: 50 Years of Medieval Archaeology* (London: Maney, 2009).

[24] N. Christie and P. Stamper (eds), *Medieval Rural Settlement: Britain and Ireland, AD 800–1600* (Oxford: Windgather, 2011).

[25] Place-names are only mentioned in reference to the study of medieval rural settlements in central southern England (David Hinton), south-west England (Sam Turner and Rob Wilson-North), and the Midlands (Richard Jones and Carenza Lewis) leaving the onomastic evidence from East Anglia, northern England, Wales, Scotland, and Ireland entirely ignored.

[26] S. Semple, 'A fear of the past: the place of the prehistoric burial mound in the ideology of middle and later Anglo-Saxon England', *World Archaeology* 30:1 (1998), 109–26; 'Defining the OE *hearg*: a preliminary archaeological and topographic examination of *hearg* place-names and their hinterlands', *Early Medieval Europe* 15:4 (2007), 364–85; 'In the open air', in M. Carver, A. Sanmark, and S. Semple (eds), *Signals of Belief in Early England: Anglo-Saxon Paganism Revisited* (Oxford: Oxbow, 2010), pp. 21–48.

[27] S. C. Turner 'Making a Christian landscape: early medieval Cornwall', in M. Carver (ed.), *The Cross Goes North: Processes of Conversion in Northern Europe, AD 300–1300* (Woodbridge: York Medieval Press, 2003), pp. 171–94; 'The Christian landscape: churches, chapels and crosses', in S. C. Turner (ed.), *Medieval Devon and Cornwall: Shaping an Ancient Countryside* (Macclesfield: Windgather, 2006), pp. 24–43.

Simon Draper's discussion of the place-name elements *burh*, *wīc* and *walh* all pay special attention to the morphology of the settlements to which these names are attached, and archaeological finds made within them.[28] Interdisciplinary collaborations have also flourished. Paul Cullen, Richard Jones and David Parsons's examination of the place-name element *thorp/throp* from linguistic, archaeological and landscape perspectives provides a methodological template for the investigation of individual name groups that others might follow.[29] Foremost among on-going examples of collaboration that are beginning to reveal exciting results are Andrew Reynolds's *Landscapes of Governance* project, where place-names and archaeology have been united to explore meeting places, execution sites, and other territorial and judicial/administrative arrangements in the early medieval countryside; and his *Beyond the Burghal Hidage: Anglo-Saxon Civil Defence in the Viking Age*, where interdisciplinary approaches are leading to important discoveries concerning the organization of integrated defensive networks linking principal strongholds with lookout posts and beacon sites and their relationship with road networks and river crossings.[30] Outside these two major projects, the work of their two principal researchers, John Baker and Stuart Brookes, each centred on a different part of the south-east,

[28] S. Draper, 'Old English *wic* and *walh*: Britons and Saxons in post-Roman Wiltshire', *Landscape History* 24 (2003), 29–43; *Landscape, Settlement and Society in Roman and Early Medieval Wiltshire*, British Archaeological Reports, British Series, 419 (Oxford: Archaeopress, 2006); 'The significance of OE *burh* in Anglo-Saxon England', *Anglo-Saxon Studies in Archaeology and History* 15 (2008), 240–53; '*Burh* place-names in Anglo-Saxon England', *Journal of the English Place-Name Society* 41 (2010), 103–17; '*Burh* enclosures in Anglo-Saxon settlements: case-studies in Wiltshire', in Jones and Semple (eds), *Sense of Place*, pp. 334–51.

[29] P. Cullen, R. Jones and D. N. Parsons, *Thorps in a Changing Landscape* (Hatfield: University of Hertfordshire Press, 2011).

[30] <www.ucl.ac.uk/archaeology/research/projects/assembly>; J. Baker, S. Brookes and A. Reynolds, 'Landscapes of governance: assembly sites in England, fifth–eleventh century', *Post-Classical Archaeology* 1 (2011), 499–502; Baker, Brookes, Reynolds, 'The law of the land: finding early medieval assembly sites', *British Archaeology* 120 (2011), 46–49. And <www.ucl.ac.uk/archaeology/research/projects/burghalhidage>; J. Baker and S. Brookes, *Beyond the Burghal Hidage: Anglo-Saxon Civil Defence in the Viking Age* (Leiden: Brill, 2013); J. Baker, S. Brookes and A. Reynolds (eds), *Landscapes of Defence in Early Medieval Europe* (Turnhout: Brepols, 2013); J. Baker and S. Brookes, 'From frontier to border: the evolution of northern West Saxon territorial delineation in the ninth and tenth centuries', *Anglo-Saxon Studies in Archaeology and History* 17 (2011), 104–19; J. Baker, 'Warriors and watchmen: place-names and Anglo-Saxon civil defence', *Medieval Archaeology* 55 (2011), 258–67. Both projects teamed UCL archaeologists with place-name scholars from Nottingham's Institute for Name-Studies.

showcases what can be achieved when different classes of evidence are brought together.[31] The sheer number of multidisciplinary studies now appearing bodes well for the future. Of those that have successfully used place-name evidence to enhance archaeological interpretation or that have used archaeology to improve understanding of naming practices we can note Mark Gardiner's examination of 'hythe' and other names associated with water transport;[32] Chris Dyer's study of names connected with the later medieval pottery industry;[33] Harold Fox's explorations of transhumance and dairying on Dartmoor (through the filter of the Old English place-name elements *smeoru*, *butere*, and *wīc*) and the Devon coastal settlement;[34] Andrew Fleming and Ros Faith's study of 'Worthy' place-names in Devon;[35] Andrew Reynolds and Sarah Semple's reassessment of the landscape around Compton Bassett (W),[36] Tania Dickinson's detailed assessment of Eastry (K),[37] and Richard Watson's reconsideration of Viking influence in Amounderness (La).[38] Meanwhile important new work continues to emerge from scholars working from historical geographical and landscape perspectives: Della Hooke's

[31] J. Baker, *Cultural Transition in the Chilterns and Essex Region, 350AD to 650AD* (Hatfield: University of Hertfordshire Press, 2006); J. Baker, 'Topographical place-names and the distribution of *tūn* and *hām* in the Chilterns and Essex region', *Anglo-Saxon Studies in Archaeology and History* 12 (2006), 50–62; S. Brookes, 'Population ecology and multiple estate formation: the evidence from eastern Kent', in N. J. Higham and M. J. Ryan (eds), *The Landscape Archaeology of Anglo-Saxon England* (Woodbridge: Boydell, 2010), pp. 65–82.

[32] M. Gardiner, 'Hythes, small ports and other landing places in later medieval England', in J. Blair (ed.), *Waterways and Canal-Building in Medieval England* (Oxford: Oxford University Press, 2007), pp. 85–109.

[33] C. Dyer, 'Place-names and pottery', in O. J. Padel and D. N. Parsons (eds), *A Commodity of Good Names: Essays in Honour of Margaret Gelling* (Donington: Shaun Tyas, 2008), pp. 44–54.

[34] H. S. A. Fox, 'Butter place-names and transhumance', in Padel and Parsons (eds), *A Commodity of Good Names*, pp. 352–64; H. S. A. Fox, 'Two Devon estuaries in the middle ages: fisheries, ports, fortifications and places of worship', *Landscapes* 8:1 (2007), 39–68.

[35] R. Faith, 'Worthys and enclosures', *Medieval Settlement Research Group Annual Report* 21 (2006), 9–14. Also J. English '*Worth*s in a landscape context', *Landscape History* 24 (2002), 45–52.

[36] A. Reynolds and S. Semple, 'Digging for names: archaeology and place-names in the Avebury Region', in Jones and Semple (eds), *Sense of Place*, pp. 76–100.

[37] T. Dickinson, 'The formation of a folk district in the kingdom of Kent and its early Anglo-Saxon archaeology', in Jones and Semple (eds), *Sense of Place*, pp. 147–67.

[38] R. Watson, 'Viking-age Amounderness: a reconsideration', in Higham and Ryan (eds), *Place-Names, Language and the Anglo-Saxon Landscape*, pp. 125–42.

extensive treatment of trees in the Anglo-Saxon countryside, for instance, Ann Cole's discussion of place-names associated with road networks and waterways, and Jill Bourne's study of Kingston-names.[39] Tom Pickles and John Blair's thought-provoking study of *Deantune* and Bishopstone (Sx), an exercise in contextualization for important recent excavations at the latter, offers an excellent example of how place-name material should be presented in archaeological reports.[40]

It is clear even from this selective list that these are exciting times for medieval archaeology and place-name studies. Collaborations are taking scholars in several directions, each throwing fresh light on a great range of aspects of medieval society, economy, and culture. In what follows discussion is limited to just two themes where advances have been made as a result of renewed dialogue between place-name scholars and medieval archaeologists. The first relates to an old question, the origin of the English village, a subject with a historiographical tradition stretching back more than a century; the second is a relatively new field of enquiry, how archaeology and place-names can be brought together to inform upon the more nebulous concept of sense of place as it manifested itself in the early medieval English countryside.

Archaeology, place-names and the origins of the English village

Arguably the most significant contribution made by medieval archaeology has been to provide a clearer picture of the chronology of, if not the processes lying behind, village creation. Before the 1960s there was little debate about their origins. It was generally held that villages had been established during the early post-Roman centuries by Anglo-Saxon settlers already familiar with these large communal centres. Villages in England were thus products of a thorough process of 'Germanization', which also brought with it changes in language and

[39] D. Hooke, *Trees in Anglo-Saxon England* (Woodbridge: Boydell, 2010); A. Cole, 'The place-name evidence for water transport in early medieval England', in Blair (ed.), *Waterways and Canal-Building*, pp. 55–84; A. Cole, 'The Anglo-Saxon traveller', *Nomina* 17 (1994), 7–18; A. Cole, '*Tūns* by the wayside', in Jones and Semple (eds), *Sense of Place*, pp. 243–59; J. Bourne, 'The place-name Kingston and its context', in Jones and Semple (eds), *Sense of Place*, pp. 260–83 (see also Bourne, 'The place-name Kingston', unpublished PhD thesis (University of Nottingham, 2012)).

[40] T. Pickles with J. Blair, '*Deantune* and Bishopstone: the estate and church under the Mercian kings and the South Saxon bishops', in G. Thomas (ed.), *The Later Anglo-Saxon Settlement at Bishopstone: a Downland Manor in the Making* (York: Council for British Archaeology, 2010), pp. 17–22.

material culture.[41] Supporting this claim was the place-name evidence: the dominance of Old English names in southern and eastern England, the 'land of villages'; and the greater survival of Brittonic names in the north and west, the 'land of hamlets'.[42] It was natural to suppose, then, that these hamlets represented the indigenous settlement archetype, forms that were able to survive in areas of late and less-dense Anglo-Saxon colonization, while it could be proposed that similar settlements had been erased and superseded by nucleated villages in those areas where Germanic peoples had settled early and in considerable numbers. Large and populous settlements implied joint enterprise, a notion that also found support in certain naming conventions, notably forms in *-ingas* relating to identifiable and discrete folk groupings. Coupled with this was the dominant idea that the introduction of the village had been accompanied by a new form of communal farming, the open fields. The onomastic and physical evidence thus seemed to point in only one direction: villages were the product of early Anglo-Saxon group settlement.

It was only as a result of two parallel developments in the 1960s that this version of events, and the inherent circularity of the evidence upon which it was based, began to be questioned seriously. The first was Joan Thirsk's re-assessment of the origins of common fields.[43] She suggested that these were the product of incremental development over long periods of time rather than systems that had been adopted at a particular moment in the forms they were later found. The Midland system represented its most mature form, and thus by implication Thirsk argued that it was in central England that communal agriculture had been first established. The less ordered field systems of East Anglia and the south east represented a less complete stage of development, systems whose origins must therefore come later than those seen in the Midlands.[44] These inferences and their implications had far reaching consequences. They opened up the

[41] For example, F. Seebohm, *The English Village Community*, 2nd edn (London: Longmans and Green, 1883); C. F. Fox, *The Personality of Britain: its Influence on Inhabitant and Invader in Prehistoric and Early Historic Times* (Cardiff: National Museum of Wales, 1932).

[42] F. M. Maitland, *Domesday Book and Beyond* (London: Collins, 1897, repr. 1960), pp. 38–39.

[43] J. Thirsk, 'The common fields', *Past and Present* 29 (1964), 3–29.

[44] For different forms of field system, see H. L. Gray, *English Field Systems* (Cambridge MA: Harvard University Press, 1915) and A. R. H. Baker and R. A. Butlin (eds), *Studies of Field Systems in the British Isles* (Cambridge: Cambridge University Press, 1973).

possibility of seeing village creation and the introduction of open-field farming as linked but separate processes; and they suggested that common agriculture did not begin in the easternmost areas most closely associated with the earliest phases of Anglo-Saxon settlement. Two years after Thirsk's article appeared, the claim to primacy of *-ingas* names was also being questioned. Dodgson argued that because such name-forms exhibited little spatial coincidence with known pre-Christian cemeteries, these names might actually belong to a secondary phase of settlement re-organization linked to the establishment of new Christian cemetery sites away from earlier pagan foci during the conversion period.[45]

It was the advent of landscape archaeology in the late 1970s, however, which ensured that the study of village origins was able to draw on solid empirical evidence for the first time. The key revelation was the existence, across substantial parts of the Midlands, of an underlying extensive pattern of dispersed settlement—essentially small farmsteads—in areas later dominated by large nucleated villages.[46] Based on the pottery record, these farmsteads could be shown to have fallen out of use by the mid-ninth century. Since many were located in places overlain by open fields—indeed memories of these lost farmsteads appeared to have been captured in some furlong-names—it was suggested that they must have already been abandoned and cleared before the fields had been laid out, their inhabitants perhaps moving to the nascent nucleation.[47]

The precise timing of this process continues to be debated. Important regional trajectories have been detected. Early investigations in Northamptonshire which gave us the idea of a 'great replanning' of both settlement and the wider landscape, and more recent studies in Dorset, Somerset and Cambridgeshire, all favour the long eighth century as the formative period.[48] Other studies in the east Midland counties such as

[45] Dodgson, 'The significance of the distribution of the English place-name in -*ingas*, -*inga*-', 1–29.

[46] G. Foard, 'Systematic fieldwalking and the investigation of Saxon settlement in Northamptonshire', *World Archaeology* 9 (1978), 357–74; D. Hall and P. Martin, 'Brixworth, Northamptonshire: an intensive field survey', *Journal of the British Archaeological Association* 132 (1979), 1–6; D. Hall, 'Survey work in eastern England', in S. Macready and F. H. Thompson (eds), *Archaeological Field Survey in Britain and Abroad* (London: Society of Antiquaries, 1985), pp. 25–44; D. Hall, 'Field surveys in Bedfordshire', *Bedfordshire Archaeology* 19 (1991), 51–56.

[47] D. Hall, *The Open Fields of Northamptonshire* (Northampton: Northamptonshire Record Society, 1995).

[48] D. Hall, 'The late Saxon countryside: villages and their fields', in D. Hooke (ed.)

Buckinghamshire, Bedfordshire, Leicestershire, and reappraisals of other parts of Northamptonshire, have pointed to a more general, prolonged, and later chronology, spanning the period from 850 to 1250, an evolutionary process dubbed the 'village moment'.[49]

If extensive survey of whole landscapes beyond the village allowed the question of nucleation to move forward in the 1980s, the key methodological breakthrough of the last two decades has been the development of sampling techniques which have enabled archaeologists to look underneath the villages themselves. Where once place-name evidence had to be compared with archaeological material gathered from outside the settlement, and where the precise relationship between the two—as *-ingas*-names and pre-Christian cemetery evidence showed—was not easily established, now there is the opportunity to compare datasets that demonstrably relate to the same place. Test-pitting within village cores has permitted the origin dates of individual settlements to be more firmly fixed, the extent of early occupation to be mapped, and the subsequent pace and direction of expansion to be traced more precisely. And as the number of such investigations continues to grow, and a statistically meaningful dataset is created, it is now possible to identify a number of emerging trends. In East Anglia and Cambridgeshire, for example, sufficient place-names in *-hām* and *-tūn* have now been explored to suggest very clear chronological distinctions between these two categories of place-name. It has been the *hām*s which have invariably produced pottery dating to the period from 450 to 720, and some Ipswich ware from AD 720, whilst it has been rare for the *tūn*s to produce any ceramic evidence predating AD 850. These findings, of course, chime well with the established chronology for these place-name types, names in *hām* having traditionally been seen as an earlier type than names in

Anglo-Saxon Settlements (Oxford: Blackwell, 1988), pp. 99–122; T. Brown and G. Foard, 'The Saxon landscape: a regional perspective', in P. Everson and T. Williamson (eds), *The Archaeology of Landscape* (Manchester: Manchester University Press, 1998), pp. 67–94; T. Hall, 'Minster Churches in the Dorset Landscape', unpublished MPhil thesis (University of Leicester, 1997); S. Rippon, *Beyond the Village: the Diversification of Landscape Character in Southern Britain* (Oxford: Oxford University Press, 2008); S. Oosthuizen, 'The origins of common fields and the Anglo-Saxon Kingdom of Mercia', *Agricultural History Review* 55:2 (2007), 153–80.

[49] C. Lewis, P. Mitchell-Fox and C. Dyer, *Village, Hamlet and Field: Changing Medieval Settlements in Central England* (Manchester: Manchester University Press, 1997; repr. Macclesfield: Windgather, 2001); Jones and Page, *Medieval Villages*.

tūn.[50] But it might be argued that the case can now be more confidently made because it is based on evidence derived directly from the settlement which carried the name.

Current archaeological understanding therefore points in two directions. First, evidence for precocious nucleation (of the eighth century) tends to be restricted to important estate centres, the very places one might expect to have attracted people to congregate around them. Secondly, beyond these central places, village formation was a more drawn out process. Consequently the emergence of new forms of settlement marches in parallel with the break-up—attested by surviving Anglo-Saxon charters from the eighth century onwards—of large, archaic estates. Settlements appear to have been reconfigured as part of this reapportionment of land and ownership, according well with the appearance of new types of place-name, particularly those combining a personal name—presumably people of thegnly rank holding local overlordship in the newly created smaller polities—with elements such as *tūn* and *lēah*. The fission of these large estates to the manorial and parochial arrangements known from the later middle ages might, however, pass through several intermediary stages (small estates), and it is clear that complete fragmentation, where fully achieved, might take considerable time to complete.[51] Domesday Book captures this process in action, revealing the survival into the late eleventh century of a number of sizable holdings—albeit often only substantial divisions of earlier, larger estates from which they had been carved—lying alongside much smaller units. And it is clear that village nucleation must also have been a phenomenon associated with these middle-sized blocks of land too.

Extensive archaeological survey of these small estates is beginning to tease out the complexities of the development of settlements found within them. On the Raunds (Nth) estate, for example, it has been shown that there was a gradual concentration of settlement at its eponymous centre across the period *c*. 800–920 before a major phase of re-planning in the mid-tenth century.[52] It was also around *c*. 950 that the first signs of

[50] B. Cox, 'The place-names of the earliest English records', *Journal of the English Place-Name Society* 8 (1975–76), 12–66. B. Cox, 'The significance of the distribution of English place-names in *hām* in the Midlands and East Anglia', *Journal of the English Place-Name Society* 5 (1972–73), 15–73.

[51] See, for example, D. Hadley, 'Multiple estates and the origins of the manorial structure in the northern Danelaw', *Journal of Historical Geography* 22 (1996), 3–15.

[52] Parry, *Raunds*, pp. 91–98, 105–06, 126–27.

nucleation at outlying places within the estate such as West Cotton and Stanwick can be detected.[53] These place-names, it will be recognized, incorporate elements suggestive of secondary or dependent status—*cot* and *wīc* and their appearance mirrors that found elsewhere. In Wicken (Nth),[54] despite both open-area excavation and the sinking of more than 50 test pits across the village, no pottery has been recovered predating *c.* 900. At Domesday, two separate five-hide manors are recorded there. Wick Dyke, the earliest of the two if we are to believe the pottery record, saw growth in the tenth century at the same time that the first signs of life in Wick Hamon emerge.[55] At the other end of the country, a later tenth- or eleventh-century date is posited for the creation, on the Glastonbury Abbey estate, of the planned village at Shapwick (So), although here establishing the precise moment that the earlier pattern of dispersed farmsteads was replaced by the nucleation is complicated by a regional absence of ninth-century ceramics.[56] The picture at Wicken Bonhunt (Ess) is also complicated. The plan of a substantial settlement dating from AD *c.* 700 has been revealed here through excavation, later re-planned on a slightly new alignment in the eleventh century. What may be significant here is a clear hiatus of activity before this redevelopment.[57] *Wicam* is first recorded as a name in the Domesday survey.[58] This clearly refers to the new Saxo-Norman settlement, but it is impossible to say whether this was a name inherited from the Middle Saxon phase or a new coinage. Although it would be unwise to generalize from only four examples, particularly using cases where the evidence is at best ambiguous, it must nevertheless be worth noting—and further testing—this possible recurrent pattern of *wīc*-names and tenth- or eleventh-century settlement establishment. There are hints, too, that *cot*-names may also exhibit

[53] Parry, *Raunds*, pp. 160–67 (Stanwick), pp. 172–77 (West Cotton); A. Chapman, *West Cotton, Raunds: A Study of Medieval Settlement Dynamics AD 450–1450. Excavation of a Deserted Medieval Hamlet in Northamptonshire, 1985–89* (Oxford: Oxbow, 2010).

[54] J. E. B. Gover, A. Mawer and F. M. Stenton, *The Place-Names of Northamptonshire* (Cambridge: Cambridge University Press, 1933), pp. 107–08.

[55] Jones and Page, *Medieval Villages*, pp. 180–81; M. Page and R. Jones, 'Stable and unstable village plans: case-studies from Whittlewood', in M. Gardiner and S. Rippon (eds), *Medieval Landscapes in Britain* (Macclesfield: Windgather, 2007), pp. 139–52.

[56] Gerrard with Aston, *Shapwick*, pp. 974–75.

[57] A. Reynolds, *Later Anglo-Saxon England: Life and Landscape* (Stroud: Tempus, 1999), pp. 140–43.

[58] Reaney, *The Place-Names of Essex*, p. 544.

similar tendencies. As at West Cotton (Nth), so at the extensively excavated deserted village of Caldecott (Hrt), the earliest medieval pottery points to a relatively late foundation, here associated with three peasant tofts of the eleventh (perhaps late tenth) century.[59]

The value of approaching the question of village origins through the filter of place-names, especially those associated with secondary or dependent settlements, has recently been shown in a comprehensive study of *thorp*s and *throp*s.[60] Whilst archaeology has occasionally been able to push back the existence of these places well beyond the date of first record—Fregthorpe (R), for example, is first attested in 1300, yet it produced quantities of tenth- and eleventh-century pottery—more generally *thorp*-places fail to produce material pre-dating the late ninth century, according well with their late appearance—in significant numbers at least—in the written record.[61] Common features of their earliest plans have also emerged. *Thorps* and *throps* were small, planned settlements from the outset regularly containing no more than a dozen house plots. The timing of their appearance, their propensity to lie beyond the main centre of populations to which they were often tenurially and administratively dependent, their association with areas dominated by open-field farming and in fact the tendency of some such fields to have borne *thorp*-names in the later medieval period,[62] suggest that these places may have been closely linked to, and perhaps played an important role in the introduction of, this type of agriculture. Indeed, *thorps*, it is suggested, may represent an intermediary stage in village nucleation, an important staging post between the abandonment of individual farmsteads dotted across the landscape and full nucleation.[63]

Archaeology, then, is bringing greater precision to the chronology of village development, and with it new insights into naming conventions. Whilst a key contribution has been to provide important antedates for settlements whose names are only known from later written sources, on occasion it has also shown that places which now carry a particular name may not have existed as settlements when they first appear in the

[59] G. Beresford, *Caldecote: the Development and Desertion of a Hertfordshire Village* (Leeds: Society for Medieval Archaeology, 2009), p. 154.

[60] Cullen, Jones, and Parsons, *Thorps*. See also Parsons above, pp. 66–69.

[61] Cullen, Jones, and Parsons, *Thorps*, pp. 98–99.

[62] See Parsons above, p. 68, n. 82.

[63] Cullen, Jones, and Parsons, *Thorps*, pp. 149–51.

historical record. A case in point is Whittlebury (Nth). Whittlebury was the venue for a royal *witan* in around 930, where King Æthelstan drew up various law codes.[64] Evidence for anything resembling a village of this date has eluded detection, despite intensive archaeological sampling across the whole of the existing settlement area. Rather it would appear that Whittlebury's 'village moment' came in the later tenth and eleventh centuries. What archaeology has demonstrated, however, is the location of an Iron Age hillfort, presumably the *burh* to which the name refers, which must have provided the setting for the council, and from which the later settlement grew.[65] It is perhaps telling that the parish church of Whittlebury was built within the ramparts of the hillfort.

Much more waits to be discovered about the origins of the English village. As recent publications have shown, interdisciplinary studies of the kind first called for in the 1960s, but which are only now beginning to be undertaken, combining the onomastic evidence—indeed led by it in some instances—with the archaeological record of the first phases of settlement, are beginning to pay dividend.

Archaeology, place-names and sense of place

To return to the beginning; Crawford's view of archaeology and its relation to place-names was not only guided by the available physical and material evidence but by prevailing interpretative structures then in vogue. He wrote at a time when archaeologists were more concerned with gathering information than wrestling with what it all meant. Those that did look for the bigger picture were keen to emphasize that particular types of artefacts, decorative motifs, monuments, settlement forms, and so forth were expressions of cultural norms, in the words of Gordon Childe, 'material expression[s] of what today would be called a "people"'.[66] It is not difficult to see, given such attitudes, how the link between the English village and incoming Anglo-Saxon settlers, dispersed settlement and indigenous British ways of life would be forged in the 1930s. Dissatisfied by the simplistic readings of the evidence

[64] D. Whitelock, *English Historical Documents, I, c. 500–1042*, 2nd edn (London: Routledge, 1979), p. 427.

[65] Jones and Page, *Medieval Villages*, p. 166, fig. 60.

[66] V. G. Childe, *The Danube in Prehistory* (Oxford: Oxford University Press, 1929), pp. v–vi, quoted in M. Johnson, *Archaeological Theory: an Introduction* (Oxford: Blackwell, 1999), p. 16.

provided by what became known as the culture-historical approach, archaeologists in the 1960s and 70s developed alternative ways of thinking, highlighting the internal dynamics of particular societies, the evolutionary and adaptive responses people made to external conditions—climate, environment and so on—and long-term processes. 'New Archaeology', as it was initially termed, morphed seamlessly into 'Processualism'. Under this paradigm medieval settlement studies shifted too, albeit slowly, moving away from further identification and recording towards attempting to trace the underlying causes of what had been found. Nucleation and desertion began to be seen as processes that could be modelled and explained. But by the 1980s the middle-range theories and systems approaches advocated by New Archaeology were themselves becoming heavily criticized in some quarters. Post-processualists argued that archaeologists should be looking for the meanings that lay behind and within the material, and should be seeking out the individual experiences that had got lost or forgotten through emphasis on the overarching systemic causes of change espoused by the processualists.[67] In particular they encouraged the acknowledgement and exploration of many—often contested and conflicting—human pasts influenced by race, religion, gender, age and many more factors besides, rather than searching for universal truths. In so doing, they introduced to archaeology a set of theoretic devices, generally borrowed from the social sciences or philosophy, as interpretative tools: agency and structure, habitus and dwelling, phenomenology, embodiment, personhood, queer theory to name just a few.

A brief review of this kind does little justice to the intellectual currents that have driven archaeology over the last century, of course, and fails to reveal just how far the discipline has travelled during that time. But it is perhaps sufficient to demonstrate why an archaeologist of the 1920s such as Crawford would not be able to recognize the subject today. Developments have been equally profound in related disciplines such as geography and its sub-discipline Cultural Geography. Here issues particularly germane to the investigation of both settlement formation and place-naming—especially notions of 'space' and 'place'—have been

[67] For overviews of post-processual ideas and their coming of age see I. Hodder, *Theory and Practice in Archaeology* (London and New York: Routledge, 1992) and M. Shanks, *Experiencing the Past: On the Character of Archaeology* (London and New York: Routledge, 1992).

thoroughly worked through.[68] However, medieval archaeologists, especially those interested in rural landscapes, have been extremely sluggish—perhaps reluctant—to embrace these more recent theoretical developments.[69] As a result their work has tended to lag behind more dynamic fields of archaeological enquiry such as prehistory by one or two decades. Into the 1990s the early medieval archaeologists' pursuit of models to explain village nucleation was still guided by the principles of the then old New Archaeology. Certainly it was grounded in the English empirical landscape tradition established by W. G. Hoskins and developed by others in the Department, now Centre, for English Local History at the University of Leicester of the 1950s.[70] It is only now, more than twenty years after post-processualism announced itself on the scene, that medieval archaeology is beginning to explore all the possibilities these new conceptualizations of the past offer.

Understanding sense of place, particularly as it developed during the formative period of settlement and landscape change witnessed during the early middle ages, is just one of several challenging issues that are now starting to be addressed as a result of these shifting intellectual parameters. Sense of place exists in the mind, but ultimately it is based upon the realities of the external world and how these were viewed, experienced, understood, and communicated. Sense of place is a corner-stone in the formation of individual and group identities, and performs an important role in establishing other related notions such as the feeling of belonging (indeed estrangement) or the sense of 'being-at-home'. Exploration of sense of place is therefore an investigation into the ways people thought, not only about themselves, but also their surrounds.

Place-names offer a way into this world. What now allows us to attempt enquiries of this sort within the context of the early medieval

[68] For an introduction to an extensive literature, see P. Hubbard, R. Kitchin and G. Valentine, *Key Thinkers on Space and Place* (London: Sage Publications, 2009). Perhaps the most influential of all books on the subject has been Y.-F. Tuan, *Space and Place: the Perspective of Experience* (Minneapolis and London: University of Minneapolis Press, 1977, repr. 2008).

[69] For a recent critique of the traditional approach to landscape studies in England see M. Johnson, *Ideas of Landscape* (Oxford: Blackwell, 2008).

[70] The canonical text is, of course, W. G. Hoskins, *The Making of the English Landscape* (London: Hodder and Stoughton, 1955). For another classic example of how place-names have been used by the Leicester school to help establish settlement chronologies and trajectories see A. Everitt, *Continuity and Colonization: the Evolution of Kentish Settlement* (Leicester: Leicester University Press, 1986).

English landscape, of course, is the foundation that previous generations of place-name scholars, historians, historical geographers, and archaeologists have laid. By combining onomastic, documentary and material evidence it is now possible to reconstruct the Anglo-Saxon landscape with some degree of confidence, either in low resolution at a national scale, or increasingly with greater clarity at regional, sub-regional or local scales.[71] It was Margaret Gelling again, working this time with Ann Cole, who advanced understanding beyond the purely empirical. *The Landscape of Place-Names* showed how the Anglo-Saxon landscape was visualized by those who lived within it (and often from where), demonstrating how intimate knowledge of the subtle variations of landforms translated into the rich toponymic language of early medieval place-names.[72]

Comprehending how people looked at the early medieval landscape is essential if we are to understand how they made sense of what they saw. But to do this, we must move beyond simply what was seen and ask why particular aspects of the landscape came to define place at all. Why were some landscape features seemingly more valued or assigned greater meaning or prominence than others, so that they became markers of place? Why was it that some place-names took their cue from the wider landscape, whilst others referred to the built environment of the villages and hamlets themselves, or even particular buildings and enclosures of which they were comprised? Why, we should be asking, did a valley or a plant or an animal come to define place in precedence over a range of other alternatives? How and why elsewhere was place-identity so closely linked with named individuals, or associated with the wider social make-up of the community as a whole, rather than some specific aspect extrapolated from the physical surroundings? Such questions open up

[71] For example, B. K. Roberts and S. Wrathmell, *An Atlas of Rural Settlement in England* (London: English Heritage, 2000); B. K. Roberts and S. Wrathmell, *Region and Place* (London: English Heritage, 2002); M. Gelling, *Place-Names in the Landscape: the Geographical Roots of Britain's Place-Names* (London: Dent, 1993); D. Hooke, *The Landscape of Anglo-Saxon England* (London: Leicester University Press, 1998); D. Hooke, *The Anglo-Saxon Landscape: the Kingdom of the Hwicce* (Manchester: Manchester University Press, 1985); J. Blair, *Anglo-Saxon Oxfordshire* (Stroud: Sutton, 1994); Jones and Page, *Medieval Villages*; Parry, *Raunds*; S. Oosthuizen, *Landscapes Decoded: the Origins and Development of Cambridgeshire's Medieval Fields* (Hatfield: University of Hertfordshire Press, 2006).

[72] M. Gelling and A. Cole, *The Landscape of Place-Names* (Stamford: Shaun Tyas, 2000). See further Cullen above, pp. 161–79.

new avenues of investigation and interpretation very different from those which have typified settlement and landscape studies of the last century. By way of illustrating the kinds of direction such studies might take, let us take just one example.

In AD 956 King Eadwig granted part of his Nottinghamshire estates centred on Southwell to Oscytel, archbishop of York.[73] This newly formed archiepiscopal holding comprised (excluding Southwell itself) eleven named land units, forming a single coherent unit stretching from the river Trent in the south-east northwards towards Mansfield. Most of these units carried names containing Old English habitative and topographical elements, whose territories were sufficiently well-defined by the mid-tenth century for their boundaries to be described in an attachment to the original grant. Three of the place-names have personal names as their first element: Gibsmere (ON *Gípr* + OE *mere* 'Gípr's pool'), Goverton (OE *Godfrið* or ON *Guðfrið* + OE *tūn* 'Godfrith's or Guthfrith's farm or estate'), and Kirklington (OE *Cyrtla* + OE *-ingtūn* 'Cyrtla's farm or estate').[74] Two place-names refer to the wider community, one defined by occupation, Fiskerton (OE *fiscera-tūn* 'the farm or estate of the fishermen'), the other defined by ethnicity, Normanton ('the farm or estate of the Northmen'). Three place-names appear to have been defined either by their topography—a topography which it might be noted is relatively subtle in this part of Nottinghamshire—or alternatively by their relative position within the land holding: Halam (OE *h(e)alh* 'nook or corner of land); Halloughton (OE *h(e)alh* + OE *tūn* 'farm or estate in the nook or corner of land'); and Upton (OE *uppe* + OE *tūn* 'the upper or higher farm or estate'). Two names paint a picture of the broader environment: Farnsfield (?OE *fearn* + OE *feld* 'open land of the ?bracken') and Morton (OE *mōr* + *tūn* 'moor farm or estate'). Finally there is the eponymous centre of this estate, Southwell (OE *sūð* + OE *wella* 'southern springs').

As we have come to expect, even a small group of place-names such as this, once set within its physical and administrative contexts, clearly informs on a whole range of issues relevant to the reconstruction of the early medieval landscape and its people. A traditional treatment of these

[73] S 659

[74] These etymologies and others that follow are taken from J. E. B. Gover, A. Mawer, and F. M. Stenton, *The Place-Names of Nottinghamshire* (Cambridge: Cambridge University Press, 1940), pp. 155–79.

names might be satisfied simply to use these twelve place-names as pointers to the state of the land, indicators of settlement hierarchies and estate organization, and markers of ethnicity and status. But could they also tell us something about local sense of place as it had developed in this small part of Nottinghamshire by the mid-tenth century? One narrative might go as follows. That these names were already coined by the time of the transfer of the estate to archiepiscopal hands means that we should probably be looking for them to make sense in the context of early royal ownership rather than later arrangements. It might be noted, for instance, that there is the strong relational naming component to be found in these names. The identity of Southwell, the 'southern springs' itself requires a northern parallel—in this instance presumably Norwell a few miles to the north-east—without which its name is rendered meaningless. This hints at the possible earlier extent of the royal estate. Other names such as Upton, Halloughton and Halam also seem to be defined as much by their geographic relationship to the estate centre than anything more locally specific, although an alternative explanation for Upton has recently been advanced.[75] This type of authoritative naming from the centre must have helped to establish the primacy of the core over the periphery whilst at the same time offering a degree of coherence to the land unit as a whole. Place-names such as these must have helped bind their communities to the much larger unity to which they ultimately belonged. The exercise of early medieval royal authority—itinerant with extensive but widespread estates—however, must have been generally light-touch in Southwell and only occasionally immediate when the royal household was in residence. Could it be that place-names such as Fiskerton suggest the importance of local resources and local services that were needed to provide for the visiting royal entourage?[76] Perhaps, but more generally as a group of names, it might be noted that they offer little idea of the economic vitality of the estate or its organization. If anything the topographical place-names describe the landscape in rather non-specific ways, open land and moors, which appear, if the interpretation of Farnsfield is correct, to have been rather wild and unkempt. But it might be argued that these too are just the kinds of name-

[75] R. Jones, 'Hunting for the meaning of the place-name Upton', in Jones and Semple (eds), *Sense of Place*, pp. 301–15.

[76] It is surely telling in this context that Fiskerton (Li) was held by the Bishops of Lincoln, providing another elite setting for this name-type.

form—generic pen-sketches of the landscape—which might be expected to be coined by those only partially or episodically familiar with these surroundings.[77]

One argument that might be advanced here, then, is that powerful yet largely removed overlordship engendered its own particular form of sense of place. This emphasized the administrative coherence of the estate but also reflected a lack of intimate knowledge of the land and its inhabitants. Absenteeism, however, leaves power vacuums. Might it be proposed that it is in this context that this space was filled by those local individuals and communities whose names became attached to smaller landholdings within the estate? Or alternatively, might it be suggested that these types of name-forms, which clearly continued to be formed after Scandinavian settlement, chart the progressive loss of direct royal control over this area, a factor that may ultimately have encouraged the king to grant this land away in the 950s?

Whatever the case, it is probable that resident groups would have had a very different relationship to the land than infrequent visitors, ensuring that a far more personal sense of place developed. This more richly named, intimate insiders' view of the landscape appears to emerge from descriptions of the boundaries of each land unit appended to the initial charter, in great contrast to the rather vague ideas conveyed by the major place-names. Through an examination of the topographical detail of these boundaries the Southwell estate comes alive, revealing a landscape full of shape, texture, water and plants, isolated trees and larger blocks of woodland, the occasional farmstead and enclosure, and signs of agricultural activity:

> These are the land-boundaries belonging to Southwell: from the ford along the Greet south-east to the new farm then straight on through new farm's brook to the Greet; up by the brook south of *sunninsale* holme: then to the broad clearing: then eastwards to the cottages; [...] along the paved way to the hollow brook: along the brook then up by the slope one furlong within the copse: then up to the oak tree: [...] keeping all the time by the headland to the more northerly thorn bush; [...] to the Greet; along the Greet and back to the ford. These are the land-boundaries belonging to Normanton: from the Greet to the corner where the vetch grows: along

[77] Alternative explanations for Morton names, as places where useful resources might be obtained for long-distance travellers, have recently been suggested by A. Cole, '*Tūns* by the wayside'.

> the enclosure to the brook; then to the valley: along the valley all the time by the headland to the Leen brook; from there to the hedge; always by the hedge to the old paved way; along the paved way and back to the Greet. These are the land-boundaries belonging to Upton: from the Greet along the old paved road by the north of Hockerwood; from the paved road across the moor to the servants' enclosure; northwards then up to the appletree: from the appletree straight across Micklebarrow Hill; onto the moor and to the little stream; along the stream and then back to the Greet. These are the land-boundaries belonging to Fiskerton; along the Greet to the Trent to Hazelford; from the ford along the paved way to Quernhill; from Quernhill straight on to new farm's brook; along the brook then east to the Greet.[78]

These boundaries' descriptions, which in comparison to others from different parts of the country are far from the most detailed we possess, nevertheless, it might be argued, evoke a sense of place founded on daily interactions with nature, a landscape shaped by communal enterprise and shared memories. They present the landscape familiar to farmers not kings, theirs not his. These richly layered living and experiential landscapes were those in which local community identities were forged and senses of belonging promoted.

Interpretative exercises such as this take us well away from the solid foundations of more traditional empirical studies; yet carefully handled, and presented with appropriate caution, they seem to offer new dimensions and exciting prospects for archaeologists and onomasts. And they reveal, of course, that the value Crawford placed on the evidence to be found in charter bounds in the 1920s was indeed well founded; for it is in their microtoponymic detail that people of the early middle ages defined space. By so doing they help us map these lost spaces; but perhaps more importantly in combination the major and minor names of England act as windows through which we can glimpse their world, revealing not only what it looked like, but how its occupants thought about it too.

[78] P. Lyth, 'The Southwell charter of 956 A.D.: an exploration of its boundaries', *Transactions of the Thoroton Society* 86 (1982), 49–61; P. Lyth and G. Davies, 'The Southwell charter of A.D. 956: a new appraisal of the boundaries', *Transactions of the Thoroton Society* 96 (1992), 125–29.

Conclusion

Archaeologists and place-name scholars are faced with the same conundrum: the primary function of their source material—whether an artefact, a landscape, or a name—was not intended to convey messages down through the centuries, even if those of us who now explore these remnants of the past wish that this was the case. Rather they were designed to communicate messages to contemporary audiences. Once divorced from their intended audiences, these messages are prone to distortion. Even when first used, their messages might be misunderstood or mistaken. The task of interpretation is therefore a complex one. Archaeologists have learned that it is insufficient simply to value a pot for its functional potential, and have begun to look for the deeper meanings these objects may have held for their users. In the same way, place-names can no longer be seen simply as convenient labels designed to differentiate settlements or parts of the landscape – even if this was one of their more important roles. The act of naming was part of a package of strategies used by people not only to make sense of their surroundings—making place from space in the jargon of cultural geographers—but to establish senses of identity and belonging. Place-names may remain meaningful in the terms they were originally intended for just a fleeting moment, perhaps no more than the life of the archaeologists' earthenware vessel. After all, it is possible to live in an Upton, an Abthorpe (Nth), or a Ringmer (Sx) as I have and still feel you belong there irrespective of whether you understand the etymological significance of these names or not. Yet, however transient, and however difficult to capture, it would be a dereliction of duty not to try to understand what people were thinking as they took their first steps towards creating and naming the very places in which we continue to live. Indeed, as Charles Frake so usefully described, one should perhaps approach a place-name just as one would an archaeological artefact:

> The semantic opacity of a placename is much like the patina on a flint tool. It covers the past of the place, hiding a story and a history. The decipherment of an English placename is rather like an archaeological dig. One strips away the deceptive superficial layers to get at the original meaning. The more stripping required, the more ancient, and thus the more interesting, the past.[79]

[79] C. O. Frake, 'Pleasant places, past times, and sheltered identity in rural East Anglia', in

In its own way, this assessment of the relationship between place-name study and the landscapes and settlements of early medieval England might be accused of being as idiosyncratic as Crawford's contribution to the *Introduction to English Place-Names* volume which it has sought to follow; and in some ways its scope is narrower than that of its predecessor. What it has tried to reflect, however imperfectly, is the double face of modern archaeology: on the one hand a powerful science that has at its disposal an armoury of techniques, even if they have not been enumerated here, which is furthering the collection of empirical data and helping to refine settlement chronologies and establish their early forms; and on the other a more free-wheeling, theoretically informed and less data-restricted enquiry which has begun to alter the kinds of questions that are being asked, particularly with regard to peoples' relationship with place. Both approaches, the practical and the theoretical, have a role to play in, indeed often rely on, the ever closer integration of place-name and material evidence to inform upon the past. Here only a fraction of that human experience has been explored, the vital moments of settlement formation in the early middle ages and the apportionment of the land. Nothing has been said, for instance, about how place-names and archaeology might be used in tandem to explore the later histories of these places, or how prehistorians and Romanists might make use of the onomastic material that has now been made available.[80] Nor has anything been said about non-mundane uses of the landscape, how, for example, archaeology and place-names can help to reveal landscapes of religion and belief. It is here that Crawford's giants and devils, sitting happily amongst the elves and spirits which inhabit the early medieval landscape revealed by linguists and archaeologists, still have much to tell us.[81] Others will have their own thoughts about how and where archaeology and place-names might fruitfully be brought together; suffice to say, future collaborations which do are to be encouraged and their results awaited with impatience.

S. Feld and K. H. Basso (eds), *Senses of Place* (Santa Fe: School of American Research Press, 1996), pp. 229–57 (p. 238).

[80] R. Jones, 'Thinking through the manorial affix', in R. Silvester and S. Turner (eds), *Life in Medieval Landscapes: People and Places in Medieval England* (Oxford: Oxbow, 2012), pp. 251–67.

[81] A. Hall, 'Are there any elves in Anglo-Saxon place-names?', *Nomina* 29 (1996), 61–80; S. Semple, 'In the open air'.

8

Personal names in place-names

John Insley

When we speak of personal names in place-names, we need to be clear about our terms of reference. By ‘place-names’ we mean here the names of parishes and townships, and not field- or minor names, and by ‘personal names’ we mean given names and not bynames and surnames. Since the majority of our parish names and township names were already in existence by 1086, the personal names found among the first elements of such names are primarily Old English with a strong concentration of Scandinavian names in the Danelaw and sporadic occurrences of British and Continental Germanic personal names. The hosts of Middle English personal names, such as *Adekin*, *Colin*, *Dande*, *Dobbin*, *Emmot* fem., *Hugge*, *Mab(be)* fem., *Sime*, *Tomkin* and *Wilkin*, which abound in field names,[1] play no part in this discussion. The same is of course true of the innumerable French personal names found in field and minor names in post-Conquest records.

Sir Frank Stenton’s account of personal names in place-names published in the *Introduction to the Survey of English Place-Names* in 1924 has stood the test of time very well.[2] Stenton had a perceptive grasp of the typological questions of personal name research and a superb

The volumes of the English Place-Name Society’s Survey are indicated by EPNS + county abbreviation as given on p. vi. Anglo-Saxon charters are indicated by S + the number in P. H. Sawyer, *Anglo-Saxon Charters: An Annotated List and Bibliography* (London: The Royal Historical Society, 1968) and the electronic version of S 1–1602 by S. E. Kelly, rev. by R. Rushworth (2006) at <http://www.esawyer.org.uk/>. In the present text, the voiced palatal fricative [j] (> [j]) is rendered by <Ġ>and <ġ>, while <G> and <g> are used to render the plosive [g] and the voiced velar fricative [ɣ]. Late Old English [tʃ] (< Germ /k/ in an original palatal environment) is rendered by <Ċ> and <ċ>. The Old English letter ‘wynn’ is rendered by <W> and <w>.

[1] For a typical list of such field namc forms, scc EPNS Ch **5.ii**, pp. 414–20.

[2] F. M. Stenton, ‘Personal names in place-names’, in A. Mawer and F. M. Stenton (eds), *Introduction to the Survey of English Place-Names*, English Place-Name Society 1.i (Cambridge: Cambridge University Press, 1924), pp. 165–89.

command of source materials, especi ally those of the Danelaw.[3] If we are now able to write a more modern survey it is because our source materials are much better and because the range of secondary literature is incomparably more comprehensive than it was in Stenton's day.[4] Alone the volumes of the English Place-Name Society's Survey (89 to the time of writing) are testimony to that. We can also mention the fifteen volumes of the British Academy's Anglo-Saxon Charter series, the collaborative edition of the Anglo-Saxon Chronicle or the excellent edition of that most intractable of texts, the *Liber Vitae* of Durham, recently edited by David and Lynda Rollason.[5] There is also much more material available for the Middle English period published by local record societies – here I think in particular of such publications as the *Early Yorkshire Charters* series, the *Registrum Antiquissimum* of Lincoln Cathedral or the series of Suffolk charters published by the Suffolk Record Society. It is easy to overlook the inadequacy of the secondary literature available when Stenton wrote. The shortcomings of W. G. Searle's Onomasticon[6] were well known, as indeed Stenton noted.[7] It is true that the Scandinavian personal name material had been competently examined by Björkman,[8] and Redin's survey of the uncompounded personal names of Old English, though in need of replacement, remains a useful tool.[9] On the other hand, a comprehensive survey of late Old English personal nomenclature only appeared in 1937 in the form of Olof von Feilitzen's seminal work on the pre-Conquest personal names of Domesday Book,[10] and while gaps have

[3] In this context, we should mention his collection of Danelaw charters, *Documents illustrative of the Social and Economic History of the Danelaw from various Collections* (London: Oxford University Press, 1920), a work which contains an important discussion of Anglo-Scandinavian personal nomenclature (at pp. cxi–cxviii).

[4] For bibliographical information on personal name research, see T. Andersson, 'Personennamen', *Reallexikon der Germanischen Altertumskunde* 22 (2003), 589–614.

[5] D. Rollason and L. Rollason (eds), *The Durham Liber Vitae: London, British Library, MS Cotton Domitian A. VII*, 3 vols (London: British Library, 2007).

[6] W. G. Searle, *Onomasticon Anglo-Saxonicum. A List of Anglo-Saxon Proper Names from the Time of Beda to that of King John* (Cambridge: Cambridge University Press, 1897).

[7] Stenton, 'Personal names in place-names', pp. 165–66, n. 1.

[8] E. Björkman, *Nordische Personennamen in England in alt- und frühmittel-englischer Zeit* (Halle a.S.: Max Niemeyer, 1910); E. Björkman, *Zur englischen Namenkunde* (Halle a.S.: Max Niemeyer, 1912).

[9] M. Redin, *Studies on Uncompounded Personal Names in Old English* (Uppsala: A.-B. Akademiska Bokhandeln, 1919).

[10] O. von Feilitzen, *The Pre-Conquest Personal Names of Domesday Book* (Uppsala: Almqvist and Wiksell, 1937).

been closed in the form of the works of Ström[11] and Anderson (Arngart)[12] on personal names and language in Bede's *Historia ecclesiastica gentis Anglorum* or those of Olof von Feilitzen,[13] Gillian Fellows-Jensen[14] and myself[15] on Scandinavian personal nomenclature or the superb collection of moneyers' names made available through the British Academy's *Sylloge of Coins of the British Isles*,[16] there remains a good deal to be done. In particular, personal name research has tended to concentrate on the late Old English and Middle English periods and little has been done on the Middle Saxon period from 700–900. My own survey of pre-Conquest personal nomenclature in Volume 23 of the Hoops *Reallexikon* at least takes these questions into account.[17]

Stenton, like Eilert Ekwall, was aware of the need to compare early English nomenclature with that of Scandinavia and with the Continental West Germanic dialects and Gothic. The Scandinavian languages were the least difficult, since Lind's compendia of medieval West Scandinavian personal names[18] provided a reliable point of reference and the earlier

[11] H. Ström, *Old English Personal Names in Bede's History: An Etymological-Phonological Investigation* (Lund: C. W. K. Gleerup, 1939).

[12] O. S. Anderson (ed.), *Old English Material in the Leningrad Manuscript of Bede's Ecclesiastical History* (Lund: C. W. K. Gleerup, 1941).

[13] O. von Feilitzen, 'Notes on some Scandinavian personal names in English 12th-century records', in R. Otterbjörk (ed.), *Personnamnsstudier 1964 tillägnade minnet av Ivar Modéer (1904–1960)* (Stockholm: Almqvist and Wiksell, 1965), pp. 52–68.

[14] G. Fellows Jensen, *Scandinavian Personal Names in Lincolnshire and Yorkshire* (Copenhagen: Akademisk forlag, 1968).

[15] J. Insley, *Scandinavian Personal Names in Norfolk: A Survey Based on Medieval Records and Place-Names* (Uppsala and Stockholm: Almqvist and Wiksell, 1994).

[16] See V. Smart, *Sylloge of Coins of the British Isles 28: Cumulative Index of Volumes 1–20* (London: Oxford University Press for The British Academy, 1981); V. Smart, *Sylloge of Coins of the British Isles 41: Cumulative Index of Volumes 21–40* (London: Oxford University Press for The British Academy, 1992).

[17] J. Insley, 'Pre-Conquest Personal Names', *Reallexikon der Germanischen Altertumskunde* 23 (2003), 367–96. For the Old English system, see also C. Clark, 'Onomastics', in R. M. Hogg (ed.), *The Cambridge History of the English Language*, I: *The Beginnings to 1066* (Cambridge: Cambridge University Press, 1992), pp. 452–89 (pp. 456–71). A fundamental account for the post-Conquest period is C. Clark, 'Onomastics', in N. Blake (ed.), *The Cambridge History of the English Language*, II: *1066–1476* (Cambridge: Cambridge University Press, 1992), pp. 542–606 (pp. 551–87).

[18] E. H. Lind, *Norsk-isländska dopnamn ock fingerade namn från medeltiden* (Uppsala: A.-B. Lundequistska Bokhandeln; Leipzig: Otto Harrassowitz, 1905–15). This was augmented in 1931 by Lind, *Norsk-isländska dopnamn ock fingerade namn från medeltiden: Supplementband* (Oslo: Jacob Dybwad, 1931).

works by Lundgren and Brate[19] and Nielsen[20] provided material for Old Swedish and Old Danish, respectively. With regard to Scandinavian material, our position today is, as one would expect, far better than it was in Stenton's day. Not only do we have much more comprehensive onomastic lexica for East Scandinavian (see notes 19 and 20) than he did, but we also have systematic surveys of the entire material.[21]

The position with regard to Continental material was far more difficult in Stenton's time. It is true that a useful compendium for the Migration period (and, therefore, for Gothic, Vandalic and the like) existed in the form of Schönfeld's *Wörterbuch der altgermanischen Personen- und Völkernamen*,[22] but otherwise scholars were largely dependent on Förstemann,[23] whose inaccuracy was even then a significant problem. Nowadays we are much better able to deal with such material. The Old

[19] M. Lundgren, E. Brate and E. H. Lind, *Svenska personnamn från medeltiden* (Uppsala: Almqvist and Wiksell, 1892–1934). This is now in the process of being replaced by *Sveriges medeltida personnamn, Förnamn* (Uppsala: Almqvist and Wiksell; Uppsala: Institutet för språk och folkminnen, 1967 ff. and in progress [by 2011 (Häfte 16), the name **Iordan** had been reached]). For the personal nomenclature of the Swedish runic inscriptions, see L. Peterson, *Nordiskt runnamnslexikon* (Uppsala: Institutet för språk och folkminnen, 2007).

[20] O. A. Nielsen, *Olddanske Personnavne* (Copenhagen: Universitets-Jubilæets danske samfund, 1883). This has now been completely replaced by G. Knudsen, M. Kristensen and R. Hornby (eds), *Danmarks gamle Personnavne*, I: *Fornavne* (Copenhagen: G. E. C. Gad, 1936–48).

[21] See in particular A. Janzén (ed.), *Nordisk Kultur* VII: *Personnavne/ Personnamn/Personnavn* (Copenhagen: J. H. Schultz; Oslo: H. Aschehoug; Stockholm: A. Bonnier, 1947). Janzén's own account of West Scandinavian personal nomenclature in this volume, 'De fornvästnordiska personnamnen', pp. 22–186, is an etymological survey of fundamental importance. The structure of Old Danish personal nomenclature in the Migration and Viking periods is covered in detail by K. Hald, *Personnavne i Danmark*, I. *Oldtiden* (Copenhagen: Dansk Historisk Fællesforening, 1971). There is an excellent general survey by E. F. Halvorsen et al. in *Kulturhistoriskt Lexikon för nordisk medeltid*, XIII: *Ormber–Regnbue* (Malmö: Allhem, 1968), cols. 198–234, s.v. *Personnavn*.

[22] M. Schönfeld, *Wörterbuch der altgermanischen Personen- und Völkernamen. Nach der Überlieferung des klassischen Altertums bearbeitet* (Heidelberg: Carl Winter, 1911). This has now been supplemented by H. Reichert, *Lexikon der altgermanischen Namen* (Vienna: Verlag der Österreichischen Akademie der Wissenschaften, 1987–1990), which provides far more material. For Ostrogothic names, see also N. Wagner, 'Ostgotische Personennamengebung', in D. Geuenich, W. Haubrichs, and J. Jarnut (eds), *Nomen et gens. Zur historischen Aussagekraft frühmittelalterlicher Personennamen* (Berlin and New York: Walter de Gruyter, 1997), pp. 41–57, and for Vandalic names, H. Reichert, 'Sprache und Namen der Wandalen in Afrika', in A. Greule and M. Springer (eds), *Namen des Frühmittelalters als sprachliche Zeugnisse und als Geschichtsquellen* (Berlin and New York: Walter de Gruyter, 2009), pp. 43–120.

[23] E. Förstemann, *Altdeutsches namenbuch*, I: *Personennamen*, 2nd edn (Bonn: Hanstein, 1900).

Low Franconian and Middle Dutch material is more accessible through the Koch-Gysseling compendium of pre-1100 charters[24] and Tavernier-Vereecken's work on Ghent names.[25] The Low German material is dealt with in the earlier work of Schlaug on Old Saxon names[26] and a series of dissertations has provided information about the personal names in use in the Hansa ports of Hamburg, Lübeck and Rostock.[27] For the High German region, we are greatly helped by the MGH editions of the great confraternity books, such as those of Reichenau[28] and St Emmeram of Regensburg.[29] The extensive early medieval material from Fulda is now available as a result of the Klostergemeinschaft von Fulda project published in 1978.[30] Recently, Wolfgang Haubrichs has presented important surveys of Alemannic[31] and Langobardic[32] personal nomenclature. The Germanic personal nomenclature of the Romance-

[24] M. Gysseling and A. C. F. Koch (eds), *Diplomata Belgica ante annum millesimum centesimum scripta*, I. *Teksten* (Brussels: Belgisch Inter-Universitair Centrum voor Neerlandistiek, 1950).

[25] C. Tavernier-Vereecken, *Gentse naamkunde van ca. 1000 tot 1253: Een bijdrage tot de kennis van het oudste Middelnederlands* (Brussels: Belgisch Interuniversitair Centrum voor Neerlandistiek, 1968).

[26] W. Schlaug, *Studien zu den altsächsischen Personennamen des 11. und 12. Jahrhunderts* (Lund: C. W. K. Gleerup; Copenhagen: Ejnar Munksgaard, 1955); Schlaug, *Die altsächsischen Personennamen vor dem Jahre 1000* (Lund: C. W. K. Gleerup; Copenhagen: Ejnar Munksgaard, 1962).

[27] G. Mahnken, *Die hamburgischen niederdeutschen Personennamen des 13. Jahrhunderts* (Dortmund: Ruhfus, 1925); A. Reimpell, *Die Lübecker Personennamen unter besondere Berücksichtigung der Familiennamenbildung bis zur Mitte des 14. Jahrhunderts* (Lübeck: Franz Westphal, 1929); H. Brockmüller, *Die Rostocker Personennamen bis 1304* (Rostock: Richard Beckmann, 1933).

[28] J. Autenrieth, D. Geuenich and K. Schmid (eds), *Das Verbrüderungsbuch der Abtei Reichenau (Einleitung, Register, Faksimile)* (Hanover: Hahnsche Buchhandlung, 1979).

[29] E. Freise, D. Geuenich and J. Wollasch (eds), *Das Martyrolog – Necrolog von St. Emmeram zu Regensburg* (Hanover: Hahnsche Buchhandlung, 1986).

[30] For the personal name part of this project, the relevant volume is K. Schmid (ed.), *Die Klostergemeinschaft von Fulda im früheren Mittelalter*, III: *Vergleichendes Gesamtverzeichnis der fuldischen Personennamen.* (Munich: Wilhelm Fink, 1978). This should be used in conjunction with D. Geuenich, *Die Personennamen der Klostergemeinschaft von Fulda im früheren Mittelalter* (Munich: Wilhelm Fink, 1976).

[31] W. Haubrichs, 'Frühe alemannische Personennamen (4.–8. Jh.). Eine komparatistische Studie', in H.-P. Naumann (ed.), *Alemannien und der Norden. Internationales Symposium vom 18.–20. Oktober 2001 in Zürich* (Berlin and New York: Walter de Gruyter, 2004), pp. 57–113.

[32] W. Haubrichs, 'Langobardic personal names: given names and name-giving among the Langobards', in G. Ausenda, P. Delogu and C. Wickham (eds), *The Langobards before the Frankish Conquest: An Ethnographic Perspective* (Woodbridge: Boydell, 2009), pp. 195–250.

speaking areas of northern Gaul still awaits a detailed investigation following up on the pioneer work done by Michaëlsson in the 1930s.[33] We do, however, have a modern edition of that most important of Carolingian sources, the *polyptyque* of Abbot Irmino of Saint-Germain-des-Prés.[34] For England, Thorvald Forssner's doctoral thesis of 1916 is still fundamental,[35] though it has been supplemented by a useful paper by Olof von Feilitzen.[36] The importance of using Continental and Scandinavian material for comparative purposes can be illustrated by reference to FINGLESHAM in Kent and WANTISDEN in Suffolk. FINGLESHAM (*Ðenglesham* *c.* 850 [contemporary] S 1195) was interpreted by Johannes K. Wallenberg as a compound of OE *þengel* 'prince, king, lord, ruler' and *hām*.[37] This etymology repeats a suggestion made by R. E. Zachrisson and has passed into accepted wisdom.[38] However, OE *þengel* and its side-form *fengel* belong to the Old English poetic language, being attested in *Beowulf* (*fengel* lines 1400, 1475, 2156, 2345; *þengel* line 1507) and *Exodus* (*þengel* line 173). The normal Old English word for this semantic field is OE *æðeling* m. which is attested as the first element of several place-names.[39] However, the Scandinavian cognate of OE *þengel*, ON *þengill*, is attested as a personal name in independent use and as the first element of Norwegian place-names.[40] An ODan **Thængil*

[33] K. Michaëlsson, *Études sur les noms de personne français d'après les rôles de taille parisiens (rôles de 1292, 1296–1300, 1313)*, I (Uppsala: Almqvist and Wiksell, 1927); Michaëlsson, *Études sur les noms de personne français d'après les rôles de taille parisiens (rôles de 1292, 1296–1300, 1313)*, II *Lexique raisonné des noms de baptême A–B* (Uppsala: A.-B. Lundequistska Bokhandeln, 1936).

[34] D. Hägermann in collaboration with K. Elmshäuser and A. Hedwig (eds), *Das Polyptychon von Saint-Germain-des-Prés,* Studienausgabe (Cologne, Weimar, Vienna: Böhlau, 1993).

[35] T. Forssner, *Continental-Germanic Personal Names in England in Old and Middle English Times* (Uppsala: K. W. Appelberg, 1916).

[36] O. von Feilitzen, 'Some Continental Germanic personal names in England', in A. Brown and P. Foote (eds), *Early English and Norse Studies, Presented to Hugh Smith in Honour of his Sixtieth Birthday* (London: Methuen, 1963), pp. 46–61.

[37] J. K. Wallenberg, *Kentish Place-Names: A Topographical and Etymological Study of the Place-Name Material in Kentish Charters dated before the Conquest* (Uppsala: A.-B. Lundequistska Bokhandeln, 1931), p. 169.

[38] It is also proposed by E. Ekwall, *Studies on English Place- and Personal Names* (Lund: C. W. K. Gleerup, 1931), p. 28, and is carried over without further comment by Ekwall, *The Concise Oxford Dictionary of English Place-Names*, 4th edn (Oxford: Clarendon, 1960) [DEPN], p. 180.

[39] D. N. Parsons and T. Styles, with C. Hough, *The Vocabulary of English Place-Names* I *(Á–Box)* (Nottingham: Centre for English Name Studies, 1997), p. 35.

[40] Lind, *Norsk-isländska dopnamn*, cols. 1122–23.

has been suggested as the first element of the lost *Thængilsthorp* on Lolland.[41] In view of the Scandinavian parallels, it would seem better to interpret the first element of FINGLESHAM as an unrecorded personal name **Þengel* derived from the poetic appellative *þengel*. WANTISDEN in Suffolk is taken by Ekwall to contain the personal name *Want*.[42] This personal name is attested independently as *Uont* in the ninth-century part of the Durham *Liber Vitae*,[43] but is otherwise not found in English sources. The great antiquity of this name is indicated by the appearance of a pre-Old Saxon cognate, **Want*, as the first element of a German place-name in *-leben*, WANZLEBEN[44] (*uillam Uuanzlouo* 947, *Uuanzleua* 956)[45] west of Magdeburg. We also have to take into account the influence of Germanic saga on Old English naming patterns. Jordanes mentions a Gothic hero named *Vidigoia*, whose name is interpreted by Schönfeld as belonging to a reconstructed form **Widu-* (*Widi-*)*-gauja*.[46] The name is attested in Old High German in such forms as *Uuitagauuo*, *Uuitigo(u)uo*, etc.,[47] and we find the form *Widicau* in a document of 713–14 from Lucca.[48] In Old English, we find *Wudgan* (acc.), *Wudga* (nom.) in *Widsith* (lines 124, 130) and *Widian* (acc.), *Widia* (nom.) in *Waldere* (II, lines 4, 9). The name is also attested independently as *Uydiga* in the ninth-century part of the Durham *Liber Vitae*[49] and *Widia*, *Widige* and *Wudia* occur among eleventh-century moneyers' names.[50] The name also

[41] A. Bjerrum and C. Lisse, *Maribo Amts Stednavne*, Danmarks Stednavne 11 (Copenhagen: G. E. C. Gad, 1954), p. 55.

[42] DEPN, p. 496.

[43] Rollason and Rollason (eds), *The Durham Liber Vitae*, II: *Linguistic Commentary*, p. 186.

[44] H. Kuhn, review of A. Bach, *Deutsche Namenkunde* II. *Die deutschen Ortsnamen* (Heidelberg: Carl Winter, 1953–54), in *Anzeiger für deutsches Altertum und deutsche Literatur* 68:4 (April, 1956), 145–70 (p. 159).

[45] For the early forms of the name, see B. Schönwälder, *Die*-leben-*Namen* (Heidelberg: C. Winter, 1993), pp. 145–46, though it should be noted that WANZLEBEN is here (p. 146) incorrectly interpreted as containing a personal name *Wandi*.

[46] Schönfeld, *Wörterbuch der altgermanischen Personen- und Völkernamen*, p. 263.

[47] See Autenrieth, Geuenich and Schmid (eds), *Das Verbrüderungsbuch der Abtei Reichenau*, p. 171.

[48] Haubrichs, 'Langobardic personal names', p. 201. Haubrichs interprets the sense of the name as 'forest barker', an old wolf kenning. He thinks that the name is probably of Gothic origin.

[49] Rollason and Rollason (eds), *The Durham Liber Vitae*, II: *Linguistic Commentary*, p. 186.

[50] Smart, *Sylloge of Coins of the British Isles 28*, p. 76; Smart, *Sylloge of Coins of the British Isles 41*, p. 109.

forms the first element of an early place-name, WITHINGTON in Gloucestershire (*Wudiandun* 736–37 [e11] S 1429, *Uuidiandun* 774 [e11] S 1255).[51] Malone took OE *Widia*, *Wudia* to be 'presumably a hypocoristic form'.[52] It is quite clearly a semantically empty form, a fossilized contracted variant of Primitive Old English **Widu-*, **Wuduġē*. OE *Widia*/*Wudia* is therefore a form of great antiquity whose continuing use must be linked to the cultivation of Germanic saga in England.[53]

Germanic anthroponymy belongs to a larger Indo-European context which can be illustrated by reference to other Indo-European dialects. The classic Germanic dithematic personal name represented by Latino-Burgundian, Latino-Visigothic *Ansemundus* (= Gothic **Ansu-munds*), OE *Ōsmund*, ON *Ásmundr* has its parallels elsewhere in Indo-European. So in Celtic, we have formations like British **Maglo-cunus* 'a prince like a wolf/dog' or Welsh *Tud-wal* < **Teuto-walos*,[54] a compound of words for 'people' and 'powerful'.[55] In Baltic, we find compound personal names like the medieval Lithuanian princes' names *Kor(y)but* (= Old Lithuanian **Kar(y)-butas*), a compound of Lithuanian *kãras*, *kãrias* 'war' and *bùtas* 'house',[56] and *Towtiwil* (= Old Lithuanian **Tauti-vilas*), a name whose first element belongs to Lithuanian *tautà* 'people, nation' and whose second is linked to *vilti-s* 'to hope' and the corresponding noun *viltis* f. 'hope'.[57] Cf. also such fourteenth-century East Prussian forms as *Thawtewille*, *Tawtewille*, *Teutewil*, etc.,[58] which stand for an exact Old Prussian counterpart of Lithuanian *Towtiwil*. Dithematic names of this

[51] EPNS Gl **1**, pp. 186–87.

[52] K. Malone (ed.), *Widsith* (Copenhagen: Rosenkilde and Bagger, 1962), p. 212.

[53] See Stenton, 'Personal names in place-names', p. 187.

[54] See K. H. Schmidt, 'Keltische Namen', in E. Eichler et al. (eds), *Namenforschung/Name Studies/Les noms propres. Ein internationales Handbuch zur Onomastik/An International Handbook of Onomastics/Manuel international d'onomastique*, 2 vols and Index (Berlin and New York: Walter de Gruyter, 1995–96), pp. 762–74 (p. 765).

[55] See K. H. Schmidt, 'Die Komposition in gallischen Personennamen', *Zeitschrift für celtische Philologie* 26 (1957), 33–301 (pp. 277–78, 284).

[56] See A. Leskien, 'Litauische Personennamen', *Indogermanische Forschungen. Zeitschrift für indogermanische Sprach- und Altertumskunde* 26 (1910), 325–52 (pp. 332–33, 340); Leskien, 'Die litauischen zweistämmigen Personennamen', *Indogermanische Forschungen. Zeitschrift für indogermanische Sprach- und Altertumskunde* 34 (1914), 296–333 (pp. 303, 317).

[57] Leskien, 'Litauische Personennamen', pp. 348, 350; Leskien, 'Die litauischen zweistämmigen Personennamen', pp. 327, 330–31.

[58] R. Trautmann, *Die altpreußischen Personennamen: Ein Beitrag zur baltischen Philologie* (Göttingen: Vandenhoeck and Ruprecht, 1925), p. 104.

kind are also attested in the medieval Slavonic languages,[59] where we find such forms as *Doberzlaus*, *Dobbroszlaus* < Polabo-Pomeranian **Dobroslav* (Primitive Slavonic **dobrЬ* 'good' + **slava* 'glory, honour')[60] and *Rademir* < Polabo-Pomeranian **Radomir* (Primitive Slavonic **radЬ* 'glad' + **mirЬ* 'peace'.[61] The correspondences within the western Indo-European anthroponymic systems should not blind us to the fact that there are important differences. For example, unlike Germanic, Slavonic has dithematic names formed from verbal bases.[62]

The basic principle of Germanic anthroponymy is that the name must be treated as a substantive arranged as to either the strong or the weak declination classes. The dithematic names in Germanic are true compounds of the type *Ælfgār* < Germanic **Albi-gaiza-*. The second element, here Germanic **gaiza-*, OE *gār* masc. *a*-declension, defines the grammatical gender and declension of the name as a whole, while the first, here Germanic **Albi-* 'elf, spirit' appears in its stem form.[63] In contrast to the rule that the second element of a compound defines its syntactic category, we find names with an adjective as second element, e.g. OE names in *-beald* 'bold', *-beorht* 'bright, *-heard* 'hard, stern', *-mǣr* 'famous'.[64] In compound Germanic personal names, the first element usually has a thematic vowel (German *Fugenvokal*), as with *-u-* in Germanic **Haþu-* and *-a-* in Germanic **Hrōþa-* and **Rēđa-*. This can be subject to a good deal of change. In the first place, it can be weakened and replaced by another vowel, ultimately by *-e-* standing for [ə], cf. OE

[59] For a useful account of the anthroponymic structure of part of the medieval Slavonic onomastic area (Polabo-Pomeranian, Old Sorbish and Old Slovene), see G. Schlimpert, *Slawische Personennamen in mittelalterlichen Quellen zur deutschen Geschichte* (Berlin: Akademie-Verlag, 1978), pp. 165–206.

[60] Schlimpert, *Slawische Personennamen*, p. 42 (for the elements, pp. 41, 127, s.nn. *Dobrita*, *Slavobor*).

[61] Schlimpert, *Slawische Personennamen*, pp. 112–13.

[62] Schlimpert, *Slawische Personennamen*, pp. 167–70,174, 177–78.

[63] See A. Greule, 'Morphologie und Wortbildung der Vornamen: Germanisch', in Eichler et al. (eds), *Namenforschung/Name Studies/Les noms, propres*, pp. 1182–87 (p. 1183), where the OHG name *Hadu-brant* is used to demonstrate these principles. An excellent survey of the principles of personal name formation in Germanic is provided in R. Schützeichel's 'Einführung in die Familiennamenkunde', in M. Gottschald, *Deutsche Namenkunde. Unsere Familiennamen. Mit einer Einführung in die Familiennamenkunde von Rudolf Schützeichel* 6th rev. edn (Berlin and New York: Walter de Gruyter, 2006), pp. 13–76 (pp. 23–39). See also S. Sonderegger, 'Prinzipien germanischer Personennamengebung', in D. Geuenich, W. Haubrichs, J. Jarnut (eds), *Nomen et gens. Zur historischen Aussagekraft frühmittelalterlicher Personennamen* (Berlin and New York: Walter de Gruyter, 1997), pp. 1–29.

[64] See Greule, 'Morphologie und Wortbildung', p. 1183.

Cynemund < earlier _Cynimund_ (Germ *_kunja-_), OE _Hilde-frið_ < *_Hildi-friþu-_. As a point of word-formation, the thematic vowel is normally syncopated when the first element is long syllabic, e.g., *_Auda-berhtaz_ > Frankish-Latin _Autbertus_, OHG _Ôtperht_, OE _Ēadbeorht_, *_Rēđa-wulfaz_ > Frankish-Latin _Râdulf(us)_, OE (Northumbrian) _Rēd-(w)ulf._ Old English generally goes much further with the loss of the thematic vowel, cf. OE _Dæġberht_, _Gūðlac_ and _Þēodrīċ_ in comparison with OHG _Tagabert_, _-breht_, _-preht_, _Tagafrid_, _Tagamâr_, Latino-Burgundian _Gundaharius_ (< Germanic *_Gunþa-harjaz_) and Latino-Frankish _Theudericus_ (< Germanic *_Þeuđa-rīkaz_), respectively.

We designate the earliest layer of Germanic personal names 'primary formations'[65] and these are defined as follows: 1) We are concerned with masculine names; 2) They are of dithematic type; 3) They have appellative compounds as their base and are formed in the same way; 4) They are morphologically and semantically motivated, that is, the names can be semantically interpreted from the appellatives which form them. The name words of the second elements include _-beald_ 'bold', _-beorht_ 'bright, shining', _-frið_ 'peace', _-gār_ 'spear', _-heard_ 'hard, stern', _-here_ 'leader of the army', _-helm_ 'helmet, protection', _-rīċ_ 'powerful', _-weard_ 'guardian', _-wulf_ 'wolf'.[66] The number of first elements greatly exceeds the number of second elements. Primarily using the Old High German system as his starting point, Greule[67] lists the following: _Ber(h)t-_ (< Germ *_berhta-_ 'bright, shining'); _Ber(n)-_ (< Germ *_beran-/*bernu-_ 'bear'); _Bil(i)-/Bill-_ (< Germ *_bilja-/ *billa-_ '(short) sword'); _Brun(i)-_ (< Germ *_brunjō_ 'corslet, coat of mail'); _Diet-_ (= OHG _Theot-_, _Thiot-_) (< Germ *_þeuđō_ 'people'); _Dōm-_ (< Germ *_dōma-_ 'court, judgement'); _Druht-/Truht-_ (< Germ *_druhti-_ 'troop, following'); _Folk-_ (< Germ *_fulka-_ 'the people at arms'); _Hah-_ (< Germ *_hanha-_ 'horse, stallion'); _Heri-_ (< Germ *_harja-_ 'army'); _Hug-_ (< Germ *_hugu-_ 'mind, sense'); _Kun(i)-_ (< Germ *_kunja-_ 'of distinguished lineage'); _Land-_ (< Germ

[65] For the distinction between 'primary' and 'secondary' formations, see O. Höfler, 'Über die Grenzen semasiologischer Personennamenforschung', in _Festschrift für Dietrich Kralik. Dargebracht von Freunden, Kollegen und Schülern_ (Horn, N.-Ö.: Berger, 1954), pp. 26–53, esp. pp. 26–35; G. Schramm, _Namenschatz und Dichtersprache. Studien zu den zweigliedrigen Personennamen der Germanen_ (Göttingen: Vandenhoeck and Ruprecht, 1957), pp. 58–60; G. Müller, _Studien zu den theriophoren Personennamen der Germanen_ (Cologne and Vienna: Böhlau, 1970), pp. 124–37; Schützeichel, 'Einführung in die Familiennamenkunde', pp. 31–32; Andersson, 'Personennamen', pp. 591–94.

[66] For the second elements and the grammatical categories of Germanic dithematic personal names, see Schramm, _Namenschatz und Dichtersprache_, pp. 39–52.

[67] Greule, 'Morphologie und Wortbildung', pp. 1183–84.

landa-* 'land, country'); *Mara(h)-* (< Germ **marha-* 'stallion, horse'); *Nor(d)-* (< Germ **norþa-* 'north'); *Rāt-* (< Germ **rēđa-* 'counsel'); *Sar(a)-* (< Germ **sarwa-* '(military) equipment'); *Sund-* (< Germ **sunþa-* 'south'); *Thing/Ding* (< Germ **þinga-* '(enclosed) assembly'); *Uodal-* (OHG) (< Germ **ōþala-* 'hereditary estate'); *Wolf-* (< Germ **wulfa-* 'wolf'). In the group of 'primary' formations, we can also reckon with copulative compounds, such as ON *Biǫrnúlfr* ('bear' + 'wolf') and with bahuvrihi formations such as OE *Wulfhelm* 'the one with a wolf-shaped helmet'.[68] There is also a secondary type consisting of dithematic names in which there was never a semantic connection between the first and second element. An example of this type is OE *H(e)ardbe(o)rht*. Dithematic names formed by the principle of variation are clearly secondary and we have the famous example of Bishop Wulfstan II of Worcester, whose father bore the name *Æthelstanus* (OE *Æðel*stān**) and whose mother's name was *Wlfgeua* (OE **Wulf***ġifu*).[69] Again, in the case of women's names, we have a group of second elements which are exclusively feminine. This group goes back to Primitive Germanic and is represented in Old English by the elements *-burh* 'protection' (< Germ **-burg-*/**-burgō* 'refuge, protection'), *-flǣd* 'the beautiful one' (< Germ **-flēdī* 'the beautiful one, the shining one'), *-rūn* (< Germ **rūnō* 'the one who makes secrets known') and *-þrȳþ* 'strength'(< Germ **-þrūþī* 'one full of strength').[70] We should note that Old English, unlike the other Germanic dialects, retained the original type of feminine name and did not create such names by the addition of a feminine suffix to a masculine second element.[71]

We should note that there is a good deal of regional variation in Germanic anthroponymy and we can perhaps speak of several subsystems branching off from a common base. If we examine the Old English (sub)system and arrange the first elements of the personal names according to semantic fields, the main protothemes of Old English dithematic personal names are as follows:

a) Religion, cult and supernatural beings: *Ælf-* ([Germ **albi-* 'elf, sprite,

[68] See Müller, *Studien zu den theriophoren Personennamen*, pp. 163, 220; Greule, 'Morphologie und Wortbildung', p. 1184.

[69] Stenton, 'Personal names in place-names', p. 169; Höfler, 'Über die Grenzen semasiologischer Personennamenforschung', pp. 27, 30.

[70] See Schramm, *Namenschatz und Dichtersprache*, pp. 157–73, for a detailed list of the second elements of feminine names in Germanic.

[71] Schramm, *Namenschatz und Dichtersprache*, pp. 120–22.

demon']: cf. OE *ylfe* m. pl. 'elves, goblins, sprites', OE *ælfsċīene* 'bright as an elf or fairy, radiant'); *(E)alh-* ([Germ **alha-* 'sacred grove'?]: OE *ealh* m. 'temple'); *God-* ([Germ **guþ-/*guđ(a)* 'divine being']: OE *god* m. 'god, image of a god'); *Ōs-* ([Germ **ansu-* 'divine being, demigod']: OE **ōs* m. 'god, divinity', more especially one of the group of gods to which Wōden belonged); *Tīu-* (cf. the name of the god OE *Tīw* [< Germ **Tīwaz* < **Teiwa-*], ON *týr* m. 'god', pl. *tívar*); *Wēoh-* ([Germ **wīha-* 'holy, consecrated']: OE *wēoh*, *wīh* n. 'idol').

b) War, battle, military bodies, weapons: *Æsċ-* ([Germ **aski-* 'ash-tree, spear whose shaft was made of ash']: OE *æsċ* m. 'ash-tree; spear, lance; ship'); *B(e)adu-* ([Germ **badwō* 'battle, struggle']: OE *beadu* f. 'war, battle, strife'); *Beorn-* ([Germ **bernu-* 'bear']: OE *beorn* m. 'man, hero, warrior');[72] *Dryht-* ([Germ **druhti-* 'troop, following']: OE *dryht* f. 'host, multitude, army, company, body of retainers, nation, people'); *Eċġ-* ([Germ **agjō* 'edge, blade, sword']: OE *eċġ* f. 'edge, blade, sword'); *Gār-* ([Germ **gaiza-* 'spear']: OE *gār* m. 'spear'); *Gūð-* ([Germ **gunþō* 'battle']: OE *gūð* f. 'combat, battle, war'); *H(e)aðu-* ([Germ **haþu-* 'conflict, discord']: cf. OE *heaðodēor* 'battle-brave', OE *heaðorinc* m. 'warrior', etc.); *Helm-* ([Germ **helma-* 'helmet, protection']: OE *helm* m. 'protection, defence, covering, crown; helmet; protector, lord'); *Heoru-* ([Germ **heru-* 'sword']: OE *heoru* m. 'sword'); *Here-* ([Germ **harja-* 'army']: OE *here* m. 'troop, army, host'); *Hild-* ([Germ **hildjō* 'war, battle', cf. OE *hildemēċe* m. 'battle-sword', OE *hilderinc* m. 'warrior', etc.]: OE *hild* f. 'war, combat'); *Ord-* ([Germ **uzđa-* 'point']: OE *ord* m. 'point, spear-point, spear'); *Siġe-* ([Germ **segiz/*segu-* 'victory']: OE *siġe* m. 'victory'); *Wīġ-* ([Germ **wīga-* 'battle, warrior']: OE *wīġ* n. 'war, battle; valour; army, troop').

c) Names of peoples: *Dene-* (cf. OE *Dene* m. pl. 'the Danes'); *Hūn-* (possibly linked to the ethnic name of the Huns, cf. Old Saxon *hūn* m. 'Hun', but note ON *húnn* m. 'bear cub' and an etymologically related word-group may have existed in West Germanic);[73] *Peht-* (OE *Pe(o)htas*, *Pihtas* m. pl. 'the Picts'); *Seax-* (OE *Seaxe* m. pl. 'the Saxons' or OE *seax* n. 'knife, dagger, short sword');[74] *Swǣf-*, *Swēf-* (OE *Swǣfe*, *Swǣfas* m. pl. 'the Swabians'); *W(e)alh-* (OE *w(e)alh* m. 'Briton, Welshman; foreigner, stranger; slave'); *Wern-* (OE *Wærnas* m. pl. 'the Warni').

d) Collective consciousness: *Cyn(e)-* ([Germ **kunja* '(of distinguished) lineage']:[75] OE *cynn* n. 'kindred'); *Þēod-* ([Germ **þeudō* 'people']: OE *þēod*

[72] For the change in meaning (from 'bear' to 'warrior') and the dissociation from the animal name in Old English, see Müller, *Studien zu den theriophoren Personennamen*, p. 12.

[73] Cf. Ström, *Old English Personal Names in Bede's History*, pp. 24–25.

[74] Cf. Ström, *Old English Personal Names in Bede's History*, p. 33.

[75] For this name element, see the discussion of Schramm, *Namenschatz und*

f. 'people, nation, tribe').

e) Personal designations: *Bregu-* (OE *brego* m. 'ruler, chief, king, lord'); *Cwēn-* fem. ([Germ **kwāni-* 'woman, wife']: OE *cwēn* f. 'woman: wife, consort; queen'); *Ġīsl-* ([Germ **gīsla-* < **geisla-* 'hostage']: OE *ġīs(e)l* m. 'hostage', but cf. Langobardic *gīsil* m. arrow-shaft');[76] *Hyse-* ([Germ **husi-* 'young man, warrior, shoot, scion']: OE *hyse* m. 'son, youth, young man, warrior; shoot, scion'); *Man(n)-* ([Germ **mann-* 'man, human being']: OE *mann* m. 'man'); *Wiht-* ([Germ **wihti-* 'thing, being']: OE *wiht* f. 'person, creature, being'); *Wine-* ([Germ **wini-* 'friend, the beloved one']: OE *wine* m. 'friend, protector, lord').

f) Animal names: *Earn-* ([Germ **arnu-* 'eagle']: OE *earn* m. 'eagle'); *Wulf-* ([Germ **wulfa-* 'wolf']: OE *wulf* m. 'wolf').

g) Designations for places, dwellings and type of ownership: *Burg-* ([Germ **burg-/*burgō* 'refuge, protection']: OE *burg*, *burh* f. 'stronghold, fortified place', perhaps used in personal names with the abstract sense 'protection');[77] *Eard-* ([Germ **arđa-* 'soil, estate, native land']: OE *eard* m. 'native land, dwelling place, estate, cultivated ground; earth, land'); *Ǣþel-*, *Ēþel-* ([Germ **ōþala-/*ōþila-* 'hereditary estate']: OE *ēðel* m. and n. 'native land, ancestral estate'); *Hǣm-* ([Germ **haima-/*haimi-* 'home, homestead, estate']: OE *hām* m. 'homestead, village, estate, manor'); *Sele-* ([Germ **sala-/*sali-* 'hall']: OE *sele* m. 'hall, house, dwelling'); *Tūn-* ([Germ **tūna-* 'fence, enclosure']: OE *tūn* m. 'enclosure, garden; farm, manor; homestead; village').

h) Miscellaneous concrete nouns: *Āc-* ([Germ **aikō* 'oak']: OE *āc* f. 'oak, ship of oak'); *Bēag-* ([Germ **bauga-* 'ring']: OE *bēag* m. 'ring, bracelet'); *Ċēol-* ([Germ **keula-* 'ship']: OE *ċēol* m. 'ship'); *Gold-* ([Germ **gulþa-* 'gold']: OE *gold* n. 'gold'); *Sǣ-* ([Germ **saiwi-* 'sea, lake']: OE *sǣ* m. and f. 'sheet of water, sea, lake, pool'); *Stān-* ([Germ **staina-* 'stone']: OE *stān* m. 'stone').

i) Abstract nouns: *Dæġ-* ([Germ **daga-* 'day']: OE *dæġ* m. 'day'); *Ēad-* ([Germ **auđa-* 'property, wealth']: OE *ēad* n. 'riches, prosperity, good fortune, happiness'); *Ēast-* ([Germ **austa-* ?'dawn']: cf. ON *austr* n. 'the east', OE *ēast* 'east, easterly'); *Hrōþ-*, *Hrǣþ-* ([Germ **hrōþa-/*hrōþi-* 'fame']: cf. ON *hróðr* m. 'praise, commendation', OE *hrēð* m. and n. 'fame, victory; honour', OE *hrōðor* m. 'solace, joy, pleasure'); *Hyġe-* ([Germ **hugu-/*hugi-* 'reason, sense']: OE *hyġe* m. 'thought, heart, mind, disposition, intention: courage'); *Nōð-* ([Germ **nanþō* 'boldness']: OE *nōð* f. 'boldness, daring'); *Rǣd-* ([Germ **rēđa-* 'counsel']: OE *rǣd* m. 'advice,

Dichtersprache, pp. 98–99.

[76] See Janzén, 'De fornvästnordiska personnamnen', p. 41.

[77] Cf. Ström, *Old English Personal Names in Bede's History*, pp. 49, 50.

counsel; deliberation, resolution; prudence, wisdom; plan; power'); *Sidu-* ([Germ **seđu-* 'custom, morality']: OE *sidu* m. 'custom, practice, manner; manners, morality, good conduct, purity'); *Tīd-* ([Germ **tīđi-* 'time']: OE *tīd* f. 'time, period, season'); *Tīr-* ([Germ **tīra-* fame, brilliance']: OE *tīr* m. 'fame, glory, honour'); *Þrȳþ-* ([Germ **þrūþī-* 'strength']: OE *þrȳð* f. 'might, power; splendour, glory'); *Wǣr-* ([Germ **wērō* 'promise, obligation, formal agreement, compact']: OE *wǣr* f. 'faith, fidelity'); *W(e)ald-* ([Germ **walda-* 'power, lordship']: OE *weald* m. 'power, dominion'); *Wil-* ([Germ **weljan-* 'will']: OE *(ġe)will* n. 'will, wish, desire', OE *willa* m. 'mind, determination, purpose; desire, wish, request; joy, pleasure'; *Wyn(n)-* ([Germ **wunjō* 'joy']: OE *wynn* f. 'joy, pleasure, delight, gladness').

j) Adjectives:[78] *Æðel-* ([Germ **aþal(j)a-* 'ancestral']: OE *æðele* 'noble, aristocratic, excellent'); *B(e)ald-* ([Germ **balþa-* 'bold']: OE *b(e)ald* 'bold, brave, confident, strong; impudent'); *Be(o)rht-* ([Germ **berhta-* 'shining']: OE *be(o)rht* 'bright, shining, clear; clear-sounding; excellent, distinguished'); *Brūn-* ([Germ **brūna-* 'glittering; red-brown']: OE *brūn* 'brown, dark; shining'); *Cœ̄n-*, *Cēn-* ([Germ **kōni-* 'experienced, bold']: OE *cēne* 'bold, brave, fierce; powerful; clever'); *Cūð-* ([Germ **kunþa-* 'known']: OE *cūð* 'known, manifest; excellent, famous'); *Dēor-* ([Germ **deuza-* 'wild']: OE *dēor* 'brave, bold; ferocious' or OE *dēore* 'dear, beloved; costly, valuable; noble, excellent'); *(E)ald-* ([Germ **alđa-* 'old']: OE *eald*, *ald* 'old, aged, ancient, eminent'); *Hēah-* ([Germ **hauha-* 'high']: OE *hēah* 'high, tall, lofty; exalted, illustrious; proud, haughty'); *H(e)ard-* ([Germ **harđu-* 'hard, raw']: OE *h(e)ard* 'hard; harsh, severe; strong, vigorous; hardy, bold'); *Lēof-* ([Germ **leuba-* 'beloved']: OE *lēof* 'dear, beloved, valued, pleasant, agreeable'); *Mǣr-* ([Germ **mǣrja-* 'famous']: OE *mǣre* 'famous, renowned, great'); *Sċīr-* ([Germ **skeiri-* 'clear, pure']: OE *sċīr* 'bright, shining'); *Swīð-* ([Germ **swenþa-* 'strong']: OE *swīð* 'strong, mighty, powerful, active'); *Tāt-* ([Germ **taita-* 'bright, shining']: OE **tāt* 'glad, merry', cognate with ON *teitr* 'glad, merry' and OHG *zeiz* 'tender', cf. OE *tǣtan* 'to gladden, cheer'); *Til-* ([Germ **tila-* 'suitable']: OE *til* 'good, useful; excellent; brave; abounding'); *Torht-* ([Germ **turhta-* 'clearly visible']: OE *torht* 'bright, radiant, beautiful, splendid, illustrious'); *Trum-* ([Germ **truma-* 'firm, strong']: OE *trum* 'firm, strong, vigorous, active; trustworthy').

k) Uncertain origin: *Ēan-* (cf. *Aune-* in Burgundian *Aunemundus*, Langobardic *Aunepertus*, *Aunipert*, *-frid*, *-gis*, etc.).

The range of second elements is far more restricted. Of the elements listed above, we find the following attested as second elements:

[78] For the etymologies of adjectives, I generally follow F. Heidermanns, *Etymologisches Wörterbuch der germanischen Primäradjektive* (Berlin and New York: Walter de Gruyter, 1993).

-bæd (cf. *B(e)adu-*); *-b(e)ald*; *-be(o)rht*; *-burh* (fem.); *-gār*; *-ġīls* (= *Ġīsl-*); *-gȳð* (< OE **gȳð* f. [< Germ **gunþjō*] 'combat, battle', side-form of OE *gūð*); *-hēah*; *-h(e)ard*; *-helm*; *-here*; *-hild* (fem.); *-hūn*; *-hyse*; *-nōð*; *-rǣd*; *-siġe*; *-swīð* (fem.); *-þrȳð* (fem.); *-w(e)ald* (as a second element *-w(e)ald* may be an original *nomen agentis* to the verb *wealdan* 'to rule, control, govern', OE **weald* m. 'ruler' cf. ON *valdr* m. 'ruler, holder of power' [< **walduʀ*], belonging to the corresponding ON verb *valda*);[79] *-w(e)alh*; *-wīġ*; *-wīh* ([<**wiha-/*wīhō*], cf. *Wēoh-*); *-wine*; *-wulf*; *-wynn* (fem.). We should also note the following frequent second elements: *-flǣd* fem. (OE **flǣd* f. 'beauty');[80] *-frið* (OE *frið* m. and n. 'peace, security'); *-ġeard* (OE *ġeard* m. 'enclosure, court, residence, dwelling land'); *-ġēat* (from the tribal-name OE *Ġēatas* m. pl. [ON *Gautar*, the inhabitants of Götaland]); *-ġifu* fem. (OE *ġ(i)efu*, *ġifu* f. 'gift'); *-lāc* (OE *lāc* n. and f. 'play, sport (probably originally connected with cultic activity); strife, battle; sacrifice, offering; gift, present');[81] *-lāf* (OE **lāf* m. 'son'); *-leofu* fem. (inflected fem. form of *lēof* 'dear' with analogical *-u*);[82] *-lufu* fem. (OE *lufu* f. 'love, affection'); *-mǣr* (cf. OE *Mǣr-* as a first element and OE *mǣre* 'famous, renowned, great'; the second element *-mǣr* represents an adjective, Germanic **mēr-a-*);[83] *-mōd* (OE *mōd* n. 'heart, mind, spirit; courage; arrogance, pride; power, violence'); *-mund* (OE **mund* m. (*a-* or *u-*declension) 'guardian');[84] *-rīċ* (probably OE **rīċ* m. 'prince, ruler', corresponding to Gothic *reiks* m. 'ruler');[85] *-rūn* fem. (OE *rūn* f. 'mystery, secret'); *-w(e)ard* (OE *weard* m. 'keeper, watchman, protector; lord, king'), *-(w)ulf* (OE *wulf* m. 'wolf').

In addition to the classic dithematic type, Germanic has a range of monothematic names. These are varied in type. We can categorize them as follows:

a) simplex original bynames formed from simplex lexical items;

b) monothematic names formed through the shortening of dithematic names;

c) lall-names;

[79] Feilitzen, *The Pre-Conquest Personal Names of Domesday Book*, p. 410; Janzén, 'De fornvästnordiska personamnen', p. 113.

[80] See Schramm, *Namenschatz und Dichtersprache*, pp. 159–60.

[81] Cf. Janzén, 'De fornvästnordiska personnamnen', p. 109, s.v. *-leikr*.

[82] Feilitzen, *The Pre-Conquest Personal Names of Domesday Book*, p. 316.

[83] Cf. Feilitzen, *The Pre-Conquest Personal Names of Domesday Book*, pp. 325–26.

[84] Feilitzen, *The Pre-Conquest Personal Names of Domesday Book*, p. 330; Janzén, 'De fornvästnordiska personnamnen', p. 109, s.v. *-mundr*.

[85] Feilitzen, *The Pre-Conquest Personal Names of Domesday Book*, pp. 348–49; Janzén, 'De fornvästnordiska personamnen', pp. 120–21, s.v. *-rekr*, *-ríkr*; W. P. Lehmann, *A Gothic Etymological Dictionary* (Leiden: Brill, 1986), p. 283 [R 18]; E. Wessén, *Nordiska namnstudier* (Uppsala: A.-B. Lundequistska Bokhandeln, 1927), pp. 33–43.

d) extended monothematic names augmented by means of diminutive and hypocoristic suffixes (*-*ja*-, -*īna*-, *-*s*-, -*(i)zo* (secondary, Continental Germanic), *-*īþa*-/-*iđa*-, *-*ika*-, *-*ila*-, *-*inga*-/-*unga*-).[86]

If we turn to the Old English subsystem, we can categorize the material as follows:

a) Simple original bynames, e.g. *Boda* (OE *boda* m. 'messenger, herald'.[87] Feilitzen unnecessarily suggests that the etymology is OE **Bodda* or *Budda* from the root **bud*- contained in OE *budda* m. 'beetle');[88] *Boga* (OE *boga* m. 'bow');[89] *Cniht* (OE *cniht* m. 'boy, youth; servant, retainer; disciple; warrior');[90] *Denisċ* (OE *denisċ* 'Danish');[91] *Derch* [Domesday Book] < **Deorc* (OE *deorc* 'dark'[92]); *Edor* (OE *eodor* m. 'hedge, boundary; enclosure; prince, lord');[93] *Snel(l)* (OE *snell* 'smart, ready, keen, fresh, brisk, active, strong, bold');[94] *Snotor* (OE *snotor* 'wise');[95] *Swift* (OE *swift* 'swift, quick');[96] OE *Wel(h)isċ* (*Velhisci* (gen.) 679 [contemporary, probably original] S 8 Ms 1), corresponding to OE *wīelisċ* 'Welsh, British' < **walχisk*).[97] This category is not free of ambiguities. For example, OE *Dēor* may be an original byname belonging to OE *dēor* 'brave, bold; ferocious', but it can also be a short form of names like *Dēorlāf*, *Dēorsiġe*, etc., while OE *Dene* might be an original byname from the name of the Danes, but can equally be a short form of such names as *Deneberht*, *Denemund*. Likewise, OE *W(e)alh*, which is attested early on in the Anglo-Saxon period, is probably best interpreted as an original byname belonging to OE *w(e)alh* m. 'Briton, Welshman; foreigner, stranger; slave', but it can also be a short form of dithematic names in *W(e)alh*-, -*w(e)alh* (Redin only gives the substantive

[86] See Greule, 'Morphologie und Wortbildung', pp. 1184–86.

[87] Redin, *Studies on Uncompounded Personal Names in Old English*, p. 45.

[88] Feilitzen, *The Pre-Conquest Personal Names of Domesday Book*, p. 204.

[89] O. von Feilitzen, 'Some Old English uncompounded personal names and bynames', *Studia Neophilologica* 40 (1968), 5–16 (p. 7).

[90] Feilitzen, *The Pre-Conquest Personal Names of Domesday Book*, pp. 216–17; Redin, *Studies on Uncompounded Personal Names in Old English*, pp. 18–19.

[91] J. Insley. 'Regional variation in Scandinavian personal nomenclature in England', *Nomina* 3 (1979), 52–60 (p. 53).

[92] Feilitzen, *The Pre-Conquest Personal Names of Domesday Book*, p. 223.

[93] Feilitzen, 'Some Old English uncompounded personal names and bynames', p. 7.

[94] Redin, *Studies on Uncompounded Personal Names in Old English*, p. 25.

[95] F. Colman, *Money Talks: Reconstructing Old English* (Berlin and New York: Mouton de Gruyter, 1992), pp. 114, 306.

[96] Redin, *Studies on Uncompounded Personal Names in Old English*, p. 26.

[97] Cf. Redin, *Studies on Uncompounded Personal Names in Old English*, p. 26.

w(e)alh as etymon).[98]

b) Original byname formations belonging to the weak *n*-declension, e.g., *Brāda* (OE *brād* 'broad, flat, open, wide; ample');[99] *Dyċġa* (< **Dug-ja-*, *nomen agentis* belonging to OE *dugan* [vb, usually impersonal] 'to avail, be worth, be capable of, competent; to thrive, be strong; to be good, virtuous, strong');[100] *Seċġa* (OE *seċġ* m. 'man, warrior, hero'; rather than OE *seċġ* f. 'sword');[101] *Wada* (*nomen agentis* from OE *wadan* 'to go, move. stride, advance');[102] *Wiċġa* (OE *wiċġ* n. 'horse');[103]

c) Simple hypocoristic forms belonging to the strong declensions (rare), e.g., *B(e)ald*,[104] short form of names in *B(e)ald-*, *-b(e)ald*; OE *Tūn*, short form of names in *Tūn-*.[105] Here again, there is the problem of ambiguity. *B(e)ald* could equally belong to the adjective *b(e)ald* 'bold'. Another example, OE *Dun(n)*, appears to be an original byname belonging to the adjective *dunn* 'dingy brown, dark coloured' and is attested early.[106] It has a number of derivatives, namely, *Dunna*, *Dunne* fem., *Dynne* (with *-e* < *-i*) and *Dunning*,[107] but we also find the dithematic names **Dunfrið*, *Dunhere* and *Dunstān*,[108] though these could well be secondary formations deriving from the simplex *Dunn(a)*. Note also the fully hypocoristic *Dunċild*, which occurs as DVNCILD, the name of a Guildford moneyer of Æthelred II.[109]

d) Simple hypocoristic forms in *-a* (fem. *-e*), e.g., *Ċēola*, *Ēada*/*Ēata*, *Goda* [fem. *Gode*], *Lēofa*, *Tīda*, *Tūna*, short forms of names in *Ċēol-*, *Ēad-*, *God-*,

[98] Redin, *Studies on Uncompounded Personal Names in Old English*, p. 8.

[99] Redin, *Studies on Uncompounded Personal Names in Old English*, p. 73.

[100] See Redin, *Studies on Uncompounded Personal Names in Old English*, p. 63.

[101] Redin, *Studies on Uncompounded Personal Names in Old English*, p. 53, mentions both alternatives, but leaves it open which is to be preferred.

[102] See Redin, *Studies on Uncompounded Personal Names in Old English*, pp. 79–80.

[103] See Rollason and Rollason (eds), *The Durham Liber Vitae*, II: *Linguistic Commentary*, p. 186.

[104] For this name see Feilitzen, *The Pre-Conquest Personal Names of Domesday Book*, p. 193.

[105] See A. S. Napier and W. H. Stevenson (eds), *The Crawford Collection of Early Charters and Documents now in the Bodleian Library* (Oxford: Clarendon, 1895), p. 131; Redin, *Studies on Uncompounded Personal Names in Old English*, p. 8.

[106] Redin, *Studies on Uncompounded Personal Names in Old English*, pp. 12–13.

[107] Redin, *Studies on Uncompounded Personal Names in Old English*, pp. 47, 114, 122, 166.

[108] Feilitzen, *The Pre-Conquest Personal Names of Domesday Book*, p. 227 and n. 4, pp. 228–29.

[109] Smart, *Sylloge of Coins of the British Isles 28*, p. 27. See further below, p. 228.

Lēof-, *Tīd-* and *Tūn-*, respectively.[110]

e) Simple hypocoristic names in *-i*, e.g., *Ēsi*, hypocoristic form of names in *Ōs-*;[111] *Tīdi*, hypocoristic form of names in *Tīd-*.[112]

f) Hypocoristic forms of dithematic names showing regressive assimilation of the first element, e.g., *Æffa* (< *Ælf-*), *Beonna* (< *Beorn-*), *Imma* (< *Irmin-*), *Odda* (< *Ord-*).[113]

g) Other assimilated forms, e.g., *Ælli* (< *Ælf-*);[114] *Beoffa* (< *Beorhtfrið* or *Beornfrið*).[115]

h) Forms with hypocoristic consonantal gemination, e.g., *Hæddi* (< *H(e)aðu* + *i*-mutation);[116] *Trymma* (< **Trymmi* < *Trum-* + *i*-mutation).[117]

i) Lall-names, e.g. *Dudd*, *Lull*, *Dudda*, *Lulla*.[118]

j) Names formed with a (diminutive) *k*-suffix, e.g., *Dēduc* (Northumbrian) (from names in *Dēd-* [OE *dǣd* f. 'deed, action'],[119] cf. *Dēda* in Bede);[120] *Brȳnca* (from names in *Brūn-*);[121] *Hereca* (from names in *Here-*).[122]

k) Names formed with the (diminutive) *l*-suffix, e.g., *Bǣsil* (Northumbrian) (< *Bōsa*);[123] *Hiddila* (< *Hidd-* [< *Hild-*] + *ilan-*);[124] *Winele* (*Wine*

[110] Redin, *Studies on Uncompounded Personal Names in Old English*, pp. 46, 47–48, 49, 51, 55, 56, 64.

[111] Ström, *Old English Personal Names in Bede's History*, p. 69.

[112] Redin, *Studies on Uncompounded Personal Names in Old English*, p. 124. *Tīdi* has been noted as the first element of TIDESWELL (Db) and TIDESLOW in the same parish (EPNS Db, pp. 172, 173).

[113] Redin, *Studies on Uncompounded Personal Names in Old English*, pp. 59, 61, 67, 68–69; Ström, *Old English Personal Names in Bede's History*, p. 71 (*Imma*).

[114] Ström, *Old English Personal Names in Bede's History*, p. 61.

[115] Feilitzen, 'Some Old English uncompounded personal names and bynames', p. 7.

[116] Ström, *Old English Personal Names in Bede's History*, pp. 69–70. Ström's alternative suggestion (p. 70) that we may be concerned here with a short form of names in *-hard* would seem less likely.

[117] Feilitzen, 'Some Old English uncompounded personal names and bynames', p. 12.

[118] Redin, *Studies on Uncompounded Personal Names in Old English*, pp. 16, 31–32, 63, 100.

[119] Redin, *Studies on Uncompounded Personal Names in Old English*, p. 152; Rollason and Rollason (eds), *The Durham Liber Vitae*, II: *Linguistic Commentary*, p. 173.

[120] Ström, *Old English Personal Names in Bede's History*, pp. 67–68.

[121] Rollason and Rollason (eds), *The Durham Liber Vitae*, II: *Linguistic Commentary*, p. 170.

[122] Redin, *Studies on Uncompounded Personal Names in Old English*, pp. 154–55.

[123] Ström, *Old English Personal Names in Bede's History*, p. 66.

[124] Ström, *Old English Personal Names in Bede's History*, p. 70.

[uncompounded from OE *wine* m. 'friend, protector, lord'] or short form of names in *Wine-* + *-il-ja-*).[125]

l) Names using the **-īna*-suffix,[126] examples being **Ē(a)dīn*, the first element of EDENSOR (Db),[127] and **Ingīn*, the first element of INGLESHAM (W).[128]

m) Forms in *-ing*, e.g., *Brūning*, *Dunning*, *Goding*, **Ording*.[129]

n) Names in *-mann*, e.g., *Dēormann*, *Dudemann*, *Godmann*.[130]

o) Forms in *-ede*, e.g., *Lēofede*, *Mon(n)ede*.[131]

p) Form in *-od*, *Æfod* fem.[132] Cf. the masc. *Æfiċ* with *k*-suffix[133] and Old Saxon *Avo*, *Avico*.[134]

q) Names with the suffix *-isa* (**-is-an-*) (rare), e.g., **Benesa* < **Ban-is-an-*, a name formed from OE *bana* m. 'killer, slayer, murderer', which forms the first element of the Oxfordshire place-name BENSON (*Bænesington* ? *c.* 1100 ASC Ms A [annal for 571], where it replaces the *(Benn)ingtun* of the first hand of Ms A [*c.* 900], *Benesingtun* 1121 [annal for 571] ASC Ms E).[135] The same suffix occurs in Visigothic *Wit(t)iza*.[136]

[125] OE *Winele* is attested as the name of a moneyer of Æthelstan; see Smart, *Sylloge of Coins of the British Isles 28*, p. 78.

[126] See the discussion in Ekwall, *Studies on English Place- and Personal Names*, pp. 2–20.

[127] EPNS Db, pp. 90–91; V. Watts, *The Cambridge Dictionary of English Place-Names* (Cambridge: Cambridge University Press, 2004) [CDEPN], p. 208.

[128] EPNS W, p. 28. See also CDEPN, p. 331.

[129] Feilitzen, *The Pre-Conquest Personal Names of Domesday Book*, p. 17; Redin, *Studies on Uncompounded Personal Names in Old English*, pp. 163–74.

[130] Feilitzen, *The Pre-Conquest Personal Names of Domesday Book*, pp. 223, 227, 265–66. For the hypocoristic function of *-man(n)* in personal names in other Germanic dialects, see the remarks of Schützeichel, 'Einführung in die Familiennamenkunde', pp. 35–36.

[131] Feilitzen, *The Pre-Conquest Personal Names of Domesday Book*, p. 322 and n. 3; Redin, *Studies on Uncompounded Personal Names in Old English*, pp. 161–62.

[132] Feilitzen, 'Some Old English uncompounded personal names and bynames', p. 7.

[133] Feilitzen, *The Pre-Conquest Personal Names of Domesday Book*, p. 172; Redin, *Studies on Uncompounded Personal Names in Old English*, pp. 150–51.

[134] Schlaug, *Die altsächsischen Personennamen vor dem Jahre 1000*, p. 54.

[135] J. M. Bately (ed.), *The Anglo-Saxon Chronicle. A Collaborative Edition, 3: MS A* (Cambridge: Brewer, 1986), p. 24 and n. 3 to the annal for 571. For a full conspectus of forms, see EPNS O, p. 116.

[136] See R. Nedoma, 'Altgermanische Anthroponyme in runenepigraphischen (und anderen) Quellen. Ein Projektbericht', in D. Geuenich, W. Haubrichs and J. Jarnut (eds), *Person und Name. Methodische Probleme bei der Erstellung eines Personennamenbuches des Frühmittelalters* (Berlin and New York: de Gruyter, 2002), pp. 105–26 (pp. 109–13,

r) The type with *-r*-extension, represented by *tepra* (witness) 716×37 (e11) S 94. As was shown by Mawer,[137] this name is a variant of **Tæppa*, **Teppa*. The <e> in **Teppa*, **Tepra* probably reflects West Mercian Second Fronting. **Tæppa* forms the first element of TAPLOW (Bu), 'Tæppa's *hlāw*', where a famous Anglo-Saxon treasure hoard was found.[138]

A final type which should be mentioned here is that compounded with *-ċild* (OE *ċild* n. 'child, infant; youth of gentle birth') and *-sunu* (OE *sunu* m. 'son, descendant'). It is possible that names of the type *Lēofsunu* began as pet forms, but later attained the status of proper baptismal names. The latter is suggested by the fact that *-sunu* appears in other compounds, e.g., **Blæcsunu*, **Mansunu*, and as the simplex *Sunu*.[139]

It should be emphasized that the Old English onomastic (sub)system is a distinct entity within Germanic. The existence of fluctuating anthroponymic (sub)systems creating diversity within a common core can be easily demonstrated on the level of onomastic lexis. So, for example, the name elements *Torht-* (as in OE [Northumbrian] *Torhthelm*, *Torhtmund*, etc.) and *Trum-* (as in OE *Trumhere*, *Trumwine*) lack Continental equivalents.[140] On the other hand, the Durham *Liber Vitae* names *Tīdcume* (fem.) and *Wīġfūs* (masc.)[141] are directly paralleled by Runic Swedish *Tīðkumi* (masc.) and ON *Vígfúss* (masc.), respectively. On another level, it is clear that the element *Þrasa-* (cf. Gothic *þrasa-balþei* f. 'quarrelsomeness'), which occurs in such 'Mediterranean' Germanic names as Latino-Visigothic *Trasimirus*, is originally East Germanic (cf. the name of the Vandal king *Thrasamund* [496–526]). The name element passed into the West Germanic language of the Langobards, but is relatively uncommon north of the Alps and the Loire. It is rare among the Franks, although it is attested in the personal name **Þrasa-walda-*, the first element of the *-ingahaima-* name DESSELGEM (*Thrassaldingehem*

esp. 112–13).

[137] A. Mawer, *Problems of Place-Name Study* (Cambridge: Cambridge University Press, 1929), pp. 108–10.

[138] EPNS Bu, pp. 231–32; CDEPN, p. 600.

[139] See Feilitzen, *The Pre-Conquest Personal Names of Domesday Book*, p. 378 and n. 1.

[140] Rollason and Rollason (eds), *The Durham Liber Vitae*, II: *Linguistic Commentary*, p. 154.

[141] For these names, see Rollason and Rollason (eds), *The Durham Liber Vitae*, II: *Linguistic Commentary*, pp. 152, 158. *Tidcume* is also paralleled by OHG *Zîtcoma* in the Fulda material, cf. Schmid (ed.), *Die Klostergemeinschaft von Fulda im früheren Mittelalter*, III, p. 337.

965 [m11]) in the Belgian province of West-Vlaanderen.[142] It does not occur in Old English or Old Norse. Again, the name-element *Thank-* is characteristically Frankish and Old Saxon, but is conspicuous by its absence in Old English and Old Norse, while dithematic names in *Grîm-* are frequent in Frankish and Langobardic, a characteristic example being *Grîmoald*, which occurs among the names of the Pippinid mayors of the palace of Austrasia and among the names of the Langobardic dukes/princes of Benevento, but have not been noted in Old English. Similarly, the name element **Hrabna-* (cf. OE *hræfn*, OHG *raben*, ON *hrafn* m. 'raven') is not found in compound names in Old English, but occurs as a second element of such compounds in Old High German, Old Saxon and (West) Frankish and as a first element in Old Norse, cf. OHG *Ôtram*, *Waltram*, OSax *Athalram*, West Frankish *Ingoramn*, ON *Hrafnkell*. A more complex case is that of Germanic **Daɣa-* (cf. OE *dæġ*, OSax *dag*, OHG *tag* m. 'day'). In Old English this only occurs as the first element of dithematic names, e.g., OE *Dæġhēah*, *-lāf*, etc., but in Old Saxon it occurs as both a first and a second element, cf. OSax *Daggrîm*, *Dagward*, *Ôsdag*, *Thiaddag*. A similarly complex case is provided by the name element **Taita-*. In Scandinavia we have only the simplex Primitive Norse runic form **tAitR** (= *TaitR*) from the rune-stone of Tveito in Telemark[143] and ON *Teitr*, but Old English has compounds such as *Tātfrið*, *Tātwine* and the monothematic *Tāta* and the extended monothematic forms *Tǣtica* and **Tǣttuca*.[144] Old High German is similar to Old English in that it has compounds of the type *Zeizfrid*, *Zeizheri*, *Zeizmâr*, but also the short form *Zeizo* and the extended *Zeizilo*. On a more regional level, research within Old English would be desirable, but unfortunately little has been done since Stenton made the observation that in place-names the name-element *Ēan-* is confined to Anglian territory and that the name-element *Tīd-* is characteristic of West Midland place-names.[145] Given the far greater amount of place-name material available nowadays, an investigation of the regional patterns taken by the Old English personal names forming the first elements of English place-

[142] M. Gysseling, *Toponymisch Woordenboek van België, Nederland, Luxemburg, Noord-Frankrijk en West-Duitsland (vóór 1226)*, 2 vols (Brussels: Belgisch Interuniversitair Centrum voor Neerlandistiek, 1960), I, p. 264.

[143] W. Krause with contributions by H. Jankuhn, *Die Runeninschriften im älteren Futhark*, 2 vols (Göttingen: Vandenhoeck and Ruprecht, 1966), I, pp. 202–03 [no. 94].

[144] Cf. [*on*] *tættucan stan* 856 (12) S 317 in the bounds of West Woolstone (Brk) which are fully discussed in EPNS Brk, pp. 680–82 (for *tættucan stan* p. 682).

[145] Stenton, 'Personal names in place-names', pp. 180–81.

names would be a desirable and feasible undertaking.

In general, the Old English (sub)system of monothematic personal nomenclature still corresponds fairly closely to its cognate (sub)systems, but there are structural differences. For example, the characteristic form for hypocoristic names formed with the *-l*-suffix in Gothic and Old High German is still the primary weakly inflected **-ilan/-ulan*, cf. Gothic *Agila*, *Ansila*, *Gundila* (= *Gunþ-ila*), *Mērila*, *Sindila* (= *Sinþ-ila*), *Theudila* (= *Þiud-ila*), OHG *Aud-*, *Ôtilo*, *Bert-*, *Birihtilo*, *Dôdilo*, *Gêrlo*, *Herilo*, *Hrôdilo*, *Liutilo*, *Theot-*, *Theudilo*, *Wânilo*, etc.[146] In England, however, the strongly inflected secondary variant is more usual and can be exemplified by **Dæġel*, the first element of DAYLESFORD (Gl)[147] and **Rendel*, the first element of RENDLESHAM (Sf).[148]

These are formal categories which tell us very little about relative chronologies. This brings us in turn to the use of a diachronic perspective in examining Old English personal nomenclature. The sources show, and this should be obvious, that the onomastic system of the seventh century is different from that of the eleventh century. Like all other aspects of linguistic systems, onomastic systems are dynamic not static. Stenton was quite clearly aware of this when he pointed out that Old English personal nomenclature among the upper echelons of Anglo-Saxon society tended to become stereotyped after the Danish wars of the late ninth and early tenth centuries, so that we have a concentration of such elements as *Ælf-*, *Æðel-*, *Beorht-*, *Ēad-*, *God-*, *Lēof-*, *Siġe-* and *Wulf-* among the names of Englishmen attesting royal charters in the last century of the Anglo-Saxon state.[149] It is clear that certain elements, such as *Æðel-* and *Ōs-*, which appear in early sources and have cognates in other Germanic dialects, are old, while others arose much later. The element *Stān-*, for example, first appears in the eleventh century.[150] There is also the question of productivity. For example, we have the Old English monothematic personal name *Deal* belonging to the adjective *deall* 'proud, bold', which is attested as the name of a Winchester moneyer of King Edgar[151] and

[146] The Old High German forms are taken from Autenrieth, Geuenich and Schmid (eds), *Das Verbrüderungsbuch der Abtei Reichenau*.

[147] EPNS Gl **1**, p. 217. We can compare OHG **Dagalo*, the first element of DALKINGEN in Württemberg, see Haubrichs, 'Frühe alemannische Personennamen', p. 80.

[148] DEPN, p. 384.

[149] Stenton, 'Personal names in place-names', pp. 176–77.

[150] Feilitzen, *The Pre-Conquest Personal Names of Domesday Book*, p. 371.

[151] O. von Feilitzen and C. Blunt, 'Personal names on the coinage of Edgar', in P. Clemoes and K. Hughes (eds), *England before the Conquest: Studies in Primary Sources*

forms the first element of DALSTON in Cumberland.[152] Ekwall postulated a weak variant **D(e)alla* as the first element of the Norfolk *-ingas*-name [FIELD & WOOD] DALLING and the Suffolk *-inga-* name DALLINGHOO.[153] As early as the eighth century, *Deal-* occurs in the compound *Dealuuino* (dat., in a letter of 743–46) and a fem. **Cynedeall* occurs in the boundary clause to S 874 *on cynedealle rodæ* 990 (12).[154] We can speak of *Deal-* /*-deall* as a productive element, but compound names formed with it belong to a semantic field and chronological framework different from those of the traditional dithematic names of ancient type. Again, the names *Dod(d)a*, *Dod(d)e*, *Dod(d)ing*, *Dud(d)*, *Dud(d)a*, *Dudde*, *Duddel*, *Dud(d)ing*, *Dudel(e)*, *Duduc* and *Dyddel* all belong to the lall-name root **dod-*/**dud-* (which appears to be Common West Germanic, cf. Old Low Franconian/Middle Dutch *Duda*, *Dudekin*, *Dudolin*, OSax *Dodica*, *Dudica*, etc.). The process is carried a step further with **dod-*/**dud-* becoming treated as if it were a normal element suitable for acting as the first element of dithematic compounds. We thus find the secondary formations *Dudemǣr*, which is attested in the form of *dudemæres hele* in the bounds of Chilton in Berkshire 1015 (*c.* 1200) S 934,[155] its side-form **Dodemǣr*, which occurs in the Leicestershire field names *Dodmerisdale* 1358 and *Dodemersdale c.* 1230,[156] and *Dudwine*, which is attested in the form DVDWINE as the name of a moneyer of Æthelberht and Alfred of Wessex and Burgred of Mercia.[157] This process may have been facilitated by the existence of the variant *Dudeman(n)*, with *-man(n)* as a hypocoristic extension, which already occurs in the ninth century as *dudemon abbas* (witness) 805 (contemporary) S 161 and as DVDEMAN, the name of a moneyer of Burgred of Mercia.[158]

The present survey has been largely concerned with the Old English anthroponymic (sub)system as a part of a wider Germanic system. It is now necessary to examine the non-English elements incorporated into this system. The British element is relatively small, but place-names

Presented to Dorothy Whitelock (Cambridge: Cambridge University Press, 1971), pp. 183–214 (pp. 192–93).

[152] EPNS Cu, pp. 130–31.

[153] DEPN, p. 138.

[154] Feilitzen and Blunt, 'Personal names on the coinage of Edgar', p. 193 and n. 1 and 2.

[155] See EPNS Brk, pp. 767, 768.

[156] EPNS Le **4**, pp. 35, 195.

[157] Smart, *Sylloge of Coins of the British Isles 28*, p. 27; Smart, *Sylloge of Coins of the British Isles 41*, p. 54.

[158] Smart, *Sylloge of Coins of the British Isles 28*, p. 27.

reveal short forms which were morphologically and phonologically integrated into English at an early date as semantically empty onomastic entities. First and foremost here is the British element **Catu-* 'battle'. This is of course contained in the name of the poet Caedmon, which is a straight loan of British *Cadμann*,[159] but also in the Bedan *Cedd* and *Ceadda*, which are fully anglicized forms borne by Englishmen and showing palatalization of the initial consonant and hypocoristic gemination of [d].[160] *Ċedda* forms the first element of CHEDWORTH (Gl)[161] and a devoiced **Ċeatta* occurs in [*on*] *ceattan broc*, [*on*] *ceattan ge mera* in the bounds of Clyffe Pypard (W) (983 [1130×50] S 848). An *-ilan-* derivative, OE **Ċeadela*, forms the first element of CHADDLEWORTH (Brk) (*ceadelanwyrð* 960 [contemporary] S 687),[162] and the secondary strong variant **Ċeadel* occurs in CHADSHUNT (Wa) ([*æt*] *ceadeles funtan* 959 [16] S 544).[163] **Ċeadel(a)* has also been noted as the first element of CHILLINGTON (D),[164] CHADLINGTON (O)[165] and CHADDENWICK (W).[166] A further fully integrated British loan is *Tūda* corresponding to Old Welsh *Tǖta*[167] and to such Gaulish formations as *Teuta*, *-ius*, *-o*, *Touta*, *-o*, etc., an onomastic complex which belongs etymologically to IE **teutā* 'people'.[168] Again, we find the typically Old English geminate forms *Tudda* and *Tutta* and suffix derivatives.[169] We should note the appearance of the Old English geminate form *Tudda* as the first element of [East and North] TUDDENHAM (Nf), TUDDENHAM (Sf) and TUDDENHAM ST. MARTIN (Sf) (< OE **Tuddanhām* 'Tudda's homestead').[170] The degree to which this name-group was integrated into

[159] K. Jackson, *Language and History in Early Britain* (Edinburgh: Edinburgh University Press, 1953), p. 244.

[160] Insley, 'Pre-Conquest personal names', p. 373.

[161] EPNS Gl **1**, p. 150.

[162] EPNS Brk, pp. 289–90.

[163] EPNS Wa, pp. 249–50.

[164] EPNS D, p. 332.

[165] EPNS O, pp. 338–39.

[166] EPNS W, pp. 178–79.

[167] See Jackson, *Language and History in Early Britain*, pp. 309, 316–17.

[168] See D. E. Evans, *Gaulish Personal Names. A Study of some Continental Celtic Formations* (Oxford: Clarendon, 1967), pp. 266–69. For the anthroponymic reflexes of Indo-European **teutā* in Illyrian, Celtic, Germanic and Baltic, see H. Krahe, *Sprache und Vorzeit. Europäische Vorgeschichte nach dem Zeugnis der Sprache* (Heidelberg: Quelle and Meyer, 1954), pp. 65–66.

[169] See Insley, 'Pre-Conquest personal names', pp. 373–74.

[170] DEPN, p. 481.

English can be illustrated by the forms [*an*] *tuddeles þorn*, [*an*] *tuddan hám* 854 (m10) S 1862 in a boundary clause probably from Wessex. Both show hypocoristic consonantal gemination, this being reinforced in the first example by the addition of a secondary -*l*-suffix. A third name of this type is OE **Wassa*, which belongs etymologically to the Celtic root **vasso*- 'servant' contained in such Continental Celtic formations as *Dago-vassus*, *Vasso-rix*, etc.,[171] and is cognate with Cornish *Wasso*. OE **Wassa* forms the first element of two early place-names with the genitive plural -*inga*-, WASHINGTON (Sx) < OE **Wassingatūn* 'the estate of the dependents of Wassa',[172] and WASHINGBOROUGH (Li [Kesteven]) < OE **Wassingaburh*, 'the fortified place of the dependents of Wassa'.[173] All the evidence suggests that the names of the *Ċead*- and *Tūda* groups and **Wassa* were taken into English at an early date. They are etymologically British, but are morphologically and phonologically integrated into the English onomastic system. Therefore they should not be regarded as straightforward direct evidence for the presence of Britons.

In comparison with the British element, the Scandinavian element is much more straightforward. The Scandinavian (sub)system of anthroponymy changed considerably between the later Migration period and the Viking period. Chief among the innovations was the emergence of the theophoric name element *Þór*-,[174] which in turn gave rise to numerous short forms of the type *Tōki*, *Tōli*, *Tōvi* in Danish.[175] We have a characteristic set of protothemes in use in Scandinavian dithematic personal names of the Viking period, e.g., *Ag*-, *Arn*-, *Ás*- (East Scandinavian *Ǣs*- from the tenth century onwards), *Auð*-, *Bjǫrn*-, *Gaut*-, *Grím*-, *Gunn*-, *Hall*-, *Hrafn*-, *Ing(i)*-, *Ketil*-, *Kol*-, *Odd*-, *Ragn*-, *Sig*-, *Stein*-, *Þjóð*-, *Þór*- (Danish *Þur*-), *Ulf*-, *Vé*-, etc..[176] There are also monothematic names. These include original bynames like *Bondi* (Danish), *Drengr*, *Ketill*, *Ormr*, *Sveinn, Úlfr* and *Þiagn* (Swedish) and short forms such as *Ási*, *Auði*, *Gunni*, *Ingi* and *Tōki*. This anthroponymic system was transferred to the Danelaw, where, as is pointed out above, it

[171] See Schmidt, 'Die Komposition in gallischen Personennamen', p. 285.

[172] EPNS Sx, pp. 240–42.

[173] K. Cameron with contributions by J. Insley, *A Dictionary of Lincolnshire Place-Names* (Nottingham: English Place-Name Society, 1998), p. 135.

[174] Hald, *Personnavne i Danmark*, I. *Oldtiden*, pp. 42–50.

[175] See Hald, *Personnavne i Danmark*, I. *Oldtiden*, pp. 86–96.

[176] See Janzén, 'De fornvästnordiska personnamnen', pp. 62–97.

has been the subject of much investigation.[177] The vigour of this system is illustrated by the existence of Anglo-Scandinavian short forms, such as *Accha*, *Acke* < ON *Áskell*, ODan *Ǣskil*, *Auca*, *Ouchi* < ON *Auðkell* (Anglo-Scandinavian *Ouðkel*), *Ogge* < ON *Oddgeirr* and *Turka*, *Turche* < ON *Þorkell*, ODan *Thurkil* (Anglo-Scandinavian *Þurcetel*, *Þurcil*).[178] We also find Scandinavian personal names which are not recorded in Scandinavia itself, but which seem to have been coined in the Danelaw, examples being *Hafgrím*, *Húnketil*, *Liðulf* and *Þornulf*.[179] There is a good deal of regional variation in Scandinavian personal nomenclature in England. For example, *Anundr*, *Bōndi* and *Hǫgni* are common in East Anglia, but rare in the Northern Danelaw, while *Ormr* is common in the North, but rare south of the Humber.[180] There are also chronological problems. The preservation of the full form *-ketill* in East Anglian forms such as *Osketel* and *Turketel* (= Anglo-Scandinavian *Þurcetel* < ON *Þorketill*) suggests that the Scandinavian settlement in East Anglia was finished earlier than in the Northern Danelaw, where the syncopated later form *-kil* (as in such names as *Askil* and *Þurkil*) is usual.[181] Similarly, East Scandinavian forms showing secondary *i*-mutation, such as *Esbern* (ODan *Ǣsbiorn*) and *Eskil*, *Æskil* (ODan *Ǣskil*) can only have been borrowed in the eleventh century in the aftermath of Cnut's invasion.[182] There is also the question of anglicization. This is manifested in the substitution of OE *Ōs-* for Scandinavian *Ās-* in Anglo-Scandinavian *Ōsgot*, *-god* < ON *Ásgautr* and Anglo-Scandinavian (mainly East Anglian) *Ōsketel* < ON *Ásketill* or OE *-stān* for ON *-steinn* in Anglo-Scandinavian *Þurstān* < ON *Þorsteinn* (Danish **Þurstæin*). It is noticeable that anglicized Scandinavian personal names are well attested in early spellings for the Grimston/Toton-hybrid place-names.[183] The

[177] For an excellent general survey of Scandinavian personal nomenclature in the British Isles, see G. Fellows-Jensen, *The Vikings and their Victims: The Verdict of the Names*, The Dorothea Coke Memorial Lecture in Northern Studies delivered at University College London 21 February 1994 (London: University College and Viking Society for Northern Research, 1995).

[178] See Feilitzen, 'Notes on some Scandinavian personal names in English 12th-century records', pp. 64–66; Insley, *Scandinavian Personal Names in Norfolk*, pp. 170–71, 303, 308, 383–85, 386–87.

[179] Fellows-Jensen, *The Vikings and their Victims*, pp. 27–28.

[180] See Insley, *Scandinavian Personal Names in Norfolk*, pp, xxxvi–xxxvii.

[181] See Insley, *Scandinavian Personal Names in Norfolk*, pp. 20–23, 54–59; Insley, 'Pre-Conquest personal names', pp. 390–91.

[182] See Insley, 'Pre-Conquest personal names', p. 390.

[183] K. Cameron, 'Scandinavian settlement in the territory of the Five Boroughs: the place-

question of anglicization leads to certain ambiguities. For example, the form *Oslac* can represent either OE *Ōslāc* or an anglicized form of ON *Áslákr*. In post-Conquest records, *Osbern* can stand for Anglo-Scandinavian *Ōsbeorn* < ON *Ásbiǫrn* or for Norman *Osbern*, which in turn is either a reflex of the Anglo-Scandinavian name or of an Ingvaeonic name (cf. OSax *Ôsbern*) brought to the coastal regions of Frankish Neustria by pre-Norman immigrants from the North Sea basin.[184] In both cases, the context is decisive and in many cases a decision is impossible.

A last category deserving of mention is that of Continental Germanic personal nomenclature. Continental Germanic personal names (usually Old Low Franconian names from the Low Countries or Old French names of West Frankish origin) abound in the Middle English period and occur in the Old English period, where they are relatively well represented among the names of moneyers. Characteristic protothemes for names of this kind found in England include *Agin-* (*Ain-*, *Ein-*), *Amal-*, *Ans-*, *Ebur-*, *Engel-* (*Ingel-*), *Erl-*, *Flod-* (< *Hlod-*), *God-*, *Goz-* (< *Gaut-*), *Hug-*, *Isen-*, *Land-*, *Odel-*, *Ragin-* (*Rain-*, *Rein-*), *T(h)ank-*, *Warin-*.[185] There are ubiquitous names, such as *Ric(h)ard*, *Roger*, *Walter* and *William* (< Old Northern French *Williaume*) and a host of short forms, such as *Drogo*, *Fulco*, *Hugo* and *Rozo*, as well as extended forms such as *Gozelin* and *Tecelin*.[186] In the late Anglo-Saxon period, we find occasional landowners with Continental Germanic personal names. Examples are the thegn Ingeram to whom King Edgar granted land at Vange in Essex in 963 (S 717) and Þeodulfus to whom Æthelred II granted five hides in 1012 (S 929). Continental Germanic personal names occur as the first elements of place-names and field- and minor names of the Middle English period. An early example is TANKERSLEY (WRY). Hugh Smith gave the etymon of the first element as 'OE *Þancrēd*',[187] though he noted elsewhere that Dorothy Whitelock took the name to be of

name evidence. Part III: the Grimston hybrids', in Clemoes and Hughes (eds), *England before the Conquest*, pp. 147–63 (p. 150); Fellows-Jensen, *The Vikings and their Victims*, pp. 17–18.

[184] See J. Insley, 'Some Scandinavian personal names from south-west England', *Namn och Bygd* 70 (1982), 77–93 (pp. 80–81).

[185] See the list given by Forssner, *Continental Germanic Personal Names*, pp. 273–76.

[186] See the list of extended forms in Forssner, *Continental Germanic Personal Names*, pp. 279–80.

[187] EPNS WRY **1**, p. 297.

Continental rather rather than of Old English origin.[188] In fact, we are concerned with a name corresponding to Latino-West Frankish *Tancredus*, a name which was used by the Normans and which goes back to Frankish **Þankrād* (cf. OHG *Thanc-*, *Dancrât*, OSax *Thancrâd*). The Tancred of Tankersley must have been a landowner of the same type as King Edgar's thegn Ingeram or Æthelred II's man Þeodulf. Interestingly, a monk named *Tancrad* occurs among the witnesses of S 1390, a charter of 1020×38 recording a lease of land belonging to St Mary's Minster at Reculver in Kent.[189] Continental Germanic personal names have been noted as the first elements in place-names in *-þorp* (ODan *thorp* 'a secondary settlement, a dependent outlying farmstead'). So, West Frankish *Gêrmund* forms the first element of GRAINTHORPE (Li [Lindsey]) and *Malbert* < West Frankish *Madalbert* that of MABLETHORPE (Li [Lindsey]).[190] Frankish *Ingulf* rather than ON *Ingólfr* may be the first element of INGOLDISTHORPE (Nf).[191] We also have the case of BUSLINGTHORPE (Li [Lindsey]) (*Esetorp* 1086, *Esatorp c.* 1115, *Buselingthorp(e)* Hy2 [1291]) in which OFr *Buzelin*, a name of Continental Germanic (West Frankish) origin, has replaced ODan *Ǣsa* (fem.) or *Ǣsi* (masc.).[192] A more complicated case is that of THEDDINGWORTH (Le). Traditionally, this name has been interpreted as a genitive plural name in *-inga-* compounded with OE *worð* nom. 'court, courtyard, enclosure, farm, village', the first element then being a personal name, OE **Þēoda* or *Tēoda*.[193] Recently (2009), Barrie Cox has suggested a new explanation.[194] On the basis of the Domesday form *Tedingesworde*, he suggests a genitival formation derived from a personal name OE **Þēoding*, **Tēoding* and *worð* 'an enclosure'. Cox reinforces his argument by pointing to the field name form *Thedyngesthorp* 1327 in the same parish. I would go a step further and suggest that the first

[188] EPNS WRY **1**, p. xi.

[189] See S. Kelly, 'Reculver Minster and its early charters', in J. Barrow and A. Wareham (eds), *Myth, Rulership, Church and Charters: Essays in Honour of Nicholas Brooks* (Aldershot: Ashgate, 2008), pp. 67–82 (p. 82).

[190] Cameron, *A Dictionary of Lincolnshire Place-Names*. pp. 52, 85.

[191] Cf. Insley, *Scandinavian Personal Names in Norfolk*, pp. 229–34 (esp. 229, 233).

[192] EPNS Li **7**, p. 24.

[193] DEPN, p. 465; B. Cox, *A Dictionary of Leicestershire and Rutland Place-Names* (Nottingham: English Place-Name Society, 2006), p. 103; CDEPN, p. 607. Watts suggests as an alternative explanation that we may be concerned with a compound of a singular (*-ing*²) OE **Þēoding* 'the place named after Þēoda' and *worð*.

[194] EPNS Le **4**, pp. 268–69.

element of THEDDINGWORTH and *Thedyngesthorp* is a Continental Germanic personal name comparable with OHG *Theoting*, OSax *Thiading*. In this context, it should be mentioned that the form *Theodingus* is attested in the eleventh century in the *Liber Traditionum Sancti Petri Blandiniensis*,[195] a source from Ghent in Flanders, an area which had close contacts to England. The importance of the regional context can also be illustrated by the case of THEDDLETHORPE (Li [Lindsey]), a name whose early forms are difficult. Here the first element is OE **Þēodlāc*.[196] There is no Continental Germanic cognate recorded in the West Frankish, Old Low Franconian and Old Saxon areas with which the English had relatively close relations in the tenth and eleventh centuries and the equivalent OHG *Theotleih* can be excluded, since it is confined to areas in south and central Germany with which the Anglo-Saxons had no direct contact.[197]

Perhaps the logical way to proceed is to examine the personal names appearing in the major types of habitational names. Following the chronology established by recent research, I will examine the names in *-hām*, *-ingas*, *-tūn* and *-bȳ*. My object is to present evidence rather than to make categorical statements. Already in the sixties and seventies of the last century, the work of such scholars as Dodgson, Cox, Gelling and Kuurman established that the names in *-hām* form the earliest layer of English habitative nomenclature.[198] The personal names forming the first elements of names in *-hām* and its somewhat later collective variant *-ingahām* are predominantly of the monothematic and extended monothematic type, but, nevertheless, they cover a broad chronological span. There are archaic names known from Germanic saga, such as *Wæls* (cf. OHG *Welisung*), the first element of [GREAT] WALSINGHAM (Nf).[199] We can note a Continental parallel in the place-name WALZEGEM (*vualzegem* 1011, *walsenghem* 1227) in the Belgian province of Oost-Vlaanderen.[200] There are also names of an ancient type with Continental

[195] Tavernier-Vereecken, *Gentse naamkunde van ca. 1000 tot 1253*, pp. 140, 187.

[196] Cameron, *A Dictionary of Lincolnshire Place-Names*, p. 124.

[197] CDEPN, p. 607.

[198] For a summary of the results of this research, see K. Cameron, 'The significance of English place-names', *Proceedings of the British Academy* 62 (1976), 135–55 (pp. 136–47). See the comments of Parsons above, pp. 50–52.

[199] E. Ekwall, *English Place-Names in* -ing, 2nd edn (Lund: C. W. K. Gleerup, 1962), p. 139; DEPN, p. 494; CDEPN, p. 647.

[200] L. van Durme, *Toponymie van Velzeke-Ruddershove en Bochoute*, 2 parts in 3 vols (Ghent: Secretariaat van de Koninklijke Academie voor Nederlandse Taal- en

Germanic and Gothic parallels, examples of which include *Ǣġel (etymologically related to pre-OHG *Aigil*, a name noted from a late sixth-century runic inscription on a buckle found at Pforzen in Bavarian Swabia, and to OHG *Eigil*)[201] in AYLSHAM (Nf),[202] **Gylla* < **Gȳðla* (corresponding to Visigothic *Gundila* and OHG *Gundilo*) in GILLINGHAM (Do),[203] (K)[204] and (Nf),[205] and **Myndel* (cf. Gothic *Mundila*) in MENDLESHAM (Sf).[206] OE *Walh*, an original byname belonging to the substantive OE *w(e)alh* m. 'Briton, Welshman; foreigner; slave' forms the first element of [NORTH and SOUTH] WALSHAM (Nf) and WALSHAM LE WILLOWS (Sf).[207] This name has an exact German parallel in the place-name WALSHEIM in the Palatinate (*Walahesheimer marca* 768–69 [*c.* 1190], *Uualaheshaim* 780–802 [*c.* 828]), which contains the cognate OHG personal name *Wal(a)h*.[208] It is also interesting to note that OHG *Wal(a)h* is attested as the first element of a name in *-leben*, WALSCHLEBEN in Thuringia (Kreis Erfurt) (*in loco Walheslebe* before 900 [12]);[209] the place-name element *-leben* is also characteristic of the Migration Period.[210] There are, however, examples of personal names belonging to later layers of nomenclature. TRIMINGHAM (Nf) contains OE **Trymma*, a regular hypocoristic form of names in *Trum-*[211] which are

Letterkunde, 1986–1991), part 2 (vol. II), p. 729. Van Durme somewhat tentatively follows Gysseling in interpreting WALZEGEM as a Germanic **Waldtsinga haim*, derived from a personal name **Waldtso* whose dental *-tso*-suffix relects Romance influence. The early forms, however, would rather suit a Frankish **Wals* corresponding to OE *Wæls*.

[201] For *Aigil* and the runic inscription of Pforzen, see R. Nedoma, *Personennamen in südgermanischen Runeninschriften* (Heidelberg: Winter, 2004), pp. 158–67 (esp. pp. 163–66).

[202] EPNS Nf **3**, p. 50, where an OE **Æġel*, corresponding etymologically to Gothic *Agila* is proposed. On formal grounds, the etymon proposed in the present article, OE **Ǣġel*, corresponding to OHG *Eigil*, is to be preferred.

[203] EPNS Do **3**, pp. 9–10.

[204] Ekwall, *English Place-Names in* -ing, p. 119.

[205] Ekwall, *English Place-Names in* -ing, p. 135.

[206] DEPN, p. 321; CDEPN, p. 407.

[207] DEPN, p. 494; CDEPN, p. 647.

[208] M. Dolch and A. Greule, *Historisches Siedlungsnamenbuch der Pfalz* (Speyer: Verlag der Pfälzischen Gesellschaft zur Förderung der Wissenschaften in Speyer, 1991), pp. 475–76.

[209] Schönwälder, *Die* -leben-*Namen*, p. 143.

[210] For a discussion of the dating of the names in *-leben*, see H. Walther, *Namenkundliche Beiträge zur Siedlungsgeschichte des Saale- und Mittelelbegebietes bis zum Ende des 9. Jahrhunderts* (Berlin: Akademie Verlag, 1971), pp. 152–56.

[211] EPNS Nf **3**, p. 45.

attested in early Northumbrian,[212] while WILLISHAM (Sf) contains the dithematic name *Wīġlāf*,[213] which occurs independently as the name of a ninth-century Mercian king. The names in *-ingas* are not habitational names in the strict sense, but originally names of groups.[214] As Kenneth Cameron pointed out,[215] these names only became place-names when the groups from whom they took their names became permanently associated with an area in which they had settled. There is a typological distinction between those *-ingas* names compounded with appellatives, such as SPALDING (Li [Holland]) < OE **spald* 'a narrow opening, slit' (used topographically),[216] or SOMPTING (Sx) < OE **sumpt*, **sunt* 'a marsh, a swamp',[217] or other non-anthroponymic specifics, which theoretically can be formed at any time during the Anglo-Saxon period, and those formed from personal names, which are generally held to be early.[218] Dodgson placed the beginning of the *-ingas* phase in the south-eastern counties to the sixth century.[219] There are also philological reasons supporting this explanation. In the first place, the *-ingas* names do not generally show *i*-mutation and Ekwall's attempt to explain this away by suggesting that we are 'to some extent' concerned with an original *-ung* that was later replaced by *-ing* is clearly unsatisfactory.[220] The personal names are also in need of reexamination and it is possible that their 'archaic' character will have to be questioned. Some of them have an original byname character, for example, **Rēad(a)* (< OE *rēad* 'red' [cf. ON *Rauðr* for a Scandinavian parallel]) in READING (Brk).[221] Dithematic names are fairly uncommon as the first elements of *-ingas* names, but such names as OE

[212] See Ström, *Old English Personal Names in Bede's History*, p. 37.

[213] DEPN, p. 520.

[214] For a survey of research into names in *-ingas*, *-inga-* and *-ing*(-) with a comprehensive bibliography, see G. Fellows-Jensen, '*Hastings*, *Nottingham*, *Mucking* and *Donnington*: a survey of research into *ing*-formations in England', *Namn och Bygd* 84 (1996), 43–60.

[215] Cameron, 'The significance of English place-names', p. 138.

[216] Cameron, *A Dictionary of Lincolnshire Place-Names*, p. 114.

[217] CDEPN, p. 560.

[218] See A. H. Smith, 'Place-names and the Anglo-Saxon settlement', *Proceedings of the British Academy* 42 (1956), 67–88 (pp. 75–76).

[219] J. McN. Dodgson, 'The significance of the distribution of the English place-name in *-ingas*, *-inga-* in south-east England', *Medieval Archaeology* 10 (1966), 1–29 (p. 17).

[220] Ekwall, *English Place-Names in -ing*, p. 80. See also R. Coates, 'On an early date for OE *i*-mutation', in A. Crépin (ed.), *Linguistic and Stylistic Studies in Medieval English* (Paris: Association des médiévistes anglicistes de l'enseignement supérieur, 1984), pp. 25–37.

[221] EPNS Brk, p. 170.

Godhelm, the first element of GODALMING (Sr),[222] and OE *Wīġmǣr*, the first element of WYMERING (Ha),[223] are not of an archaic type. Again, in dealing with the age of hypocoristic names formed with the *-l*-suffix, a differentiated approach is appropriate. Some of these names appear to be of ancient type, e.g., OE **Bǣrla*, the first element of BARLING (Ess),[224] BARLINGS (Li [Lindsey])[225] and BIRLING (K),[226] is a hypocoristic form based on OE *bār* m. 'boar' and may be a personal name with originally heathen cultic significance, and OE **Ǣsla*, *Ēsla*, the first element of EASTLING (K),[227] which is cognate with Gothic, Vandalic Ansila. Likewise of ancient type, is **Hǣsta,* the first element of HASTINGS (Sx).[228] This name is not attested in independent use in Old English sources, but is etymologically identical with Frankish/Langobardic **hai(f)sti-* 'quarrel, zeal', the first element of the name of the Langobardic king *(H)aistulf* (749–56).[229] On the other hand, we find *Dyd(d)el*, which is characteristic of the Middle Saxon period, as the first element of DIDLING (Sx).[230] The name occurs in independent use as *Dyddel* in the witness list of S 1510, the will of Badanoth Beotting, a contemporary Kentish record of the period 845×53. Note also DVDEL, the name of an Exeter moneyer of Æthelred II.[231] An unvoiced variant, **Dyttel*, occurs as the first element of DETLING (K).[232]

The most frequent term used for habitational names in English is OE *tūn* m. 'enclosure; homestead; village; manor, estate', a term which remained productive until after the Norman Conquest. Hugh Smith noted that from 'a fairly extensive sample' of names in *-tūn* and *-ingtūn*, just

[222] EPNS Sr, pp. 195–96.

[223] Ekwall, *English Place-Names in -ing*, pp. 43–44; CDEPN, p. 707.

[224] EPNS Ess, pp. 178.

[225] EPNS Li 7, pp. 5–6.

[226] Ekwall, *English Place-Names in -ing*, p. 9; CDEPN, p. 59.

[227] Ekwall, *English Place-Names in -ing*, p. 11; CDEPN, p. 205.

[228] See Ekwall, *English Place-Names in -ing*, pp. 35–36.

[229] See Haubrichs, 'Langobardic Personal Names', pp. 200, 203.

[230] EPNS Sx, p. 34.

[231] Smart, *Sylloge of Coins of the British Isles 28*, p. 27.

[232] Ekwall, English *Place-Names in -ing*, p. 11; CDEPN, p. 185. For a conspectus of forms, see J. K. Wallenberg, *The Place-Names of Kent* (Uppsala: Appelberg, 1934), p. 136, though Wallenberg's derivation (p. 137) of the name from an OE **Dyttelingas* 'the men of a lumpy, rounded stature' can be rejected out of hand as a classic piece of Zachrissonian exposition in favour of the personal name **Dyttel*, (Old Kentish **Dettel*) which is a quite regular devoiced variant of *Dyddel*.

over 50% are compounded with personal names (about 30% with *-tūn*, about 20% with *-ingtūn*).[233] The personal names compounded with the element *-tūn* are of the following types:[234] a) Simple monothematic personal names, as in DEDDINGTON (O) (OE *Dǣda*),[235] DUNSTON (Li [Kesteven]),[236] (St) (OE *Dunn*),[237] ECTON (Nth) (OE *Ecca*);[238] b) Extended monothematic personal names, as in DERRINGSTONE (K) (OE *Dēoring*),[239] DODLESTON (Ch) (OE *Dod(d)el*),[240] HARLTON (Ca) (OE **Herela*);[241] c) Dithematic personal names, as in CHELMONDISTON (Sf) (OE *Ċēolmund*),[242] DARLASTON (St) (OE *Dēorlāf*),[243] DENNINGTON (Sf) (OE **Deneġifu* fem.),[244] EARDISTON (Wo) (OE *Eard(w)ulf*),[245] HUNSTANTON (Nf) (OE *Hūnstān*),[246] OSBALDESTON (La) (OE *Ōsb(e)ald*)[247] and WOOLSTASTON (Sa) (OE *Wulfstān*);[248] d) Scandinavian personal names, as in ASLOCKTON (Nt) (ON *Áslákr*),[249] THURMASTON (Le) (ON *Þormóðr*),[250] TOTON (Nt) (ODan *Tōvi*)[251] and THELVETON (Nf) (OSwed *Þjálfi*);[252] e) Continental Germanic personal names, as in OGSTON (Db) (*Oggod*, corresponding to such Continental forms as

[233] A. H. Smith, *English Place-Name Elements*, 2 vols, English Place-Name Society 25–26 (Cambridge: Cambridge University Press, 1956) [EPNE], II, p. 192.

[234] For a list more extensive than that given here, see EPNE, II, pp. 197–98. For examples of personal names combined with *-ingtūn*, see EPNE, I, p. 297.

[235] EPNS O, p. 256.

[236] Cameron, *A Dictionary of Lincolnshire Place-Names*, p. 39.

[237] EPNS St **1**, p. 84; D. Horovitz, *The Place-Names of Staffordshire* (Brewood: the author, 2005), p. 241.

[238] EPNS Nth, pp. 138–39.

[239] Wallenberg, *Kentish Place-Names*, p. 189; CDEPN, p. 184.

[240] EPNS Ch **4**, pp. 156–57.

[241] EPNS Ca, pp. 76–77.

[242] DEPN, p. 99; CDEPN, p. 129.

[243] Horovitz, *The Place-Names of Staffordshire*, p. 224; CDEPN, p. 179.

[244] DEPN, p. 142; CDEPN, p. 183.

[245] EPNS Wo, p. 58.

[246] DEPN, p. 257; CDEPN, p. 323.

[247] E. Ekwall, *The Place-Names of Lancashire* (Manchester: Manchester University Press, 1922), p. 70; CDEPN, p. 453.

[248] EPNS Sa **1**, pp. 323–24.

[249] EPNS Nt, p. 219.

[250] EPNS Le **3**, p. 237.

[251] EPNS Nt, p. 152.

[252] DEPN, p. 465. For the specifically Swedish character of the personal name *Þjálfi*, see Insley, *Scandinavian Personal Names in Norfolk*, p. 390.

Odgaudus, *Otgaudus*, *Otgotus* < Frankish **Auđ-gaut*).[253] Some consideration should also be given to the morphology of the names formed from a personal name + *-tūn*. We find the normal genitival type represented by such names as EDLASTON (Db) (*Edolves-*, *-ues-*, *-vis-*, *-tun*, *-ton(am) c.* 1141) < OE **Ēad(w)ulfestūn* (OE *Ēadwulf* + *tūn*)[254] and THULSTON (Db) (*Turulvestun*, *Torulfestune* 1086) < Anglo-Scandinavian **Þurulfestūn* (ON *Þórólfr* + *tūn*).[255] However, there are also names in which the personal name would appear to be uninflected and to have an attributive function, as in the Nottinghamshire place-names EDWALTON (*Edvvoltone*, *Edwoltun* 1086) < OE *Ēadw(e)ald* + *tūn*[256] and THOROTON (*Turuertune* 1086) < Anglo-Scandinavian *Þurferð* < ON **Þorfrøðr* + *tūn*.[257] The second of these names should be compared with the etymologically identical Derbyshire place-name THURVASTON (*Turverdestune* 1086) < Anglo-Scandinavian **Þurferðestūn*,[258] a name of the normal genitival type.

The place-name type personal name + *tūn* and the place-names in -*ing*(*a*)*tūn* are exclusively Anglo-Saxon, the -*ing*(*a*)*tūn* names in the northern French *département* of Pas-de-Calais being the result of Kentish immigration in this area in the Middle Saxon period.[259] The personal names occurring as the first elements of these northern French names are typical of the Middle Saxon period, e.g., OE *Bacga* in BAINCTHUN,[260] OE (Kentish) *Dīorw(e)ald* in DIRLINCTHUN,[261] OE *Goda* in GODINCTHUN,[262] OE *Tōta* in TODINCTHUN,[263] OE *Wada* in WADENTHUN,[264] WAINCTHUN[265]

[253] EPNS Db, pp. 217–18.

[254] EPNS Db, p. 557.

[255] EPNS Db, p. 462.

[256] EPNS Nt, p. 246.

[257] EPNS Nt, p. 229.

[258] EPNS Db, pp. 593–94.

[259] See J. Insley, 'Otlinga Saxonia', *Reallexikon der Germanischen Altertumskunde* 22 (2003), 387–91. See also H. Ehmer, *Die sächsischen Siedlungen auf dem französischen „Litus Saxonicum"* (Halle (Saale): Max Niemeyer, 1937), pp. 9–48.

[260] Insley, 'Otlinga Saxonia', pp. 387–88. See also Ehmer, *Die sächsischen Siedlungen*, pp. 21–22, where the base is wrongly given as 'OE *Baga*'.

[261] Insley, 'Otlinga Saxonia', p. 388. See also Ehmer, *Die sächsischen Siedlungen*, p. 22.

[262] Ehmer, *Die sächsischen Siedlungen*, p. 22.

[263] Insley, 'Otlinga Saxonia', p. 388. See also Ehmer, *Die sächsischen Siedlungen*, p. 23, where the personal name is rendered as 'OE *Tota*'.

[264] Insley, 'Otlinga Saxonia', p. 388; Ehmer, *Die sächsischen Siedlingen*, p. 23.

[265] Ehmer, *Die sächsischen Siedlungen*, p. 24.

and WARINCTHUN,[266] and OE *Wǣrwulf* (Kentish *Wērwulf*) in VERLINCTHUN.[267] Ekwall believed that English *-ingtūn* reflected an original collective *-ingatūn* with genitive plural *-inga-*, medial *-a-* being lost in the inflected form *-ingatūne*.[268] English research, as manifested in the early volumes of the English Place-Name Society's Survey, generally treated the medial *-ing-* in the *-ington* names as corresponding to a regular genitive. For example, the editors of the Nottinghamshire Survey, writing in 1940, interpreted DALLINGTON (lost) (*Dallintune* 1086) and RUDDINGTON (*Roddintone* 1086) as 'Dealla's farm' and 'Rudda's farm', respectively.[269] It is clear that the variant *-ingatūn* does exist, examples being the form [*æt*] *Tudincgatunæ* (? TEDDINGTON Mx) *c*. 968×71 (12) S 1485, which stands for an OE **Tūdingatūn* 'homestead, village of the followers of Tūda',[270] and the Staffordshire place-name ESSINGTON < OE **Esningatūn* 'homestead, village of the followers of Esne'.[271] It is equally clear however that this type, which is rare, cannot account for the majority of names in *-ingtūn*. A. H. Smith interpreted the *-ing-* in *-ingtūn* as a connective particle (*-ing*[4]), and he took it to have an associative function in place-names like TEDDINGTON (Wo) < OE **Teotta* + *ingtūn*, this name then having the sense 'farmstead or village associated with a man named Teotta' rather than 'Teotta's farmstead or village'.[272] The difficulty with this is that we find place-names in which early forms in *-ingtūn* alternate with those with a genitival ending. TIDDINGTON (Wa), which contains the Old English personal name *Tīda* as first element, occurs as [*æt*] *Tidinctune* in 969 and as the gentival form *Tidantun* in 985,[273] while BRIGHTWALTON (Brk), a name containing OE *Beorhtweald*

[266] Ehmer, *Die sächsischen Siedlungen*, p. 24.

[267] Ehmer, *Die sächsischen Siedlungen*, p. 25, gives the following forms: *Verlingtun* 1173, *Werlinghetun* 1199, *Vrelinguethun* 1392. He proposes a short form of OE *Wernbeald*, *Wernbeorht* as first element, whilst, at the same time, allowing for the possibility that we are concerned with a short form of *Wǣrbeald*, *-beorht*, etc. formed with the *-l*-suffix. In this context, his remark that in the case of the latter, *i*-mutation could have been operative is irrelevant, because the Old Kentish form of the prototheme is *Wēr-*. We can reckon here with an OE (Kentish) *Wērulf* < *Wērwulf*, with reduction of the first medial syllable in the place-name form (**Wērulfing(a)tūn* > **Wereling(a)tūn* > **Werling(a)tūn*.

[268] DEPN, p. 264.

[269] EPNS Nt, pp. 214, 248–49.

[270] EPNS Mx, p. 24 and n. 1.

[271] EPNS St **1**, pp. 49–50; Horovitz, *The Place-Names of Staffordshire*, p. 249.

[272] Cf. EPNE, I, p. 295; Smith, 'Place-names and the Anglo-Saxon settlement', pp. 79–80 (p. 80).

[273] EPNS Wa, p. 232.

as first element, occurs as [*æt*] *Beorhtwaldingtune* in 939 and as *Bristoldestune* in 1086.[274] A way round this would perhaps be that the association suggested by the medial *-ing-* is seignorial, while the use of the genitive indicates possession. This is perhaps too categoric. We can perhaps come a little closer to the truth by examining the two genitival formations UFFINGTON (Brk) < OE **Uffantūn* 'Uffa's village, estate'[275] and WOOLSTONE (Brk) < OE **Wulfrīċestūn* 'Wulfrīċ's village, estate'.[276] Sir Frank Stenton believed we are concerned with possession here, but possession with rights over the land and the peasants who tilled it, either in the form of services or dues, the Uffa of Uffington then being 'the great man and leading settler of the township'.[277] Margaret Gelling has shown that the reality is more complex. She demonstrated that the estates which were named UFFINGTON and WOOLSTONE from the middle of the tenth century onwards had formerly been part of a larger territorial complex which the English named *Æscesbyrig* (*Æscesburh*) (after an ancient hill fort on the boundary between Woolstone and Uffington), a land-unit which had probably been in existence since the Iron Age or even earlier.[278] In other words, Uffington and Woolstone were *seigneuries* resulting from the carve-up of an ancient territory in the middle of the tenth century and Uffa and Wulfric were the respective *seigneurs*. We can identify the Wulfric of Woolstone with the thegn of that name who acquired the two parcels of land in *Æscesburh* which later became Woolstone in 944 and 958.[279] In S 687, an original charter of 960,[280] King Edgar restored the estate at *Æscesburuh* and fourteen other estates to Wulfric, Wulfric having forfeited these properties for some undisclosed offence apparently between 958 and 960.[281] The forfeiture and the restoration, for which Wulfric had to pay 120 mancuses of gold, make it

[274] EPNS Brk, p. 237. Cf. EPNE, I, p. 294.

[275] EPNS Brk, p. 379.

[276] EPNS Brk, p. 383.

[277] F. M. Stenton, *The Place-Names of Berkshire: An Essay* (Reading: University College, 1911), p. 25.

[278] EPNS Brk, p. 824. For *Æscesburh*/*-byrig*, see EPNS Brk, p. 380.

[279] See EPNS Brk, p. 675.

[280] S. E. Kelly (ed.), *Charters of Abingdon Abbey, Part II* (Oxford: British Academy, 2001), no. 86 (pp. 351–55).

[281] For the date, see Kelly (ed.), *Charters of Abingdon Abbey, Part II*, p. 355. For a discussion of the estates in this charter and for Wulfric, whom Susan Kelly identifies with the Wulfric Cufing of S 1491, a Winchester charter of 958, see Kelly (ed.), *Charters of Abingdon Abbey, Part I* (Oxford: British Academy, 2000), pp. clxxiii–clxxxv, and *Part II*, pp. 354–55.

clear that Wulfric's rights of possession were limited by the royal power. Woolstone is recorded as *Olvricestone* in Domesday Book,[282] so that at some juncture between 960 and 1086, the estate must have taken the name of the tenant Wulfric and perhaps the renaming of that part of *Æscesburh* which had passed into Wulfric's possession to **Wulfrīċestūn* may indeed imply something more substantial, perhaps the status of *bōcland*. It should be noted that the seignoral implication is also inherent in the Grimston/Toton-hybrid type of place-name and here we must quote Kenneth Cameron:

> If my interpretation of these hybrids is correct, and most people seem now to accept that it is, their significance may be even greater than Sir Frank Stenton thought back in 1940, when he said that it was at least possible that they denoted English villages "acquired by a Danish owner at the time when the Great Army of the Danes divided out the land which it had chosen for settlement" [EPNS Nt, p. xix]. I suggest, therefore, very tentatively indeed, that not only are names like Aslockton, Car Colston and Colston Bassett, Gamston, Gonalston and Toton, for example, "manorial" in type, but that they have also for nearly 1,100 years concealed the names of *Áslakr*, *Kolr*, *Gamall*, *Gunnulf* and *Tovi*, men of the *micel here*, the extent and density of whose settlements have exercised, and will, it seems, continue in the future to exercise, the academic mind, as I have suggested elsewhere [Cameron, 'The Significance of English Place-Names'].[283]

The connective *-ing-* also occurs in conjunction with elements other than personal names, as in the case of SINNINGTON (NRY), whose first element is the river-name SEVEN.[284] Arngart has a different interpretation of the personal name + *ingtūn* type. He suggests that names of the type *Eadbrihtincgtun* (ABBERTON, Wo) and *Eadbaldingtun* (ABLINGTON, Gl) have the sense '*tūn* called *Eadbrihtincg* (Ēadbeorht's place)', '*tūn* called Eadbalding', etc.[285] In Arngart's scheme of things, we are concerned with

[282] EPNS Brk, p. 383.

[283] K. Cameron, 'The Scandinavian settlement of eastern England: the place-name evidence', *Ortnamnssällskapets i Uppsala årsskrift* (1978), 7–17 (pp. 16–17). For further views on Grimston-type names see Fellows-Jensen above, pp. 98–99 and Townend above, pp. 117–20; for the suggestion that some Grimston-names are late formations see G. Fellows-Jensen, 'Scandinavian settlement names in East Anglia: some problems', *Nomina* 22 (1999), 45–60 (pp. 58–60), and G. Fellows-Jensen, 'Grimston revisited', in O. J. Padel and D. N. Parsons (eds), *A Commodity of Good Names: Essays in Honour of Margaret Gelling* (Donington: Shaun Tyas, 2008), pp. 125–35.

[284] Smith, 'Place-names and the Anglo-Saxon settlement', p. 80.

[285] O. Arngart, 'On the *ingtūn* type of English place name', *Studia Neophilologica* 44

singular names in *-ing* to which the habitative generic *-tūn* has been added. It should also be noted that there are examples of designations for natural features in *-ing* to which *-tūn* has been added,[286] an example being the hill-name RIVINGTON [PIKE] (La) (< OE **hrēofing* 'the rough, the rugged one' + *tūn*).[287] The numerous examples of the English place-name DOD(D)INGTON were traditionally interpreted as containing the Old English personal name *Dodda*, though it has also been suggested that they reflect a hill-name **dod(d)ing*, **dud(d)ing* + *tūn*.[288] Though specifically Anglo-Saxon and without parallels elsewhere in Germanic toponymy, it would seem that the *-ingtūn* group includes names which are relatively early. Certainly some of them contain personal names of an archaic character. Examples are **Benesa*, a name formed with the *-isa*-suffix, in BENSON in Oxfordshire,[289] and **Dryhtel*, **Dryhtla*, a name etymologically identical with OHG **Truhtilo*,[290] in DRIGHLINGTON (WRY).[291] There are forms which present considerable difficulties. Ekwall proposed an OE **Trost(a)*, a personal name which he compares to 'O[ld] G[erman] *Trostila*, *Trostheri*', as the first element of TROSTON (Sf) ([*æt*] *Trostingtune* 975×1016 [contemporary] S 1487).[292] Förstemann gives the forms *Traostilo*, *Trostila* (fem.), *Trostheri*, *Trosthad*, *Trostmar* and *Tr(a)ostolf*, and quite correctly takes the first element to belong to OHG *trôst* m. 'solace, help; confidence'.[293] OHG *trôst* goes back to Germanic **trausta-*,[294] and since Germanic /au/ became /æ:ɑ/ in Old

(1972), 263–73 (pp. 268–69).

[286] EPNE, I, p. 296.

[287] Ekwall, *The Place-Names of Lancashire*, pp. 28, 48; CDEPN, pp. 502–03.

[288] See G. Fellows Jensen, 'English place-names such as Doddington and Donnington', *Sydsvenska ortnamnssällskapets årsskrift* (1974), 26–65 (pp. 37–38).

[289] EPNS O, p. 116 (see also above and note 135).

[290] OHG **Truhtilo* has been suggested as the first element of the place-name Treuchtlingen in Middle Franconia, see W.-A. Frhr. v. Reitzenstein, *Lexikon bayerischer Ortsnamen: Herkunft und Bedeutung*, Zweite, verbesserte und erweiterte Auflage (Munich: C. H. Beck, 1991), p. 382. However, N. Wagner, 'Zu ungeklärten Personennamen in süddeutschen Ortsnamen', *Beiträge zur Namenforschung*, n.s. 37 (2002), 371–407 (pp. 403–04), has shown that there are cogent phonological reasons for taking the first element of TREUCHTLINGEN to be **Trūtilo*, an extended short form of such names as *Trūt-bert*, *Trūt-man*, *Trūt-mār*, *Trūt-munt*, *Trūt-win*. This has been recently accepted by Frhr. v. Reitzenstein in his *Lexikon fränkischer Ortsnamen: Herkunft und Bedeutung, Oberfranken, Mittelfranken, Unterfranken* (Munich: C. H. Beck, 2009), p. 223.

[291] EPNS WRY **3**, pp. 19–20.

[292] DEPN, p. 481.

[293] Förstemann, *Altdeutsches namenbuch*, I: *Personennamen*, col. 1399.

[294] *Kluge: Etymologisches Wörterbuch der deutschen Sprache*, Bearbeitet von Elmar

English, it is impossible that the first element of TROSTON is an archaic Old English personal name cognate with OHG names in *Trôst-*. We are rather concerned with a reflex of the Scandinavian byname *Trausti*[295] which has been extended by means of the OE *-ing*/ON *-ingr* suffix. Hence, we are concerned here with an Anglo-Scandinavian personal name/byname **Trousting*/**Trōsting* used adjectivally as the first element of a place-name in *-tūn*.

The characteristic Scandinavian habitative element in the Danelaw is ODan *bȳ*, ON *býr* m. 'settlement, village', which seems to have been normally applied to nucleated villages and occasionally to towns (most notably in the case of Derby, where the Scandinavian name replaced OE *Norðworðiġ*),[296] and hamlets. The place-name type in which *-bȳ* is compounded with a personal name is much more ubiquitous in the Danelaw than in Denmark itself, where it is only found sporadically, apart from a group of names in Angeln on both sides of the Schlei.[297] Hugh Smith estimated that approximately two-thirds of the English names in *-bȳ* are compounded with personal names.[298] We find typically Danish names, such as *Tōki* in TUGBY (Le)[299] and *Wraghi* in WRAWBY (Li [Lindsey]),[300] but there are also names which have a predominantly West Scandinavian distribution in the Viking period, such as ON *Áslákr* in ASLACKBY (Li [Kesteven])[301] and ON *Þorgrímr* in THORGANBY (Li [Lindsey]),[302] (ERY).[303] ON *Vífill*, the first element of WEELSBY (Li [Lindsey])[304] is exclusively West Scandinavian, while **Tīdhe*, the first element of TITHBY (Nt),[305] has East Scandinavian parallels and would be

Seebold, 25, erweiterte Auflage (Berlin and New York: Walter de Gruyter, 2011), p. 932, s.v. *Trost*.

[295] E. H. Lind, *Norsk-isländska personbinamn från medeltiden* (Uppsala: A.-B. Lundequistska Bokhandeln, 1920–21), col. 386.

[296] EPNS Db, p. 446.

[297] For names in *-bȳ* in Denmark compounded with personal names, see B. H. Pedersen, 'Bebyggelsesnavne på -by sammensat med personnavn', in *Ti Afhandlinger* (Copenhagen: G. E. C. Gad, 1960), pp. 10–46.

[298] EPNE, I, p. 68.

[299] EPNS Le **3**, p. 254.

[300] EPNS Li **2**, pp. 307–08.

[301] Cameron, *A Dictionary of Lincolnshire Place-Names*, p. 5.

[302] EPNS Li **3**, pp. 157–58.

[303] EPNS ERY, pp. 263–64.

[304] EPNS Li **5**, pp. 165–66.

[305] EPNS Nt, p. 242.

an acceptable short form of Runic Swedish *Tīðkumi*. There are also names showing Scandinavian inflectional morphology. BRANSBY (Li [Lindsey]) and RAUCEBY (Li [Kesteven]), whose first elements are the Scandinavian personal names *Brandr* and *Rauðr*, respectively,[306] both preserve the Danish genitive in *-s* of the *a*-declension, while AISMUNDERBY in the West Riding of Yorkshire, whose first element is ON *Ásmundr*,[307] preserves the genitive in *-ar* of the ON *u*-declension. We also find the uninflected type, as in THEALBY (Li [Lindsey]) (*Tedulfbi* 1086) < ON *Þjóðólfr* + *bȳ*.[308] The element *-bȳ* also occurs with Old English personal names, as in AUDLEBY (Li [Lindsey]) < OE (Anglian) *Ald(w)ulf* + *bȳ*,[309] DUNSBY (Li [Kesteven: 2×]) < OE *Dun(n)* + *bȳ*[310] and WARTNABY (Le) < OE **Wrac-*, **Wræcnōð* + *bȳ*.[311] Barrie Cox suggests that the first element here is an unrecorded OE **Wærcnōð*,[312] but a name **Wrac-*, **Wræcnōð*, the early forms of whose first element had undergone metathesis of **Wrac-/*Wræc-* > **Warc-/*Wærc-*, would make better etymological sense. The first element of this name can be linked etymologically to OE *wracu* f. 'revenge, punishment, enmity', OE *wræc* n. (? f.) 'misery, persecution, vengeance, exile' and we can compare such Continental Germanic personal names as OSax *Wrakhard*, *Wrakheri*,[313] latinized West Frankish *Uuaraculfus* (< **Wraki-wulf*)[314] and Alemannic *Uuaracco*, *Uuarachio*, etc..[315] In the North and North-West, there are also examples of names in *-bȳ* compounded with Old Irish personal names. Examples are DOVENBY (Irish *Dubhán*)[316] and MELMERBY (Irish *Máelmuire*)[317] in Cumberland. In Cumberland and Dumfriesshire, there is a group of names in *-bȳ* compounded with Continental personal names, e.g., AGLIONBY (Cu) (OFr *Agyllun*),[318] BOTCHERBY (Cu) (OFr *Bochard* <

[306] Cameron, *A Dictionary of Lincolnshire Place-Names*, pp. 19, 100.

[307] EPNS WRY **5**, p. 168.

[308] EPNS Li **6**, pp. 44–45.

[309] EPNS Li **2**, p. 88.

[310] Cameron, *A Dictionary of Lincolnshire Place-Names*, p. 39.

[311] For the early forms, see EPNS Le **2**, p. 165.

[312] EPNS Le **2**, p. 166.

[313] Schlaug, *Die altsächsischen Personennamen vor dem Jahre 1000*, pp. 180–81.

[314] Hägermann (ed.), *Das Polyptychon von Saint-Germain-des-Prés*, p. 317.

[315] Autenrieth, Geuenich and Schmid (eds), *Das Verbrüderungsbuch der Abtei Reichenau*, p. 176.

[316] EPNS Cu, p. 284.

[317] EPNS Cu, pp. 223–24.

[318] EPNS Cu, p. 158.

Frankish **Burg-harđu-*),[319] ROBBERBY (Cu) (OFr *Robert* < Frankish **Hrōđa-berhta-*)[320] and WIGGONBY (Cu) (OBret *Uuicon*).[321] Gillian Fellows-Jensen believes that these personal names had been substituted for earlier specifics after the Norman occupation of Carlisle in 1092,[322] but one could rather argue that *-bȳ* was still a living element in this region in the twelfth century and that such names were coined by an Anglo-Scandinavian population which probably still spoke a Scandinavian language.

[319] EPNS Cu, p. 42.

[320] EPNS Cu, p. 208.

[321] EPNS Cu, p. 120.

[322] G. Fellows-Jensen, *Scandinavian Settlement Names in the North-West* (Copenhagen: C. A. Reitzel, 1985), pp. 21–24, esp. pp. 22, 24.

9

Women in place-names

Carole Hough

The first 100 entries in Ekwall's historical dictionary of English place-names include 72 references to people, of which 9 or possibly 10 are to females.[1] Another 100 entries from the beginning of letter *M* include 41 references to people, of which 10 are to females, and another 100 entries from the beginning of letter *W* include between 54 and 57 references to people, of which 2 are to females.[2] The lower figures are used for the percentages in Table 1 (p. 252). The pattern reflects both the high incidence of references to people in English place-names, and the minority status of women in the toponymicon, as indeed in most other types of historical record. As regards the epigraphic material from Anglo-Saxon England, for instance, Okasha notes that '[t]he 136 vernacular personal names divide into approximately 4.5 male names to every female name'.[3]

This situation is not necessarily paralleled elsewhere, even in other parts of mainland Britain. A similar exercise undertaken with recent dictionaries of Welsh and Scottish place-names yielded much lower results.[4] Samples from Wales contained on average 26.5 references to

The volumes of the English Place-Name Society's Survey are indicated by EPNS + county abbreviation as given on p. vi.

[1] E. Ekwall, *The Concise Oxford Dictionary of English Place-Names*, 4th edn (Oxford: Clarendon, 1960) [DEPN]. Cross references and entries for place-name elements were ignored.

[2] Samples were taken from different sections to counteract the potential influence of a high incidence of individual personal name themes or appellatives.

[3] E. Okasha, 'Anglo-Saxon women: the evidence from inscriptions', in J. Higgitt, K. Forsyth and D. N. Parsons (eds), *Roman, Runes and Ogham: Medieval Inscriptions in the Insular World and on the Continent* (Donington: Shaun Tyas, 2001), pp. 79–88 (p. 81).

[4] H. W. Owen and R. Morgan, *Dictionary of the Place-Names of Wales* (Llandysul: Gomer, 2007); A. Grant, *The Pocket Guide to Scottish Place-Names* (Glasgow: Richard Drew, 2010). The higher incidence in Wales and Scotland of Celtic place-names, often with the generic element in initial position, leads to some clustering within the

people per 100 entries, with an average of 2 being to females, while corresponding samples from Scotland contained on average 21 references to people per 100 entries, with an average of 1 being to a female. The contrast may serve to highlight the major part played in the formation of English place-names by the social environment, alongside the natural and built environments.

Table 1. Average references in sample dictionary entries

	people	women
England	**55.7%**	**7%**
Wales	**26.5%**	**2%**
Scotland	**21%**	**1%**

This chapter has two main aims. Firstly, to discuss the place-names relating to women in their legal and historical contexts, with particular reference to the Anglo-Saxon period from which most of our major place-names survive. Secondly, to discuss the place-names relating to women in their linguistic contexts, with reference to the history of English through to the later periods represented in the minor names and field-names that make up the majority of English Place-Name Society material. Although the focus will be on English place-names, comparative evidence from Scotland and Wales will also be relevant.

Previous research

Allusions to women in place-names can take various different forms, and the 21 secure instances mentioned above from Ekwall's *Dictionary* comprise 10 personal names, 5 saints' names, and 6 appellatives. They suggest a range of potential approaches. One is to examine occurrences of individual (or groups of) appellatives in order to establish geographical distribution and semantic range. Some progress along these lines was made by an analysis of three terms found in the legal as well as toponymic corpora—Old English (OE) *gift* and *morgengifu*, both referring to a marriage portion, and OE *mægden* 'young woman'—which also identified a number of recurrent name-types on the basis of place-

alphabetical sequence of place-names from the same generic, some more likely than others to combine with references to people. These sections were avoided so as not to skew the results.

name surveys completed up to 1995.[5] Subsequent work has investigated individual terms and types in greater detail. The name-type Maiden Castle, with 21 known occurrences mainly in northern England and in Scotland, has been identified as a medieval literary topos, stimulated by Geoffrey of Monmouth's use of the phrase *Castellum Puellarum* 'girls' castle' to refer to Edinburgh Castle or Rock.[6] The name-type Maid(en)well, with 21 known occurrences mainly in the south and midlands of England and in Wales, has been interpreted as a dedication to the Virgin Mary parallel to the ubiquitous Lady Well.[7]

References to women are often difficult to differentiate from other types of place-name element, and in some instances, closer investigation has suggested alternative interpretations for appellatives previously included within this group. The term *mother* in the place-names of northern England and Scotland is now considered to be a reference to a type of water-course rather than the kinship term,[8] while the distinguishing feature of the fords at Bridford, Britford and Birdforth may have been a plank bridge rather than a bride.[9] Even where a female referent is generally agreed, the type of woman may be uncertain. The first element of Portinscale (Cu) refers either to townswomen or to prostitutes, and cases have been made for both interpretations.[10]

Another focus of research is personal names. The following discussion will draw on a corpus of over 500 feminine personal names in place-names from the Anglo-Saxon and early medieval periods, compiled from EPNS and other major surveys published up to the end of the twentieth

[5] C. Hough, 'Place-name evidence relating to the interpretation of Old English legal terminology', *Leeds Studies in English* 27 (1996), 19–48.

[6] R. Coates, 'Maiden Castle, Geoffrey of Monmouth and Hārūn al-Rašīd', *Nomina* 29 (2006), 5–60.

[7] C. Hough, 'The name-type Maid(en)well', *Nomina* 33 (2010), 27–44.

[8] M. Scott, 'Unsung etymologies: lexical and onomastic evidence for the influence of Scots on English', in M. Mooijaart and M. van der Wal (eds), *Yesterday's Words: Contemporary, Current and Future Lexicography* (Newcastle: Cambridge Scholars Publishing, 2008), pp. 187–98 (pp. 195–97).

[9] C. Hough, 'The place-names Bridford, Britford, and Birdforth', *Nottingham Medieval Studies* 39 (1995), 12–18.

[10] The traditional interpretation 'prostitutes' was challenged by C. Hough, 'The ladies of Portinscale', *Journal of the English Place-Name Society* 29 (1997), 71–78. The most recent and authoritative discussion, D. Whaley, *A Dictionary of Lake District Place-Names* (Nottingham: English Place-Name Society, 2006), p. 267, remains agnostic.

century.[11] This revealed a number of interesting patterns, as well as highlighting advances in place-name scholarship since the pioneering work of Sir Frank Stenton.[12] Some additions to the corpus are suggested in a subsequent study of Scandinavian feminine personal names in English place-names,[13] and others have come to light in later EPNS volumes. Less attention has so far been paid to eponymous women from the later medieval and early modern periods, but the potential of this line of research is illustrated by the section on 'Field-name references to women' in Field's *A History of English Field-Names*.[14]

Regional studies, looking at the full range of references to women in the place-names of a particular area, may give a more rounded picture. This has been attempted for north-west England, where a substantial body of evidence has been assembled as part of an investigation of the role of women in the historical landscape.[15] The bulk of the material comprises personal names from the Anglo-Saxon through to the early modern periods, but appellatives and dedications are also strongly represented. This more holistic methodology is in keeping with the general approach taken by the EPNS Survey of English Place-Names, progressing as it does through the systematic analysis of place-names on a county-by-county basis. The present chapter will utilize data from the studies mentioned above, but will also take much of its material from three of the most recent EPNS volumes, all published as part of the AHRC-funded project 'Perceptions of Place'. As envisaged in the original grant application, these volumes advance the Survey on various fronts while illustrating regional variation in naming practices. It therefore seems

[11] C. Hough, 'Women in English place-names', in C. Hough and K. A. Lowe (eds), *'Lastworda Betst': Essays in Memory of Christine E. Fell with her Unpublished Writings* (Donington: Shaun Tyas, 2002), pp. 41–106.

[12] F. M. Stenton, 'The historical bearing of place-name studies: the place of women in Anglo-Saxon society', *Transactions of the Royal Historical Society*, 4th series 25 (1943), 1–13. Reprinted in D. M. Stenton (ed.), *Preparatory to Anglo-Saxon England: Being the Collected Papers of Frank Merry Stenton* (Oxford: Clarendon, 1970), pp. 314–24. Page numbers are cited from the reprint.

[13] J. Jesch, 'Scandinavian women's names in English place-names', in O. J. Padel and D. N. Parsons (eds), *A Commodity of Good Names. Essays in Honour of Margaret Gelling* (Donington: Shaun Tyas, 2008), pp. 154–62.

[14] J. Field, *A History of English Field-Names* (London and New York: Longman, 1993), pp. 166–67.

[15] C. Hough, 'Women in the landscape: place-name evidence for women in north-west England', *Nomina* 31 (2008), 45–66.

appropriate to consider the extent to which they advance our knowledge of women in place-names, and how far they illustrate regional variation in this type of naming practice.

Regional variation

Table 2. Place-names relating to women

	EPNS Du **1**	EPNS Le **4**	EPNS Sa **5**
women total	**83**	**49**	**80**
gazetteer page total	**233**	**300**	**298**
women per page	**0.356**	**0.163**	**0.268**

The three EPNS volumes in question are Part 5 of Margaret Gelling's *The Place-Names of Shropshire*, covering the hundreds of Pimhill and Bradford North (EPNS Sa **5**), Part 1 of Victor Watts's *The Place-Names of County Durham*, covering Stockton Ward (EPNS Du **1**), and Part 4 of Barrie Cox's *The Place-Names of Leicestershire*, covering Gartree Hundred (EPNS Le **4**). With one county bordering on Wales, another close to Scotland, and the third in the heart of the Danelaw, they reflect different cultural as well as linguistic influences. EPNS Sa **5** contains around 80 place-names relating in some way to women. EPNS Du **1** contains around 83, and EPNS Le **4** contains around 49. These figures exclude transferred or derived names, where existing place-names are used as qualifiers in new formations,[16] and also exclude the names of churches, inns and streets, which are treated differently by the three editors.[17] Even so, the statistics are not directly comparable. Most obviously, the volumes are of different lengths. In EPNS Sa **5**, the place-name gazetteer runs to 298 pages. In EPNS Du **1**, it runs to 233 pages, and in EPNS Le **4**, to 300 pages. Moreover, different practices are followed by the different editors. Gelling adopts a non-inclusive policy towards field-names, resulting in the exclusion of potentially relevant examples with personal name qualifiers:

[16] For instance, the figures include Lady Wood in Kissington and Cold Overton parish, Leicestershire, but not Lady Wood Close or Lady Wood Meadow (EPNS Le **4**, pp. 147, 149).

[17] As regards names relating to women, EPNS Sa **5** has no church names, no inn names and 2 street-names. EPNS Du **1** has 10 church names, no inn names and 21 street-names. EPNS Le **4** has 8 church names, 10 inn names and 8 street-names.

> The (a) list presented here [for Dudleston] is not a complete tally of the names of these fields. Categories omitted are: Welsh names in which Cae is qualified by personal names or surnames (e.g. Cae Davee, ~ Beddow, ~ Dicken); English names in which Field is similarly qualified (e.g. Harpers ~, Parry's ~); and names like Field below Barlows, ~ by Jenny Jones, ~ facing the Tailor's. (EPNS Sa **5**, p. 38)

It is worth noting, however, that the effect of this should be to depress the number of references to women, making the high tally of 80 in EPNS Sa **5** all the more striking, while EPNS Du **1**, with the smallest gazetteer, has the highest number of references to women. These will need to be unpacked below with regard to different historical periods and types of name. The vast majority are medieval or early modern, with fewer than half a dozen relevant names in each volume likely to date from the Anglo-Saxon period. Viewed in their historical and linguistic contexts, they have much to tell us.

Anglo-Saxon law

The position of women in Anglo-Saxon England is highly controversial. There exists a range of evidence in the form of charters, laws, wills and other documents, but much of it offers difficulties of interpretation, and almost all is hotly disputed. A Google search for *Women in Anglo-Saxon England* produces 1,040,000 results, with the first two webpages listed offering the following opposing viewpoints:

> For many women, Anglo-Saxon England was a golden age of power and wealth, culture and education; women's role in marriage had (for the free-born) immense potential.[18]

> Women's social position was at the bottom of the scale; they were forced into an arranged marriage and they had abusive husbands on whom they were completely dependent.[19]

Oddly, both cite as an authority Christine Fell, whose 1984 book *Women in Anglo-Saxon England* remains a classic text.[20] Although the case for the legal independence of Anglo-Saxon women was persuasively set out

[18] <hullwebs.co.uk/content/c-anglo-saxon/home-life/anglo-saxon-women.htm>, accessed 28 May 2010.

[19] <csis.pace.edu/grendel/projf20004g/womenAnglo.html>, accessed 28 May 2010.

[20] C. Fell, C. Clark and E. Williams, *Women in Anglo-Saxon England and the Impact of 1066* (Oxford: Blackwell, 1984).

by Fell, and has been substantially supported by a systematic analysis of all clauses relating to women in the early Old English law-codes,[21] there remain many areas of contention. Part of the problem is that the evidence is fragmentary. From the seventh century we have three sets of laws from the kingdom of Kent, and a lengthy and probably composite series issued by the West Saxon king Ine. The first national law-code was issued by Alfred the Great towards the end of the ninth century and supplemented by later kings in a succession of additional enactments culminating in two major law-codes issued by the Danish conqueror Cnut in the early eleventh century.[22] The majority of laws relating to women occur in the laws of Æthelberht of Kent, Ine, Alfred and Cnut, but not only are these widely disparate in terms of time and space, they are also often cryptically worded, requiring background information now difficult to reconstruct. The problem may be illustrated by the variety of interpretations offered for a short sequence of clauses from the laws of Æthelberht, dealing respectively with the three main categories of women in Anglo-Saxon society – married, unmarried and widowed:[23]

> Æbt 73. Gif fri wif locbore leswæs hwæt gedeþ xxx scłł gebete.
>
> If a freewoman, with long hair, commits any misconduct, she is to pay 30 shillings compensation.[24]
>
> If a free woman in control of the keys does anything seriously dishonest she is to pay thirty shillings compensation.[25]
>
> If a free woman in a position of responsibility commits any violence, she is to pay 30 shillings compensation.[26]

[21] C. Hough, 'Women and the law in seventh-century England', *Nottingham Medieval Studies* 51 (2007), 207–30.

[22] The standard edition of the Anglo-Saxon law-codes, including variant readings from all extant manuscripts, is F. Liebermann, *Die Gesetze der Angelsachsen*, 3 vols (Halle: Max Niemeyer, 1903–1916). An introductory account is C. Hough, 'Legal and documentary writings', in P. Pulsiano and E. Treharne (eds), *A Companion to Anglo-Saxon Literature* (Oxford: Blackwell, 2001), pp. 170–87.

[23] The Old English text is from the semi-diplomatic edition presented in Hough, 'Women and the law in seventh-century England'.

[24] D. Whitelock, *English Historical Documents* I, c. *500–1042*, 2nd edn (London and New York: Eyre Methuen and Oxford University Press, 1979), p. 393.

[25] C. Fell, 'A *friwif locbore* revisited', *Anglo-Saxon England* 13 (1984), 157–65.

[26] C. Hough, 'Two Kentish laws concerning women: a new reading of Æthelberht 73 and 74', *Anglia* 19 (2001), 554–78.

Æbt 74. Mægþbot sy swa friges mannes.

The compensation for [injury to] a maiden is to be as for a freeman.[27]

The compensation payable by an unmarried girl is to be the same as that payable by a free woman.[28]

Æbt 75. Mund þare betstan widuwan eorlcundre L scillinga gebete. Ðare oþre xx scłł, ðare þriddan xii scłł. Þare feorðan vi scłł.

[Breach of] guardianship over a noble-born widow of the highest class is to be compensated for with 50 shillings; that over one of the second class, with 20 shillings; over one of the third class, with 12 shillings; over one of the fourth, with six shillings.[29]

The right of protection of a widow of the highest class of nobility is to be compensated for at 50 shillings; that of one of the second class, at 20 shillings; of one of the third class, at 12 shillings; of one of the fourth class, at 6 shillings.[30]

Æthelberht 73 has been variously taken to refer to a long-haired woman committing a sexual offence, a woman in a position of responsibility committing a financial offence, and a woman in a position of responsibility committing an act of violence. Æthelberht 74 has been taken to refer to injuries inflicted *against* or *by* an unmarried girl, aligned with those relating to a free *man* or a free *woman*, and Æthelberht 75 has been taken to refer to the right of protection exerted *over* a dependent widow, or *by* an independent one.

In short, the same evidence can be—and has been—used to support widely differing views of the position of women. In this context, the place-name corpus provides a valuable source of additional information.

Anglo-Saxon personal names

With the exception of the maiden, to whom we shall return, the three-fold categorization of women used as the basis for legal distinctions rarely occurs in the place-name corpus. A. H. Smith's *English Place-Name Elements* has no entry for OE *widuwe*, and identifies only four potential

[27] Whitelock, *English Historical Documents* I, c. *500–1042*, p. 393.

[28] Hough, 'Two Kentish laws concerning women'.

[29] Whitelock, *English Historical Documents* I, c. *500–1042*, p. 393.

[30] C. Hough, 'The widow's *mund* in Æthelberht 75 and 76', *Journal of English and Germanic Philology* 98 (1999), 1–16.

occurrences of OE *wīf*: Westoe (Du), Westow (ERY), Winestead (ERY) and Wyton (ERY).[31] All are open to challenge. Watts considers the derivation of Westoe to be ambiguous between the genitive plural *wīfa* and a feminine personal name OE **Wīfe*.[32] The same alternatives are given by Mills for Westow and Winestead,[33] and appear to be consistent with the available evidence for Wyton (EPNS ERY, p. 52). Although other relevant names have come to light since publication of EPNE in 1956, they are vanishingly few. Perhaps the most secure are Woodyhyde 'widow's hide of land' (*Wodewehide* 1311) in Dorset, with reference to the widow of a Domesday landholder (EPNS Do **1**, p. 66), and a lost field-name *Wiueneleche c.* 1200 'the women's boggy stream' in Durham, from the genitive plural form of *wīf* (EPNS Du **1**, p. 174).

By contrast, over 500 occurrences of Old English feminine personal names in place-names had been identified by the turn of the century,[34] and the number is still rising. This in itself appears to suggest that women enjoyed some prominence in Anglo-Saxon society. The corpus includes examples from all the historical counties of England except Durham, for which no EPNS Survey was then available. EPNS Du **1**, p. 77 contributes one potential occurrence: a lost field-name *meldrespot*, *Meldrespol'*, *meldrychepolflatt' c.* 1250, for which a derivation from OE *Mildþrȳð* is tentatively proposed. The 13 examples already on record for Shropshire are supplemented by Ollerton (*Alvereton* 1284–85) from OE *Ælfwaru* (EPNS Sa **5**, p. 224). EPNS Le **4**, p. 35 adds a lost field-name *Goldiuethorn* 12, *Goldiuethornwang* 12, *c.* 1200 from OE *Goldgifu*, and the same volume brings to light a previously unrecorded personal name OE **Dryhtburh* as the qualifier of a lost field-name *Drihtburhlawe* Hy 3 (EPNS Le **4**, pp. 123–24).

Although again interpretation can be problematic, considerable advances have been made in recent years. Whereas Stenton considered feminine personal names in place-names to reflect the involvement of women in the early Anglo-Saxon settlements, the growing recognition

[31] A. H. Smith, *English Place-Name Elements*, 2 vols, English Place-Name Society 25–26 (Cambridge: Cambridge University Press, 1956) [EPNE].

[32] V. Watts with contributions by J. Insley, *A Dictionary of County Durham Place-Names* (Nottingham: English Place-Name Society, 2002), pp. 135–36.

[33] A. D. Mills, *A Dictionary of British Place-Names* (Oxford: Oxford University Press, 2003), pp. 492, 502.

[34] A total of 543 are identified in Hough, 'Women in English place-names', but these include doubtful instances flagged with a question mark.

that toponyms were unstable during the Middle Ages, with estates being renamed after successive owners, means that some of the eponymous women may be identified with land-holders from the tenth or eleventh centuries. As Gelling has pointed out:

> It is possible to point to a growing and quite impressive number of instances in which an 'x's *tūn*' place-name is firmly connected with a man or woman mentioned in a charter of tenth- or eleventh-century date, or with an overlord who appears in the Domesday Survey.[35]

An example is Aughton in Wiltshire from OE *Æffe*, the name of a widow to whom the estate was bequeathed in 931 by her husband Wulfgar (EPNS W, p. 344).[36] Similarly in Dorset and Devon, Afflington (EPNS Do **1**, pp. 6–7), Goodcott (EPNS D, p. 355) and Lovacott (EPNS D, p. 108), are named from women who held the manors during the reign of Edward the Confessor (1042–66).

In other instances the link may not be manorial but based on rights associated with the land. This may account in part for a high incidence of topographical generics, as Fell suggests:

> Crofts, cottages, fields, woods and streams linked with female personal names abound, and again it is hard to know quite what the links imply. In the case of cottage and field, land-holding is a reasonable proposition; in the case of a wood, the woman may simply have had rights of collecting fuel.[37]

Fell also argues strongly that some place-names reflect administrative responsibilities, showing women capable of holding the same roles in estate management as men:

> It is obvious that the combination of women's names with elements implying land-holding and manorial status (*tun* and *burh*), with land-clearance (*leah*), with church, road and bridge-building or repair (*cyrice*, *stræt*, *ford*, *brycg*), suggests a reasonable range of administrative responsibilities.[38]

[35] M. Gelling, *Signposts to the Past: Place-Names and the History of England*, 3rd edn (Chichester: Phillimore, 1997), p. 181. As Gelling goes on to demonstrate, the phenomenon is not limited to formations with OE *tūn*.

[36] Gelling, *Signposts*, p. 124.

[37] Fell, *Women in Anglo-Saxon England*, p. 99.

[38] Fell, *Women in Anglo-Saxon England*, p. 100.

Table 3. Elements combined more than once with OE feminine personal names

OE *tūn* 'farmstead, estate'	52 (70)
OE *lēah* 'wood, clearing, pasture, meadow'	28 (38)
OE/ME *croft* 'small enclosed field'	21 (24)
OE *w(i)elle* 'spring, stream'	13 (18)
OE *denu* 'valley'	11 (18)
OE *land* 'land'	11 (14)
OE *burh* 'fortified place, manor house'	10 (12)
OE *hām* 'homestead'	9 (14)
OE *brycg* 'bridge'	9
OE *cot* 'cottage, shelter'	8 (9)
OE **rod* 'clearing'	7
OE *-ingtūn* 'farmstead associated with ...'	6 (15)
OE *hyll* 'hill'	6 (7)
OE *hlāw* 'hill, barrow'	6
OE *mǣd* 'meadow'	6
OE *þorn* 'thorn-tree, hawthorn'	6
OE *wīc* 'specialized farm'	6
OE *feld* 'open country'	5 (8)
OE *ford* 'ford'	5 (8)
OE *hamm* 'land hemmed in by water or marsh, water-meadow'	5 (8)
OE *cumb* 'valley	5 (6)
OE *ēg* 'island'	5 (6)
OE *haga* 'hedge, enclosure'	5
OE *worð* 'enclosure'	4 (9)
OE *grāf*, *grǣfe* 'grove, copse'	4 (8)
OE *trēow* 'tree'	4 (6)
OE *(ge)mǣre* 'boundary'	4 (5)
OE *(ge)hæg* 'fence, enclosure'	4
OE *sīc* 'small stream, meadow along a stream'	4
OE *dūn* 'hill'	3 (6)
OE *brōc* 'brook, stream'	3 (4)
OE *æcer* 'plot of cultivated land'	3
OE *cross* 'cross'	3
OE *dīc* 'ditch, dike'	3
OE *mōr* 'moor, marshland'	3
OE *strǣt* 'Roman road'	3

OE *wang* 'piece of meadowland / ON *vangr* 'garden, in-field'	3
OE *weg* 'way, path'	3
OE *hyrst* 'hillock, copse'	2 (6)
OE *stān* 'stone'	2 (5)
OE *lane* 'lane'	2 (4)
OE *pōl* 'pool'	2 (4)
OE *stoc* 'place'	2 (4)
OE *h(e)alh* 'nook, water-meadow'	2 (3)
OE *hrycg* / ON *hryggr* 'ridge'	2 (3)
OE *wudu* 'wood'	2 (3)
OE *bece* 'stream, valley	2
OE *be(o)rg* 'hill, mound, tumulus'	2
OE *cirice* 'church'	2
ON *garðr* 'enclosure	2
OE *geat* 'gate, opening'	2
ON *haugr* 'hill, burial mound'	2
OE *hlid-geat* 'swing-gate'	2
OE *(ge)lād* 'small water-course, crossing-place'	2
OE *lǣs* 'pasture, meadow land'	2
OE *mersc* 'watery land, marsh'	2
OE *mynster* 'monastery'	2
OE **ryding* 'clearing'	2
ON *skáli* 'hut, shieling'	2
ON *þorp* 'secondary settlement'	2

It is indeed the case that certain generics are very strongly represented. Table 3 sets out, in descending order of frequency, all generics with at least two secure occurrences in combination with Old English feminine personal names.[39] Figures in brackets include doubtful occurrences.[40]

[39] The figures are based on the index in Hough, 'Women in English place-names', pp. 98–104, with the addition of a lost Cumberland field-name *Alditcroft* 1261–72 'Aldgȳþ's *croft*' (EPNS Cu, p. 450) that was overlooked in that study, and the following names that have come to light more recently: *Alyeuelidieht c.*1225 'Ælfgifu's *hlid-geat*' (EPNS Sa **4**, p. 88), *Drihtburhlawe* Hy 3 '*Dryhtburh's *hlāw*' (EPNS Le **4**, pp. 123–124), *Godrenelonde* 1321'Godrūn's *land*' (EPNS Do **4**, p. 487), *Goldiuethorn* 12 'Goldgifu's *þorn* (EPNS Le **4**, p. 35), *Meldrespol*' *c.* 1250 ?'Mildþrȳð's *pōl*' (EPNS Du **1**, p. 77) and Ollerton 'Ælfwaru's *tūn*' (EPNS Sa **5**, p. 224).

[40] These are names flagged with a question mark to indicate uncertainty in Hough,

Between 52 and 70 compounds of Old English feminine personal names with OE *tūn* have been identified, alongside 28 (38) with OE *lēah* and 10 (12) with OE *burh* – almost half the number (25) of Old English masculine personal names with OE *burh* listed in VEPN.[41] In some instances, occurrences of feminine names may have implications for the function of masculine names in corresponding formations. If Fell is correct in suggesting that compounds of Old English feminine personal names with OE *brycg* and OE *ford*—totalling 9 and 5 (8) respectively in the present corpus[42]—are to be understood in terms of responsibility for the upkeep of the bridge or ford, it appears to follow that the same may apply to masculine personal names. This is a possibility only considered by VEPN (s.v. *brycg*) for appellatives:

> Pers.ns are presumably owners or builders, [...] Other terms for people—**cyning**, probably also **gilda** and perhaps **cēap-mann**—denote owners and/or those responsible for the bridge's upkeep.[43]

However, it should be noted that 2 compounds with OE *cirice* and 3 with OE *strǣt* make up a much smaller proportion of the total, and offer scant support for Fell's interpretation. Although possible as an explanation for the eponymous Ælfgȳð of Alvechurch (EPNS Wo, pp. 332–33), Ælfwaru (or Æðelwaru) of a lost *Aylwarstrete* 1279 (Ha),[44] Bōthild of a lost *Bothildestrete* (EPNS BdHu, p. 298), and Burghild of Buckle Street (EPNS Wo, p. 2; EPNS Gl **1**, pp. 15–16), it can be ruled out as regards Peakirk, where the allusion is to St Pega, the sister of St Guthlac, 'who is reputed to have established a cell here' (EPNS Nth, p. 241).

The range of generics found with feminine personal names combines with other types of evidence to indicate a wide chronological span.

'Women in English place-names', pp. 98–104.

[41] VEPN = D. Parsons and T. Styles with C. Hough, *The Vocabulary of English Place-Names* I *(Á–Box)* (Nottingham: Centre for English Name-Studies, 1997); D. N. Parsons and T. Styles, *The Vocabulary of English Place-Names* II *(Brace–Cæster)* (Nottingham: Centre for English Name-Studies, 2000); D. N. Parsons, *The Vocabulary of English Place-Names* III *(Ceafor–Cock-pit)* (Nottingham: English Place-Name Society, 2004).

[42] These figures are higher than was previously realized, since M. Gelling and A. Cole, *The Landscape of Place-Names* (Stamford: Shaun Tyas, 2000), identify only one occurrence of OE *brycg* with a feminine personal name (p. 69), and comment that '[w]ith only two exceptions', personal names in combination with *ford* are masculine (p. 72).

[43] VEPN has not yet reached letter *F*, but the entry for *ford* in EPNE comments: 'The exact significance of such compounds [with personal names] is not clear; they may be named after individuals who owned them or had had them made or to whose property they gave access'.

[44] R. Coates, *The Place-Names of Hampshire* (London: Batsford, 1989), p. 22.

Notable are 9 (14) occurrences of feminine personal names in combination with the early place-name forming element OE *hām*, alongside 6 (15) from the slightly later OE *-ingtūn* 'farmstead associated with ...' and 6 from OE *wīc* 'specialized farm'. Moreover, of the 73 Old English personal names in Cox's corpus of place-names recorded by the early eighth century,[45] at least 2 are those of women: OE *Bebbe* in Bamburgh (Nb) and OE *Flǣde* in Fladbury (Wo).[46] Both combine with OE *burh*, raising the possibility that some of the other 8 (10) names within this group may similarly be early.[47] Bibury (Gl) certainly is, since the eponymous Bēage is named as joint grantee of the estate in an eighth-century charter (S 1254).[48] The nature of the association between other women and the places named from them is less clear, as is the identification of the women themselves. According to the *Historia Brittonum* (traditionally ascribed to Nennius), Bamburgh was given to Queen Bebba by her husband, King Æthelfrith of Northumbria (r. 592–616), and Fell speculates that it may have comprised her *morgengifu* 'morning-gift'.[49] However, this is not suggested by the text, and indeed it contains no indication that the gift was made at an early stage of the marriage:

> Eadfered Flesaurs regnavit duodecim annis in Berneich et alios duodecim in Deur, viginti quattuor annis inter duo regna regnavit et dedit uxori suae Dinguoaroy, quae vocatur Bebbab, et de nomine suae accepit nomen, id

[45] B. Cox, 'The place-names of the earliest English records', *Journal of the English Place-Name Society* 8 (1976), 12–66. Not counted here are the putative personal names **Hagustald* (Hexham) and **Strēon* (*Streanaeshalch*), which are included (with queries) within Cox's list but are now thought more likely to represent vocabulary words. See V. Watts, 'The place-name Hexham: a mainly philological approach', *Nomina* 17 (1994), 119–36, and C. Hough, 'Strensall, *Streanaeshalch* and Stronsay', *Journal of the English Place-Name Society* 35 (2003), 17–24.

[46] Less certain is OE *Hēahburh* in a lost *Hebureahg* (K), which, as Cox notes, might alternatively derive from a compound appellative OE *hēah-burh* 'chief stronghold' ('The place-names of the earliest English records', p. 22). The same ambiguity applies to Highborough in the same county (J. K. Wallenberg, *The Place-Names of Kent* (Uppsala: Appelbergs, 1934), p. 580).

[47] Adderbury (O), Alberbury (Sa), Alderbury (W), Bibury (Gl), ?Binbury (K), Bucklebury (Brk), ?Godbury (Hrt), Harbury (Wa), Heytesbury (W) and Tetbury (Gl).

[48] S = P. H. Sawyer, *Anglo-Saxon Charters: An Annotated List and Bibliography* (London: Royal Historical Society, 1968). The charter survives only in an eleventh-century copy: London, British Library MS Cotton Tiberius A xiii.

[49] Fell, *Women in Anglo-Saxon England*, p. 57.

est Bebbanburth.[50]

Eadfered Flesaurs reigned for twelve years in Bernicia and for twelve more in Deira; he reigned for twenty-four years altogether and gave the town of Dynguoaroy to his wife, who was called Bebba, and it is named Bebbanburg after her.

A further problem—as Fell acknowledges—is that the reliability of *Historia Brittonum* is highly uncertain.[51] Corroborative evidence that Æthelfrith had a wife called Bebba (or Bebbe) is lacking, and it may be significant that whereas Bede twice mentions that Bamburgh was called after a queen with this name, no more precise identification is made:

Denique in urbe regia, quae a regina quondam uocabulo Bebba cognominatur, loculo inclusae argenteo in ecclesia sancti Petri seruantur ac digno a cunctis honore uenerantur.

[T]hey [Oswald's hand and arm] are in fact preserved in a silver shrine in St. Peter's church, in the royal city which is called after Queen Bebbe (Bamburgh) and are venerated with fitting respect by all.[52]

Nam tempore episcopatus eius hostilis Merciorum exercitus Penda duce Nordanhymbrorum regiones impia clade longe lateque deuastans peruenit ad urbem usque regiam, quae ex Bebbae quondam reginae uocabulo cognominatur, eamque, quia neque armis neque obsidione capere poterat, flammis absumere conatus est;

During the time of his [Aidan's] episcopate a hostile Mercian army, under the leadership of Penda, which had been cruelly devastating the kingdom of Northumbria far and wide, reached the royal city called after a former queen Bebbe (Bamburgh). As he could not capture it by assault or siege, he attempted to set it on fire.[53]

Thus although Nennius' identification has generally been accepted by place-name scholars,[54] it seems unlikely that the putative link with

[50] T. Mommsen (ed.), *Historia Brittonum* <www.thelatinlibrary.com/histbrit.html>.

[51] See e.g. D. N. Dumville, 'The historical value of the *Historia Brittonum*', in R. Barber (ed.), *Arthurian Literature* VI (Cambridge: D. S. Brewer, 1986), pp. 1–26.

[52] Bede, *Historia Ecclesiastica Gentis Anglorum* [*HE*], iii, 6; B. Colgrave and R. A. B. Mynors (eds), *Bede's Ecclesiastical History of the English People* (Oxford: Clarendon Press, 1969), pp. 230–31.

[53] *HE*, iii, 16; Colgrave and Mynors (eds), *Bede's Ecclesiastical History*, pp. 262–63.

[54] E.g. A. Mawer, *The Place-Names of Northumberland and Durham* (Cambridge: Cambridge University Press, 1920), p. 10; DEPN, p. 24; K. Cameron, *English Place Names*, new edn (London: Batsford, 1996), p. 61; V. Watts, *The Cambridge Dictionary of*

Æthelfrith was known to Bede, much less any tradition that the city had formed (part of) his wife's *morgengifu*. It does, however, appear from the context of the second extract in particular that Bamburgh represented a fortified settlement – one of several possible interpretations of OE *burh*. Bibury and Fladbury, on the other hand, may refer to manor houses,[55] while Tetbury (Gl) was a monastic foundation, described in the earliest source as *Tettan monasterium* (EPNS Gl **1**, pp. 109–10). Again the identity of the eponymous *Tette* is unclear. One possibility is that the church was founded by Tette, sister of the seventh-century King Ine of Wessex, but alternatively, the place-name may commemorate the mother of St Guthlac, or—as is so often the case—an otherwise unknown woman.

In other instances, feminine personal names are combined with generics mainly associated with the later Anglo-Saxon period. These include OE *lēah* and OE *tūn*, the most common topographical and habitative elements respectively in Table 3 (pp. 261–62). Even these figures are unlikely to be comprehensive. A concentration of women's names with OE *tūn* in Kent was already noted by Stenton,[56] and major advances on this front may be expected from the inauguration of the Kent Survey under the editorship of Paul Cullen. Taken in conjunction with the tenth- and eleventh-century identifications discussed above, they testify to the continuing practice of naming places after women up to the Norman Conquest and beyond.

Anglo-Scandinavian and medieval personal names

Table 4. Elements combined more than once with ON feminine personal names

Element	Count
OE/ME *croft* 'small enclosed field'	20 (22)
ON *þorp* 'secondary settlement'	6 (7)
OE *brycg* 'bridge'	5
ON *haugr* 'hill, burial mound'	4 (5)
OE *land* 'land'	4 (5)
ON *bý* 'farmstead, village'	3 (4)
OE *w(i)ella* 'spring, stream'	3 (4)
OE *æcer* 'plot of cultivated land'	3
OE *lacu* 'stream, water-course'	3

English Place-Names (Cambridge: Cambridge University Press, 2004), p. 33.

[55] As suggested by Gelling, *Signposts to the Past*, p. 182.

[56] 'The historical bearing of place-name studies', p. 319.

ODan / late OE *toft* 'curtilage'	3
ON *bekkr* 'stream'	2
ON *deill* 'share, portion of land'	2
OE *grāfa* 'grove, copse'	2
OE *haga* / ON *hagi* 'hedge, enclosure'	2
OE *hop* 'secluded valley'	2
OE *pōl* 'pool'	2
OE **ryding* 'clearing'	2
OE *wang* 'piece of meadowland' / ON *vangr* 'garden, in-field'	2

Generic elements are also significant in the interpretation of place-names from Scandinavian women's names. Table 4 sets out, in descending order of frequency, all generics with at least two secure occurrences in combination with Scandinavian (or in some instances, Scandinavian-derived) feminine personal names.[57] Here the most striking feature is the absence of OE *tūn*, overwhelmingly the most common generic in Table 3, and also found in combination with Scandinavian masculine personal names in a large number of formations of the so-called Grimston hybrid type.[58] This absence forms a significant contrast with the 3 (4) occurrences of women's names with ON *bý*, and the 6 (7) with ON *þorp*. The pattern appears to support Cameron's contention that such formations belong to different stages of settlement, with the personal names found in the Grimston hybrids representing those of Scandinavian military leaders and those in ON *bý* and ON *þorp* reflecting later phases of colonization.[59]

[57] Again, the figures are based on the index in Hough, 'Women in English place-names', pp. 104–06, with the addition of *Becstervild* 1210 'Hildr's *bekkr*' (EPNS Cu, p. 218), *Gunildebrigge* [n.d.] 'Gunnhildr's *brycg*' (E. Ekwall, *The Place-Names of Lancashire* (Manchester: Manchester University Press, 1922), p. 255), Motherby 'Móðir's *bý*' (EPNS Cu, p. 198), *Sighrethcroft* [n.d.] 'Sigríðr's *croft*' (EPNS Cu, p. 281), *Sirithlandes* 1338 'Sigríðr's *land*' (EPNS Cu, p. 383) and *yngfirthop*, *Yngfrithop c.* 1250 'Ingifríðr's *hop*' (EPNS Du **1**, p. 75).

[58] The corpus assembled for 'Women in English place-names' contains only half-a-dozen dubious examples of Scandinavian personal names with *tūn*, all potentially attributable to alternative etymologies or later time-periods. The implications for women's involvement in the Scandinavian settlements are discussed at pp. 66–68.

[59] *Scandinavian Settlement in the Territory of the Five Boroughs: The Place-Name Evidence* (Nottingham: University of Nottingham, 1965); 'Scandinavian settlement in the territory of the Five Boroughs: the place-name evidence. Part II: place-names in *thorp*', *Mediaeval Scandinavia* 3 (1970), 35–49; 'Scandınavian settlement in the territory of the Five Boroughs: the place-name evidence. Part III: The Grimston-hybrids', in P. Clemoes and K. Hughes (eds), *England Before the Conquest: Studies in Primary Sources Presented*

Particularly significant is the higher incidence of women's names with *þorp* than with *bý*, despite the higher frequency of *bý* overall in English place-names and a strong tendency for it to combine with personal names.[60] As Table 4 shows, Scandinavian-derived feminine personal names occur more frequently with *þorp* than with any other generic except *croft*, an element most productive during the post-Conquest period. Although ON *þorp* also continued in use after the Conquest, an Anglo-Scandinavian origin for the names represented in Table 4 is more likely since recent research has demonstrated that 'the densest evidence of personal names as *þorp*-qualifiers is very predominantly Scandinavian in linguistic origin and early in date'.[61] Indeed, this research has associated *þorp*-names with the spread of open-field agriculture from the ninth century, although the high incidence in the Danelaw of (masculine) personal names qualifying *þorp* may suggest that the course of open-field farming ran somewhat differently there than further south and west.

Since reflexes of many Anglo-Saxon and Scandinavian personal names were in use during the medieval period, they present many difficulties of dating. It is often impossible to ascertain whether a name was created contemporaneously with its earliest record, or centuries before. The only Scandinavian feminine personal name to be identified in the three EPNS volumes under special consideration here is a possible occurrence of ON *Ingifriðr* in a lost Durham field-name *yngfirthop*, *Yngfrithop c.* 1250 (EPNS Du **1**, p. 75). Even this might rather be a post-Conquest formation, as appears to be the case with a lost Shropshire field-name *Ingriythemedewe* 1269–82, explained as 'Ingrith's meadow' from the Middle English reflex (EPNS Sa **5**, p. 212).

In some instances, personal names can help to date the place-names, whether directly through identification with a woman on documentary record, or indirectly from names fashionable at different times. An

to Dorothy Whitelock (Cambridge: Cambridge University Press, 1971), pp. 147–63; all reprinted in K. Cameron (ed.), *Place-Name Evidence for the Anglo-Saxon Invasion and Scandinavian Settlements* (Nottingham: English Place-Name Society, 1975), pp. 115–38, 139–56 and 157–71.

[60] Cameron, *English Place Names*, pp. 81–82, describes *bý* as '[t]he commonest by far of all the Scandinavian elements in English place-names', and estimates that 'no less than 192 out of the 303 recorded in DB in the territory of the Five Boroughs' have a Scandinavian personal name as the first element.

[61] P. Cullen, R. Jones and D. N. Parsons, *Thorps in a Changing Landscape* (Hatfield: University of Hertfordshire Press, 2011), p. 153. Cullen, Jones, and Parsons also calculate that around 46 per cent of pre-1300 thorp-qualifiers are personal names (p. 46).

example of the former is Aughton (W) mentioned above. Although first recorded in 1346 (EPNS W, p. 344), the place-name can be dated to the tenth century on the basis of the identification with Wulfgar's widow Æffe. As regards the latter, the high incidence of a small number of personal names in field-names suggests a derivation from the medieval reflexes of Anglo-Saxon or Scandinavian names rather than from the pre-Conquest etymons. The corpus drawn up at the turn of the century contains a small group of Old English and Old Norse personal names that together account for between a quarter and a third of minor and field-names, pointing to a date during the later Anglo-Saxon or early medieval period when the personal name stock in general use had diminished.[62] Of the 20 (22) instances of *croft* in Table 4, no less than 15 are in combination with the personal name *Gunnhildr*, strongly suggesting a medieval rather than Anglo-Scandinavian derivation.[63]

Similarly in Durham, two occurrences of *Emma* in twelfth- and thirteenth-century field-names may be almost contemporary with the date of record,[64] while the *Maud* of the lost field-name *Mauldeflat* 1316 (EPNS Du **1**, p. 36) is again clearly medieval. On the other hand, a lost field-name *Godrenelonde* 1321 in Godderthorn Hundred, Dorset (EPNS Do **4**, p. 487), seems likely to be named after the same woman as the hundred-name itself *Goderonestona hundret c*. 1086 (EPNS Do **4**, p. 467), and hence to represent a pre-Conquest formation from OE *Godrūn*.

Post-medieval personal names

Table 5. Women's names in field-names and minor toponyms

	EPNS Du **1**	EPNS Le **4**	EPNS Sa **5**
pers.n. only	**27**	**3**	**32**
Dame + pers.n.	**1**	**1**	**0**
pers.n. + surname	**8**	**7**	**4**
Lady + surname	**0**	**1**	**0**
Miss + surname	**0**	**1**	**0**
Mrs + surname	**0**	**5**	**0**
Widow + surname	**3**	**6**	**0**

[62] 'Women in English place-names', p. 51.

[63] This pattern is not reflected by the *þorp* compounds, where the only personal name represented more than once is ON *Ragnhildr*.

[64] *Emmestode* late 13th (EPNS Du **1**, p. 77); *unam carrucatam terre de dominio eiusdem Emme* 1157 (EPNS Du **1**, p. 131).

The majority of new discoveries coming to light in successive EPNS volumes are from later field-names and minor names, often testifying to the role of women in the agrarian economy of post-medieval England. Again, most are identified by personal names rather than—as is not infrequently the case with men—by occupation or social position. But with the rise of surnames, there is now a wider choice of name form, and a variety of practices in different areas. In EPNS Le **4**, unmodified personal names account for only 3 field- or minor names, one of which is commemorative—Elizabeth Plantation, referring to the present queen (EPNS Le **4**, pp. 209–10)—while another has been reduced from the fuller description *Susanna Freyers headland*, *Widow Freers Head Land* recorded in 1715 to become Susans Headland in 1771 (EPNS Le **4**, p. 161). There is also one instance where the personal name is modified by a title: *Dame Margarete thyng* 1424 (EPNS Le **4**, p. 195). The form personal name + surname, as with Poll Bird's Meadow and Jane Bates's Headland (EPNS Le **4**, pp. 63, 189), accounts for a further 7, and the form title + surname, as with Miss Ingrams Farm and Widow Knights Orchard (EPNS Le **4**, pp. 166, 122), for a further 13. EPNS Du **1**, on the other hand, has some 27 unmodified personal names, alongside one preceded by *Dame*, 8 in combination with a surname, and only 3 where the surname is preceded by a title, which in each case is *Widow*. The respective figures for EPNS Sa **5** are 32, 0, 4 and 0.

Clearly there are substantial variations here. A high incidence of unmodified personal names in certain areas may suggest a more intimate form of naming within families, in contrast with formal statements of ownership. There is also a contrast with street-names, a more public form of naming with a much higher proportion of commemorative names. EPNS Le **4** contains 8 street-names referring to women, of which 4 appear to be commemorative. EPNS Du **1** contains 21, of which around 8 are commemorative, and EPNS Sa **5** only 2, at least one of them commemorative. They include appellatives as well as personal names, but there are no occurrences here of women's names in any format other than unmodified personal name. Typical examples are Ethel Road, Judith Drive and Susan Avenue (EPNS Le **4**, p. 44), Ida Street, Jane Street and Lucy St (EPNS Du **1**, p. 157). These contrast not only with the variety found in field- and other minor names, but with practices elsewhere. Særheim's study of urban naming in Norway discusses differences in the representation of men and women in the street-names of Stavanger, where titles are less common with women's names than with men's names for chronological as well as social reasons, but do occur (*Botaniker Rescolls gate*, *Dr. Martha Persens gate*), as does the use of personal name + surname (*Bolette Wieses gate*).[65]

Table 6. Women in street-names

	EPNS Du **1**	EPNS Le **4**	EPNS Sa **5**
commemorative	**8**	**4**	**1**
non-commemorative	**13**	**4**	**1**
total	**21**	**8**	**2**

A common theme in most previous research into women in place-names is the difficulty of differentiating references to women from other types of element.[66] With Anglo-Saxon and Anglo-Scandinavian personal names, there is often a risk of confusion between masculine and feminine names, and between elements used to form personal names and cognate lexical items. The uncertainty in the opening sentence of this chapter as to whether the first 100 entries in Ekwall's *Dictionary* include 9 or 10 references to women is because the first element of Abingdon (Brk) is ambiguous between a masculine personal name OE *Æbba* and a feminine personal name OE *Æbbe*. Similarly, EPNS Le **4**, p. 147 treats Rickleburrow Hill as ambiguous between OE *Ricel* (masculine) and OE *Ricola* (feminine), but prefers the former, while EPNS Du **1**, p. 37 explains a lost field-name *Wiveshope* 1359 as 'Wif or Wifa's enclosure' without further discussion. Even the unrecorded personal name OE **Dryhtburh* in *Drihtburhlawe* Hy 3 mentioned above might theoretically represent a compound appellative **Dryhtnesburgeshlaw* 'the hill of the lord's stronghold', which is considered but ruled out on the grounds that it 'would suppose the unlikely loss of *n* as well as that of two gentival [sic] composition joints)' (EPNS Le **4**, pp. 123–24).

The problem is equally acute in later periods. In the case of surnames derived from personal names, a place-name qualifier may be ambiguous between the personal name and its surname reflex. Examples are Kates Hill and Alices Close in Leicestershire (EPNS Le **4**, pp. 5, 148). Equally, some surnames may refer to women. In Scotland, place-names from a woman's maiden surname include Petley in Tarbat parish, Ross and

[65] I. Særheim, 'Official urban naming: cultural heritage and identity', *Onoma* 42 (2007), 171–87 (pp. 180–82).

[66] See e.g. Hough, 'Women in English place-names', pp. 46–51.

Cromarty, '[s]o called [...] by Sheriff Macleod of Geanies, who married Miss Jane Petley',[67] and Renton in Dumbartonshire, named by Alexander Smollett in honour of his wife, Cecilia Renton.[68] It is fully possible that the same practice may account for some English place-names, while in other instances an eponymous surname may refer to a female rather than a male family member. This appears to be the case with Crossbys Cottage in Durham—'Mary *Crossby* owner' (EPNS Du **1**, p. 159)—while King's Close in Leicestershire is first recorded in 1844 as Nanny King's Close, from the pet-form of *Anne* (EPNS Le **4**, p. 291). A feminine indicator has also disappeared from Wadlands in Leicestershire, recorded in 1762 as *Mrs Wadlands Headland* – but previously as *Mr Wadlands Headland* (EPNS Le **4**, p. 194). Without documentary information, it is usually impossible to ascertain. Indeed, it may sometimes be a false distinction, with surnames alluding to ownership by a family that includes women as well as men.

Appellatives

In comparison with the number of feminine personal names in place-names, the number of feminine appellatives from any period is tiny. It is fully possible—indeed likely—that many general references to people in place-name qualifiers encompass both genders. In Anglo-Saxon times, women no less than men belonged to a class such as *eorl* or *ceorl* – hence the provision for different classes of widows in Æbt 75 quoted above. It therefore seems reasonable to assume that formations such as Carlton in Durham (EPNS Du **1**, p. 164) and Carlton Curlieu in Leicestershire (EPNS Le **4**, p. 27), from a Scandinavianized form of OE **ceorlena tūn* 'farmstead, village of the free peasants', refer to people of *ceorl* rank rather than specifically to men.[69] Terms referring unequivocally to women, on the other hand, are very sparse. Pre-Conquest examples in EPNS Du **1** and EPNS Sa **5** are limited to OE *wīf* 'woman' in the Durham field-name mentioned above. EPNS Le **4** may have one occurrence each of OE *brȳd* 'bride', OE *cwēn* 'queen' and OE *frēo* 'woman, lady', but

[67] W. J. Watson, *Place-Names of Ross and Cromarty* (Inverness: Northern Counties Printing and Publishing, 1904), p. 47.

[68] I am grateful to Peadar Morgan for drawing these to my attention.

[69] Recent discussions of this common name-type appear in VEPN, s.v. *ceorl* (i), and C. Hough, 'Commonplace place-names', *Nomina* 39 (2007), 101–20 (pp. 117–19); see also Parsons above, pp. 46, 47–48, 50, 51–53.

none is secure. The field-name Birdwell is not recorded until 1934, making it difficult to establish an Old English etymon, which might in any case be an adjective **brȳd* 'surging' rather than the noun *brȳd* 'bride' (EPNS Le **4**, p. 270). The lost Saddington field-name *Quen furlong(e)* 1601, 1638, m17, *Queenes furlong* 1679, *Quens furlonge* 1700, may plausibly be linked with Queen Edith, wife of Edward the Confessor, who owned Saddington from 1066 to 1075, but alternatively the first element may be the surname *Queen* (EPNS Le **4**, p. 227).[70] Another lost field-name, *Frewell* ~ 1707, *Free Well Close* 1714, in Hallaton parish, may derive either from OE *frēo* 'woman, lady' or from OE *freht* 'augury, divination' (EPNS Le **4**, p. 102). The latter is almost certainly to be preferred, as this sense of OE *frēo* is attested only as a nonce occurrence in the poem *Genesis B*,[71] while a derivation from OE *freht* would have the advantage of fitting into an established name-type.[72]

Table 7. Appellatives referring to women

	EPNS Du **1**	EPNS Le **4**	EPNS Sa **5**
countess	**1**	**1**	**1**
dame	**0**	**0**	**1**
daughter	**2**	**0**	**0**
granny	**1**	**0**	**1**
housewife	**2**	**0**	**0**
kerling	**1**	**0**	**0**
lady	**13**	**16**	**25**
madam	**0**	**0**	**1**
maid(en)	**2**	**3**	**4**
niece	**1**	**0**	**0**
queen	**0**	**0**	**1**
sister	**1**	**0**	**1**
virgin	**0**	**0**	**1**
wench	**1**	**0**	**0**
widow	**1**	**0**	**2**
wife	**4**	**0**	**0**
woman	**0**	**0**	**2**

[70] As Cox notes, a derivation from OE *cwene* 'woman' is unlikely.

[71] *Dictionary of Old English A–G*, version 2.0, CD-ROM (Toronto: Pontifical Institute of Mediaeval Studies, 2008), s.v. *frēo* noun[1].

[72] Cf. C. Hough, 'The place-name Fritwell', *Journal of the English Place-Name Society* 29 (1997), 65–70, and 'The name-type Fritwell', *Journal of the English Place-Name Society* 42 (2010), 87–89.

Later examples are also few and far between. Excluding the commemorative Queens, Princesses and so on found in street-names, and occurrences of *Lady* and *Widow* as titles modifying a surname, the only appellatives found in these three EPNS volumes are as shown in Table 7.[73] Again these require unpacking. There is a notable tendency for the more general terms to be modified. Three occurrences of *wife* are *Old Wife* (EPNS Du **1**, pp. 42, 141, 148) and the fourth is *fowlers wyfe* (EPNS Du **1**, p. 19), while the two occurrences of *woman* are *Blind Woman* and *Old Woman* respectively (EPNS Sa **5**, pp. 39, 222). Niece appears in the minor name Neasless, recorded earlier as *Nieceless* 1838×39, *Neseless* 1863 (EPNS Du **1**, p. 194).[74] This is a formation of which I can make no sense, although there may be a connection with Fatherless Field in the same volume (EPNS Du **1**, p. 159).[75] It is fully possible that other names may not be what they seem. Whereas the Shropshire field-name Granny's Yard (EPNS Sa **5**, p. 222) is paralleled by Grandfather's Croft in the same volume (EPNS Sa **5**, p. 296), Granny Hill in Greatham parish, Durham appears alongside Granary Bottom and Granary Hill (EPNS Du **1**, p. 85), suggesting the influence of folk etymology – perhaps helped along by the association with kinship terms represented by Sisters Hospital, also in Greatham and presumably referring to nuns (EPNS Du **1**, p. 85). In other instances, the operation of folk etymology may serve to obscure female appellatives or personal names. This appears to be the case with the Durham field-name Piggy Pasture, recorded in 1714–20 as *Peggys Pasture* (*alias Leonards field*) (EPNS Du **1**, p. 42). The lost *Kerlingescros* 1198×1204 (EPNS Du **1**, p. 77) is one of several place-names predating the *Oxford English Dictionary* entry for *carline* 'old woman', while a parallel to the Northamptonshire field-name *Dedquenesike* 13th 'dead woman's stream' (EPNS Nth, p. 275) is offered by *where the wench was slaine* 1673 (EPNS Du **1**, p. 32).[76]

[73] Figures include one occurrence of *housewife* in a Durham street-name.

[74] Four occurrences of Neiceless / Nieceless Field (EPNS Du **1**, p. 197) are excluded from the count as derived names, as explained above.

[75] The two names are not geographically contiguous. Neasless is in Sedgefield parish, Fatherless Field in Norton parish. No explanation is offered for either.

[76] EPNS Nth, p. 275 notes that references to the finding of dead men, and the like, are '[c]uriously common'. Another example is *Deadmans grave* 1601 in Leicestershire (EPNS Le **4**, p. 102). Cameron, *English Place Names*, p. 239, draws attention to a number of such field-names that 'commemmorate a now long-forgotten tragedy', including *Thertheoxlaydede* 13th century 'where the ox lay dead' in Buckinghamshire. This is the

Table 8. Generics combined with *lady*

	EPNS Du **1**	EPNS Le **4**	EPNS Sa **5**
close	3	2	0
land	2	2	0
meadow	0	3	10
piece	0	0	4
well	0	2	1
others	8	7	10

The most obvious patterns displayed by Table 7 are the sparsity of female appellatives in EPNS Le **4** in comparison with the other two volumes, and the overwhelming preponderance of names from *lady* in all three. As shown in Table 8, this too forms characteristic combinations in different areas, most notably with *meadow* in EPNS Sa **5**. Occasionally the lady in question can be identified with a woman on historical record, as with a lost field-name *leleuedygarthe* 1349 in Durham, representing 'four messuages and a croft assigned to Alice, widow of Leo de Claxton' (EPNS Du **1**, p. 81). Even where no identification can be made, a living referent may be indicated, as with a lost field-name *My Ladies hedge* 1679, *c.* 1690 in Leicestershire (EPNS Le **4**, p. 200). In other instances, a dedication to the Virgin Mary is indicated, as with the lost field-names *terr voc' our lady lande* 1535 in Durham (EPNS Du **4**, p. 128) and *Our Ladyes Meadow* 1587 in Leicestershire (EPNS Le **4**, p. 78). Other saintly virgins might also be considered. Although the lost *Lady Hill* [1749] after 1785 in the parish of Sedgefield, Durham, is tentatively explained as 'possibly land dedicated to the upkeep of a shrine of the Virgin Mary' (EPNS Du **1**, p. 198), the proximity of *Graysland* 1434×35, also in Sedgefield and described as 'appropriated and amortised to the chantry of the Blessed Virgin Katherine in the parish church' (EPNS Du **1**, p. 198), leads one to wonder whether *Lady Hill* might also refer to Katherine. Another possibility for some of these names is an allusion to rent payable on Lady Day, as with the field-name Ladies Ground in Leicestershire (EPNS Le **4**, p. 217).

Many of the names, however, are ambiguous between a secular and a religious interpretation. In a recent study of English and Scottish place-names, I have suggested that the term *lady* is more likely to have religious connotations in onomastic than in non-onomastic language,

closest parallel of which I am aware to *where the wench was slaine* in Durham.

highlighting differences between the onomasticon and the lexicon.[77] Such differences have been established for early stages of the Germanic and other Indo-European languages,[78] and I have argued that they are also identifiable in later stages of English, extending to place-name qualifiers as well as to generics.[79] This is reflected in name-types such as Lady Well, long recognized as a dedication to the Virgin Mary, and Maid(en)well, for which I have proposed the same interpretation.[80] Further occurrences of each are still coming to light, with two instances each of Lady Well and Maid(en)well in EPNS Le **4** (pp. 125, 175, 204, 207), and one of each in EPNS Sa **5** (pp. 151, 286).

The dearth of other terms for women shown in Table 7 appears to support a specialized use of *maid(en)* and *lady*, especially as both occur with generics found elsewhere with the names of female saints. The latter group includes many references to springs and wells, as discussed by Scherr,[81] and are represented here by St Ann's Well (EPNS Le **4**, p. 37) and two occurrences of St Helen's Well (EPNS Du **1**, pp. 111, 114). Other references to saints are Main St. Mary's Meadow (EPNS Le **4**, p. 80), *Seyntmarecroft* 1477 (e16) (EPNS Le **4**, pp. 126), St Ann's Hill (EPNS Du **1**, p. 217) and St Mary Magdalen's Farm (EPNS Du **1**, p. 102).

Marriage and inheritance

Except where records survive documenting the grant or bequest of land to a woman, the procedure that led to the association between an

[77] C. Hough, '"Find the lady": the term *lady* in English and Scottish place-names', in W. Ahrens, S. Embleton and A. Lapierre with the assistance of G. Smith and M. Figueredo (eds), *Names in Multi-Lingual, Multi-Cultural and Multi-Ethnic Contact: Proceedings of the 23rd International Congress of Onomastic Sciences, August 17–22, 2008, York University, Toronto, Canada* (Toronto: York University, 2009), pp. 511–18.

[78] Cf. W. F. H. Nicolaisen, 'Is there a Northwest Germanic toponymy? Some thoughts and a proposal', in E. Marold and C. Zimmermann (eds), *Nordwestgermanisch* (Berlin and New York: Walter de Gruyter, 1995), pp. 103–14; P. R. Kitson, 'British and European river-names', *Transactions of the Philological Society* 94 (1996), 73–118; J. Insley, 'Early Germanic personal names and onomastic dialects', in A. J. Johnston, F. von Mengden and S. Thim (eds), *Language and Text: Current Perspectives on English and Germanic Historical Linguistics and Philology* (Heidelberg: Winter, 2006), pp. 113–31.

[79] C. Hough, *Toponymicon and Lexicon in North-West Europe: 'Ever-Changing Connection'*, E. C. Quiggin Memorial Lectures 12 (Cambridge: University of Cambridge, Department of Anglo-Saxon, Norse and Celtic, 2010).

[80] 'The name-type Maid(en)well'.

[81] J. Scherr, 'Names of springs and wells in Somerset', *Nomina* 10 (1986), 79–91 (pp. 82–87).

eponymous woman and the place-name is often uncertain. In later names, some may represent dower land, a conclusion supported by the recurrence of the term *widow*. In Anglo-Saxon times, the marriage contract included a settlement or 'morning-gift' made by the bridegroom to the bride on the morning after the wedding, which was regarded as her property after his death, and probably during his lifetime.[82] This settlement is referred to in two marriage agreements dating from the early eleventh century (S 1459; S 1461):

> Her swutelað on ðysum gewrite ymbe ða forwerda ðe Wulfric ⁊ se arcebisceop geworhtan ða he begeat ðæs arceb. swuster him to wife · þ is ðæt he behet hyre þ land æt Ealretune ⁊ æt Ribbedforda hire dæg . ⁊ he behet hire þ land æt Cnihtewican · þ he wolde hit hire begytan ðreora manna dæg æt ðam hirede on Wincelcumbe . ⁊ sealde hyre þ land æt Eanulfintune to gyfene ⁊ to syllenne ðam ðe hire leofest wære on dæge ⁊ æfter dæge · ðær hire leofest wære · ⁊ behet hire .L. mances goldes . ⁊ xxx. manna · ⁊ xxx. horsa.
>
> Here in this document is stated the agreement which Wulfric and the archbishop made when he obtained the archbishop's sister as his wife, namely he promised her the estates at Orleton and Ribbesford for her lifetime, and promised her that he would obtain the estate at Knightwick for her for three lives from the community at Winchcombe, and gave her the estate at Alton to grant and bestow upon whomsoever she pleased during her lifetime or at her death, as she preferred, and promised her 50 mancuses of gold and 30 men and 30 horses.[83]

> Her swutelaþ on þysan gewrite þa foreward þe Godwine worhte wið Byrhtric þa he his dohter awogode, þ is ærest þ he gæf hire anes pundes gewihta goldes wið þonne þe heo his spæce underfenge, ⁊ he geuþe hire þæs landes æt Stræte mid eallan þon þe þærto herð, ⁊ on Burwaramersce oðer healf hund æcera, ⁊ þærto þrittig oxna, ⁊ twentig cuna, ⁊ tyn hors . ⁊ tyne ðeowmen.
>
> Here is declared in this document the agreement which Godwine made

[82] M. A. Meyer, 'Land charters and the legal position of Anglo-Saxon women', in B. Kanner (ed.), *The Women of England from Anglo-Saxon Times to the Present: Interpretive Bibliographical Essays* (London: Mansell, 1980), pp. 62–63, argues that this property would not have been treated as a separate holding during the husband's lifetime, drawing attention to post-obit bequests which affirm the woman's possession of her morning-gift. In my view, however, such bequests do not constitute a regranting of the estates, but a straightforward statement of ownership.

[83] A. J. Robertson, *Anglo-Saxon Charters*, 2nd edn (Cambridge: Cambridge University Press, 1956), pp. 148–49.

> with Brihtric when he wooed his daughter. In the first place he gave her a pound's weight of gold, to induce her to accept his suit, and he granted her the estate at Street with all that belongs to it, and 150 acres at Burmarsh and in addition 30 oxen and 20 cows and 10 horses and 10 slaves.[84]

It also appears in a late tenth- or early eleventh-century text known as *Wifmannes Beweddung* 'Woman's Betrothal':

> 3. Đon*ne* syððan cyþe se brydguma, hwæs he hire geunge, wið ðet heo his willan geceose, ⁊ hwæs he hire geunge, gif heo læng sy ðonne he.[85]
>
> 3. Then afterwards the bridegroom is to make known what he grants her in return for her acceptance of his proposal, and what he grants her if she should live longer than he.

An indication that the practice was current throughout the Anglo-Saxon period is provided by references in both the seventh-century laws of Æthelberht and the eleventh-century laws of Cnut:

> Æbt 81. Gif hio bearn ne gebyreþ fæderingmagas fioh agan, ⁊ morgengyfe.
>
> If she does not bear a child, the paternal relatives are to have the property and the morning-gift.[86]

> II Cnut 73. ⁊ sitte ælc wudowe werleas XII monað, ceose syððan þ*æt* heo sylf wylle.
> 73a. ⁊ gif heo binnan geares fæce wer geceose, þonne þolige heo þære morgengyfe ⁊ ealra þæra æhta, þe heo þurh ærran wer hæfde; ⁊ fon þa nehstan frynd to ða*m* landan ⁊ to þan æhtan, þe heo ær hæfde.[87]
>
> And every widow is to remain without a husband for twelve months, and afterwards she is to choose what she herself wishes.
> 73a. But if she chooses a husband within a year, then she is to forfeit her morning-gift and all the possessions that she had from her first husband, and his nearest relatives are to take the land and the possessions that she had had.

It is also mentioned in a small number of charters, including S 1445, where a dispute over ownership of an estate at Fonthill includes a clear

[84] Robertson, *Anglo-Saxon Charters*, pp. 150–51.

[85] Liebermann, *Die Gesetze der Angelsachsen*, I, p. 442.

[86] Hough, 'Women and the law in seventh-century England', p. 213.

[87] Liebermann, *Die Gesetze der Angelsachsen*, I, p. 360.

statement of a woman's right to dispose of property acquired as her morning-gift:

> Ða reahte heora aegðer his spell ða ðuhte us eallan ðæt Helmstan moste gan forð mid ðon bocon ⁊ geagnigean him ðæt lond ðæt he hit hæfde ƿpa Æðeldryð hit Osulfe on æht gesealde ƿið gemedan feo ⁊ heo cƿæð to Osulfe ðæt heo hit ahte him ƿel to syllanne forðon hit ƿæs hire morgengifu ða heo æ[*re*]st to Aðulfe com.
>
> Then each of them related his version; then it seemed to us all that Helmstan might proceed with the books [*i.e. land-charters*] and state his claim for the estate: [namely] that he had it just as Ætheldryth had given it into Oswulf's ownership for a fair price; and that she had declared to Oswulf that she possessed it with the full right to give [it away], since it was her morning-gift when she first came to Athulf.[88]

The most substantial body of evidence, however, is the place-name corpus. As mentioned above, OE *gift* and OE *morgengifu* in place-names both refer to land given as part of the marriage settlement, and Coates has suggested a similar interpretation for a putative OE **munddenn* in a group of names on the southern border of Kent.[89] By far the most common of these elements is OE *morgengifu*, and a selection of 36 place-names containing the term were included in the study cited above.[90] Many are Middle English field-names, as also noted in EPNE, s.v. *morgen-gifu*.[91] They tend to cluster in southern England, but the geographical range may now be extended by two possible occurrences in Shropshire and one in Durham: Morrey (EPNS Sa **5**, pp. 184–85), Murray (EPNS Sa **5**, p. 282) and Morrington (EPNS Du **1**, p. 42).

I should like to make two main points with regard to this group of names. Firstly, none of the estates identified within documentary sources as having formed part of a woman's marriage settlement contains the element *morgengifu* within the place-name. This may suggest that, as Rumble has pointed out with regard to OE *bōc-land*, only a small

[88] N. P. Brooks, 'The Fonthill Letter, Ealdorman Ordlaf and Anglo-Saxon law in practice', in S. Baxter et al. (eds), *Early Medieval Studies in Memory of Patrick Wormald* (Farnham: Ashgate, 2009), pp. 301–17 (p. 303).

[89] R. Coates, 'Towards an explanation of the Kentish *-mondens*', *Journal of the English Place-Name Society* 18 (1986), 40–47.

[90] Hough, 'Place-name evidence relating to the interpretation of Old English legal terminology', pp. 30–31.

[91] EPNE, II, 43, s.v. *morgen-gifu*.

proportion of land-holdings of this type used the term.[92] We may therefore be looking at the tip of the iceberg.

Secondly, no occurrence of *morgengifu* in place-names combines it with a feminine personal name. In view of the nature of the land-holding, and the high incidence of feminine personal names with other generics, this is surprising. An explanation may be suggested by the fact that—in marked contrast to names from OE *gift* and OE **munddenn*—*morgengifu* does not combine with any type of qualifying element. So far as I have been able to ascertain, it invariably functions either as a simplex name, or as the qualifier in combination with another generic. The pattern may suggest that where it appears to function as a qualifier, as in combination with generics such as *croft*, *feld* and *land* in Middle English field-names, the first element is in fact an earlier place-name, not an appellative. If this suggestion is correct, it would push back the formation of this group of names to the pre-Conquest period from which there is documentary evidence for the role of *morgengifu* within the marriage contract, and it would confirm that the practice was widespread throughout large areas of Anglo-Saxon England.[93]

Conclusion

In conclusion, there remain many uncertainties concerning the origins, motivation and purpose of place-name references to women throughout English history. As hinted at the beginning of this chapter, they need to be compared directly with place-name references to men in order to ascertain both statistical salience and contextual relevance. Without computerized searching facilities, this is impractical.[94] Even viewed in isolation, however, the range and scale of references to women of all social classes, from all parts of the country and from all historical periods, is staggering. A constant factor is the high incidence of personal names as opposed to appellatives, suggesting that women feature in

[92] A. R. Rumble, 'Old English *boc-land* as an Anglo-Saxon estate-name', *Leeds Studies in English* 18 (1987), 219–29.

[93] In 'Place-name evidence relating to the interpretation of Old English legal terminology', I followed EPNE in accepting the Middle English field-names as evidence that the practice continued into the later Middle Ages. I no longer believe this to be the case.

[94] The material for this chapter, as for my earlier study 'Women in English place-names', was obtained by trawling page-by-page through all the relevant place-name surveys – a method not only time-consuming but prone to human error.

place-names as individuals, not as groups or categories. With few exceptions, each place-name within the corpus represents a direct link between a certain woman and a certain place. Collectively, they reflect the extent of female influence on English place-nomenclature from Anglo-Saxon times up until the present day. The final word should go to Christine Fell, whose inspiring research and inspirational teaching did so much to advance scholarship in this area:

> Of course the personal names of men in similar formations occur more often, but it is significant that women's names appear as frequently as they do.[95]

[95] *Women in Anglo-Saxon England*, p. 100.

10

Many strata: English and Scots place-names in Scotland

Thomas Owen Clancy

Historically, the activities of the Survey of English Place-Names have not crossed the border into Scotland, except incidentally. This is unremarkable, since the Survey takes its remit as a geographical one, relating to the place-names of England's historical counties. Asking wider questions, as this volume does, about 'English place-names' across Britain and Ireland in a linguistic sense, the lack of investigation or comparative work across the Scottish border becomes more problematic. As Maggie Scott has shown, there are many ways in which awareness of the Scottish evidence of the place-names deriving from the English-language continuum can extend our understanding of the richness and diversity of the English toponymicon, and indeed of the lexicon lying behind the names.[1] Some of the basis for the lack of comparison is easily explicable. In contrast to the majority of English counties whose place-names have, since the inception of the Survey, received in-depth collection and analysis, Scotland until recently had only one published county survey approaching the methodological standards of the English Place-Name Society, that by Angus MacDonald for West Lothian.[2] For

[1] M. R. Scott, 'The Germanic Toponymicon of Southern Scotland: Place-Name Elements and their Contribution to the Lexicon and Onomasticon', unpublished PhD thesis (University of Glasgow, 2003); cf. Scott, 'Place-names and the Scots language: the marches of lexical and onomastic research', *Scots Language* 26:1 (2008), 85–98; and further, C. Hough, *Toponymicon and Lexicon in North-West Europe: 'Ever-Changing Connection'*, E. C. Quiggin Memorial Lecture, 12 (Cambridge: Department of Anglo-Saxon, Norse and Celtic, 2010).

[2] A. MacDonald, *The Place-Names of West Lothian* (Edinburgh: Oliver and Boyd, 1941); J. B. Johnston's preliminary survey of Berwickshire harvests much data but his analysis is problematic: *The Place-Names of Berwickshire* (Edinburgh: Royal Scottish Geographical Society, 1940). This was optimistically subtitled 'The Place-Names of Scotland Series, no. 1'. The beginnings of a survey of Berwickshire are underway under the auspices of the 'Scottish Toponymy in Transition' project at the University of Glasgow, Berwickshire work being undertaken by Carole Hough, Leonie Dunlop, and Eila Williamson. See n. 6. For a survey of dictionaries, surveys and approaches, see C. Hough, 'Dictionaries of place-names', in A. P. Cowie (ed.), *The Oxford History of English Lexicography* (Oxford: Oxford University Press, 2009), pp. 94–121.

those in the know, there was also the 1947 PhD thesis of Norman Dixon, a robust survey of the place-names of Midlothian undertaken employing English Place-Name Society methodology; this now has been made available online by the Scottish Place-Name Society.[3] Much has changed with the recent publication of the five-volume county survey *The Place-Names of Fife* by Simon Taylor with Gilbert Márkus,[4] and of *The Place-Names of Bute*, by Gilbert Márkus,[5] to which surveys of Kinross-shire, Clackmannanshire and Menteith (historically part of Perthshire) are soon to be added:[6] all these give hope that serious survey of Scotland's place-names is underway anew. Despite this, as the authors of EPNS surveys have compiled their volumes, there has been little for them to turn to easily for comparison north of the border. May Williamson's important PhD on 'The Non-Celtic Place-Names of the Scottish Border Counties' was until recently difficult of access,[7] whilst its title reflects the fact that the dominant research tool for Scottish toponymists for long years was W. J. Watson's *A History of the Celtic Place-Names of Scotland*.[8] W. F. H. Nicolaisen gave us a new overview and many new perspectives on place-name studies in his *Scottish Place-Names*,[9] which incorporated all the linguistic dimensions of the Scottish landscape, including of course both English and Scots. Further work has been done incipiently in articles and importantly in Maggie Scott's unpublished PhD thesis, which built

[3] N. Dixon, 'The Place-Names of Midlothian', unpublished PhD thesis (University of Edinburgh, 1947); see <www.spns.org.uk/Dixon_Prelims.html>; also published as hard copy by the Scottish Place-Name Society, 2011.

[4] S. Taylor with G. Márkus, *The Place-Names of Fife*, 5 vols (Donington: Shaun Tyas, 2006–12).

[5] G. Márkus, *The Place-Names of Bute* (Donington: Shaun Tyas, 2012).

[6] Thanks to the work of Simon Taylor, Peter McNiven and Eila Williamson, under the auspices of the AHRC-funded project 'Scottish Toponymy in Transition: Progressing County Surveys of the Place-Names of Scotland' at the University of Glasgow. The author (as Principal Investigator) is grateful to the AHRC for its funding of this, and a previous project, 'The Expansion and Contraction of Gaelic in Medieval Scotland: The Onomastic Evidence', during the final phase of which this paper, and the research which it draws upon, was originally done. Vols II–V of *Place-Names of Fife* (see n. 4) were researched, written and published under the auspices of that project.

[7] M. G. Williamson, 'The Non-Celtic Place-Names of the Scottish Border Counties', unpublished PhD thesis (University of Edinburgh, 1942); now available online via the SPNS website: <www.spns.org.uk/resources09.html>.

[8] W. J. Watson, *A History of the Celtic Place-Names of Scotland* (Edinburgh: Oliver and Boyd, 1926; repr. with revised introductions by Simon Taylor, Edinburgh: Birlinn, 2004, 2011).

[9] W. F. H. Nicolaisen, *Scottish Place-Names* (London: Batsford, 1976; rev. edn, Edinburgh: Birlinn, 2001).

substantially on the survey work of MacDonald, Dixon and Williamson; but the problem remains that the raw data, being differentially surveyed, must of necessity be difficult to compare.

Beyond survey, studies of Scottish place-names have moreover concentrated on other linguistic strands than that deriving from varieties of English. W. J. Watson's foundational *Celtic Place-Names of Scotland* has already been mentioned, and a fair amount of work has been devoted to aspects of the Celtic contribution to Scottish place-names, and beyond that to the Scandinavian dimension, particularly in work on the Western and Northern Isles.[10] The theses of Williamson and Scott have been noted already as providing a stable basis from which to discuss the English and Scots strands in Scottish toponymy, these concentrating on Scotland south of the Forth. This is the region which claimed Nicolaisen's attention for the most part in the English chapters of his *Scottish Place-Names*.[11] There he focused particularly on the chronology and distribution of what he saw as the earliest English place-names, and this has remained a focus for comment on such in later publications. G. W. S. Barrow's work on the twelfth and thirteenth centuries has employed place-name analysis in important and influential ways, but since much of this is situated in the work of an historian it has not always claimed the attention it richly deserves.[12] Simon Taylor in his study of linguistic transformation in medieval Fife employed similar evidence and techniques to good effect in a context more apparent to toponymists.[13]

[10] A full bibliography is beyond the remit of this article; for work on the western and northern isles, however, see for instance R. A. Cox, *The Place-Names of Carloway, Isle of Lewis: Their Structure and Significance* (Dublin: Dublin Institute for Advanced Studies, 2002); A.-B. Stahl, 'Place-Names of Barra in the Outer Hebrides', unpublished PhD thesis (University of Edinburgh, 1999); B. Sandnes, *From Starafjall to Starling Hill: An Investigation of the Formation and Development of Old Norse Place-Names in Orkney* (<www.spns.org.uk/Starafjall.pdf>, Scottish Place-Name Society e-book, 2010); for Scandinavian dimensions elsewhere see for instance G. Fellows-Jensen, 'Scandinavians in Southern Scotland?', *Nomina* 13 (1989–90), 41–60; S. Taylor, 'The Scandinavians in Fife and Kinross: the onomastic evidence', in B. E. Crawford (ed.), *Scandinavian Settlement in Northern Britain* (London: Leicester University Press, 1995), pp. 141–67.

[11] In particular, Nicolaisen, *Scottish Place-Names*, pp. 22–43, 88–108.

[12] For instance, in G. W. S. Barrow, 'The uses of place-names and Scottish history: pointers and pitfalls', in S. Taylor (ed.), *The Uses of Place-Names* (Edinburgh: Scottish Cultural Press, 1998), pp. 54–74; Barrow, *The Anglo-Norman Era in Scottish History* (Oxford: Clarendon Press, 1980), esp. ch. 2 'The pattern of settlement'.

[13] See S. Taylor, 'Babbet and Bridin Pudding or polyglot Fife in the Middle Ages', *Nomina* 17 (1994), 99–118; Taylor with Márkus, *Place-Names of Fife*, v; see also G. Márkus, 'Gaelic under pressure: a 13th-century charter from east Fife', *Journal of Scottish Name Studies* 1 (2007), 77–98.

These studies are crucial to some of the aspects of the place of English and Scots in the Scottish landscape I wish to discuss below. But we so far lack a published attempt at a full overview of the English and Scots dimension of Scottish place-names.

The foregoing suggests that fundamentally what lies behind a comparative failure of interchange over the place-names of Scotland and England is simply the pace and chronology of the two nations' projects of survey, and to a lesser extent a difference of focus in analytical work. I would suggest, however, that this diagnosis underestimates the differences between the situations of the two countries, and in particular the place of what we could initially term 'English place-names' within Scotland. There are two dimensions in particular worth highlighting. One is the controversial matter of language and terminology. The other is the issue to which my title alludes: the very complex stratification of the English contribution to Scottish toponymy. I will treat the first issue briefly, and then dwell in a bit more detail on the problems of stratification, before turning to the evidence in particular of south-west Scotland in order to explore more deeply some aspects of English place-names in Scotland.

Terminology

What do you call an English place-name in Scotland? What terminology do you use to describe the language in which it was coined? This is a problem intimately caught up with the historical development of the English language in Scotland, with modern linguistic sensibilities and protocols, and with issues of scholarly coherence and transparency. Varieties of English have been spoken within the borders of what is now Scotland since at least the seventh, and probably since the sixth century. For the English spoken in south-eastern Scotland we must for historical reasons posit continuity through time (that is, an essentially unbroken development of the language in these counties) and also continuity with the English of neighbouring counties in what became England (especially Northumberland). Large parts of southern Scotland were for a considerable time within the same kingdom as parts of northern England, though the nature of that relationship is very varied.[14] At its earliest

[14] Several kingdoms must be invoked here, incorporating English and Scottish border counties in different arrangements, e.g. the kingdom of Bernicia; the composite kingdom of Northumbria; the kingdom of Cumbria or Strathclyde; the territory of the rulers of Bamburgh; and for a century and a half, the kingdom of the Scots. For discussion of some

stages no one would object to terming this variety of English 'Old English', though other names such as 'Northumbrian' and 'Anglian' have been used (partly to reflect the dialectal differences from southern varieties of Old English, though there may also be modern political emphases underlying these choices, perhaps not always consciously). Yet by the fourteenth century at the very latest, scholars of language and also those of place-names would see this language as distinct, drawing its lexis and morphology from different sources than southern English dialects, and would emphasize both its geographical continuities to the north with the variety of English implanted there, and its increasing prominence as a national language of literature and law, by describing it as 'Older Scots'. The chronological divide between Old English and Older Scots lies in the centuries of intense linguistic and cultural change that are the twelfth and thirteenth centuries, a period for which Maggie Scott and others have used the term 'pre-literary Scots' to describe the language in question.[15] The same period which for England separates Old English from Middle English, then, in Scotland separates 'Old English' (or 'Anglian') from 'pre-literary Scots' and 'Older Scots'. While one stays on one side of that chronological divide or the other there are few problems, but once one crosses it, as with place-names, there can be confusion. Moreover, the twelfth and thirteenth centuries are ones in which English speech expanded dramatically in Scotland, particularly in the south-west and in eastern Scotland benorth the Forth. This is a period during which English speech was still appreciably an immigrant language in many of these areas; but conversely during this same period south-eastern Scotland could be thought of as being in England, despite its political status within the Scottish kingdom.[16] The language was regularly called *Inglis* and place-names in this language were referred to in Latin as

of these issues, see for instance G. W. S. Barrow, *The Kingdom of the Scots*, 2nd edn (Edinburgh: Edinburgh University Press, 2003), pp. 112–47; A. Woolf, *From Pictland to Alba, 789–1070* (Edinburgh: Edinburgh University Press, 2007), pp. 232–40.

[15] Scott, 'Germanic Toponymicon', p. 64, following the usage of M. Robinson (ed.), *The Concise Scots Dictionary* (Aberdeen: Aberdeen University Press, 1987), p. xiii.

[16] See for instance, D. Broun, *Scottish Independence and the Idea of Britain from the Picts to Alexander III* (Edinburgh: Edinburgh University Press, 2007), pp. 165 and 184 n. 18, citing Adam of Dryburgh's description of that monastery in Roxburghshire as *in terra Anglorum, et in regno Scotorum*. For a slightly dated but still helpful summary of the evolution of Scots in Scotland, see D. Murison, 'Linguistic relationships in medieval Scotland', in G. W. S. Barrow (ed.), *The Scottish Tradition* (Aberdeen: Scottish Academic Press, 1974), pp. 71–83; a brief but useful summary history of Scots is also to be found in *The Concise Scots Dictionary*, pp. ix–xiii.

being *anglice* until the fifteenth century.[17] To be sure, however, this was already substantially a different language from that of England to the south, heavily influenced by what has been termed the 'Scandinavianised Northern English [...] of the early Scottish burghs'.[18] As such, terminologically the scholar of this period is in something of a cleft stick. 'Scots' does not do full justice to the social and cultural context of the language at the time; 'English' downplays the extent to which this same language would evolve to become a national language of Scotland, and also obscures both its actual linguistic differences from southern English dialects, and its clear continuities with modern spoken Scots.

The problem is to some extent accentuated by the practices of the different place-name surveys in England and Scotland. The Survey of English Place-Names early took the decision—which is only in recent years being inflected—to employ Old English or Old Norse base-forms of the elements of names (with the exception of words which could not have existed in English at that period, for instance, loan-words from French), even where those *names* may have been coined in the Middle English period or later, or indeed, where the use of the word in question in toponymy is limited to the Middle English or Early Modern English period.[19] My purpose is not to take issue with this, but to point to the problems this causes for describing, for instance, the place-names of Aberdeenshire. Here, a variety of (Northern) English was certainly not spoken until after the Old English period, rendering a description of relevant place-name elements as 'English', or the use of Old English base-forms highly problematic. Here, surely, the only sensible way to describe such names and elements is as Scots, in other words, under the sign of the variety of English then developing in Scotland?

This is the choice taken by the most recent and authoritative surveys in Scotland, those by Taylor and Márkus. The terminology employed in these surveys is 'Scots', not 'English', though 'Scottish Standard English' is used to describe the northern variety of the normative dialect of Modern English which has been moderately influential on names, and more influential on official name-forms over the past two centuries. There is another way in which these recent surveys differ from the EPNS volumes (as also from earlier Scottish surveys, such as those of Dixon

[17] Murison, 'Linguistic relationships', p. 81.

[18] *Concise Scots Dictionary*, p. ix.

[19] See discussion of this issue by Simon Taylor in his review of V. Watts, *The Place-Names of Co. Durham, Part 1: Stockton Ward*, *Nomina* 32 (2009), 186–93 (pp. 191–92).

and MacDonald, which based their protocols more closely on the EPNS system). Taylor and Márkus employ modern base-forms for elements, where possible, rather than the earlier roots of those base forms. For Scots, the standard is determined (where possible) by the headwords of the *Concise Scots Dictionary*; for Gaelic, at present, by modern dictionary forms subjected to the revised version of the Gaelic Orthographical Conventions.[20] What these protocols emphasize for the reader is the continuity of the elements with the languages still spoken in Scotland, as a way of enfranchising readers to understand, interrogate and incorporate the toponymic landscape as part of their own linguistic environment.

The result of this, and the reason for dwelling on these differences here, is that current surveys of place-names progress from two distinctive positions as regards linguistic protocols and terminology. Linguists and place-name scholars should, of course, know that a Scots element and an English element are related, that what is given in *The Place-Names of Fife*, for instance, as Sc. *haugh*, is the element that EPNS volumes, including Smith,[21] would call OE *halh*. Both positions are utterly reasonable, and yet the disparity does not aid cross-border comparison of names derived from varieties of English. I should underline here that I am not advocating change, still less criticising the protocol decisions of the respective surveys and their authors. I am, rather, pointing out that there exist and will remain integral barriers to easy and fruitful cross-border comparative work.

Strata

A second aspect in which the place-names derived from varieties of English present themselves distinctly in Scotland relates to the geographical and chronological coordinates of the progress of English and Scots in Scotland during medieval and modern times. As noted above, in south-eastern Scotland, a variety of English has been spoken continuously since the sixth or seventh centuries. This part of Scotland is thus in many ways fully analogous with many English counties. Yet

[20] For the latter, see *SQA: Gaelic Orthographic Conventions* (Glasgow: Scottish Qualifications Authority, 2009), <www.sqa.org.uk/sqa/45356.2871.html?lang=G#>. See <www.gaelicplacenames.org/orthographic.php> for toponymic adaptation of these conventions.

[21] A. H. Smith, *English Place-Name Elements*, English Place-Name Society 25–26 (Cambridge: Cambridge University Press, 1956). For the beginnings of a Scottish equivalent, see Taylor with Márkus, *Place-Names of Fife*, V, elements glossary.

many other parts of Scotland experienced varieties of English first at much later dates. For instance, the twelfth and thirteenth centuries saw the first major impact of Northern English in much of eastern Scotland north of the Forth, partly through the settlement of 'Anglo-French' landowners and their followers, and more especially through the advent of burghs with a burgess class drawn mainly from the north-eastern English market towns and bearing with them their varieties of English speech.[22] In Caithness, Orkney and Shetland, however, the impress of Scots and later Scottish Standard English belongs to the much later middle ages and the early modern period, and in Orkney and Shetland is largely confined to the period after the Scottish acquisition of the Northern Isles in 1468.[23] In the Outer Hebrides, in the isle of Lewis for instance, although local Gaelic-speaking kindreds had for centuries employed Scots as a language of law and diplomacy,[24] nonetheless Scots made no substantial impact on the toponymy of the island until the eighteenth century, and even then we might prefer to speak of the influence of Scottish Standard English (SSE).[25] Unlike the situation for much of England, then, in different regions of Scotland the first impact of English or Scots was in each case of an English or Scots at a very different phase of development. This said, those who brought English and Scots into these areas also often brought previous toponymic habits; they were not inventing naming systems anew. The implications of these observations for understanding the nature of the English-based toponymy of Scotland have barely begun to be explored.

Added to this diverse chronological stratification is the differential nature of the linguistic context of that stratification. When Scots began to affect the toponymy of Orkney, it intruded into a toponymic context

[22] See Taylor 'Babbet and Bridin Pudding'; Taylor with Márkus, *Place-Names of Fife*, V; Márkus 'Gaelic under pressure'; and also Murison, 'Linguistic relationships'.

[23] For an excellent external linguistic overview of the period of Scots contact and subsequent take-over in Orkney, see Sandnes, *From Starafjall to Starling Hill*, pp. 15–30; see also Sandnes, 'What is Norse, what is Scots in Orkney place-names?', in P. Gammeltoft, C. Hough and D. Waugh (eds), *Cultural Contacts in the North Atlantic Region: The Evidence of Names* (Lerwick: NORNA, 2005), pp. 173–80.

[24] A. MacCoinnich, 'Where and how was Gaelic written in late medieval and early modern Scotland? Orthographic practices and cultural identities', in C. Ó Baoill and N. McGuire (eds), *Caindel Alban. Fèill-Sgrìobhainn do Dhòmhnall E Meek* (= *Scottish Gaelic Studies* 24) (Aberdeen: University of Aberdeen, 2008), pp. 309–56.

[25] I am not counting here influence through the use in place-names of words fully part of the Scottish Gaelic lexicon that were derived from Scots, for which see for instance Cox, *Place-names of Carloway*, pp. 107–08.

which was then almost exclusively Scandinavian.[26] On the island of Lewis, Scots or SSE inflected a landscape whose names were substantially coined in Old Norse, but which had subsequently been taken into, adapted, and very significantly supplemented by Gaelic, which completely replaced Old Norse as the island's language during the central to later middle ages.[27] In Fife or Aberdeenshire, on the other hand, the advent of Scots was into a landscape substantially Gaelic but with a deeper substrate of Pictish names.[28] The south-west, as we shall see, presents even more complexities. These different linguistic contexts had effects on English and Scots place-names in a variety of ways, amongst which we may include the way in which previously existing names from older linguistic strands were incorporated into new Scots or English names, for instance, Meikle Camaloun, Crofts of Yonder Bognie, Kingskettle, Brig o' Turk, The Lydes of Orquil.[29] The extent of such name patterns in Scotland, of older names and languages preserved in new Scots contexts, creates the distinctive warp and weft of Scottish place-names in many regions, and must be part of how we understand the English and Scots contribution to the toponymic tapestry.

The present chapter cannot hope to explore all the varieties of these contexts and their results. Instead, I turn now to illustrate a number of features of the strata and contexts of varieties of English in Scottish toponymy, the ways in which interrogating the Scottish data might be of use to English place-name research, and what due attention to the context of the strata can tell us about language contact and change, through a closer examination of one region of Scotland, the south-west.

South-West Scotland: Some Preliminaries

The area for investigation essentially encompasses the historical counties of Renfrewshire, Ayrshire, Wigtownshire, Kirkcudbrightshire and Dumfriesshire, though I shall stray briefly into Lanarkshire as well. There is nothing particularly historical about this catchment of counties,

[26] Sandnes, *From Starafjall to Starling Hill*.

[27] Cox, *Place-Names of Carloway*, is the best guide to this process; see also his 'Towards a taxonomy of contact onomastics: Norse place-names in Scottish Gaelic', *Journal of Scottish Name Studies* 3 (2009), 15–28.

[28] See Taylor with Márkus, *Place-Names of Fife*, V; Taylor, 'Pictish place-names revisited', in S. T. Driscoll, J. Geddes and M. A. Hall (eds), *Pictish Progress. New Studies on Northern Britain in the Early Middle Ages* (Leiden and Boston: Brill, 2011), pp. 67–118.

[29] On the last of these, see Sandnes, *From Starafjall to Starling Hill*, p. 221.

although all of these areas were capable of being described during the twelfth century as within something called Gall-Ghàidheil or *Galweia*, 'Galloway', a term later restricted to the counties of Wigtownshire and Kirkcudbrightshire.[30] They also share a considerable uncertainty surrounding historical and linguistic development. A few things are clear: at various points during the early middle ages, as the place-name record indicates, this area was host to speakers of what I will call Northern British (often referred to as Cumbric), of English, Norse, and Gaelic. From the twelfth century on, the two languages that influenced it most were Gaelic and the local development of the English continuum which would come to be termed Older Scots, with the latter coming to predominate, at dates that vary across the area. Carrick in Ayrshire was still significantly Gaelic-speaking in the sixteenth century;[31] it is likely that Gaelic was gone or going from Renfrewshire by the thirteenth century.

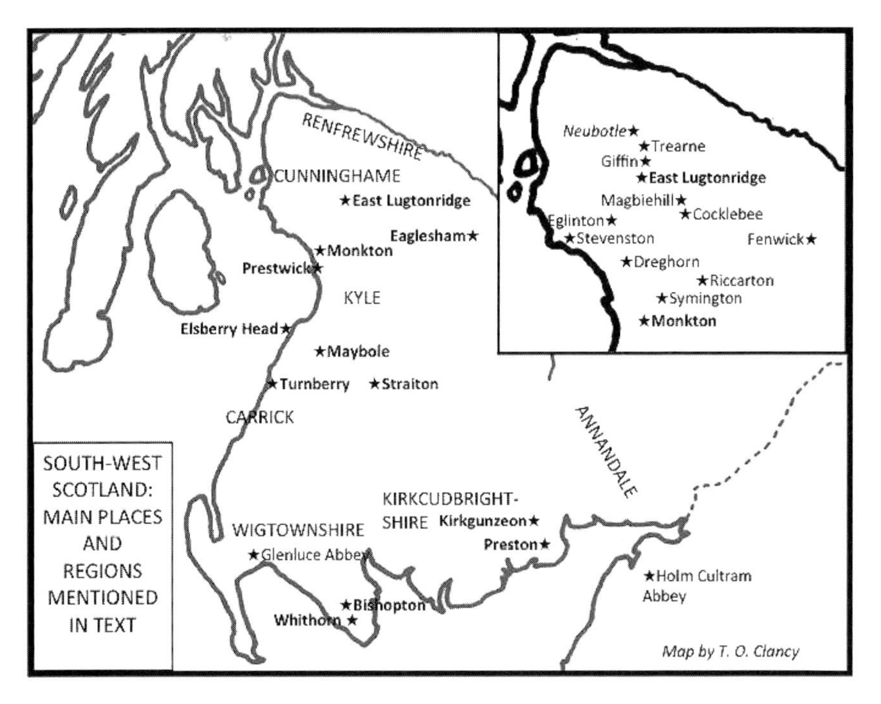

[30] On this development T. O. Clancy 'The Gall-Ghàidheil and Galloway', *Journal of Scottish Name Studies* 2 (2008), 19–50, which provides a review of previous scholarship on the issue.

[31] W. L. Lorimer, 'The persistence of Gaelic in Galloway and Carrick', *Scottish Gaelic Studies* 6 (1949), 114–36.

As far as external English influence on the region is concerned, we may notice that Whithorn was an English bishopric by the early eighth century; and that Eadberht of Northumbria made conquest of the plain of Kyle by 750, and was battering on the doors of Dumbarton by 756.[32] Alex Woolf has recently suggested, however, that English influence in the area may antedate 700.[33] This western region of Bernician power seems, however, to have collapsed under various types of pressure from Scandinavian power in the late ninth century. From 900 to 1100 it is hard to say anything terribly intelligent about the area, at least with the backing of genuine evidence. Unfortunately, it is during this period that both Norse (to a limited degree) and Gaelic (in the main) affected the area. Gaelic provided the bulk of the place-names in the landscape in many of these counties, a contribution that only seems to begin during this period, though Gaelic was still a language productive of place-names well into the later middle ages in some areas. There has been a tendency to see these different languages as affecting the area sequentially, but I suspect that during the crucial period 900–1100 we are dealing with all four languages, Northern British, English, Norse and Gaelic, being spoken concurrently in different degrees in different locations, some of these regions contiguous with each other, or even linguistically mixed. Alex Woolf has used the term 'Balkanisation' to describe this arrangement,[34] but I suspect that may not quite carry the right message (though I agree with what he intends by the term). Thus, unlike English place-names in the south-east of Scotland, we are here dealing with linguistic interventions and local continuities that may be quite complex and stratified. From the early twelfth century a number of regions within our area were subject to intensive settlement of new lords and their followers (I will use the term Anglo-Norman to describe them, in default of something better; the toponymic evidence suggests their followers were largely speakers of English dialects). This affected Renfrewshire,

[32] See Bede, *Historia Ecclesiastica Gentis Anglorum*, v, 23; B. Colgrave and R. A. B. Mynors (eds), *Bede's Ecclesiastical History of the English People* (Oxford: Clarendon Press, 1969), pp. 558–60, also pp. 574–75 for Kyle; for the Dumbarton reference, see K. Forsyth, 'Evidence of a lost Pictish source in the *Historia Regum Anglorum* of Symeon of Durham', in S. Taylor (ed.), *Kings, Clerics and Chronicles in Scotland, 500–1297* (Dublin: Four Courts, 2000), pp. 19–34 (p. 29); J. E. Fraser, *From Caledonia to Pictland: Scotland to 795* (Edinburgh: Edinburgh University Press, 2009), pp. 308–19.

[33] See his forthcoming 2011 Whithorn lecture: 'Conquest and Cohabitation: Britons, Saxons and the Church of Whithorn'.

[34] Woolf, *From Pictland to Alba*, p. 294.

Ayrshire (Cunninghame and parts of Kyle), and Dumfriesshire (Annandale) particularly.[35] English/Older Scots naming took on new pace from this period, though evidence may suggest that the key period is the later twelfth and early thirteenth centuries.

East Lugtonridge

To illustrate the complexities of the linguistic and toponymic stratification of the area, and by way of orientation, I would like to pay some attention to a farm in the parish of Beith, in what is now called 'North Ayrshire', roughly identical with Cunninghame, one of the historical divisions of Ayrshire. The farm is now called East Lugtonridge (NGR NS379494), but locally, Little or Wee Lugtonridge, by way of contrast with the adjoining farm of Lugtonridge, often called 'the Big Lugtonridge' (NGR NS377492), which was run as part of the same farm throughout much of the twentieth century, under the auspices of James S. Goldie and Sons. These are two of a number of farms called Lugtonridge (see for instance NS370493, 365491 on OS 1st edition 6", the latter is 'High Lugtonridge' on later maps), once part of a single estate which was divided in early modern times. I give forms for both names below:

EAST LUGTONRIDGE (NS379494)
Ludgar-little 1604×08 Pont[36]
Little Lugdrig 1654 Blaeu
William Johnstone in *Little Ludnerrige* 1663 *RMS* xi no. 518
John Shaddaw in *Litle Ludnerrigge* 1663 *RMS* xi no. 518
Wee Lugtonridge 1999 Mr J. Goldie (farmer)

LUGTONRIDGE (NS377492)
Ludgar meikle 1604×08 Pont
Luderigs 1654 Blaeu
Meikle Lugdnerig 1663 *RMS* xi no. 518
Meikle Lugdounridge 1743 Charter in possession of Mrs J. Goldie, East Lugtonridge [within lordship and barony of Giffen]

[35] See Barrow, *Anglo-Norman Era*, pp. 30–60.

[36] This is Timothy Pont's 'Cunningham Topographized', a prose MS underlying the (lost) map originals which in turn partly underlay Blaeu's map of Cunninghame, 1654. It was edited by J. Fullarton, *Topographical Account of the District of Cunningham, Ayrshire, compiled about the year 1600 by Mr Timothy Pont* (Glasgow: Maitland Club, 1858). For this form, see p. 26. For the date range of Pont's *Cunningham*, see J. Stone, 'Timothy Pont: three centuries of research, speculation and plagiarism', in I. C. Cunningham (ed.), *The Nation Survey'd: Timothy Pont's Maps of Scotland* (Edinburgh: Birlinn, 2006), p. 7.

Luggtonrigge 1791 Nicolaisen 1958, 199
Lugtonridge 1999 Mr J. Goldie (farmer)

The name is a palimpsest of moments of naming: at its base is the name of the burn which bounds the farm to the south-east, the Lugton Water. This burn name was subject to a thorough and useful analysis by W. F. H Nicolaisen.[37] It has at its root a British hydronym, the same found in names like the Lugg in Herefordshire, and the Luggie Water which flows into the Kelvin,[38] and various versions of Llugwy in Wales.[39] In earliest forms it appears as *Lugdur* 1604×08 (Pont, p. 5), *Ludgar fluvius* 1604×08 (Pont, p. 26) and *Lugdwrr* 1654 (Blaeu), suggesting, like its neighbour to the south the Glazert (*Glashdwrr*, Blaeu 1654), that it contains a Northern British reflex of what became in Welsh the word *dŵr* 'water'.[40]

And indeed, East Lugtonridge itself is *Litle Lugdrig* or *Ludgar Littil* (showing metathesis or printing error) in the earliest sources so far uncovered (see above), suggesting that the form *Lugdwrr* represents the compound which lies at the base of the name (originally probably **Lugdur-rigg* 'the ridge of the **Lugdur*/the **Lug* water'). A settlement upstream was later established (it does not exist on maps until the mid-nineteenth century), and named 'Lugton'. It is difficult to be certain whether this was simply assimilation of an unfamiliar burn name **Lugdur* to a more familiar pattern in *-ton*, or whether it was an active coining in **Lug* + Scots *toun*. Either way, this name seems to have had a subsequent knock-on effect on the name of the Lugton Water, and thence on the Lugtonridges. (We cannot rule out assimilation of an earlier **Lugdur* to a more explicable *Lugton* for the burn name independent of, and prior to the establishment of, the settlement.[41]) Also affecting the development of the name Lugtonridge is the Englishing of Scots names in official contexts in the modern era: for the earlier Scots *-rigg*, by the late

[37] W. F. H. Nicolaisen, 'Notes on Scottish place names: 8 Lugton Water', *Scottish Studies* 2:2 (1958), 189–205.

[38] Dixon, *Place-Names of Midlothian* shows there to be a different derivation for the Midlothian Lugton: p. 183 (p. 113 in the online pdf).

[39] See H. W. Owen and R. Morgan, *Dictionary of the Place-Names of Wales* (Llandysul: Gomer, 2007), p. 294.

[40] On this element, see A. James, 'Brittonic Language in the Old North' (BLITON), <www.spns.org.uk/bliton/blurb.html> s.v. *dußr*; cf. the entry on *lūch*, *lūɣ*.

[41] This may be supported by the recording in 1829 of *Lugtonbridge Inn* to the north of Lugton, on Robert Aitken's *New Parish Atlas of Ayrshire: Vol. I, Cunninghame* (Beith: Robert Aitken, 1829), sheet 3.

eighteenth-century we find SSE *-ridge* fairly consistently.[42] But as well as being a variant in speech, the Scots form Lugtonrigg survived (or rather, was revived) in the name of the farm's dairy herd,[43] and so both Lugtonridge and Lugtonrigg existed as official names side-by-side for many years.

Before leaving the modern nomenclature, it is worth mentioning two very modern farm-name responses to the Lugtonridge name-cluster. The farm of Merryridge (NS363486) was once (frustratingly for postmen) also called Lugtonridge, and was in the 1950s renamed for clarity, its name suggested by amalgamating Lugtonridge with the name of the neighbouring Merryhagen,[44] owned by the same family. Finally, in 1972, a bungalow was built on the land of Lugtonridge (NS377492), and called Rigton; it is now an independent dwelling marked on OS maps.[45] The name was invented through rearrangement of the apparent constituent

[42] The Ordnance Survey Name Books comment interestingly on the nature of this written standard / speech dichotomy, as also on the large number of farms in this small area called simply 'Lugtonridge': 'There are 6 Farm houses bearing this name, only one of which is distinguished from the others, by the name "High Lugton~~ridge~~" The Occupiers of all the Farms have it "Lugtonridge" in their Tacks, it so painted on their Carts, and letters from their different Landlords and Agents are addressed "Lugtonridge" but the country people pronounce it invariably "Lugtonrig". I considered the former the better name to use having so many proprietors and occupiers as authority.' *Ordnance Survey Name Books*, Ayrshire (1855–57), XII, p. 148. The Name Books for Ayrshire are now available online via <www.scotlandsplaces.gov.uk/digital_volumes/type.php?type_id=5>.

[43] The Lugtonrigg herd was sold in 2002, but the name survives in pedigree books. See for example the progeny of the bull Moscow Highland Laddie at: <ukcow.com/Holsteinuk/publicweb/AnimalData/data/SelectableProgenyList.aspx?AnimalID=65816>.

[44] *Merryhagen* is itself of interest as a name. I have yet to find an earlier record for it than the OS 6" 1st edn (1858: *Merryhagan*), but if the name is not a strange modern confection, it is best analyzed as containing the OE element *hægen/hagen* 'fence, enclosure' (see Smith, *English Place-Name Elements*, s.vv.), in a northern dialect form showing the same phonological distinction we see in e.g. Dreghorn (whether this is due to influence of Old Norse or not is arguable). The first element might be either OE *(ge)mǣre* 'border, boundary' (it lies at the boundary of Kilwinning and Beith parish), or something related to Sc. *mirie*, an adjective based on 'mire, moss', since it is surrounded by Cockinhead Moss, Sidehead Moss and Auchintiber Moss (cf. Taylor with Márkus, *Place-Names of Fife*, I, p. 338 for Merryhill, and V, Elements Glosssary, *mirie*, for suggested specific). Supporting the derivation 'boundary fence/enclosure' might be the fact that this section of the border between the parishes seems not to be based on natural features. If this is OE *hægen/hagen*, it would be a significant and unusual element to find in this region, especially alongside local use of, for example, *ærn* in Trearne. For parallels in England to this proposed derivation, see B. Jepson, *English Place-Name Elements Relating to Boundaries* (Lund: Centre for Languages and Literature, Lund University, 2011), pp. 26, 54.

[45] The foregoing via James Goldie, farmer, East Lugtonridge (pers. comm.).

elements in the name Lugtonrigg. These naming processes show the dynamic nature in the modern period of the use of the dialect continuum encompassing Scots and Scottish Standard English. Given the relative lateness of the documentary record in this part of Scotland, this dynamism is a salutary warning. The names Lugton and Rigton, here, are of modern and very recent vintage, but might easily pass muster for older names in OE *tūn* or Sc. *toun*. That element in fact is not ultimately present in the underlying history of either name.

If we pan out from East Lugtonridge to consider its local context, we can see that this is an area that has long been of fitful interest to those investigating the earliest strata of English place-names in southern Scotland. Cunninghame, the name of the region of Ayrshire in which East Lugtonridge is situated, has been disputed both as a potential *hām*-name, and as being the location of Dryhthelm's vision of the afterlife in Bede's *Ecclesiastical History*.[46] Here, and in immediately neighbouring regions, are the locations of a number of English place-names which have been understood as potentially early: Fenwick and Prestwick, Eaglesham in Renfrewshire. Somewhere in Beith parish was the site of a lost *Neubotle*, a probably Old English *bōðl* name, recorded on Blaeu's map of 1654.[47] I have recently suggested that the name Trearne (the lands of which, like Lugtonridge, were part of the original estate of Giffen), contains the Old English element *ærn* 'dwelling, building'; and that it joins in this a number of others, including Dreghorn, also in Cunninghame (another is in Midlothian) and Cleghorn in Lanarkshire.[48] If this is so, these names join Whithorn in suggesting a particular northern inflection to the use of *ærn*, one which should perhaps be allowed to influence VEPN's entry on the term.[49] The investigation of English place-names in south-west

[46] Nicolaisen, *Scottish Place-Names*, pp. 91–92; A. James, 'Scotland's *-ham* and *-ingham* names: a reconsideration', *Journal of Scottish Name Studies* 4 (2010), 103–30, esp. pp. 120–23; Bede, *HE*, v, 12, Colgrave and Mynors (eds), *Bede's Ecclesiastical History*, pp. 488–99.

[47] See Nicolaisen, *Scottish Place-Names*, pp. 102–03, 99; James, 'Scotland's *-ham* and *-ingham* names', pp. 123–24; Barrow, 'Uses', p. 68.

[48] T. O. Clancy, 'Two Ayrshire place-names: 1. Pulprestwic; 2. Trearne', *Journal of Scottish Name Studies* 2 (2008), 99–114 (pp. 106–07).

[49] D. Parsons and T. Styles with C. Hough, *The Vocabulary of English Place-Names* I *(Á–Box)* (Nottingham: Centre for English Name Studies, 1997) [vol. I of VEPN], pp. 31–32. It is worth noting that the early form of Whithorn in the Old English translation of Bede (*æt tham Hwitan Ærne*) represents one of the earliest attestations of the element; see J. MacQueen, *Place-Names of the Wigtownshire Moors and Machars* (Stranraer: Stranraer and District Local History Trust, 2008), pp. 25–26.

Scotland partially represents a chance to see familiar elements in unfamiliar surroundings, and the differences as we shall see may shed light on the core data.

Those surroundings include Celtic and also potentially Scandinavian place-name neighbours. Just as the water-system of Cunninghame is based partly on Brittonic linguistic roots (Lugton, Glazert), so too are some of the major estates and parishes. Lugtonridge was in Giffen estate, as was Trearne, and *Giffen* is probably from the Northern British equivalent of Welsh *cefn*, 'ridge, back', judging by its placement in the landscape.[50] The estate of Giffen contained some holdings with Gaelic names (Drumbuie), but many more with names from the English-Scots continuum (Hessilhead, Broadstone, Roughwood, Nettlehurst). Trearne, if rightly construed here, and if an early name, suggests, alongside the nearby lost *Neubotle*, and more distant names like Fenwick, Prestwick, that we may be dealing with multiple pulses of English naming in this region. As well as the impact of English and Scots on the area from the twelfth century, we must allow for the potential presence of an earlier English stratum in a landscape originally linguistically British, and subsequently for a time linguistically Gaelic. This makes names like Hessilhead and Nettlehurst difficult to securely place, chronologically. This is of course where making the precise distinction between 'Early English names' and 'Scots names' runs into problems, and making choices of nomenclature can obscure uncertainties.[51]

There is apparent Scandinavian influence on the area as well. Cunninghame shows hardly any Scandinavian place-names, but does play host to two of the important clusters of names in central Scotland employing the element *bý* (with a further several *bý*-names in neighbouring Kyle), clusters discussed by the likes of Gillian Fellows-Jensen, Simon Taylor, and Alison Grant.[52] There has been some dispute about the nature and origins of these clusters, an issue I would like to

[50] Clancy, 'Two Ayrshire place-names', p. 101, n. 1.

[51] In the forthcoming volumes on Kinross-shire and Clackmannanshire, it has been proposed that we adopt for this continuum, especially for names where it is impossible to decide either way, the term 'Scots English' (ScEng).

[52] G. Fellows-Jensen, 'Scandinavians in Southern Scotland?', *Nomina* 13 (1989–90), 41–60; Fellows-Jensen, *Scandinavian Settlement Names in the North-West* (Copenhagen: C. A. Reitzel, 1985), esp. pp. 10–43; S. Taylor, 'Scandinavians in Central Scotland: *bý*-place-names and their context', in G. Williams and P. Bibire (eds), *Sagas, Saints and Settlements* (Leiden: Brill, 2004), pp. 125–46; A. Grant, 'The origin of the Ayrshire *bý* names', in Gammeltoft, Hough and Waugh (eds), *Cultural Contacts*, pp. 127–40.

return to. In the area around Stewarton, to the south of East Lugtonridge, are several of these names, most prominently Busbie in Kilmaurs, but also Magbie(hill) north of Stewarton.[53] To these names discussed in the literature to date, I can add a further not-quite lost name, Cocklebee (NS417461: still known locally, and on the OS first edition 6" and third edition 1", it is also recorded on Blaeu as *Cocleb*, and there is good documentation of it in the late medieval and early modern period). Almost certainly the qualifying element here is OE *coccel* (Sc. *cokle*) 'cockle(weed), corn-cockle', interestingly in light of the debate on the date and nature of these *bý*-names, not an element attested in the Scandinavian languages, and therefore to be assigned to Old English/ Scots, with implications I will return to.

tūn and *bý*

I wish now to turn to examine two place-name elements whose position in south-west Scotland can inform and inflect our understanding of their usage in Scotland as a whole, and also in England. Examining such elements should give some insight into the potential advantages of cross-border comparative work. The first of these is one of the most common English and Scots place-name generics, OE *tūn*, Sc. *toun*. As we have already seen, it is an element which continued to be understood and productive into contemporary times, the creation of the new settlement name Rigton in 1972 having been based on an appreciation of the malleable (apparent) constituent parts of the earlier name-set Lugtonridge, Lugtonrigg. Although we must thus contend with a potential date-range for the creation of names in *tūn*/*toun* stretching from the present back to the early middle ages,[54] nonetheless south-west Scotland presents us with some very precisely dateable examples of *tūn*/*toun*, with contexts and individuals involved, and this can shed light on one phase of the impact of English on the area.

As a first illustration of this, it may be instructive to collate the south-west Scottish record against a recent important article investigating and providing some cautious chronological anchorage for a set of English place-names, those which generally appear as Preston, Monkton, and

[53] For documentation, see Taylor, 'Scandinavians', pp. 140, 143.

[54] John MacQueen has suggested that some names in *tūn* in Wigtownshire are of perhaps eighth-century date: *Place-Names of the Moors and Machars*, pp. 33–34.

Bishopton.[55] Tom Pickles sets out the grounds for thinking that these three items, which have different but distinctive distributions in England, and also representation in the historical record, are likely to have their origins as terms in current use during a period between the eighth and the eleventh centuries, with his preferred context being the reorganization of ecclesiastical land-holding related to the Benedictine reforms of the middle of that period. As he puts it in his conclusion: 'Consideration of the wider historical context of ecclesiastical property management and individual instances of [these place-names] suggests that a large proportion of these names were coined in the late eighth, ninth, tenth or eleventh century as a result of the reorganization of estates to provide a separate endowment for bishops or for parts of a religious community'.[56] It is not my purpose to dispute his analysis as it relates to the English record, and in particular the well-evidenced instances he explores as test cases. Rather, my concern is with instances of place-names formed on these patterns present in the south-western Scottish record, but clearly dateable to later in the middle ages, and capable of somewhat different interpretation. The concern is thus that clear Scottish records can show that, whatever the validity of Pickles's conclusions, names in this pattern should be treated individually and circumspectly; there is no exportable paradigm here.

To take each of my three instances in turn, we are looking at Preston in Kirkbean parish, Kirkcudbrightshire (roughly NX962563); Monkton in Prestwick (formerly Monkton) parish in Ayrshire (NS357276); and finally Bishopton near Whithorn in Wigtownshire (NX437409). Preston, the first of these, appears in a charter of 1176×85 from Roland, Lord of Galloway and Constable of Scotland to Holm Cultram abbey, a Cistercian foundation in Cumberland established by David I (along with his son, Henry), when it was within his kingdom.[57] The charter grants two

[55] T. Pickles, '*Biscopes-tūn*, *muneca-tūn* and *prēosta-tūn*: dating, significance and distribution', in E. Quinton (ed.), *The Church in English Place-Names* (Nottingham: English Place-Name Society, 2009), pp. 39–108.

[56] Pickles, '*Biscopes-tūn, muneca-tūn* and *prēosta-tūn*', p. 84.

[57] For the text, see K. J. Stringer, 'Acts of Lordship: the records of the Lords of Galloway to 1234', in T. Brotherstone and D. Ditchburn (eds), *Freedom and Authority: Historical and Historiographical Essays Presented to Grant G. Simpson* (East Linton: Tuckwell, 2000), pp. 203–34, (pp. 217–18). On Holm Cultram itself and general context, see further K. J. Stringer, *The Reformed Church in Medieval Galloway and Cumbria: Contrasts, Connections and Continuities*, The Eleventh Whithorn Lecture (Whithorn: Friends of Whithorn Trust, 2003).

different sets of items, the first being the *villa* (later church and parish) of Kirkgunzeon; the latter being usage rights, including 'easements of my wood in *Preston* and in *Lochildela* as far as *Pollesteresheued* of material and wood and other things necessary for the house of Holm and its own use'. This has the appearance of bringing together two grants previously separate. The first set of items employs names in its boundary clauses almost without exception Celtic (mostly Gaelic) in language, with only one or two names out of seventeen being English (*Grenethfalde*; and perhaps the rather mangled looking *Haclthetofte*). In the second section, only Preston and *Pollesteresheued* are mentioned; this latter looks like the old name for Airds Point, where what is now the New Abbey Pow (elsewhere *Polster*[58]) empties into the estuary of the Nith. *Pollesteresheued* must be an English name in *hēafod* 'head(land)', incorporating an existing Gaelic name for the New Abbey Pow. The context suggests, though cannot confirm, that the name Preston for the estate wherein Holm had easement rights, related to the monks of the new establishment of Holm,[59] rather than having any longer standing usage. Names in *tūn/toun* in this area show no signs of being particularly early, though English was undoubtedly present in this general area from the seventh century on. Conversely, we might wish to take a lead from the name Prestwick (discussed below), which has because of its generic element been seen as an early (Old English) name, and wonder about whether OE *prēost* 'cleric' could readily apply to the monks of a Cistercian monastery like Holm.[60] On this reading, Preston might refer to an earlier phase in the relationship between church and land in Kirkcudbrightshire. Technically, then, absence of records and the nature of the name mean that Preston KCB could have been named any time between the seventh and the twelfth century, with the balance of probability favouring the new context of the relationship between the estate and the monastery of Holm, with this being most favourable to the introduction of English-language names into the area.

[58] B. Webster (ed.), *Regesta Regum Scottorum* VI, *The Acts of David II* (Edinburgh: Edinburgh University Press, 1982), no. 235, p. 264. The name is Gaelic *pol(l)* + an undetermined element, perhaps *stair* 'path over a bog'.

[59] It should be noted that, *c.* 1176×96, Alan of Galloway further granted a salt-pan in Preston (which is on the Solway) as well as rights to extract wood to burn for salt making, to Melrose Abbey: see Stringer, 'Acts', p. 219 (no. 17).

[60] Though Pickles shows that the term was a flexible one which could incorporate any cleric ('*Biscopes-tūn*, *muneca-tūn* and *prēosta-tūn*').

We are on surer ground with our second example. Monkton in Kyle, in Ayrshire, is so called because it was an estate belonging to the Cluniac monks of Paisley Abbey. We can follow the emergence of this name over the course of the twelfth to fourteenth centuries. The church of Monkton, and hence perhaps also the estate it served, was in fact probably the original *Prestwic*, which, as we have seen, looks to belong to an older stratum of English nomenclature in the region. We first hear of this estate 1165×73, when Walter fitz Alan, the Steward, granted to Paisley:

> the church of *Prestwic*, with all of that land which Dovenaldus filius Yweni perambulated between the land of Simon Loccard [= *Symington*] and the land of *Prestwic* as far as *Pulprestwic* and along *Pulprestwic* as far as the sea, and from the sea along the burn between the land of Arnaldus and the land of *Prestwic*, as far as the boundaries of Simon Loccard; and that church of my burgh of *Prestwic*.[61]

There are a number of very interesting items in this grant, but two should draw our attention. I have already written about the name *Pulprestwic*, which demonstrates the incorporation of an existing English name within a Gaelic name in *pol(l)* 'burn' (now the Pow Burn which divided the formerly independent parishes of Prestwick and Monkton).[62] The main issue however is the extensiveness of Prestwick in this grant, and the distinction made between the two churches, one of *Prestwic*, the other of 'my burgh of *Prestwic*'. By 1226, this distinction had been crystallized to one between the churches *de Prestwic burgo* and *de altera Prestwic*.[63] This latter (in essence the original Prestwick estate and church) was at the same date also referred to as *nunc dicitur villa monachorum*, which probably bears testimony to the emergence of the name 'Monkton'. By the end of the fourteenth century, we hear in the same register of 'the mill of Monkton', and by 1400 of 'the church of Monkton'.[64] 'Monkton' thus is a name which emerges for an older estate, to describe the *toun* belonging to the monks of Paisley Abbey, while the name Prestwick becomes firmly attached to the burgh of that name and its parish church.

[61] *Registrum Monasterii de Passelet,* (Paisley: Maitland Club, 1877) [hereafter *Paisley Reg.*], [no. 8] p. 6, cf. [no. 12] p. 12. For dates and numbering, see the Syllabus of Scottish Charters: Paisley Reg. is at <www.arts.gla.ac.uk/scottishstudies/charters/index.htm>.

[62] T. O. Clancy, 'Two Ayrshire Place-Names', p. 99.

[63] *Paisley Reg.*, [no. 362] p. 412; see also 1265 confirmation on p. 309.

[64] *Paisley Reg.*, [no. 320] p. 364, dated 1390; [no. 323] p. 369, dated 1400. For a parallel case, see Friarton (Forgan) in Fife, Taylor with Márkus, *Place-Names of Fife*, IV, pp. 413–15.

'Monkton' was thus a fully functional and lexically meaningful name in south-western Scotland in the thirteenth and fourteenth centuries, and its purpose here was not to represent reorganization of ecclesiastical property as such (though its existence is a consequence of such reorganization in the twelfth century), but to distinguish the property of Paisley from other local properties.

My final example is later and more precise. Bishopton, near Whithorn, is a name which emerges in the late fifteenth or early sixteenth century. In the fifteenth century we find the bishops of Galloway complaining that, because the buildings at Whithorn belonged primarily to the Premonstratensian monks of that monastery, they had no official residence in Whithorn, nominally the location of their see. By 1502 at the latest this had been rectified, when we hear of 'castellans and keepers of the palace and fortalice of *Balnespyk* at the church of Candida Casa, granting to them the 100 shilling lands of *Balnespik* of old extent'.[65] This residence, a striking new coinage in Gaelic (i.e., *baile an easbuig*, 'the fermtoun of the bishop'), was known either simultaneously or shortly thereafter in Scots as Bishopton,[66] the name by which it is still known.

The Scottish evidence from the south-west, therefore, shows that these names or name-types, Preston, Monkton, and Bishopton, were in active use in this region between 1100 and 1500. The names were used with precision, to describe estates with proprietary relationships to clerics, monks and bishops. That this is so does not negate the conclusions of Pickles's investigation of these name-types in England, where his evidence clearly suggests an earlier horizon for many of the names there; but it should inflect any discussion of such names, and make us aware of the continuing validity of these name-types into the later middle ages.

So far this discussion has confined itself to a small subset of name-types employing the generic *tūn/toun*. As has long been recognized, however, the activities of rulers and the major nobility in the twelfth and thirteenth centuries have left an indelible chronological mark on the toponymic landscape. Where these phenomena have been sufficiently

[65] R. C. Reid (ed.), *Wigtownshire Charters*, Publications of the Scottish History Society, 3rd Series, vol. 51 (Edinburgh: Scottish History Society, 1960), pp. 19–20 (no. 2), 25–26 (no. 14). I discuss this name in more detail in my forthcoming Whithorn lecture, *Gaelic in Medieval Galloway: The Evidence of Names* (Whithorn: Friends of Whithorn Trust, 2013).

[66] Reid (ed.), *Wigtownshire Charters*, p. 107 (no. 75), which records it as *Beschoptoun* in 1521.

studied, it has become clear that new or newly-acquired settlements gained names in *tūn/toun* modified by the names of the individuals holding these estates during this period. These names are dateable by the nature of the names involved, mainly Norman or Flemish names, or those of a related continental name-stock; and many of the individuals are known from charters of the period and other sources.[67] Simon Taylor, building on work done elsewhere by Geoffrey Barrow, has shown the way in which, in Fife, previously existing estates were renamed for the settlements of the new landholding class. Names such as Otterston (named for an Othere who lived *c.* 1190, and formed from the lands of Cockairnie); and Thomastoun (named for Thomas of Cupar, *fl.* 1170 and probably created from the lands of Cupar) demonstrate this well. As with the Lothians, however, this new class, holding land or perhaps conceptualizing landholding in a distinct way, also included men with Gaelic names, such as Gille Girg, *fl.* 1215, who was probably the eponym of Greigston, formed, probably, from the lands of Denork.[68] Perhaps the best Fife demonstration of these toponyms as a way into the history of regional landholding and cultural change is the case of Mastertown near Dunfermline, named for the landholder, Master Ailric the mason, *fl.* 1150, but formerly a Gaelic name possessing a kinship ownership modifier, **Ledmacdu(n)gal* 'the settlement of the sons of Dúngal or Dubgall'.[69]

The recent findings in Fife to a certain extent reinforce observations made earlier about the south-west of Scotland. Geoffrey Barrow demonstrated that the twelfth-century resettlement under royal patronage of areas such as Cunninghame in the south-west left behind distinctive toponymic traces. Individuals, some of whom we can identify, are the eponyms of a series of names in *tūn*. We might highlight amongst these particularly Stevenston, whose eponym is Stephen Loccard, a Fleming prominent amongst those associated with both court and higher nobility; Symington, named from a kinsman, Simon Loccard; Riccarton, probably to be associated with Richard Wallace;[70] and Eglinton, named from an

[67] Dixon, 'Place-names of Midlothian', pp. 50–56 (online pdf, pp. 19–21); see also Barrow, *Anglo-Norman Era*, pp. 35–50; Nicolaisen, *Scottish Place-Names*, pp. 30–43.

[68] Taylor with Márkus, *Place-Names of Fife*, v, ch. 6, and elements glossary, s.v. *toun*; i, pp. 263, 274 (Otterston); iv, p. 318 (Thomastoun); iii, pp. 104–05 (Greigston).

[69] Taylor with Márkus, *Place-Names of Fife*, i, pp. 337–38; see also discussion in vol. v, p. 236.

[70] Barrow, *Anglo-Norman Era*, pp. 46, 66; Barrow, *Kingdom*, p. 323.

Eglun whose son Brice was active in (probably) 1255.[71] The settlements and activities, as well as the relatively early attestations of these names in relation to their probable coining, gives this sequence a particular significance for understanding the linguistic history of this part of Scotland. The names seem to be coinages of the period on either side of 1200, and refer back to individuals granted these estates in the previous two generations. They seem to mark a new injection of language into the area, though as we have seen, unlike Fife, this is an area with some significant traces of previous phases of English influence as revealed by the toponyms. I will return below to the way these names articulate with ones in *bý* both in Cunninghame and, in a different way, in Dumfriesshire and Cumberland.

Peter McNiven's recent research on the region of Menteith (formerly in Perthshire, and now largely in Stirling district) also ties the coining of names in Sc. *toun* with holders' names to the injection of new language into a region. Here, he has revealed the employment of the generic *toun* in the fifteenth century, at a point at which Scots becomes effectively the dominant language in a previously largely Gaelic-speaking district, representing the divisions of larger former estates (or, possibly, land newly reclaimed for agricultural use), and named for the kindreds or individuals holding the lands. McNiven notes, for instance, 'The earliest of the *toun*-names is the ephemeral *Donald-youngistoun* which is on record in 1488–9, and which then disappears when Donald Young's portion of Cessintully is sold to someone else. This exchange of lands is one reason for the appearance of new names in new languages'.[72] He

[71] For the eponym of Eglinton as *Eglun*, and the dating, see J. Shedden-Dobie (ed.), *Muniments of the Royal Burgh of Irvine*, 2 vols (Edinburgh: Ayrshire and Galloway Archaeological Association, 1890–91), I, no. 1, pp. 1–4 (*Bricium de Eglunstone filium quondam Eglun domini de Eglunstone*; the existence of a seemingly contemporary *Hugo dominus de Eglunstone* might suggest that the eponym might be another generation or two back); for re-dating (from 1205 to 1255), with consequences for the floruit of this individual, see PoMs database <www.poms.ac.uk>, document 4/26/10 and discussion. The name is probably Norman Fr. *Agyllun*, met in the Cumberland place-name Aglionby. The eponym of that place-name is possibly the Aguillon, father of Lawrence, who was active in the 1170s, though the personal name forms are complicated. See J. B. Prescott (ed.), *Register of the Priory of Wetherhal* (London: Elliot Stock, 1897), p. 83 and note. See also Fellows-Jensen, *Scandinavian Settlement Names in the North-West*, p. 25, and A. M. Armstrong, A. Mawer, F. M. Stenton, and B. Dickins, *The Place-Names of Cumberland*, 3 vols, English Place-Name Society 20–22, p. 158. There may be a link between these, something I hope to explore in the near future.

[72] McNiven, 'Gaelic Place-Names and the Social History of Gaelic Speakers in Medieval Menteith', unpublished PhD thesis (University of Glasgow, 2011), p. 125.

details the emergence of a restricted series of *toun*-names in the area around Thornhill in the late fifteenth and early sixteenth century. One of the most intriguing such is Watston in Kilmadock parish, which is:

> on record from at least 1491 as *Wat Doggistoun* and *Wat Smy[tht]toun* (NAS, PA2/6, 1st part, f.28v). Walter Dog was '*camerarii de Menteith*' in 1471 and it was probably he who had been husband to Elizabeth Nory of Boquhapple in 1480 (ER ix, 563). Walter Smyth was a tenant in *Collach*, probably Coldoch, or part of it, in 1480 (ER ix, 563). It is not clear which 'Wat' was the tenant at Watston, and indeed it is not clear if the specific, i.e. 'Wats', is a genitive singular or plural; it may be that Watston was farmed by both men.[73]

What this demonstrates is that our historical data allow us to use, for parts of Scotland, even such a common generic as *tūn/toun* as a tool for understanding language change. Nonetheless, it also highlights that in Scotland the history of *tūn/toun* as a place-name element may be distinct and productively much later than is usually seen to be the case in England. To that extent, the chronological range of *tūn* as a place-name generic in Scotland needs to be folded into the understanding of this term in the work of the Survey of English Place-Names.

bý

Bound up with the new coining of *tūn*-names in the twelfth and thirteenth centuries, in Ayrshire at least, is another set of names, those employing the Scandinavian generic *bý*, 'farm, settlement'. These names have been much debated, particularly in terms of chronology and the nature of the settlement they are testimony to.[74] Are the names in *bý* in south-west Scotland testimony to Scandinavian settlement, or to the importation from parts of England of habits of naming generated by the previous domination of Scandinavian speech in those areas? There has been considerable debate on this subject, and there is not space here to rehearse it in full. Some considerations are in order. First, the bulk of the place-names using *bý* in southern Scotland are in Dumfriesshire where, along with a large cluster in northern Cumberland, they form a distinct group, both geographically and in the nature of their specific elements. Crucially, most of these names employ personal names well attested in the late eleventh and early twelfth century, in particular as land-holders

[73] McNiven, 'Gaelic Place-Names', p. 127.

[74] See note 52.

and witnesses of charters, in precisely this area. This has suggested that these names are the product of the redistribution of lands in this period, including the famous immigration to the area in the wake of the 1092 conquest under Ranulf de Meschin.[75] I would concur in this view, and reject the view that these are older places in *bý* where personal names have been substituted for previous specifics.[76] The evidence and the context do not support this view. But the distribution nonetheless prompts the as yet unanswered question, why *bý*, and why mostly here? Is this the result of folk taken from other parts of England bringing an onomastic habit with them? Were southern Dumfriesshire and northern Cumberland still fundamentally Scandinavian localities in language, in which *bý* remained a live part of the naming habit, to be employed by local speakers consequent on the arrival of new land-holders during the late eleventh and twelfth centuries?[77] This latter explanation would perhaps accord better with the presence in this area of some names with rarer, and possibly Scandinavian, specifics (e.g. Mabie in Kirkcudbrightshire) which look to be older than the main group. This issue is more difficult to resolve, but that the period, say, 1050–1200 sees a large number of names in *bý* created in this area, defined by the names of men linked proprietorially to these settlements, is hard to question. Equally, it becomes difficult to describe these names, precisely, as 'Scandinavian', if they are rather local reflections, within a largely English-language naming environment, of originally Scandinavian names and naming habits.[78]

If this is so, does this reorientation have any knock-on effect for the analysis of *bý*-names elsewhere, particularly in south-western Scotland? I

[75] See B. K. Roberts, 'Late *-bý* names in the Eden Valley, Cumberland', *Nomina* 13 (1989–90), 25–39; the best map of these names is to be found in J. G. Scott, 'The partition of a kingdom: Strathclyde 1092–1153', *Transactions of the Dumfriesshire and Galloway Natural History and Antiquarian Society*, 3rd series, 72 (1997), 11–40 (p. 20).

[76] Fellows-Jensen, 'Scandinavians in Scotland?', pp. 44–45, though see Taylor, 'Scandinavians', n. 15.

[77] See D. N. Parsons, 'On the origin of "Hiberno-Norse Inversion Compounds"', *Journal of Scottish Name Studies* 5 (2011), 115–52 (p. 126 and n. 31).

[78] See the comments of Williamson, 'Non-Celtic Place-Names', p. 281 (online version p. 112): 'The element persisted in living use in ME into the 11th and 12th centuries [...] Several names in Dumfriesshire seem to have been formed about this time, when *-by* had become an element in the local ME speech: cf Albie, Canonbie, Mumbie, Sibbaldbie. Lindkvist notes that the term may have been in use in the Northern ME dialect, and that unless the first element of a name ending in *-by* is Scandinavian, the compound may well be of English formation'.

should note that I do not fundamentally disagree with, for instance, Simon Taylor on the likely tenth-century background to the *bý*-names in eastern central Scotland.[79] But the ones in Ayrshire do not display the same traits as those which prompted his dating of the names in Fife and the south-east. The Ayrshire names, also studied by Grant, are a notably limited selection: Crosby/-ie (×2), Busby/-ie (×3,[80] and note one also in East Kilbride), Sorbie; with a few more unusual instances (Magbiehill; Cocklebee). All scholars have noted the absence of any other Scandinavian names in the vicinity of these *bý*-names. I would rather side with Geoffrey Barrow in thinking them to be product of the further importation of naming habits by folk granted lands in Cunninghame in the twelfth century.[81] Two sets of names demonstrate interesting overlaps between the naming-world of the southern *bý*-names in Dumfriesshire and Cumberland, and the environment of those in Ayrshire. This includes the employment of the same personal-name specifics in turn for *bý*-names in the south and *tūn*-names in Ayrshire (for instance, Lockerbie is named from a Loccard kinsman of the eponyms of both Stevenston and Symington, if it is not for one of these individuals themselves; we have already noted Eglinton and Aglionby). Beyond this, the zone of proven late-twelfth- and early-thirteenth-century *tūn*-names in Ayrshire overlaps at a detailed level with where *bý*-names are found. For instance, Crosby and Busby are found in Ardrossan parish, neighbouring Stevenston, named from Stephen Loccard, kinsman as we have seen of the Loccard whose name is preserved in Lockerbie. Busbie in Kilmaurs parish neighbours Warwickhill (which is in Dreghorn), probably named from Richard de Warwick, of Cumberland; Kilmaurs itself was granted to a Fleming, Robert son of Wernembald.[82] Crosbie in Dundonald parish, a medieval chapel, lies very close to Symington, as also to a landholding which never gained a *tūn*-name, 'the land of Arnald'.[83]

[79] Taylor, 'Scandinavians'.

[80] This includes the recently noted Busby or Bushby Wood, Mauchline parish (NS478262), recorded on OS 6" 1st edition (1857). I have not yet found it attested before this date.

[81] See Barrow, *Anglo-Norman Era*, pp. 47–48; 'Uses', pp. 70–72.

[82] Barrow, *Anglo-Norman Era*, pp. 83–84 and n. 198.

[83] See n. 52. Grant, 'Origin', p. 139, misplaces Crosbie (Dundonald parish) in Prestwick parish, and also misses its early documentation in the Paisley Register: (chapel of) *Crosby* 1208×14; (chapel of) *Crosseby* 1230; (mill of) *Corsby* 1371; (Adam de Fullarton, lord of) *Corsby* 1392. It may alternatively be that she has misplaced some of the early forms under

As noted above, Cocklebee seems to have a specific element derived from Old or Middle English, not Old Norse, and this aligns this name with some Dumfriesshire examples, also derived from Old or Middle English.[84] As a name, it seems to align well with the many Busbie and Sorbie names in describing a property claimed or reclaimed from disuse (judging from the specifics 'bush, undergrowth', 'sour, difficult', and 'cockleweed').[85] We are at least I think obliged to orient ourselves in understanding this complex of names within a dataset that encompasses north-western England, rather than one that looks to the west and north in Scotland, as suggested partly by Grant. And this is surely the right thing to do in general with respect to the English place-names of southern Scotland. In particular, only Barrow has championed, though some others such as Gillian Fellows-Jensen have acknowledged, the potential for the transfer of personnel and naming habits posed by the cross-border land-ownership of the nobility during the period before the wars of independence.[86] Obviously, what we would be dealing with in Ayrshire, if we look to a twelfth-century context for the names in *bý*, would be distinct from what we see in Dumfriesshire and Cumberland. Instead of *bý*-names being employed by local populations to name new settlements for incoming landholders, instead we would have to envisage two processes, one the importation of 'standard' *bý*-names like Busbie, Sorbie, Crosby by people (of a lower standing, hence farming more difficult land?) attached to those landholders, whose personal names were then instead employed in the creation of new names in *tūn*. Fundamentally, what we need is serious, detailed, and systematic and

Crosby, West Kilbride. In Taylor, 'Scandinavians', p. 141, Crosbie (Dundonald parish) has been entirely omitted in the editorial/printing process.

[84] Fellows-Jensen, 'Scandinavians in Southern Scotland?', pp. 42–43 (Canonbie, Appleby, Newbie; perhaps Mabie); Williamson, 'Non-Celtic place-names', p. 284 (online version p. 113): Mumbie (*Monkeby*), Mumbiehirst (*Monkebyhirst*), missed out in the review by Fellows-Jensen. There may also be some significance in the potential correlation of Mabie in KCB and Magbiehill AYR. See Taylor, 'Scandinavians', p. 127, 142–43, on the etymologies. Grant, 'Origin', pp. 134–35, seems inclined to exclude Magbiehill as a *bý*-name, but it seems to me reinforced by its proximity to Cocklebee.

[85] See Taylor, 'Scandinavians', p. 135. It should be noted that such places, once reclaimed, could become very fertile, giving them a status/yield belying their names: see Fellows-Jensen, *Scandinavian Settlement Names*, p. 40.

[86] Barrow, 'Uses', pp. 70–72; Fellows-Jensen, 'Scandinavians in Southern Scotland?'.

historically contextualized work on English place-names of south-western Scotland.[87]

Contextualising the strata

In the final part of this contribution, I wish to explore some ways in which context may be informative, in trying to understand both the lingering presence of an earlier stratum of English place-names in some areas of south-west Scotland, and the way in which new strands of English and Scots contributions emerged in this area during the period after 1100. In particular, this final section explores the 'neighbours' of English/Scots names: the context of the first appearance of certain names, and the languages of the other place-names that English names accompany within early bounds and charters. One of the real advantages in the Fife volumes has been the demonstration of the way in which boundary texts can reveal the shifting linguistic patterns in a dynamic landscape.[88] Gilbert Márkus's study of the bounds of Caiplie is an excellent explication of this methodology, showing the predominance of Scots (English) names on the east side of the estate adjoining the burgh of Crail, as opposed to the predominance of Gaelic on the west side, away from the influence of the burgh.[89] For the south-west of Scotland, though, this is a complex matter, as the presence of English/Scots in this region does not necessarily follow the same patterns, and there are some impressive counter-examples. The foundation-charter of the burgh of Ayr, from *c.* 1205, for instance, shows at best one out of over a dozen names in it to be English – and that one (Corton, in document *Crottun*) could well be an older (Old English) name.[90]

I begin, however, with the famous confirmation of properties in 1161 or 1162 by Malcolm IV, king of Scots, of grants made by David I to Walter fitz Alan, the Steward – the making of the fortunes of the family whose descendants would one day inherit the kingship of Scotland (and indeed, later, England). Here he received a series of properties: in the

[87] I am engaged in preliminary work towards a survey of Cunninghame, as part of the AHRC-funded 'Scottish Toponymy in Transition' project.

[88] See especially the exploration in vol. V, ch. 7.

[89] Márkus, 'Gaelic under pressure', building on work by Taylor, incorporated in *Place-Names of Fife*, III, pp. 329–33.

[90] G. W. S. Barrow (ed.), *Regesta Regum Scotorum* II, *The Acts of William I* (Edinburgh: Edinburgh University Press, 1971), no. 462, pp. 426–28. I am grateful to Dauvit Broun for a copy of his unpublished discussion of the boundary text.

south-west, these included *Reinfreu* (Renfrew), *Passeleth* (Paisley), *Polloc* (Pollock), *Talahret*, *Ketkert* (Cathcart), *le Drep* (Dripps), *le Muerne* (Mearns), *Egglesham* (Eaglesham), and *Louhenauhe* (Lochwinnoch).[91] What is notable in this rather bare list of estates is the dominance of Northern British names: Renfrew, Paisley, Cathcart, Pollock, the unlocated, but linguistically probably Brittonic *Talahret* (probably from the equivalent of Welsh *tal y rhyd* 'the brow of the ford', but there are other possibilities). The list does, of course, contain one of our putatively early English names, Eaglesham. But it also contains—marked out as a vernacular word—*le Drep*, now Dripps. This belongs to a large number of names in Scotland related to OE *þrēap* 'dispute', mapped and discussed all too briefly by Geoffrey Barrow.[92] It is interesting to see this name intrude itself here at this macro-level of major and probably old estates given to a rising lord within the Scottish court – it suggests one place in which the coining of new English/Scots names in the twelfth century in place of or in distinction to older estate names was in areas of dispute. Notable in this context is the presence of *Busby* within what was presumably the estate of *le Drep*. Given the relationship I have posited above between the names in Ayrshire in *bý* and twelfth-century settlement, there may also be a relationship here. What that relationship might be is not clear, but the proximity is suggestive and worth further investigation.

My second example comes from a document edited in 1955, held in The National Archives in Kew, but of Scottish provenance.[93] It relates to Carrick, the southernmost part of Ayrshire, and the least subject to the sort of infeftment of incoming nobles that can be seen in Cunningham

[91] G. W. S. Barrow (ed.), *Regesta Regum Scotorum* I, *The Acts of Malcolm IV* (Edinburgh: Edinburgh University Press, 1960), no. 184, pp. 225–26.

[92] Barrow, 'Uses', p. 68, map p. 71. The evidence from Scotland should reasonably be used to augment the record in Smith, *English Place-Name Elements*, p. 312 (and in future volumes of VEPN). The (fairly frequent) simplex usage in Scotland is notable, and it is not clear if this is replicated in English counties.

[93] TNA C 145/10/21. I. A. Milne, 'An extent of Carrick in 1260', *Scottish Historical Review* 34 (1955), 46–49; see also notes and clarifications by A. McKerral in the same volume, pp. 189–90; and especially identifications in J. Fergusson, also in the same volume, pp. 190–92. That some at least of these lands were core lands of the earls of Carrick earlier is shown by the granting of the churches of Turnberry and Straiton, along with Dailly (*Dalmakeran*) to Paisley in 1236; they later became churches pertaining to the daughter foundation of Crossraguell. See *Paisley Reg.*, p. 427; F. C. Hunter Blair (ed.), *Charters of the Abbey of Crossraguell* (Edinburgh: Ayrshire and Galloway Archaeological Association, 1886), nos 2, 22.

and Annandale and Clydesdale in the twelfth and thirteenth centuries. It describes the extent of the lands pertaining to the earldom of Carrick directly, during a period when the earl had died without heir and the arrangements regarding the lands had not yet been resolved, with the result that the king took the lands temporarily into crown possession. It is a century later, of course, but in a sense we are seeing a range of 'core' holdings by a major magnate within the Scottish kingdom, similar to those granted to the Steward. These are:

> *Straton* (Straiton), *Turnebyri* (Turnberry), *Drumfad, Bennan* (Bennan Head), *Glenop* (Glen App[94]), *Cunray* (Conray/Cundry; assoc. with Straid), *Dalachoran* (Dalquharran), *Glenkenith* (Glengennet).

The list of jurors for the proceedings (in the genitive singular) is also instructive: *Rolandi de Carric, Murthach mac Kenedy, Samuel mac Kenedy, Dunegal mac Gilendres, Sufne mac Ragnell, Macrath mac Nell, Henrici de Ros, Murthach filii Sumerlech, Roberti de Castello, Andree tal[li]atoris senescalli, Henrici mac Kenedy, et Gilmur Iudicis.* Notice the high proportion with Gaelic names – in contrast to the witness list of the grant to the Steward in 1161/62, the audience and indeed to some extent the constructors of this document are Gaelic-speakers. In that case, it may be doubly significant that amongst the largely Gaelic names of estates that pertained to the earldom were Turnberry and Straiton. Turnberry, of course, is well known as one of the names that scholars have noted as belonging to an early strand of English place-names, ones suggestive of lordly power.[95] Indeed, Turnberry, together with the likes of Borgue and Buittle, provide the ingredients from which this equation has been made – names based (apparently) on either OE *burh* or *bōðl*, which appear as major administrative centres of lordships in the twelfth or thirteenth centuries. It is also the persistence of Turnberry as a name, in amongst a sea of Gaelic names, in a lordship dominated by Gaels, that strengthens the notion that it is early, to my mind. And it participates in a cluster of names locally which all tend in this direction. Amongst these we should count Maybole, a *bōðl* name which, when first recorded, is incorporated into a Gaelic form (see below), and Kirkoswald, the church of Turnberry,

[94] Fergusson disputes the identification with Glenapp, but it seems hard to avoid. 'Extent', p. 191.

[95] Barrow, 'Uses', pp. 67–69. On this aspect of English place-names within the context of earlier Northumbrian power, see D. Brooke, 'The Northumbrian settlements in Galloway and Carrick: an historical assessment', *Proceedings of the Society of Antiquaries of Scotland* 121 (1991), 295–327.

a probable Gaelic name incorporating a Northumbrian saint.[96] Both the parishes of Maybole and Straiton (and Monkton, originally *Prestwic*, for that matter), are dedicated to Cuthbert, another Northumbrian saint. All these speak additionally of the potential depth of English toponymy in the region. In that context we should consider the presence of *Straton* (Straiton), here. Despite the apparent absence of Roman roads in the area, it seems likely that this place-name is to be referred to the various other Scottish and English names of this sort, meaning primarily 'steading near a (Roman) road'. The name and the location deserve closer scrutiny, both because of the likely age of the name, to judge by context, and because of its potential meaning.

This region provides a further, and rather different, set of examples in charters from the Melrose Cartulary. The estate of *Meibothelbeg* was granted in 1193 along with *Bethoc* (Beoch) to the monks of Melrose.[97] The name is a Gaelic incorporation of an existing English name, 'little Meibothel', the name itself being probably OE *mǣge* + *bōðl*. This estate was later called simply Grange (from its functional status in relation to the monks of Melrose; the modern High Grange farm is at NS303124), to be distinguished from *Meibothelmor* 'big Meibothel', which is modern Maybole itself. Again, although Maybole has often been invoked as an early English place-name, we benefit from seeing it as the only stable and prominent English name in an otherwise fairly solidly Gaelic set of boundary texts, those preserved in *Melrose Lib.* nos 29 and 30, and even at that, one which presents itself having been augmented by Gaelic modifiers. That said, there are some nuanced readings of the boundary texts available on comparison of *Melrose Lib.* no. 29 with no. 30. It is not clear what the distinction between these two texts is—they have mostly the same witnesses, for instance—but it is noticeable that no. 30 supplies a slightly different set of bounds (or perhaps rather, describes the bounds differently), and that it includes a few English (or possibly Norse in one instance) names in amongst them: *Scipsate* (possibly a translation of the Gaelic *Lemenluing* 'leap of the ship' – itself a seemingly odd use of the

[96] There is not space here to discuss my view that names in *kirk-* in SW Scotland are fully Gaelic names employing an Old English or Old Norse loan-word, rather than 'inversion compounds'; for a précis of this view, see Parsons, 'On the origin', p. 118.

[97] C. Innes (ed.), *Liber Sancte Marie de Melros: munimenta vetustiora Monasterii Cisterciensis de Melros* (Edinburgh: Bannatyne Club, 1837) [hereafter *Melrose Lib.*], nos 29, 30.

generic *leum* 'leap'), and *Brocklaue*, now Brockloch.[98] This may perhaps suggest that English was beginning to be a new force in the toponymy of the area again in the late twelfth century, though we can hardly rule out some much more complex explanation.

Likewise, in charters regarding lands to the north-west of Maybole given between 1188 and 1196 by Roger de Scalebroc, or Skelbrook, who came from a Norman family with estates in Yorkshire near Pontefract, the dominant language of both place-names and witnesses seems to be Gaelic,[99] but here there are even more key names that are English. In *Melrose Lib.* no. 31, granting 'the whole estate of *Drumceisuiene* and *Alesburc* and *Auchenphur*' to Melrose, we see not only *Alesburc*, later Elsberry Head (now Bower Hill), which we should add to the list of early *burh* names, but also *Farnlei* and *Gilliforde*, as well as the 'Englished' Gaelic name *Largas*, in which G. *lairg* 'pass' is supplied with an English plural. It may be important that, similar to the case of the Carrick extent, we are dealing with an estate name in English alongside two Gaelic names.[100]

Although there is not space to review them in detail here, these texts from Carrick provide an interesting contrast to a series of documents pertaining to Kirkcudbrightshire, further south and east. They relate to lands of Kirkgunzeon (a grange and later church, though judging by the place-name an earlier church settlement); the lands of Mabie and

[98] 1193 grant by Duncan earl of Carrick of *Meibothelbeg* (now Grange) and *Beoch* to Melrose Abbey (*Melrose Lib.* nos 29, 30). [I give important variants from no. 30 in square brackets; → is used to indicate the progression of the perambulation, without detailing precise wording or orientation]:

Moybothelbeg [Meibothelbeg] (by these bounds): Crumder [Crubder] → Culelungford → Polnetiber → Don → Polgarroh [Polnegarrah] → Polnecog- [Polcog-] → Duuah → Enahconecal → Crumder [30: Dufah inter Meibothelbeg et Meibothelmor] → Brockelaue→ Crubder]

Bethoc (by these bounds):

Lemenlung → Neskecokeri → Croah → Gallan → Tunregaith → Polnesalahart → Polnetyberes

[30: Scipsate →Altecreue → Cragan → Tunregaid → Polsalacharic → Polnetybered]

[99] Witnesses include: Gillenem Accoueltan, Gilledouengart (frater eius), Gillecrist mac Makin, Murdac mac Gillemartin, Gilleasald mac Gilleandris, Gillemernoch (frater eius).

[100] 1188×96 grant by Roger de Scalebroc of 'Drumceisuiene' to Melrose Abbey (*Melrose Lib.* no. 31), listing, inter alia:

Totam terram de Drumeceisuiene et Alesburc et Auchenphur.

Largas, Bethoc, Dunduf, Drumceisuiene

Alesburc → Auchnephur → Gilliforde → Farnleie → Polnesalahari → Hauenegaith

Achencork; and the boundary between Kirkgunzeon and Colvend.[101] All of these are found in the register of Holm Cultram Abbey, which we have seen as a force in the area already. It is impressive that the names in this effectively 'English' set of landholdings (in terms of their primary landholders) are Gaelic. Out of a series of very detailed boundary texts, the language of the micro-toponymy is very strongly Gaelic, even extending to the new coining of names in Gaelic in one charter. This said, across the texts, there are some English place-names apparent, and the nature and context of these names suggest not long-standing older names embedded in a landholding landscape, but rather some local and (roughly) contemporary use of English to name minor features. These include, in the boundaries of Kirkgunzeon (from 1174×85), *Grenethfalde* (*Grenefaude* in 1203×34); in the boundaries of Kirkconnell (from 1235×53) *Grenesiche*. By the 1280s, strongly English aspects of these lands are in evidence, with *le Kyrkfrerd* in Kirkconnell (1280×90), whilst a delineation of the boundary between Kirkgunzeon and Colvend proceeds at its southern end as follows (I have left English names unglossed):

> up to *le Bathepot*, up by a sike to *le Bracanhirst*, then southwards to *le Stanrayse* and then to a hummock on the moss called *Moynhonyld* [= G. *móine* 'bog, peatmoss' + pers.n. *Conaill*?]; and so west to another hummock in the same moss, and thence to *le Broue* on *le Gile* called *Tauenaherothery* [= G. *tamhnach* '(green) clearing' + pers.n. *Ruaidhri*]; and so straight down to the *Pollenhaune* [G. *poll* 'burn' + ?], and by it until it falls into the moss; and by the moss to the great white rock in the moss, and so straight west to *le Birkeheved*, then to a fallen oak and to *Stodfald*...[102]

There is presumably a story to be told here about progressive encroachment of English on an otherwise Gaelic landscape, but it seems unlikely that this would represent the full story. Throughout these documents, the Gaelic names in them represent locations (burns, hills) which now possess other names, themselves often derived from Gaelic

[101] F. Grainger and W. G. Collingwood (eds), *Register and Records of Holm Cultram* (Kendal: Cumberland and Westmorland Antiquarian and Archaeological Society, 1929) [henceforth RHC]: Kirkgunzeon and Colvend: RHC nos 121, 130, 255; Kirkconnell: RHC nos 116, 117, 149; Mabie and Achencork: RHC nos 142 and 154. See also Stringer, 'Acts of Lordship', nos 15, 25, 50, 47. On the Kirkgunzeon lands, see also R. C. Reid, 'The early ecclesiastical history of Kirkgunzeon', *Transactions of the Dumfriesshire and Galloway Natural History and Antiquarian Society*, 3rd Series, 14 (1926–28), 201–15.

[102] RHC no. 255.

(i.e., different Gaelic names than appear in the boundary clauses). I have suggested that this suggests in some areas a period of displacement and re-naming, with the re-naming (probably after the Wars of Independence caused severe changes to landholding patterns) happening in Gaelic.[103] The complexity of the stratification of names in south-west Scotland does not end in the thirteenth century by any means.

One final selection of texts, which I elsewhere examine from a different perspective,[104] may be a salutary reminder about the lateness and lack of centrality of English/Scots in the toponymy of much of the south west during the central and later middle ages. These are accounts of the properties held by various major ecclesiastical institutions in Wigtownshire in the later middle ages. In Wigtownshire we lack anything by way of extensive records before the late fifteenth century. Nonetheless, these lists of lands from the later middle ages give a sense of the linguistic landscape occupied by each establishment. The first we may consider is the list of the lands of Glenluce Abbey, in 1573.[105] I have placed in italics those names where the underlying name is probably derived from English/Scots:

> Barquhaskin; Culroy; Auchmaulg; Creauchchis; Hidder *Synnonis*; Kirkcrist; Auchinfad; Litil-Barloccart; Meikle Barloccart; Dirwardis; Wod de Dirwardis; Dirgollis; Blairdirry; Cassinginzell; Barnesalye; Glenjorie; Glenhouill; Caskilloch (Cascreoch or Crescreauch); Anabaglische; Dernegormoir; Knok; Dirsculbeyne; Dirnone; Craiginweauch; Grenane; Glenschammer; Gas; Glennarne; Kilchyrne; Balneill; Drumgangewir; Kilmakfadzeane; Dougrie; Dirnemow; Glenquhillie; Marclauch; Markdow; Glenkittin; Cragach; Dalnigep; Kilfedder; Cragberinoch; Barluyir; Barnesangand; Knoktebey; Areawland; Crag; Arehamyne; Litill Dunraggit; Ganoch; *Quhitecruk*; Challoch; Clannarie; Balnab; Barnis; Multonische; Poltduff; Balmurra; *Artfeild*; Garvellen; Hidder Torris; Ovir Torris; Balmasche; Drochdule; Gallaspik; Cragnargit; Colquossoun; Machriemoir; Nethir *Synnonis*; Meikle Dunraggit; Galdenoch; Cameray; Ballincarrie; Kilphillane;

[103] T. O. Clancy, 'Gaelic in medieval Scotland: advent and expansion' (The Sir John Rhŷs Memorial Lecture, 2009), *Proceedings of the British Academy* 167 (2011), 349–92 (p. 388).

[104] Clancy, *Gaelic in Medieval Galloway.*

[105] J. M. Thomson (ed.), *Registrum Magni Sigilli Regum Scotorum. The Register of the Great Seal of Scotland,* IV, *AD 1546–1580* (repr. Edinburgh: Clark Constable, 1984), no. 2202, pp. 580–81.

> Challochmwn; *Park*; *Cultstoun*; *Blakmark*; Bailcaill; Ballinlauch; Drumpaill cum molendino de Clauchean de Glenluce

Note, there are only approximately six names (*Synnonis; Quhitecruk*; *Artfeild*; *Park*; *Cultstoun*; *Blakmark*) deriving from English / Scots or Old Norse out of eighty-four: that is, less than 10%. Here I am not including names that derive from Gaelic or British but which have been 'Scotticized' by the addition of a Sc. modifier or affix, such as *Meikle Dunragit*, or where a Gaelic name incorporates and English/Scots loan-word, as in *Markdow,* though we could no doubt by including these produce a more nuanced analysis.[106]

Second in this selection, and slightly different in being a modern compilation from diverse medieval sources, is the list of the lands of the Bishops of Galloway, as assembled by R. C. Reid:[107]

> Inch; Killinpoti; Culeady; Balyett; Innermessan; Dalzarrane; Little *Tung*; Meikle *Tung* of le *Seuchance*; Marsalloch; Kirrunray; Clannery; Achrocher; *Penninghame*; Clarie; Over Bar; Barchelauchlyne; Barquharrane; Baltersan; Barvanan; *Bordland*; Carnestik; Polchullie; Balschalloch; *Grange* (Kirkcolm); Trave; Bartrachane; Lekkingurum; Achyfe; Clachanis; Auchtafie; Ervie; Knokcowat; Kairomannock; *Bischoptoun*/Balnespik; Balyequhoir; Rispyne; Craig; Balcray; Kirkcrist; *Nuntoun*; *Bischoptoun*; Kirkeoch; Auchengassil; *Newtoun*; *Endrig*.

Again the number of Old English/Scots or Old Norse names is strikingly low, only around nine or ten out of about forty-six, around 20% (the names are Little Tung; Meikle Tung of le Seuchance; Penninghame; Bordland; Grange; Bischoptoun/Balnespik; Nuntoun; Bischoptoun; Newtoun; Endrig).

Finally though, by contrast, the lands pertaining to the priory of Whithorn show a different picture. There are many fewer lands, but nonetheless it is instructive. These come from a 1325 charter of confirmation of churches and lands pertaining to the Priory of Whithorn:[108]

[106] John MacQueen discusses some of the names deriving from this charter in *Place-Names in the Rhinns of Galloway* (Stranraer: Stranraer and District Local History Trust, 2002), pp. 64–77 (some hunting is needed; *Synnonis* is discussed under *Sinniness*, p. 88, and analyzed as Old Norse though the connection with the forms here is missed).

[107] Reid, *Wigtownshire Charters*, pp. 2–6.

[108] A. A. M. Duncan (ed.), *Regesta Regum Scotorum* V, *The Acts of Robert I* (Edinburgh: Edinburgh University Press, 1988), no. 275; discussed from a different perspective in R. Oram, *A Monastery and its Landscape: Whithorn and Monastic Estate Management in Galloway (c. 1250–c. 1600)*, Thirteenth Whithorn Lecture (Whithorn: Friends of the

> (ecclesiam Sancte Kener de) *Karnesmoll*; (ecclesiam sancti Machuti de) *Wygtoune*; (ecclesiam sancti Michaelis de) *Geuellstoune*; (quatuor quarterias de) *Oton* in *Farines*; Malmene; Glens*winton*; *Parton*; (toft in Kirkcudbrycht); Donarhahualf; Beath; Drumdath; Drumkell; *Cregilton*; *Soreby*; Clachhane; *Mochrome*.

Around nine of these names may be from Old English/Scots or Old Norse, out of about seventeen, that is, around 50% (the names in question: Karnesmoll;[109] Wygtoune; Geuellstoune; Oton (+ Farines); Glenswinton; Parton; Cregilton; Soreby; Mochrome[110]).

Elsewhere I explore these data with respect to the status of Gaelic in Galloway during the middle ages,[111] but they have much to tell us also about the status of the Germanic languages, and in particular English and Scots. We have, of course, to make allowances for different factors at work here. The properties in the first two lists (for Glenluce and for the Bishops of Galloway) lie across a swathe of territory in the middle and upper lands of Wigtownshire, whereas the Whithorn Priory lands and churches are mainly situated within the Whithorn peninsula itself. That Old English/Scots and Old Norse has more prominence here thus may either be geographically determined, or be a feature relating to the long-standing land-holding arrangements of the abbots and priors of Whithorn. Was Whithorn from its inception as a Northumbrian see in the eighth century a vector of linguistic change and influence, and its land-holding a conservative force for preservation of Old English in the vicinity? Or was this peninsula less subject to the intensive Gaelicization in the years after 900 that we see elsewhere in Galloway? Or should we seek explanations at a later stage in the region's history, during the twelfth and thirteenth centuries, for instance? Given the state of our evidence, it will be difficult to answer fully these questions.

In conclusion then, this chapter suggests a number of pressing issues in understanding the role of English (and Scots) in the formation of the place-names of south-west Scotland. Key among them is the historical

Whithorn Trust, 2005). He there compares a further feu charter of 1569, which I have not space to discuss here.

[109] MacQueen, *Place-Names of the Wigtownshire Moors and Machars*, p. 86 suggests a Br. derivation for this name.

[110] Comment on some of these names may be found in MacQueen, *Place-Names of the Wigtownshire Moors and Machars*; for discussion of Mochrum (*Mochrome*) as an Old English or Old Norse name, see pp. 45–48.

[111] Clancy, *Gaelic in Medieval Galloway*.

contextualization of the documentary witnesses to these names, where it is possible. Alas, it is not very often possible to get a firm fix on the documentary history of the area, since we lack so much. To return to Cunninghame, however, it is clear to me that detailed study would show the dating horizons for many further sets of names – such as the families behind names like Robertland, Kelsoland, and similar names, who appear as owners of these lands in the early modern period. The main lesson to me is that the appeal of the early in place-names in Scotland has obscured the later medieval and early modern contribution, and left us guessing when it may be possible to know. But of course, what we need above all is the sort of survey work which would provide the robust data on which that knowledge might be based.[112]

[112] I am indebted to Simon Taylor for his comments on a draft of this chapter, as too for many discussions of matters in it. Material relating to Cunninghame, especially to East Lugtonridge and environs, benefited from the local knowledge of Dr Anne Scott Goldie, Mrs Joan Goldie, and especially that of my father-in-law, Mr James S. H. Goldie, farmer of East Lugtonridge, who died suddenly in 2011 during work on this contribution. This chapter is dedicated to his memory.

11

English place-names in Wales

Hywel Wyn Owen

Introduction

In 1938 B. G. Charles published his *Non-Celtic Place-Names in Wales*.[1] Twenty years later Gwynedd Pierce published a detailed analysis of non-Welsh place-names in Wales,[2] which was written in Welsh and for that reason did not reach as wide an audience as it most certainly deserved, but his 'Some aspects of English influence on place-names in Wales' did achieve a wider audience.[3] In 2007 Richard Morgan and I published the *Dictionary of the Place-Names of Wales* which covered the names of all the major and minor settlements in Wales (as well as selected topographical names).[4] DPNW, therefore, not only updates toponymic interpretation but provides the first opportunity to bring together a comparative analysis of all the significant place-names of Wales of

[1] B. G. Charles, *Non-Celtic Place-Names in Wales* (London: University College London, 1938).

[2] G. O. Pierce, 'Enwau lleoedd anghyfiaith yng Nghymru' ['Alien place-names in Wales'], *Bulletin of the Board of Celtic Studies* 18 (1958–60), 252–65.

[3] G. O. Pierce, 'Some aspects of English influence on place-names in Wales', *Onoma* 17 (1972–73), 173–91, originally presented as a paper at the annual conference of the Council for Name Studies in Great Britain and Ireland at Bangor, Wales, in 1972.

[4] H. W. Owen and R. Morgan, *Dictionary of the Place-Names of Wales* (Llandysul: Gomer, 2007; reprinted with corrections 2008) [DPNW]. The historical forms cited in this chapter are taken mostly from this volume. As in DPNW place-names in this chapter are assigned to their pre-1974 historical counties which are abbreviated thus:

Angl	Anglesey	Glam	Glamorganshire
Brec	Breconshire	Mer	Merionethshire
Caern	Caernarfonshire	Monm	Monmouthshire
Card	Cardiganshire	Mont	Montgomeryshire
Carm	Carmarthenshire	Pemb	Pembrokeshire
Denb	Denbighshire	Radn	Radnorshire
Flints	Flintshire		

whatever linguistic origin. It allows us to observe patterns in the later phonological and sociological development of settlement names, migration, language shift, dialectal variants, bilingualism, anglicization and cymricization and national consciousness. It also provides an opportunity to plot the distribution of the English names in DPNW.[5] This chapter, which also includes a number of minor and local names not in DPNW, will be the first opportunity to set out the findings of such an analysis. With its 3000 place-names, 2086 places and 1060 elements, DPNW provides quantitative place-name evidence to examine these features comparatively.

The definition 'English' will be seen to be contentious in itself. In Wales, whether we like it or not, and rightly or wrongly, frequently 'English' implies 'not Welsh'. In casual unguarded conversation in Welsh, people find themselves describing acquaintances as 'English' when they mean 'they don't speak Welsh'. That is socially and linguistically indefensible, and leads to prejudice and resentment. However, this broad-brush approach has always applied to place-names. Place-name evidence shows English-speakers using 'Welsh' to describe not only people who spoke Welsh but places with Welsh tenurial practices. Many English settlers of whatever period have pronounced Welsh names in their own fashion, and this anglicization has allowed names to follow a different phonological path to the regular Welsh pronunciation. This is particularly true of the more anglicized areas of Wales where the scarcity or absence of the Welsh language in a community over a long period has not provided a corrective pronunciation. It is only the toponymist who knows that the names could be Latin, Irish, Anglo-Saxon, Scandinavian, French, Flemish or Modern English. Conversely, many 'English' names (of whatever origin) have been readily adapted to follow cymricized phonological routes different from the regular development of similar names when they occur in England. For the purposes of this chapter, therefore, and following the studies of Gwynedd Pierce and B. G. Charles, I intend to allow the term 'English' to encompass names which are simply not Welsh in origin. However, the discussion within the chapter will make it clear when the actual derivation is, say, Old Norse.

Of the 2086 places in DPNW 76% have Welsh names only. The others

[5] Place-name evidence can only be a guide to settlement history in Wales and frequently does not provide contemporary corroboration. Scandinavian place-name evidence, for example, has to be judiciously interpreted since most documentation postdates the early Middle Ages.

can be classified into three categories:

i. places with English names only;
ii. places with English and Welsh names (dual naming);
iii. places with phonological adaptations (cymricization or anglicization).

Category i, those places with exclusively English names, contains 157 names which represents 7.5% of the places in DPNW. Category ii, those places with English names side by side with Welsh names, contains 110 names which represents 5.3%. The combined English component from categories i and ii is 267 places with English names, representing 12.8% of the place-names in DPNW.

English place-names

Later in this chapter I will look in detail at the distribution of those names regarded as being English of whatever origin and at the phonological processes which have given those place-names an identity peculiar to Wales. At this point I shall give an overview of the 267 English names together with other local names which illustrate the same features.[6] Discussion of features of dual naming and of phonology are largely omitted in this first section which concentrates on the English (or pseudo English) place-names themselves. Readers will need to suspend curiosity on the linguistic aspects of what appear to be highly un-English names (such as Gwesbyr and Gwersyllt) until later sections of the chapter.

We have first to get past the name Wales itself. Fortunately the issues, linguistic and ethnic, are well-known to all toponymists. Cymru (the country) and Cymry (the people), a distinction of spelling which emerged in the Middle Ages, derive from two Brittonic or Brythonic words **kom-brogī* 'fellow countrymen' with the element *brog*, fossilized in Pembroke and found in modern Welsh *bro* 'region, neighbourhood'.[7] It is also found in Cumbria, Cumberland and the Latinized Cambria(n), as well as in individual place-names: Comberbatch and Comber Mere (Ch), Comberhalgh (La), Comberton (He), Cumberwell (W), Cumberwood (Gl) and Cumberworth (WRY), as well as others in eastern England.[8]

[6] Such a survey can only be completed when an exhaustive survey of all the counties in Wales has been undertaken along the lines of the English Place-Name Society survey volumes.

[7] J. M. Jones, *A Welsh Grammar* (Oxford: Clarendon, 1931), p. 4.

[8] M. Gelling, *Signposts to the Past*, 3rd edn (Chichester: Phillimore, 1997), pp. 97–98, noting that the term is best represented in the west Midlands and north-west.

Much has been made of the distinction between the neighbourly inclusivity of the name Cymru, the name Welsh people use of themselves, compared with Wales and Welsh, the label imposed by others. In the politically sensitive twentieth century, the widespread belief, now considered mistaken, that 'Wales' and 'Welsh' denoted 'foreign(ers)' in early usage, led to some unease.[9]

Margaret Gelling has shown that OE *walh* or *wealh*, plural *walas* or *wealas*, meant 'Welshman'.[10] The other meaning of OE *walh* 'slave' was, according to J. R. R. Tolkien in 1963, simply the result of many serfs being Welsh speakers.[11] A thorough examination of the evidence by Margaret Faull supports Tolkien's view that *walh* meant 'Celtic speaker' at the time of the Anglo-Saxon occupation from the fifth century onwards, because many slaves would be from Celtic-speaking tribes, and that ninth-century laws of Wessex used *walh* or *wealh* specifically of a Welsh rather than an English slave.[12] By the eleventh century, *Wealas* was being used solely of inhabitants of Wales and Cornwall.

This is perhaps the occasion to consider Bretton, a Flintshire place-name very close to the Cheshire border. The first recorded form, *Edritone* 1086, should be interpreted as '*Britone*' and the second, *Brecton* 13th cent., probably has *-ct-* for *-tt-*, while the third, *Bretton c.* 1310, puts us on safer ground to interpret the name as ON *Bretar* 'Britons', genitive plural *Breta*, combined with OE *tūn*. On the assumption that the settlement was distinguished as being Welsh in some way, the challenge is to explain why Bretton is not 'Walton' or 'Comberton'. Why does Bretton have the same Scandinavian name for the Welsh as occurred in ON *Bretland* 'Wales' and Bretby (Derbyshire)? There was certainly a heavy Scandinavian presence in north Wirral, and Norse settlers were granted

[9] B. L. Jones, *Enwau* (Llanrwst: Carreg Gwalch, 1991), p. 4, referred to the distant Germanic connotations of *walh* to indicate someone who spoke a foreign tongue: 'Estron oeddem ni yng ngolwg y Saeson cynnar, hyd yn oed yn ein gwlad ein hunain' ('In the eyes of the early English, we were foreigners even in our own land'). In fact, it can be argued, with Tolkien, that common Germanic usage suggests its original adoption (apparently from a Celtic tribal name) as an 'ethnic' label for Romanized Celts (J. R. R. Tolkien, 'English and Welsh', in *Angles and Britons: O'Donnell Lectures* (Cardiff: University of Wales, 1963), pp. 1–41 (p. 26)).

[10] Gelling, *Signposts*, pp. 95–97.

[11] Tolkien, 'English and Welsh', p. 27.

[12] M. L. Faull, 'The semantic development of Old English *wealh*', *Leeds Studies in English* 8 (1975), 20–44.

land near Chester which is only three miles away;[13] we also know that the Scandinavians had Welsh and Britons from the north of England in their armies.[14] The conclusion seems to be that Bretton was settled by Scandinavianized Welsh speakers, and that the Mercians adopted the Scandinavians' ethnic descriptor.

A fair number of coastal names fall into the all-inclusive 'English' group regardless of their specific linguistic origin, particularly those Scandinavian names which were absorbed into a maritime lingua franca and thence into local usage. The generally accepted view is that the Scandinavian sea-routes from Ireland and the Isle of Man can be traced along the north and west coast of Wales as well as along the south and south-west coast. Anglesey itself probably combines the Scandinavian personal name *Ǫngull* and ON *ey* 'island', despite the early evidence already betraying the perception that it was the 'isle of the Angles' (*Anglesege* 1098, *Anglorum insula* 12th cent., *Ongulsey* 13th cent., *Angleseye* 1248, *Engleseye* 1353). Bardsey (Caern) (*Berdeseie c.* 1191, *Bardesey* 1277), an island off the tip of the Llŷn peninsula, is similar to Anglesey in the sense that it involves a Scandinavian personal name, *Barðr*.

Off the south-east coast of Anglesey is Priestholm 'priest island' with ON *prestr* and ON *holmr*, a reference to the sixth-century church of Seiriol and the monastic settlement on the island (in Welsh Ynys Seiriol). The 'English' name is admittedly recorded very late (*Prestholme* 1468, *Prest-holm* 1478) but with the Old Norse element *holmr*, and in the context of the other Scandinavian island-names around the coast, its origin is almost certainly much earlier. The existence of several other aliases such as Ynys Lannog (*Enislannach id est insula ecclesiastica c.* 1191, *Onyslannauc* 1258, *Prestholme alias Evys Llanoc* 1468), with the personal name *Glannog*, and Ynys Seiriol (*Ynys Seiriol* mid-16th cent.), with the personal name Seiriol, suggests that they were more widely used ecclesiastically and locally than Priestholm, that the Scandinavian name may have been unrecorded for several centuries in official documentation, and that it may owe its survival to maritime use. A modern name Puffin Island (*Puffin island or Priest holm* 1797) has

[13] P. Cavill, S. E. Harding and J. Jesch, *Wirral and its Viking Heritage* (Nottingham: English Place-Name Society, 2000).

[14] H. W. Owen, *The Place-Names of East Flintshire* (Cardiff: University of Wales, 1994), pp. 20–21.

perhaps more currency with tourists.

We need to be careful in ascribing a Scandinavian origin to (The) Skerries (Angl), the series of interconnecting reefs or low crags which explains the plural usage. The Skerries are the first landmark off Anglesey and the north-west coast on the sea route from the Irish Sea, a role reinforced by the modern lighthouse. The belief has been that this is ON *sker* 'rock', seen at least twice in Glamorganshire as Sker (Point) (*Bla(c)kescerre* 1158–83, *Skarre* 1536, *Scerr c.* 1700) and as Sker (*Skerra* 1173–78, *Skarra or Sker c.* 1291). However, there is no record of the Skerries with the form 'Sker' (*le Skerry* 15th cent., *the Skerres* 16th cent., *Scerries* 1761, *Skerry I.* 1805, *The Skerries* 1818). The conclusion must be that this is not ON *sker* but English *skerry* 'rugged sea-rock, stretch of rocks, reef'. Interestingly, the documentation of *skerry* in Anglesey's Skerries predates usage elsewhere in Britain.[15]

Another trace of an Anglo-Scandinavian name along the north Wales coast is the extensive promontory of the (Great) Orme (Caern) (*Ormeshead insula* 15th cent., *Ormeheade point* 1610, *Gt Ormes Head* 1805). We cannot discount the Old Norse personal name *Ormr* but the distinctive shape seen from sea and land makes it more likely to be ON *ormr* 'serpent'. It bears comparison with the equally striking Worm's Head (Glam) on the Gower coast which is a distinctive island at mid and low tide (*Wormeshed* 1400, *insula Wormyshede* 1478, *Wormes hedd* 1562, *Wormesheade Poynt, Wormeshead, a little iland* 1578). On the basis of the documentary evidence this seems to be OE *wyrm* 'snake' rather than ON *ormr* or *Ormr*.[16]

Two other Scandinavian traces are in the Flintshire Point of Ayr and Axton/Acstyn. Now largely sand-dunes and marsh on the Dee coast, Point of Ayr (*Point of Eyrre* 1558, *Poynt of Ayre* 1656, *Point of aire* 1689) is ON *eyrr* 'gravel, sand bank'; cf. a similar place-name in the Isle of Man. Once again, its location suggests the low headland's function as a Scandinavian navigational landmark still maintained by its modern lighthouse (*Point of Ayr lighthouse* 1834). Axton/Acstyn (*Asketone* 1086,

[15] OED s.v. *skerry*[2] has 'Orkney dialect from ON sker' but first dated 1616, and 'with reference to Scotland, esp. those parts of it under Scandinavian influence'; the first record of it in 'general use' is 1853.

[16] One Welsh form was Ynysweryn with *gweryn* 'snake', a word which is probably cognate with *wyrm*. A more recent Welsh name for Worm's Head is Penrhyn Gŵyr, 'Gower promontory'. See G. O. Pierce, *Place-Names in Glamorgan* (Cardiff: Merton Priory, 2002), pp. 219–21.

Axton 1242, *Axtyn* 1569, *Axton*, *Acstson*, *Actsyn c.* 1700) is also a coastal name a few miles from Point of Ayr but in this instance ON *askr* with OE *tūn* 'ash farm' suggests more than a landmark, perhaps toponymic evidence of a minor Scandinavian settlement.

The late date for the appearance of some of these Scandinavian/English names can be accounted for by postulating their regular use by seafarers, and their gradual drift from general maritime parlance to acceptance in documentation as local and national names.

In south Wales, Scandinavian/English settlement names are more numerous than on the north coast. Fishguard (Pemb) (*Fiscard* late 12th cent., *Fissigart* 1200, *Fissegard* 1210 [late 13th cent.]) provides evidence of a fisheries-based commercial enterprise with ON *fiskr* 'fish' and ON *garðr* 'yard'. Milford Haven (Pemb) ((*de*) *Milverdico portu c.* 1191, *Mellferth* 1207, *Milford* 1219, *Milford Haven* 1394) is 'harbour of the fjord by the sand-bank' with ON *melr*, ON *fjǫrðr* and ME *haven*. In this instance, when the significance of *melr* and *fjǫrðr* had long disappeared the subsequent development of the name was probably influenced by the English elements *mill* and *ford*.

As far as we know, there are only three examples of ON *bý*, tellingly the three being in Cardiff (Glam) itself.[17] Womanby, a Cardiff street name, was *Hundemanby c.* 1283, from ON *hundemaðr* 'houndsman', Lamby, preserved in another street name, was *Langby c.* 1401, from ON *langr* 'long', and Homri, a farm name, was *Horneby* 1382–83, from either the ON personal name **Horny* or ON *horn* 'horn-shaped piece of land'. Their late appearance does not help to identify or date a specific Viking settlement near or at Cardiff, but on the other hand we must acknowledge the existence of the cluster of *bý*-names.

There are several *-ey* names off the Pembrokeshire coast. Ramsey (*Ramesey* 1293, *Ramsey* (*Iland*) 1385) may contain the Scandinavian personal name *Hrafn*. The preference for a personal name is influenced by the pattern of personal name + *-ey* seen in Anglesey and Bardsey, but ON *hramsa* 'garlic' can be supported by the existence of wild garlic on the island and by its headland called Trwyn Garlic (Welsh *trwyn* 'point'). The small exposed island of Caldey (*Caldea* 1100–35, *Caldei c.* 1191, *Kaldey, Caldey* 1291, *the Ieland of Cauldey* 1566) is 'cold island' with ON *kald.* Skomer (*Skalmey*(*e*) 1324, *Scalmey* 1387, *Skalemay* 1592, *Scomer* 1761, *Skomar I* 1777) despite its modern spelling and

[17] Pierce, 'Some aspects', p. 173.

pronunciation, is 'cleft island' with ON *skálm* and *-ey*, the form Skomer probably the result of loss of *-l-* before *-m-*, subsequent rounding of *-a-* > *-o-* and the reduction of the final unstressed syllable to a neutral vowel. Close by is Skokholm (*Scogholm* 1219–31, *Stokholm* 1275, *Scokholm* 1324, *Stokeholme* 1376, *Stokeholme alias Scolcam* 1592, *Scockholme* 1599, *Scokum* 1761) 'island of the sound' with ON *stokkr* and ON *holmr.* The original 'Stok-holm' became 'Skok-holm' by assimilation and by analogy with the adjacent Skomer, with the *stokkr* 'sound' separating them (now Broad Sound). Gateholm (*Gateholme* 1480, *Insula de Getholme* 1482, *Gatholme*, *Gateholme Insul'* 1578) is 'goat island' with ON *geit* and ON *holmr* the earlier development of which was possibly influenced by the OE cognate *gāt* 'goat' and later by English *gate* referring to the very narrow channel between the island and Gateholm Stack on the mainland. In Wales generally Swnt (English 'sound') refers to a 'sound, strait'.

Stack 'tall column of rock' itself appears twice in north Wales, as North Stack and South Stack, on Anglesey's precipitous cliffs near Holyhead, but the appearance is late (*Nth. Stack* 1777, *The north Stack* 1818, *South Stack* 1805, *The south Stack (The light house)* 1818). The late appearance, and the fact that *stack* is not recorded elsewhere in English on the north Wales coast (not that there are many similar cliff locations), points not to ON *stakkr* but to a late generic term in English for a coastal feature given by seafarers. In Pembrokeshire, *stack* is a common name for cliff rocks and insular rocks such as several called Stack Rock (*Ye stack rock* 1578, *the Stacke* 1594) and Stackpole (*Stakepol* 1230) and Stackpool (Mill) (*Stackpooles-Mylle* 1594). Its prevalence is confirmed by the cymricized *stac* with diminutive *stacen* (as in Stacen y Brenin).

A number of Pembrokeshire's prominent headlands are English, not necessarily the direct result of maritime usage but simply influenced by English settlement. Angle is '(land in an) angle' with ME *angle*, referring to the safe haven in what is now Angle Bay on the south shore of the Milford Haven estuary; the adjacent extensive peninsula is now also known by the name Angle ((*de*) *Angulo* 1291, *le Angle* 1272–1307, with *le Nangle* 1325, *nangel c.* 1566 deriving from ME *atten angle* 'at the Angle'). Hook 'hooked spit of land' is located on a promontory within the Western Cleddau river (*West Hooke* 1601, *easthooke* 1612). Wooltack Point (*Wiltock* 1610, *Wilthooke alias Wildhook* 1630, *Wooltack* 1729) is 'wild hook', one of the most exposed westerly headlands in Pembrokeshire. Strumble Head is slightly more obscure but may well be 'storm bill' with English *strom*, an obsolete and rare variant of *storm*, and

English *bill* 'narrow promontory'. Local usage is simply Strumble, reinforcing the probability that it was originally 'Strom Bill' with Head being a later addition (*Strumble heade* 1578). The Dale peninsula in the Milford Haven estuary takes its name from the small valley between Dale village and Westdale Bay. Early references to this valley are (*de*) *Valle* 1207, *Val* 1290 probably given by Norman French settlers and reinforced in Latin documents, but the existence of Dale (*Dale* 1293 [16th cent.], *Ladale* 1307, *le Dale* 1423, *the Dale* 1539) raises the possibility that *Dale* was the original local name, possibly ON *dalr* 'dale'. There is a narrow headland a mile east called Dale Point, formerly *the Dale Poynte alias the Dale-word or castle-word, Dale worde* 1595, which seems to have ME *worde* 'point' (a variant of OE *ord*), an element found several times in Pembrokeshire such as Small Word Point on Caldey island and Mowingword by Stackpole Head; remains of a fort were recorded here in 1595. Newgale/Niwgwl ((*sabulum de*) *Nivegal* 1197, *Neugyll* 1291, *Newgall* 1568, *Newgull* 1590, *Newgol Haven* 1602, *Newgal Sands* 1824) is obscure but possibly 'new lane' with OE *nīwe* 'new' and ON *geil* 'ravine, narrow lane', a reference to steep hills on either side providing access to the wide sandy bay. Forms have been heavily influenced by English *gale*. Attempts have been made to point to toponymic and linguistic similarities with Neigwl (Caern).

Wick 'bay' appears several times as the common dialectal name for a bay, possibly from ME *wick* 'bay', but equally possibly directly from its etymon ON *vík* 'bay'. Examples are Musselwick (Pemb) (*Mussellvick* 13th cent.) with OE *muscle* 'mussel', and Gelliswick (Pemb) (*Gelliswyck* 1539) with ON personal name *Gelli*.

Several names in ME *brode* 'broad' indicate favourable navigation around the Pembrokeshire coast such as Broadhaven (*Brode Hauen* 1578, *Broade haven* 1602) and Broad Sound (*Broad sound* 1748) between Skokholm and Skomer islands. The attraction of what is now Whitesands Bay was recorded in Welsh as Porth Mawr and with the Latin gloss *Porthmawr* [...] *id est Portu magno* 1194, *Porthmaur* 1200, *Whitesand Bay* 1578.

In Flintshire, there are a few estuarine names relating to the river Dee. Saltney (*Salteney c.* 1230, *Saltney* 1379) is 'salty marshland' with OE *saltan* and OE *ēg*, dry land within tidal marshland (*Salteney Marshe* 1249, *Mariscus de Salteneya* 1250). The Dee was formerly tidal up to Chester (under two miles up-river from Saltney) until the gradual silting resulted in the river changing its course, leaving a *great pasture called Salteney* 1639 and *Saltney moore* 1652. Canalization of the Dee in 1737 placed the village of Saltney on the banks of the Dee. The land and village called Sealand (*Sealand* 1726) was also the direct result of reclamation of the former tidal basin, a name which appeared before completion of the actual canalization.

Neyland (Pemb) is also 'at the low-lying marsh' with ME *atten* and OE *ēg-land*. Although the recorded forms (*Neyland* 1508, *Nailand* 1596, *Nayland* 1773) are very late for us to postulate an OE derivation, the location on low-lying land close to the estuary of Milford Haven points to a much older name than the attestation dates suggest, an argument supported by the ME *atten*. Slebech (Pemb) (*Slebyche c.* 1170 [*c.* 1600], *Slebech* 1270, with the occasional cymricization Slebets (*Slebets* 15th cent.) is a 'muddy stream' (OE **slǣpe* and *bece*) in an angle of the Eastern Cleddau river. The Mumbles (Glam) (with the Welsh adaptation Y Mwmbwls) are two small islands and adjoining rocks off Mumbles Head (*Mumbles poynt* 1578), a name which continues to perplex but could be 'the mumbling rocks' with ME *momele* 'mumble' (*Mummess* 1536–39, *Mommulls* 1549, *Mombles* 1580, *y Mwmlws* 1609, *Mumbles* 1650).

Tusker Rock (Glam) 'projecting reef' is a prominent isolated rock with two Old Norse elements, ON *skot* and ON *sker*: *groundes called Skuttskeir* 1596–1600, *Skuscar I.* 1745, *Skuskar* 1777, *Tusker Rock* 1813–14, with the latter form influenced by *tusk* or by *tusker* 'elephant, wild boar'. Burry Holms (Glam), a small island and rocks at the west end of Gower, was originally *Holms* (*Holmes* 1398, *Le Holm, insula Holmys* 1478, *the Holmes* 1583, *Holmes Isle* 1813, *Burry Holmes* 1832). Burry is a late qualifier taken from the Burry River (*Borry* 1318, *Burry* 1323, *Byrri* 14th cent.), a name transferred to the whole of the Loughor estuary (*the Creeke of Burrey* 1562), probably OE *burh* 'fort' in its dative form *byrig*, referring to a small fort at North Hill Tor.

Pill from English *pill* (OE *pyll*) 'tidal stream or creek' appears several times, a word associated with the Bristol Channel and the Severn estuary for a tidal creek, a pool in a creek or stream or in the confluence of a stream with a larger river. Its Welsh adaptation *pil* occurs along the coast of Glamorganshire and Monmouthshire for small streams flowing through marine marshland, but there appears to be a regional variant with a long vowel to give Welsh *pîl*. In turn *pîl* seems to have produced the diphthongized Pyle (twice in Glam) (*The Pile* 1536, *y pil c.* 1566, *pîl* 1803), although both of these are now some distance inland which has raised questions as to whether they are in fact *pîl* names.

Fortifications of various types feature in Wales's English names, not surprising given the early Mercian occupation of some parts of Wales. Flintshire, on one of the major Mercian routes, is particularly prominent in that respect. Basingwerk is 'Basa's fortification' with the OE personal name *Basa*, and *-ing* 'associated with' and OE *weorc* 'fortification, building structure'. It has been linked to the earthwork of Wat's Dyke but is more likely to be a fort associated with *Basa* (*Basinwerch* 1148, *Basinwerk* 1188, *Basingwerk* 1279–80). It was later translated as Dinas Basing (*Dinas Bassin c.* 1350) with Welsh *dinas* 'fortress, stronghold'.

It has recently been argued that Gwesbyr (Flints), whose early forms (*Waestbyrig* 1053, *Wesberie* 1086, *Westbury*, *Gwespur* 1332, *Gwesbyr*, *Gwespyr (Westbury) c.* 1700) suggest 'west fort', should be identified with the *Weardbyrig* 'lookout fort' mentioned in the Anglo-Saxon Chronicle (under the year 915) and on coins of Athelstan (927–39).[18] It is suggested that the first element, OE *weard* 'ward, watch', was replaced with OE *west* 'west' and the resulting compound cymricized. The fort was probably a strategic Mercian lookout for the Dee estuary to the north and the Gwynedd-Powys kingdom to the west and south. The development of a fortified Rhuddlan (Flints) six miles south west on the river Clwyd in 921 may have reduced the importance of the lookout fort which soon came to be interpreted as the 'west fort', the westernmost fort in Mercia, perceived as offering garrisoned protection against the Welsh who had by then occupied Rhuddlan. It was this Welsh presence which contributed to the later cymricization of *Westbury* to Gwesbyr (for a discussion of the phonology see below). Several garrisoned settlements had a 'lookout hill' (OE *tōt-hyll*) which has survived as Welsh Twtil (or the like) in Rhuddlan, Caernarfon, Conwy, Wrexham and Harlech. It is perhaps an open question as to whether Rhyl (Flints) fits in here. Rhyl (*Hulle* 1292, *Hul* 1296, *Ryhyll* 1301, *the hill, Yrhill* 1578, *Rhyll* 1660, *Rhil* 1706, *Rhyl* 1840) is the Welsh definite article *yr* and OE *hyll*. The *hyll* was a specific feature, probably military, in an otherwise flat landscape, called 'The Hill' in English and 'Yr Hill' in Welsh (because of its English associations). The exact site, indeed any feature which could be deemed a hill, has long been eroded. It is this later lack of a visible elevation which probably explains why the name did not settle down as 'Rhill' and lent itself easily to the cymricized Rhyl and Y Rhyl.

[18] R. Coates, 'Æthelflæd's fortification of Weardburh', *Notes & Queries* 243 (1998), 9–12. For an alternative view, see J. Carroll, 'Coins and the Chronicle: mint-signatures, history, and language', in A. Jorgenson (ed.), *Reading the Anglo-Saxon Chronicle: Language, Literature, History* (Turnhout: Brepols, 2010), pp. 243–73 (pp. 251–54).

The Welsh definite article also appears in Flint/Y Fflint (Flints) itself. The castle built at Flint (between 1277 and 1284) is ME *flint* 'hard rock', the stony platform jutting into the river Dee. That it was a specific feature explains the definite article in French (*le Flynt* 1277, *le Fflynt* 1300), in Welsh (*y flynt* 14th cent.) and in English (*the Flynte* 1527) with attempts at rendering it with a French translation (*Le Cayllou* 1278). Hawarden (Flints) (*Haordine* 1086, *Hauardina* 1093, *Hawurdin* 1250, *Hawarden* 1439, *Harden otherwise Howarden* 1839) is a 'high enclosure' above the Dee estuary with OE *hēah* and OE *worðign* (the phonology of which is discussed below). In Flintshire's Maelor district, Worthenbury is 'manor-house within an enclosure', with OE *worðign* 'enclosure' and OE *burh*, dative *byrig*, which commonly refers to a fortified place but here the most appropriate meaning is 'manor-house or estate' surrounded by a fence or palisade. Caergwrle (Denb) (*?Kaeirguill* 1277–78, *Caergorlei* 1327–28, *Caergurley* 1601–02, *Caer Gwrle c.* 1700) is a hybrid, meaning 'fort at Corley'. We can postulate a Mercian settlement called 'Corley' on the banks of the river Alun, with OE *corn* or *cron* 'crane' and OE *lēah* 'river meadow'. Edward I built a castle here *c.* 1278, which Welsh speakers referred to as a *caer* 'fort'; 'Caer Gorley' then eventually became *Caergwrle.* An alias for Caergwrle was *Queen's Hope* 1398, *Quene hope als Kaer gorley* 1580, a reference to the nearby Mercian settlement of Hope/Yr Hôb (*Hope* 1086, *Hopp* 1283–84). This is OE *hop* in the sense 'enclosed land in a marsh' (rather than 'small, remote valley' which is the prevailing sense in the Shropshire *hop*-names). Edward I presented the castle and parish to his wife Eleanor in 1282, hence Queen's Hope.

One interesting group of English names comprises those which reflect the introduction of new agrarian practice and land management, or new English terms for existing rural terminology. The obvious example is ME *frith* (OE *fyrhðe*) 'land overgrown with brushwood, scrubland on the edge of forest' seen in various place-name combinations of Frith in Lancashire, Derbyshire, Middlesex and Lincolnshire.[19] The word *frith* appeared in north Wales as the cymricized *ffrith* before the fourteenth century through association with hunting, possibly as a semi-legal description of the status of the *ffrith.* Certainly, 'waste land' is abundantly apparent in the early Welsh documentation, as well as the expression 'forest or frith'. But land clearance was moving apace and meanings vary between *pasture called*

[19] M. Gelling and A. Cole, *The Landscape of Place-Names* (Stamford: Shaun Tyas, 2000), pp. 224–26.

the common fryth (1563), *plowed land lately taken out of a mountain* (1688), and *enclosed rough mountain pasture* (1918). *Geiriadur Prifysgol Cymru* lists the following meanings s.v. *ffrith*: 'moorland; frith, rough mountain pasture, sheep walk; woodland, forest, park'.[20] The pronunciation and spelling *ffrith* is found in north-east Wales, but as it spread across north Wales it was cymricized further as the final *-th* [θ] of *ffrith* became the voiced [ð] of *ffridd* found in north-west Wales.[21] Curiously, *ffridd/ffrith* seems to be very scarce indeed outside north Wales. Examples are Ffrith (Flints) (*Ffrîdh c.* 1700, *Ffrith* 1871), Bwlch-y-ffridd (Mont) (*Bwlchyffridd* 1800) and in very many minor names.[22]

The introduction of English terms for existing Welsh agricultural words explains the emergence of *acr*. Historically, the Welsh measure *erw* varied in size in different parts of Wales but was considered to be approximate to a bovate (though its modern use has been as the equivalent of *acre*). The English measure is recorded in Wales from the fourteenth century as English *acre* and Welsh *acr*, *acer* or *acar*, plurals *aceri*, *acrau*. It emerges twice in north-east Wales place-names with the plural *acrau* in its dialectal form *acre*: Acre-fair (Denb) (*Yr Acrefair* 1795) 'Mary's acres', and Talacre (Flints) (*Tallacre* 1381–82, *Taleacrey* 1569, *Talacre* 1840) 'end of the acres', applied to the extensive pasture land of the Point of Ayr. Hedges could be *gwrych* or *perth* but in Montgomeryshire and south Wales the English term *setting* 'planting' (as in 'quickset' hedge) was adopted for enclosure purposes, appearing (from the fifteenth to sixteenth centuries) in the cymricized form *sietin* in many minor names. The English *outrake* (OE *ūt* 'out' and *hraca* 'rough path') means 'path from the enclosed cultivated pasture to common land or hill pasture'[23] and also appears in many minor names in Montgomeryshire from the sixteenth century as *wtra* 'country lane, track, path, (narrow) road'. The cymricization was probably via the Middle English pronunciation of *outrake* > *wtrag* > *wtra*, with *wtrag* surviving in the

[20] *Geiriadur Prifysgol Cymru*: *A Dictionary of the Welsh Language* (Cardiff: University of Wales, 1950–2002). A review of the distribution and range of meanings of *ffrith* and *ffridd* in Wales can be seen in H. W. Owen, 'Ffridd', *Y Naturiaethwr* 2:3 (June 1998), 5–9.

[21] For a similar unvoiced/voiced distinction between forms, compare *stryt* 'street' in the north east and *stryd* in the rest of Wales.

[22] There is an extensive list in M. Richards, '*Ffridd*/*ffrith* as a Welsh place-name', *Studia Celtica* 2 (1967), 29–90.

[23] H. D. G. Foxall, *Shropshire Field-Names* (Shrewsbury: Shropshire Archaeological Society, 1980), p. 35.

plural *wtregydd* (with *i*-affection of *-a-* to *-e-* before *-y-*). The village green appears at least four times as *Y Grîn*, in Cricieth (Caern), Beaumaris (Angl), Denbigh (Denb) and Llanbryn-mair (Mont). *Lloc* 'pen, fold' is the cymricized version of ME *loc* 'enclosure, fold', found in Lloc (Flints) (*Llok* 1479, *Y Llocke* 1517).[24] *Parsel* 'part, portion, piece' (from ME *parcel*) appears in several minor names, and in southern and parts of mid Wales it is also used of a division of a large parish. *Clos* is 'close, enclosed space' (from ME *clos*(*e*)); it also has the meaning 'farmyard' in south Wales.

One of the more interesting appearances of OE *feld* 'open country' is Englefield (Flints) (*Englefeld* 1086, *Anglefeld* 1247, *Englefield* 1299, *Ingelfeld* 1322), a territorial descriptor that did not survive the Middle Ages (at least there are no records beyond 1431).[25] It describes, broadly, the north-west part of Flintshire, where the presence of the English was more unusual than in the more heavily colonized south east. The Welsh name was Tegeingl (*Tegeigyl* 1157, *Tegeingyl* 1160, *Tegeingl* 1318), believed to be derived from the tribal name *Deceangli*, evidenced in inscriptions on lead pigs dated AD 74 at Chester.[26] Its similarity to Englefield has prompted the interpretation of Tegeingl as *teg* 'fair, pleasant' and *Eingl* 'English'. It may well be that the name Englefield was modelled on Tegeingl.

Much later in Flintshire history *feld* appears again in Gwernaffield (*Gwernaffeld* 1477, *Gwernaffild* 1486, *Gwernaffield* 1598). In Welsh, the terms which generally correspond to English *field* are *maes* 'open land' and *cae* 'enclosed field'. However, in Gwernaffield (with medial stress) we have what appears to be a very early use of *field* 'cultivated arable land' as if it were a Welsh element **ffild*. The name Gwernaffield means 'alder-grove of the field' with *gwern* and the definite article *y*. There are several *gwern* place-names in the area (such as Gwernymynydd 'alder-grove of the mountain'). The tentative conclusion is that it is, once again, an English term introduced through custom and practice perhaps by one of the adjoining Rhual or Gwysaney estates, otherwise we would have expected 'Gwern-y-cae'. This 'field', it seems, was a significant feature

[24] Although *Geiriadur Prifysgol Cymru* s.v. *lloc* has it recorded only from the seventeenth century and in south and west Wales.

[25] The name appears formally identical with Englefield (Berkshire).

[26] A. L. F. Rivet and C. Smith, *The Place-Names of Roman Britain* (London: Batsford, 1979), p. 331.

of the agricultural landscape introduced by the English-run estate and therefore known locally (in English) as 'the Field' and (in Welsh) as 'y Ffîld'. 'Gwern-y-ffîld' (with final stress) eventually became Gwernaffield with stress-shift to the penultimate syllable, the stressed medial syllable being represented by *-a-*.

Other minor names found frequently throughout Wales which are adaptations of English land management terms and sometimes associated with nearby estates are *parrog* 'stretch of flat land by the sea-shore' (English *parrock* 'small enclosure'), *parwg* 'field' (English *parrock*), *parc* 'field, enclosed land' plural *parciau* or *perci* (English *park*), *padog* (English *paddock*), *clwt* 'patch of land' (English *clout*), *lôn* (English *lane*), *sling* 'long narrow piece of land, roadside verge' (English *sling*), *comin(s)* (English *common(s)*), *gât* or *giât* (English *gate*) and *iet* (ME *yatt* 'gate, pass'), *helm* 'open shed, shed in the fields' (dialectal English *helm*), *fforest*, *cocsut* or *cocsiwt* (English *cockshoot*), *crofft*, *grofft*, *rofft* plural *crofftydd*.

The suffix *-ws* appears several times in specific terminology arising from estate management such as Gatws, Getws (English *gatehouse*) and Storws (English *storehouse*) both found in many minor names, and reflecting the OE and ME pronunciation of *hūs*. The most intriguing *hūs* compound has nothing to do with estate management. Betws, 'house of prayer, chapel of ease', is very common such as Y Betws (Monm) (*Bettus* 1476), Betws Garmon (Caern) (*Betous Carmon* 1303–04, with the personal name *Garmon*) and Betws-y-coed (Caern) (*Betus* 1254). It is contentious only because Welsh *betws* is derived from OE *bēd-hūs* 'bead house', a term which has not survived in England as a major settlement name as such, but which did occur in several minor names.[27] The general view is that the English designation was the term used by ecclesiastical authorities to describe a small isolated cell which reflected the Celtic rather than the Anglo-Norman church. The more conventional representatives of the church are represented by Spittal (Pemb) ((*de*) *Ospitali* 1259, *Spital* 1319, *Spyttel* 1393, *Spyttel otherwise manerium de Hospitali* 1541), and Cheriton (Glam) (*Cheriton* 1387) and (Carew)

[27] The *-ws* suffix appears to have become a common rendering of English *-house*, because it occurs in words with no known Old or Middle English origin such as *wyrcws* (English *workhouse*), *warws* (English *warehouse*) and *rheinws*, *rhinws* 'lock-up'(English *arraign house*). For examples of *bēd-hūs* in England, see D. Parsons and T. Styles, with C. Hough *The Vocabulary of English Place-Names* I *(Á to Box)* (Nottingham: Centre for English Name-Studies, 1997), p. 70

Cheriton (Pemb) (*Churcheton* 1346), both of which combine OE *cirice* and OE *tūn*.

Landshipping (Pemb) (*Langshipping* 1554, *Longshippinge* 1588, *Longeshippen* 1614) is 'long cow-shed' (OE *lang*, *scipen*). Eyton (Denb) (*Eytune* 1286, *Eyton* 1315) is a 'farm overlooking a flood plain' with OE *ēg* 'island, well-watered land' and *tūn*, a reference to its location at a wide loop of the river Dee. Oxwich (Glam) (*Oxen wiche* 1176–98, *Oxewyche* 1306) is 'ox farm' with forms in *Oxen*- and *Ox*- coexisting until the seventeenth century. Saundersfoot (Pemb) (*Saunders foot* 1607) is 'hill of Saunders', still locally stressed on the final syllable. Ewloe (Flints) (*Ewlawe* 1281) is 'hill at the source of a stream' with OE *ǣwell* and OE *hlāw*. Goldcliff (Monm) (*Goldclyviœ* 1072–1104, *Goldclif* 1245–53) 'gold cliff' with OE *gold* and OE *clif* was supposed by Gerald of Wales to refer to the colour of the rocks (*Goldclive, hoc est, rupea aurea c.* 1191) but might also describe areas where there were marigolds (OE *golde*). Holt (Denb) (*Holte* 1326, *le Holt* 1347, *the holt* 1535, *yr holt c.* 1566) 'wood', with OE *holt* with the definite article in three languages, reinforced the significance of the area probably for timber in building the castle here. Houghton (Pemb) (*Holton* 1541, *Houton* 1680, *Howton* 1683, *Houghton* 1708) was also a *holt* with a *tūn* nearby. Hay-on-Wye (Brec) ((*Castello de*) *haia taillata* 1121, *Haya c.* 1135–47, *La Haye* 1299, *Hay c.* 1570) was certainly an 'area within a fence' with OE *hæg* possibly '(part of a forest) fenced off for hunting' but more likely simply 'enclosure' or 'defensive enclosure'. In Welshpool (Mont), the original name appears to have been *Pool* (*Pole* 1190, *la Pole* 1197) to which was added *Welsh* (*Pole in Wales* 1477, *Walshepole* 1478, *Welshe Poole* 1577) to distinguish it in legal documents from places in England, notably Poole in Dorset, but Pool did survive in local usage for Welshpool (*Pool* 1774) and is found in Pool Quay (*New Quay* 1608, *the quay of Welsh Poole* 1774, *Pool Quay* 1784), the name of the head of navigation for barges on the river Severn. Porth-cawl (Glam) (*Portcall* 1632, *Porth Cawl* 1825) is 'sea-kale harbour' (*porth* 'harbour, cove', *cawl* 'sea-kale'). The anglicized pronunciation as 'Porthcall' is influenced by ME *cole* 'sea-kale'. It is worth noting that while English *port* and Welsh *porth* are phonologically and semantically close, Welsh *porth* has the additional meaning of 'landing-place, ferry, cove, small bay'. Halkyn (Flints) (*Helchene* 1086, *Alkyn* 1284, *Halkyn* 1360) is OE *halc* pl. *halcen(a)* 'cavity', with reference to extensive mining activity; the *-yn* ending was probably influenced by Prestatyn and Mostyn, etc., while the Welsh form Helygen (*Helegen* 1254, *Helygen* 1315) was influenced by *helygen* the diminutive of *helyg* 'osier'.

In-migration occasionally brought with it dialectal features. One area of Cardiff is known as Splot (*Splot* 1392), *splot* being a variant of *plot* (OE *plot*) 'small plot of land', found in the south of England.[28] Its appearance in some eight field or farm names outside Cardiff, in the Vale of Glamorgan and in Gower and Pembrokeshire such as in Penmark's Splott (*ye Splot* 13th cent.), points to a more general use of the dialectal *splot* in the area. It also became cymricized as Y Sblot with the definite article, which also featured in some of the English forms (*the Splott* 1542–43). Drope (Glam) (*Le Thrope*, *Thorpe* 1540, *y Drop c.* 1780, *Drope* 1799) is OE *throp* 'outer farmstead, hamlet'; so well established is it that it has a cymricized form Y Drôp and a consciously feminine form as Y Ddrôp.[29] In north-east Wales, Derbyshire miners came to work and live in what is now Licswm/Lixwm (Flints) and were sufficiently impressed by the location to describe it as *licksome*, a dialectal variant of *likesome* 'pleasant, agreeable'. The original description was of a 'Licksome Green' recorded as *Lixwm Green* 1733–34, *Luxum*, *Luxwm* 1801–02, *Lixwm Green* 1825, *Licswm* 1838). A few miles away, on the outskirts of industrial Buckley, there was another, similarly pleasant plot called *Lixwmgreen* 1800, *Lixwm Green* 1803–04. Red Wharf Bay/Traeth Coch (Angl) was originally *Red Warth*, *warth* being a common enough west of England word for 'shore, strand, stretch of coast' which frequently alternated with *wharf* along the Monmouthshire side of the Bristol Channel, especially if there was a commercial development there involving a wharf or quay. This was the case in Anglesey, so evidently this maritime term *warth* had extended to north Wales. Hundleton (Pemb) (*Hundenton* 1475, *Hondelton* 1573) where the hounds were kept, appears to be *hunden*(*e*) a dialectal genitive plural variant of ME *hund* associated with the south-west of England.

Three names appear to be local in south-west Wales. Cidell, Cidel, Gidel, Gudel (Pemb and Carm) is 'blind alley; narrow passageway leading down to a stream; uncultivated or awkward corner of a field' linked in some way to English *kiddle* 'dam, weir'. The Drang (Pemb) is a 'narrow passage, lane; long narrow field, field to which a narrow lane

[28] For a further discussion of this name, see Pierce, *Place-Names in Glamorgan*, pp. 179–80.

[29] Pierce, 'Some aspects', p. 190, and Pierce, *The Place-Names of Dinas Powys Hundred* (Cardiff: University of Wales, 1968), pp. 253–56.

leads' (English dialectal *drong*, *drang* 'narrow lane or passage'). Slade (Pemb and Glam) is 'valley, hollow depression in the side of a hill' (OE *slæd* 'valley').

Some names are transferred from outside Wales. Battle (Brec) ((*de*) *Bello* 1222–24, *Battle* 1527, *y battel c.* 1566) was named after Battle Abbey in Sussex which held the advowson of the church. Montgomery (Mont) (*Muntgumeri*, *Montgomeri* 1086, *Monte Gomeri* 1166) was first applied to the motte-and-bailey castle (at Hen Domen near the river Severn) and named after Sainte-Foy-de-Montgommery or Saint-Germain-de-Montgommery in Normandy, and then transferred to the new castle built in 1223–24. Morville (Pemb) (*Morvin* 1291, *Moruile* 1397, *Morvill* 1488) was named after one of several places called Morville in France and Normandy; it was cymricized as Morfil (*y morfil c.* 1566), heavily influenced by Welsh *morfil* 'whale'.

In modern times, New Brighton (Flints) (*New Brighton* 1850) was named after New Brighton (Cheshire), indicating incoming workers, as was also the case of the *New Brighton* which was part of Bagillt (Flints). Garden Village appears on the outskirts of several towns such as Gorseinon (Glam), Wrexham (Denb), Treharris (Glam) and Machynlleth (Mont) and there was a Garden City near Queensferry (Flints), all in the wake of the Garden City Movement of 1901, but particularly after the Second World War. Chatham (Caern) was the ironic name given to a small boatyard near Caernarfon, whose seafarers knew of the naval dockyards in Kent. Common enough field and minor names such as Greenland, Sebastopol, Bunkers Hill, Talavera, Vinegar Hill, Table Mountain and Abyssinia indicate an awareness of world affairs, while Jericho, Babylon and Sodom are biblical names which came directly into community use from biblical study and memorable preaching in the Welsh language (and strictly speaking have no real place in this chapter).

Naturally, personal names of settlers feature in place-names. They are plentiful in Pembrokeshire for example, evidence of early colonization (English, Scandinavian, Flemish and French) as the discussion of phonology below shows, many of them in OE *tūn* or ON *tún* compounds such as Bosherston (*Bosher*), Canaston (*Canan*), Clarbeston (*Clarenbald*), Gumfreston (*Gunfrid*), Haroldston (*Haraldr*), Herbrandston (*Herbrand*), Hodgeston (*Hodge*), Lambston (*Lambert*), Moylgrove (*Matilda*), Reynalton (*Reynold*), Rudbaxton (*Rudepac*), Waterston (*Walter*), Uzmaston (*Osmund*), Yerbeston (?*Gerbard*). Freystrop (*Freistr*, OE *throp* 'hamlet') may offer another example of personal name + habitative generic element in a Pembrokeshire place-name, although it has recently been argued that the personal name was that of a pagan divinity, compounded with ON *þorp*.[30] Topographical generics are found in Gelliswick (*Gelli*, ME *wick* or ON *vík* 'bay'), Lydstep (*Hlūd*, ON *hóp* 'inlet') and Wolfsdale (*Wulf*, OE *dæl* 'valley').

In the industrial period, personal names were commonly combined with the *-ton* and *-town* suffix becoming a useful habitative marker for industrial complexes or associated hamlets for workers built by entrepreneurial developers such as in Morriston/Treforys (Glam), Butetown (Glam), Johnstown (Denb), Dukestown (Monm), Griffithstown (Monm), Tylorstown (Glam), Hopkinstown/Trehopcyn (Glam). Other industrial related personal compounds are Wattsville (Monm), Connah's Quay (Flints), Port Talbot (Glam), Port Tennant (Glam), Cendl (Monm, from the personal name Kendall), Porthmadog and Tremadog (Caern). A considerable number of these industrialists, however, would not have responded kindly to being described as incomers, since they were already well-established gentry or wealthy developers. Seven Sisters (Glam) (*Seven Sisters* 1882) is a modern name for the colliery said to be named after the seven sisters of the son of one of the colliery owners; colloquially it was Y Sefn 'the seven', although the village then took its Welsh name from a much older name for the general area, Blaendulais (*Blayth Tulleys* 1296, *Blaen dilas* 1631) 'headwaters of (the river) Dulais'.

One interesting feature of personal name compounds is the way in which their names were transformed by local usage (the phonology of which is dealt with below). Examples are the mountain Cnicht (Caern) (*Knight*), Cichle (Angl) (*Keighley*), Maesincla (Caern) (*Hinckley*, with *maes* 'open land'),[31] Bisla (Caern) (*Bisley*), Gallt y Sil (Caern) (*Sill*). Llys Fasi (Denb) 'court of Massy' was named after the Norman family of *Mascy*, *Massy*, *Massie*, Cheshire.

Tourism plays a part in modern naming. The inhabitants of Llandrillo-yn-Rhos (Denb) (*Lantreullo* 1245, *llan drillo yn Ros* 1565–87) evidently felt that the Welsh name did not provide a sufficiently clear message about the attractions of its location and so coined Rhos-on-Sea

[30] See P. Gammeltoft, 'Freystrop: a sacral Scandinavian place-name in Wales?', in O. J. Padel and D. N. Parsons (eds), *A Commodity of Good Names* (Donington: Shaun Tyas, 2008), pp. 136–46.

[31] For a discussion of some English personal names in Caernarfon and environs see G. Carr, *Hen Enwau o Arfon, Llŷn ac Eifionydd* (Caernarfon: Gwasg y Bwthyn, 2011), passim.

(*Llandrillo yn Rhos* (*Rhos-on-Sea*) 1898). This also accounts for the nineteenth- and early-twentieth-century addition of *Bay* to places that had previously no need to promote their attractions: Cemaes (Angl) became Cemaes Bay, though it is now restored to Cemaes; Colwyn Bay (Denb) was based on the original settlement of Colwyn which is now called Old Colwyn. Mineral wells turned villages into spa towns although the designation Wells is now becoming less prominent in local usage. Examples are Builth (Wells) (Brec), Llandrindod (Wells) (Radn) and Llanwrtyd Wells (Brec). Fairbourne (Mer) was coined as a name for a new resort in 1898–99. Pen-y-Pass (Caern) is at the head of the pass from Llanberis to Snowdon. Similarly, in Penmaenpool (Mer) (*Penmaen Pool* 1838) Penmaen was the name of the prominent outcrop (*penmaen*) near which was a pool in a wide section of the river Mawddach, the Welsh name of which was Llyn y Penmaen (*Llyn y penmaen* 1796). The addition of English *pool* is ascribed to the station and the popularity of the area for tourism. By now a cymricized Penmaenpŵl is commonly used (cf. Pontypŵl, below).

Commerce accounts for Chepstow (Monm) (*Chepestowe* 1308) 'market-place' with OE *cēap* and *stōw*, reflecting the importance of the castle, the town and its markets. Connah's Quay (Flints) (*the New Quay, a very handsome pier* 1773, *Conna's Quay* 1791, *Connah's Quay* 1818) was built by James Connah to sustain commerce in the face of canalization of the Dee. Several halts or stations were located at or near railway crossings which in turn grew into hamlets and villages such as Cemaes Road (Mont) and Clarbeston Road (Pemb). Newbridge (Denb, Monm, Radn), Fourmile Bridge (Angl) and Menai Bridge (Angl) show routes being upgraded. Queensferry (Flints), now two bridges, arose from silting of the Dee and the canalization of 1737. Previous names were *Lower Ferry* (1726), *Lower King's Ferry* (1826) and *King's Ferry* (1828) in honour of George IV's accession in 1820, and finally Queensferry at the coronation of Victoria in 1837.

Other industrial names are Rasau (Monm) (*Rhas-y-mwyn* 1697, *Rhasau'r mwyn* 1778, *the Race mine works* 1810), a reference to the water-course called a 'race' in an industrial context; there are several minor names with *Ras*, *Rhas* or *Race* in Glamorganshire and Carmarthenshire. In Pont-y-pool (Monm) (*Pont y poole* 1614, *Pontipool* 1682 , *Pontypool* 1718, *Pontypwl* 1834) 'bridge at the pool', *pool* is used in a specialist sense connected with industrial works, probably the iron forges there recorded from the late sixteenth century. The use of English *pool* (as opposed to Welsh *pwll*) indicates that this was the term used by everyone regardless of mother tongue; this is reaffirmed by the cymricized Pontypŵl. In Furnace/Ffwrnes (Card) (*Furnace* 1763, *Dovey Furnace* 1803, *Pentre'r Ffwrnes* 1841, *Furnace* 1837) the river Einion powered several smelting works (of lead, silver and iron) from the seventeenth century (such as *The Silver Mills, with 5 Furnices* 1699); the actual works which gave the village its name was the blast furnace erected *c.* 1755. Forge (Mont) (*Forge* 1813–34) was the site of a small forge. Cadole (Flints) (*Catshole* 1795, *Cat hole Mine* 1840) was 'cat-hole', the name given to the hole for a chain or rope from a ship, but here a description of the narrow entrance through which workmen were let down into the mine. Local sensitivity to such a name ensured it was changed in the 1950s to Cadole. Y Grango (Denb) was originally 'crank-coal', a particularly rich seam of coal which was brought to the surface using a crank system from 1791 and was the name of the shaft, the colliery and the immediate area; the phonological development was probably *crank-coal* > *Cranko* > Y Grango, later the name of the local secondary school.

The distribution of English names

Of the 157 places with English names only, 44% are in Pembrokeshire, no surprise given its history of colonization as the 'little England beyond Wales' with waves of English, Norse, Norman and Flemish migration. After Pembrokeshire, there is a dramatic drop to three counties statistically close together, between 9% and 11%, for Monmouthshire, Flintshire and Glamorganshire. There is a further drop to around 5% in Denbighshire, Montgomeryshire and Carmarthenshire. Radnorshire has 3.8%. Then a fall to between 1% and 2% for Cardiganshire, Breconshire and Merionethshire. The tail-enders are Caernarfonshire and Anglesey with 0.6%.

Accounting for the types and distribution of the English names provides an interesting challenge. For example, why are there so few English-only names in counties we now regard as heavily anglicised, such as Radnorshire and Breconshire? The answer is that these were mainly rural counties where the major settlements had already been established by the Middle Ages when the Welsh language was far more dominant. There were far fewer early modern settlements or industrial developments in these counties than in Monmouthshire, Flintshire and Glamorgan.

Another question worth examining is why there were any English-only place-names at all in the more Welsh counties. Analysis of the place-names of those counties reveals three features. One is that they are all late names, mainly from the eighteenth and nineteenth centuries. The second is that most are tavern names, which in Wales have traditionally been English in the vast majority of cases. Some taverns were at strategic locations for travel, others were the focal points of industrial hamlets (vying with chapels), occasionally some way from the original village and built, almost as shanty towns, to house workers for the slate or coal industry to enable them to stay close to the quarry or colliery. In Carmarthenshire, for example, of the seven English settlement names, six are tavern names: Cross Hands (twice), Trap, Halfway, New Inn and Tumble. In other counties too (including more anglicized ones) we have villages called Four Crosses (several), Cross Inn (Card), Cross Keys (Monm), Valley (Angl), Stepaside (Pemb), Star (Pemb and Angl), Square and Compass (Pemb), Stop-and-Call (Pemb), Nelson (Glam) and Loggerheads (Denb). The point is that English tavern names represent a significant proportion of the few English names in more Welsh counties.

The third characteristic of such late English names in these predominantly Welsh-speaking counties is that they are related to transport and travel, commerce and improved communications, in settlement names such as Broadway (Carm twice, Pemb), Crossgates (Radn), Cross Lanes (Denb) and Clatter(-gate) (Mont). Tyrpeg from English *turnpike* appears frequently in minor names. They were all introduced in an English industrial context, perhaps with non-Welsh speaking engineers and with publicity in English newspapers. We can link these names to a number of London place-names in two counties in particular, Cardiganshire and Carmarthenshire, names such as Llundain Fach 'little London', Bow Street, Temple Bar, Chancery and Piccadilly, some of them ironic names for small commercial or financial establishments, others traditionally linked to drover routes.

Pembrokeshire has a high proportion of personal name compounds. Of the 69 non-Welsh place-names in that county, 42% contain personal names (mostly Continental), almost all with *tūn*, and most being twelfth- to fourteenth-century: Bosherston, Uzmaston, Gumfreston, Herbrandston, Robeston and so on.[32] Once again, an analysis of place-name distribution

[32] Pierce, 'Some aspects', pp. 178–79, has pointed out that *-ton* (rather than *tūn*) had become an 'active name-forming element for a considerable period after the eleventh century'. Indeed of the 340 *-ton* names counted by him (in settlement and minor names) the majority occur first in the late thirteenth and fourteenth centuries. No *-ton* names are found in the north west and the west. The meaning is probably 'estate, manor'.

in Wales serves to provide additional evidence of personal names + *tūn* as convenient settlement descriptors. What is remarkable is the 42% cited for Pembrokeshire matches the 41% of the *tūn*-names recorded in the Domesday Book entry for Flintshire,[33] two counties part of whose settlement history is illustrated by the significant number of *tūn*-clusters.

This in turn reminds us of Margaret Gelling's comment about 'the extraordinary degree of repetition of some recurrent *tūn* compounds in Shropshire'.[34] She concluded that *tūn*-compounds were:

> originally convenient labels used by Mercian administrators when referring to the component parts of large estates. These names could have originated in the speech of Mercian administrators. Such appellatives might gradually have come to be perceived as place-names and ousted earlier British names of the places.

B. G. Charles called the Pembrokeshire pattern 'a Mercian plantation'.[35] Significantly there are no *hām*-names in Pembrokeshire or Flintshire, nor, for that matter, in the rest of Wales. As John Dodgson put it, *hām* was used of a place 'historically distinguished as an important centre of settlement',[36] and which marked 'a recognition of social permanence in territorial possession by the English community'.[37] It would seem that *hām* had fallen into disuse before Flintshire and certainly Pembrokeshire were colonized. The few examples of place-names ending in *-ham* in Denbighshire (such as Wrexham and Bersham) turn out to be the topographical element *hamm* 'enclosure, water-meadow'.

Dual naming

I now turn to the second category of English names, the dual category, where the location has an English name alongside a Welsh name. In this

[33] H. W. Owen, 'Old English place-name elements in Domesday Flintshire', in A. Rumble and A. D. Mills (eds), *Names, Places and People: An Onomastic Miscellany in Memory of John McNeal Dodgson* (Stamford: Paul Watkins, 1997), pp. 269–78.

[34] M. Gelling, *The Place-Names of Shropshire*, Part 1 (Nottingham: English Place-Name Society, 1990) [EPNS Sa **1**], p. xiv.

[35] Charles, *Non-Celtic Place-Names*, pp. xxii–iv.

[36] J. McN. Dodgson, 'Place-names from *hām*, distinguished from *hamm* names, in relation to the settlement of Kent, Surrey and Sussex', *Anglo-Saxon England* 2 (1973), 1–50 (p. 7). Compare also D. Kenyon, 'The antiquity of *hām* place-names in Lancashire and Cheshire', *Nomina* 10 (1986), 11–27.

[37] J. McN. Dodgson, 'The English arrival in Cheshire', *Transactions of the Historic Society of Lancashire and Cheshire* 119 (1968 for 1967), 1–37 (p. 15).

category, there are 110 names in all, representing some 5.3% of the place-names in DPNW.

In one sub-set of this category the Welsh and English names are entirely independent of each other, probably having evolved at different periods or referring to slightly different features of the same landscape but over time coming to refer to the one place. Occasionally we cannot be sure whether the Welsh or the English name came first. In the case of Cowbridge/Y Bont-faen (Glam) we know that *Covbruge c.* 1262 preceded *Bontvaen c.* 1500 (with *pont* 'bridge' and *maen* 'stone'). Swansea (Glam) (*Swensi c.* 1140, *Sweynesse* 1153–84 [14th cent.], *Sweyneseye* 1277, *Swannesey* 1505) referred to the island (ON *ey*) associated with *Sveinn*, while its Welsh name Abertawe (*Abertawe c.* 1191, *Abertawi* 1192 (*c.* 1286)) refers to the estuary (*aber*) of the river Tawe. In Pembrokeshire, several originally Old Norse names fall into this group. Grassholm (*insula Grasolm* 15th cent., *Gresse Holme* 1536–39, *Grasholme* 1699), the island seven miles off the coast, is Scandinavian but the Welsh name Gwales (*Gwalas*, *Gwales* 12th cent.) means 'refuge', a name venerated in Welsh literary legend. Milford Haven ((*de*) *Melverdico portu c.* 1191, *Milford* 1219, *Milford Haven* 1394) is a 'fjord, or inlet, by a sandbank' (ON *melr*, ON *fjǫrðr*) whereas Aberdaugleddau (*Aber-Deu-gledyf* late 13th cent., *Aber Dau Gleddau* 15th cent.) is the 'estuary of the two rivers called Cleddau'. Fishguard (*Fiscard* late 12th cent., *Fissegard* 1200) is 'fish enclosure' (ON *fiskr*, *garðr*) while Abergwaun (*Aber gweun* 1210 [late 13th cent.]) is 'estuary of the Gwaun (river)'. Ramsey (*Ramesey* 1293) is an island probably associated with the Scandinavian *Hrafn*, while Ynys Dewi (*Ynys Dewi* 1825) is a recent coinage associating the island with St David's/Tyddewi. In the north, Snowdon (Caern) (*Snawdune* 1095, *Snaudon* 1284, *Snowdon* 1341) is the 'snow-covered hill' (OE *snāw*, OE *dūn*) while Yr Wyddfa (*Weddua vaur* 1284, *wedua vaur* 13th cent. [14th cent.]) means 'the prominent place' (with *yr* 'the' and *gwyddfa* 'high, eminent place' and the occasional *mawr*, feminine *fawr*, 'great, big'). Knighton (Radn) (*Chenistetone* 1086, *Cnicheton* 1193, *Knighton* 1536–39) is the '*tūn* of the youths or retainers' (OE *cniht*), while Trefyclawdd, or Trefyclo (*Trebuclo* 1536–39, *Treficlaudh* 1586) is 'settlement at the dyke' (Offa's Dyke/Clawdd Offa).

In the dual category, another sub-set is when both languages refer to the same topographical feature but in slightly different ways. Then the correlation is closer. Interestingly a significant number are ecclesiastical names. Holyhead/Caergybi (Angl) (*Haliheved* 1315, *Le Holyhede* 1394, *the holihed* 1565, *Karkeby* 1225, *Caerkeby* 1352, *kaer gybi c.* 1566,

Holihead called Caergyby 1684) is the 'holy headland' on Holy Island/Ynys Cybi with its monastic settlement dedicated to the sixth-century Cybi located within the Roman fort (*caer*). Holywell/Treffynnon (Flints) (*Haliwel* 1093, *Holywell* 1465, *Treffynnon* 1329) is still the site of a curative well (*ffynnon*) and centre of pilgrimage dedicated to Gwenfrewi/Winifred. St Asaph/Llanelwy (Denb) (*Lanelvensis Ecclesiae* 1143, *Asavensi ecclesia* 1284, *Ecclesia Cathedralis de Sancto Asaph* c. 1191, *Lanhelewey* 1345, *Lanelwy* 1365, *Llan Elwy alias S. Asaphe* 1536) is the church (*llan*), now a cathedral, dedicated to Asaph beside the river Elwy.[38] Whitchurch (Glam) is 'white' (*Witechurche* 13th cent., *Whytechurche* 1376) and also 'new' in Eglwys Newydd (*Newchurch* 1472, *Egluis Newith* 1536–39) although the two names record different chronological stages. Monknash/Yr As Fawr (Glam) (*Aissa c.* 1140, *Asse* 1291, *Nashe magna* 1578, *Monken Ashe alias Magna Aish* 1607, *Race vawor* 1670) was 'atten ash of the monks' in English and 'the big ash' in Welsh with *As* being an interesting cymricization of *ash* rather the standard *onnen* 'ash'. Priestholm/Ynys Seiriol (Angl) has been dealt with above. The Scandinavian island-name Bardsey has also been dealt with above, while the Welsh name, Ynys Enlli, is 'strong current' with the intensive prefix *en-* and *llif*, a reference to the particularly challenging sound between island and mainland.

There is intriguing evidence to suggest that Welsh *llan* and OE *stōw* in the sense 'holy place' may have been interchangeable.[39] Llanddingad (Monm) (*Landinegath c.* 1191) exists alongside Dingestow (*Denstow* 1290, *Dyngarstowe* 1395), and Llanwarw (*Lanngunguarui* 1136–54) beside Wonastow (*Wonewarstawe* 1292). St David's/Tyddewi (Pemb) itself may have had an alternative *Dewstow* (late 13th cent.) similar to Dewstow (Monm) (*Dewystowe* 1219–75, with the alternative *Llandewy* 1539 which does not seem to have survived). In Chepstow/Cas-gwent (Monm), of course, OE *stōw* means more generally 'site, place', with OE *cēap* 'market'.

Newport (Monm) (*Novi Burgi* 1072–1104, *Neuburc* 1262, *Neweporte* 1265) has *port* in the sense of town, while Casnewydd (*Castell Newyd ar wysc* 14th cent., *y castell newyd ar wysc c.* 1400) has *castell* later *cas* 'castle', *newydd* 'new', located on the river Usk/Wysg. Newport (Pemb)

[38] The Celtic church did not as a rule prefix a holy man or women with 'Saint'. That was a post-Conquest convention.

[39] Pierce, 'Some aspects', pp. 176–77.

((*de*) *Novo burgo* 1231, *Nuport* 1282) was a borough and new castle replacing an earlier settlement around an older castle nearer the sea and destroyed in 1195, while Trefdraeth (*Trefdraeth* 1215) 'settlement by the shore' probably referred to the older site on the south side of Newport Sands near the estuary of the river Nyfer. Menai Bridge (Angl) dates from the building of the bridge over the Menai Strait in 1826 and gave the town its English name, while the Welsh name Porthaethwy (*Porthaethay'* 1190–99, *Porthaethwy* 1316) is the *porth* 'cove' (and twelfth-century 'ferry') near the fort of the *Daethwy* tribe.

Some later dual names are very close parallels, some conscious translations. We have already seen the industrial Morriston/Treforys (*Morriston* 1780, *Morristown* 1792, *Treforris* 1870). Nine Wells (Pemb) (*the Nine Wells c.* 1600) was given a Welsh translation Naw Ffynnon. Newquay (Card) (*New Key* 1700, *New Quay* 1798) exists side by side with Ceinewydd (*Cai newydd* 1762, *Cei Newydd* 1831) for the expanded fishing port and later pier. Others are Wolfscastle (Pemb) (*Woolfes castell* 1588, *Wolfes castle* 1602) with the well-attested Pembrokeshire personal name *Wolf*, despite attempts at translating it as the animal name *Castrum Lupi* in 1291 and early modern Welsh Cas-blaidd (*blaidd* 'wolf'). St Clears (Carm) co-exists with Sanclêr (*Seint Cler* 1189 [*c.* 1400], *Sencler c.* 1386–87). In Valle Crucis/Glyn-y-groes (Denb) and Strata Florida/ Ystrad Fflur (Card) we have ecclesiastical sites whose Latin designations were renderings of Welsh names.

Further examples involve the regular substitution of one element for an equivalent. Thus Allington (Denb) (*Aluntune* 1086, *Alynton* 1315, *Allington* 1391) the '*tūn* beside the Alun (river)', became Trefalun (*Trefalyn* 1383, *Trevallin* 1561, *Trevallen otherwise Allington* 1653) with *tref* 'farm'. Other examples, notably with personal name + *tūn*, are Cadoxton/Tregatwg (Glam), Siginstone/Tresigin (Glam), Laleston/ Trelales (Glam), Flemingston/Trefflemin (Glam), Colwinston/Tregolwyn (Glam), Letterston/Treletert (Pemb), Bishton/Trefesgob (Monm). Evidently, *tref* had become a regular substitute for the older *tūn*.

The place-name evidence from border counties in particular points to a surge in English place-names, a density which we can possibly ascribe to an administrative influence. The English language, more than we have ever thought, was becoming the language of commerce, officialdom and public administration, and the preferred language of officials and of record-keeping. This in itself might well have encouraged the disuse of Welsh names, simply because they found no favour with English administration. Certainly, the names of new settlements in the east of

Wales after the Conquest tended to be English. It is most probable that, in some cases, existing but unrecorded Welsh names of expanding settlements were supplanted with new or alternative English names. The repossession by Welsh princes of parts of Wales during the twelfth and thirteenth centuries could have led to the reinstatement of Welsh names for settlements but that did not happen, at least on any significant scale. Place-names had become fixed, and adaptation was the main indicator of a linguistically mixed community.

Phonological and scribal adaptation

So far we have looked at the English place-names as they appear either as the sole name of a place or as the English half of dual naming. There is a third category, that of phonological adaptation. Category iii, in which names are adapted by usage into either language, has 146 names, 7% of the names in DPNW.

Such adaptation is a regular feature of most place-names in any bilingual community, where the subsequent development of a name undergoes changes in phonology, stress or spelling in accordance with a variety of factors. In Wales, many English place-names show similar developments to their counterparts in England but a small group of names displays specific phonological preferences characteristic of the Welsh language. Many of these belong to the dual category in the sub-set in which the Welsh name and the English name of a place are phonological variants of the same name. This adaptation has been dealt with as it applies to English words (rather than place-names) in the important but largely forgotten 1923 publication *The English Element in Welsh* by Sir T. H. Parry-Williams.[40] It was B. G. Charles and Gwynedd Pierce who pioneered the methodical analysis of phonological patterns as it applied to place-names, a methodology followed by subsequent scholars.

Welsh toponymists have coined the term 'cymricization' to describe the naturalization of English place-names in Wales, whereby place-names of whatever linguistic origin behave as if they were native Welsh names. Melville Richards suggested that, in north-east Wales for example, this naturalization could reflect military repossession with much territory

[40] T. H. Parry-Williams, *The English Element in Welsh* (London: Honourable Society of the Cymmrodorion, 1923). Aspects of the book were delivered as the O'Donnell Lecture which was published as T. H. Parry-Williams, 'English–Welsh loan-words', in *Angles and Britons: O'Donnell Lectures* (Cardiff: University of Wales, 1963), pp. 42–59.

being regained by Welsh princes in the eleventh century.[41] However, the reconquest was military not linguistic. There had never been linguistic capitulation. There may have been changes in military allegiance and occupation, but this in itself did not prompt language-shift. Daily speech within the community would have been Welsh, and in most cases in the Middle Ages, exclusively so. What we have in this section is the result of linguistic interplay within a community which used the two languages, though most individuals were monolingual. In time, the Welsh speakers became bilingual and the English speakers remained monolingual. The Welsh speakers became more conditioned to assimilating English names and pronouncing them as English names or as cymricizations. Monolingual English speakers did what they could with unfamiliar sounds with their rendering, conditioned by English phonology, becoming generally accepted as the standard name, even by Welsh speakers.

Most of the examples cited here are chosen to illustrate some of the phonological processes of cymricization, whereby English names were modified by the Welsh sound-system. Then there is a selection of names to show what English-speakers made of Welsh names. Some have already been referred to above to illustrate different features.

One of the characteristic features of the Welsh language is the velar fricative [x] represented in modern Welsh as <ch> but also as <gh> in earlier documents. The fate of the velar fricative elsewhere is varied, from its clear enunciation in, say, Scottish *loch* to its non-existence in modern English pronunciation (*bough*) or its substitution as [f] (*cough*) but with the historic [x] often preserved in spelling as <gh>. The Anglesey place-name Newborough/Niwbwrch illustrates the point. When Edward I established the castle and fortified town of Beaumaris in 1284, he downgraded the existing settlement of nearby Llan-faes, but to appease the burgesses of Llan-faes he established for them a new borough twelve miles to the west, variously described in documentation as *Villa de Nouo Burgo*, *Novus Burgus*, *Neuburgh* 1304–05, *Newborough* 1497, *Nuburche* 1496–97, *Nuburch* 1536–39. The modern English form Newborough follows the regular development in English spelling, whereas the Welsh form Niwbwrch retains the [x] of medieval English. Other examples of [x] are Soughton/Sychdyn (*Sutone* 1086, *Sychtun, Sychton* 1271, *Soughton* 1363, *Sughton* 1446–47, *Syghtyn* 1539, *Sychdyn*

[41] 'Welsh influence on some English place-names in north east Wales', in *Otium et Negotium* (Stockholm: Kungl. Boktr, 1973), pp. 216–20.

c. 1700) which is OE **sōg* (ME *sogh*) 'bog' and *tūn*.[42] The personal name *Knight* was preserved in the mountain name Cnicht (Caern). Cichle (Angl) records a settler from Yorkshire's Keighley.

It is worth digressing briefly to draw attention to Beaumaris/ Biwmares (Angl) (*Beaumaris* 1296, *Beaumareys* 1301, *Bewemarrras* 1489, *Bewmaris* 1610) from Norman French *beau* and *marais* 'fair marsh'. The Welsh pronunciation and form Biwmares more closely replicates the medieval French pronunciation of *beau*, while the modern pronunciation of Beaumaris has been influenced by standard modern pronunciation of *beau*. Compare Beaupre/Y Bewpyr (Glam) (*Bewerpere* 1376, *Y Bewper* 1485–1515, *the Bewpere* 1526) with OFr *beau* and OFr *repaire* 'place of retreat', later confused with French *pré* 'meadow'; the local pronunciation is close to 'Bewper'.

The Welsh [x] also replicates the aspirated OE *hw-* seen in the Flintshire Whitford/Chwitffordd (OE *hwīt*, *ford* 'white ford'). The original pronunciation, probably seen in *Quitfordia* (1240 [1285]), is preserved in the historical Welsh forms *Chwitforth* 1284, *Chwytffordd* 1373, *Chwitfford* 1550–62. Here, there is the additional feature of the semantic adaptation of English *ford* as Welsh *ffordd* 'way, route'. Old English initial, medial and final *-l-* is occasionally adapted as Welsh *-ll-*, the voiceless postdental lateral (heard, for example in Llan- names). One example is OE *lēah* which, rather than ending up as *Leigh* perhaps, becomes Llai (Denb). The same element survives in Leeswood/Coed-llai (Flints). We can postulate a Welsh element **llai* 'river meadow', borrowed from English and unrecorded outside place-names.

Initial OE *w-* is sometimes taken as the lenition of Welsh initial *gw-* as in Gwersyllt (Denb) (*Wersull*, *Wersullt* 1315, *Gwersild* 1393, *Gwersyllt* 1402) from the personal name **Wērsige* and OE *hyll* (ME *hull*), with final OE *-l* becoming first Welsh *-ll* in pronunciation and spelling, and then the common colloquial *-llt*. In Gwesbyr (Flints) (OE *west*, *burh* dat. *byrig*, 'west fort') documentation traces the phonological development through *Waestbyrig* 1053, *Westbury*, *Gwespur* 1332, *Gwespyr* (*Westbury*)

[42] Compare Sychtyn (Shropshire) in EPNS Sa **1**, pp. 289–90. Margaret Gelling conceded that there was a comparison with the Flints Sychdyn and that the general opinion of that name had hitherto derived it from OE *sūð* 'south' with substitution of [x] for [ð]. This was the view which I followed in several publications (for example in Owen, 'Old English place-name elements', p. 274, in 1997). However, Margaret Gelling went on to argue (ibid.) that this interpretation was 'not certain to be correct' and proposed OE **sōg* and ME *sogh*. I became convinced by Margaret Gelling's arguments and have followed that in subsequent publications including DPNW.

c. 1700. 'Westbury' did not survive.

In Gwesbyr (Flints) there is another Welsh influence at work, which is the inclination to penultimate stress.[43] Where there is conflict between existing English initial stress and the Welsh preference for penultimate stress, the issue is usually resolved by stress-shift in Welsh, generally entailing apocope to accommodate the shift. In Gwesbyr, we assume the three-syllable English *Westbury* had initial stress. Welsh tongues retained the initial stress but transformed it into penultimate stress through loss of the final syllable, hence *Westbury* > *Westbur* > Gwesbyr. Similarly in Borras (Denb) (*Boresham*, *Borasham* 1315, *Bor(r)as* 1550) with the Old English personal name *Bār* and *hamm*, 'Bār's river meadow', and Erddig (Denb) (*Eurdicote* 1315, *Eurthyg, Erthigge* 16th cent.) from OE *hierde* and *cot* 'herdsman's hut'). Prestatyn (Flints) (*Prestetone* 1086, *Prestattune* 1257, *Presaton* 1305, *Prystatun* 1325, *Prestatyn* 1536) from OE *prēosta* (gen. pl.) and *tūn*, giving 'farm of priests', is an interesting case because its counterpart in England regularly became Preston, but in Flints the conflict was resolved by stress-shift from the initial stress to the medial syllable.

The final syllable of Prestatyn also reveals the Flintshire inclination to have ME *-u-* fall in with Middle Welsh *-u-* to become *-y-*, to produce a suffix characteristic of the more Welsh parts of Flints and Shropshire, which has Brogyntyn (OE personal name *Porca*, *-ing-*) and Selattyn (*sulh* 'gully', gen. plural *sūla*). In Flintshire we have Kelsterton/Celstryn (OE personal name *Cweldhere*) with syncope to resolve penultimate stress, Mostyn (OE *mos* 'bog'), Estyn (OE *ēast* 'east), Mertyn (OE *mere* 'sea pool'), Sychdyn (OE **sōg* 'bog'), Axtyn (ON *askr* 'ash'), Golftyn (OE personal name *Wulfwine*). In Broughton/Brychdyn (OE *brōc* 'brook') the Welsh form is not historical in this part of east Flintshire but is a recent analogous coinage. In south Wales *tūn* more conservatively remained as *-twn*, particularly in Glamorganshire's Broughton/Brychdwn, Gileston/Silstwn, Ifton/Ifftwn, and in alternatives that did not survive such as Wrinstone/*Wrinstwn* (Glam), Nurston/*Nyrstwn* (Glam), Crosstown/*Crostwn* and Burton/*Britwn*.[44]

Another example of stress-shift is Hawarden (Flints) which is 'Harden' in modern pronunciation but has retained the three-syllable spelling. The derivation is OE *hēah* and OE *worðign* 'high enclosure'

[43] For a detailed discussion, see H. W. Owen, 'English place-names and Welsh stress-patterns', *Nomina* 11 (1987), 99–114.

[44] Pierce, 'Some aspects', p. 180.

(*Haordine* 1086, *Hawurdin* 1250, *Hawarden* 1439, *Harden* 1545). The latter historical form is the expected English development; cf Harden (St), Carden (Ch) and Marden (He). However, alongside the English pronunciation with initial stress there existed a Welsh pronunciation with medial, penultimate stress, these forms reflecting the local and regional pronunciation outside the town. Historical forms provide evidence of the pronunciation variant as late as the nineteenth century: *Howarden alias Hawarden or Harden* 1828, *Harden otherwise Howarden* 1839. The Welsh name is Penarlâg 'height rich in cattle' (Welsh *pennardd*, Welsh *alawg*) which is first recorded later than Hawarden (*Pennardlawwc*, *Pennardlaoc* 14th cent., *pennarddlac* 16th cent., *Pen ar lag* 1566, *Penarlâg c.* 1700) but we can safely assume that it was the Anglo-Norman and then English clerks who exclusively used Hawarden in early records at the expense of the much older Penarlâg. It has also been suggested that Penarlâg originally referred to the forested area around Hawarden.[45]

Another feature of the Welsh language is to give unstressed final syllables clearer enunciation. Bangor, for example, in Welsh speech has [gɔr] as the final syllable, whereas the anglicized pronunciation is [gə] with a neutral vowel and no [r]. One term used for such clarity of tone is pitch-prominence. Consequently, some Middle English place-names which developed unstressed final syllables in standard English speech retain a clearer enunciation of the final syllable in cymricized pronunciation. This is the explanation for the Carmarthenshire village of Alltwalis (*allt* 'hill'), the Pembrokeshire village of Wallis (earlier *Walles* 1572) and several minor place-names called *Wal(l)is* in the same two counties. They can all be ascribed to the disyllabic ME *walles* 'walls', referring to defensive ramparts (archaeologically evidenced in these places). Interestingly, the village Wallis has always retained the confusing *-ll-* spelling. The prevalence of the name is an argument for postulating an otherwise unrecorded Welsh element **walis* 'ramparts'.

These place-names sound and look as if they were native Welsh place-names. For the casual enquirer it is a remarkably challenging feature of Welsh toponymy to have to accept that such names as Bagillt, Gwersyllt, Gwesbyr, Sychdyn and Prestatyn are in fact English names. It is not surprising that the anglicized colloquial pronunciation [baglt] and [gwərslt] is heard locally.

[45] Owen, *Place-Names of East Flintshire*, pp. 60–63.

To finish, perhaps we should also look at standard anglicized versions of Welsh place-names because they too reveal the interplay of two languages within one community. They also reveal scribes and administrators struggling to accommodate what was to them an alien phonology, and rendering names in some semblance of English orthography.[46] Additionally they provide a comparison with the development of English place-names outside Wales. In time, given exhaustive place-name surveys of all areas in Wales, it will be possible to describe in detail the phonology of place-name adaptation.

Initial Welsh *Ll-* becomes *L-* as in *llethr* 'slope' > Lether (Glam) (to be compared with Leather Tor D), and several Llanbedr/Lampeter names, and Llandimôr/Landimore (Glam). Initial Welsh and English initial *cn-* (as in English *knave*/Welsh *cnaf*) is retained in the medieval period only to disappear in the modern English pronunciation such as Cnwclas/Knucklas (Radn) (Welsh *cnwc*, *glas* 'verdant hillock'). Initial Welsh *rh-* becomes anglicized as *r-* as in Rhuthun/Ruthin (Denb) (Welsh *rhudd*, *hin* 'red edge'), Rhiwabon/Ruabon (Denb) (Welsh *rhiw*, personal name *Mabon* 'Mabon's hill') and Rhaglan/Raglan (Monm) (Welsh **rhaglan* 'rampart').

Final Welsh *-g* becomes anglicized as *-c(k)* as in Llangatwg/Llangattock (Brec and Monm) 'church of Cadog', and Tryleg/Treleck (Monm) (Welsh *try*, *lleg* 'conspicuous stone').

The development of [x] is perhaps predictable. Lacharn (Carm) (Welsh ?*llachar* 'bright rock') has the regular anglicized Laugharne (pronounced 'Larne'). More often than not the final unstressed [x] was lost as in Solfach/Solva (Pemb) (Welsh *salw*, *-ach* 'mean, discoloured river') and Dinbych/Denbigh (Denb) (Welsh *din*, *bych* 'little fort') and Dinbych(-y-pysgod)/Tenby (Pemb); the northern Denbigh retains the spelling but not the pronunciation of Dinbych, whereas the spelling Tenby is probably influenced by the Scandinavian *-bý*.

Metanalysis explains Sain Tathan/St Athan (Glam) (personal name *Tathan*) and Arberth/Narberth (Pemb) ('in Arberth'). In Caerdydd/Cardiff (Glam) the English version is closer to the original *Caer Dyf* 'fort of (the

[46] Pierce, 'Some aspects', p. 183, draws attention to the notable example of Talyllychau (Carm) 'end of the stone slabs' whose Welsh form presented such a challenge that fairly early in its history versions such as *Tallagh*, *Talley* 1382 became common, possibly as a clerical abbreviation, but just as likely because 'the combination of *-ll-* and *-ch-* apparently proved too much [...] the Englishman seems to have given up in despair'. Hence Talyllychau/Talley. One is reminded of *Lani* as a local familiar contraction of Llanidloes, and *Landod* for Llandrindod.

river) Taf' with the Welsh version having later substitution of *-f-* and *-dd-*. Morgannwg/Glamorgan shows, in Welsh, the personal name *Morgan* and the territorial suffix *-wg*, while the name regarded as English is simply two Welsh words *gwlad Morgan* 'land of Morgan'.

Finally, it is worth drawing attention to ways in which anglicizations actually preserve Welsh dialectal variants. In the Gwentian dialect of Glamorgan, the diphthong *ae* and the long vowel *â* frequently became [ɛ:] so that Llys-faen 'stone court' is also Lisvane, and Aberdâr 'mouth of the (river) Dâr' has the anglicized spelling Aberdare, and the same Welsh vowel is found in the 'much maligned and misunderstood pronunciation of Cardiff'[47] as [kɛ:dif] and [kæ:dif].

Summary

Place-names perceived to be not Welsh represent just over a tenth of the names in Wales, although those names which are genuinely English in origin are somewhat fewer. Analysis of the place-name elements extends our understanding of English place-name elements generally. Coastal names record access routes to Wales as well as being tokens of trade and the common stock of maritime terms. Some settlement names reflect deliberate implantation, and some record the personal names of settlers; others are the by-products of military occupation, religion, industry, tourism, commerce, transport, travel and agriculture. Dual names of places record the presence of two languages at various periods. A considerable number of place-names provide valuable evidence of phonological adaptation. The density of English names in certain areas marks the English encroachment stabilizing, with English becoming the dominant language of that society. The administrative status of the English language over the centuries has promoted many English names exclusively, regardless of colloquial usage locally or cultural custom nationally. In recent years, however, legal parity for both languages has ensured a greater awareness of the political and cultural significance of place-names, leading to the restoration of the status of Welsh place-names.[48]

[47] Pierce, 'Some aspects', p. 189.

[48] I am very grateful to Gwynedd Pierce and to Richard Morgan for detailed comments on this chapter. Their helpful suggestions have been silently incorporated into the text.

12

English place-names in Ireland

Kay Muhr

Historical framework

The earliest language documented in Ireland, and the language in which most of its place-names are coined, is a type of Celtic. Irish Gaelic, often referred to simply as Irish, derives from the same branch of Indo-European as Welsh. It is traditionally thought to have been taken from Ireland to western Scotland, where it became Scottish Gaelic, at about the same time as Angles and Saxons brought the Germanic language to southern and eastern Britain.[1] Manx Gaelic, in the Isle of Man, may also have been established at the same period or possibly later.

Although there was early contact between Ireland and Britain, most would have been between Ireland and western Wales or Scotland. The Irish borrowed a personal name *Conaing*, first attested in the *Annals of Ulster* under the year AD 622, from Old English *cyning* 'king'. However, there is no clear evidence of Old English borrowing in the vocabulary of Irish place-names,[2] despite the late-seventh-century foundation of the

PNI = *The Place-Names of Northern Ireland* (Belfast: The Queen's University Belfast): Vol. 1: Co. Down I, Newry and South-West Down, by G. Toner and M. B. Ó Mainnín (1992); Vol. 2: Co. Down II, The Ards, by A. J. Hughes and R. J. Hannan (1992); Vol. 3: Co. Down III, The Mournes, by M. B. Ó Mainnín (1993); Vol. 4: Co. Antrim I, The Baronies of Toome, by P. McKay (1995); Vol. 5: Co. Derry I, The Moyola Valley, by G. Toner (1996); Vol. 6: Co. Down IV, North-West Down / Iveagh, by K. Muhr (1996); Vol. 7: Co. Antrim II, Ballycastle and North-East Antrim, by F. Mac Gabhann (1997); Vol. 8: Co. Fermanagh I, Lisnaskea and District: the Parish of Aghalurcher, by P. McKay (2004). *GÉ* = *Gasaitéar na hÉireann / Gazetteer of Ireland: ainmneacha ionad daonra agus gnéithe aiceanta* (Dublin: Oifig an tSoláthair, 1989). *Fiants Eliz.* = 'Calendar and index to the fiants of the reign of Elizabeth I', appendix to the *11th–15th, 15th–18th and 21st–22nd Reports of the Deputy Keeper of Public Records in Ireland* (Dublin: Thom, 1879–81, 1883–86, 1889–90).

[1] Argyll and the north of Ireland may have shared language and culture from a very early date: see T. O. Clancy, 'Gaelic in medieval Scotland: advent and expansion', *Proceedings of the British Academy* 167 (2011), 349–92 (pp. 355–58).

[2] For discussion of suggested Old English origins for *drong* 'assembly place' and *sráid* 'street' see K. Muhr, 'Place-names of Germanic origin in Ireland', *Reallexikon der Germanischen Altertumskunde* 22 (2002), 302–04 (pp. 302–03).

monastery of Mayo 'of the Saxons' in Ireland, linked with Northumbria. The first Germanic-speaking culture to influence Irish place-names appears to be that of the Vikings.

Places in Ireland directly named by Scandinavian raiders and subsequently settlers, from the late eighth century to the twelfth, have been studied by Dónall Mac Giolla Easpaig.[3] There are thirty-two surviving names, all coastal but for the village of Leixlip 'salmon leap' in Co. Dublin. As well as naming islands the Scandinavians founded trading centres which developed into some of the earliest towns in Ireland: Limerick, Wexford, Wicklow and Arklow. In addition, some Scandinavian personal names were borrowed by the Irish, eventually appearing in surnames. Many of the Scandinavian place-names are paralleled by different Irish names for the same place. In some cases there is evidence for language interplay between the two forms, sometimes correspondence of meaning, and sometimes correspondence of sound. However, Mac Giolla Easpaig concludes that 'all trace of Scandinavian place-names, however numerous they may have been, would have disappeared with the disappearance of Scandinavian as a spoken language in Ireland, were it not for the fact that a number of them had been borrowed into English'.[4] In some cases, such as Olderfleet, Strangford, Carlingford, Ireland's Eye, and Waterford, the names now look so much like combinations of English or Scots words that these coinages in Norse, a language related to English, may be considered among the earliest English names. This process of adaptation set a pattern for the treatment of place-names in Ireland.

Evidence for cultural contact also appears in the much larger set of place-names in Ireland given by the Anglo-Norman knights (French and English-speaking) who arrived in the late twelfth century from Britain, and colonized the south and east of the island. They built castles and founded or refounded monasteries on the continental model, sometimes with Latin names. Eventually they established marriage alliances with the

[3] D. Mac Giolla Easpaig, 'L'influence scandinave sur la toponymie irlandaise', in É. Ridel (ed.), *L'héritage maritime des Vikings en Europe de l'Ouest* (Caen: Presses Universitaires de Caen, 2002), pp. 441–82. Mac Giolla Easpaig is Chief Placename Officer of the Republic of Ireland.

[4] 'Toute trace de toponymes scandinaves aurait disparu, aussi nombreux qu'ils aient pu être, lorsqu'on cessa de parler le scandinave en Irlande, si certains d'entre eux n'avaient pas été empruntés par l'anglais'; Mac Giolla Easpaig, 'L'influence scandinave', p. 446; also Muhr, 'Place-names of Germanic origin', p. 303.

native Irish and learned the Irish language, often resulting in place- and family names with English and Irish versions.

The Norman lords apportioned land to their followers and to the church apparently using the Irish townland system,[5] and many Anglo-Norman place-names follow the pattern of a Norman personal name, indicating the new holder of the land, plus Old English *tūn* 'farmstead', and its later forms. Éamonn de hÓir noted that in the first two centuries after the Norman invasion '[f]ar the most common type of English name coined is that of personal name + *town*',[6] and he gave a number of ownership place-name examples from the Pale: Craddockstown, Co. Kildare (*Cradokeston* 1297), Blakestown, Co. Wicklow (*Blakyston* 1373), Bellewstown, Co. Meath (*Bellewyston* 1381), Backweston, Co. Dublin (*Backbyestoun* 1395).[7] Further examples survive in concealed or altered forms. Thus Mornington, a townland and town in the parish of Colp, Co. Meath, was *villa Roberti Marinerii* 1211, 'Robertus le Mariner in *villa de Mariners*' 1234, *Marinerston* 1343, *Mornanston* 1552, *Mornanton or Marinerston* 1604 and *Morningtown* in 1777 (<www.logainm.ie>). It thus began as an ownership name, misinterpreted in the eighteenth century.

By the fourteenth century many of these coinages were gaelicized by replacing word-final *tūn* with word-initial *baile*, since Irish *baile*, basically an 'occupied place', has had the same range of meanings as *tūn*/*town* (farmstead > settlement > town) and is still used as the Irish-language equivalent of the Plantation administrative term townland. Examples from the Ards peninsula, Co. Down, include Ballyfounder in Ballytrustan parish, Ballynichol in Ballytrustan parish and Ballyfrenis in Donaghadee parish, recorded in 1333 as *Punyertoun, Nicholtown* and *Frenestoun* respectively.[8] The parish of Ballyphilip maintained its English name, *Philiptown*, on Mercator's map of 1595: it was taxed as 'the church of *Feliptone*' *c.* 1306, but called *Ba[lly] Philip* in 1601.[9]

In fact Liam Price has suggested that the proliferation of the use of the word *baile* in place-names was a result of the arrival of settlers and their

[5] C. Doherty, 'Settlement in early Ireland: a review', in T. Barry (ed.), *A History of Settlement in Ireland* (London and New York: Routledge, 2000), pp. 50–80 (p. 79). The townland system is discussed further below.

[6] É. de hÓir, 'The anglicisation of Irish place-names', *Onoma* 17 (1972/73), 192–204 (pp. 193, 196).

[7] De hÓir, 'The anglicisation', pp. 196–97.

[8] Muhr, 'Place-names of Germanic origin', p. 303; *PNI* 2, pp. 57, 59, 183.

[9] Muhr, 'Place-names of Germanic origin', p. 303; *PNI* 2, pp. 41.

use of the word *town* in giving names to their lands, noting that the proportion of *baile* names is greatest in those parts of Ireland which had been ruled by the Anglo-Normans but subsequently gaelicized, and is lowest in the counties of mid-Ulster in which there was little or no English settlement.[10] However, Charles Doherty has argued that it is not clear whether *baile* or *tūn* preceded as an administrative unit,[11] and *baile* referring to a settlement first appears in AD 1011, well before the Normans.[12] Fergus Kelly deduced, from the early Irish legal term *fintiu* 'kin-land', that ownership names were unlikely to be a new invention,[13] and many thousands of townlands bear the name of the family which at one time held the land.[14]

The equivalence of *tūn* and *baile* did not help in a law-case of 1307 'in which Gerald son of Nicholas Tancard lost his case for the restoration of his lands in Co. Limerick because he described them as being in *Balytancard* instead of *Tancardeston*'.[15] Although this is the only example of such harsh discrimination in land-naming that has come to light, it illustrates how English culture was officially preferred to Irish.

De hÓir also noted that another Irish settlement term *ráth*, the native Irish name for a farm dwelling in an earthen ring-fort, had been adopted in place-names in English word-order coined by the Anglo-Normans. As he said of Baggot Rath in Dublin 'from the word order it must be an English coinage and it indicates that the Ir. *ráth* (applied to an earthen ringwork indicating an early homestead) was borrowed into English'.[16] The Irish Government's Placenames Branch has studied the surviving townland names of this type (occurring especially in Co. Kilkenny) and shown that the associated individuals or families tend to date back to the

[10] L. Price, 'A note on the use of the word *baile* in place-names', *Celtica* 6 (1963), 119–126 (pp. 124–25).

[11] Doherty, 'Settlement in early Ireland', p. 67.

[12] G. Toner, '*Baile*: settlement and landholding in medieval Ireland', *Éigse* 34 (2004), 25–43 (p. 31).

[13] F. Kelly, *Early Irish Farming: A Study Based Mainly on the Law-Texts of the 7th and 8th Centuries AD* (Dublin: Dublin Institute for Advanced Studies, 1997), p. 402.

[14] For numerous examples of *baile* followed by an Irish family name in townland-names, see, e.g., the Co. Down parish of Magheralin; *PNI* 6, pp. 218–26. About 10% of Irish-language place-names contain a personal or family name.

[15] J. Mills (ed.), *Calendar of the Justiciary Rolls II* (Dublin: Thom, 1914), p. 431; de hÓir, 'The anglicisation', p. 194.

[16] De hÓir, 'The anglicisation', p. 197. The point had earlier been observed by John O'Donovan: see S. Ó Cadhla, *Civilizing Ireland: Ordnance Survey 1824–1842, Ethnography, Cartography, Translation* (Dublin: Irish Academic Press, 2007), p. 220.

thirteenth and fourteenth centuries, while the anglicized order of the *ráth*-names is at least as old as the fifteenth:

> Archersrath, Co. Kilkenny (*Archerstoun* 1356, Walter Archer there in 1586)
>
> Cotterellsrath, Co. Kilkenny (Griffin Coterell there in 1369, *Coterellsrath* 1441)
>
> Griffinrath, Co. Kildare (*Griffynrath* 1540)
>
> Holde[r]nsrath, Co. Kilkenny (Robert Howlyn, rector de *Inchyholleghan* 1376, *Fowlingrath* 1556, *Holdingsrath* 1655)
>
> Marshallrath, Co. Louth (*Rathmarchal* 1301, *Marshallrath* 1594)
>
> Shellumsrath, Co. Kilkenny (Walter de Schuldham, sheriff of Kilkenny 1294, *Shulhames raith* 1434)
>
> Suttonsrath, Co. Kilkenny (Nicholas Suttoun in Kilkenny 1383, *Sottounsrathe* 1526)

No earlier place-names for these townlands are known, and in all cases, *ráth* followed by the surname in Irish spelling has now been given as the official Irish form.[17]

Many of the coastal place-names created by Scandinavian and Norman settlers seem to have survived in English usage among seafarers, often with an Irish alternative used on land. Thus the name of the first Anglo-Norman landing-place, Baginbun in Co. Wexford, can be considered a maritime name. D. Ó Murchadha criticized the Irish historian Keating's attempt to gaelicize the name Baginbun, preferring the historian Orpen's suggestion that it represents the names of two ships that made landfall there.[18]

Other English maritime place-names on maps include Fair Head, Co. Antrim, which was shown as *Faire forlande* on sixteenth-century maps of Ireland, long before there is any evidence for the Irish name Benmore, *An Bhinn Mhór* meaning 'the big cliff'.[19] Mizen Head has been applied to

[17] E.g. *Ráth an tSutúnaigh* for Suttonsrath, <www.logainm.ie> [accessed 18 August 2011].

[18] D. Ó Murchadha, 'A review of some placename material from *Foras Feasa ar Éirinn*', *Éigse* 35 (2005), 81–97 (p. 84). The name is shown on Boazio's map (Fig. 1) as three words: *Bagg and Bonne*. See M. T. Flanagan, 'Baginbun', in S. J. Connolly (ed.), *The Oxford Companion to Irish History* (Oxford: Oxford University Press, 2007), p. 33. The official place-name website <www.logainm.ie> gives only the unrelated Irish name of the headland, *Ceann Bhanú*.

[19] *Fayre forland* (Goghe 1567), *Faire forlande* (Nowel *c.* 1570), *the faire foreland* (Jobson's Ulster *c.* 1590: TCD 1209/17); see K. Muhr, 'Place-names and Scottish clan traditions in north-east County Antrim', in J. D. McClure, J. M. Kirk, and M. Storrie (eds), *A Land That Lies Westward: Language and Culture in Islay and Argyll* (Birlinn, Edinburgh: John Donald, 2009), pp. 79–102 (p. 87).

two headlands, in Cos Cork and Wicklow, with 'Mizen', a type of sail, presumably referring to the headlands' triangular profiles.[20] Two other English names are translations: Loop Head, Co. Clare, represents *Lyme Concollen* 'the leap of Cú Chulainn', the legendary Irish warrior, with a Scots/English dialect variant *loup* 'leap' (*GÉ*, p. 247); and Hook Head, Co. Wexford, stands for *Rinn Duáin*, where *Duán* 'little black one' is both the name of a local saint and a word for a hook, a metaphor for its shape.[21]

The Elizabethan conquest of Ireland regained control of the Anglo-Norman territory, and was extended by James I into Ulster and established by a Plantation there of English and Scottish settlers. All of Ireland was thus brought under English administration, culminating in the Act of Union in 1707 and only broken when the Republic of Ireland gained its independence in 1922.

What sort of names exist?

The basic place-name framework in Ireland was established in Gaelic-speaking times. Major water features, mountain ranges, and secular and ecclesiastical settlements had their names written down in Irish in the first millennium, especially those used as locations in the Irish Annals and records of the early saints.[22] As well as topographic and settlement names, there is early evidence in Ireland for a developed system of administrative names, for larger and smaller land-units.

There were five provinces or major over-kingdoms, in Irish *cúige* 'a fifth' followed by the genitive of an Irish plural population name: *Connacht, Laighean, Mumhan, Uladh*. Of the present forms in English—Connaught, Leinster, Munster and Ulster—the latter three were apparently first created by the Scandinavian colonists from the plural population name followed by Norse genitive *-s* and then the Irish word *tír* 'land'.[23] In early historic times Munster might have been divided in two, but it seems that the original fifth province was Meath, in Irish *An Mhí*[*dhe*] meaning 'the middle'.[24] Within the provincial kingdoms in

[20] See OED <www.oed.com>, s.v. mizzen [accessed 18 November 2012].

[21] <www.logainm.ie> [accessed 15 August 2011]; K. Muhr, Reviews, *Ainm* 8 (2000), 214–24 (p. 217).

[22] *Pace* J. H. Andrews, '"More suitable to the English tongue": the cartography of Irish placenames', *Ulster Local Studies* 14:2 (1992), 7–21 (p. 12).

[23] A. Sommerfelt, 'The English forms of the names of the main provinces of Ireland', *Lochlann* 1 (1958), 223–27.

[24] *PNI* 6, p. 364.

Ireland were many smaller population groups ruled as chieftainships or petty kingdoms, and these might also be grouped into regional alliances. It appears that the incoming Anglo-Norman and Tudor rulers and administrators used these smaller groups and their territories in creating barony and county divisions. Baronies frequently bear the names of local chieftain families. Some Irish counties also have such names, but many bear the names of Irish towns, often those that had grown up around long-established Irish monasteries, which commanded allegiance over a wide area. Despite being units imposed from outside, baronies and counties still tend to have Irish-language names, although counties are named from several of the Scandinavian trading towns: Dublin, Waterford, Wexford, and Wicklow.

Early church foundations in Ireland often continued to use a pre-existing place-name, and only sometimes were named with ecclesiastical elements or with a dedication to the founding saint. Parishes in the ecclesiastical administrative system, recorded in a papal taxation *c.* 1306, were based on these ancient churches and took on their names. Thus although the parish divisions were adopted in the seventeenth century as part of the civil administration, all but 314 of over 3000 parishes bear Irish-language names. Most of the English-language parish names were taken from a local castle or village established by settlers, while a third involve saints' names. There are sometimes differences between ecclesiastical and secular traditions in the naming of parishes and lands belonging to the Church, an intriguing example being the civil parish of Ballyaghran in Co. Derry. This is Irish *Baile Uí Eachráin* 'holding of O Haughran', which was recorded in Anglo-Norman anglicization in 1306 as *Ecclesia de Hathranton*, and the Church of Ireland continued to refer to it as *Agherton*.[25] Other translations, such as *Ywes* for the parish of Ballynure 'settlement of the yew-tree' in Co. Antrim, did not survive.[26]

The smallest unit in the system consolidated by the English administrators was the townland, itself an English or Scottish term for a native land unit with various Irish local names. Evaluating earlier studies (including those by Patrick Duffy and Thomas McErlean in the early 1980s), Charles Doherty concluded that 'a uniform system of land

[25] W. Reeves (ed.), *Ecclesiastical Antiquities of Down, Connor and Dromore, consisting of a taxation of those dioceses compiled in the year 1306* (Dublin: Hodges and Smith, 1847), p. 75, note k. The Roman Catholic parish system, not rebuilt until after the repeal of the Penal Laws in 1829, has sometimes restored Irish spelling of names.

[26] The form again comes from the 1306 papal taxation: Reeves (ed.), *Ecclesiastical Antiquities*, p. 68 and note.

division lies behind the townland unit and that it was well in place by the 12th century'.[27] Townlands were mapped for use in re-distributing land in the Plantation, and Andrews commented, '[o]nce this was done, the English colonists of the seventeenth century would be just as willing to accept the native territorial structure as their Norman predecessors seem to have been'.[28] There are currently about 62,000 townlands in Ireland as a whole, smaller on good land, larger on poor, but—with some regional variation—on average about 325 acres.[29] The standard descriptive work by McErlean deals also with the complexity of different terms and units.[30] In 1691 the surveyor Sir William Petty referred to the uncontrolled variety of the Irish 'town-lands, plow-lands, colps, gneeves, bullibos, ballibetaghs, twos, horsesmen's beds etc',[31] and in many of the eastern counties the Plantation administrators used the term ploughland for what is now termed the townland, showing their familiarity with a unit recognized in England since the Domesday Book.[32] Some of Petty's terms are clearly Irish: the bullibo, or ballyboe, is Ulster *baile bó* 'farmstead of a cow', and ballibetagh is *baile biataigh* 'land of a food-provider,[33] while gneeve (recorded in the south and west) seems to derive from the Irish word *gnímh* 'work', and colp (recorded in the west) from *colpach* 'heifer or bullock'. The latter is perhaps translated in cowland or martland (recorded in the south-east), and there are other regional terms

[27] Doherty, 'Settlement in early Ireland', p. 69.

[28] J. H. Andrews, *A Paper Landscape* (Oxford: Clarendon, 1975), p. 32.

[29] W. Reeves, 'On the townland distribution of Ireland', *Proceedings of the Royal Irish Academy* 7 (1861), 473–90 (p. 490).

[30] T. McErlean, 'The Irish townland system of landscape organisation', in T. Reeves-Smyth and F. Hamond (eds), *Landscape Archaeology in Ireland* (Oxford: British Archaeological Reports, 1983), pp. 315–39. A hypothetical table printed in the introduction to the Townland Index for 1901 appears to have misled scholars more recently: see K. Muhr, Reviews, *Ainm* 8 (2000), 214–24 (pp. 218–19); Ó Cadhla, *Civilizing Ireland*, p. 230.

[31] Sir William Petty, *The Political Anatomy of Ireland* [1691], reprinted in *A Collection of Tracts and Treatises Illustrative of the Natural History, Antiquities, and the Political and Social State of Ireland at Various Periods prior to the Present Century*, 2 vols (Dublin: Thom, 1860–61), II, pp. 1–142 (at pp. 72–73).

[32] McErlean, 'Irish townland system', pp. 317, 319, 320, 328.

[33] In the (over-simplified) system described by Geoffrey Keating in his seventeenth-century history of Ireland, the *baile biataigh* was a subdivision of a subdivision of a province consisting of twelve *seisreachs* or 'plough-teams', each of 120 acres (G. Keating, *Foras Feasa ar Éirinn I*, ed. D. Comyn, repr. with new introduction by B. Ó Buachalla (Dublin: Royal Irish Academy, 1987 [1901]), p. 122; the text is also available at <www.ucc.ie/celt/online/G100054/>). At this estimate the *seisreach* would broadly equate to an Ulster ballyboe or townland.

for land units which are apparently borrowed from English: the poll[e], gallon, pottle and pint in Co. Cavan, and the tate in Cos Fermanagh and Monaghan.[34]

Large estates were built up from multiples of townlands, but a comfortably-off family might hold or control a whole one. Townland units had names, as can be seen from those listed in the foundation grants of Anglo-Norman monasteries,[35] but colonists sometimes considered that ownership of land included the right to change its name to English. Legal provision for this was made under Charles II in the *Act of Settlement and Explanation* [1665]:

> His Majesty [Charles II] taking notice of the barbarous and uncouth names by which most of the towns and places in his kingdom of Ireland are called […], for remedy thereof is pleased that it be enacted […], how new and proper names more suitable to the English tongue may be inserted with an alias for all towns, lands, and places in that kingdom, that shall be granted by letters patents; which new names shall thenceforth be the only names to be used, any law, statute, custom or usage to the contrary notwithstanding.[36]

This was then justified by Petty:

> The last Clause of the Explanatory Act, enabled men to put new Names on their respective Lands, instead of those uncouth, unintelligible ones yet upon them. And it would not be amiss if the significant part of the *Irish* Names were interpreted, where they are not, or cannot be abolished.[37]

However in general settlers kept the names of the townland units granted them as they were, albeit in an anglicized spelling.

The six-inch mapping by the Ordnance Survey in the 1830s extended the townland system from cultivable land across the entire landscape,[38] and this restructuring of formerly marginal land, together with the improvement in economic land use since Petty's survey, provided an

[34] McErlean, 'Irish townland system', pp. 317, 328; Reeves, 'On the townland distribution', p. 484.

[35] For examples from the north see *PNI* 1, p. 1, and J. F. Rankin, *Down Cathedral: The Church of Saint Patrick of Down* (Belfast: Ulster Historical Foundation, 1997), pp. 176–77 and map p. 213. The situation can be compared with Gaelic Scotland (G. W. S. Barrow, *Kingship and unity: Scotland 1000–1306* (London: Edward Arnold, 1981), p. 15) and the Isle of Man (G. Broderick, *Place-Names of the Isle of Man*, VI (Tübingen: Niemeyer, 2002), pp. xiv, xvi).

[36] Quoted from T. Crowley, *The Politics of Language in Ireland 1366 1922: A Sourcebook* (London: Routledge, 2000), p. 76.

[37] Petty, *Political Anatomy*, p. 73.

[38] Andrews, *A Paper Landscape*, p. 6.

opportunity for the names of units which had begun as townland subdivisions to enter an official Topographic Index of townlands. Some of these names gained an English qualifier, and others were entirely English.

One noticeable feature of English names for townlands is the presence in them of words for land-divisions. Townland names which consist of a specified number of acres are not uncommon: there are four Irish townlands named Twentyacres, eleven named Fortyacres and seven named Hundredacres. In Co. Antrim there is a (now obsolete) townland named Two Acres and Half, as well as two named Twenty Acres, one named Five Acres and another named Four Score Acres. In Co. Donegal there is a Sixty Acres and in Co. Meath an Eightyeight Acres. John Andrews comments that such names 'probably originat[ed] before the age of exact admeasurement [...] Very few of these names get within 10 per cent of the truth on any known numerical definition of an acre'.[39]

The term *poll*[40] appears in a townland name in Co. Meath, in Irish *Baile an tSléibhe* 'townland of the upland', but translated as Mountainpole.[41] Other terms are also borrowed from (Scandinavian-influenced) English or Scots: *stang*, a land-division name from ON *stǫng*, E dial. *stang*, 'pole, pointed ridge, ?bridge', forms part of the name of fourteen townlands.[42] In the sixteenth century this term appears to have been used as a subdivision of an acre in the Pale.[43]

Maps of the Plantation period

The linguistic range of place-names found *c.* 1600 can be demonstrated on maps of the Plantation period, which were created by the non-Gaelic administrators since there was no native Irish cartographic tradition. A range of manuscript maps of Ireland from the period has recently (2009) been put online by the United Kingdom National Archives.[44] Unfortunately the introduction to these maps, by Rose Mitchell of the National Archives map collection, states that '[p]lace-names are those

[39] Andrews, *A Paper Landscape*, p. 24, n.: table 4, p. 16, shows 'Varieties of Acre'.

[40] Poll, *n.*[3] <www.oed.com> [accessed 5 November 2012].

[41] P. Walsh, 'Irish Ms Egerton 208' (1932), reprinted in N. Ó Muraíle (ed.), *Irish Leaders and Learning through the Ages* (Dublin: Four Courts, 2003), pp. 277–78.

[42] *PNI* 3, pp. 93–94; on the element in north-west England see D. Whaley, *A Dictionary of Lake District Place-Names* (Nottingham: English Place-Name Society, 2006), p. 419.

[43] *Fiants Eliz.* §3319 (1578, Meath) and §4169 (1583, Co. Dublin).

[44] <www.nationalarchives.gov.uk/documentsonline/irishmaps.asp>.

used at the time and are generally old English ones rather than native Irish'. Most of the place-names shown are in fact native Irish—the maps being earlier than the large post-Plantation increase in English-language names—but in English transliterations.[45] It seems one cannot expect expert cartographers to be precise when talking about language, and in her book on the Ordnance Survey Rachel Hewitt also confuses transliteration, finding equivalent spellings to represent the sounds, with translation, using another language to express the meaning.[46]

The place-names of Ireland on maps of *c.* 1600 reflect a majority of Gaelic names, together with some pre-Gaelic, all respelled as if English. There are some Norse names, also spelled as English (much as Norse place-names in England), and some Anglo-Norman English names. Finally, some English names are either translations from Gaelic or reinterpretations from Gaelic where the sounds suggested English words to English-speaking users. Occasionally, however, these still use Gaelic word order.

Some representative examples of English-language names follow, taken from different parts of Ireland shown on four maps of the period:

1. Baptista Boazio, *Irelande* (1599; see Fig. 1):[47] Cos Waterford and Wexford in the south-east.
   Newtown, Waterford, Newtown, Milck Ca., Whit Ca., Ca. Roche
   Lough miles, Crooke passage, Waterford hauen, Mowntgaret [twice], Stonhouse, Polford, Bagg and Bonne, Rosegarlande, Bridwel, C. Browne, Iland Saltes, Forte Wexford, Brandiren, Blackrock, Castleton, Ampton pool.

[45] I have written to Rose Mitchell to suggest that 'ones' in the phrase above should be altered to 'spellings': 'old English spellings rather than native Irish'. So far (September 2012) the point has not been taken.

[46] R. Hewitt, *Map of a Nation: A Biography of the Ordnance Survey* (London: Granta, 2010), p. 277.

[47] Baptista Boazio's *Irelande* published separately in London in 1599, and in Ortelius' atlas *Theatrum Orbis Terrarum* from 1606 on. The 1606 copy from Neptune Gallery, Dublin, was printed in 1990 as appendix to J. O'Donovan (ed.), *Annála Ríoghachta Éireann: Annals of the Kingdom of Ireland by the Four Masters from the Earliest Period to the Year 1616*, 7 vols (Dublin: Hodges, Smith and Co, 1848–51, repr. Dublin: de Búrca, 1990). (Names transcribed following their order on the map.)

Fig. 1: English and Irish place-names on *Irelande,* by Baptista Boazio (London, 1599) a published compiler's map drawing on surveys of Ireland in the 1560s by Robert Lythe, although the 'line of descent cannot now be traced'.[48] John Andrews commented on Lythe's surviving manuscript maps, 'although at first sight his map seems dominated by densely massed settlements of Anglo-Norman origin [...] Gaelic names abound'.[49] Excerpt showing coastal part of counties Wexford and Waterford.

2. Francis Jobson, *Ulster* (1590):[50] excerpt from Co. Tyrone.
   O'Donell his fort, a forte, Betwene the waters, Neuetun [= Newtownstewart], The stone whereon they make ye Onels, ye forte, Iland Sydney, the abbey [in W], S. Patricke his Purgatorie, fort of Blackwater, Fortobrassel.
3. Gerard Mercator, *Ulster* (1595; see Fig. 2):[51] the north-east coast, including—underlined below—some Irish names with English translations, either on the map itself or in the margin.

[48] J. Andrews, *Shapes of Ireland* (Dublin: Geography Publications, 1997), p. 75.

[49] Andrews, *Shapes of Ireland*, p. 69.

[50] Unpublished: TCD MS 1209/17.

[51] *Ultoniae Orientalis Pars*, by Gerard Mercator, first published in his atlas entitled *Atlas sive Cosmographicae Meditationes de Fabrica Mundi et Fabricati Figura* (Duisburg, 1595).

Stone Otor, The Maydens, Olderflet hauen, Maghees ile, ye Kow, Blak head, ye caue, Woodborne abb., Kinbaune or whit head, Crosse Ile, Freerstone, Holywod ab., Copland Iles, Newtoun abb., Black abbaye, Graye abb, North rock, Whites ca., Whites ile, Blakstaffe, Spordes castel, Talbots cort, South Rock, St Iohans towne, Smites castel, S. Patriks rock, Swans Ile, Philipstown, New castel, C. Walche, C. Audelay, Strangford, Tarragh alias Bull, Bishops Court, Dunesforte, Angwys rok.
[margin:] Kerne Shalgue or huntinghill, Belwharsakel or Marshalltown.

4. John Speed, *Leinster* (1610):[52] the Co. Dublin coast.
   Garmerston, Hol[m]e Patrick / Iland Patrik, Gareston, Holywood, Skires, Baron, Rogers, Leniston, Cabelston, Seaton, Newton, St Boneis Isle, Anna Hill, Poures Court.

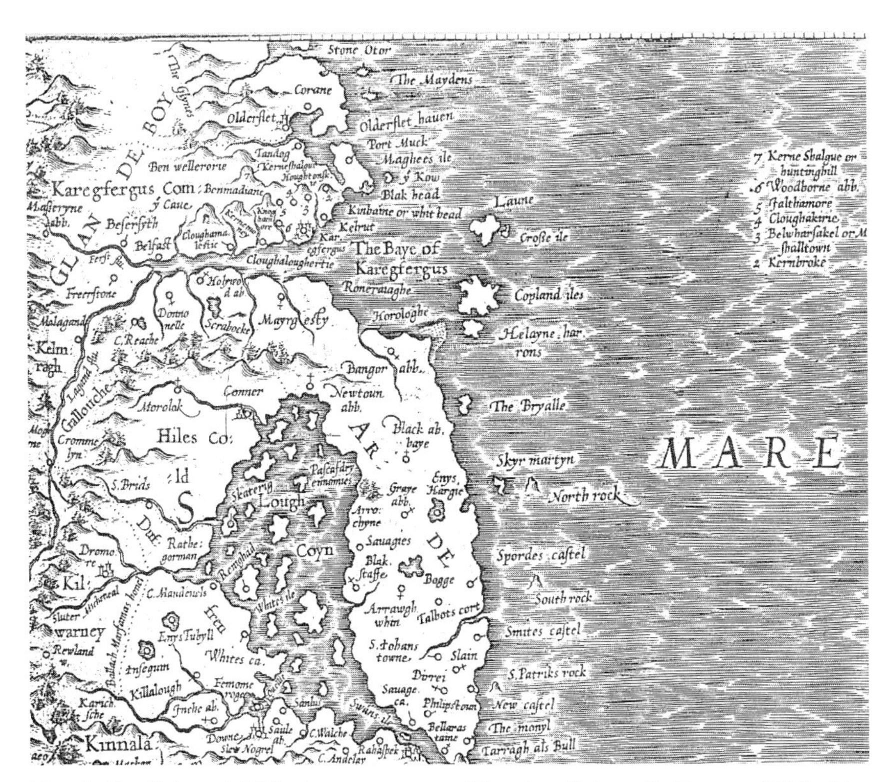

Fig. 2: English and Irish place-names on *Ultoniae Orientalis Pars*, published by Gerard Mercator (Duisburg 1595); map compiled from various earlier surveys.[53] Excerpt showing coastal parts of counties Antrim and Down.

[52] Published in his atlas *The Theatre of the Empire of Great Britain*, and Latin edition: *Theatrum imperii magnae Britanniae* (London: Sudbury and Humble, 1616).

[53] Andrews, *Shapes of Ireland*, pp. 73, 75, 87 n. 30.

The maps reveal the difference in approach to different parts of Ireland: Jobson in only partly-explored mid-Ulster was providing descriptions rather than actual place-names, while Mercator and Speed on the east coast opposite Scotland and England were providing information and place-names for mariners as much as for those on land. On the south-east coast in Co. Wexford, Boazio was recording the area initially reached by the Anglo-Normans, the first English-using conquerors and settlers of the island, who first made landfall at Baginbun (*Bagg and Bonne*, see above, p. 359) in 1170.

The English names listed all occur amid place-names in Irish, still the original language of the majority of place-names in Ireland. Some of the English names show Irish word order: Ca.[stle] Roche, Iland Saltes, Forte Wexford on Boazio; Iland Sydney on Jobson; C. Walche, C. Audelay on Mercator; Iland Patrik on Speed. Mercator's map offers some English translations, while an earlier map, Jodocus Hondius's 'A new description of Ireland' (1591), neatly filled part of unexplored Tyrone with a table giving English equivalents of some recurring place-name elements in Irish: *Nomina haec quae passim reperiuntur, ita Anglice intellige* 'these names which are found everywhere, understand thus in English'.[54] Such recurring place-name elements noted by the map-makers must be the 'significant part of the Irish Names' suggested for translation by Sir William Petty (above, p. 363).

Hondius gives his elements in two columns headed *Hibernice* ('in Irish') and *Anglice* ('in English'), although the words that follow are not all aligned:

Can	Head lant
Enie[s]	Iland
Knok	hyll, Rok
C. Carick	Castel
B. Bali	Towne
L. Logh	Lake

[54] Manuscript map *Hyberniae Novissima Descriptio*, AD 1591, drawn up by Jodocus Hondius and engraved by Pieter van den Keere, reprinted by the Linen Hall Library, Belfast in 1983, with note to facsimile by J. H. Andrews. Table also discussed in J. H. Andrews, '"More suitable to the English tongue": the cartography of Irish placenames', *Ulster Local Studies* 14: 2 (1992), 7–21 (p. 14); K. Muhr, 'Ulster place-name links between Gaelic, English and Scots', in J. M. Kirk and D. P. Ó Baoill (eds), *Language Links: The languages of Scotland and Ireland* (Belfast: Queen's University Belfast, 2001), pp. 257–72 (p. 257).

Kil.	Parishe. tou[n]
Slagho	Montains
Glin. Can	Valley
Bog	Bog marish

The Irish elements are presented in an anglicized spelling. *Ceann* <Can> which means 'head' is translated 'headland', frequently the meaning in place-names. *Inis* (read <Enis>) is 'island', and *cnoc* <Knoc> 'hill' – the initial combination of consonants was still pronounced [kn] in English *c.* 1600. It later became pronounced [kr] in northern Irish,[55] so that minor place-names, anglicized later, may now have the element spelled as *crock*. The translation <Rok> more likely belongs with the next word, since Irish *carraig* <Carick> 'rock' may have connotations of 'castle' in place-names, as in the Co. Antrim town of Carrickfergus, and C. is a convenient abbreviation in both languages. However, any of *caiseal, caisleán* and *caisteal*, the Irish words for 'stone fort' or 'castle', are normally translated into English 'castle' in the anglicized form of Irish place-names. *Baile* <Bali> is the Irish semantic equivalent of Old English *tūn*, although in translating *Towne* Hondius gives the same 'urban' connotations that have puzzled many English visitors since (for the term townland, see above). The word (*baile* / bally) became so familiar in both languages that it was often added to another place-name to signify that it was a townland.[56] The Gaelic words *loch* <Logh> for lake, *gleann* <Glin> for valley, and *bog* 'soft' for marsh have been borrowed into English, at least in Scotland and Ireland, as in parts of Ireland was *daire* 'oakwood', another common place-name element strangely absent from Hondius's list. *Ceall* or *cill* 'church' is explained as naming the parish around it, or maybe the village around the parish church. *Sliabh* <Slagho> 'upland, mountain' is now usually anglicized as Slieve. The alternative *can* for 'valley' appears to be a mistake, misplaced from the beginning of the list.

Explanatory translations as on Mercator's map were also sometimes used in Plantation documents, alongside the name in Irish, for example:

> 'lands called *Ferrenemanaghe* alias *Monckeslandes*' (*Fiants Eliz.* §2903, 1576). Ir. *Fearann na Manach.*
>
> '*Carnehushoke alias* Larckes hill' (*Fiants Eliz.* §6620, 1594; Carrickfergus, Co. Antrim). Ir. *Carn na hUiseóige.*

[55] Ó Cadhla, *Civilizing Ireland*, p. 236.

[56] D. Flanagan, 'Places and their names', *Bulletin of the Ulster Place-Name Society*, 2nd series, 1 (1978), 44–52 (p. 52)

'the Yellow stream otherwise *Owenboye* ... the Red river otherwise *Dearge*' (1602; Termonmagrath, Co. Tyrone).[57] Ir. *An Abhainn Bhuí / Dhearg.*

'*Lemneneigh*, in English the Horse Leap' and '*Agh Fowke,* in English the Dyvell's Foarde' (1618/1623; Co. Down).[58] Ir. *Léim an Eich, Áth an Phúca.*

'*Aghduff* or Blackford' (Co. Wexford; bounds of barony of Bargy).[59] Ir. *An Áth Dubh.*

'Ye foard called *Aghaleyme* or Leapford' (Co. Wexford; bounds of Carnagh parish, barony of Dunbrody).[60] Ir. *Áth an Léim.*

However, translation of Irish place-names for use in English was never widespread, despite the wider implications for cultural change in native Irish society referred to by the modern playwright Brian Friel's metaphor 'Translations'.[61] The late-seventeenth-century Act of Settlement and Explanation had permitted or indeed encouraged changes which were not practical. The versions of place-names cited in the eighteenth-century Registry of Deeds show the importance of correct naming of the land for legal title, so that changing the wording of a name was a serious matter. Although suggesting translation, Sir William Petty had to ask that:

> the Names of all publick Denominations according as they are spelled in the latest Grants, should be set out by Authority to determine the same for the time to come. And that where the same Land hath other Names, or hath been spelled with other Conscription of Letters or Syllables, that the same be mentioned with an *alias*.[62]

Where translations existed, the 1830s Ordnance Survey quite often felt compelled to include alternative place-names, anglicized Irish and English, in its Topographical Index, and the Griffith Valuation in the later nineteenth century preferred to use (anglicized) Irish names 'in order to facilitate the continued use of old documents in modern legal

[57] *Irish Patent Rolls of James I: Facsimile of the Irish Record Commissioner's Calendar Prepared Prior to 1830*, with a foreword by M. C. Griffith (Dublin: Stationery Office for the Irish Manuscripts Commission, 1966), 48a.

[58] J. Hardiman (ed.), *Inquisitionum in officio rotulorum cancellariae Hiberniae asservatorum repertorium*, 2 vols (Dublin: Irish Record Commission, 1826–29), II (Ulster), App IV, p. xliii.

[59] R. C. Simington (ed.), *The Civil Survey, AD 1654–6*, 10 vols (Dublin: Irish Manuscripts Commission, 1931–61), IX, Co. Wexford 1655c, 126.

[60] Simington (ed.), *Civil Survey*, IX, Co. Wexford 1655c; 186.

[61] B. Friel, *Translations* (London: Faber, 1981); Andrews, '"More suitable to the English tongue"', pp. 18–20; Ó Cadhla, *Civilizing Ireland*, pp. 72, 220–26.

[62] Petty, *Political Anatomy of Ireland*, p. 73.

proceedings'.[63] Some statistics on the number and type of names in English will follow, but it is important to remember that the present discussion, of names apparently English, deals with only a small part of the current Irish namescape.

The effect of English on Irish place-names

English is now the dominant language in Ireland, and within Ireland, north and south, local 'English place-names' are those place-names which now appear to be in the English language. Many of the names that appear English in origin, however, are actually phonetic adaptations or translations of Irish Gaelic, as well as other languages known in Ireland, including Latin, Scandinavian, French, and Scots. Almost all the 'Irish' names generally published, in maps or guides for locals and visitors alike, are adaptations, with the place-names written as one word whatever their origin. Both place-names and surnames generally represent Irish Gaelic spelled as if it were English, a practice firmly established since the Plantation but widely used by earlier administrators dealing with Ireland. This was all long before Thomas Larcom of the Irish Ordnance Survey in the 1830s employed a Gaelic scholar, John O'Donovan, to research the Irish versions and standardize the anglicized spellings to those which most accurately reflected the original.[64] Irish independence, and the revival of Irish as the first national language, led to the restoration of some Irish spellings on bilingual road signs. Within the Republic of Ireland, the bilingual place-name policy is visible to all, emphasizing older Irish-language names rather than recent names in English. However bilingual or Irish-language maps are still a minority,[65] while the focus on Irish origins means less study of the effect of English.

[63] Andrews, *A Paper Landscape*, p. 119.

[64] Andrews, *A Paper Landscape*, pp. 122–25; C. Nash, 'Irish placenames: post-colonial locations' *Transactions of the Institute of British Geographers* new series, 24:4 (1999), 457–80 (p. 466).

[65] The Placenames Branch of the Civil Service was founded in 1946 to research and provide authentic Irish-language versions of place-names, while in Northern Ireland the voluntary Ulster Place-Name Society was founded in 1952. Research to rediscover the origin of names long-anglicized requires time and expertise. The official findings of the Dublin Placenames Office are being published in books, on maps, and on the website <www.logainm.ie>, while Northern Ireland, gaining the university-based Northern Ireland Place-Name Project in 1987, has produced a journal, books, and the website <www.placenamesni.org>. The recent attractive laminated map of the island *An Léarscáil Bheag Mhór: Éire* boasts painstaking research, largely drawn from these organizations.

There were three strategies by which the historically Irish-language namescape of Ireland was altered.[66] Éamonn de hÓir, when head of the Dublin Placenames Office, set out a scheme which can be summarized as follows, observing that '[t]he English adopted all three courses in Ireland to varying extents':[67]

1. transliterate from the sounds;
2. translate the meaning (which requires some understanding of the source language);
3. rename.

The map scholar John Andrews similarly listed three processes different from recording place-names in the original language, which he called substitution, translation, and dictation (meaning listening to and representing the sounds).[68]

I will be re-ordering their categories, dealing first with substitute or replacement names, next transliteration (Andrew's 'dictation process'), and finally translation.

Strategy 1: Replacement with transferred or new names

Replacing the original name made Irish language issues irrelevant, but in a country where the majority of the population were Irish-speaking, the introduction of English names needed considerable effort and personnel to enforce. Besides renaming existing land-units, it was new settlements created by English speakers which were probably the chief source of English-language coinages: townland sub-divisions, and house-names, as well as Plantation towns and villages.

A. Transferred names

A series of examples will show the range. Dunsfort parish in Co. Down, first recorded in 1178, was apparently given the name by its new Norman landlord *Rogerus de Dunsforthe* from Dunsforth, in Yorkshire.[69] Tintern, the name of a townland and parish in Co. Wexford was borrowed from

[66] To the two studies mentioned in this paragraph can be added K. Muhr, Introduction to 'Irish and Scottish Gaelic family names', in P. Hanks (ed.), *Dictionary of American Family Names* (New York: Oxford University Press, 2003), pp. xxxvi–xliii. The suggestion is made there that Gaelic surnames were adapted by English-speakers in the same three ways as the place-names.

[67] De hÓir, 'The anglicisation', p. 195.

[68] Andrews, '"More suitable to the English tongue"', p. 13.

[69] Flanagan, 'Places and their names'; Muhr, 'Place-names of Germanic origin', p. 303.

the Cistercian Abbey in Monmouthshire, a Welsh name apparently meaning 'fort of Dwrn', while the monastic charter from William Marshall to Tintern Abbey in Ireland was in AD 1200.[70] Acton, townland and village, Co. Armagh, grew up around the house and bawn of Lieutenant Charles Poyntz, who successfully defended the nearby Poyntz Pass against Hugh O'Neill, Earl of Tyrone, and was granted land there in 1600. It was named from Lieutenant Poyntz's native village of Iron Acton (OE *āc-tūn* 'oak-tree farmstead') in Gloucestershire.[71] Saint Johnstown townland and village in Co. Donegal was named from Saint Johnstone in Scotland, the old name of the town of Perth. It was founded *c.* 1618 on lands granted to Ludovic Stewart, second Duke of Lennox (recorded as *St Johnston c.* 1655). St Johnstown is adjoined on the north by a townland named Dundee, also borrowed from Scotland.[72] Virginia townland and town in Co. Cavan is based on a town founded on lands granted to Captain John Ridgeway in 1611, and originally named from *Lough Ramor* beside it. It was re-named Virginia from the newly-established colony of Virginia in America which was named from Queen Elizabeth I, the 'Virgin Queen'.[73] New Birmingham, a village in Glengoole townland Co. Tipperary, appears in a patent for holding fairs there in 1802, in which it was called New Birmingham or Glengoole. Abington is now a parish and townland straddling the counties of Limerick and Tipperary, but the earliest record of this name is *Abingtown* in 1752, replacing *Mainistir Uaithne* in Irish. (There are villages called Abington in Cambridgeshire and Dumfries, and the town of Abingdon south of Oxford.) The name of Salisbury, a townland in Kildare apparently named from the Wiltshire town, appears first in 1763.[74] Ashbourne, a village in Co. Meath, in the parish and townland of Killegland, 'St Declan's church', was first recorded in 1836 as a 'small town, the property of Mr Bourne of Dublin'.[75] Although Mr Bourne may have been thinking of his own name, there is a town called Ashbourne in England west of Derby.

[70] B. Colfer, 'The ethnic mix in medieval Wexford', *History Ireland* (Spring 2002), 19–23 (p. 19). There are no notes on <www.logainm.ie> on the name Tintern.

[71] P. McKay, *A Dictionary of Ulster Place-Names* (Belfast: The Queen's University Belfast, 1999), p. 1.

[72] McKay, *Dictionary*, p. 128.

[73] McKay, *Dictionary*, p. 145.

[74] From the bound mss volumes (1708–1832) in the Registry of Deeds, Henrietta Street, Dublin.

[75] In the Ordnance Survey Name-Books (1827–35) [OSNB], National Archives, Dublin.

As well as the transferred names of major settlements, there are also minor name types that were apparently imported by Scottish or English settlers. The name Bessy Bell is attested for the hill above Newtownstewart in Tyrone from the late eighteenth century, replacing *Sliabh Truim* 'elder-tree mountain'.[76] The rector of Ardstraw, Dr Fitzgerald, commented in 1814 that it and its companion Mary Grey bore 'names that are celebrated in old Scotch ballads'.[77] The relevant verse was quoted in a squib in 1688 beginning:

Bessy Bell and Mary Grey,
Those famous bonny lasses.

In 1719 Allan Ramsay wrote a popular drawing room song of the same title keeping the first verse, and by the nineteenth century the verse was also in print as a nursery rhyme.[78] The name was given presumably by the Scottish Plantation landowners of the area, which became the Abercorn estate of Baronscourt.

As with Bessy Bell, other names in Ulster were introduced from Scotland. There are more than ten examples of the place-name Calhame and variants occurring in the north of Ireland, several of them townlands, considered as a 'transplant of English or Scottish Coldhame, Coldham, Cauldham' meaning 'cold (inhospitable) dwelling', like Coldham in Cambridgeshire or Cauldham in Kent. John O'Donovan assumed it was Lowland Scots,[79] where Caldhame has the specialized meaning of 'poor, marshy farm', and this is the current explanation.[80] It is not clear if Caldhame was directly borrowed from another place by Scottish or English settlers or simply transferred because its meaning was both transparent and seemed appropriate. Cold is also a frequent element in

[76] K. Muhr, 'The mountain of *Slewtrim* or Bessy Bell', *West Tyrone Historical Society Journal* 1 (2007), 72–90.

[77] W. Shaw Mason, *A Statistical Account, or Parochial Survey of Ireland, drawn up from the Communications of the Clergy*, 3 vols (Dublin: Graisberry and Campbell; London: Longman, Hurst, Rees, Orme, and Brown; Edinburgh: Archibald Constable, 1814–19), I, p. 109.

[78] I. Opie and P. Opie (ed.), *Oxford Dictionary of Nursery Rhymes*, rev. edn (Oxford: Clarendon, 1952), p. 71 (poem 39).

[79] J. B. Arthurs, 'The element Cal- in place-names', *Bulletin of the Ulster Place-Name Society*, series 1, 4 (1956), 28–31 (p. 29).

[80] P. McKay, 'Scots elements in townland names', *Ainm* 10 (2009), 1–26 (p. 3). Simon Taylor found Scottish examples of Scots *cauld* + *hame* 'cold home or dwelling' in Fife: Caldhame and Cadham (*Caldhame* 1497) in the parishes of Kettle and Leslie: S. Taylor with G. Márkus, *The Place-Names of Fife*, 5 vols (Donington: Shaun Tyas, 2006–12), II, pp. 262, 368.

names of English origin for townlands in other parts of Ireland, with names such as Coldblow, Coldcut, Coldfields, Coldharbour, Coldwells, and Coldwinter.

B. New creations in English

As suggested by de hÓir and Price, language shift in the east of Ireland encouraged by Scandinavian and then Norman settlers, especially in the area around Dublin called the Pale, meant that new names were created in English from early in the second millennium. New English-speaking owners following the Plantation created many more ownership names, first for their new dwellings, and then market towns and villages. By the eighteenth century established English-speaking landlords were developing and naming their houses and demesnes with names currently in fashion in England, some of which replaced the original townland names. (The fashion was not always for names in English – numerous houses were given French names such as Belvue, Belmont etc.)

The majority of new names were created for new entities, without previous existence in the Irish administrative system, such as new towns, villages, houses with demesnes, and townland subdivisions established by incoming landlords. As already mentioned, Éamonn de hÓir noted the frequency from Anglo-Norman times of place-names formed with a personal name + *town*.[81] It is clear from his examples that de hÓir included surnames among his 'personal names', and comparable Irish types have already been discussed above. Ownership place-names were not a new invention: only the language was new.

At the Plantation this pattern was still often used for the names of new towns:

> Mitchelstown in Co. Cork was *Ballyvestela* in 1589 (*Fiants Eliz.*), but the 'king's castle of *Michelstown* alias *Ballyvisteal'* in 1618. A suggestion has been made that it was called after a Norman, Mitchell Condon, who had held the castle <www.logainm.ie>.
>
> Lanesborough, a townland and town in Co. Longford, in the parish of Rathcline, was in 1617 a 'castle and fort of *Ballyleigg al. Bealaleig*', on the Roscommon bank of the Shannon. However, in the 1660s Sir George Lane was granted the 'manor of Lanesborough' intending him to found a town, and this seems to be the origin of the English name <www.logainm.ie>.
>
> Castleblayney town in Co. Monaghan takes its name from Sir Edward Blayney, governor of Monaghan, who was granted land by James I in the

[81] De hÓir, 'The anglicisation', pp. 193, 196.

early seventeenth century. Sir Edward built a small castle, no trace of which now remains, but the site of which is close to the eighteenth-century mansion originally known as Blayney Castle.[82]

The villages of Waringsford in the eighteenth century (originally a house name, in the parish of Garvaghy) and Waringstown, in the parish of Donaghcloney, Co. Down, were named from the family of a Cromwellian general who settled in Waringstown in 1666.[83]

Ballymena original townland and town in Co. Antrim was intended to be replaced by *Kinhiltstown*, drawing on the place of origin of the Adair family from Scotland, the seventeenth-century landlords.[84]

Edgeworthstown, Co. Longford, was created by Richard, father of the authoress Maria Edgeworth, in the late eighteenth century, and his family grew up on the estate. The original townland and parish name, anglicized as Mostrim, was partly supplanted by the name of the village. Both have continued in use.

In addition to the coining of new town and estate names, place-names were also susceptible to change and sometimes 'improvement' on grounds of taste. John O'Donovan was moved to comment on the replacement of minor place-names by the names of the Scottish landlord's three daughters on the Baronscourt estate, Co. Tyrone, in his edition of an Irish poem on the death of Brian Ó Néill, *c.* 1260. The poem praised this chieftain as 'Brian of *Loch Laeghaire*', and O'Donovan explained the background: 'the lake of *Laeghaire*. This lake was called after *Laeghaire Buadhach*, or Leary the victorious, one of the champions of the *Craebh Ruadh* or Red Branch in Ulster in the first century, who had his residence at it [...] The name of this lake is now corrupted to Lough Mary'. Commenting upon the transferred name Bessy Bell mentioned above, he continued: 'The change of names in this part of Ireland is remarkable, as appears from ancient maps of Ulster, such as *Sliabh Truim* to Bessy Bell, *Loch Laeghaire* to Lough Mary &c. &c. They will be restored when the Irish become national and rational, by the force of education and true taste'.[85]

However, incoming landlords were likely to prefer place-names in their own language, and also to see changes made by themselves as for

[82] McKay, *Dictionary*, p. 37.

[83] *PNI* 6, pp. 210, 100–01; McKay, *Dictionary*, p. 145.

[84] *PNI* 4, pp. 234–35.

[85] J. O'Donovan, *Miscellany of the Celtic Society* (Dublin: Celtic Society, 1849), pp. 162–63, note d (to l. 174).

the better. De hÓir included in his study of early anglicized place-names in Ireland the Latin names of Cistercian monasteries founded by the Normans, saying that '[i]n a number of cases […] names seem to be based on a form of punning – or possibly improvement'. One of his examples was that of *Rosea Vallis* ('rosy valley') which replaced the Irish name *Ros Glas* 'grey grove', Co. Laois,[86] a replacement term already noted in Rosegarland on Boazio's map.

Townlands and towns with two surviving names, Irish and English, may show anglophile aesthetic discrimination in replacing one with the other:

Townland	*Parish (County)*	*Meaning of Irish name*
Annaghboy or Rosebrook	Armagh (Armagh)	*eanach buí* 'yellow marsh'
Drishoge or Strawberryhill	Gallen (Kings)	*driseog* 'bramble, briar'
Pollaturk or Newgarden	Belclare (Galway)	*poll an tuirc* 'hollow of the boar'
Rathcam or Lemongrove	Enniscoffey (WMeath)	*ráth cam* 'crooked fort'
Breandrum or Windsor	Breaghwy (Mayo)	*bréandroim* 'stinking ridge'
Aughatubbrid or Chatsworth	Castlecomer (Kilkenny)	*achadh na tiobraide* 'field of the well'
Lecarrow Glebe or Britannia	Reynagh (Kings)	*leath-cheathramh* 'half-quarterland'
Ballyslattery or Newgrove	Tulla (Clare)	Does the English name resist Slattery ownership?
Tonlegee or Moorerow	Kilbride (WMeath)	*tón le gaoith* 'bottom to the wind'; the English attests to Moore ownership.

Townland names of Gaelic origin were also frequently replaced by the house name of the later landlord, and many of the examples above are no doubt house names in origin. Gardenhill townland, originally a house name in Fermanagh, seems to improve an earlier *Garbhchoill* 'rough wood'. Goldengrove in Co. Tipperary was in Irish *An Garrán* meaning simply 'the grove'. Goldengrove or Knocknamase townland in the parish of Ettagh, Co. Offaly, apparently gained its English name from a house

[86] De hÓir, 'The anglicisation', p. 200.

first appearing on Taylor and Skinner's road maps in 1777.[87] In Co. Down, Springvale (now called Ballywalter Park) is a house name which then became used as a townland name.[88] The townland name *Templecrone* 'St Crón's church' in Greyabbey parish was superseded by Mount Stewart, which was applied to the house built there in the late eighteenth century.[89] While Florencecourt in Fermanagh replaced the uncomfortable townland name Mullynashangan 'hill of the ants', Brookeborough is situated in the townland of Aghalun, much more charmingly *Achadh na Lon* 'field of the blackbirds'.[90]

Examination of townlands with dual names in north-west Co. Armagh reveals Bondville (from the landlord surname Bond) in the north of Tullybrick Etra or Bondville, Mount Irwin demesne in the north of Lissmeagh or Mount Irwin, Wood Park demesne in Ballynameta or Wood Park, and Ashford demesne in the north of Unshog – this time a part translation (*uinseog* 'ash-tree place') which did not displace the townland name.[91]

An English-language house name which became a townland name in fourteen instances across the island is Snugborough, which must have had considerable appeal in Ireland. The Snugborough in Co. Mayo appears to have been built in 1765 (<www.landedestates.ie>). The name Snugborough, however, is rare in England: Snugborough Mill in the parish of Blockley, Gloucestershire, appears to have been relatively recently bestowed, which may suggest the name's movement from Ireland to England rather than the other way round.[92]

A few supplanting names were those of public houses. The townland of Redcow, Co. Louth, was in Irish *Lios Bhaile Uí Réigín* 'O'Regan's ringfort', but gained its Irish name, according to John O'Donovan of the Ordnance Survey, from a 'public house having the sign of the red-cow'.[93]

An interesting feature in Ireland was the survival of a traditional Gaelic genre of stories about place-names, using place-names introduced in English or Scots as well as Irish: for example of the hunting down of a

[87] G. Taylor and A. Skinner, *Maps of the Roads of Ireland, Surveyed 1777* (London and Dublin: [published for the authors], 1778), pp. 97, 207.

[88] *PNI* 2, pp. 71–72.

[89] *PNI* 2, p. 208.

[90] McKay, *Dictionary*, pp. 29, 70.

[91] Armagh 6" sheet no. 15.

[92] It is not listed in A. H. Smith, *The Place-Names of Gloucestershire*, 4 vols (Cambridge: Cambridge University Press, 1964–65).

[93] <www.logainm.ie>.

magic cat—the house name Mount Panther in Co. Down[94]—and local battles in Co. Antrim: the Bloody Hill, Cork Hill, Breakback Hill, Slaughterford, Burnt House, Horse Loup, Wine Hill.[95]

Some English names were not considered socially acceptable. Oatencake townland, parish of Mogeesha Co. Cork (94 acres) was recorded as '4 acres of the Oaten Cake land' in the late eighteenth century, while an agent in 1844 said it 'originally took its name from the shape'. Griffith's Valuation objected to it as an 'unseemly name'.[96] John O'Donovan (whose dislike of imposed English names has already been noted) called Mockbeggar, the name of a small townland of 27 acres in the parish of Galloon, Fermanagh, an 'odious name', while he criticized Hurtletoot in Co. Antrim as 'some Scottish barbarism' (OSNB).[97]

Many minor names must have been given in English in recent centuries, and share in the range of minor names known in England. An example shown in Co. Wexford on Boazio's map is Bridewell, originating from the prison of the name in London. John Timbs, in the mid-nineteenth century, explained this common transferral: 'Bridewell is named from the famous well in the vicinity of St. Bride's Church; and this prison being the first of its kind, all other houses of correction, upon the same plan, were called Bridewells. In the *Nomenclator*, 1585, occurs "a workhouse where servants be tied to their work at *Bridewell*; a house of correction; a prison." We read of a treadmill at work at Bridewell in 1570'.[98] In Ireland there are many other examples, including in Carlow town, Cork city, Tarbert, North Kerry and a police (*garda*) station in Dublin.[99]

The battle against rebellious Americans at Bunker's Hill [Bunker Hill] near Boston, Massachusetts, in 1775, was a British victory but with heavy losses. Bunker seems to have been the surname of the American landowner, but popular interest from Ireland resulted in the name

[94] K. Muhr, 'Where did the Brown Bull die? An hypothesis from Ireland's epic *Táin Bó Cúailnge* version I', in R. Ó hUiginn and B. Ó Catháin (eds), *Ulidia 2: Proceedings of the Second International Conference on the Ulster Cycle of Tales, Maynooth 24–27 June 2005* (Maigh Nuad [Maynooth]: An Sagart, 2009), pp. 121–39 (pp. 138–39).

[95] Muhr, 'Place-names and Scottish clan traditions', pp. 80–82, 89, 91–92.

[96] Andrews, *A Paper Landscape*, p. 119.

[97] Probable translation 'hunched projection' in McKay, *Dictionary*, pp. 5–6.

[98] John Timbs, *Curiosities of London* (1867), text quoted from <www.victorianlondon.org/prisons/citybridewell.htm>. See also D. N. Parsons and T. Styles, *The Vocabulary of English Place-Names* II *(Brace–Cæster)* (Nottingham: Centre for English Name-Studies, 2000), p. 30.

[99] Pers. comm. Paul Tempan.

Bunker's Hill being given to a hill near Belfast. Contributors to 'Notes and Queries' in the *Ulster Journal of Archaeology* also informed readers that the Irish Bunker's Hill was so called by a family living there who were the first to hear about the battle, and that a local ballad commemorating the name-change had been composed in 1776.[100] As well as this example in Co. Down (grid J 3435) there are four others in Northern Ireland: in Co. Antrim at J 1098 and J 1467, in Co. Derry at C 5020, and Co. Tyrone at H 7057. There were also a number of examples in England.[101]

A local Irish creation was Bully's Acre, a name made the subject of a thesis and published article by Gary Dempsey.[102] Dempsey has found examples on local maps all over Ireland, generally referring to a burial site for the destitute, but the explanation seems to lie in the meaning of bully as a rough 'common man', and the sites often as unclaimed common ground.

Strategy 2: Transliteration and re-interpretation of place-names

The major place-names of Ireland had long been written down in Irish by the learned class, secular and ecclesiastical, who recorded not only the location of mythological and historical events but also the stories of place-name origins. Although Plantation surveyors recorded boundary descriptions from local members of learned families, they rarely noted the Irish spellings which these informants could have supplied. To add to its strangeness to an English reader, Irish in the Tudor period and much later was written in a manuscript hand with unfamiliar letter shapes.

Altering Irish spelling for outside use happened over a long period, and was well established long before the 1830s Ordnance Survey, although the Ordnance Survey has been complimented for becoming less draconian in its treatment of non-English place-names in Scotland and Wales.[103] The real cause was a perceived hierarchy of languages, and anglicization in Ireland the result of the 'wild' status accorded the Irish in Tudor times, when Ireland was a newly-conquered colony. However,

[100] See the various contributions in *Ulster Journal of Archaeology* series 2, 4 (1898), pp. 195, 263.

[101] See J. Field, *English Field-Names: A Dictionary* (Newton Abbott: David and Charles, 1972), pp. 32–33.

[102] G. Dempsey, 'In search of the "Bully's Acre"', *Archaeology Ireland* 23:3 (2009), 9–10.

[103] Andrews, '"More suitable to the English tongue"', p. 17; Ó Cadhla, *Civilizing Ireland* , pp. 220–21, 240, 245; Hewitt, *Map of a Nation*, pp. 191–94.

concern about the status of the Irish spelling of names compared with Latin had been expressed in the early ninth century by the scribe of the Book of Armagh, writing on names of churches believed to have been founded by St Patrick.[104] Likewise the papal taxation in 1302–06 did not attempt to record the names of parishes in their Irish spelling.

Most Gaelic place-names are formed of noun phrases, occasionally a noun alone, or with a preposition, but most often a noun defined by an adjective or another noun or name in the genitive. In the grammar of the Irish noun phrase, any adjective or descriptive genitive followed the noun, rather than preceded it as with word order in English. The spelling system of Irish was based on the Roman alphabet, but it did not make use, as English did, of the later variant letter shapes <j k v w y z>, while it extended the digraphs <ph th ch> for fricatives borrowed from Greek to their voiced equivalents as <bh dh gh>.

Irish has roughly the same phonemic set of stops used in English [p t k b d g] but also has a second palatalized set. The palatalized consonants were expressed by additional vowels. Early Irish also had all the complementary (place of articulation) fricatives and nasals for each of these stops, either within words or alternating as mutations of the radical within the noun phrase. These sounds include the velar fricatives and nasal [x] [γ] and [ŋ], which are restricted in range in English. Although some of the Irish fricatives ([β θ ð γ]) have now become semivowels or vowels, attempts to spell their earlier sound can still be found in anglicized place-names. Other sounds could also occur in combinations not now found in English, such as [kn]—current in both languages in the seventeenth century—and [sr]. Some consonant combinations had developed 'epenthetic' glide vowels between them, as in the stage-Irish pronunciation of film as 'fillum'. All of this, Irish words, grammar and sounds, required to be represented in any English transliteration of Irish place-names.

Only early anglicizations recorded Irish dental fricatives (voiceless [θ] and voiced [ð], as with the English spelling <th>) because this sound was lost in Irish in the thirteenth century.[105] However, the voiceless velar fricative [x] existed in both languages in the seventeenth century (surviving, unweakened, in Scottish Gaelic and Scots), and was

[104] L. Bieler, *Additamenta* 172, in L. Bieler (ed.), *The Patrician Texts in the Book of Armagh* (Dublin: Dublin Institute for Advanced Studies, 1979), pp. 11–26.

[105] T. F. O'Rahilly, 'Notes on Middle Irish pronunciation', *Hermathena* 20 (1930), 152–95.

anglicized in Ireland with the spelling <gh>, including in the middle of names like Ahoghill. The later English development of this sound to [f], as in rough and cough, had some influence in Ireland, as one can see in the surname Murphy anglicized from *Ó Murchú*. Anglicized spellings of place-names never attempted the palatalised /t/ still locally pronounced in the middle of Kiltymagh Co. Mayo, Meenatotan Co. Donegal, Gortin or Tattyreagh Co. Tyrone (*Coillte Mach, Mín an Toitín, Goirtín, An Táite Riabhach*), or the velar nasal in Cloghernagore Co. Donegal, Irish *Clochar na nGabhar*. Like Classical Irish spelling, early anglicizations (such as townland names) rarely attempted to spell the epenthetic vowel, although this does appear occasionally, as in the name of Limerick (with its part-Scandinavian history) and sometimes in minor names.

However, despite the variation in anglicized spellings 1600–1800, some regular conventions and correspondences emerge. Irish [kn] was anglicized <kn>, although the [n] alone is now pronounced in English. (Much later, when the Irish pronunciation had become [kr], the anglicized spelling <cr> was used.) As for the vowels, *a, i* followed by 'silent e' originally meant [a:] [i:], whatever changes have happened since; <ea> meant [e:] (a pronunciation which lasted for words so spelled in Irish English, like tea, beat, and beagle); and <oe> often meant [u:] as in shoe. The frequent anglicized spelling <y> was used for schwa [ə], the unstressed 'second vowel in Adam', for which there is no established spelling in English. It is worth noting that the same convention was adopted in the seventeenth-century anglicized spelling devised for Manx Gaelic.

The most far-reaching effect of anglicizing Irish place-names was to write them as one word instead of several, confusing the accent in the Irish noun-phrase, in which the first syllable of an adjective or descriptive genitive following the noun bore the main stress. (Individual words in Irish are mostly stressed on the first syllable.) Examples in earlier sources, such as the Tudor Fiants, are sometimes in two or more words:

> *Baelle Iossey* Fermanagh (for *Baile Uí Eodhusa* 'Hussey's holding', *Fiants Eliz.* §4810);
>
> *Neadd ne viagh*, West Connaught (for *Nead na bhFiach*, 'nest of the ravens', *Fiants Eliz.* §5808);
>
> *Avan na loggan boy*, a river in Tyrone (*Abhainn an Lagáin Bhuí* 'river of the yellow hollow', *Fiants Eliz.* §5993);
>
> a monastery of friars preachers, Co. Donegal, with the lands of *Kyllenne Crosse* (*Cill na Croise* 'church of the cross') and Ramullen alias *Farren ne*

braher (*Fearann na mBráthar* 'land of the Brothers') in the same country (*Fiants Eliz,* §6653).

Not all of these have yet been identified.

Local pronunciation often still preserves the stress pattern of the original Irish, as in the town names Ballinamore, Borrisokane, Carrigaline, Maghera,[106] but more urban, 'educated' or outside speakers may shift the stress to make it more like English. Partly because of the difficulty in determining the original word division, the process of researching back through anglicized forms of place-names to find the original Irish is not open to everyone. A feature sometimes regarded as quaint by English speakers is the (unofficial) use of the English article 'the' with place-names, which in most cases reflects and preserves usage in Irish, such as (The) Moy, Co. Tyrone.

While it may please modern enthusiasts for the Irish language to hear aspects of traditional pronunciation faithfully preserved, the same has not always been true. In the eighteenth century Jonathan Swift asked:

> How is it possible that a gentleman who lives in those parts where the *town lands* (as they call them) of his estate produce such odious sounds from the mouth, the throat and the nose, can be able to repeat the words without dislocating every muscle that is used in speaking, and without applying the same tone to all other words, in every language he understands?[107]

John O'Donovan in the nineteenth century also complained, although from a very different perspective, of the effect of supposed refinement in altering the pronunciation of Irish names, among both gentry and farmers.[108]

Over time many transliterated Irish place-names came to be spelled more and more as if they contained word-elements in English, probably partly as a mnemonic,[109] but also because of the intermittent desire of

[106] *Baile an Átha Móir* 'settlement of the big ford', *Buiríos Uí Chéin* 'O'Kean's burgage', *Carraig Uí Léighin* 'O'Leyne's rock', *Machaire Rátha* 'plain of the ringfort', stressed in each case on the final syllable of the anglicized form.

[107] J. Swift, 'On barbarous denominations in Ireland', in H. Davis (ed.), *The Prose Works of Jonathan Swift*, 16 vols (Oxford: Blackwell, 1941–74), IV, p. 280; quoted by A. J. Bliss, 'The emergence of modern English dialects in Ireland', in D. Ó Muirithe (ed.), *The English Language in Ireland* (Dublin: Mercier Press, 1977), pp. 7–19 (pp. 14–15).

[108] Ó Cadhla, *Civilizing Ireland*, p. 240, from A. Day and P. McWilliams (eds), *Ordnance Survey Memoirs of Ireland* (Belfast: The Queen's University Belfast, 1990–), vol. 36, p. 60.

[109] As suggested by Andrews, '"More suitable to the English tongue"', p. 13.

inhabitants to make linguistic sense of their place-name environment. English-speakers have thus to cope with the intriguing connotations of names such as Boolawater (Fermanagh), Finny (Meath), Lough Shark (Down), the Oily river (Donegal), Maze (Down), Muff (Derry), Muck (Kilkenny), Clay (Down), Quilty (Clare), Raw (several northern townlands), Rush (Dublin), Screen (Wexford), Trim (Meath), Smarmore, Yellowbatter (Louth). Themes appear to include avarice—Golden (Tipperary), Moneygold (Sligo), Moneysterlin (Derry), Moneymore (Derry), Derry Moneynick (Antrim), Moneydig (Down)—and violence—the Ow river (Wicklow), Batterjohn townland (Meath), Drumaknockan (Down), Swords (Dublin), Lough Arrow (Sligo), Dart Mountain (Derry/Tyrone), Skull (Cork, when not spelled Schull), several townlands called Scalp, many names beginning Kill, and Finish Island (Galway).

Talking about the dictation process of name transmission, described as 'a non-Celtic monoglot recording what he heard', Andrews says:[110]

> One bizarre and admittedly uncouth feature of this adaptive process [...] involves the use not just of English letter-sequences but of complete English words that partially match the sounds of the Irish name elements while carrying entirely different connotations. We have already met the examples of money [*muine*, 'thicket'] and beg [*beag*, 'little']. Others are batter (*bóthar*, 'road'), boy (*buidhe*, 'yellow'), [...] drum (*druim*, 'ridge'), glass (*glas*, 'green'), inch (*inis*, 'island'), kill (*cell*, 'church'), knock (*cnoc*, 'hill'), letter (*leitir*, 'slope'), more (*mór*, 'big'), muck (*muc*, 'pig'), roe (*ruadh*, 'red'), ton (*tón*, 'back'), Anna (*eanach*, 'marsh'), Garry (*garrdha*, 'garden'), Owen (*abhainn*, 'river'), Ross (*ros*, 'wood'), Terry (*tír*, 'land')

The history of individual anglicized place-names can reveal the wider processes at work. Early transliterated forms may be copied from other written documents, sometimes introducing alterations in the process. The more foreign the phonology of the original Irish, the more spelling variations there are likely to be, as can be seen in the recurring Irish placenames *Creamhchoill*, 'garlic wood', and *Leamhchoill*, 'elm wood', which in some cases ended up anglicized as Cranfield and Longfield.[111]

In general, of course, such anglicized names are entirely misleading. Drumaknockan in Co. Down refers to 'the ridge of the little hill',[112] although locally associated with the drums of an Orange band, and the

[110] Andrews, '"More suitable to the English tongue"', p. 13 – Irish length-marks restored.

[111] Muhr, 'Ulster place-name links', pp. 266–71.

[112] *PNI* 6, p. 120.

recurring place-name Kilmore is a ‘big church’, not an invitation to murder.[113] A number of further names, where the processes of anglicization have produced misleading English forms, follow:

The name of the Bush river, Co. Antrim, is derived from Irish *bó* ‘cow’.[114]

The Curlew Mountains in Cos Roscommon and Sligo represent Irish *An Corrshliabh* ‘the prominent or peaked upland’ (*GÉ*, p. 211).

Drains Bay in Co. Antrim takes its first element from Ir. *draighean* ‘blackthorn’.

The small rivers anglicized Flurry in Cos Armagh/Louth, and Fury and Fairy Water in Tyrone, come from *Fliuchraidh* ‘the wet one’, and a name *An Fheoraí* ‘the stream, rivulet’, possibly related to Early Irish *feraid* ‘pours’.[115]

Fourknocks, Co. Dublin, and the Foreglen, Co. Derry, take their first elements not from English ‘four’ or ‘fore’ but from Irish *fuar* ‘cold’.[116]

Glenlark in the Sperrin Mountains, Co. Tyrone, is ‘glen of forking streams’.[117]

Golden in Tipperary is from *Gabhailín* ‘little forking stream’, and Irish *gabhal* ‘[stream-]fork’ was regularly anglicized as gold, using a conventional addition of a final *-d* to a syllable closing in *l, n* or *r*, which occurs in anglicized forms of both place and family names, but has not been satisfactorily explained. In place-names the result is often the English ‘words’ gold, field, island, or land.

Lowertown townland in Skull parish, Co. Cork, was suggested as deriving from *Lubhghortán* ‘herb garden’ by John O’Donovan (OSNB); this also likely for Lowertown townland in Killyman, Tyrone which was spelled *Lourtan* in 1609. (Skull itself is completely misleading, since it means ‘school’, while Scalp is from a word meaning ‘fissure’.)

Man o’ War, a minor name in Co. Armagh, is believed to be anglicized from *Méan an Bhóthair* ‘the middle of the road’.

Longford, a county town which like Waterford does not derive from an early monastery, is an anglicized form of *longphort*, ‘ship encampment’, usually referring to a Scandinavian settlement.[118]

Money is the usual anglicization of Irish *muine* ‘thicket’ or *móineadh* ‘bog’,

[113] Muhr, ‘Ulster place-name links’, p. 259.

[114] McKay, *Dictionary*, p. 31.

[115] McKay, *Dictionary*, pp. 70–71.

[116] *Na Fuarchnoic* ‘the cold hills’ <www.logainm.ie>.

[117] McKay, *Dictionary*, p. 76.

[118] Mac Giolla Easpaig, ‘L’influence scandinave’, pp. 468–69.

but people were misled in nineteenth-century Co. Antrim into digging the cairn in Carnmoney, or the 'money cairn', in hopes of finding money inside![119]

Ovens, Co. Sligo, is from Irish *Na hUamhanna,* which means 'the caves' (*GÉ*, p. 261).

Raw or Ray, the name of a number of townlands (Armagh, Tyrone, Donegal) is from Irish *Ráth* 'a ringfort'.

Rosegarland townland in Ballylannan parish, Co. Wexford, had already been thus adapted from Irish *Ros Carlann* 'wooded height of the rocky place' on Boazio's map of Ireland mentioned earlier, while the townland of Rosgarran in Co. Derry, probably 'wooded height of horses', is sometimes also pronounced Rosegarland, via a frequent phonetic interchange in Irish of *r* and *l*.[120]

The 'smell and taste' townland name of Roselick in Ballyaghran parish, Co. Derry, has been shortened from the original anglicization, which was from 1306 until 1780 *Rosrelick*, from Irish *ros reilige* 'wooded height of the graveyard'. There is still a graveyard in the townland. Similarly, Lickmolassy parish in Galway is from *Leac Molaise* 'St Molaise's flagstone'.

Turbot Island, Co. Galway is from Irish *Tairbeirt* 'isthmus, place for carrying across' (*GÉ*, p. 279).

Upperland, townland and village, Co. Derry, arose as a peculiar anglicization of Irish *Áth an Phoirt Leathain* 'ford of the broad (river) bank' which became *Upperlane* and Upperland in some late-eighteenth-century parish registers but was still *Ampurtain* on Sampson's map in 1813.[121] The gradual corruption can be seen in the historical evidence: *aghfortlauy* 1609, *Aportlaughan* 1654, *Apportlane* 1793.[122]

Yellowbatter Park, Co. Louth, introduces two new categories of anglicization. It derives from *Páirc an Bhóthair Bhuí* 'field of the yellow road' (*GÉ*, p. 283), and is therefore partly a translation. 'Batter' can then be considered an anglicized respelling of *bóthar*, comparable with many of the examples above. However, *batter* became a loanword into English, as can be seen in names like Stonybatter, Magheralin, Co. Down, and Yellowbatter Park is to be analysed as translation plus loanword, as O'Rahilly

[119] Day and McWilliams (eds), *Ordnance Survey Memoirs of Ireland*, II, p. 70.

[120] *PNI* 5, pp. 103–05, quoting *PNI* 1, p. 154. The Norman surname Gernon had already become *Gernún* in Irish, but a variant in *-l-*, Garland, appears early, for example in 1560: George Garland alias Garnon, of the [...] lands of [...] Parysrath, Co. Meath (*Fiants Eliz* §280).

[121] *PNI* 5, p. 201; McKay, *Dictionary*, p. 144.

[122] *PNI* 5, p. 201, with full forms and sources.

recognized.[123]

Related to such processes are some modern unofficial name adaptations which are humorous, like Money-fer-nuthin for Mullaghfernaghan townland, Co. Down,[124] and Scare-the-Devil for Skerryravel townland, Co. Antrim. John O'Donovan showed this process—but in French—in his musing on the minor name Anwee in Ravara townland, Co. Down: 'Well might it be called *ennui*'.[125] A few are euphemistic: Devilsmother, a mountain or mountain range in Co. Galway, was in Irish *Magairlí an Deamhain* 'testicles of the Devil'.[126]

In the 1830s the Ordnance Survey attempted to standardize the anglicized spelling of names by employing the Irish scholar John O'Donovan to refer back to the original elements in Irish, but the strength of established convention often prevented any reform.[127] Nevertheless attempts at standardizing spellings have made possible books such as Tom Burnell's *The Anglicized Words of Irish Placenames*.[128] This is basically an attempt at a dictionary of anglicized elements, given in alphabetical order. Burnell represents the Irish originals of the names with dashes between the elements. Unfortunately he calls the Irish versions 'translations'.[129]

Strategy 3: Translation

Transliterated place-names could be erroneously interpreted as English words in the minds and mouths of English speakers, but, as presaged by early map-makers and suggested by Sir William Petty, some names are deliberate translations from the Irish. Some examples of explanatory translations offered in Plantation documents were given above; such instances are very rare, but one needs some documentary evidence of the Irish version to determine if a name in English is a translation or not. Some elements and equivalents seem to have been particularly transparent, usually either because the Irish and English terms had been borrowed from a common source (Latin or French) or the Gaelic word

[123] *PNI* 6, p. 254; O'Rahilly, 'Notes', pp. 180–81.

[124] *PNI* 6, p. 266.

[125] OSNB 35/56 Killinchy.

[126] <www.logainm.ie>. There is a similar name in Man.

[127] Andrews, *A Paper Landscape*, pp. 122–25.

[128] T. Burnell, *The Anglicized Words of Irish Placenames* (Dublin: Nonesuch, 2006).

[129] Burnell, *The Anglicized Words*, p. 7.

had been borrowed into English ('brae', 'cairn', 'glen', 'lough') or the native term was recognizably close to its English equivalent ('cat', 'new'). Words such as 'castle', 'cross', 'desert', 'park', 'port', and 'temple' were normally simply transferred from their Irish equivalents, since these were recognizable although in some cases slightly different in meaning ('castle' could represent Irish *caiseal*, a stone ringfort, as well as a later fortified dwelling, Irish *díseart* was a monastic site and *teampall* a Christian church, 'park' any field and 'port' an embankment or settlement not necessarily near the sea).

The Latin loan-word *mainistir* ('monastery') was regularly equated with 'abbey'. In the names Abbeydorney, Abbeyfeale, Abbeylara, Abbeyleix, only the first element has been translated, and Irish word order has been retained. A townland named *Shanvanister alias Old Abbaye* in Co. Kilkenny, in 1567 had a full translation, although no such townland survives.[130] Similarly, *muileann* from Latin *molendinum* is frequently rendered 'mill', as in Millwood townland in Aghalurcher, Co. Fermanagh, which was *Kilmillen* in 1659, *Kilnamullin* in 1668, and thus originally *Coill an Mhuilinn* 'wood of the mill'.[131] Again, *airgead*, Latin *argentum*, is commonly translated 'silver'. Thus Silverhill in Kilfarboy parish, Co. Clare, which is by a stream called Knockanarragid River (*Cnoc an Airgid* 'hill of the silver', with an epenthetic vowel represented in *-arragid*); while the Silverhand River, from Lough Owel to Lough Iron, Co. Westmeath, was in 1568 'the river called *Lawargitt*'.[132] The equivalence of *baile* and 'town', and their interchange from the Anglo-Norman period have already been illustrated.

An interesting article by Alan Crozier, comparing the transparency of place-names in England, Sweden and Ireland to their own native-speaker inhabitants, suggests that the translatable-ness of Irish-language names means that they must be relatively recent, so that the language had changed less from the date of coinage than typical place-names in the other languages. It is true that the lack of a native written genre of charter or survey means that few townland names were recorded before the Plantation, but the names of many churches and later parishes were recorded in the first millennium, and exist updated today. The difference appears to be cultural – names were considered significant and

[130] *Fiants Eliz.* §1175. Cf. Greyabbey, p. 397 below.

[131] *PNI* 8, p. 147.

[132] *Fiants Eliz.* §1240. It has a counterpart in the document in 'the water called *Lawore*', the 'golden hand' (Irish *lámh airgid, lámh óir*).

dindsenchas or expertise in explaining place-names was expected of the native learned class. Thus place-names and their etymological structure continued 'a living part of [...] speech',[133] and the interest and expectation of meaning were taken over by the English-speaking settlers. However, as already mentioned, the transparency of Irish place-names has been overrated.

Sometimes, as noted by de hÓir, the translation is not exact:[134]

> Kingscourt, Co. Cavan, is in the townland of Dunaree, *Dún an Rí*, meaning 'hillfort of the king'.[135]
>
> The hilltop monument called Vicars Carn, Co. Armagh, seems to be a translation of the townland name Carnavanaghan, in Irish *Carn an Mhanacháin*, 'cairn of the little monk'.[136]
>
> Woodend in Leckpatrick, Co. Tyrone, seems to be a translation name for the townland earlier called *Conkill* in 1654,[137] in Irish *Ceann Coille*, 'headland of the wood', since Irish *ceann* 'head' also means 'end'.
>
> Freshford, Co. Kilkenny, from *Achadh Úr* 'fresh field' (*GÉ*, p. 223).
>
> Roundstone, Co. Galway, from *Cloch na Rón* 'stone of the seals' (*GÉ*, p. 268).
>
> Watergrasshill, Co. Cork, from *Cnocán na Biolraí* 'little hill of the watercress' (*GÉ*, p. 281).
>
> Bettystown, Co. Meath, from *Baile an Biataigh* 'farmstead of the food-provider' (*GÉ*, p. 190).

Most current names of hostelries were coined in English. However, Twopothouse townland and village Co. Cork was *Teach an dá Phota* 'house of the two pots' in a poem by Dáibhídh Ó Bruadair who flourished *c.* 1625–97,[138] although it had been translated by 1755 (Newtwopothouse in *GÉ*, p. 259).

Many of these translated names must have been created as explanations, and one can see further illustration of the process in

[133] A. Crozier 'On the transparency of place-names in Ireland, England and Sweden', *Norna-Rapporter* 34 (1985), 33–50 (p. 37).

[134] De hÓir, 'The anglicisation', p. 199.

[135] McKay, *Dictionary*, p. 90.

[136] Irish attested earlier, on R. Bartlett, 1602–03, SE Ulster map, map 2 in *Barony maps of the escheated counties in Ireland, AD 1609*, 28 maps, PRO, published as *The Irish Historical Atlas* (Southampton: Ordnance Survey, 1861).

[137] Simington (ed.), *Civil Survey*, III, p. 392.

[138] J. McErlean (ed.), *Duanaire Dháibhidh Uí Bhruadair: The Poems of David Ó Bruadair*, 3 vols (London: Irish Text Society, 1910–17), II, p. 68.

townlands that were recorded in the townland index as having two current names, English and Irish. The following table, extracted from the Topographic Index, lists those townland name alternatives where the two names are apparently related by translation. (Inexact translations are corrected by the versions supplied at the end of the line.)

Townland and alias	*Civil Parish*	*County*	*Literal translation*
Abbeygrey or Monasternalea	Killeroran	Galway	
Abbeygrey or Monasternalca	Athleague	Galway	
Aghadrumgowna or Calf Field	Larah	Cavan	'field of the ridge of the calf'
Aghateggal or Ryefort	Denn	Cavan	'ford or field of the rye'
Ashglen or Glennafunshoge	Woolengrange	Kilkenny	
Ashtown or Ballinafunshoge	Derrylossary	Wicklow	
Ballinaspick or Bishopstown	Killare	Westmeath	
Ballindoo or Doocastle	Kilturra	Mayo	'townland of the black place'
Ballinkeeny or Mosstown	Killare	Westmeath	
Ballinriddery or Knightstown	Ardea	Queen's	
Balloughter or Hightown	Killucan	Westmeath	'upper settlement'
Ballynahoogh or Cavetown	Estersnow	Roscommon	
Barefield or Gortlumman	Templemaley	Clare	
Barratrough or Streamstown	Omey	Galway	'top of the stream'
Birchhall or Curraveha	Kilcummin	Galway	'marsh of the birch'
Bushfield or Maghernaskeagh	Aghaboe	Queen's	'plain of the thorn'

Castlecarragh or Castlerock	Kilmacteige	Sligo	'rocky castle' (note Irish word order)
Cloggernagh or Bellmount	Lissonuffy	Roscommon	'bell noise'
Cloverhill or Knocknashammer	Kilmacowen	Sligo	
Davidstown or Ballydaw	Monart	Wexford	(Daw is a pet form of David)
Deerfield or Gortnavea	Moycullen	Galway	
Drumalough or Lough Hill	Inishkeel	Donegal	
Drumanilra or Mounteagle	Tumna	Roscommon	
Drumsawry or Summerbank	Loughcrew	Meath	
Drumsillagh or Sallybank (Merritt)	Kilseily	Clare	
Drumsillagh or Sallybank (Parker)	Kilseily	Clare	
Dunanore or Goldentown	Oldross	Wexford	'fort of the gold'
Falnasoogaun or Ropefield	Kilvarnet	Sligo	
Feebrack or Nutgrove	Tynagh	Galway	'speckled wood'
Foorkill or Coldwood	Athenry	Galway	
Fordstown or Ballaghboy	Balrathboyne	Meath	'approach to the yellow ford'
Gallowstown or Lisnacroghy	Roscommon	Roscommon	'fort of the gallows'
Gallowstown or Ballynacroghy	Kilbixy	Westmeath	
Gardenham or Garrymore	Annaghdown	Galway	'big kitchen garden'
Gardenham or Garrymore	Lackagh	Galway	'big kitchen garden'

Glennameeltoge or Midgefield	Cloonfinlough	Roscommon	'glen of the midges'
Gortrory or Rogersfield	Killeany	Galway	Rory = 'Roger'
Gowel or Forkfield	Aghagower	Mayo	*gabhal* a 'forking stream'
Greyfield or Clylea	Kilmainemore	Mayo	'grey trench'
Hagfield or Treanacally	Kilbeagh	Mayo	'*trian*/third of the old woman'
Hollyfield or Edencullentragh	Rossinver	Sligo	'hillbrow of the holly place'
Hollymount or Knockaculleen	Ardcarn	Roscommon	'hill of the holly'
Kilstraghlan or Ragwood	Kilfree	Sligo	'wood of the tatter'
Knocknakillew or Woodhill	Cloonoghil	Sligo	
Lowtown or Balleighter	Killucan	Westmeath	
Mullyknock or Topped Mountain	Enniskillen	Fermanagh	
Oakfield or Gortnandarragh	Killannin	Galway	'field of the oaks'
Oakfield or Derrydarragh	St. Johns	Sligo	'oakwood of oak-trees'
Oldrock or Shancarrigeen	Cloonoghil	Sligo	
Owenavaddy or Riverstick	Killaan	Galway	'river of the "footstick"'
Roadstown or Ballinvally	Cloonoghil	Sligo	
Rochestown or Raheenarostia	Newbawn	Wexford	'Roches' little rath'
Runnateggal or Ryefield	Creeve	Roscommon	'portion of the rye'
Thornhill or Mullandreenagh	Killinagh	Cavan	
Tinakilly or Woodhouse	Kilmolash	Waterford	'house of the wood'
Trouthill or Knockbrack	Kilbcagh	Mayo	'speckled (= trout) hill'

Walshstown or Ballynabranagh	St. Mullin's	Carlow	*Breatnach* 'Welsh' (the Irish form of the surname Walsh)
Whitehill or Knockanbaun	Clonbroney	Longford	'little white hill'

The nature and frequency of English place-names in Ireland

In general the Ireland described in English-language place-names (of any origin) is rather different from its depiction in place-names in Irish, more built-up, more cultivated and managed. From analysis of the townlands of Ireland that appear to have English names we learn the following.

Of English name-elements that begin five or more townland names, the themes deal with:

<u>Landscape and nature</u>: ash, badger, beck, birch, bird, bloom, bog, briar, brook, broom, calf, cave, cherry, coney, dog, eagle, elm, flower, forest, fountain, fox, furze, grouse, hawk, hazel, heath, hill, holly, horse, lake, mead/ow, moss, mountain, oak, pigeon, rabbit, rose, rush, stream, sally, salt, sand, sea, sheep, spring, stone, sun, thorn, warren, water, well, wind.[139]

<u>Cultivation, agriculture, the managed environment</u>: acres, barley, bleach, brick, butter, common, corporation, dairy, deerpark, demesne, hay, hunt, manor, mill, orchard, paddock, pea, quarry, racecourse, rye, stang, stripe, town.

<u>The church</u> is mentioned, via the names of saints (though not so titled) Bride (Bridget) and Patrick, and Saint John; abbey (often translating Irish *Mainistir*), chapel, church, spital; bishop, dean, friar, monk, parson, priest, prior, vicar. Lady is also frequent, though probably not in a religious sense, and more likely to be matched with earl.

Other <u>buildings</u> are barn, bawn (a borrowing from Irish *bó-dhún*), cabin, castle, college, cottage, court, fort, gallows, lodge, and moat (in the sense of 'mound').

[139] It is notable that English-language place-names include a range of tree-species that were introduced and/or favoured by gardeners, including cherry, beech, chestnut, fir, larch, laurel, lime, maple, pear, rose and sycamore. Irish-language names naturally record many varieties of native trees and shrubs, including alder, apple, arbutus, ash, birch, elder, elm, gorse, hawthorn, hazel, holly, juniper, oak, rowan, whitethorn and yew, as well as ivy, bog-myrtle and woodbine. See further K. Muhr, 'Trees in Ireland in early tradition and place-names' (2005), online at <http://homepage.eircom.net/~archaeology/two/trees>.

There are also adjectives – of colour—black, brown, green, grey, red, white, yellow—and size—big, broad, great, high, little, long, low—and direction—top, upper, west—and age—new and old—and numerals—half, three, nine, twenty, forty, hundred.

House names that recur are Snugborough as already mentioned, Hermitage, and Prospect, but also names beginning Court or Mount (especially Mount Catherine, Mount Pleasant, Mount Prospect, Mount Sion), or many names based on Spring (plus -field, -grove, -hall, -hill, -mount, and -vale). Summerhill is also popular.

Personal names and surnames also feature as a significant element, those that recur being:

> Adams, Baggot, Baldwin, Baron, Barrett, Bell, Bennett, Bess, Blake, Blessington, Brown, Burton, Butler; Charles, Cook, Daly, David, Dawson, Edmond, Fanning, Fleming, Frank, French, Gibbons, Griffin, Hacket, Hammond, Harris, Herbert, Higgins, Hore, James, John, Jordan, Julian, Marshall, Mary, Miler/Myler, Mitchel, Moore, Nicholas, Paine, Palmer, Pembroke, Peppar, Philip, Pierce, Piper, Power, Punch, Randal, Richard, ?Rivers, Robert, Robin, Roche, Roger, Russell, Scot, Simon, Smith, Stafford, Staples, Stephen, Stokes, Tankard, Taylor, Thomas, Tyrell, Wall, Walsh, Walter, Ward, Warren, White, Williams, Wills.

Of these only Daly (*Ó Dálaigh*) is of Irish-language origin, although Higgins, Power and Ward may represent the Irish surnames *Ó hUiginn, de Paor,* and *Mac an Bhaird.*

Of course the Irish and English languages lived side by side for hundreds of years and any of these names could be translations, leaving none of the clues that can be seen in the 'reverse language order' English names commented on on Plantation maps (see Figs 1 and 2, pp. 366–67), and the half-translated abbey names mentioned above.[140]

The statistics for the proportion of English place-names in Ireland are not fully available, but some estimates have been made. Éamonn de hÓir presented several. In his opinion '[i]n the current place-names of the country as a whole English coinages are not too common and most of those are quite late names, often as late as the 18th century'.[141] However, '[i]n the small area of the Pale [...] there is a considerable number of English coinages, many of which date back to the period up to *c.* 1350'.

[140] See De hÓir, 'The anglicisation', p. 197 for the history of Castlewarden, Dublin.
[141] De hÓir, 'The anglicisation', p. 196.

He counted those in the *Calendar of Documents for Ireland*.[142] For all Ireland, he estimated 10% English coinages in the sources covering the period 1171–1250, and found a similar number in the late thirteenth century. As he says, these documents probably reflect the most Normanized parts of the island. De hÓir then quoted the place-name scholar Liam Price's estimate for the townland names of Co. Wicklow, part of the English-speaking Pale. Price says that 300–400 (25%) of the 1400 Wicklow townland names were 'first formed in the centuries following the Norman invasion'.[143] De hÓir thought the estimate 'rather high', but had no time to check. He continued, '[o]f the 860 or so townlands in the county [Dublin], about ⅔rds are of English and ⅓rd of Irish origin'. However, of the English two thirds, 'many are clearly late' and '[f]ar the most common type of English name coined is that of personal name + *town*'.[144]

The Northern Ireland Place-Name Project's base gazetteer was constructed initially from administrative names (townlands, parishes and baronies) combined with the place-names on the 1:50,000 map of the six counties of Northern Ireland. At this stage the research team made a rough estimate of the place-names not in Irish; the figures are no longer to hand, but the principal finding was that a small proportion of townland names were English, as against a large proportion of towns, villages and minor settlement names. My rough count of the number of parishes in Ireland agreed with an estimate seen elsewhere of a total of 3000 parishes overall, while English-language parish-names throughout Ireland came to about 300, equating to 10%. However, this count of parishes rather challenged my impression gained from Ulster that parish-names were less likely to be changed than those of townlands, since a number of parishes in provinces further south took their names from new villages founded and named in English, or they had been given English parish-names from church dedications, amounting to 10% of the whole. As for townland names, adding up the data for recurring initial themes (four, five or more names) in English, the figure arrived at was 3291, thus about 5% of the all-Ireland total of 62,000, though once the less-popular English initial elements were added the proportion might rise closer to 10%.

[142] Vols I (AD 1171–1250) and II (AD 1252–84) of H. S. Sweetman and G. F. Handcock (eds), *Calendar of Documents relating to Ireland*, 5 vols (London: Longman, 1875–86).

[143] L. Price, *The Place-Names of Co. Wicklow*, 7 fascicles (Dublin: Dublin Institute for Advanced Studies, 1945–67), I, p. lxxxv.

[144] De hÓir, 'The anglicisation', pp. 195–96.

Thus although the proportion of place-names of English origin in Ireland is clearly significant, it is not the dominant part of the namescape, as is immediately obvious to visitors and name-scholars alike. Moreover, from experience to date, further research is likely to reveal that a greater number of the apparently English names are derived from an Irish original, either by adaptation or translation. Hen Mountain in the Mourne Mountains (*Boirche*), Co. Down, was thought to be an English name, before the 1682 reference *sleaghnekirk* ('mountain of the hen', Irish *sliabh na circe*) made it clear that the name was originally Irish, and might be linked to an even earlier reference to the legendary *cearc Boirche* 'hen of Boirche'.[145] Another minor name Todd's Leap, in south Co. Tyrone, was thought possibly to contain a surname before the 1654 reference *Lemontony* ('leap of the fox', Irish *léim an tsionnaigh*) was discovered.[146] The translation *tod* uses a dialect word in Scots and English meaning 'fox', which is the origin of the surname.

Afterword: the complexity of language-contact

We have been dealing with the anglicization of Irish place-names, both those created in English and those which became English. However this happened over centuries (the actual date for individual names often being unknown) and the linguistic background was complex, reflecting interaction between speakers of several languages. Christianity ensured familiarity with Latin among the educated. It has been mentioned how the Scandinavian place-names indicate some influence from Irish, and the Anglo-Normans brought some French as well as English to the mix. The history of two townland names in Ulster will serve to demonstrate some of the possibilities for language contact.

The present name of Groomsport in Bangor, Co. Down, was represented in eighteenth-century Irish as *Port an Ghiolla Ghruama* 'the port of the gloomy fellow or attendant', but in 1333 it was *Mollerytoun,* probably containing the surname Mallory derived from French *le Malheureux* 'the unhappy one'. *Gilgroomes* appeared in 1620, *Ballymulleragh al Gilgrooms-Port* in 1623 and *Portgillegroome* in 1633. It appears that Irish *Giolla Gruama* is an Irish translation of the Norman-French surname (at first transliterated to Irish as *Mulleragh*), and that Groom is an English translation of the servant aspect of *Giolla Gruama,*

[145] *PNI* 1, p. 141.

[146] Simington (ed.), *Civil Survey*, III, p. 325.

compare Scots *gillie*.[147] A similar story can be told about the village and former monastery of Greyabbey: founded with a Latin name in 1193, *c.* 1580 it was described in English on a map as *Graye Abbaye,* and in English and anglicized Irish in 1585 as *Hore abbey alias Leighe* ('hoar' or *liath* 'grey' abbey). In 1603 it was *Monesterlee, Mainistir Liath* 'the grey abbey', a term used in Irish *c.* 1700, and all these terms, Latin, English and Irish, were recited in 1662 and 1717, before the present English name was settled upon.[148] Further research is needed before all the place-names of Ireland give up their stories.

[147] *PNI* 2, pp. 163–64.
[148] *PNI* 2, pp. 199–200.

Bibliography

Abrams, L., and D. N. Parsons, 'Place-names and the history of Scandinavian settlement in England', in J. Hines, A. Lane and M. Redknap (eds), *Land, Sea and Home: Proceedings of a Conference on Viking-period Settlement, at Cardiff, July 2001* (Leeds: Maney, 2004), pp. 379–431.

Adigard des Gautries, J., 'Études de toponymie Normannique II. Les *Caudecote*', *Études Germaniques* 8 (1953), 1–5.

Ainiala, T., 'Place names in the construction of social identities: the uses of names of Helsinki', in W. Ahrens et al. (eds), *Names in Multi-lingual, Multi-cultural and Multi-ethnic Contact* (Toronto: York University, 2009), pp. 67–75.

Aitken, R., *New Parish Atlas of Ayrshire: Vol. 1, Cunninghame* (Beith: Robert Aitken, 1829).

Allcroft, A. H., *Earthwork of England* (London: MacMillan, 1908).

Anderson, J. M., *The Grammar of Names* (Oxford: OUP, 2007).

Anderson, O. S. (ed.), *Old English Material in the Leningrad Manuscript of Bede's Ecclesiastical History* (Lund: C. W. K. Gleerup, 1941).

Andersson, T., '*Tuna*-problem', *Namn och Bygd* 56 (1968), 88–124.

Andersson, T., 'The origin of the *Tuna*-names reconsidered', in I. Wood and N. Lund (eds), *People and Places in Northern Europe 500–1600: Essays in Honour of Peter Hayes Sawyer* (Woodbridge: Boydell Press, 1991), pp. 197–204.

Andersson, T., 'Personennamen', *Reallexikon der Germanischen Altertumskunde*, 2nd edn, 22 (2003), 589–614.

Andrews, J. H., *A Paper Landscape* (Oxford: Clarendon, 1975).

Andrews, J. H., '"More suitable to the English tongue": the cartography of Irish placenames', *Ulster Local Studies* 14:2 (1992), 7–21.

Andrews, J. H., *Shapes of Ireland* (Dublin: Geography Publications, 1997).

Anttila, R., *Historical and Comparative Linguistics*, 2nd edn (Amsterdam and Philadelphia: John Benjamins, 1989).

Armstrong, A. M., A. Mawer, F. M. Stenton and B. Dickins, *The Place-Names of Cumberland*, 3 parts, EPNS 20–22 (Cambridge: CUP, 1950–52).

Armstrong, A. M., M. Gelling and K. Cameron, 'Some notes on the history of the EPNS', *JEPNS* 25 (1992–93), 1–8.

Arngart, O., 'On the *ingtūn* type of English place name', *Studia Neophilologica* 44 (1972), 263–73.

Arthurs, J. B., 'The element *Cal-* in place-names', *Bulletin of the Ulster Place-Name Society*, series 1, 4 (1956), 28–31.

Atkin, M., 'Viking race-courses? The distribution of *skeið* place-name elements in northern England', *JEPNS* 10 (1977–78), 26–39.

Autenrieth, J., D. Geuenich and K. Schmid (eds), *Das Verbrüderungsbuch der Abtei Reichenau (Einleitung, Register, Faksimile)* (Hanover: Hahnsche Buchhandlung, 1979).

Baker, A. R. H., and R. A. Butlin (eds), *Studies of Field Systems in the British Isles* (Cambridge: CUP, 1973).

Baker, J., *Cultural Transition in the Chilterns and Essex Region, 350AD to 650AD* (Hatfield: University of Hertfordshire Press, 2006).

Baker, J., 'Topographical place-names and the distribution of *tūn* and *hām* in the Chilterns and Essex region', *Anglo-Saxon Studies in Archaeology and History* 12 (2006), 50–62.

Baker, J., 'The language of Anglo-Saxon defence', in J. Baker, S. Brookes, and A. Reynolds (eds), *Landscapes of Defence in Early Medieval Europe* (Turnhout: Brepols, forthcoming 2013).

Baker, J., 'Warriors and watchmen: place-names and Anglo-Saxon civil defence', *Medieval Archaeology* 55 (2011), 258–67.

Baker, J., and S. Brookes, 'From frontier to border: the evolution of northern West Saxon territorial delineation in the ninth and tenth centuries', *Anglo-Saxon Studies in Archaeology and History* 17 (2011), 104–19.

Baker, J., S. Brookes and A. Reynolds, 'Landscapes of governance: assembly sites in England, fifth–eleventh century', *Post-Classical Archaeology* 1 (2011), 499–502.

Baker, J., S. Brookes and A. Reynolds, 'The law of the land: finding early medieval assembly sites', *British Archaeology* 120 (2011), 46–49.

Baker, J., and S. Brookes, *Beyond the Burghal Hidage: Anglo-Saxon Civil Defence in the Viking Age* (Leiden: Brill, 2013).

Barnes, M., 'Standardisation and variation in Migration- and Viking-Age Scandinavian', in K. Árnason (ed.), *Útnorður: West Nordic Standardisation and Variation* (Reykjavík: University of Iceland Press, 2003), pp. 47–66.

Barnes, M. P., and R. I. Page, *The Scandinavian Runic Inscriptions of Britain*, Runrön 19 (Uppsala: Uppsala Universitet, 2006).

Barrow, G. W. S. (ed.), *Regesta Regum Scotorum vol. I, The Acts of Malcolm IV* (Edinburgh: Edinburgh UP, 1960).

Barrow, G. W. S. (ed.), *Regesta Regum Scotorum vol. II, The Acts of William I* (Edinburgh: Edinburgh UP, 1971).

Barrow, G. W. S., *The Anglo-Norman Era in Scottish History* (Oxford: Clarendon, 1980).

Barrow, G. W. S., *Kingship and Unity: Scotland 1000–1306* (London: Arnold, 1981).

Barrow, G. W. S., 'The uses of place-names and Scottish history: pointers and pitfalls', in S. Taylor (ed.), *The Uses of Place-Names* (Edinburgh: Scottish Cultural Press, 1998), pp. 54–74.

Barrow, G. W. S., *The Kingdom of the Scots*, 2nd edn (Edinburgh: Edinburgh UP, 2003).

Bately, J. (ed.), *The Old English Orosius* (London: OUP for the Early English Text Society, 1980).

Bately, J. M. (ed.), *The Anglo-Saxon Chronicle: A Collaborative Edition. Volume 3 MS A* (Cambridge: Brewer, 1986).

Bately, J., 'Ohthere and Wulfstan in the Old English Orosius', in J. Bately and A. Englert (eds), *Ohthere's Voyages* (Roskilde: The Viking Ship Museum, 2007), pp. 10–58.

Beam, A., et al., *The People of Medieval Scotland, 1093–1314* (Glasgow and London, 2012) <www.poms.ac.uk>.

Beresford, G., *Caldecote: The Development and Desertion of a Hertfordshire Village* (Leeds: Maney, 2009).

Beresford, M., *Lost Villages of England* (London: Lutterworth Press, 1954).

Beverley Smith, Ll., 'Yr Iaith Gymraeg cyn 1536', in G. H. Jenkins (ed.), *Y Gymraeg yn ei Disgleirdeb* (Cardiff: University of Wales Press, 1997), pp. 15–44.

Bieler, L., *Additamenta* 172, in L. Bieler (ed.), *The Patrician Texts in the Book of Armagh* (Dublin: Dublin Institute for Advanced Studies, 1979), pp. 11–26.

Billy, P.-H., *Dictionnaire des noms de lieux de la France* (Paris: Errance 2011).

Birch, W. de Gray, *Cartularium Saxonicum*, 4 vols (London: Whiting, 1885–99)

Bjarni Aðalbjarnarson (ed.), *Heimskringla*, 3 vols, Íslenzk Fornrit 26–28 (Reykjavík: Íslenzka Fornritafélag, 1941–51).

Bjarni Einarsson (ed.), *Ágrip af Nóregskonunga Sǫgum. Fagrskinna – Nóregs Konunga Tal*, Íslenzk Fornrit 29 (Reykjavík: Íslenzka Fornritafélag, 1985).

Bjerrum, A., and C. Lisse, *Maribo Amts Stednavne*, Danmarks Stednavne 11 (Copenhagen: G. E. C. Gad, 1954).

Björkman, E., *Scandinavian Loan-Words in Middle English* (Halle: Niemeyer, 1900–02).

Björkman, E., *Nordische Personennamen in England in alt- und frühmittel-englischer Zeit* (Halle: Niemeyer, 1910).

Björkman, E., *Zur englischen Namenkunde* (Halle: Niemeyer, 1912).

Blair, J., *Anglo-Saxon Oxfordshire* (Stroud: Sutton, 1994).

Blake, M., '*W(e)alh tūn*: balancing the probabilities', in R. Jones and S. Semple (eds), *Sense of Place in Anglo-Saxon England* (Donington: Shaun Tyas, 2012), pp. 284–300.

Bleach, J., and R. Coates, 'Three more Walcots', *Journal of the English Place-Name Society* 19 (1986–87), 56–63;

Bliss, A. J., 'The emergence of modern English dialects in Ireland', in D. Ó Muirithe (ed.), *The English Language in Ireland* (Dublin: Mercier Press, 1977), pp. 7–19.

Bourne, J., 'Kingston place-names: an interim report', *JEPNS* 20 (1987–88), 13–37.

Bourne, J., 'The Place-Name Kingston and its Context', unpublished PhD thesis (University of Nottingham, 2012).

Bourne, J., 'The place-name Kingston and its context', in R. Jones and S. Semple (eds), *Sense of Place in Anglo-Saxon England* (Donington: Shaun Tyas, 2012), pp. 260–83.

Brink, S., 'Land, bygd, district och centralort i Sydsverige: Några bebyggelsehistoriska nedslag', in L. Larsson and B. Hårdh (eds), *Central Platser Centrala Frågor* (Stockholm: Almqvist and Wiksell, 1998), pp. 297–326.

Brockmüller, H., *Die Rostocker Personennamen bis 1304* (Rostock: Richard Beckmann, 1933).

Broderick, G., *Place-Names of the Isle of Man*, VI (Tübingen: Niemeyer, 2002).

Brooke, D., 'The Northumbrian settlements in Galloway and Carrick: an historical assessment', *Proceedings of the Society of Antiquaries of Scotland* 121 (1991), 295–327.

Brookes, S., 'Population ecology and multiple estate formation: the evidence from eastern Kent', in N. J. Higham and M. J. Ryan (eds), *The Landscape Archaeology of Anglo-Saxon England* (Woodbridge: Boydell Press, 2010), pp. 65–82.

Brooks, N. P., 'England in the ninth century: the crucible of defeat', *Transactions of the Royal Historical Society* 5th Series 29 (1979), 1–20.

Brooks, N. P., 'The Fonthill Letter, Ealdorman Ordlaf and Anglo-Saxon law in practice', in S. Baxter et al. (eds), *Early Medieval Studies in Memory of Patrick Wormald* (Farnham: Ashgate, 2009), pp. 301–17.

Brotherton, P., 'Celtic place-names and archaeology in Derbyshire', *Derbyshire Archaeological Journal* 125 (2005), 100–37.

Broun, D., *Scottish Independence and the Idea of Britain from the Picts to Alexander III* (Edinburgh: Edinburgh UP, 2007).

Brown, T. and G. Foard, 'The Saxon landscape: a regional perspective', in P. Everson and T. Williamson (eds), *The Archaeology of Landscape* (Manchester: Manchester UP, 1998), pp. 67–94.

Burnell, T., *The Anglicized Words of Irish Placenames* (Dublin: Nonesuch, 2006).

Byock, J., *Viking Age Iceland* (Harmondsworth: Penguin, 2001).

Cameron, A., et al., *Dictionary of Old English A–G*, version 2.0, CD-ROM (Toronto: Pontifical Institute of Mediaeval Studies, 2008).

Cameron, K., *The Place-Names of Derbyshire*, 3 parts, EPNS 27–29 (Cambridge: CUP, 1959).

Cameron, K., *Scandinavian Settlement in the Territory of the Five Boroughs: The Place-Name Evidence* (Nottingham: University of Nottingham, 1965).

Cameron, K., 'Scandinavian settlement in the territory of the Five Boroughs: the place-name evidence. Part II: place-names in *thorp*', *Mediaeval Scandinavia* 3 (1970), 35–49.

Cameron, K., 'Scandinavian settlement in the territory of the Five Boroughs: the place-name evidence. Part III: The Grimston-hybrids', in P. Clemoes and K. Hughes (eds), *England Before the Conquest: Studies in Primary Sources Presented to Dorothy Whitelock* (Cambridge: CUP, 1971), pp. 147–63.

Cameron, K., 'Eccles in English place-names', in K. Cameron (ed.), *Place-Name Evidence for the Anglo-Saxon Invasion and Scandinavian Settlements* (Nottingham: EPNS, 1975), pp. 1–7.

Cameron, K., (ed.), *Place-Name Evidence for the Anglo-Saxon Invasion and Scandinavian Settlements* (Nottingham: EPNS, 1975).

Cameron, K., 'The significance of English place-names', *Proceedings of the British Academy* 62 (1976), 135–55 [also published separately as the Sir Israel Gollancz Memorial Lecture].

Cameron, K., 'The Scandinavian settlement of eastern England: the place-name evidence', *Ortnamnssällskapets i Uppsala årsskrift* (1978), 7–17.

Cameron, K., 'The meaning and significance of Old English *walh* in English place-names', *Journal of the English Place-Name Society* 12 (1979–80), 1–53;

Cameron, K., with J. Field and J. Insley, *The Place-Names of Lincolnshire*, parts 1–7, EPNS 58, 64–65, 66, 71, 73, 77, 85 (Nottingham: EPNS, 1985–).

Cameron, K., 'Stenton and place-names', in D. Matthew (ed.), *Stenton's* Anglo-Saxon England *Fifty Years On: Papers Given at a Colloquium Held at Reading 11–12 November 1993* (Reading: University of Reading, 1994), pp. 31–48.

Cameron, K., *English Place-Names*, new edn (London: Batsford, 1996).

Cameron, K., 'The Scandinavian element in minor names and field-names in north-east Lincolnshire', *Nomina* 19 (1996), 5–27.

Cameron, K., with contributions by J. Insley, *A Dictionary of Lincolnshire Place-Names* (Nottingham: EPNS, 1998).

Campbell, A., *Old English Grammar* (Oxford: Clarendon 1959).

Campbell, A., (ed.), *The Chronicle of Æthelweard* (London: Nelson, 1962).

Campbell, J., 'Bede's words for places', in P. H. Sawyer (ed.), *Names, Words, and Graves: Early Medieval Settlement* (Leeds: University of Leeds, 1979), pp. 34–51.

Campbell, J., 'Stenton's *Anglo-Saxon England*, with special reference to the earlier period', in D. Matthew (ed.), *Stenton's* Anglo-Saxon England *Fifty Years On* (Reading: University of Reading, 1994), pp. 49–59.

Carr, G., *Hen Enwau o Arfon, Llŷn ac Eifionydd* (Caernarfon: Gwasg y Bwthyn, 2011).

Carroll, J., 'Coins and the Chronicle: mint-signatures, history, and language', in A. Jorgensen (ed.), *Reading the Anglo-Saxon Chronicle: Language, Literature, History* (Turnhout: Brepols, 2010), pp. 243–73.

Carroll, J. and D. N. Parsons, *Anglo-Saxon Mint-Names:* I. *Axbridge–Hythe* (Nottingham: EPNS, 2007).

Cavill, P., S. E. Harding and J. Jesch (eds), *Wirral and its Viking Heritage* (Nottingham: EPNS, 2000).

Chapman, A., *West Cotton, Raunds: A Study of Medieval Settlement Dynamics AD 450–1450.* (Oxford: Oxbow, 2010).

Charles, B. G., *Non-Celtic Place-Names in Wales* (London: UCL, 1938).

Charles, B. G., 'The Welsh, their language and place-names in Archenfield and Oswestry', in H. Lewis (ed.), *Angles and Britons* (Cardiff: University of Wales Press, 1963), pp. 85–110.

Charles, B. G., *The Place-Names of Pembrokeshire*, 2 vols (Aberystwyth: National Library of Wales, 1992).

Charles-Edwards, T. M., 'The distinction between land and moveable wealth in Anglo-Saxon England', in P. H. Sawyer (ed.), *Medieval Settlement: Continuity and Change* (London: Arnold, 1976), pp. 180–87.

Childe, V. G., *The Danube in Prehistory* (Oxford: OUP, 1929).

Chomsky, N., and M. Halle, *The Sound Pattern of English* (New York: Harper and Row, 1968).

Christensen, A. E., and E. Moltke, 'Hvilken (kong) Svend belejrede Hedeby', *Historisk Tidsskrift* 12 Række V, Hæfte 2 (1971), 297–236.

Christie, N., and P. Stamper (eds), *Medieval Rural Settlement: Britain and Ireland, AD 800–1600* (Oxford: Windgather, 2011).

Clancy, T. O., 'The Gall-Ghàidheil and Galloway', *Journal of Scottish Name Studies* 2 (2008), 19–50.

Clancy, T. O., 'Two Ayrshire place-names: 1. Pulprestwic; 2. Trearne', *Journal of Scottish Name Studies* 2 (2008), 99–114.

Clancy, T. O., 'Gaelic in medieval Scotland: advent and expansion' (The Sir John Rhŷs Memorial Lecture, 2009), *Proceedings of the British Academy* 167 (2011), 349–92.

Clancy, T. O., *Gaelic in Medieval Galloway: The Evidence of Names* (Whithorn: Friends of Whithorn Trust, 2013).

Clark, C., 'Towards a reassessment of "Anglo-Norman Influence on English Place-Names"', in P. Sture Ureland and G. Broderick (eds), *Language Contact in the British Isles: Proceedings of the Eighth International Symposium on Language Contact in Europe, Douglas, Isle of Man, 1988* (Tübingen: Niemeyer, 1991), pp. 275–95, repr. in P. Jackson (ed.), *Words, Names and History: Selected Papers of Cecily Clark* (Cambridge: Brewer 1995), pp. 144–55.

Clark, C., 'Domesday Book – a great red-herring: thoughts on some late-eleventh-century orthographies', in C. Hicks (ed.), *England in the Eleventh Century: Proceedings of the 1990 Harlaxton Symposium* (Stamford: Paul Watkins, 1992), pp. 317–31, repr. in P. Jackson (ed.), *Words, Names and History: Selected Papers of Cecily Clark* (Cambridge: Brewer 1995), pp. 156–67.

Clark, C., 'Onomastics', in R. M. Hogg (ed.), *The Cambridge History of the English Language*, I: *The Beginnings to 1066* (Cambridge: CUP, 1992), pp. 452–89.

Clark, C., 'Onomastics', in N. Blake (ed.), *The Cambridge History of the English Language*, II: *1066–1476* (Cambridge: CUP, 1992), pp. 542–606.

Clark, C., 'The myth of "the Anglo-Norman scribe"', in M. Rissanen et al. (eds) *History of Englishes: New Methods and Interpretations in Historical Linguistics* (Berlin: Mouton de Gruyter, 1992), pp. 117–29, repr. in P. Jackson (ed.), *Words, Names and History: Selected Papers of Cecily Clark* (Cambridge: Brewer 1995), pp. 168–78.

Coates, R., 'The Status of Rules in Historical Phonology', unpublished PhD thesis (University of Cambridge, 1977).

Coates, R., 'On an early date for OE *i*-mutation', in A. Crépin (ed.), *Linguistic and Stylistic Studies in Medieval English* (Paris: Association des médiévistes anglicistes de l'enseignement supérieur, 1984), pp. 25–37.

Coates, R., 'Towards an explanation of the Kentish *-mondens*', *JEPNS* 18 (1986), 40–47.

Coates, R., 'Pragmatic sources of analogical reformation', *Journal of Linguistics* 23 (1987), 319–40.

Coates, R., *Toponymic Topics: Essays on the Early Toponymy of the British Isles* (Brighton: Younsmere, 1988).

Coates, R., *The Place-Names of Hampshire* (London: Batsford, 1989).

Coates, R., 'Æthelflæd's fortification of Weardburh', *Notes & Queries* 243 (1998), 9–12.

Coates, R., 'Heel your ho, boys....', *Locus Focus: Forum of the Sussex Place-Names Net* 4:1 (2000), 16.

Coates, R., 'Singular definite expressions with a unique denotatum and the limits of properhood', *Linguistics* 38:6 (2000), 1161–74.

Coates, R., 'The significances of Celtic place-names in England', in M. Filppula et al. (eds), *The Celtic Roots of English* (Joensuu: Joensuu UP, 2002), pp. 47–85.

Coates, R., 'Microdialectological investigations in the English south-east', *Locus Focus: Forum of the Sussex Place-Names Net* 7:1/2 (2003–07), 62–80.

Coates, R., 'Chesterblade, Somerset, with a reflection on the element *chester*', *JEPNS* 38 (2006), 5–12.

Coates, R., 'Maiden Castle, Geoffrey of Monmouth and Hārūn al-Rašīd', *Nomina* 29 (2006), 5–60.

Coates, R., 'Properhood', *Language* 82:2 (2006), 356–82.

Coates, R., 'Some consequences and critiques of The Pragmatic Theory of Properhood', *Onoma* 41 (2006), 27–44.

Coates, R., 'The pre-English name of Dorchester on Thames', *Studia Celtica* 40 (2006), 51–62.

Coates, R., 'Invisible Britons: the view from linguistics', in N. J. Higham (ed.), *Britons in Anglo-Saxon England* (Woodbridge: Boydell, 2007), pp. 172–91.

Coates, R., 'Invisible Britons: the view from toponomastics', in P. Cavill and G. Broderick (eds), *Language Contact in the Place-Names of Britain and Ireland* (Nottingham: EPNS, 2007), pp. 43–55.

Coates, R., 'South-West English *dumball*, *dumble*, *dunball* "pasture subject to (occasional) tidal flooding"', *JEPNS* 39 (2007), 59–72.

Coates, R., 'Reflections on some major Lincolnshire place-names, part 1: Algarkirk to Melton Ross', *JEPNS* 40 (2008), 35–95.

Coates, R., 'A glimpse through a dirty window into an unlit house: names of some north-west European islands', in W. Ahrens et al. (eds), *Names in Multi-lingual, Multi-cultural and Multi-ethnic Contact* (Toronto: York University, 2009), pp. 228–42 [CD-ROM].

Coates, R., 'A strictly Millian approach to the definition of the proper name', *Mind and Language* 24:4 (2009), 433–44.

Coates, R., 'Reflections on some major Lincolnshire place-names, part 2: Ness wapentake to Yarborough', *JEPNS* 41 (2009), 57–102.

Coates, R., 'The sociolinguistic context of Brunanburh', in M. D. Livingston (ed.), *The Battle of Brunanburh: A Casebook* (Exeter: University of Exeter Press, 2011), pp. 365–84.

Coates, R., '*to þære fulan flóde óf þære fulan flode*: on becoming a name in Easton and Winchester, Hampshire', in D. Denison et al. (eds), *Analysing Older English* (Cambridge: CUP, 2011), pp. 28–34.

Coates, R., '"Agricultural" compound terms and names in *tūn* like *Acton* and *Barton*', in R. Jones and S. Semple (eds), *Sense of Place in Anglo-Saxon England* (Donington: Shaun Tyas, 2012), pp. 211–37.

Coates, R., and A. Breeze, *Celtic Voices, English Places: Studies of the Celtic Impact on Place-Names in England* (Stamford: Shaun Tyas, 2000).

Cole, A., 'Topography, hydrology, and place-names in the chalklands of southern England: *cumb* and *denu*', *Nomina* 6 (1982), 73–87.

Cole, A., 'Topography, hydrology and place-names in the chalklands of southern England: **funta*, *ǣwiell* and *ǣwielm*', *Nomina* 9 (1985), 3–19.

Cole, A., 'The distribution and usage of the OE place-name *cealc*', *JEPNS* 19 (1986–87), 45–55.

Cole, A., 'The meaning of the Old English place-name element *ōra*', *JEPNS* 21 (1988–89), 15–22.

Cole, A., 'The origin, distribution and use of the place-name element *ōra* and its relationship to the element *ofer*', *JEPNS* 22 (1989–90), 26–41.

Cole, A., '*Burna* and *brōc*: problems involved in retrieving the Old English usage of these place-name elements', *JEPNS* 23 (1990–91), 26–48.

Cole, A., 'Distribution and use of the Old English place-name *mere-tūn*', *JEPNS* 24 (1991–92), 30–41.

Cole, A., 'The distribution and use of *mere* as a generic in place-names', *JEPNS* 25 (1992–93), 38–50.

Cole, A., 'The Anglo-Saxon traveller', *Nomina* 17 (1994), 7–18.

Cole, A., '*Flēot*: distribution and use of this OE place-name element', *JEPNS* 29 (1996–97), 79–87.

Cole, A., '*Cisel*, *grēot*, *stān* and the four U's', *JEPNS* 31 (1998–99), 19–30.

Cole, A., '*Ersc*: distribution and use of this Old English place-name element', *JEPNS* 32 (1999–2000), 27–40.

Cole, A., 'The place-name evidence for water transport in early medieval England', in J. Blair (ed.), *Waterways and Canal-Building in Medieval England* (Oxford: OUP, 2007), pp. 55–84.

Cole, A., '*Weg*: a waggoner's warning', in O. J. Padel and D. N. Parsons (eds), *A Commodity of Good Names: Essays in Honour of Margaret Gelling* (Donington: Shaun Tyas, 2008), pp. 345–49.

Cole, A., '*Tūns* by the wayside', in R. Jones and S. Semple (eds), *Sense of Place in Anglo-Saxon England* (Donington: Shaun Tyas, 2012), pp. 243–59.

Colfer, B., 'The ethnic mix in medieval Wexford', *History Ireland* (Spring 2002), 19–23.

Colgrave, B., and R.A.B. Mynors (eds), *Bede's Ecclesiastical History of the English People* (Oxford: Clarendon, 1969).

Collingwood, R. G., *The Idea of History*, rev. edn (Oxford: OUP, 1993).

Collingwood, W. G., *Scandinavian Britain* (London: SPCK, 1908).

Collingwood, W. G., 'Mountain-names', *Transactions of the Cumberland and Westmorland Antiquarian and Archaeological Society* New Series 18 (1918), 93–104.

Colman, F.,'The name-element *Æðel-* and related problems', *Notes and Queries*, n.s., 28 (1981), 295–301.

Colman, F., *Money Talks: Reconstructing Old English* (Berlin and New York: Mouton de Gruyter, 1992).

Cooper, C., *Grammatica linguae anglicanae* (London, 1685; repr. Menston: Scolar Press, 1968).

Coplestone-Crow, B., *Herefordshire Place-Names* (Oxford: BAR, 1989).

Costen, M., 'The field names of Shapwick', in C. Gerrard with M. Aston, *The Shapwick Project, Somerset: a Rural Landscape Explored* (Leeds: Maney, 2007), pp. 1078–83.

Cox, B., 'The significance of the distribution of English place-names in *hām* in the Midlands and East Anglia', *JEPNS* 5 (1972–73), 15–73.

Cox, B., 'The place-names of the earliest English records', *JEPNS* 8 (1975–6), 12–66.

Cox, B., *The Place-Names of Rutland*, EPNS 67–69 (Nottingham: EPNS, 1994).

Cox, B., *The Place-Names of Leicestershire*, parts 1–5, EPNS 75, 78, 81, 84, 88 (Nottingham: EPNS, 1998–).

Cox, B., *A Dictionary of Leicestershire and Rutland Place-Names* (Nottingham: EPNS, 2006).

Cox, B., 'Dimmingsdale', in O. J. Padel and D. N. Parsons (eds), *A Commodity of Good Names: Essays in Honour of Margaret Gelling* (Donington: Shaun Tyas, 2008), pp. 350–51.

Cox, R. A., *The Place-Names of Carloway, Isle of Lewis: Their Structure and Significance* (Dublin: Dublin Institute for Advanced Studies, 2002).

Cox, R.A., 'Towards a taxonomy of contact onomastics: Norse place-names in Scottish Gaelic', *Journal of Scottish Name Studies* 3 (2009), 15–28.

Crawford, O. G. S., *Notes on Archaeological Information Incorporated in the Ordnance Survey Maps, Part 1: Long barrows and Stone Circles*, OS Professional Paper 6 (London: HMSO, 1922).

Crawford, O. G. S., *Notes on Archaeological Information Incorporated in the Ordnance Survey Maps, Part 2: Long Barrows and Megaliths*, OS Professional Paper 8 (London: HMSO, 1924).

Crawford, O. G. S., 'Place-names and archaeology', in A. Mawer and F. M. Stenton (eds), *Introduction to the Survey of English Place-Names*, EPNS 1.i (Cambridge: CUP, 1924), pp. 143–64.

Crawford, O. G. S., 'Air photograph of Gainsthorpe, Lincolnshire', *Antiquaries Journal* 5 (1925), 432–33.

Croft, W., *Radical Construction Grammar: Syntactic Theory in Typological Perspective* (Oxford: OUP, 2001).

Crowley, T., *The Politics of Language in Ireland 1366–1922: A Sourcebook* (London: Routledge, 2000).

Crozier, A., 'On the transparency of place-names in Ireland, England and Sweden', *Norna-Rapporter* 34 (1985), 33–50.

Crumlin-Pedersen, O., *Viking-Age Ships and Shipbuilding in Hedeby/Haithabu and Schleswig* (Schleswig and Roskilde: Archäologisches Landesmuseum/The Viking Ship Museum, 1997).

Cullen, P., '*Vagniacis* and Winfield: the survival of a British place-name in Kent', in O. J. Padel and D. N. Parsons (eds), *A Commodity of Good Names: Essays in Honour of Margaret Gelling* (Donington: Shaun Tyas, 2008), pp. 95–100.

Cullen, P. 'The place-names of the Lathes of St Augustine and Shipway, Kent' unpublished PhD thesis (University of Kent, 1997).

Cullen, P., R. Jones and D. N. Parsons, *Thorps in a Changing Landscape* (Hatfield: University of Hertfordshire Press, 2011).

Darby, H. C., 'Place-names and the geography of the past', in A. Brown and P. Foote (eds), *Early English and Norse Studies Presented to Hugh Smith* (London: Methuen, 1963), pp. 6–18.

Day, A., and P. McWilliams (eds), *Ordnance Survey Memoirs of Ireland* (Belfast: The Queen's University Belfast, 1990–).

de hÓir, É., 'The anglicisation of Irish place-names', *Onoma* 17 (1972/73), 192–204.

Dempsey, G., 'In search of the "Bully's Acre"', *Archaeology Ireland* 23:3 (2009), 9–10.

De Stefani, E., and N. Pepin, 'Une approche interactionniste de l'étude des noms propres: Les surnoms de famille', *Onoma* 41 (2006), 131–62.

Dickinson, T., 'The formation of a folk district in the kingdom of Kent and its early Anglo-Saxon archaeology', in R. Jones and S. Semple (eds), *Sense of Place in Anglo-Saxon England* (Donington: Shaun Tyas, 2012), pp. 147–67.

Dixon, N., 'The Place-Names of Midlothian', unpublished PhD thesis (University of Edinburgh, 1947) [available online at < www.spns.org.uk/Dixon_Prelims.html>].

Dodgson, J. McN., 'The significance of the distribution of the English place-name in *-ingas*, *-inga-* in south-east England', *Medieval Archaeology* 10 (1966), 1–29.

Dodgson, J. McN., 'The English arrival in Cheshire', *Transactions of the Historic Society of Lancashire and Cheshire* 119 (1968 for 1967), 1–37.

Dodgson, J. McN., 'Place-names from *hām*, distinguished from *hamm* names, in relation to the settlement of Kent, Surrey and Sussex', *Anglo-Saxon England* 2 (1973), 1–50.

Dodgson, J. McN., *The Place-Names of Cheshire*, 5 parts, EPNS 44–47, 48, 54, 74 (Cambridge: CUP, 1970–97).

Doherty, C., 'Settlement in early Ireland: a review', in T. Barry (ed.), *A History of Settlement in Ireland* (London and New York: Routledge, 2000), pp. 50–80.

Dolch, M., and A. Greule, *Historisches Siedlungsnamenbuch der Pfalz* (Speyer: Verlag der Pfälzischen Gesellschaft zur Förderung der Wissenschaften in Speyer, 1991).

Dolley, R. H. M., and F. Elmore Jones, 'The mints "Æt Gothabyrig" and "Æt Sith(m)estebyrig"', *British Numismatic Journal* 28 (1957), 279–82.

Draper, S., 'Old English *wic* and *walh*: Britons and Saxons in post-Roman Wiltshire', *Landscape History* 24 (2002), 29–43.

Draper, S., *Landscape, Settlement and Society in Roman and Early Medieval Wiltshire* (Oxford: Archaeopress, 2006).

Draper, S., 'The significance of OE *burh* in Anglo-Saxon England', *Anglo-Saxon Studies in Archaeology and History* 15 (2008), 240–253.

Draper, S., '*Burh* place-names in Anglo-Saxon England', *JEPNS* 41 (2010), 103–117.

Draper, S., 'Language and the Anglo-Saxon landscape: towards an archaeological interpretation of place-names in Wiltshire', in N. J. Higham and M. J. Ryan (eds), *Place-Names, Language and the Anglo-Saxon Landscape* (Woodbridge: Boydell Press, 2011), pp. 85–104.

Draper, S., '*Burh* enclosures in Anglo-Saxon settlements: case-studies in Wiltshire', in R. Jones and S. Semple (eds), *Sense of Place in Anglo-Saxon England* (Donington: Shaun Tyas, 2012), pp. 334–51.

Dumville, D. N., 'The atheling: a study in Anglo-Saxon constitutional history', *Anglo-Saxon England* 8 (1979), 1–33.

Dumville, D. N., 'The historical value of the *Historia Brittonum*', in R. Barber (ed.), *Arthurian Literature VI* (Cambridge: D. S. Brewer, 1986), pp. 1–26.

Duncan, A. A. M. (ed.), *Regesta Regum Scotorum vol. V: The Acts of Robert I* (Edinburgh: Edinburgh UP, 1988).

Dyer, C., 'Place-names and pottery' in O. J. Padel and D. N. Parsons (eds), *A Commodity of Good Names: Essays in Honour of Margaret Gelling* (Donington: Shaun Tyas, 2008), pp. 44–54.

Edmonds, F., 'A twelfth-century migration from Tegeingl to Lancashire', in T. M. Charles-Edwards and R. J. W. Evans (eds), *Wales and the Wider World: Welsh History in an International Context* (Donington: Shaun Tyas, 2010), pp. 28–56.

Ehmer, H., *Die sächsischen Siedlungen auf dem französischen „Litus Saxonicum"* (Halle: Niemeyer, 1937).

Eilersgaard Christensen, L., *Stednavne som kilde til yngre jernalders centralpladser* (Copenhagen: Det Humanistiske Fakultet, 2010).

Ekwall, E., *Contributions to the History of Old English Dialects* (Lund: C. W. K. Gleerup, 1917).

Ekwall, E., *Scandinavians and Celts in the North-West of England* (Lund: Gleerup, 1918).

Ekwall, E., *The Place-Names of Lancashire* (Manchester: Manchester UP, 1922).

Ekwall, E., 'The Celtic element', in A. Mawer and F. M. Stenton (eds), *Introduction to the Survey of English Place-Names*, EPNS 1.i (Cambridge: CUP, 1924), pp. 15–35.

Ekwall, E., 'The Scandinavian Element', in A. Mawer and F.M. Stenton (eds), *Introduction to the Survey of English Place-Names*, EPNS 1.i (Cambridge: CUP, 1924), pp. 55–92.

Ekwall, E., *English River-Names* (Oxford: Clarendon, 1928).

Ekwall, E., *Studies on English Place- and Personal Names* (Lund: C. W. K. Gleerup, 1931).

Ekwall, E., 'The Scandinavian settlement', in H. C. Darby (ed.), *An Historical Geography of England Before AD 1800: Fourteen Studies* (Cambridge, 1936), pp. 133–64.

Ekwall, E., 'The proportion of Scandinavian settlers in the Danelaw', *Saga-Book of the Viking Society* 12 (1937–45), 19–34.

Ekwall, E., *Early London Personal Names* (Lund: C. W. K. Gleerup, 1947).

Ekwall, E., *The Concise Oxford Dictionary of English Place-Names*, 4th edn (Oxford: Clarendon, 1960).

Ekwall, E., *English Place-Names in* -ing, 2nd edn (Lund: C. W. K. Gleerup, 1962).

Ellwood, T., *The Landnama Book of Iceland as it Illustrates the Dialect, Place Names, Folklore, & Antiquities of Cumberland, Westmorland and North Lancashire* (Kendal: Wilson, 1894).

Ellwood, T. (trans.), *The Book of the Settlement of Iceland, Translated from the Original Icelandic of Ari the Learned* (Kendal: Wilson, 1898).

English, J., '*Worth*s in a landscape context', *Landscape History* 24 (2002), 45–52.

Evans, D. E., *Gaulish Personal Names: A Study of Some Continental Celtic Formations* (Oxford: Clarendon, 1967).

Everitt, A., 'Place-names and *pays*: the Kentish evidence', *Nomina* 3 (1979), 95–112.

Everitt, A., *Continuity and Colonization: the Evolution of Kentish Settlement* (Leicester: Leicester UP, 1986).

Everitt, A., 'Common land', in J. Thirsk (ed.), *The English Rural Landscape* (Oxford: OUP, 2000), pp. 210–35.

Everson, P., and D. Stocker, *Custodians of Continuity? The Premonstratensian Abbey at Barlings and the Landscape of Ritual* (Sleaford: Heritage Trust of Lincolnshire, 2011).

Faith, R., *The English Peasantry and the Growth of Lordship* (London: Leicester UP, 1997).

Faith, R., 'Worthys and enclosures', *Medieval Settlement Research Group Annual Report* 21 (2006), 9–14.

Falileyev, A. et al., *Dictionary of Continental Celtic Place-Names* (Aberystwyth: CMSC, 2010).

Faull, M. L., 'The semantic development of Old English *wealh*', *Leeds Studies in English* 8 (1975), 20–44.

Fell, C., 'A *friwif locbore* revisited', *Anglo-Saxon England* 13 (1984), 157–65.

Fell, C., C. Clark and E. Williams, *Women in Anglo-Saxon England and the Impact of 1066* (Oxford: Blackwell, 1984).

Fellows Jensen, G., *Scandinavian Personal Names in Lincolnshire and Yorkshire* (Copenhagen: Akademisk Forlag, 1968).

Fellows Jensen, G. 'The scribe of the Lindsey Survey', *Namn och Bygd* 57 (1969), 58–74.

Fellows Jensen, G., *Scandinavian Settlement Names in Yorkshire* (Copenhagen: Akademisk Forlag, 1972).

Fellows-Jensen, G., 'English field-names and the Danish settlement', in P. Andersen et al. (eds), *Festskrift til Kristian Hald: navneforskning, dialektologi, sproghistorie* (Copenhagen: Akademisk Forlag, 1974), pp. 45–55.

Fellows Jensen, G., 'English place-names such as Doddington and Donnington', *Sydsvenska ortnamnssällskapets årsskrift* (1974), 26–65.

Fellows-Jensen, G., 'The Vikings in England: a review', *Anglo-Saxon England* 4 (1975), 181–206.

Fellows-Jensen, G., 'A Gaelic-Scandinavian loan-word in English place-names', *JEPNS* 10 (1977–78), 18–25.

Fellows Jensen, G., *Scandinavian Settlement Names in the East Midlands* (Copenhagen: Akademisk Forlag, 1978).

Fellows-Jensen, G., *Scandinavian Settlement Names in the North-West* (Copenhagen: Reitzels Forlag, 1985).

Fellows-Jensen, G., 'Danish lake- and river-names in England', in V. Dalberg and G. Fellows-Jensen (eds), *Mange Bække Små: Til John Kousgård Sørensen på tresårsdagen 6.12.1985* (Copenhagen: Reitzels Forlag, 1986), pp. 59–74.

Fellows-Jensen, G., 'The Vikings' relationship with Christianity in the British Isles: the evidence of place-names containing the element *kirkja*', in J. E. Knirk (ed.), *Proceedings of the Tenth Viking Congress: Larkollen, Norway, 1985* (Oslo: Universitetets Oldsaksamling, 1987), pp. 295–307.

Fellows-Jensen, G., 'To divide the Danes from the Norwegians: on Scandinavian settlement in the British Isles', *Nomina* 11 (1987), 35–60.

Fellows-Jensen, G., 'Scandinavians in Southern Scotland?', *Nomina* 13 (1989–90), 41–60.

Fellows-Jensen, G., 'Place-names in *-þorp*: in retrospect and turmoil', *Nomina* 15 (1991–92), 35–51

Fellows-Jensen, G., 'Tingwall, Dingwall and Thingwall', *North-Western European Language Evolution* 21/22 (1993), 53–67.

Fellows-Jensen, G., 'Les noms de lieux d'origin scandinave et la colonisation viking en Normandie. Examen critique de la question', *Proxima Thulé* 1 (1994), 63–103.

Fellows-Jensen, G., *The Vikings and their Victims: The Verdict of the Names* (London: University College and Viking Society for Northern Research, 1995).

Fellows-Jensen, G., '*Hastings*, *Nottingham*, *Mucking* and *Donnington*: a survey of research into *ing*-formations in England', *Namn och Bygd* 84 (1996), 43–60.

Fellows-Jensen, G., 'Little Thwaite, who made thee?', in W. F. H. Nicolaisen (ed.), *Proceedings of the 19th International Congress of Onomastic Sciences. Aberdeen, August 4–11, 1996*, II (Aberdeen: University of Aberdeen, 1998), pp. 101–06.

Fellows-Jensen, G., 'Scandinavian settlement names in East Anglia: some problems', *Nomina* 22 (1999), 45–60.

Fellows-Jensen, G., '*Torp*-navne i Norfolk i sammenligning med *torp*-navne i andre dele af Danelagen', in P. Gammeltoft and B. Jørgensen (eds), *Nordiske torp-navne*, NORNA-rapporter 76 (Uppsala, 2003), pp. 47–59.

Fellows-Jensen, G., 'The Anglo-Scandinavian street-names of York', in R. A. Hall et al., *Aspects of Anglo-Scandinavian York* (York: York Archaeological Trust, 2004), pp. 357–71.

Fellows-Jensen, G., 'Grimston revisited', in O. J. Padel and D. N. Parsons (eds), *A Commodity of Good Names: Essays in Honour of Margaret Gelling* (Donington: Shaun Tyas, 2008), pp. 125–35.

Fellows-Jensen, G., 'A few more words on place-names in *thorp* in England', in P. Dam et al. (eds), *Torp som ortnamn och bebyggelse*, Tvärvetenskaplig torp-konferens Malmö, 25–27 april 2007 (Lund: Dialekt- och ortnamnsarkivet i Lund, 2009), pp. 43–53.

Ferguson, R., *The Northmen in Cumberland and Westmoreland* (London: Longman, 1856).

Fergusson, J., 'An extent of Carrick in 1260', *Scottish Historical Review* 34 (1955), 190–92.

Field, J., *English Field-Names: A Dictionary* (Newton Abbott: David and Charles, 1972).

Field, J., *The Place-Names of Greater London* (London: Batsford, 1980).

Field, J., *A History of English Field-Names* (London and New York: Longman, 1993).

Finberg, H. P. R., 'Charltons and Carltons', in his *Lucerna: Studies of Some Problems in the Early History of England* (London: Macmillan, 1964), pp. 144–60.

Finberg, H. P. R. (ed.), *The Agrarian History of England and Wales: Volume I, ii A.D. 43–1042* (Cambridge: CUP, 1972).

Flanagan, D., 'Places and their names', *Bulletin of the Ulster Place-Name Society*, 2nd series, 1 (1978), 44–52.

Flanagan, M. T., 'Baginbun', in S. J. Connolly (ed.), *The Oxford Companion to Irish History* (Oxford: OUP, 2007), p. 33.

Foard, G., 'Systematic fieldwalking and the investigation of Saxon settlement in Northamptonshire', *World Archaeology* 9 (1978), 357–74.

Förstemann, E., *Altdeutsches namenbuch*, I: *Personennamen*, 2nd edn (Bonn: Hanstein, 1900).

Forssner, T., *Continental-Germanic Personal Names in England in Old and Middle English Times* (Uppsala: K. W. Appelberg, 1916).

Forster, K., *A Pronouncing Dictionary of English Place-Names* (London: Routledge 1982).

Forsyth, K., *Language in Pictland: The Case Against Non-Indo-European Pictish* (Utrecht: de Keltische Draak, 1997).

Forsyth, K., 'Evidence of a lost Pictish source in the *Historia Regum Anglorum* of Symeon of Durham', in S. Taylor (ed.), *Kings, Clerics and Chronicles in Scotland, 500–1297* (Dublin: Four Courts, 2000), pp. 19–34.

Forward, E., 'Place-Names of the Whittlewood Area', unpublished PhD thesis (University of Nottingham, 2007).

Fowler, F. G., *The King's English* (Oxford: Clarendon, 1906).

Fox, C. F., *The Personality of Britain: its Influence on Inhabitant and Invader in Prehistoric and Early Historic Times* (Cardiff: National Museum of Wales, 1932).

Fox, H. S. A., 'Two Devon estuaries in the middle ages: fisheries, ports, fortifications and places of worship', *Landscapes* 8:1 (2007), 39–68.

Fox, H. S. A., 'Butter place-names and transhumance', in O. J. Padel and D. N. Parsons (eds), *A Commodity of Good Names: Essays in Honour of Margaret Gelling* (Donington: Shaun Tyas, 2008), pp. 352–64.

Fox, H. S. A., *Dartmoor's Alluring Uplands: Transhumance and Pastoral Management in the Middle Ages* (Exeter: Exeter UP, 2012).

Foxall, H. D. G., *Shropshire Field-Names* (Shrewsbury: Shropshire Archaeological Society, 1980).

Frake, C. O., 'Pleasant places, past times, and sheltered identity in rural East Anglia', in S. Feld and K. H. Basso (eds), *Senses of Place* (Santa Fe: School of American Research Press, 1996), pp. 229–57.

Fraser, J. E., *From Caledonia to Pictland: Scotland to 795* (Edinburgh: Edinburgh UP, 2009).

Freise, E., D. Geuenich and J. Wollasch (eds), *Das Martyrolog – Necrolog von St. Emmeram zu Regensburg* (Hanover: Hahnsche Buchhandlung, 1986).

Fridriksson, S., 'Grass and grass utilization in Iceland', *Ecology* 53 (1972), 785–96.

Friel, B., *Translations* (London: Faber, 1981).

Fulk, R. D., 'Old English poetry and the alliterative revival: on Geoffrey Russom's "The evolution of Middle English alliterative meter"', in A. Curzan and K. Emmons (eds), *Studies in the History of the English Language II: Unfolding Conversations* (Berlin: Mouton de Gruyter, 2004), pp. 305–12.

Fullarton, J., *Topographical Account of the District of Cunningham, Ayrshire, Compiled About the Year 1600 by Mr Timothy Pont* (Glasgow: Maitland Club, 1858).

Gammeltoft, P., 'Freystrop: a sacral Scandinavian place-name in Wales?', in O. J. Padel and D. N. Parsons (eds), *A Commodity of Good Names: Essays in Honour of Margaret Gelling* (Donington: Shaun Tyas, 2008), pp. 136–46.

Gammeltoft, P., and B. Jørgensen (eds), *Names through the Looking-Glass: Festschrift in Honour of Gillian Fellows-Jensen* (Copenhagen: C. A. Reitzels forlag, 2006).

Gardiner, M. and R. Coates, 'Ellingsdean, a Viking battlefield identified', *Sussex Archaeological Collections* 125 (1987), 251–52.

Gardiner, M., 'Hythes, small ports and other landing places in later medieval England', in J. Blair (ed.), *Waterways and Canal-Building in Medieval England* (Oxford: OUP, 2007), pp. 85–109.

Gelling, M., 'Place-names as clues to history', *The Amateur Historian* 1:2 (1952), 51–59.

Gelling, M., *The Place-Names of Oxfordshire*, 2 vols, EPNS 23–24 (Cambridge: CUP, 1953–54).

Gelling, M., 'Place-names and Anglo-Saxon paganism', *University of Birmingham Historical Journal* 8 (1961), 7–25.

Gelling, M., 'English place-names derived from the compound *wīchām*', *Medieval Archaeology* 11 (1967), 87–104.

Gelling, M., 'Further thoughts on pagan place-names', in F. Sandgren (ed.), *Otium et Negotium: Studies in Onomatology and Library Science Presented to Olof von Feilitzen* (Stockholm: Norstedt, 1973), pp. 109–28.

Gelling, M., 'Some notes on Warwickshire place-names', *Transactions of the Birmingham and Warwickshire Archaeological Society* 86 (1974), 59–79.

Gelling, M., 'The chronology of English place-names', in T. Rowley (ed.), *Anglo-Saxon Settlement and Landscape* (Oxford: BAR, 1974), pp. 93–101.

Gelling, M., 'The place-names of the Mucking area', *Panorama* 19 (1975), 7–20.

Gelling, M., *The Place-Names of Berkshire*, 3 parts, EPNS 49–51 (Nottingham: EPNS, 1973–76).

Gelling, M., 'Latin loan-words in Old English place-names', *Anglo-Saxon England* 6 (1977), 1–13.

Gelling, M., 'Topographical settlement-names', *The Local Historian* 12:6 (1977), 273–77.

Gelling, M., 'The effect of man on the landscape: the place-name evidence in Berkshire', in S. Limbrey and J. G. Evans (eds), *The Effect of Man on the Landscape: The Lowland Zone* (London: Council for British Archaeology, 1978), pp. 123–25.

Gelling, M., *Signposts to the Past: Place-Names and the History of England*, (London: Dent, 1978; 2nd edn Chichester: Phillimore, 1988; 3rd edn Chichester: Phillimore, 1997).

Gelling, M., 'On looking into Smith's *Elements*', *Nomina* 5 (1981), 39–45.

Gelling, M., *Place-Names in the Landscape: the Geographical Roots of Britain's Place-Names* (London: Dent, 1984; repr. 1993).

Gelling, M., 'Towards a chronology for English place-names', in D. Hooke (ed.), *Anglo-Saxon Settlements* (Oxford: Blackwell, 1988), pp. 59–76.

Gelling, M., 'The historical importance of English place-names', in J.-C. Boulanger (ed.), *Proceedings of the XVth International Congress of Onomastic Sciences* (Quebec: Université de Laval Press, 1990), pp. 85–104.

Gelling, M., *The Place-Names of Shropshire*, parts 1–6, EPNS 62–3, 70, 76, 80, 82, 89 (Nottingham: EPNS, 1990–2012).

Gelling, M., with illustrations by A. Cole, 'Place-names and landscape', in S. Taylor (ed.), *The Uses of Place-Names* (Edinburgh: Scottish Cultural Press, 1998), pp. 75–100.

Gelling, M., and A. Cole, *The Landscape of Place-Names* (Stamford: Shaun Tyas, 2000, repr. with corrections 2003).

Gelling, M., 'The landscape of *Beowulf*', *Anglo-Saxon England* 31 (2002), 7–11.

Gelling, M., 'English place-name studies: some reflections', *JEPNS* 35 (2002–03), 5–16.

Gelling, M., 'Anglo-Norse place-names on the Yorkshire Wolds', in P. Gammeltoft and B. Jørgensen (eds), *Names through the Looking-Glass: Festschrift in Honour of Gillian Fellows-Jensen* (Copenhagen: Reitzels Forlag, 2006), pp. 85–93.

Gerrard, C., *Medieval Archaeology: Understanding Traditions and Contemporary Approaches* (London and New York: Routledge, 2003).

Gerrard, C., with M. Aston, *The Shapwick Project, Somerset: A Rural Landscape Explored* (Leeds: Maney, 2007).

Geuenich, D., *Die Personennamen der Klostergemeinschaft von Fulda im früheren Mittelalter* (Munich: Wilhelm Fink, 1976).

Gilchrist, R., and A. Reynolds (eds), *Reflections: 50 Years of Medieval Archaeology* (Leeds: Maney, 2009).

Gover, J. E. B., A. Mawer and F. M. Stenton, *The Place-Names of Devon*, 2 parts, EPNS 8–9 (Cambridge: CUP, 1931–32).

Gover, J. E. B., A. Mawer and F. M. Stenton, *The Place-Names of Northamptonshire*, EPNS 10 (Cambridge: CUP, 1933).

Gover, J. E. B., A. Mawer and F. M. Stenton, *The Place-Names of Surrey*, EPNS 11 (Cambridge: CUP, 1934).

Gover, J. E. B., A. Mawer and F. M. Stenton, *The Place-Names of Hertfordshire*, EPNS 15 (Cambridge: CUP, 1938).

Gover, J. E. B., A. Mawer and F. M. Stenton, *The Place-Names of Wiltshire*, EPNS 16 (Cambridge: CUP, 1939).

Gover, J. E. B., A. Mawer and F. M. Stenton, *The Place-Names of Nottinghamshire*, EPNS 17 (Cambridge: CUP, 1940).

Gover, J. E. B., A. Mawer and F. M. Stenton *The Place-Names of Middlesex*, EPNS 18 (Cambridge: CUP, 1942).

Gover, J. E. B., A. Mawer and F. M. Stenton, in collaboration with F. T. S. Houghton, *The Place-Names of Warwickshire*, EPNS 13 (Cambridge: CUP, 1936).

Grainger, F., and W. G. Collingwood (eds), *Register and Records of Holm Cultram* (Kendal: Cumberland and Westmorland Ant. and Arch. Society, 1929).

Grane, T, 'Did the Romans really know (or care) about Southern Scandinavia? An archaeological perspective', in T. Grane (ed.), *Beyond the Roman Frontier: Roman Influences on the Northern Barbaricum* (Roma: Edizione Quasar, 2007), pp. 19–25.

Grant, A., 'The origin of the Ayrshire *bý* names', in P. Gammeltoft, C. Hough and D. Waugh (eds), *Cultural Contacts in the North Atlantic Region: The Evidence of Names* (Lerwick: NORNA, 2005), pp. 127–40.

Grant, A., *The Pocket Guide to Scottish Place-Names* (Glasgow: Richard Drew, 2010).

Gray, H. L., *English Field Systems* (Cambridge MA: Harvard UP, 1915).

Greule, A., 'Morphologie und Wortbildung der Vornamen: Germanisch', in E. Eichler et al. (eds), *Namen-forschung/Name Studies/Les noms propres. Ein internationales Handbuch zur Onomastik/ An International Handbook of Onomastics/Manuel international d'onomastique*, 2 vols and Index (Berlin and New York: Walter de Gruyter, 1995–96), pp. 1182–87.

Guinet, L., *Contribution à l'étude des établissements saxons* (Caen: Publications de la Faculté des lettres et sciences humaines de l'université de Caen, 1967).

Gysseling, M., *Toponymisch Woordenboek van België, Nederland, Luxemburg, Noord-Frankrijk en West-Duitsland (vóór 1226)*, 2 vols (Brussels: Belgisch Interuniversitair Centrum voor Neerlandistiek, 1960).

Gysseling, M., and A. C. F. Koch (eds), *Diplomata Belgica ante annum millesimum centesimum scripta*, I. *Teksten* (Brussels: Belgisch Inter-Universitair Centrum voor Neerlandistiek, 1950).

Hadley, D., 'Multiple estates and the origins of the manorial structure in the northern Danelaw', *Journal of Historical Geography* 22 (1996), 3–15.

Hadley, D. M., '"And they proceeded to plough and to support themselves": the Scandinavian settlement of England', *Anglo-Norman Studies* 19 (1997), 69–96.

Hadley, D. M., *The Vikings in England: Settlement, Society and Culture* (Manchester: Manchester UP, 2006).

Hägermann, D., in collaboration with K. Elmshäuser and A. Hedwig (eds), *Das Polyptychon von Saint-Germain-des-Prés,* Studienausgabe (Cologne, Weimar, Vienna: Böhlau, 1993).

Hald, K., *Vore Stednavne*, 2nd edn (Copenhagen: Gad, 1965).

Hald, K., *Personnavne i Danmark*, 2 vols (Copenhagen: Dansk Historisk Fællesforening, 1971–74).

Hall, A., 'Are there any elves in Anglo-Saxon place-names?', *Nomina* 29 (1996), 61–80.

Hall, D., and P. Martin, 'Brixworth, Northamptonshire: an intensive field survey', *Journal of the British Archaeological Association* 132 (1979), 1–6.

Hall, D., 'Survey work in eastern England', in S. Macready and F. H. Thompson (eds), *Archaeological Field Survey in Britain and Abroad* (London: Society of Antiquaries, 1985), pp. 25–44.

Hall, D., 'The late Saxon countryside: villages and their fields', in D. Hooke (ed.), *Anglo-Saxon Settlements* (Oxford: Blackwell, 1988), pp. 99–122.

Hall, D., 'Field surveys in Bedfordshire', *Bedfordshire Archaeology* 19 (1991), 51–56.

Hall, D., *The Open Fields of Northamptonshire* (Northampton: Northamptonshire Record Society, 1995).

Hall, D. N., 'The open fields of Raunds and its townships', in S. Parry, *Raunds Area Survey: An Archaeological Survey of the Landscape of Raunds, Northamptonshire, 1985–94* (Oxford: Oxbow Books, 2006), pp. 116–26.

Hall, D. N., R. Harding and C. Putt, *Raunds: Picturing the Past* (Raunds: F. W. March, 1988).

Hall, T., 'Minster Churches in the Dorset Landscape', unpublished MPhil thesis (University of Leicester, 1997).

Halvorsen, E. F., et al., *Kulturhistoriskt Lexikon för nordisk medeltid,* XIII: *Ormber–Regnbue* (Malmö: Allhem, 1968).

Hansen, Å. K., *Språkkontakt i gammelt koloniområde. En studie av normannerbosetningens stedsnavn, med særlig vekt på navnegruppa* -tuit (Bergen: Universitetet i Bergen, 1998).

Hansen, A. M., *Landnåm i Norge* (Kristiania [Oslo]: Fabritius, 1904).

Hardiman, J. (ed.), *Inquisitionum in officio rotulorum cancellariae Hiberniae asservatorum repertorium*, 2 vols (Dublin: Irish Record Commission, 1826–29).

Härke, H., 'The debate on migration and identity in Europe' (review), *Antiquity* 78 (2004), 453–56.

Haskett Smith, W. P., 'Wastdale Head 600 years ago', *The Climbers' Club Journal* 5 (1903), 3–15.

Haubrichs, W., 'Geschichte der deutsch-romanischen Sprachgrenze im Westen', article 214 in W. Besch, A. Betten, O. Reichmann and S. Sonderegger (eds), *Sprachgeschichte: ein Handbuch zur Geschichte der deutschen Sprache und ihrer Erforschung*, 2nd edn, 4 vols (Berlin and New York: Walter de Gruyter, 1998–2000), IV, pp. 3331–46.

Haubrichs, W., 'Frühe alemannische Personenennamen (4.–8. Jh.). Eine komparatistische Studie', in H.-P. Naumann (ed.), *Alemannien und der Norden. Internationales Symposium vom 18.–20. Oktober 2001 in Zürich* (Berlin and New York: Walter de Gruyter, 2004), pp. 57–113.

Haubrichs, W., 'Langobardic personal names: given names and name-giving among the Langobards', in G. Ausenda, P. Delogu and C. Wickham (eds), *The Langobards Before the Frankish Conquest: An Ethnographic Perspective* (Woodbridge: Boydell Press, 2009), pp. 195–250.

Heather, P., *Empires and Barbarians: Migration, Development and the Birth of Europe* (London: Macmillan, 2009).

Heidermanns, F., *Etymologisches Wörterbuch der germanischen Primäradjektive* (Berlin and New York: Walter de Gruyter, 1993).

Hewitt, R., *Map of a Nation: A Biography of the Ordnance Survey* (London: Granta, 2010).

Hey, G., *Yarnton: Saxon and Medieval Settlement and Landscape* (Oxford: Oxford University School of Archaeology, 2004).

Higham, M., 'The *-erg* place-names of Northern England', *JEPNS* 10 (1977–78), 7–17.

Higham, N. J., (ed.), *Britons in Anglo-Saxon England* (Woodbridge: Boydell Press 2007),

Higham, N. J., and M. J. Ryan (eds), *The Landscape Archaeology of Anglo-Saxon England* (Woodbridge: Boydell Press, 2010).

Higham, N. J., and M. J. Ryan (eds), *Place-Names, Language and the Anglo-Saxon Landscape* (Woodbridge: Boydell Press, 2011).

Hjorth-Pedersen, B., 'Bebyggelsesnavne på -bý sammensat med personnavn', in *Ti Afhandlinger. Udgivet i anledning af Stednavneudvalgets 50 års jubilæum* (Copenhagen: Gad, 1960), pp. 10–46.

Hock, H. H., *Principles of Historical Linguistics* (Berlin: Walter de Gruyter, 1986).

Hodder, I., *Theory and Practice in Archaeology* (London and New York: Routledge, 1992).

Hoffman, E., 'Namen politischer Ereignisse', in A. Brendler and S. Brendler (eds), *Namenarten und ihre Erforschung: Ein Lehrbuch für das Studium der Onomastik* (Hamburg: Baar-Verlag, 2004), pp. 655–70.

Höfler, O., 'Über die Grenzen semasiologischer Personennamenforschung', in *Festschrift für Dietrich Kralik. Dargebracht von Freunden, Kollegen und Schülern* (Horn, N.-Ö.: Berger, 1954), pp. 26–53.

Hogg, A. H. A., 'The survival of Romano-British place-names in southern Britain', *Antiquity* 38 (1964), 296–69.

Hogg, R. M., and R. D. Fulk, *A Grammar of Old English*, 2 vols (Oxford: Wiley-Blackwell, 1992–2011).

Holmberg, K. A., *De svenska Tuna-namnen* (Uppsala: AB Lundequistska Bokhandel, 1969).

Hooke, D., 'Open-field agriculture: the evidence from the pre-Conquest charters of the West Midlands', in T. Rowley (ed.), *The Origins of Open-Field Agriculture* (London: Croom Helm, 1981), pp. 39–63.

Hooke, D., *The Anglo-Saxon Landscape: the Kingdom of the Hwicce* (Manchester: Manchester UP, 1985).

Hooke, D., *The Landscape of Anglo-Saxon England* (London: Leicester UP, 1998).

Hooke, D., *Trees in Anglo-Saxon England* (Woodbridge: Boydell Press, 2010).

Horovitz, D., *The Place-Names of Staffordshire* (Brewood: the author, 2005).

Hoskins, W. G., *The Making of the English Landscape* (London: Hodder and Stoughton, 1955).

Hoskins, W. G., *Local History in England* (London: Longmans, 1959).

Hough, C., 'The place-names Bridford, Britford, and Birdforth', *Nottingham Medieval Studies* 39 (1995), 12–18.

Hough, C., 'Place-name evidence relating to the interpretation of Old English legal terminology', *Leeds Studies in English* 27 (1996), 19–48.

Hough, C., 'The ladies of Portinscale', *JEPNS* 29 (1997), 71–78.

Hough, C., 'The place-name Fritwell', *JEPNS* 29 (1997), 65–70.

Hough, C., 'The place-name Kingston and the laws of Æthelberht', *Studia Neophilologica* 69 (1997), 55–57.

Hough, C., 'The widow's *mund* in Æthelberht 75 and 76', *Journal of English and Germanic Philology* 98 (1999), 1–16.

Hough, C., 'Legal and documentary writings', in P. Pulsiano and E. Treharne (eds), *A Companion to Anglo-Saxon Literature* (Oxford: Blackwell, 2001), pp. 170–87.

Hough, C., 'Two Kentish laws concerning women: a new reading of Æthelberht 73 and 74', *Anglia* 19 (2001), 554–78.

Hough, C., 'Women in English place-names', in C. Hough and K. A. Lowe (eds), *'Lastworda Betst': Essays in Memory of Christine E. Fell with her Unpublished Writings* (Donington: Shaun Tyas, 2002), pp. 41–106.

Hough, C., 'Strensall, *Streanaeshalch* and Stronsay', *JEPNS* 35 (2003), 17–24.

Hough, C., review of V. Watts, *The Cambridge Dictionary of English Place-Names*, *Nomina* 27 (2004), 133–42.

Hough, C., 'Commonplace place-names', *Nomina* 39 (2007), 101–20.

Hough, C. 'Women and the law in seventh-century England', *Nottingham Medieval Studies* 51 (2007), 207–230.

Hough, C., 'Women in the landscape: place-name evidence for women in north-west England', *Nomina* 31 (2008), 45–66.

Hough, C., 'Dictionaries of place-names', in A. P. Cowie (ed.), *The Oxford History of English Lexicography* (Oxford: OUP, 2009), pp. 94–121.

Hough, C., 'Eccles in English and Scottish place-names', in E. Quinton (ed.), *The Church in English Place-Names* (Nottingham: EPNS, 2009), pp. 109–24.

Hough, C., '"Find the lady": the term *lady* in English and Scottish place-names', in W. Ahrens et al. (eds), *Names in Multi-Lingual, Multi-Cultural and Multi-Ethnic Contact* (Toronto: York University, 2009), pp. 511–18 [CD-ROM].

Hough, C., 'The name-type Fritwell', *JEPNS* 42 (2010), 87–89.

Hough, C., 'The name-type Maid(en)well', *Nomina* 33 (2010), 27–44.

Hough, C., *Toponymicon and Lexicon in North-West Europe: 'Ever-Changing Connection'*, E. C. Quiggin Memorial Lectures 12 (Cambridge: University of Cambridge, Department of Anglo-Saxon, Norse and Celtic, 2010).

Hubbard, P., R. Kitchin and G. Valentine, *Key Thinkers on Space and Place*, repr. (London: Sage Publications, 2009).

Hughes, A. J., and R. J. Hannan, *The Place-Names of Northern Ireland, Vol. 2: Co. Down II, The Ards* (Belfast: The Queen's University Belfast, 1992).

Hunter Blair, F. C., (ed.), *Charters of the Abbey of Crossraguell* (Edinburgh: Ayrshire and Galloway Archaeological Association, 1886).

Hussey, A., 'Eastry wills', *Archaeologia Cantiana* 39 (1927), 77–90, and 40 (1928), 35–47.

Hyenstrand, Å., *Centralbygd – Randbygd*, Acta Universitatis Stockholmiensis. Studies in North-European Archaeology 5 (1974).

Innes, C. (ed.), *Liber Sancte Marie de Melros: munimenta vetustiora Monasterii Cisterciensis de Melros* (Edinburgh: Bannatyne Club, 1837).

Insley, J., 'Regional variation in Scandinavian personal nomenclature in England', *Nomina* 3 (1979), 52–60.

Insley, J., 'The continental evidence: OHG *wal(a)h*, OSax *walh*', *Journal of the English Place-Name Society* 12 (1979–80), 50–53;

Insley, J., 'Some Scandinavian personal names from south-west England', *Namn och Bygd* 70 (1982), 77–93.

Insley, J., *Scandinavian Personal Names in Norfolk: A Survey Based on Medieval Records and Place-Names* (Uppsala and Stockholm: Almqvist and Wiksell, 1994).

Insley, J., 'Grimston-hybrids', in *Reallexikon der Germanischen Altertumskunde* 13 (1999), 49–56.

Insley, J., 'Otlinga Saxonia', *Reallexikon der Germanischen Altertumskunde* 22 (2003), 387–91.

Insley, J., 'Pre-Conquest personal names', *Reallexikon der Germanischen Altertumskunde* 23 (2003), 367–96.

Insley, J., 'Early Germanic personal names and onomastic dialects', in A. J. Johnston, F. von Mengden and S. Thim (eds), *Language and Text: Current Perspectives on English and Germanic Historical Linguistics and Philology* (Heidelberg: Winter, 2006), pp. 113–31.

Insley, J., 'Wealh', *Reallexicon der Germanischen Altertumskunde* 33 (2006), 319–22.

Irish Patent Rolls of James I: Facsimile of the Irish Record Commissioner's Calendar Prepared Prior to 1830, with a foreword by M. C. Griffith (Dublin: Stationery Office for the Irish Manuscripts Commission, 1966).

Jackson, K., *Language and History in Early Britain* (Edinburgh: Edinburgh UP, 1953).

Jackson, K., 'Angles and Britons in Northumbria and Cumbria', in H. Lewis (ed.), *Angles and Britons* (Cardiff: University of Wales Press, 1963), pp. 60–94.

Jackson, K., Addenda and corrigenda in *JEPNS* 1 (1968–9), 43–52; 2 (1969–70), 73–4; 3 (1970–1), 50; and 6 (1973–4), 52.

Jacobsen, L., and E. Moltke, with A. Bæksted and K. M. Nielsen (eds), *Danmarks Runeindskrifter I–II* (Copenhagen: Munksgaard, 1941–42).

Jakob Benediktsson (ed.), *Íslendingabók. Landnámabók*, Íslenzk Fornrit 1 (Reykjavík: Íslenzka Fornritafélag, 1968).

James, A. G., 'Brittonic language in the Old North' (BLITON), available at <http://www.spns.org.uk/bliton/blurb.html>.

James, A., review of R. Coates and A. Breeze, *Celtic Voices, English Places, Nomina* 27 (2004), 147–50.

James, A., 'A Cumbric diaspora?', in O. J. Padel and D. N. Parsons (eds), *A Commodity of Good Names: Essays in Honour of Margaret Gelling* (Donington: Shaun Tyas, 2008), pp. 187–203.

James, A., '**Eglēs*/*Eclēs* and the formation of Northumbria', in E. Quinton (ed.), *The Church in English Place-Names* (Nottingham: EPNS, 2009), pp. 125–50.

James, A., review of P. Cavill and G. Broderick (eds), *Language Contact in the Place-Names of Britain and Ireland*, *Journal of Scottish Name Studies* 3 (2009), 135–58.

James, A., 'Scotland's *-ham* and *-ingham* names: a reconsideration', *Journal of Scottish Name Studies* 4 (2010), 103–30.

Janzén, A., 'De fornvästnordiska personnamnen', in A. Janzén (ed.), *Nordisk Kultur* VII: *Personnnavne/ Personnamn/Personnavn* (Copenhagen: J. H. Schultz; Oslo: H. Aschehoug; Stockholm: A. Bonnier, 1947), pp. 22–186.

Janzén, A. (ed.), *Nordisk Kultur* VII: *Personnnavne/ Personnamn/Personnavn* (Copenhagen: J. H. Schultz; Oslo: H. Aschehoug; Stockholm: A. Bonnier, 1947).

Jenkins, J. G., *Ceredigion: Interpreting an Ancient County* (Llanrwst: Gwasg Carreg Gwalch, 2005).

Jensen, J. S., 'The introduction and use of runic letters on Danish coins around the year 1065', in M. Stoklund et al. (eds), *Runes and their Secrets: Studies in Runology* (Copenhagen: Museum Tusculanum Press, 2006), pp. 159–68.

Jepson, B., *English Place-Name Elements Relating to Boundaries* (Lund: Centre for Languages and Literature, Lund University, 2011).

Jesch, J., 'Scandinavian Wirral', in P. Cavill, S. E. Harding and J. Jesch (eds), *Wirral and its Viking Heritage* (Nottingham: EPNS, 2000), pp. 1–10.

Jesch, J., 'Skaldic verse in Scandinavian England', in J. Graham-Campbell et al. (eds), *Vikings and the Danelaw* (Oxford: Oxbow Books, 2001), pp. 313–25.

Jesch, J., 'Scandinavian women's names in English place-names', in O. J. Padel and D. N. Parsons (eds), *A Commodity of Good Names: Essays in Honour of Margaret Gelling* (Donington: Shaun Tyas, 2008), pp. 154–62.

Johnson, M., *Archaeological Theory: An Introduction* (Oxford: Blackwell, 1999).

Johnson, M., *Ideas of Landscape* (Oxford: Blackwell, 2008).

Johnston, J. B., *Place-Names of Scotland*, 3rd edn (London: Murray, 1934).

Johnston, J. B., *The Place-Names of Berwickshire* (Edinburgh: Royal Scottish Geographical Society, 1940).

Jones, B. L., *Enwau* (Llanrwst: Carreg Gwalch, 1991).

Jones, J. M., *A Welsh Grammar* (Oxford: Clarendon, 1931).

Jones, R., 'Hunting for the meaning of the place-name *Upton*', in R. Jones and S. Semple (eds), *Sense of Place in Anglo-Saxon England* (Donington: Shaun Tyas, 2012), pp. 301–15.

Jones, R., 'Thinking through the manorial affix', in R. Silvester and S. Turner (eds), *Life in Medieval Landscapes: People and Places in Medieval England* (Oxford: Oxbow Books, 2012), pp. 251–67.

Jones, R., and M. Page, *Medieval Villages in an English Landscape: Beginnings and Ends* (Macclesfield: Windgather Press, 2006).

Jones, R., and S. Semple, 'Making sense of place in Anglo-Saxon England', in R. Jones and S. Semple (eds), *Sense of Place in Anglo-Saxon England* (Donington: Shaun Tyas, 2012), pp. 1–15.

Jones, R., and S. Semple (eds), *Sense of Place in Anglo-Saxon England* (Donington: Shaun Tyas, 2012).

Jørgensen, B., 'The degree of onomastic coverage within various categories of denotata', in E. Brylla and M. Wahlberg (eds), *ICOS 2002*, I (Uppsala: Språk- och folkminnesinstitutet, 2005), pp. 196–206.

Jørgensen, B., *Danske Stednavne*, 3rd edn (Copenhagen: Gyldendal, 2008).

Karlsson, G., *Iceland's 1100 Years: The History of a Marginal Society* (London: Hurst, 2000).

Kay, C., et al., *Historical Thesaurus of the Oxford English Dictionary*, 2 vols (Oxford: Oxford University Press, 2009).

Keating, G., *Foras Feasa ar Éirinn I*, ed. D. Comyn, repr. with new introduction by B. Ó Buachalla (Dublin: Royal Irish Academy, 1987 [1901]).

Kelly, F., *Early Irish Farming: A Study Based Mainly on the Law-Texts of the 7th and 8th Centuries AD* (Dublin: Dublin Institute for Advanced Studies, 1997).

Kelly, S. E. (ed.), *Charters of Selsey* (Oxford: British Academy, 1998).

Kelly, S. E. (ed.), *Charters of Abingdon Abbey, Part I*, Anglo-Saxon Charters 7 (Oxford: British Academy, 2000).

Kelly, S. E. (ed.), *Charters of Abingdon Abbey, Part II*, Anglo-Saxon Charters 8 (Oxford: British Academy, 2001).

Kelly, S., 'Reculver Minster and its early charters', in J. Barrow and A. Wareham (eds), *Myth, Rulership, Church and Charters: Essays in Honour of Nicholas Brooks* (Aldershot: Ashgate, 2008), pp. 67–82.

Kemble, J. M., *Codex diplomaticus ævi Saxonici* (London: English Historical Society, 1839–48).

Kenyon, D., 'The antiquity of *hām* place-names in Lancashire and Cheshire', *Nomina* 10 (1986), 11–27.

Kershaw, J. F., 'Culture and gender in the Danelaw: Scandinavian and Anglo-Scandinavian brooches', *Viking and Medieval Scandinavia* 5 (2009), 295–325.

Keynes, S., *The Diplomas of King Æthelred 'the Unready' 978–1016: A Study in their Use as Historical Evidence* (Cambridge: CUP, 1980).

Keynes, S., and M. Lapidge (trans.), *Alfred the Great: Asser's* Life of King Alfred *and Other Contemporary Sources* (Harmondsworth: Penguin, 1983).

King, R., and S. Öberg, 'Introduction: Europe and the future of mass migration', in R. King (ed.), *Mass Migrations in Europe: The Legacy and the Future* (London: Belhaven Press, 1993), pp. 1–4.

Kitson, P. R., 'Quantifying qualifiers in Anglo-Saxon charter boundaries', *Folia Linguistica Historica* 14 (1993), 29–82.

Kitson, P. R., 'The nature of Old English dialect distributions, mainly as exhibited in charter boundaries', in J. Fisiak (ed.), *Medieval Dialectology* (Berlin and New York: Mouton de Gruyter, 1995), pp. 43–135.

Kitson, P. R., 'British and European river-names', *Transactions of the Philological Society* 94 (1996), 73–118.

Kitson, P. R., 'Fog on the Barrow-Downs?', in O. J. Padel and D. N. Parsons (eds), *A Commodity of Good Names: Essays in Honour of Margaret Gelling* (Donington: Shaun Tyas, 2008), pp. 382–94.

Kitson, P. R., *A Guide to Anglo-Saxon Charter Boundaries* (Nottingham: EPNS, forthcoming).

Kluge, F., *Etymologisches Wörterbuch der deutschen Sprache*, 25th edn, rev. E. Seebold (Berlin and New York: Walter de Gruyter, 2011).

Knudsen, G., M. Kristensen and R. Hornby (eds), *Danmarks gamle Personnavne*, I: *Fornavne* (Copenhagen: G. E. C. Gad, 1936–48).

Kousgård Sørensen, J., *Danske sø-og ånavne*, 8 vols (Copenhagen: Akademisk Forlag, 1968–96).

Kousgård Sørensen, J., 'Place-names and settlement history', in P. H. Sawyer (ed.), *Names, Words, and Graves: Early Medieval Settlements* (Leeds: Leeds University School of History, 1979), pp. 14–17.

Krahe, H., *Sprache und Vorzeit. Europäische Vorgeschichte nach dem Zeugnis der Sprache* (Heidelberg: Quelle and Meyer, 1954).

Krause, W., with contributions by H. Jankuhn, *Die Runeninschriften im älteren Futhark*, 2 vols (Göttingen: Vandenhoeck and Ruprecht, 1966).

Kripke, S., *Naming and Necessity*, 2nd edn (Oxford: Blackwell, 1980).

Kristensson, G., *A Survey of Middle English Dialects* (Lund: New Society of Letters 1967–2002).

Kuhn, H., review of A. Bach, *Deutsche Namenkunde* II. *Die deutschen Ortsnamen* (Heidelberg: Carl Winter, 1953–54), in *Anzeiger für deutsches Altertum und deutsche Literatur* 68:4 (April, 1956), 145–70.

Kurath, H., and S. M. Kuhn (eds), *Middle English Dictionary* (Ann Arbor: University of Michigan Press, 1952–2001).

Kuurman, J., 'An examination of the *-ingas*, *-inga-* place-names in the east midlands', *JEPNS* 7 (1975), 11–44.

Laing, M., *A Linguistic Atlas of Early Middle English, 1150–1325*, <http://www.lel.ed.ac.uk/ihd/laeme1/laeme1.html> (Edinburgh: University of Edinburgh, 2008–).

Lavelle, R., 'Geographies of power in the Anglo-Saxon Chronicle: the royal estates of Anglo-Saxon Wessex', in A. Jorgensen (ed.), *Reading the Anglo-Saxon Chronicle: Language, Literature, History* (Turnhout: Brepols, 2010), pp. 187–219.

Leahy, K., 'The contents of the [Staffordshire] hoard', available at <http://finds.org.uk/staffshoardsymposium/>.

Leahy, K., and R. Bland, *The Staffordshire Hoard* (London: British Museum Press, 2009).

Leahy, K., and C. Paterson, 'New light on the Viking presence in Lincolnshire: the artefactual evidence', in J. Graham-Campbell et al. (eds), *Vikings and the Danelaw* (Oxford: Oxbow Books, 2001), pp. 181–202.

Lehmann, W. P., *A Gothic Etymological Dictionary* (Leiden: Brill, 1986).

Leino, A., *On Toponymic Constructions as an Alternative to Naming Patterns in Describing Finnish Lake Names* (Helsinki: Finnish Literature Society, 2007).

Lerche Nielsen, M., *Vikingetidens personnavne i Danmark belyst gennem runeindskrifternes personnavne og stednavne på* -torp *sammensat med personnavneforled* (Copenhagen: Københavns Universitet, 1997).

Lerche Nielsen, M., 'Runefund fra Hedeby og Slesvig', in *Enogtyvende tværfaglige Vikingesymposium* (Højberg: Forlaget Hikuin, 2002), pp. 53–71.

Leskien, A., 'Litauische Personennamen', *Indogermanische Forschungen. Zeitschrift für indogermanische Sprach- und Altertumskunde* 26 (1910), 325–52.

Leskien, A., 'Die litauischen zweistämmigen Personennamen', *Indogermanische Forschungen. Zeitschrift für indogermanische Sprach- und Altertumskunde* 34 (1914), 296–333.

Lewis, C., P. Mitchell-Fox and C. Dyer, *Village, Hamlet and Field: Changing Medieval Settlements in Central England*, 2nd edn (Macclesfield: Windgather Press, 2001).

Liebermann, F., *Die Gesetze der Angelsachsen*, 3 vols (Halle: Niemeyer, 1903–16).

Lind, E. H., *Norsk-isländska dopnamn ock fingerade namn från medeltiden* (Uppsala: A.-B. Lundequistska Bokhandeln; Leipzig: Otto Harrassowitz, 1905–15).

Lind, E. H., *Norsk-isländska dopnamn ock fingerade namn från medeltiden: Supplementband* (Oslo: Jacob Dybwad, 1931).

Lindkvist, H., *Middle-English Place-Names of Scandinavian Origin: Part I* (Uppsala: Uppsala UP, 1912).

Lindkvist, H., 'A study on early medieval York', *Anglia* 50 (1926), 345–94.

Lorimer, W. L., 'The persistence of Gaelic in Galloway and Carrick', *Scottish Gaelic Studies* 6 (1949), 114–36.

Lowth, R., *A Short Introduction to English Grammar* (London, 1762; repr. Menston: Scolar Press, 1967).

Loyn, H., *The Vikings in Wales* (London: Viking Society for Northern Research, 1976).

Lund, N., '*Thorp*-names', in P. H. Sawyer (ed.), *Medieval Settlement: Continuity and Change* (London: Arnold, 1976), pp. 223–25.

Lundgren, M., E. Brate and E. H. Lind, *Svenska personnamn från medeltiden* (Uppsala: Almqvist and Wiksell, 1892–1934).

Lyth, P., 'The Southwell charter of 956 A.D.: an exploration of its boundaries', *Transactions of the Thoroton Society* 86 (1982), 49–61.

Lyth, P., and G. Davies, 'The Southwell charter of A.D. 956: a new appraisal of the boundaries', *Transactions of the Thoroton Society* 96 (1992), 125–29.

MacCoinnich, A., 'Where and how was Gaelic written in late medieval and early modern Scotland? Orthographic practices and cultural identities', in C. Ó Baoill and N. McGuire (eds), *Caindel Alban. Fèill-Sgrìobhainn do Dhòmhnall E Meek* (Aberdeen: University of Aberdeen, 2008), pp. 309–56.

MacDonald, A., *The Place-Names of West Lothian* (Edinburgh: Oliver and Boyd, 1941).

Mac Gabhann, F., *The Place-Names of Northern Ireland, Vol. 7 Co. Antrim II, Ballycastle and North-East Antrim* (Belfast: The Queen's University Belfast, 1997).

Mac Giolla Easpaig, D., 'L'influence scandinave sur la toponymie irlandaise', in É. Ridel (ed.), *L'héritage maritime des Vikings en Europe de l'Ouest* (Caen: Presses Universitaires de Caen, 2002), pp. 441–82.

MacQueen, J., *Place-Names in the Rhinns of Galloway and Luce Valley* (Stranraer: Stranraer and District Local History Trust, 2002).

MacQueen, J., *Place-Names of the Wigtownshire Moors and Machars* (Stranraer: Stranraer and District Local History Trust, 2008).

Mahnken, G., *Die hamburgischen niederdeutschen Personennamen des 13. Jahrhunderts* (Dortmund: Ruhfus, 1925).

Maitland, F. M., *Domesday Book and Beyond* (London: Collins, 1897, repr. 1960).

Malone, K. (ed.), *Widsith* (Copenhagen: Rosenkilde and Bagger, 1962).

Márkus, G., 'Gaelic under pressure: a 13th-century charter from east Fife', *Journal of Scottish Name Studies* 1 (2007), 77–98.

Márkus, G., *The Place-Names of Bute* (Donington: Shaun Tyas, 2012).

Marslen-Wilson, W. D., 'Functional parallelism in spoken word recognition', *Cognition* 25 (1987), 71–102.

Mawer, A., *The Place-Names of Northumberland and Durham* (Cambridge: CUP, 1920).

Mawer, A., *Place-Names and History*, Robert Spence Watson Memorial Lecture (Liverpool: UP of Liverpool, 1922).

Mawer, A. (ed.), *The Chief Elements used in English Place-Names*, EPNS 1.ii (Cambridge: CUP 1924).

Mawer, A., *Problems of Place-Name Study* (Cambridge: CUP, 1929).

Mawer, A., 'The study of field-names in relation to place-names', in J. G. Edwards, V. H. Galbraith, and E. F. Jacob (eds), *Historical Essays in Honour of James Tait* (Manchester: printed for subscribers, 1933), pp. 189–200.

Mawer, A., and F. M. Stenton (eds), *Introduction to the Survey of English Place-Names*, EPNS 1.i (Cambridge: CUP 1924).

Mawer, A., and F. M. Stenton, *The Place-Names of Buckinghamshire*, EPNS 2 (Cambridge: CUP, 1925).

Mawer, A., and F. M. Stenton, *The Place-Names of Bedfordshire and Huntingdonshire*, EPNS 3 (Cambridge: CUP, 1926).

Mawer, A., and F. M. Stenton *The Place-Names of Worcestershire*, EPNS 4 (Cambridge: CUP, 1927).

Mawer, A., and F. M. Stenton, with J. E. B. Gover, *The Place-Names of Sussex*, 2 parts, EPNS 6–7 (Cambridge: CUP, 1929–30).

McClure, P., 'Names and landscapes in medieval Nottinghamshire, with particular attention to Lindrick and lime woods', in O. J. Padel and D. N. Parsons (eds), *A Commodity of Good Names: Essays in Honour of Margaret Gelling* (Donington: Shaun Tyas, 2008), pp. 395–409.

McErlean, J. (ed.), *Duanaire Dháibhidh Uí Bhruadair: The Poems of David Ó Bruadair*, 3 vols (London: Irish Text Society, 1910–17).

McErlean, T., 'The Irish townland system of landscape organisation', in T. Reeves-Smyth and F. Hamond (eds), *Landscape Archaeology in Ireland* (Oxford: British Archaeological Reports, 1983) pp. 315–39.

McIntosh, A., M. L. Samuels, and M. Benskin, A *Linguistic Atlas of Late Middle English, 1350–1450* (Aberdeen: Aberdeen UP; Edinburgh: Mercat Press, 1986); the revised online edition [*eLALME*, 2013] is available at <www.lel.ed.ac.uk/ihd/elalme/elalme.html>.

McKay, P., *The Place-Names of Northern Ireland, Vol. 4: Co. Antrim I, The Baronies of Toome* (Belfast: The Queen's University Belfast, 1995).

McKay, P., *A Dictionary of Ulster Place-Names* (Belfast: The Queen's University Belfast, 1999).

McKay, P., *The Place-Names of Northern Ireland, Vol. 8: Co. Fermanagh I, Lisnaskea and District: the Parish of Aghalurcher* (Belfast: The Queen's University Belfast, 2004).

McKay, P., 'Scots elements in townland names', *Ainm* 10 (2009), 1–26.

McKerral, A., 'An extent of Carrick in 1260', *Scottish Historical Review* 34 (1955), 189–90.

Meyer, M. A., 'Land charters and the legal position of Anglo-Saxon women', in B. Kanner (ed.), *The Women of England from Anglo-Saxon Times to the Present: Interpretive Bibliographical Essays* (London: Mansell, 1980), pp. 62–63.

Michaëlsson, K., *Études sur les noms de personne français d'après les rôles de taille parisiens (rôles de 1292, 1296–1300, 1313)* 2 vols (Uppsala: Almqvist and Wiksell/A.-B. Lundequistska Bokhandeln, 1927–1936)

Mills, A. D., *The Place-Names of Dorset*, parts 1–4, EPNS 52–53, 59–60, 86–87 (Nottingham: EPNS, 1977–).

Mills, A. D., *The Place-Names of the Isle of Wight* (Stamford: Paul Watkins, 1996).

Mills, A. D., *A Dictionary of English Place-Names*, 2nd edn (Oxford: OUP, 1998).

Mills, A. D., *A Dictionary of British Place-Names* (Oxford: OUP, 2003).

Mills, A. D., *A Dictionary of London Place-Names*, 2nd edn (Oxford: OUP, 2010).

Mills, J., (ed.), *Calendar of the Justiciary Rolls II* (Dublin: Thom, 1914).

Milne, A., 'An extent of Carrick in 1260', *Scottish Historical Review* 34 (1955), 46–49.

Moltke, E., *Runes and their Origin: Denmark and Elsewhere* (Copenhagen: The National Museum of Denmark, 1985).

Müller, G., *Studien zu den theriophoren Personennamen der Germanen* (Cologne and Vienna: Böhlau, 1970).

Muhr, K., *The Place-Names of Northern Ireland, Vol. 6: Co. Down IV, North-West Down / Iveagh* (Belfast: The Queen's University Belfast, 1996).

Muhr, K., 'Ulster place-name links between Gaelic, English and Scots', in J. M. Kirk and D. P. Ó Baoill (eds), *Language Links: The Languages of Scotland and Ireland* (Belfast: Queen's University Belfast, 2001), pp. 257–72.

Muhr, K., 'Place-names of Germanic origin in Ireland', *Reallexikon der Germanischen Altertumskunde*, 2nd edn, 22 (2002), 302–04.

Muhr, K., Introduction to 'Irish and Scottish Gaelic family names', in P. Hanks (ed.), *Dictionary of American Family Names* (New York: OUP, 2003), pp. xxxvi–xliii.

Muhr, K., 'Trees in Ireland in early tradition and place-names' (2005), available online at <http://homepage.eircom.net/~archaeology/two/trees.htm>.

Muhr, K., 'The mountain of *Slewtrim* or Bessy Bell', *West Tyrone Historical Society Journal* 1 (2007), 72–90.

Muhr, K., 'Place-names and Scottish clan traditions in north-east County Antrim', in J. D. McClure, J. M. Kirk and M. Storrie (eds), *A Land That Lies Westward: Language and Culture in Islay and Argyll* (Edinburgh: John Donald, 2009), pp. 79–102.

Muhr, K., 'Where did the Brown Bull die? An hypothesis from Ireland's epic *Táin Bó Cúailnge* version I', in R. Ó hUiginn and B. Ó Catháin (eds), *Ulidia 2: Proceedings of the Second International Conference on the Ulster Cycle of Tales, Maynooth 24–27 June 2005* (Maigh Nuad [Maynooth]: An Sagart, 2009) pp. 121–39.

Murison, D., 'Linguistic relationships in medieval Scotland', in G. W. S. Barrow (ed.), *The Scottish Tradition* (Aberdeen: Scottish Academic Press, 1974), pp. 71–83.

Musset, L., 'Pour l'étude comparative de deux fondations politiques des vikings: le royaume d'York et le duché de Rouen', *Northern History* 10 (1975), 40–54.

Napier, A. S., and W. H. Stevenson (eds), *The Crawford Collection of Early Charters and Documents Now in the Bodleian Library* (Oxford: Clarendon, 1895).

Nash, C., 'Irish placenames: post-colonial locations' *Transactions of the Institute of British Geographers*, new series, 24:4 (1999), 457–80.

Nedoma, R., 'Altgermanische Anthroponyme in runenepigraphischen (und anderen) Quellen. Ein Projektbericht', in D. Geuenich, W. Haubrichs and J. Jarnut (eds), *Person und Name. Methodische Probleme bei der Erstellung eines Personennamenbuches des Frühmittelalters* (Berlin and New York: de Gruyter, 2002), pp. 105–26.

Nedoma, R., *Personennamen in südgermanischen Runeninschriften* (Heidelberg: Winter, 2004).

Nicolaisen, W. F. H., 'Notes on Scottish Place Names: 8 Lugton Water', *Scottish Studies* 2:2 (1958), 189–205.

Nicolaisen, W. F. H., *Scottish Place-Names* (London: Batsford, 1976; rev. edn, Edinburgh: Birlinn, 2001).

Nicolaisen, W. F. H., 'Is there a Northwest Germanic toponymy? Some thoughts and a proposal', in E. Marold and C. Zimmermann (eds), *Nordwestgermanisch* (Berlin and New York: Walter de Gruyter, 1995), pp. 103–14.

Nicolaisen, W. F. H., *The Picts and their Place Names* (Rosemarkie: Groam House Museum, 1996).

Nielsen, O. A., *Olddanske Personnavne* (Copenhagen: Universitets-Jubilæets danske samfund, 1883).

Nurminen, T., 'Hill-terms in the Place-Names of Northumberland and County Durham', unpublished PhD thesis (Newcastle University, 2012).

Oakden, J. P., *The Place-Names of Staffordshire*, part 1, EPNS 55 (Nottingham: EPNS, 1984).

Ó Cadhla, S., *Civilizing Ireland: Ordnance Survey 1824–1842, Ethnography, Cartography, Translation* (Dublin: Irish Academic Press, 2007).

O' Donovan, J., *Miscellany of the Celtic Society* (Dublin: Celtic Society, 1849).

O' Donovan, J. (ed.), *Annála Ríoghachta Éireann: Annals of the Kingdom of Ireland by the Four Masters from the Earliest Period to the Year 1616*, 7 vols (Dublin: Hodges, Smith and Co, 1848–51; repr. Dublin: de Búrca, 1990).

Okasha, E., *Hand-list of Anglo-Saxon Non-Runic Inscriptions* (Cambridge: CUP, 1971).

Okasha, E., 'Anglo-Saxon women: the evidence from inscriptions', in J. Higgitt, K. Forsyth and D. N. Parsons (eds), *Roman, Runes and Ogham: Medieval Inscriptions in the Insular World and on the Continent* (Donington: Shaun Tyas, 2001), pp. 79–88.

Ó Mainnín, M. B., *The Place-Names of Northern Ireland, Vol. 3: Co. Down III, The Mournes* (Belfast: The Queen's University Belfast, 1993).

Ó Murchadha, D., 'A review of some placename material from *Foras Feasa ar Éirinn*', *Éigse* 35 (2005), 81–97.

Oosthuizen, S., *Landscapes Decoded: The Origins and Development of Cambridgeshire's Medieval Fields* (Hatfield: University of Hertfordshire Press, 2006).

Oosthuizen, S., 'The origins of common fields and the Anglo-Saxon Kingdom of Mercia', *Agricultural History Review* 55:2 (2007), 153–80.

Opie, I., and P. Opie (ed.), *Oxford Dictionary of Nursery Rhymes*, rev. edn (Oxford: Clarendon, 1952).

Oppenheimer, S., *The Origins of the British* (London: Robinson, 2006).

O'Rahilly, T. F., 'Notes on Middle Irish pronunciation', *Hermathena* 20 (1930), 152–95.

Oram, R., *A Monastery and its Landscape: Whithorn and Monastic Estate Management in Galloway (c.1250–c.1600)*, Thirteenth Whithorn Lecture (Whithorn: Friends of the Whithorn Trust, 2005).

Osthoff, H., and K. Brugmann, *Morphologische Untersuchungen auf dem Gebiete der indogermanischen Sprachen* (Leipzig: S. Hirzel, 1878).

Owen, G., *The Description of Penbrokshire*, ed. H. Owen, 4 vols (London: Honourable Society of Cymmrodorion, 1892–1936).

Owen, H. W., 'English place-names and Welsh stress-patterns', *Nomina* 11 (1987), 99–114.

Owen, H. W., *The Place-Names of East Flintshire* (Cardiff: University of Wales Press, 1994).

Owen, H. W., 'Old English place-name elements in Domesday Flintshire', in A. Rumble and A. D. Mills (eds), *Names, Places and People: An Onomastic Miscellany in Memory of John McNeal Dodgson* (Stamford: Paul Watkins, 1997), pp. 269–78.

Owen, H. W., 'Ffridd', *Y Naturiaethwr* 2:3 (June 1998), 5–9.

Owen, H. W., and R. Morgan, *Dictionary of the Place-Names of Wales* (Llandysul: Gomer, 2007; repr. with corrections 2008).

Oxford English Dictionary Online edition at <http://www.oed.com>.

Padel, O. J., *Cornish Place-Name Elements*, EPNS 56–57 (Nottingham: EPNS, 1985).

Padel, O. J., *A Popular Dictionary of Cornish Place-Names* (Penzance: Alison Hodge, 1988).

Padel, O. J., 'Fields called *Denabole*', *Devon and Cornwall Notes and Queries* 36 (1987–91), 145–47.

Padel, O. J., 'Place-names and the Saxon conquest of Devon and Cornwall', in N. J. Higham (ed.), *Britons in Anglo-Saxon England* (Woodbridge: Boydell Press 2007), pp. 215–30.

Padel, O. J., 'Two Devonshire place-names', *JEPNS* 41 (2009), 119–26.

Padel, O. J., 'Christianity in medieval Cornwall: Celtic aspects', in N. Orme (ed.), *Victoria County History of Cornwall* II: *Religious History to 1560* (Woodbridge: Boydell and Brewer for the Institute of Historical Research 2010), pp. 110–25.

Padel, O. J., 'Aneirin and Taliesin: sceptical speculations', in A. Woolf (ed.), *Beyond the Gododdin: Dark Age Scotland in Medieval Wales* (St Andrews: University of St Andrews Press, 2013), pp. 115–52.

Padel, O. J., and D. N. Parsons (eds), *A Commodity of Good Names: Essays in Honour of Margaret Gelling* (Donington: Shaun Tyas, 2008).

Page, M., and R. Jones, 'Stable and unstable village plans: case-studies from Whittlewood', in M. Gardiner and S. Rippon (eds), *Medieval Landscapes in Britain* (Macclesfield: Windgather Press, 2007), pp. 139–52.

Page, R. I., review of I. Wood and N. Lund (eds), *People and Places in Northern Europe 500–1600: Essays in Honour of Peter Hayes Sawyer*, *Saga-Book of the Viking Society* 23 (1993), 529–35.

Parry, S., *Raunds Area Survey: An Archaeological Study of the Landscape of Raunds, Northamptonshire* (Oxford: Oxbow Books, 2006).

Parry-Williams, T. H., *The English Element in Welsh* (London: Honourable Society of the Cymmrodorion, 1923).

Parry-Williams, T. H., 'English–Welsh loan-words', in *Angles and Britons: O'Donnell Lectures* (Cardiff: University of Wales, 1963), pp. 42–59.

Parsons, D. N., 'Classifying Ptolemy's English names', in D. N. Parsons and P. Sims-Williams (eds), *Ptolemy: Towards a Linguistic Atlas of the Earliest Celtic Place-Names of Europe* (Aberystwyth: CMCS, 2000), pp. 169–78.

Parsons, D. N., 'How long did the Scandinavian language survive in England? Again', in J. Graham-Campbell et al. (eds), *Vikings and the Danelaw* (Oxford: Oxbow Books, 2001), pp. 299–312.

Parsons, D. N., 'Old English **lōt*, dialect *loot*, a salt-maker's "ladle"', in C. Hough and K. A. Lowe (eds), *'Lastworda Betst': Essays in Memory of Christine E. Fell* (Donington: Shaun Tyas, 2002), pp. 170–88.

Parsons, D. N., *The Vocabulary of English Place-Names* III (*Ceafor–Cock-pit*) (Nottingham: English Place-Name-Society, 2004).

Parsons, D. N., 'Field-name statistics, Norfolk and the Danelaw', in P. Gammeltoft and B. Jørgensen (eds), *Names through the Looking-Glass: Festschrift in Honour of Gillian Fellows-Jensen, July 5th 2006* (Copenhagen: Reitzels Forlag, 2006), pp. 165–88.

Parsons, D. N., 'On the origin of "Hiberno-Norse Inversion Compounds"', *Journal of Scottish Name Studies* 5 (2011), 115–52.

Parsons, D. N., 'Sabrina in the thorns: place-names as evidence for British and Latin in Roman Britain', *Transactions of the Philological Society* 109 (2011), 113–37.

Parsons, D. N., 'The name "Hammerwich"' <finds.org.uk/staffshoardsymposium/>.

Parsons, D. N., and T. Styles, *The Vocabulary of English Place-Names* II (*Brace–Cæster*) (Nottingham: Centre for English Name-Studies, 2000).

Parsons, D. N., and T. Styles, with C. Hough, *The Vocabulary of English Place-Names* I (*Á–Box*) (Nottingham: Centre for English Name-Studies, 1997).

Partridge, E., *A Dictionary of Slang and Unconventional English*, 8th edn rev. P. Beale (London: Routledge, 1984, repr. 2003).

Payling, L. W. H., 'Geology and place-names in Kesteven (S.W. Lincolnshire)', *Leeds Studies in English and Kindred Languages* 4 (1935), 1–13.

Pedersen, B. H., 'Bebyggelsesnavne på -by sammensat med personnavn', in *Ti Afhandlinger* (Copenhagen: G. E. C. Gad, 1960), pp. 10–46.

Peterson, L., *Nordiskt runnamnslexikon* (Uppsala: Institutet för språk och folkminnen, 2007).

Petty, Sir William, *The Political Anatomy of Ireland* [1691], repr. in *A Collection of Tracts and Treatises Illustrative of the Natural History, Antiquities, and the Political and Social State of Ireland at Various Periods Prior to the Present Century*, 2 vols (Dublin: Thom, 1860–61), II, pp. 1–142.

Pickles, T., '*Biscopes-tūn*, *muneca-tūn* and *prēosta-tūn*: dating, significance and distribution', in E. Quinton (ed.), *The Church in English Place-Names* (Nottingham: EPNS, 2009), pp. 39–108.

Pickles, T., with J. Blair, '*Deantune* and Bishopstone: the estate and church under the Mercian kings and the South Saxon bishops' in G. Thomas (ed.), *The Later Anglo-Saxon Settlement at Bishopstone: A Downland Manor in the Making* (York: Council for British Archaeology, 2010), pp. 17–22.

Pierce, G. O., 'Enwau lleoedd anghyfiaith yng Nghymru' ['Alien place-names in Wales'], *Bulletin of the Board of Celtic Studies* 18 (1958–60), 252–65.

Pierce, G. O., *The Place-Names of Dinas Powys Hundred* [Glamorganshire] (Cardiff: University of Wales Press, 1968).

Pierce, G. O., 'Some aspects of English influence on place-names in Wales', *Onoma* 17 (1972–73), 173–91.

Pierce, G. O., *Place-Names in Glamorgan* (Cardiff: Merton Priory, 2002).

Prescott, J. B. (ed.), *Register of the Priory of Wetherhal* (London: Elliot Stock, 1897).

Preston-Jones, A., 'Decoding Cornish churchyards', *Cornish Archaeology* 33 (1994), 71–95.

Price, L., *The Place-Names of Co. Wicklow*, 7 fascicles (Dublin: Dublin Institute for Advanced Studies, 1945–67).

Price, L., 'A note on the use of the word *baile* in place-names', *Celtica* 6 (1963), 119–126.

Probert, D., 'Mapping early medieval language change in south-west England', in N. Higham (ed.), *Britons in Anglo-Saxon England* (Woodbridge: Boydell Press, 2007), pp. 231–44.

Probert, D., 'Towards a reassessment of "Kingston" place-names', *JEPNS* 40 (2008), 7–22.

Pulman, G. P. R., *Local Nomenclature: A Lecture on the Names of Places, Chiefly in the West of England, Etymologically and Historically Considered* (London: Longman, Brown, Green, Longmans and Roberts, 1857).

Rackham, H. (ed. and trans.), *Pliny: Natural History. II. Libri III–VII*, Loeb Classical Library (London: Heinemann, 1924).

Rackham, O., *The History of the Countryside* (London: J. M. Dent, 1986).

Rankin, J. F., *Down Cathedral: The Church of Saint Patrick of Down* (Belfast: Ulster Historical Foundation, 1997).

Reaney, P. H., *The Place-Names of Essex*, EPNS 12 (Cambridge: CUP, 1935).

Reaney, P. H., *The Place-Names of Cambridgeshire and the Isle of Ely*, EPNS 19 (Cambridge: CUP, 1943).

Redin, M., *Studies on Uncompounded Personal Names in Old English* (Uppsala: A.-B. Akademiska Bokhandeln, 1919).

Redknap, M., *Vikings in Wales: An Archaeological Quest* (Cardiff: National Museums and Galleries of Wales, 2000).

Reeves, W. (ed.), *Ecclesiastical Antiquities of Down, Connor and Dromore, Consisting of a Taxation of Those Dioceses Compiled in the Year 1306* (Dublin: Hodges and Smith, 1847).

Reeves, W., 'On the townland distribution of Ireland', *Proceedings of the Royal Irish Academy* 7 (1861), 473–90.

Reichert, H., *Lexikon der altgermanischen Namen* (Vienna: Verlag der Österreichischen Akademie der Wissenschaften, 1987–1990).

Reichert, H., 'Sprache und Namen der Wandalen in Afrika', in A. Greule and M. Springer (eds), *Namen des Frühmittelalters als sprachliche Zeugnisse und als Geschichtsquellen* (Berlin and New York: Walter de Gruyter, 2009), pp. 43–120.

Reid, R. C., 'The early ecclesiastical history of Kirkgunzeon', *Transactions of the Dumfriesshire and Galloway Natural History and Antiquarian Society*, 3rd series, 14 (1926–28), 201–15.

Reid, R. C. (ed.), *Wigtownshire Charters*, Publications of the Scottish History Society, 3rd series, vol. 51 (Edinburgh: Scottish History Society, 1960).

Reimpell, A., *Die Lübecker Personennamen unter besondere Berücksichtigung der Familiennamenbildung bis zur Mitte des 14. Jahrhunderts* (Lübeck: Franz Westphal, 1929).

Reynolds, A., *Later Anglo-Saxon England: Life and Landscape* (Stroud: Tempus, 1999).

Reynolds, A., and S. Semple, 'Digging for names: archaeology and place-names in the Avebury Region', in R. Jones and S. Semple (eds), *Sense of Place in Anglo-Saxon England* (Donington: Shaun Tyas, 2012), pp. 76–100.

Richards, J. D., *Viking Age England*, rev. edn (Stroud: Tempus, 2000).

Richards, M., '*Ffridd/ffrith* as a Welsh place-name', *Studia Celtica* 2 (1967), 29–90.

Richards, M., *Welsh Administrative and Territorial Units* (Cardiff: University of Wales Press, 1969).

Richards, M., 'Some Welsh place-names containing elements which are found in Continental Celtic', *Études celtiques* 13 (1972–3), 364–410.

Richards, M., 'Welsh influence on some English place-names in north east Wales', in F. Sandgren (ed.), *Otium et Negotium: Studies in Onomatology and Library Science Presented to Olof von Feilitzen* (Stockholm: Norstedt, 1973), pp. 216–20.

Richards, M., *Archif Melville Richards Database*, available at <www.e-gymraeg.co.uk/enwaulleoedd/amr>.

Rippon, S., *Beyond the Village: the Diversification of Landscape Character in Southern Britain* (Oxford: OUP, 2008).

Rivet, A. L. F., and C. Smith, *The Place-Names of Roman Britain* (London: Batsford, 1979).

Rivet, A. L. F., 'Celtic names and Roman places', *Britannia* 11 (1980), 1–19.

Roberts, B. K., 'Late *-bý* names in the Eden Valley, Cumberland', *Nomina* 13 (1989–90), 25–39.

Roberts, B. K., and S. Wrathmell, *An Atlas of Rural Settlement in England* (London: English Heritage, 2000).

Roberts, B. K., and S. Wrathmell, *Region and Place* (London: English Heritage, 2002).

Robertson, A. J., *Anglo-Saxon Charters*, 2nd edn (Cambridge: CUP, 1956).

Robinson, M. (ed.), *The Concise Scots Dictionary* (Aberdeen: Aberdeen UP, 1987).

Roesdahl, E., and D. M. Wilson, 'The Århus rune-stones', in P. Gammeltoft and B. Jørgensen (eds), *Names through the Looking-Glass: Festschrift in Honour of Gillian Fellows-Jensen, July 5th 2006* (Copenhagen: Reitzels Forlag, 2006), pp. 208–209.

Rollason, D., and L. Rollason (eds), *The Durham Liber Vitae: London, British Library, MS Cotton Domitian A. VII*, 3 vols (London: British Library, 2007).

Ronneberger-Sibold, E., 'Warennamen', in A. Brendler and S. Brendler (eds), *Namenarten und ihre Erforschung: Ein Lehrbuch für das Studium der Onomastik* (Hamburg: Baar-Verlag, 2004), pp. 557–603.

Round, J. H. (ed.), *Calendar of Documents Preserved in France 918–1206* (London: Stationary Office, 1899).

Rowley, T. (ed.), *The Origins of Open-Field Agriculture* (London: Croom Helm, 1981).

Rumble, A. R., 'Old English *Bōc-land* as an Anglo-Saxon estate-name', *Leeds Studies in English* 18 (1987), 219–29.

Russell, P., 'The suffix *-āko-* in Continental Celtic', *Études celtiques* 25 (1988), 131–73.

Særheim, I., 'Official urban naming: cultural heritage and identity', *Onoma* 42 (2007), 171–87.

Sandnes, B., 'What is Norse, what is Scots in Orkney place-names', in P. Gammeltoft, C. Hough and D. Waugh (eds), *Cultural Contacts in the North Atlantic Region: The Evidence of Names*, (Lerwick: NORNA, 2005), pp. 173–80.

Sandnes, B., *From Starafjall to Starling Hill: An Investigation of the Formation and Development of Old Norse Place-Names in Orkney* (Scottish Place-Name-Society, 2010, available at <http://www.spns.org.uk/Starafjall.pdf>).

Sandred, K. I., *English Place-Names in -stead* (Uppsala: Almqvist and Wiksell, 1963).

Sandred, K. I., 'The element *hamm* in English place-names: a linguistic investigation', *Namn och Bygd* 64 (1976), 69–87.

Sandred, K. I., 'Language contact in East Anglia: some observations on the Scandinavian place-names in *-thwaite* in Norfolk', in E. M. Närhi (ed.), *ICOS 1990 Helsinki. Proceedings of the XVIIth International Congress of Onomastic Sciences* (Helsinki, University of Helsinki, 1990), pp. 310–17.

Sandred, K. I., 'Nordiskt i Norfolk. Ortnamn och bebyggelsehistoria i en del av Danelagen', *Kungl. Humanistiska Vetenskaps-Samfundet I Uppsala Årsbok* (1994), 129–54.

Sandred, K. I., and B. Lindström, *The Place-Names of Norfolk*, parts 1–3, EPNS 61, 72, 79 (Nottingham: EPNS, 1989–2002).

Saussure, F. de, *Cours de linguistique générale*, ed. by C. Bally and A. Sechehaye (Paris: Payot, 1916).

Sawyer, P. H., 'The density of the Danish settlement in England', *University of Birmingham Historical Journal* 6 (1957), 1–17.

Sawyer, P. H., *The Age of the Vikings* (London: Arnold, 1962).

Sawyer, P. H., *Anglo-Saxon Charters: An Annotated List and Bibliography* (London: Royal Historical Society, 1968); Revised version available online: 'The Electronic Sawyer: online catalogue of Anglo-Saxon Charters' (King's College London, 2006–) <http://www.esawyer.org.uk>.

Sawyer, P. H., 'Baldersby, Borup and Bruges: the rise of Northern Europe', *The University of Leeds Review* 16 (1973), 75–96.

Sawyer, P. H., *From Roman Britain to Norman England* (London: Methuen, 1978).

Sawyer, P. H., *Kings and Vikings: Scandinavia and Europe AD 700–1100* (London: Routledge, 1982).

Scarfe, N., *Suffolk in the Middle Ages* (Woodbridge: Boydell Press, 1986).

Scherr, J., 'Names of springs and wells in Somerset', *Nomina* 10 (1986), 79–91.

Scheuringer, H., 'Geschichte der deutsch-ungarischen und der deutsch-slawischen Sprachgrenze im Südosten', article 216 in W. Besch, A. Betten, O. Reichmann and S. Sonderegger (eds), *Sprachgeschichte: ein Handbuch zur Geschichte der deutschen Sprache und ihrer Erforschung*, 2nd edn, 4 vols (Berlin and New York: Walter de Gruyter, 1998–2000), IV, pp. 3365–79.

Schlaug, W., *Studien zu den altsächsischen Personennamen des 11. und 12. Jahrhunderts* (Lund: C. W. K. Gleerup; Copenhagen: Ejnar Munksgaard, 1955).

Schlaug, W., *Die altsächsischen Personennamen vor dem Jahre 1000* (Lund: C. W. K. Gleerup; Copenhagen: Ejnar Munksgaard, 1962).

Schlimpert, G., *Slawische Personennamen in mittelalterlichen Quellen zur deutschen Geschichte* (Berlin: Akademie-Verlag, 1978).

Schmid, K. (ed.), *Die Klostergemeinschaft von Fulda im früheren Mittelalter*, III: *Vergleichendes Gesamtverzeichnis der fuldischen Personennamen.* (Munich: Wilhelm Fink, 1978).

Schmidt, K. H., 'Die Komposition in gallischen Personennamen', *Zeitschrift für celtische Philologie* 26 (1957), 33–301.

Schmidt, K. H. 'Keltische Namen', in E. Eichler et al. (eds), *Namen-forschung/Name Studies/Les noms propres. Ein internationales Handbuch zur Onomastik/ An International Handbook of Onomastics/Manuel international d'onomastique*, 2 vols and Index (Berlin and New York: Walter de Gruyter, 1995–96), pp. 762–74.

Schönfeld, M., *Wörterbuch der altgermanischen Personen- und Völkernamen. Nach der Überlieferung des klassischen Altertums bearbeitet* (Heidelberg: Carl Winter, 1911).

Schönwälder, B., *Die* -leben-*Namen* (Heidelberg: C. Winter, 1993).

Schramm, G., *Namenschatz und Dichtersprache. Studien zu den zweigliedrigen Personennamen der Germanen* (Göttingen: Vandenhoeck and Ruprecht, 1957).

Schützeichel, R., 'Einführung in die Familiennamenkunde', in M. Gottschald, *Deutsche Namenkunde. Unsere Familiennamen. Mit einer Einführung in die Familiennamenkunde von Rudolf Schützeichel*, 6th rev. edn (Berlin and New York: Walter de Gruyter, 2006), pp. 13–76.

Scott, J. G., 'The partition of a kingdom: Strathclyde 1092–1153', *Transactions of the Dumfriesshire and Galloway Natural History and Antiquarian Society*, 3rd series, 72 (1997), 11–40.

Scott, M. R., 'The Germanic Toponymicon of Southern Scotland: Place-Name Elements and their contribution to the Lexicon and Onomasticon', unpublished PhD thesis (University of Glasgow, 2003).

Scott, M. R., 'Place-names and the Scots language: the marches of lexical and onomastic research', *Scots Language* 26:1 (2008), 85–98.

Scott, M. [R.], 'Unsung etymologies: lexical and onomastic evidence for the influence of Scots on English', in M. Mooijaart and M. van der Wal (eds), *Yesterday's Words: Contemporary, Current and Future Lexicography* (Newcastle: Cambridge Scholars Publishing, 2008), pp. 187–98.

Scott, W. W., *Syllabus of Scottish Charters: Paisley Reg,* ed. M. Hammond available at <http://www.arts.gla.ac.uk/scottishstudies/charters/index.htm>.

Searle, W. G., *Onomasticon Anglo-Saxonicum* (Cambridge: CUP, 1897).

Sedgefield, W. J., 'Methods of place-name study', in A. Mawer and F. M. Stenton (eds), *Introduction to the Survey of English Place-Names*, EPNS 1.i (Cambridge: CUP, 1924), pp. 1–14.

Seebohm, F., *The English Village Community*, 2nd edn (London: Longmans and Green, 1883).

Semple, S., 'A fear of the past: the place of the prehistoric burial mound in the ideology of middle and later Anglo-Saxon England', *World Archaeology* 30:1 (1998), 109–26.

Semple, S., 'Defining the OE *hearg*: a preliminary archaeological and topographic examination of *hearg* place-names and their hinterlands', *Early Medieval Europe* 15:4 (2007), 364–85.

Semple, S., 'In the open air', in M. Carver, A. Sanmark and S. Semple (eds), *Signals of Belief in Early England: Anglo-Saxon Paganism Revisited* (Oxford: Oxbow Books, 2010), pp. 21–48.

Shanks, M., *Experiencing the Past: On the Character of Archaeology* (London and New York: Routledge, 1992).

Shaw Mason, W., *A Statistical Account, or Parochial Survey of Ireland, Drawn up from the Communications of the Clergy*, 3 vols (Dublin: Graisberry and Campbell; London: Longman, Hurst, Rees, Orme, and Brown; Edinburgh: Archibald Constable, 1814–19).

Shedden-Dobie, J. (ed.), *Muniments of the Royal Burgh of Irvine*, 2 vols (Edinburgh: Ayrshire and Galloway Archaeological Association, 1890–91).

Simington, R. C. (ed.), *The Civil Survey, AD 1654–6*, 10 vols (Dublin: Irish Manuscripts Commission, 1931–61).

Sims-Williams, P., 'Dating the transition to Neo-Brittonic: phonology and history, 400–600', in A. Bammesberger and A. Wollmann (eds), *Britain 400–600: Language and History* (Heidelberg: Carl Winter Universitätsverlag, 1990), pp. 217–61.

Sims-Williams, P., 'Genetics, linguistics, and prehistory: thinking big and thinking straight', *Antiquity* 72 (1998), 505–27.

Sims-Williams, P., *Ancient Celtic Place-Names in Europe and Asia Minor* (Oxford: Blackwell, for the Philological Society, 2006).

Sims-Williams, P., 'Bronze- and Iron-Age Celtic-speakers: what don't we know, what can't we know, and what could we know? Language, genetics and archaeology in the twenty-first century', *The Antiquaries Journal* 92 (2012), 427–49.

Skånes ortsnamen, Serie A. Bebyggelsenamn, 1 ff. (Lund: Institutet för Språk och Folkminnen, Dialekt- och Ortnamnsarkivet i Lund, 1958 ff.).

Smart, V., *Sylloge of Coins of the British Isles 28: Cumulative Index of Volumes 1–20* (London: OUP for The British Academy, 1981).

Smart, V., 'Variation between *ÆTHEL-* and *ÆGEL-* as a name-element on coins', *Nomina* 7 (1983), 91–96.

Smart, V., *Sylloge of Coins of the British Isles 41: Cumulative Index of Volumes 21–40* (London: OUP for The British Academy, 1992).

Smith, A. H., *The Place-Names of the North Riding of Yorkshire*, EPNS 5 (Cambridge: CUP, 1928).

Smith, A. H., *The Place-Names of the East Riding of Yorkshire and York*, EPNS 14 (Cambridge: CUP, 1937).

Smith, A. H., *English Place-Name Elements*, 2 vols, EPNS 25–26 (Cambridge: CUP, 1956; repr. Nottingham: EPNS, 2008).

Smith, A. H., 'Place-names and the Anglo-Saxon settlement', *Proceedings of the British Academy* 42 (1956), 67–88.

Smith, A. H., *The Place-Names of the West Riding of Yorkshire*, 8 parts, EPNS 30–37 (Cambridge: CUP, 1961–63).

Smith, A. H., *The Place-Names of Gloucestershire*, 4 parts, EPNS 38–41 (Cambridge: CUP, 1964–65).

Smith, A. H., *The Place-Names of Westmorland*, 2 parts, EPNS 42–43 (Cambridge: CUP, 1967).

Smith, C., 'The survival of Romano-British toponymy', *Nomina* 4 (1980), 27–40.

Smith, J. J., *Sound Change and the History of English* (Oxford: OUP, 2007).

Smyth, A. P., *King Alfred the Great* (Oxford: OUP, 1995).

Sommerfelt, A., 'The English forms of the names of the main provinces of Ireland', *Lochlann* 1 (1958), 223–27.

Sonderegger, S., 'Prinzipien germanischer Personen-namengebung', in D. Geuenich, W. Haubrichs, J. Jarnut (eds), *Nomen et gens. Zur historischen Aussagekraft frühmittelalterlicher Personennamen* (Berlin and New York: Walter de Gruyter, 1997), pp. 1–29.

Stahl, A.-B., 'Place-Names of Barra in the Outer Hebrides', unpublished PhD thesis (University of Edinburgh, 1999).

Stenton, D. M., 'Frank Merry Stenton', *Proceedings of the British Academy* 54 (1968), 315–423.

Stenton, D. M. (ed.), *Preparatory to Anglo-Saxon England: Being the Collected Papers of Frank Merry Stenton* (Oxford: Clarendon, 1970).

Stenton, F. M., *The Place-Names of Berkshire: An Essay* (Reading: University College, 1911).

Stenton, F. M., *Documents Illustrative of the Social and Economic History of the Danelaw from Various Collections* (London: OUP, 1920).

Stenton, F. M., 'Personal names in place-names', in A. Mawer and F. M. Stenton (eds), *Introduction to the Survey of English Place-Names*, EPNS 1.i (Cambridge: CUP, 1924), pp. 165–89.

Stenton, F. M., 'The English Element', in A. Mawer and F. M. Stenton (eds), *Introduction to the Survey of English Place-Names*, EPNS 1.i (Cambridge: CUP, 1924), pp. 36–54.

Stenton, F. M., 'The Danes in England', *Proceedings of the British Academy* 13 (1927), 203–46.

Stenton, F. M., 'Sir Allen Mawer', *Proceedings of the British Academy* 29 (1943), 433–39.

Stenton, F. M., 'The historical bearing of place-name studies: the place of women in Anglo-Saxon society', *Transactions of the Royal Historical Society*, 4th series, 25 (1943), 1–13.

Stenton, F. M., *Anglo-Saxon England*, 3rd edn (Oxford: Clarendon, 1971).

Stevenson, W. H. (ed.), *Asser's Life of King Alfred* (Oxford: Clarendon, 1904).

Stiles, P., 'Old English *halh*, "slightly raised ground isolated by marsh"', in A. R. Rumble and A. D. Mills (eds), *Names, Places and People: An Onomastic Miscellany in Memory of John McNeal Dodgson* (Stamford: Paul Watkins, 1997), pp. 330–44.

Stoklund, M., 'Chronology and typology of the Danish runic inscriptions', in M. Stoklund et al. (eds), *Runes and their Secrets: Studies in Runology* (Copenhagen: Museum Tusculanum Press, 2006), pp. 355–83.

Stone, J., 'Timothy Pont: three centuries of research, speculation and plagiarism', in I. C. Cunningham (ed.), *The Nation Survey'd: Timothy Pont's Maps of Scotland* (Edinburgh: Birlinn, 2006), pp. 1–26.

Streatfeild, G. S., *Lincolnshire and the Danes* (London: Kegan Paul, Trench and Co, 1884).

Stringer, K. J., 'Acts of lordship: the records of the Lords of Galloway to 1234', in T. Brotherstone and D. Ditchburn (eds), *Freedom and Authority: Historical and Historiographical Essays Presented to Grant G. Simpson* (East Linton: Tuckwell, 2000), pp. 203–34.

Stringer, K. J., *The Reformed Church in Medieval Galloway and Cumbria: Contrasts, Connections and Continuities*, The Eleventh Whithorn Lecture (Whithorn: Friends of Whithorn Trust, 2003).

Ström, H., *Old English Personal Names in Bede's History: An Etymological-Phonological Investigation* (Lund: C. W. K. Gleerup, 1939).

Sundby, B., *Studies in the Middle English Dialect Material of the Worcestershire Records* (Bergen and Oslo: Norwegian Universities Press, 1963);

Sutherland, E., *In Search of the Picts: A Celtic Dark Age Nation* (London: Constable 1994).

Sveriges medeltida personnamn, Förnamn (Uppsala: Almqvist and Wiksell; Uppsala: Institutet för språk och folkminnen, 1967–).

Sweetman, H. S., and G. F. Handcock (eds), *Calendar of Documents relating to Ireland*, 5 vols (London: Longman, 1875–86).

Swift, J., 'On barbarous denominations in Ireland', in H. Davis (ed.), *The Prose Works of Jonathan Swift*, 16 vols (Oxford: Blackwell, 1941–74), IV, p. 280.

Tait, J., 'The feudal element', in A. Mawer and F. M. Stenton (eds), *Introduction to the Survey of English Place-Names*, EPNS 1.i (Cambridge: CUP, 1924), pp. 115–32.

Tanguy, B., *Les Noms de lieux bretons* I, *Toponymie descriptive* (Rennes: Centre Régional de Recherche et de Documentation Pédagogiques, 1975).

Tanguy, B., *Dictionnaire des noms de communes, trèves et paroisses du Finistère* (Douarnenez: Le Chasse-Marée, 1990).

Tanguy, B., *Dictionnaire des noms de communes, trèves et paroisses des Côtes d'Armor* (Douarnenez: Le Chasse-Marée, 1992).

Tavernier-Vereecken, C., *Gentse naamkunde van ca. 1000 tot 1253: Een bijdrage tot de kennis van het oudste Middelnederlands* (Brussels: Belgisch Interuniversitair Centrum voor Neerlandistiek, 1968).

Taylor, G., and A. Skinner, *Maps of the Roads of Ireland, Surveyed 1777* (London and Dublin: [published for the authors], 1778).

Taylor, S., 'Babbet and Bridin Pudding or polyglot Fife in the Middle Ages', *Nomina* 17 (1994), 99–118.

Taylor, S., 'The Scandinavians in Fife and Kinross: the onomastic evidence', in B. E. Crawford (ed.), *Scandinavian Settlement in Northern Britain* (London: Leicester UP, 1995), pp. 141–67.

Taylor, S., 'Scandinavians in Central Scotland: *bý*-place-names and their context', in G. Williams and P. Bibire (eds), *Sagas, Saints and Settlements* (Leiden and Boston: Brill, 2004), pp. 125–46.

Taylor, S., 'Pictish place-names revisited', in S. T. Driscoll, J. Geddes and M. A. Hall (eds), *Pictish Progress: New Studies on Northern Britain in the Early Middle Ages* (Leiden and Boston: Brill, 2011), pp. 67–118.

Taylor, S., and G. Márkus, *The Place-Names of Fife*, 5 vols (Donington: Shaun Tyas, 2006–12).

Thirsk, J., 'The common fields', *Past and Present* 29 (1964), 3–29.

Thomas, R. J., 'Enwau afonydd â'r ôl-ddodiad *-wy*', *Bulletin of the Board of Celtic Studies* 7 (1933–5), 117–33; and 8 (1935–7), 27–43.

Thomas, R. J., *Enwau Afonydd a Nentydd Cymru* (Cardiff: University of Wales Press, 1938).

Thomas, R. J., G. A. Bevan, and P. J. Donovan (eds), *Geiriadur Prifysgol Cymru: A Dictionary of the Welsh Language*, 4 vols (Cardiff: University of Wales Press, 1950–2002).

Thomson, J. M. (ed.), *Registrum Magni Sigilli Regum Scotorum. The Register of the Great Seal of Scotland IV, AD 1546–1580* (repr. Edinburgh: Clark Constable, 1984).

Thrane, T., *Referential-Semantic Analysis: Aspects of a Theory of Linguistic Reference* (Cambridge: CUP, 1980).

Thurneysen, R., *A Grammar of Old Irish* (Dublin: Dublin Institute for Advanced Studies, 1946).

Tolkien, J. R. R., 'English and Welsh', in *Angles and Britons: O'Donnell Lectures* (Cardiff: University of Wales, 1963), pp. 1–41.

Tomasson, R. F., *Iceland: The First New Society* (Minneapolis: University of Minnesota Press, 1980).

Tomlin, R. S. O., 'Was ancient British Celtic ever a written language? Two texts from Roman Bath', *Bulletin of the Board of Celtic Studies* 34 (1987), 18–25.

Todd, M., 'The archaeological significance of place-names in *walh*', *Journal of the English Place-Name Society* 12 (1979–80), 47–50;

Toner, G., *The Place-Names of Northern Ireland, Vol. 5: Co. Derry I, The Moyola Valley* (Belfast: The Queen's University Belfast, 1996).

Toner, G., '*Baile*: settlement and landholding in medieval Ireland', *Éigse* 34 (2004), 25–43.

Toner, G., and M. B. Ó Mainnín, *The Place-Names of Northern Ireland, Vol. 1: Co. Down I, Newry and South-West Down* (Belfast: The Queen's University Belfast, 1992).

Townend, M., 'Viking Age England as a bilingual society', in D. M. Hadley and J. D. Richards (eds), *Cultures in Contact: Scandinavian Settlement in England in the Ninth and Tenth Centuries* (Turnhout: Brepols, 2000), pp. 89–105.

Townend, M., *Language and History in Viking Age England: Linguistic Relations between Speakers of Old Norse and Old English* (Turnhout: Brepols, 2002).

Townend, M., 'Contacts and conflicts: Latin, Norse, and French', in L. Mugglestone (ed.), *The Oxford History of English* (Oxford: OUP, 2006), pp. 61–85.

Townend, M., *Scandinavian Culture in Eleventh-Century Yorkshire* (Kirkdale: The Trustees of the Friends of St Gregory's Minster, 2007), pp. 4–6.

Townend, M., *The Vikings and Victorian Lakeland: the Norse medievalism of W. G. Collingwood and his contemporaries* (Kendal: Cumberland and Westmorland Antiquarian and Archaeological Society, 2009).

Trafford, S., 'Ethnicity, migration theory, and the historiography of the Scandinavian settlements of England', in D. M. Hadley and J. D. Richards (eds), *Cultures in Contact: Scandinavian Settlement in England in the Ninth and Tenth Centuries* (Turnhout: Brepols, 2000), pp. 17–39.

Trautmann, R., *Die altpreußischen Personennamen: Ein Beitrag zur baltischen Philologie* (Göttingen: Vandenhoeck and Ruprecht, 1925).

Tristram, H., 'Why don't the English speak Welsh?' in N. J. Higham (ed.), *Britons in Anglo-Saxon England* (Woodbridge: Boydell Press 2007), pp. 192–214.

Tuan, Y.-F., *Space and Place: the Perspective of Experience*, (Minneapolis and London: University of Minneapolis Press, 1977; 6th repr. 2008).

Turner, S. C., 'Making a Christian landscape: early medieval Cornwall', in M. Carver (ed.), *The Cross Goes North: Processes of Conversion in Northern Europe, AD300–1300* (Woodbridge: York Medieval Press, 2003), pp. 171–94.

Turner, S. C., 'The Christian landscape: churches, chapels and crosses', in S. C. Turner (ed.), *Medieval Devon and Cornwall: Shaping an Ancient Countryside* (Macclesfield: Windgather Press, 2006), pp. 24–43.

Turville-Petre, T., 'The etymology of *road*', *Notes and Queries* 55:4 (2008), 405–06.

Ureland, P. S., and G. Broderick (eds), *Language Contact in the British Isles: Proceedings of the Eighth International Symposium on Language Contact in Europe, Douglas, Isle of Man, 1988* (Tübingen: Niemeyer, 1991).

Van Durme, L., *Toponymie van Velzeke-Ruddershove en Bochoute*, 2 parts in 3 vols (Ghent: Secretariaat van de Koninklijke Academie voor Nederlandse Taal- en Letterkunde, 1986–1991).

Van Langendonck, W., *Theory and Typology of Proper Names* (Berlin and New York: Walter de Gruyter, 2007).

Vendryes, J., et al., *Lexique étymologique de l'irlandais ancien* (Dublin and Paris: Dublin Institute for Advanced Studies/Centre National de la Recherche Scientifique, 1959–).

Vohra, P., 'Kinship in the Viking Diaspora: Icelanders and their Relations across the North Atlantic', unpublished PhD thesis (University of York, 2008).

Von Feilitzen, O., *The Pre-Conquest Personal Names of Domesday Book* (Uppsala: Almqvist and Wiksell, 1937).

Von Feilitzen, O., 'Some Continental Germanic personal names in England', in A. Brown and P. Foote (eds), *Early English and Norse Studies, Presented to Hugh Smith in Honour of his Sixtieth Birthday* (London: Methuen, 1963), pp. 46–61.

Von Feilitzen, O., 'Notes on some Scandinavian personal names in English 12th-century records', in R. Otterbjörk (ed.), *Personnamnsstudier 1964 tillägnade minnet av Ivar Modéer (1904–1960)* (Stockholm: Almqvist and Wiksell, 1965), pp. 52–68.

Von Feilitzen, O., 'Some Old English uncompounded personal names and bynames', *Studia Neophilologica* 40 (1968), 5–16.

Von Feilitzen, O., and C. Blunt, 'Personal names on the coinage of Edgar', in P. Clemoes and K. Hughes (eds), *England Before the Conquest: Studies in Primary Sources Presented to Dorothy Whitelock* (Cambridge: CUP, 1971), pp. 183–214.

Von Reitzenstein, W.-A. Frhr., *Lexikon bayerischer Ortsnamen*: *Herkunft und Bedeutung*, 2nd edn (Munich: C. H. Beck, 1991).

Von Reitzenstein, W.-A. Frhr., *Lexikon fränkischer Ortsnamen: Herkunft und Bedeutung, Oberfranken, Mittelfranken, Unterfranken* (Munich: C. H. Beck, 2009).

Vuolteenaho, J., and T. Ainiala, 'Slang toponyms in early twentieth century Helsinki', in W. Ahrens et al. (eds), *Names in Multi-lingual, Multi-cultural and Multi-ethnic Contact* (Toronto: York University, 2009), pp. 1030-35 [CD-ROM].

Wagner, N., 'Ostgotische Personennamengebung', in D. Geuenich, W. Haubrichs and J. Jarnut (eds), *Nomen et gens. Zur historischen Aussagekraft frühmittelalterlicher Personennamen* (Berlin and New York: Walter de Gruyter, 1997), pp. 41–57.

Wagner, N., 'Zu ungeklärten Personen-namen in süddeutschen Ortsnamen', *Beiträge zur Namenforschung*, n.s., 37 (2002), 371–407.

Wahlberg, M., *Svenskt Ortnamnslexikon* (Uppsala: SOFI, 2002).

Wainwright, F. T., *Archaeology and Place-Names and History: An Essay on Problems of Co-ordination* (London: Routledge, 1962).

Wakeford, J., 'Two *walh* names in the fields of Kingston', *Surrey Archaeological Collections* 75 (1984), 251–56;

Wallace-Hadrill, J. M., review of P. H. Sawyer, *The Age of the Vikings*, *English Historical Review* 79 (1964), 818–19.

Wallenberg, J. K., *Kentish Place-Names: A Topographical and Etymological Study of the Place-Name Material in Kentish Charters Dated before the Conquest* (Uppsala: A.-B. Lundequistska Bokhandeln, 1931).

Wallenberg, J. K., *The Place-Names of Kent* (Uppsala: Appelberg, 1934).

Walsh, P., 'Irish Ms Egerton 208' (1932), repr. in N. Ó Muraíle (ed.), *Irish Leaders and Learning through the Ages* (Dublin: Four Courts, 2003), pp. 277–78.

Walther, H., *Namenkundliche Beiträge zur Siedlungsgeschichte des Saale- und Mittelelbegebietes bis zum Ende des 9. Jahrhunderts* (Berlin: Akademie Verlag, 1971).

Watson, R., 'Viking-age Amounderness: a reconsideration', in N. J. Higham and M. J. Ryan (eds). *Place-Names, Language and the Anglo-Saxon Landscape* (Woodbridge: Boydell, 2011), pp. 125–42.

Watson, W. J., *Place-Names of Ross and Cromarty* (Inverness: Northern Counties Printing and Publishing, 1904).

Watson, W. J., *A History of the Celtic Place-Names of Scotland,* (Edinburgh: Oliver and Boyd, 1926; repr. with revised introductions, Edinburgh: Birlinn, 2004, 2011).

Watson, W. J., *The History of the Celtic Place-Names of Scotland* (Edinburgh: Blackwood, 1926).

Watts, V., 'The place-name Hexham: a mainly philological approach', *Nomina* 17 (1994), 119–36.

Watts, V., 'Some place-name distributions', *JEPNS* 32 (1999–2000), 53–72.

Watts, V., *A Dictionary of County Durham Place-Names* (Nottingham: EPNS, 2002).

Watts, V. (ed.), *The Cambridge Dictionary of English Place-Names* (Cambridge: CUP, 2004).

Watts, V., *The Place-Names of County Durham,* Part 1, EPNS 83 (Nottingham: EPNS, 2007).

Watts, V., and E. Prince,. 'OE *walh* in place-names: an addendum', *Journal of the English Place-Name Society* 14 (1981–82), 32–36;

Wawn, A., 'Hereward, the Danelaw and the Victorians', in J. Graham-Campbell et al. (eds), *Vikings and the Danelaw* (Oxford: Oxbow, 2001), pp. 357–68.

Weber, E., 'Hausnamen', in A. Brendler and S. Brendler (eds), *Namenarten und ihre Erforschung: Ein Lehrbuch für das Studium der Onomastik* (Hamburg: Baar-Verlag, 2004), pp. 469–90.

Webster, B. (ed.), *Regesta Regum Scottorum vol. VI, The Acts of David II* (Edinburgh: Edinburgh UP, 1982).

Wenzel, W., 'Familiennamen', in A. Brendler and S. Brendler (eds), *Namenarten und ihre Erforschung: Ein Lehrbuch für das Studium der Onomastik* (Hamburg: Baar-Verlag, 2004), pp. 705–42.

Wessén, E., *Nordiska namnstudier* (Uppsala: A.-B. Lundequistska Bokhandeln, 1927).

Whaley, D., 'Trusmadoor and other Cumbrian "pass" words', *Nomina* 24 (2001), 77–95.

Whaley, D., *A Dictionary of Lake District Place-Names* (Nottingham: EPNS, 2006).

Whitelock, D., *Anglo-Saxon Wills* (Cambridge: CUP, 1930).

Whitelock, D., 'Recent work on Asser's *Life of Alfred*', in W. H. Stevenson (ed.), *Asser's Life of King Alfred* (Oxford: Clarendon, 1959), pp. cxxxii–clii.

Whitelock, D., 'The EPNS 1923–1973', *JEPNS* 5 (1972–73), 5–14.

Whitelock, D. (ed.), *English Historical Documents* c. *500–1042*, 2nd edn (London: Eyre Methuen, 1979).

Whitelock, D. (ed. and trans.), with D. C. Douglas and Susie I. Tucker, *The Anglo-Saxon Chronicle: A Revised Translation* (London: Eyre and Spottiswoode, 1961).

Williamson, M. G., 'The Non-Celtic Place-Names of the Scottish Border Counties', unpublished PhD thesis (University of Edinburgh, 1942; available at <http://www.spns.org.uk/resources09.html>).

Williamson, T., *Shaping Medieval Landscapes: Settlement, Society, Environment* (Macclesfield: Windgather, 2003).

Wilson, D. M., review of P. H. Sawyer, *The Age of the Vikings*, *Saga-Book of the Viking Society* 16 (1962), 103–08.

Wilson, J., 'Antiquities found at Woodperry', *Archaeological Journal* 3 (1846), 116–28.

Wmffre, I., *The Place-Names of Cardiganshire*, 3 vols (Oxford: Archaeopress, 2004).

Woolf, A., *From Pictland to Alba, 789–1070* (Edinburgh: Edinburgh UP, 2007).

Woolf, A., 'Conquest and Cohabitation: Britons, Saxons and the Church of Whithorn', 20th Whithorn lecture, 2011 (Whithorn: Friends of Whithorn, forthcoming).

Wormald, C. P., 'Viking Studies: whence and whither?', in R. T. Farrell (ed.), *The Vikings* (Chichester: Phillimore, 1982), pp. 128–53.

Worsaae, J. J. A., *An Account of the Danes and Norwegians in England, Scotland, and Ireland* (London: Murray, 1852).

Wright, J. (ed.), *The English Dialect Dictionary* (London: Henry Frowde, 1898–1905).

Yeates, S., 'River-names, Celtic and Old English: their dual medieval and post-medieval personalities', *JEPNS* 38 (2006), 63–81.

Zachrisson, R. E., *A Contribution to the Study of Anglo-Norman Influence on English Place-Names* (Lund: University of Lund, 1909).

Zachrisson, R. E., 'The French element', in A. Mawer and F. M. Stenton (eds), *Introduction to the Survey of English Place-Names*, EPNS 1.i (Cambridge: CUP, 1924), pp. 93–114.

Index of place-names

General index

For place-names see the separate index, above pp. 441–61. Alphabetical order is here assimilated to modern English usage, so, e.g., Old English *æ* and *ð*/*þ* are listed as if *ae*, *th* respectively, Welsh *rh* and *ll* are not kept separate; Danish *å* is treated as *a*. Note the abbreviations Sc. for Scots and Gael. for both Irish and Scots Gaelic.